JA954.03/

Subalterns and Raj

The field of modern South Asian history has grown rapidly over the last fifteen years. A great deal of new writing has been encouraged by the subaltern studies school, which has had a major impact, not only within India, but in the historical discipline generally and within the field of post-colonial studies.

Subalterns and Raj, reflecting these historiographical changes, presents an innovative and iconoclastic account that begins before the period of British rule, and pursues the continuities within that history right up to the present day. Its coverage ranges from Mughal India to post-independence Pakistan, Bangladesh and Sri Lanka, with a focus on the 'ordinary' people of India and South Asia, and overlooked issues in Indian social history. Key issues addressed include:

- the history of peasants, tribals and workers of the subcontinent
- women's history
- popular and local politics
- religious, revolutionary and social movements.

Subalterns and Raj is a stimulating and controversial read, and with a detailed bibliography for further reading, it is an excellent guide for all students of the Indian subcontinent.

Crispin Bates is Reader in Modern South Asian History at the University of Edinburgh. His publications include, with S. Basu, *Community, Empire and Migration: South Asians in Diaspora* (2001), *Rethinking Indian Political Institutions* (2005), and *Beyond Representation: Constructions of Identity in Colonial and Post-Colonial India* (2006).

Subalterns and Raj
South Asia since 1600

Crispin Bates

Routledge
Taylor & Francis Group

LONDON AND NEW YORK

First published 2007
by Routledge
2 Park Square, Milton Park, Abingdon, Oxon OX14 4RN

Simultaneously published in the USA and Canada
by Routledge
270 Madison Ave, New York, NY 10016

Routledge is an imprint of the Taylor & Francis Group, an informa business

Typeset in Baskerville by
RefineCatch Limited, Bungay, Suffolk
Printed and bound in Great Britain by
MPG Books Ltd, Bodmin, Cornwall

British Library Cataloguing in Publication Data
A catalogue record for this book is available from the British Library

Library of Congress Cataloging in Publication Data
Bates, Crispin, 1958–
    Subalterns and Raj : South Asia since 1600 / Crispin Bates.
    p. cm.
    Includes bibliographical references.
    1. South Asia–History–Textbooks. I. Title.
    DS340.B385 2007
    954.03–dc22
                                        2006101852

ISBN10: 0–415–21483–1 (hbk)
ISBN10: 0–415–21484–X (pbk)

ISBN13: 978–0–415–21483–4 (hbk)
ISBN13: 978–0–415–21484–1 (pbk)

8109 C

Contents

Figures

Maps

Preface

Subalterns and Raj was conceived as an introductory text for my own students and others starting out on the study of the modern subcontinent of South Asia, covering key events, together with some marginal and ignored aspects of the same, from Mughal times right up to the present. Its first publication, in a year that coincides with the 150th anniversary of the Indian uprising of 1857 and the 60th anniversary of Indian independence, offers a particularly appropriate time for reflection upon the connections between the history of the recent past and that of the present, which it is hoped this volume might encourage and permit. The volume was also conceived as offering something of a riposte to the sentimental, colonialist recollections of the British *raj* in India, always beginning in 1757 and ending in 1947, which still plague popular history writing in Britain. Such writing, which pays attention only to feats and never failures, obscures the British conception of their real place in the world and encourages the irresponsibilities of foreign policy in the present. It is a perpetual myopia, writ large by national prejudice to which all countries are victim, though some rather more than most. I have endeavoured as far as possible to correct this by a serious and sincere reflection of subaltern and South Asian nationalist perspectives on the history of the subcontinent. At the same time, I have tried to hold onto what for most readers will be the recognisable signposts of South Asian history, most often deriving from the machinations of elites. This is unavoidable, but I have sought to maintain throughout a critical perspective, combined with a sympathy for the victims of history, which hopefully carries the narrative through some of the knottier issues of interpretation. The contemporary history chapters were the most difficult to write, since there is nothing like the same volume of secondary historical material that might assist in historicising events and putting them into some sort of perspective. There is a heavy reliance here on the work of political and social scientists, which may all too soon become out of date. It is nonetheless hoped that by providing a largely narrative survey of (primarily political) change in the subcontinent that crosses over the 1947 divide, together with copious references to further reading, this volume will help guide students of history, politics and related disciplines, and also the general reader who seeks to understand and contextualise historically the problems and dilemmas of the present.

Even as I was writing this book the names of principal cities and even states in

India were changing. Without intending any disrespect I have nonetheless mainly employed contemporary usages of place names when referring to, and quoting those involved in, events up until the present. Hence, for the most part, Bombay instead of Mumbai, Calcutta instead of Kolkatta, Madras instead of Chennai, and Bangalore instead of Bengalooru. Exceptions have been made with a few of the more unhelpful instances of colonial usage (hence Awadh has been adopted instead of Oudh and Kanpur instead of Cawnpore). I have used Ceylon and Sri Lanka interchangeably up until 1972, and then only Sri Lanka thereafter. I have been similarly liberal with transliterations, for which I have avoided diacritics and have employed the simplest recognisable English spellings that phonetically approximate the pronunciation in use in recent times. For dates in the Gregorian calendar BCE (Before Common Era) and CE (Common Era) are used rather than BC and AD, for obvious reasons. A special thanks must go to Anona Lyons (mapsatanona@btinternet.com) for the maps that accompany the volume and to Sunil Janah (sjanah1@aol.com) for a delightful correspondence and access to his magnificent collection of photographs, too few of which I was able to use. The maps in this book are nonetheless drawn approximately for illustrative purposes alone and should not be taken as accurate interpretations of geographic or political features. By way of apologies, I necessarily regret the paucity of coverage given to Sri Lankan history prior to 1948 and the neglect of minor South Asian states such as Bhutan and Nepal, to which only passing reference is made. For reasons of space the stories of Pakistan and Bangladesh are also entirely enfolded into the larger states of which they were a part prior to their independence. Such compromises are unavoidable in a volume of this nature, but will hopefully not limit its utility.

The writing of this book took far longer than originally planned and was formed at various times in various places. I am especially grateful for the comments I have received from readers at different stages. For early input I am indebted to the patient reading and comments of David Hardiman and Subho Basu. Later on I received invaluable corrections and suggestions from Satadru Sen, Roger Jeffery and David Ludden, as well as several anonymous independent referees commissioned by Routledge. I also received a helpful reminder of the 'fire in the blood' of nationalists in the late 1930s from a lengthy and inspiring conversation with Gyan Pandey, which helped in the reworking of the chapter on that period. For other chapters I am grateful for the thoughts and comments of Nira Wickramasinghe, Harinda Vidanage, David Washbrook and Suranjan Das, and especially for the assistance of Markus and Umbreen Daechsel and Sudhir Chandra, who provided the translations of Ustad Daman and Ghalib, respectively. I am heavily indebted to Marina Carter for her encouragement, suggestions and careful reading and re-reading of every chapter in the book from its very inception until the end. My own dear parents, and the Vaudescal and Ikegame families have all borne the afflictions of this book, for which I am hugely grateful. However, I must thank Aya Ikegame above all for her understanding and support in the final stages, without which it might not have been completed.

1 History, society and culture of the Indian subcontinent

I do not idealise the conception of the masses and, as far as possible, I try to avoid thinking of them as a theoretical abstraction. The people of India are very real to me in their great variety and, in spite of their vast numbers, I try to think of them as individuals rather than as vague groups. Perhaps it was because I did not expect much from them that I was not disappointed . . . I grew to know the sturdy Jat of the northern and western districts, that typical son of the soil, brave and independent looking . . .; the Rajput peasant and petty landholder, still proud of his race and ancestry, even though he might have changed his faith and adopted Islam; the deft and skilful artisans and cottage workers, both Hindu and Moslem; the poorer peasantry and tenants in their vast numbers, especially in Oudh [Awadh] and the eastern districts, crushed and ground down by generations of oppression and poverty . . . yet hoping and full of faith.

(Nehru, *Discovery of India*)[1]

It is easy to forget that [history] is a humanistic discipline, that it can, like literature, indicate alternative possibilities of existence. The studies of Indian politics under the Raj are seldom a pleasure to read. Anyone with a memory of those exciting days would find it difficult to recognise the hopes, passions and heartbreak of millions in the endless narratives of factional squabbles and the fact that not so very long ago to countless Indians nationalism was a fire in the blood.

(Tapan Raychaudhuri)[2]

Introduction: subalternity and historiography

The term 'subaltern' was coined in the 1930s by the Italian Marxist Antonio Gramsci to refer collectively to the oppressed or subordinated classes of a society (Arnold 1984). It was revived in recent years by a group of Indian historians keen to place renewed emphasis on this neglected section of Indian society (Guha 1981), and, in so doing, to change our way of writing about the past (Prakash 1994). Subaltern perspectives are sometimes described as 'post-orientalist', referring to the influential critique of Eurocentrism by Edward Said, or otherwise 'post-modern', indicating a desire to shed the shackles of 'essentialising' and reductive empiricism associated with traditional European scholarship.[3] However, the key characteristic is a desire for differentiation from the tired and worn historiography of colonial apologists, nationalists, and orthodox Marxist traditions, which all in some way enshrined an elitist view of Indian history and society, a point of view that lives on into the present day and persistently forgets the 'fire in the blood' of the millions of people who participate in great historical events.

The great tragedy of modern South Asian history is that for all the vitality and creativity of its masses, the subcontinent has been dominated and controlled, for better and for worse, by a handful of elites. This elite dominance, and the extreme inequality that goes along with it, has persisted well into the era of apparently democratic politics. Unlike many other societies, the vast majority of the Indian subcontinent has failed to experience either a thoroughgoing middle-class (bourgeois) or a working-class revolution to bring to an end the influence of feudal elites and with it the idea that but a few had the right to rule in their own interests. For this reason, whilst fiercely defensive of their democratic rights, the citizens of present-day South Asia are commonly disenchanted with the state of their politics: a phenomenon that has resulted in some of the most dramatic see-saws in political life.

South Asia's sometimes flawed democracies are in many ways a legacy of its extraordinary experience of colonial rule.[4] For a period of 150 years, the subcontinent was administered both directly and indirectly, under a single government, by a country thousands of miles away on the other side of the globe: England or, as it was after 1707, the united kingdom of England, Scotland and Wales. Colonial rule, whilst ushering in significant aspects of westernisation – some fruitful, others less so – at the same time stymied the possibilities for radical political change seen elsewhere in the world in this period. South Asia thus became strikingly modernised in many aspects, but carrying with it a great many customs and practices of pre-modern times, including the dominance and abuse of power, intentionally or otherwise, by a variety of elites: landowners, business families, and political dynasties in the cities, and landowners, princely chiefs, bureaucrats, and rich and high-caste peasants elsewhere, allied with a powerful middle class that emerged in the nineteenth century and has grown steadily ever since. This paradox explains many of the peculiarities of South Asian society today, and is an important focus of this book. It has also generated some of the greatest false debates amongst historians: between those, for example, who see continuities as a major feature in Indian history (an approach associated with the so-called Cambridge school of Indian historians), and others – including both Marxists and orthodox nationalists – who see the colonial period as being one of extraordinary transformation and the colonised most often as victims in this process. The two positions are not so far apart as both contain elements of orientalism and neither allows much of a role for the achievements and actions (or 'agency') of ordinary Indians.[5] On the one hand, the nations of South Asia are viewed as permanently steeped in ancient customs, prejudices, and religious traditions, incapable of ever truly engaging with the modern world; on the other, they are depicted as static and backward cultures until the advent of colonial rule brought about capitalism and most of the trappings of modernity. All too easily this debate becomes tangled up in a confused defence of the indefensible: colonial rule itself. This volume takes an unequivocally anti-colonial stance and the view that the continuity versus change positions are both fatally flawed by their political origins and their dependence upon each other.[6]

The colonial regime first established by the East India Company in India was not an anomalous or curious invention of the time and circumstances but, as Sudipta Sen (1998, 2002) has argued, an extraterritorial apparatus of the British state, legitimated by ideologies of liberty and property and protected by chartered rights, that founded an indirect rule in defence of a commercial enterprise. The interpenetration of state formation at home and in the colony was thus 'strikingly consistent with the overall paradigm of political culture in contemporary England' and owed much to the aggressive national imperialism and commercialism of the Georgian state. Although transformed dramatically in many ways as a consequence, the Indian subcontinent under colonial rule was nonetheless often deliberately preserved unchanged in others, where it suited the interests of the colonial rulers. It was a case of colonial dominance in terms of coercion but without hegemony in ideological terms, as Ranajit Guha has argued (1997a). The mapping of South Asian geography, languages and society, the establishment of laws and educational institutions and even the writing of history itself, all became part of the means by which the Indian empire sustained itself, but colonialism lacked hegemony in many practical areas of daily and personal life. Religion, for example, was one of the fields in which Indians were permitted for the most part to articulate their views. It is for this reason, as well as in straightforward reaction to the violations of colonial rule, that the political movements to overthrow colonial government were powerfully rooted in ideas and traditions of the imagined past (Chatterjee 1993). Of course, even radical visions of the future often contain elements of cultural resuscitation, but in India the past was commonly seen through the distorting prism of colonialism's culture (Inden 1986, 1990). Indian nationalism was thus often expressed in terms of reified notions of pre-colonial culture and religious belief (with important exceptions we shall come to), rather than attempting – as in China, Russia, France and the United States of America – to define itself in terms of an entirely novel (albeit sometimes wildly misconceived) vision of the future. This phenomenon remains a part of politics in the present day. The conflict between India's subalterns and those who exercise the power to rule (*raj*) is thus one in which ideas of an imagined past continue to play a powerful role in shaping the politics and society of the present. So it is that divisive social institutions such as caste still persist, albeit in modified form, and the teaching of Vedic mathematics and Sanskrit are important ideas in the political ideology of certain sections of the Indian elite, whilst the meanings of modernity, and the indigenous roots of ideals such as socialism, secularism and democracy, continue to be argued over and contested (Madan 1998; Ludden 2005; Vanaik 1990).

The elimination or evasion of embarrassing or inconvenient historical facts in historical writing is characteristic of anti-democratic and authoritarian regimes, like spots in a disease such as measles. Colonial South Asia had a very bad case of historiographical measles and the symptoms have not entirely disappeared. In order to understand those missing events and explanations in the long-term history of the Indian subcontinent, it is necessary to transcend the conventional periodisations into pre-colonial and colonial history, the 'modern' and the pro-modern, the history of Indian nationalism, and that of independent South Asia, and to offer a narrative that ties these units together and in doing so reveals their intimate dependence and interconnection. We begin with a brief summary of ancient history, and social and religious practices, as best they can be understood. In subsequent chapters the roots of that great contradiction that governs the subcontinent today, the colonial legacy, are discussed. The focus then shifts to the political movements that threw off the colonial yoke, and the course of history (largely, but not exclusively political) in the various independent nations that subsequently came into being. In this time the subalterns of colonial South Asia (or at least the elite amongst them) become the rulers and beneath them, in turn, new subalterns emerged. Of the four principal countries that today comprise South Asia, only Sri Lanka, formerly Ceylon, was treated as a distinct territory in the colonial period. Thus, whilst separate consideration is given to each of the principal nations of South Asia post-1947, in discussions of the colonial period the term 'India' covers also Pakistan and Bangladesh, today separate from India, but which in the colonial period were part of that colonial entity. Although Afghanistan and the minor states of Nepal and Bhutan are sometimes included in discussions of 'South Asia' they are not the central focus of this book, which concentrates on the region conceived since ancient times as 'Bharat' and which has in more recent centuries been imagined as a territorially defined productive space (Goswami 2004); they are mentioned therefore only indirectly.

Throughout this book, subalternity is treated as a relational concept, focusing our attention on transformative institutions and movements of both repression and resistance. Thus the term 'subaltern' does not simply connote the poor and the wretched, but all those placed in relations of subordination and domination to superordinate classes. This definition could of course at times encompass the entire population of the Indian subcontinent, including the wealthiest sections, in their relationships with the British colonial regime, as well as post-independence societies in relation to anti-democratic elements amongst their landed, business, and governing elites. This book does not claim to speak directly for those who have been marginalised in this history (a dangerous claim in any circumstances as Spivak [1988, 1999] has argued) but aims to re-present that history in a fashion that is keenly aware of their difficulties and dilemmas. The focus will not be on theorisation, of which there is abundance already available (Chaturvedi 1999; Ludden 2001), but will remain as far as possible fixed on identifiable historical characters, events, and processes, eschewing the essentialising of groups, including that of 'the subaltern'. Fortunately, subalternity has now woven itself so far into the mainstream of South Asian history that it is unnecessary to indicate the ideological or theoretical slant of each and every secondary source upon which this book is based. It is sufficient to note that the most innovative, important and recent historiographical contributions on key topics are referenced throughout for the purpose of further reading and research and that on many of these the critical concept of 'the subaltern' has enjoyed a profound influence which this history will endeavour to reflect.

Ancient Indian civilisation

The population of South Asia today is often described as Indo-Aryan, the popular belief being that Indian civilisation only began after the invasion of Aryan peoples from the north some time around the second millennium BCE.[7] The discovery of the ruins of the cities of Mohenjo-Daro and Harappa in the 1920s, however, led to the view that sophisticated societies existed there as far back as the fourth millennium, thus making Indian civilisation the oldest in the world. The cities of the Harappan civilisation were built of standard-sized bricks, were laid out on a grid plan and had a sophisticated water supply and sewerage works, as well as granaries, meeting halls, and hard roads connecting them to the surrounding countryside. Copper items, and ornaments made with gold, silver and precious stones were found by archaeologists, along with similar items believed to originate in Mesopotamia, thus indicating that the population engaged in international trade. Coins and weights and measures were also found, suggesting that the two cities shared a uniform system of exchange based on binary numbers and the decimal system. Subsequent investigations have reinforced the view that these two cities lay at the centre of an extensive civilisation covering an area larger than Western Europe. In recent years attempts have been made to claim Mohenjo-Daro as the ancient cultural ancestor of the modern state of Pakistan (Ahsan 1997), but it is surely more accurate to state that the influence of the city-states spread over the whole of northern India.

The earliest traces of the civilisation, dating from the sixth millennium, found in the hills of Eastern Baluchistan, indicate that the Harappan was one of the earliest civilisations to effect the transition from nomadic to settled cultivation, the twin cities of Mohenjo-Daro and Harappa themselves flourishing long before the era of Sumerian and Mesopotamian civilisation. The reasons for the decline of this ancient culture are, however, shrouded in mystery. At Mohenjo-Daro there is evidence of a great catastrophe some time between 1800 and 1700 BCE, believed by many to have been perpetrated by Aryan warriors from the north. Evidence for this is to be found in ancient Indian texts, known as the Vedas, which speak of the 'Arya' and include descriptions of the Aryan warrior god Indra, who is portrayed as a destroyer of forts. The evidence for some great conflict, however, is not very substantial. There is no record that the Harappans had an army, so it is more likely that the cities were abandoned peacefully. Climatic evidence suggests that in fact migration southwards, as well as the decline of the Harappan civilisation, is more likely to have been the consequence of a prolonged drought. The same drought also probably caused the decline of the great forests in the Indo-Gangetic Plain, thus allowing northern, migratory tribes to move eastwards into this region. Although artefacts remain suggestive of religious practices under the Harrapans, we have no idea as to the exact nature of their beliefs.

References to the Aryans in ancient texts were interpreted by colonial orientalists in the nineteenth century as delineating a tribe or 'race' of people (which had a powerful impact on popular understanding of the term). However, most present-day archaeologists and Indologists argue that 'Aryan' rather implied a status achieved by individuals for the performance of meritorious acts and was not therefore a racial category at all (Ballantyne 2002; Trautmann 1997; Hock 1999). The word 'Aryan' has an etymological origin in *Arya* from Sanskrit, meaning noble, and some Vedic texts explicitly describe leading Aryans as dark-skinned, including Krishna, Draupadi, Arjuna (in spite of his name, 'pale'), Nakula and Damayanti. Vedic texts suggest, nonetheless, that it was these 'Aryans' dwelling in the north of the subcontinent who developed and systematised religious practices in the second half of the second millennium into a form that bore many of the elements of what in the present day is described as 'Hinduism'. Some would claim (particularly religious nationalists) that this makes Hinduism the oldest and most long-lasting religion in the world. It should be noted nonetheless that this 'Hinduism' was far more complex and variegated in its forms than that characterised (and commonly received today) from nineteenth-century colonial texts (King 1999).

Caste, Hinduism, and other religions

There are numerous forms of social differentiation in South Asia. In ancient times, the *gana*, *sabha*, *samiti* and *Parishad* in the north and the *nadu*, *brahmadeya* and *periyanadu* in southern India were political or social communities enjoying a degree of autonomy (Stein 1980; Thapar 1984). In other parts of the continent different terms to describe social entities are used, such as *bhaiband* to describe 'brotherhoods' in the villages of the Bombay Deccan or *nurwa* and *patidar* in Gujarat. All of these are communities amongst which various forms of endogamy, or intra-marriage, may be practised as well as other means of maintaining social and political unity. Family ties, marriage practices and socio-political groupings, customs of language, religion, gender – and obviously economics – all play an important part in differentiating groups of Indians one from another. However, one of the most important forms of differentiation found amongst the majority population of Hindus is that commonly referred to as 'caste'. This is not an indigenous term, since it derives from the Portuguese word *casta* (race or breed). The appropriate Indian word is *jati* – a blanket term for a variety of social groupings within which (or subsections of which) endogamy is commonly practised.

Jatis are subdivisions of the *varna* system of social division. There are a number of interpretations of the meaning of *varna*, including form, quality, class, category, race, merit and virtue, but it is most commonly taken to mean colour in Sanskrit and explained as referring to the symbolic colours attributed to the three cosmological qualities (*guna*). Thus white corresponds to *sattva* (clarity), red to *rajas* (energy) and black to *tamas* (darkness), following the pattern of daylight, twilight and nightly darkness. The four major social divisions of the *varna* hierarchy are: the Brahmin, Kshatriya, Vaishya, and Shudra; the menial Shudras being symbolically black, the heroic Kshatriyas red, and the truth-loving (*sattvika*) Brahmins white. In addition, the entrepreneurial Vaishyas are considered to have a mixture of qualities, and are allotted the colour yellow. According to Hindu tradition every *varna* and *jati* has its own *dharma* or duty to perform and members must adhere to this throughout their lives. Broadly speaking, the Brahmin are supposed to be priests; the Kshatriya, warriors; the Vaishya, commonly artisans, traders and agriculturists; and the Shudra, peasants or labourers. Apart from the Brahmin, those living in the south of India, the Dravidians – so-called because they generally spoke a range of languages (including Tamil, Telugu, Malayalam and Kannada) unrelated to those of the north (including Hindi, Gujarati, Bengali and Punjabi) – were slow to adopt this *varna/jati* system but in time did so as well – although the Vaishya category in the south is far less common than in the north.

The high-caste Brahmin, Kshatriya and Vaishya are known as the 'twice born' since they have been through the *upanayanam* or thread ceremony, signifying the commencement of their 'studenthood' (of the Vedas) following which they are permitted amongst other things to perform Vedic sacrifice. Initially both men and women could take part in this ceremony, but by the time the 'Laws of Manu' were written (*c.* 200 BCE–200 CE) it had become an exclusively high-caste male preserve. The Shudras are described (in the Vedas) as their servants and are merely once-born. To signify this distinction the high castes wear a sacred thread. Through regular prayer, the performance of appropriate rituals, and close adherence to their *dharma*, all castes can hope to escape *samsara*, the cycle of rebirth, and achieve *moksha*, or union with the supreme divine power (otherwise *nirvana* in Buddhism), although not until they have passed through many incarnations on this earth.

The *varna* or 'caste' system, as we shall call it for the sake of convenience, constitutes a status hierarchy based upon religious notions of purity and impurity, occupation and politics – defining the difference between the rulers and the ruled. The *varna* system is thus a complex social hierarchy unlike the Western notion of class, which it is possible to define in very narrow economic terms according to a person's income or, in the Marxist sense, 'control over the means of production'. Attempts to define caste in equally simple terms (for example, by the famous French anthropologist Louis Dumont [1980]) have generally failed. However, Western notions of class also sometimes refer to a person's status, religion, occupation or race. It is, therefore, often possible to talk about caste differences as being similar to differences of 'class', since being high caste and/or 'upper class' both ensure superior access to power – culturally, materially, politically and socially.

How do Indians themselves see the question of caste? The answer is different at different times and in different places, and it can include some, more or all the elements mentioned above. In ancient times, when India was a land of warring tribes, the Kshatriyas (or warrior castes) had the highest status. In medieval times, however, as societies became more stable, the status of Brahmins (the priestly caste) increased, because their role as preservers and interpreters of the culture meant that their approval and guidance became an important source of legitimacy for *rajas* or kings. Since the eighteenth century, rapid economic change has helped to raise the status of the lower castes who have often thereby been able to either change their caste or to improve its position, in the process challenging the authority of the Brahmins and Kshatriyas (Bayly 1999). More recently still, the castes have become economic competitors to a considerable extent, and certain Vaishyas (such as the Marwaris) have become important employers – examples include the Birla family – whilst their workforces have come to include penniless Kshatriyas and Brahmins as well as Shudras. In these cases the traditional caste hierarchy has lost all meaning (at least as far as the Kshatriyas and Brahmins are concerned). In social and religious terms, however, Brahmins and Kshatriyas have retained their status, with Brahmins in particular still being revered as the descendants of 'holy' men and wielding considerable influence.

Whilst Kshatriyas today are no longer kings and princes, many have instead become landlords and landowners, the Shudras (including castes such as Kunbi, Lodhi and Patidar) becoming their tenants. In such cases the status hierarchy has been simply translated into a class hierarchy and the terms 'caste' and 'class' become virtually interchangeable. In general the lowliest and most menial of social tasks, such as street sweeping, tanning of leather, and cleaning of latrines, continue to be performed by a group accounting for nearly a third of the population who lie at the very bottom, or rather outside of the caste hierarchy. They are the so-called *harijans* (a term preferred by Gandhi), outcastes, untouchables, or *dalits* (meaning 'the oppressed') – the label frequently preferred today by members of this community themselves (Joshi 1986; Mendelsohn and Vicziany 1998). Strict rules of commensality traditionally forbade the sharing of food and social mixing between castes, but so strong has been the prejudice against *dalits* that they were commonly obliged to live in a separate community from the main village, to drink from separate wells, and to avoid even their shadow falling upon members of a higher caste. This community includes castes such as the Chamars (traditionally leather workers) and the south India 'sweeper' caste of Pariahs, who rarely own land. However, to every such rule there is always an exception. In Chhattisgarh in central India, for example, Chamars owned and farmed land for several centuries and claim a higher status as Kshatriyas, as commonly do most outcaste and low-caste migrants who have settled overseas. Due to positive discrimination measures in India since independence *dalits* are increasingly found in all walks of life, particularly in government service.

Another group we shall encounter, who have a slightly higher status but who lie outside the caste system, is that of the *adivasis* or 'tribals' (the word '*adi*', meaning 'beginning' or 'of earliest times', and '*vasi*' meaning 'resident of'). The term *adivasi* was first used in Chotanagpur in the 1930s and has since become the favoured label. The *adivasis* are, supposedly, the original inhabitants of South Asia, predating the bulk of the population, who are described as Indo-Aryan, and even the Dravidian peoples of the south. The labels *adivasi* or 'tribal' are, however, merely blanket terms to describe a collection of different polities and social groups with their own rulers, who for one reason or another are conceived of as outside the mainstream of Indian society. Commonly this has been due to their geographical isolation, although it is believed that tribal and nomadic groups dominated the plains of India in pre-modern times, in sometimes large and powerful kingdoms, and were only gradually forced over time into hillier and more isolated regions, or else were conquered and incorporated, thereby losing their separate status in the process (Bates 1995). According to some, this process of incorporation, known as 'Sanskritisation' has been going on for centuries, as people are converted to supposedly higher status Brahminical forms of Hinduism and brought into the mainstream of Hindu society. Others have argued that the complexity of Hindu beliefs is itself an indication of the incompleteness of this process. Rather than being converted, tribal people are often simply co-opted and their gods and religious rituals added to the Hindu pantheon such that Hinduism represents little more than a formal collection of animist beliefs (Singh 1985). This might explain the great variety of Hindu gods, and the fact that these gods often have many incarnations, appearing in completely different guises in different parts of the country, even though ostensibly still the same divine being. Strictly speaking, *adivasis* are completely outside of the Hindu system and are not recognised as Hindus – being referred to as the *dasyus* in certain Vedic texts – and due to their alleged wildness they are regarded with a certain amount of awe, occasionally playing a marginal but magical role in certain religious rituals and festivals (including marriage ceremonies).

The other main religions of South Asia, apart from Hinduism, include Islam, Buddhism, Jainism, Sikhism, Zoroastrianism and Christianity. Jainism could be described as an ascetic variation of Hinduism, placing particular emphasis on *ahimsa* or non-violence – extending even to the injury of insects – for which reason Jains consider agriculture to be impure; thus they are found mostly to be working in commercial and mercantile professions. Jainism dates from the sixth century BCE, the same era in which Greek philosophy, and Confucianism in China were developing. It was also during this period that Zoroastrianism was developing in Iran, a variant of which became established among the community known as Parsis in western India. Buddhism was also established at this time, the Buddha – Siddaratha Gautama – being born in the Terai area of Nepal around 550 BCE. The Buddha was born into the Hindu faith, but founded his own sect and went on to have a major impact through wandering and preaching around northern India for some 45 years and his foundation of a *sangha* or monastic order to carry on the preaching of his beliefs. The Buddha's first sermon described the Four Noble Truths that were the nucleus of his teaching: that the world is full of suffering, that suffering is caused by craving, that suffering can be ended by the renunciation of craving, and that the way to renunciation is by following the Eightfold Path of Righteousness – this consisting of a balanced, moderate life based upon right views, resolves, speech, conduct, livelihood, effort, mindfulness, and meditation. The revolutionary aspect of his philosophy lay in the Buddha's argument that by devotion to this path his disciples might achieve *nirvana*, or union with the divine power, sooner rather than later and regardless of one's caste origins – thereby avoiding the endless cycles of reincarnation. Many of the Buddha's ideas and tenets were incorporated into Hinduism, as well as spreading in their own right throughout South-East and East Asia. Buddhism flourished particularly in Sri Lanka, where it became established as the principal religion between the third and fifth centuries BCE (see the later discussion of Sri Lanka in Chapter 16). Its great appeal lay partly in its eschewal of notions of caste and its emphasis, at least in its earlier *theravada* phase, on individual salvation. Buddhism's later *bodhisattva* phase, with its emphasis on the Buddha as saviour, encouraged deification and rendered it more vulnerable to assimilation; but although its influence was extinguished in central Asia by Islam, and by Brahminical revival in India between the seventh and eleventh centuries CE (Common Era), Buddhism continued to spread eastwards and was revitalised in China and Japan by development of the Chan and Zen schools.

Islam was founded by the Prophet Muhammad who was born in 570 CE in Mecca in Arabia, a highly cosmopolitan town, where Sabaeans, and Muhammad's tribe, the Quraysh, worshipped a black stone representing the moon (said to be a meteorite), named Al-ilah or Allah, and a variety of other gods. Around the year 610, when he was forty years old, Muhammad claimed he had a visitation from the angel Gabriel when he was meditating, soon after which he began to preach that there was no God but Allah and that all must submit to him. Further revelations followed and were transcribed and compiled by his followers into the 114 *suras* or chapters of the Qur'an (Koran). After the death of his wife and uncle (who raised him), and persecuted for his beliefs, Muhammad moved 280 miles north to the city of Yathrib, later renamed Medina ('City of the Prophet'). This northern migration called the 'hegira' started on 24 September 622 and marks the beginning of Islam. After this, Muhammad embarked upon a series of military campaigns, expanding his territory until he conquered Mecca itself in 630, in the process converting all of the tribes to his beliefs. Muhammad died in 632, by which time he controlled much of Arabia. His successors were known as the *Caliphs*, but after 30 years the state was split between the followers of Uthman, the third *Caliph*, and those of Ali, the fourth, Muhammad's son-in-law. This division led to the two great religious sects that still exist – the Sunni (who go back to Uthman's followers) and the Shia (who go back to Ali's).

Islam arrived in western and southern India initially through trade between Arabia and India via the Persian Gulf. Other diverse routes for its transmission included the territorial conquest of north India and the Deccan plateau by a succession of Turkish, Persian and Afghan rulers from the eighth century onwards (Robinson 1982). At a popular level Sufism was one of the most formative later movements to develop. The best-known orders of Sufism – the Chisti, Qadriya, Naqshbandiya and Suhrawardiya – all trace their origins to the period between 1100 and 1600 CE, and north India is still the largest centre of Sufism in the world. The most dominant sect however was Sunni Islam, which grew in influence in north India under the patronage of the Mughal empire (1526–1858). Over the subcontinent as a whole (according to 1999 statistics) there are some 372 million Muslims, divided mostly between India, Pakistan and Bangladesh. Some

120 million Muslims reside in India (12 per cent of the total population of 1 billion), making India's the third largest Muslim population in the world after Indonesia and Pakistan, and Islam the second most important religion. In many Indian states such as West Bengal, Karnataka, Assam, Uttar Pradesh, Kerala and Bihar, Muslims are a significant minority, accounting for between 10 and 20 per cent of the population. In the independent nation-states of Pakistan and Bangladesh some 96 per cent and 86 per cent are Muslim out of the total populations of 146.5 and 126 million respectively, the majority being Sunni Muslim and 17 per cent and 9 per cent of them Shia. In the Himalayan kingdom of Nepal there are 1 million Muslims in a total population of 24 million. In the island of Sri Lanka too there is an important Muslim population – concentrated mostly in the centre and east of the island – amounting to some 1.7 million or 9 per cent of the total population of 19 million.

Sikhism did not develop until the very end of the fifteenth century, being founded by Guru Nanak (the first of ten Sikh gurus) in the Punjab. The term 'Sikh' derives from *sishya*, meaning discipline, and its founder was a key figure of the passionate *bhakti* devotional movement within Hinduism, which was critical of Brahminic ritual and exclusiveness and emphasised the unity of God and the equality of all human beings. Nanak believed in one, formless, creator God, rejected ritual and caste hierarchy, and enjoined his followers to form a community who worshipped together using a single body of devotional hymns. It is the religious verses he wrote that form the holy scriptures, the Guru Granth Sahib, of Sikhism, and it is in the Golden Temple of Amritsar that the holy scriptures are preserved. A populist religion, Sikhism is mystical, monotheistic, evangelical and egalitarian: thus whilst it incorporates the ideas of reincarnation and *karma*, Sikhism rejects the worship of a multiplicity of gods and idols, along with the caste system, that is characteristic of Hinduism.

Initially Sikhism flourished peaceably within the fold of the Mughal empire, until the torture and execution of the fifth Guru Arjun by Emperor Jahangir forced it to develop an altogether more militaristic and defensive style: an army of the faithful being formed to defend the holy scriptures and the Temple of Amritsar. The ninth guru, Tegh Bahadur, was martyred by the Mughal emperor Aurangzeb, after which his son Gobind Singh (1666–1708) – the tenth and last guru – ordered the army of the faithful, whom he called the *khalsa* or pure ones, to give up smoking and alcohol and other drugs. He also told them to never cut their hair (*kesh*), to wear long breeches (*katch*), and always carry a dagger (*kirpan*), comb (*kanga*) and steel bangle (*kara*). These five features, the five k's, became symbolic of those who were the most loyal, faithful and ardent protectors of the Sikh religion. The wearing of a turban to cover the hair became a further, later marker of Sikh identity under the influence of the colonial military. Men who joined Guru Gobind Singh's army took on the name of the guru himself – 'Singh' which means 'lion'. Upon his death Guru Gobind Singh was declared to be the last of the gurus so that none could follow him. Following further persecution and division, Ranjit Singh united the Sikhs and established an empire in the Punjab that lasted until the British annexation in 1849: to this day Sikhs remain concentrated in the Punjab, although migration and the division of the state during the Partition of India between India and Pakistan in 1947 have caused Sikhs to disperse across the subcontinent, and throughout Europe, South-East Asia, and the Americas (Singh 1963). The fate of the Sikhs in India since independence is described in detail in Chapter 14.

Christianity arrived in the subcontinent, according to popular tradition, with a visit by the Apostle Thomas to southern India in the first century CE, the descendants of his followers, known as Syrian Christians, being found mostly in Kerala. With the Portuguese came the Jesuits in the fifteenth century, who undertook mass conversion to the Roman Catholic Church in Sri Lanka and Goa in western India. Saint Francis of Xavier came to Goa in 1542, where his embalmed body is the object of pilgrimage for Christians. However, Christianity did not begin to gain really substantial numbers of converts until the arrival of Protestant and Catholic missionaries in the eighteenth and nineteenth centuries, who enjoyed particular success in converting outcastes and the poorest of the poor in southern India (Bayly 1990). In the present day there are approximately 16 million Christians in India (according to the census of 1981), some 3 million more than the population of Sikhs, and a further 8 million (mostly Catholic) in Sri Lanka. Although numerically a small community, the cultural, social and political impact of Christianity on the subcontinent has been profound, provoking both rivals and imitators, as well as encouraging the spread of English amongst the poorer sections of society through a network of missionary schools. Christian missionaries are regarded by many *dalits* as 'liberators' from Hindu oppression who opened up opportunities through education, never previously available to them. They also, however, gave a powerfully conservative and puritanical impulse to Indian middle-class culture and provoked reactionary movements of religious revivalism and counter-conversion, such as the Arya Samaj, in the north of India. This is discussed further in Chapter 6.

Hinduism is arguably older than all of the above-mentioned faiths – the earliest texts that are associated with it originating sometime between 3000 and 1500 BCE (Flood 1996). However, most of the devotional aspects of modern Hinduism did not begin to emerge until the second half of the first millennium CE. Even the term 'Hindu' did not then exist, and it was not widely adopted until the British censuses of the late nineteenth century obliged Indians to categorise their faith. The modern name derives from the Sanskrit word 'Sindu' (the River Indus), which was used by the earliest Persian-speaking Muslim travellers to describe all those whom they encountered in the geographical area near the River Indus, regardless of their religious beliefs. Portuguese and British travellers of the same period referred to the Indians as 'gentoos', meaning 'gentile' or 'heathen'. Not until around the fifteenth century did the name 'Hindu' begin to be appropriated by north Indian Hindus to describe themselves. The term 'Hindu' is then encountered in the writings of *bhakti* (devotional) sects that were influenced by Islamic thought. However, there was no uniformity implied by the concept, the term simply being adopted to distinguish themselves from Muslims. At this time, Hinduism shared much in common with the practices of other religions (notably Islam) that were developing within the Indian Ocean region. These shared practices are nicely captured in images of the Sufi (follower of mystical Islam), monk, saint or preacher of *bhakti*, and the *sanyasi* (wandering renouncer) that dominated the religious culture of the pre-modern period. In the modern era, however, due to the pressure of economic and social and political change, and whilst still retaining a great many popular and regional variations, Hinduism developed the characteristics of the entirely distinct cultural complex that makes it by far the most important religion in the subcontinent today – being espoused by more than three-quarters of the population (700 to 800 million people).

One of the great strengths of Hinduism is that it does not have one or two sacred texts but a great number of them, produced at various times, and thus also reflecting changes in social and religious rituals and beliefs at the time they were written. Most of the texts, known as Vedas, were originally composed by sages who handed them down by word of mouth to their followers, or priests, the Brahmins. The lines of text were learnt and recited in rhyming cycles and some-times survived in this form for a considerable time before being committed to paper in the ancient language of Sanskrit. In the absence of printing presses the myths were then often learnt and repeated again and again before being once more committed to paper. A tremendously complex variety of beliefs are, there-fore, to be found in these texts and, in turn, were created by them. The result, in Hinduism, is a religion of great complexity and flexibility in which, at least in earlier times, a variety of beliefs and forms of worship were tolerated. These include the worship of the sun, the moon, rivers, fire, rocks and trees, as well as the reverence of spirits and saints and the worship of the holy places where they were born or died.

The earliest of the four Vedas, the Rig-Veda, was simply a collection of *mantras*, or holy words, and hymns addressed to elemental powers. However the later commentaries, the *Brahmanas* and *Upanishads* (otherwise known as Vedantas, being the conclusion to the Vedas) contained considerable philosophical speculation and theorising about religious practice (including Yoga) and the ideal structure of society, along with information on basic Hindu beliefs, including belief in a uni-versal spirit and creator of the universe, *Brahman*, and an individual soul, *atman*, which is at death subject to reincarnation. The most important distinction to be found in these ancient texts is that between conquered peoples and the bearers of the Hindu religion coming from the north. These conquering peoples described themselves as being paler in colour than the indigenous population. It was British Orientalists of the nineteenth century, however, who judged these Aryans (on the basis of rather shaky linguistic evidence) to be connected to central Asian tribes, who they argued probably migrated to Western Europe at the same time, explain-ing thereby the affinities between the languages of Europe, central and southern Asia. Such a migration may have taken place, but it was more likely one simply of language, as a consequence of trade and cultural exchange, rather than any actual movement of people: a cultural conquest rather than the creation of a physical empire (Renfrew 1990). If such a physical movement did take place there is no other evidence for it, and it must furthermore have been at a time so remote as to have no genetic significance in the present, since none have been found. Claims to authentic Aryan 'racial' origin, a popular assertion of supremacists in central Europe in the 1930s and 1940s and in India too, are therefore completely bogus.

The ordering of people according to caste is an important practice in Indian society which, as has been observed, is linked to occupational specialisation, and which has been developed and maintained by exclusive marriage practices. Of course, the reality is rather different and one of the most enduring features of Indian society concerns the constant attempts by families and caste groups to raise their status by 'marrying up', a practice known as hypergamy, whereby the payment of extravagant dowries or (less commonly) bride price enabled newly prosperous families to seek alliances for their sons and daughters with higher status groups. Hence, although theoretically this was not the case, caste status was always highly mutable over time and heavily influenced by cultural contexts, and even Muslims in South Asia have developed forms of social hierarchy akin to caste (Ahmad 1978; Barth 1962).

The theoretically exclusive marriage practices of Hindus led many colonialists to believe that differences of caste were comparable to the differences of race, as popularly theorised at the time, and great efforts were made to rank and distinguish castes by their skin colour and other physical characteristics in the belief that this might, amongst other things, indicate their suitability for different forms of employment. Race and caste thus became crucial elements in the ideology and epistemology of colonial rule (Bates 1996). These ideas became widespread, not least of all because British comparisons between themselves and their high-caste Brahmin collaborators in the colonial administration (sometimes referred to by lower caste activists as the 'the Anglo-Brahmin Raj') flattered a few, whilst usefully shifting some of the blame and responsibility for colonialism onto indigenous peoples. The link between skin colour, caste, race, and supposed common central Asian origin for Europeans and high-caste Indians is still widely believed and fuels not only caste discrimination but also rivalries between northerners and southerners in India, whose languages and thereby 'ethnicity' are described as 'Dravidian'. This rivalry spawned a number of important political movements in the late colonial period and after, which are discussed in Chapters 6 and 14. Notwithstanding these imputed racialised differences, individuals who are construed as Brahmins in India may still frequently be dark-skinned, while working-class, low-caste or *adivasi* Indians are often lighter in skin colour (especially in the north). As always, questions of 'race' and status are relative and very much a matter of perspective.

Some have argued that caste was never more than a method of social control by elites and that in colonial times it was rendered less fluid through its use as a mechanism to divide and rule (Dirks 2001). At the very least it has been suggested that the nature of caste was misrepresented in the orientalist accounts of Hinduism purveyed by Europeans, whose exotic depictions of the 'mystic East' continue to play a role in the Western imagination to this day (King 1999; Sugirtharajah 2003). Others nonetheless maintain that caste is quintessentially rooted in Indian religious belief (Dumont 1980). Regardless of these differences, ideas of caste have endured as, in Partha Chatterjee's description, 'the general cultural form of legitimising and ordering the relations of identity and difference between several kinds of social groupings' (1993: 165), and although there are important popular forms and variations upon this hierarchical system (Fuller 1992), the traditional Brahminical system is to some degree recognisable almost everywhere. In accordance with this system each member of a caste (including the king) must follow his or her particular *dharma* or duty, if they are to sustain their *karma* or spiritual fate. Failure to do so means that he or she will be reincarnated after death into a lower caste or a lower form of life than a human being (such as a frog). In this way religion, everyday life and nature are intimately ordered and connected.

The authors of the Vedas described themselves as the *jana* or 'the people'. They were, however, divided into numerous 'tribes' or clans and numerous sub-'tribes', each with its own chief, or *raja*, and its own ruling council or *sabha*. This itself is one aspect of the origin of certain caste divisions. Needless to say, as a warlike people the highest status was initially given to the *raja* and the Kshatriya warriors and this is reflected in the earliest Vedas (3000–1500 BCE). As warriors they revered, particularly, the chariot wheel (which has a great many symbolic associations in Hinduism), but also the cow, regarded as a sacred animal in India since ancient times right up to the present day.

As society became more stable from the tenth century BCE onwards, the four divisions of the *varna* system became more minutely divided into castes, each caste (and there are dozens of them) reflecting the relative status of different occupations and effectively preventing the downward mobility of the high-caste Kshatriya and Brahmin elite. As warfare declined, however, so did the importance of the Kshatriya or warrior. In the earliest Vedic text, the Rig-Veda, it is the Kshatriyas who feature most of all, but in the later Brahmana texts it is the priests, or Brahmins, who are given the greatest importance. Later still, post-Vedic historical texts, or Puranas, gave importance not only to the rituals, rights and functions of the Brahmins but also greatly elaborated the description of the duties and responsibilities of the *rajas*, or kings. The most important and one of the most popular of these was the Mahabharata written sometime between 400 and 800 BCE. This formed the blueprint or model for the management of the Hindu kingdoms that flourished in the north of India from the fourth century right up until the invasion of the Mughals a thousand years later. The text itself runs to some 106,000 verses and tells of the battles between two 'Aryan' tribes – the Pandavas and the Kauravas and their allies among the indigenous peoples – battles fought out on the plains between the Ganga and Yamuna rivers in the north-west of India between about 1000 and 700 BCE. Stories from the Mahabharata, as well as from other sources, have been told and re-told (mostly by Brahmin priests) throughout the past 2,000 years and are popular in India to this day. It is from this source that the majority of the population learn of the duties and powers of rulers and the rights of the people, as well as the status, responsibilities and customs of each of the castes into which they are born. It is from the Mahabharata too that Hindu Indians learn of the rights and responsibilities of male and female and of the superior position of the male, who alone is permitted to perform sacrifices to the gods. Women in Hindu tradition are invariably depicted in this subordinate role: thus patriarchy in South Asia has no need of the typical Western legitimation of women's second-class status through their alleged physical weakness. Women, female gods and feminised icons, such as Bharat Mata (Mother India) or the Goddess Durga (the world mother, an incarnation of Parvati, the consort of Shiva) in India are seen as powerful and strong, and ordinary women are revered for their endurance and ability to perform heavy tasks. In terms of political, social and economic power, however, they remain subordinate to men, a position maintained by both custom and coercion where necessary.

Today, the most popular of ancient texts is the Ramayana, the life history of the God-King Ram, an incarnation of Vishnu and ruler of the kingdom of Ayodhya. It is worth describing in some detail because of its popularity and importance in late twentieth-century political conflicts and because it illustrates the reality of dynamism and change within Hindu tradition. There are many versions of the tale, the earliest version in Sanskrit being by Valmiki and later rewritings including Goswami Tulsidas's Ramacharitmanas, written in Hindi in 1574 CE, and the Kamban Ramayana, which is popular in Tamil Nadu. There are strongly egalitarian elements in the Ramayana, in which all the peoples of India, including those led by the monkey-king Hanuman (believed by some to be a representation of the tribal peoples of India) unite to aid Ram in his battle to recover his kidnapped wife Sita from the demon king Ravana in the southern kingdom of 'Lanka'. The different versions of this tale enjoyed popularity in different times and places, and not only amongst Hindus. The Tulsidas version has Sita playing a somewhat heroic role, while the Valmiki version (preferred by many conservatives and militant Hindu organisations) depicts Sita as a rather more submissive character who at the end of the tale, in response to doubts about her 'purity', having been rescued from Ravana's clutches, banishes herself in a forest the better to preserve her husband's honour. Many versions include a closing episode in which Sambuka, a Shudra (in some versions an untouchable), is killed by Ram for performing *tapasya* or ascetic exercises that are the province of Brahmins alone. In other versions his crime is the simple act of learning to read, which violation brought about the death of two Brahmin boys. Sambuka having been executed, harmony is restored. Thus even in the more egalitarian tale of the Ramayana caste discrimination is still sometimes affirmed.[8]

At the root of both Hinduism and Buddhism is a belief in the interconnectedness of all things – a notion that helps to explain Mahatma Gandhi's conviction that ends do not justify means and his espousal of non-violent methods of resistance to British rule. Interconnectedness helps to explain the tremendous variety of Indian gods, many of which are reincarnations (or different faces) of the same divinity. It also accounts for the fact that in Hindu belief the gods have frequently visited the earth in the form of human beings (such as the King Rama: an incarnation of Vishnu), as animals (such as the elephant: in the case of Ganapati) or as inanimate objects such as trees and rocks.

In ancient times the two most popular gods were Varuna and Indra. Both are much less popular in modern India, where the minor Vedic gods Vishnu and Rudra (also known as Shiva – the omnipresent and all-knowing god of creation, destruction, and maintenance) are better known. Shiva is most popular in eastern India, and Vishnu (the protector of the universe) and his consort Lakshmi (goddess of wealth) are more popular in the west of India, in the south, and in rural areas. Vishnu has ten major avatars or incarnations, including Rama and Krishna, although some believe he has 22 incarnations, one of them being the Buddha. Both Shiva and Vishnu have many other forms. Parvati is Shiva's consort in mythical tradition, but otherwise merely another aspect of the same god, who is both male and female. A well-known incarnation of Parvati is Kali, the goddess of destruction, or Durga in eastern India, whilst another – in many Brahminical interpretations – is the popular village goddess Mariamma in the south of India. Parvati is associated with nature and all its produce and is characterised by her devotion to Shiva and care for the unfortunate, whilst in Gujarat in western India in the earlier part of the twentieth century Shiva was incarnated as the goddess Devi who urged the tribals to give up smoking and drinking and to free themselves from the grip of landlords and moneylenders. Equally popular is their son, Ganesha, the elephant-headed god, who removes obstacles and brings good fortune. In Indian villages today one can find temples devoted to some or all of these gods, and in medieval times local kings would build temples devoted to different gods and supply them with land, tax free, to maintain the temples and priests. In this way kings, or *rajas*, would win both the support of the god and that of the people. Similarly in tribal areas, Rajput Kshatriya kings would often be forced to worship tribal gods in order to win the support of the population, in the long term incorporating them into the broader Hindu pantheon as 'incarnations' of established Hindu gods in order to legitimise this practice. In this way the variety of gods grew more diverse as the area influenced by Hindu rulers expanded, and Hinduisation of the local population and tribalisation of the Hindu population went hand in hand throughout the medieval period (Singh 1985).

Pre-modern kingdoms

The largest and most sophisticated of the pre-modern Hindu kingdoms was that of Magadha, the later rulers of which, the Maurya dynasty, turned it into an empire that, in the second, third and fourth centuries BCE covered most of northern India. One of the last and most famous Maurya emperors, Ashoka (who ruled from 269 to 232 BCE), was converted to Buddhism, and this played an important role in assisting the spread of Buddhism throughout the subcontinent. However, after the collapse of the Maurya empire the smaller kingdoms that took its place, as well as the later empire of the Guptas, which flourished between the fourth and sixth centuries CE, all adhered to Hinduism; this remained the dominant religion in the subcontinent despite repeated invasions and migrations from the north of the Huns and other nomadic groups.

The Gupta dynasty (*c.* 320–547 CE) led the most advanced of all the Hindu empires, applying the sciences of astronomy and mathematics, borrowed from the Arabs, to the development of navigation and trade throughout the Indian Ocean. Their ships regularly sailed from Bengal, or from Surat on the west coast of India, to places as far off as Canton, carrying jewels and manufactured goods. It was also at this time that through trade, Hinduism and Buddhism were spread to South-East Asia, where they became the principal religions from about the fifth century CE onwards. The rule of the Guptas in the north was paralleled, though less spectacularly, by the Chola dynasty in the south centred on Tanjore, who dominated the Tamil country from about 100 CE until the thirteenth century, when its power and influence were supplanted by the Bahmani sultanate in the Deccan and the Vijayanagar empire in the south.

The first Arab invasion of the Indian subcontinent came in 711 CE when Muhammad Bin Qasim was sent by the Ummayid dynasty (based in Syria) to occupy the area of Sindh, principally for the purposes of trade. He was followed at the end of the tenth century by Sultan Mahmud of Ghazni (in Afghanistan) who occupied the Punjab and Sindh in 1186. In the eleventh and twelfth centuries north India was invaded by Afghan and Turk armies, the most successful being under the command of Muhammed Ghor, who defeated the powerful Rajput dynasty of Priviraj Chauhan upon their second encounter at Tarain in 1192. The assassination of this last great Ghorid sultan in 1206 led to the independence of the north Indian territories, which flourished as an autonomous sultanate, initially under the rule of Qutbuddin Aibak (one of Muhammed Ghor's generals at Tarain), who built the famous Qutb Minar tower in honour of his achievement. There followed five successive dynasties (Turki, Khalji, Tughlaq, Sayyid and Lodi) until 1398, when Delhi, the capital, was sacked by the central Asian conqueror, Timur. Timur's descendant, Babur (1483–1530), the ruler of Kabul, then invaded the north of India in 1526, defeating the Lodi rulers of Delhi and Agra on the battlefield of Panipat, and also a confederacy of Rajput princes, thereafter establishing the empire of his own Mughal dynasty. Babur's son, Humayun, was forced to retreat from Delhi in 1540 by the Afghan warlord Sher Shah – who proved an efficient administrator of the empire – but the Mughal dynasty was restored by Humayun in 1555, who died the year after and left the empire to his young grandson the Emperor Akbar (1542–1605) and the regent Bairam Khan.

Under Akbar, trade, the arts and sciences flourished, the capital was moved from Delhi to Agra, the territory of the empire was expanded and it began to acquire fabulous wealth. With the Mughals came a myriad of new social practices and traditions. Not all of these customs were Islamic, but were often merely characteristic of the culture of Afghanistan from where the Mughals originated. For example, the practice of *purdah*, or the veiling of women, came to be widely practised amongst Muslims in north India at this time and was even adopted by many elite Hindus, although there is no mention of it in the Vedas or Koran. Akbar himself was a syncretist. He married the Hindu daughter of a Rajput king who helped him to establish control over his empire at an early stage in his career, he abolished the *jizya* (a tax on non-Muslims), and attempted to combine

Hinduism and Islam in the theology of his state. This won him many allies among local Hindu princes, who were incorporated into a hierarchy of ruling Mughal nobility, the *mansabhdars* (derived from the word for 'dignity', *mansab*). In this way there was extensive overlapping and convergence between Indic and Islamic world-views in north India at this time (Gilmartin and Lawrence 2000).

Southern expansion of Muslim rule was facilitated by the collapse of the 200-year-old Hindu Vijyanagar empire in 1565 under the weight of an alliance of five Deccan sultanates, including the Shia kingdoms of Bijapur and Golconda (successor states to the Muslim Bahmani kingdom), which were themselves in turn defeated and finally succumbed to Mughal rule in 1686. Akbar's successors Jahangir and Shah Jahan were responsible for consolidating and expanding the Mughal empire to the south (Map 1). Under these two seventeenth-century emperors the Mughal nobility, which ruled over the provinces of the empire, was drawn largely from the ruling families of the adjacent Safavid and Ottoman empires in Iran and the Middle East. Akbar's eldest son Prince Salim assumed the name Jahangir (meaning 'conqueror of the world') upon ascending the Peacock throne and immediately faced a revolt from his eldest son Khusrau, whom he blinded and kept in prison, at the same time executing the fifth Sikh guru, Arjun, with whom he had allied. A fantasised story of Jahangir's youth is told in the famous 1960 Hindi film *Mughal-e-Azam*. Under his rule, for the first time, large

Figure 1 Akbar's arrival in Surat in 1572 (from a fifteenth-century painting by Farrukh Beg). © M.D. Carter.

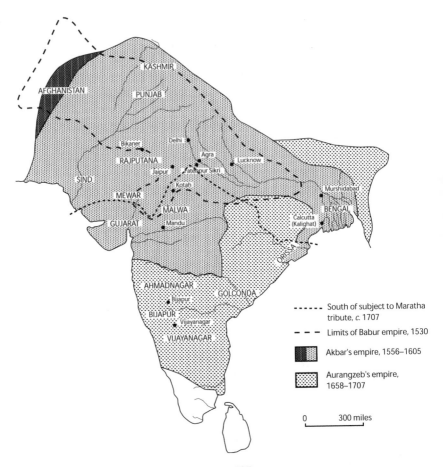

Map 1 Limits of the Mughal empire, *c.* 1524–1707.

numbers of low-caste Hindus, particularly in the cities, began to convert to Islam in order to raise their status and to gain promotion (for example) in the Mughal army. Jahangir is famous for having signed a treaty with the East India Company allowing them to trade, for the first time, within the subcontinent. His twentieth and last wife was the legendary Nur Jehan, who exercised considerable influence in the closing years of his reign.

After the death of Jahangir in 1627, his second son Prince Khurram (1592–1666) seized power and took the name Shah Jahan ('Ruler of the World') following a fratricidal war with his younger brother (such conflicts being characteristic of most Mughal successions). Shah Jahan was something of a megalomaniac, who drained his empire of funds by waging war in Afghanistan and central Asia and harrying the Shia kingdoms of the Deccan. At great expense he moved the capital from Agra back to Delhi – building the famous Red Fort (Lal Qila) and the Jama Masjid. It was he who built the Taj Mahal in Agra, supposedly a last resting place for his beloved wife Mumtaz, although it has been argued that it may have been more than that, being designed as an architectural representation of paradise, or 'the throne of God', as described in the Koran (Richards 1993). By the beginning of the eighteenth century this empire had begun a slow but terminal process of decline due to over-expansion, continuing war in the Deccan, and internal factionalism under the rule of the last great Mughal emperor Aurangzeb (1618–1707). Aurangzeb came to power in 1658 by fighting and killing his brothers and imprisoning his aged father in Agra. During his reign he turned to a strict interpretation of Islam and Shariah law, reimposing (amongst other things) the unpopular *jizya*: a tax on non-Muslims. The earliest European traders, the Portuguese, had begun to visit the shores of India on a regular basis even before the sixteenth century, during the time of Akbar, but it was only after the death of Aurangzeb that the Europeans began to make their influence significantly felt in the subcontinent; this is the subject of the next chapter.

It may be deduced from the above summary that the Indian subcontinent, like Europe, has a varied history of conflict and conquest and is a society divided between many regions, religions, languages and cultures. Given its semi-tropical climate and vast and fertile plains, washed each summer by the rain of the monsoons, the subcontinent is capable of sustaining considerable populations and generating substantial agricultural wealth: a great prize to any would-be ruler. There are a total of nine major languages, each with many dialects, and according to some estimates more than 200 minor or local languages. Each language group reflects the hegemony of a particular socio-political community – whether it be a tribe, chiefship, kingdom or empire. Until very recent times people have thus owed allegiance to a great variety of overlords and faiths that have ebbed and flowed across the land over time. This is perhaps why most inhabitants of the subcontinent have little difficulty in identifying themselves in several ways: as Tamil or Gujarati (for example), Muslim, Hindu, Parsi or Jain, as well as members of wider communities of caste, class and nation. In modern times people are increasingly pressurised to declare their loyalty to a single, unitary (and unifying) identity (usually of state or religion), and the diversity of identities in South Asia has been a source of conflict. That same diversity also made this a richly complex society with remarkable resources and opportunities, as European traders of the early modern period were quick to discover.

2 The decline of Mughal India and rise of European dominion

Agra and Fatehpore are two very great cities, either of them much greater than London and very populous. Between Agra and Fatehpore are twelve miles, and all the way is full of victuals and other things, as full as though a man were still in a town, and so many people as if a man were in a market. They have many fine carts, and many of them carved and gilded with gold . . . which be drawn with two little bulls . . . They are covered with silk or very fine cloth . . . Here is great resort of merchants from Persia and beyond India, and very much merchandise of silk and cloth, and of precious stones, both rubies, diamonds, and pearls.

(Ralph Fitch, 1583)[1]

The Great Moghul, considering his territories, his wealth, and his rich commodities, is the greatest known King of the east, if not of the world . . . This wide monarchy is very rich and fertile; so much abounding in all necessaries for the use of man as that it is able to subsist and flourish of itself, without the help of any neighbour.

(Father Edward Perry, 1616–1619)[2]

The history of the decline of the Mughals and the rise of British dominion in the eighteenth century is a subject about which there are perhaps more misconceptions than any other in the field of Indian historical writing. It is no coincidence that this was also the period in which the history of Britain and India first became inextricably linked. Indian history as a whole is notoriously prone to misconceptions, not only because, after the loss of the Americas, it was the first and largest British imperial possession – the 'jewel in the crown' of the British empire – but because India itself was a vast and complex society. India was furthermore of such importance to Britain that Indian history and conceptions of India became as much a part of British national identity as they have been a part of Indians' understanding of who they are and where they come from (Majeed 1992; Clarke 1997; Trautmann 1997). This has not prevented Indians and the British from presenting very different understandings of the same events. The conventional interpretation of the rise of British dominion sees it as a glorious episode, a product of the superiority of British firepower, man management, morale and even, possibly, religious or divine inspiration. This view is lamentably ahistorical, and suggests, to begin with, a complete neglect of the economic history of India in the sixteenth, seventeenth and eighteenth centuries, when it was a far more prosperous place than Europe. The earliest European explorers went to India less to exploit, than to admire, and paid dearly in silver bullion for the luxury goods they purchased. It was only later in the eighteenth century, following the establishment of formal territorial control by the British, that the terms of trade were reversed, and the British began to use taxes levied on Indian peasants to pay for the goods that they shipped abroad. Later still, in the early nineteenth century, the onset of the Industrial Revolution meant that the British could flood the Indian market with goods produced much more cheaply than they were manufactured indigenously, and the terms of trade worsened still further. By the 1930s the combination of high unemployment and population growth was established; which, combined with gross inequality, has created the erroneous modern-day Western image of India as a historically 'backward' and impoverished society, together with parallel assumptions about the exclusively Western origins of modernity (Parthasarathi 2001; Chakrabarty 2000).

Those who visit India today are often surprised at how economically and technologically advanced the subcontinent is, despite the extreme inequalities. In the eighteenth century and earlier most European visitors were absolutely stunned by India's wealth, especially when compared with Europe. Travellers such as Marco Polo in the fifteenth century and Sir Thomas Roe, ambassador of James I at the court of Jahangir between 1615 and 1619, returned from South Asia with fabulous stories of the wealth of the Indian kings and princes. India was a major supplier of textiles, including fine cloths as well as textiles for the masses, to the whole of South-East Asia, Iran, the Arab countries and East Africa. With the advent of the European, this trade later extended as far as the Americas, the Philippines and Japan, as well as to Europe itself. It was a desire for access to the enormous wealth that this trade generated, that first inspired Europeans to seek to develop a route to India by sea. Before the sixteenth century Indian goods came predominantly overland, on the silk route issuing from the Levant and Egypt, and finding a route to Europe via Venice. Europeans had by this means become accustomed to goods from the Orient, but it was not until the sixteenth century that a means was found of obtaining these valued goods more cheaply and easily with the development of a sea-going trade with the East Indies.

It was sufficient for European trade to flourish for there to be security on the high seas: territorial control was unnecessary. Therefore to understand the move from trade to dominion by the British one has to look at events internal to South Asia rather than the activities of European merchants and adventurers. Far from being simply a feat of conquest by British arms, there were a great many other, more important, factors involved in the acquisition of territory by the English East Indian Company in South Asia. Even at the height of empire, the British never directly controlled more than two-thirds of the subcontinent – hence the role of collaborators of one sort or another was of fundamental importance. Vast tracts remained at least nominally independent, governed by local Indian rulers and princes who had signed treaties with the East India Company; indeed, up until 1858 the British were mostly found in eastern India, concentrated in Bengal and along the coast at Bombay and Madras. Even in British-controlled territories the emperor's face still appeared on coins minted by the East India Company, and both British and Indian peoples were regarded as subjects of the Mughal emperor right up until 1857 when he was finally deposed. Thus Indian rule in India persisted very much longer than is usually realised. How and why the English East India Company came to dominate these local rulers is a complicated matter. The first and most important reason was the decline of the Mughal empire itself.

The Mughal empire was a predominantly (although by no means exclusively) Muslim polity, originating in Afghanistan, which ruled over some two-thirds of India from the sixteenth century onwards. It was not the first great empire in the north of India, but it was by far the largest, being comparable in size and indeed related to the Safavid and Ottoman empires in the Near East. It was stable, powerful and still well entrenched when the British arrived on the scene. The strength and power of the Mughal empire had helped to provide India with its tremendous wealth. How then did the British come to supplant it? In many cases the British were invited in: they became involved in territorial control of India by treaty and by alliance with local Indian rivals of the Mughals, and in other cases they simply walked in and took control of territories at the invitation of Mughal nobility and merchants. How they were able to do this, under the feet of one of the world's largest and most powerful Islamic empires, necessitates an understanding of the weaknesses and vulnerabilities in the Mughal system that were becoming apparent by the dawn of the eighteenth century. These weaknesses revealed themselves most strongly in the form of declining revenues, the increasing frequency of movements of secessionism and revolt, and the empire's inability to resist three crushing invasions by Afghans and Persians from the north-west, which critically undermined the military might and hence credibility of the imperial system.

Later on in the eighteenth century, British territorial ambitions in India were encouraged by rivalry with France. Like the 'scramble for Africa' in the period before the First World War, India became an arena in which European rivalries confronted one another. Thus a great deal of territory in British India was acquired simply in order to limit the imagined threat of French aggrandisement, or to act as a bulwark against French attacks, rather than because the English East India Company wanted control of it in the first place. After the loss of the American colonies in the mid-eighteenth century the British crown was reluctant to acquire any further overseas territories, while the corporation of the East India merchants was answerable to the crown and parliament for the continuation of its charter. When the first Indian territories were acquired in Bengal in the 1750s, Sir Robert Clive – who took control over this area – offered them to parliament, only to be told by William Pitt the Younger (who was then prime minister) that the crown wanted nothing to do with it. The Indian territories were consequently ruled by the East India Company, a trading corporation, not the British government, until 1858, the corporation paying an annual tribute to parliament for the continuation of this privilege. Trade was encouraged by the British government of the eighteenth century, but territorial control was another matter. Glorying in territorial conquest for its own sake was very much a nineteenth-century concept, and this did not emerge until quite late on in the relationship between Britain and India.

A third factor that favoured the acquisition of territory by the East India Company was the nature of the treaty system it established with Indian princes. Christopher Bayly, an eminent historian of eighteenth-century India, highlights the subsidiary treaty system as one unintended means by which British involvement in India, and their alliances, had a powerful destabilising influence on the finances of formerly independent Indian states (Bayly 1988). The subsidiary treaty system entailed the stationing of British troops on the borders of Indian kingdoms for their defence, paid for out of the revenues of those kingdoms. By the late eighteenth century the British army was rather more successful than many of its rivals in the subcontinent, encouraging Indian princes to enter into alliances with the East India Company, according to which they borrowed British trained Indian troops to defend their territories. The nature of these alliances placed huge strains on the exchequers and tax systems of these princes, leading to destabilisation, and the East India Company then took over their territories by default in payment of their debts. It was thus the quest for alternative sources of revenue to pay for the hire of mercenary troops to protect trade, primarily against the French and their allies, rather than the desire for territory itself, that led the East India Company to acquire control over a number of Indian kingdoms.

The final and key factor in the decline of the Mughals and the rise of British territorial control was the growth of a prosperous and independent Indian merchant class. This is discussed by Christopher Bayly (1983, 1988) and in a seminal article by Karen Leonard (1979). These authors make the point that the British were often drawn into territorial control at the invitation of Indian merchants who were often already fabulously powerful and wealthy, and had been so for many centuries, and who had assumed a dominant role in the escalating growth of trade between Britain and India. These merchants acted as intermediaries with the English, making alliances with the *videshis* (foreigners) for their own self-interest and regardless of the political consequences elsewhere. This research is substantiated by a growing body of evidence, albeit controversial, that suggests that in the late eighteenth century India was a developing capitalist economy with an increasingly substantial trading class, sophisticated accounting practices, credit networks and transcontinental means of exchange (Das Gupta 1994; Subrahmanyam and Bayly 1988; Bayly 1983; Perlin 1983).

First contacts

The earliest transoceanic encounters between Europe and India took place through the intermediary of Portuguese traders in the sixteenth century, who acquired a commanding position in the Indian Ocean trade in spices and other luxury goods. This trade began in 1499 when Vasco de Gama's exploratory expedition returned loaded with pepper. The sale of this pepper brought huge profits for the Portuguese king who made it a royal monopoly. In the mid-sixteenth century warfare between Venice and the Turkish empire, which disrupted the silk trade overland, made the Portuguese sea trade even more profitable. In 1580, however, the Ottoman–Venetian Wars ended and Philip II, the Portuguese king, became bankrupt. After this, the Portuguese role in East Indies trade declined, to be supplanted soon after by the Dutch and then the British.

The Dutch were far more efficient traders than the Portuguese. They developed streamline production techniques for the large ships required to engage in the East India trade, so that from a very early stage they could send a greater number of ships across the sea. So successful were the Dutch in acquiring a monopoly of the trade that they were able to raise the price of pepper from 3 to 8 shillings a pound. It was this tremendous increase in price that ultimately encouraged a group of English merchants involved in the East India trade to band together to form the East India Company, which was incorporated by royal charter in 1600. In response to this the Dutch set up their own East India Company in 1602. Thus at the beginning of the seventeenth century there were at least two major rivals in the East India trade. The Dutch quickly began to turn their attention towards Indonesia, rather than India, as a source of supply. The British were also interested in this region, but in 1623 a large party of English merchants was massacred by the Dutch at Amboyna in the Molluccas islands, and after that the British concentrated their efforts largely on South Asia. The rivalry between the two meant that there was a rapid growth in the supply of silk and spices to Europe, and, as prices fell, Indian goods began to become affordable for the middle classes.

Although based in London and described as the 'English' East India Company, Scottish and other British merchants and seamen began to play a part after an unsuccessful attempt to set up a rival organisation based in Edinburgh in 1695. The Scottish Africa and India Company, as it was called, was founded by Sir William Paterson and raised the enormous sum of £400,000 by public subscription in Scotland. All of this was lost after vigorous lobbying against it by the East India Company in London and an ill-conceived attempt to found a colony at Darien on the isthmus of Panama (and thereby pioneer a new route to India), which was attacked by Spain, its inhabitants subsequently starving to death. The Scottish Company limped on but was virtually bankrupt by 1706. The tragic demise of the Darien scheme was a contributory factor in the decision of the Scottish parliament to vote for union with England in 1707, but it was not until well after the passage of the Act of Union that Scots were accepted as partners rather than rivals of the English. By the late eighteenth century, however, Scots had become an important element in the Company hierarchy as it expanded to become the largest single European enterprise in the East India Trade.

In the late seventeenth and early eighteenth centuries most Europeans led simple lives, wearing rough linen and woollen clothes. Their food was salted, but with few condiments to add flavour, and eaten off crude earthenware, using tin utensils. The great change that the Indian trade brought to Europe was to transform cuisine and the art of dining through the use of spices and china table-ware goods. Clothing was revolutionised with the import of washable and durable cotton trousers and shirts. Tea and coffee were also added to the European diet. A parallel revolution was produced by the cultivation of sugar in the Caribbean. The cotton piece goods arriving from India were a particularly popular item of consumption. It was not until the early nineteenth century that British manu-facturers later began to imitate the texture of Indian cloth and to flood the market with machine-made cotton goods in exchange for raw cotton. In the eighteenth century and before, India was a supplier of finished cotton goods and produced some 25 per cent of the world's manufactured output.[3]

With the arrival of china and cotton goods, not only was the European lifestyle transformed but a great admiration for all things oriental developed in Europe. Poets and writers like Samuel Taylor Coleridge and Robert Southey extolled the achievements and culture of Kubla Khan and other mythical rulers of the East. A fascination for acquiring oriental produce and manufactures followed (Majeed 1992; Mackenzie 1995). With the demand for Indian goods far outstripping the supply, one way in which the British managed to increase the shipment of pro-duce was by leasing privately owned ships. By adopting this practice, the English East India Company was soon able to outdo the Dutch, who continued to manu-facture their own ships, and the East India Company was set to become the largest supplier of East Indies goods to the European market.

Initially English ships would purchase goods at the western port of Surat from Indian merchants, then sail southwards to pick up spices from the Malabar coast before returning to Britain. The first permanent English bases were established in Bengal in eastern India at Ballasore and Hugli (a former Portugese base) in 1636 and 1637, and from there a flourishing trade developed – not only in textiles and spices but also in dyes, such as indigo, and in saltpetre, this latter being an essential constituent in the manufacture of gunpowder. Following the success of these 'factories', as they were then called (i.e. bases for the factoring of Indian produce), another was set up in Madras in 1640. Everything went well for the Europeans until the middle of the seventeenth century when the Mughal emperor Aurangzeb came to the throne (Figure 2). The Mughal emperors were generally successful in augmenting their dominions, but Aurangzeb was by far the most adventurous of them all. He seized the throne in 1658, moved his capital from Agra to Delhi, and thereafter embarked on an ambitious programme of imperial expansion. Within a short time, the East India Company became embroiled in a dispute with Aurangzeb after he had driven the Mughal borders down almost to the tip of India. English, Dutch, French and Portuguese traders were all subjected to taxes by the emperor and his governors to help pay for this warfare, and when a group of Company merchants refused to pay customs duties on their trade from Bengal, they were driven out of the province. It was this conflict between the East India Company and Aurangzeb's local governor in Bengal, the *nawab*, that revealed one of the fundamental weaknesses of the Mughal empire. Like all of the Muslim empires, it was predominantly land based. Its huge armies could completely overwhelm any opposition put to them on land, but at sea, since they never had

Figure 2 Emperor Aurangzeb enthroned (Khemanand, *c.* 1660). © British Library.

any need to engage in naval conflict, they were completely helpless, and soon after the English were driven from Bengal an English fleet was sent to blockade the coast. The blockade caused a loss of revenue to the governor of Bengal by disrupting the flourishing local trade being carried on between southern and eastern Asia. After the sinking of several Indian vessels, the governor of Bengal decided to rid himself of this nuisance by allowing the British to return, and in 1690 a new base was established in Bengal by an English merchant, Job Charnock, at the anchorage of Sultanuti between the villages of Kalikata and Govindapur. This site was later to become the capital city of Calcutta. It was not a healthy spot, and many residents died from malaria, dysentery and other diseases. But despite these disadvantages, trade flourished both with Europe and with the East through the subcontracting of space on Company ships to Indian merchants engaged in the country trade along the coast and farther afield. This relationship was mutually beneficial both to the Indian merchants and to British navigators.

Mughal decline

Despite their comings and goings, the activities of the Europeans were entirely confined to trade until the end of the seventeenth century, and they only occupied a few bases on the Indian coast (Map 2). They had no interest in the interior. The

Map 2 India, *c.* 1785.

acquisition of the goods they purchased and paid for was made by Indian merchants acting on their behalf. Inland the country was dominated by the Mughals. However, by the end of the eighteenth century, and particularly after the death of Aurangzeb in 1707, there were increasing signs of instability within the Mughal empire. A not unbiased commentator, the English Whig historian T.B. Macaulay (1800–59), described the emperors of the subsequent four decades as 'a succession of nominal sovereigns sunk in indolence and debauchery, sauntering away life in secluded palaces, chewing *bhang*, fondling concubines and listening to buffoons'[4] – a possible description of the symptoms rather than of the disease itself. What were the causes of this sudden collapse of Mughal power? Aurangzeb ran a highly centralised regime, but many have suggested that the Mughal empire itself was nothing but a confederacy of princes, with the emperor in a somewhat nominal position as sovereign (Heesterman 1985: 16–17).[5] To begin with, the emperor was apparently dependent on the willing co-operation of the Mughal nobility (known as *mansabdars*). The significance of this was that as long as everyone prospered from the system, they were happy to co-operate with it, to supply the Mughal army and to pay taxes to the Delhi emperor. But as soon as the empire became less prosperous, and less beneficial for all concerned, it was susceptible to rapid disintegration, not unlike the later empire of the British (although the decline of the Mughals was comparatively less catastrophic).

If one accepts the theory that the Mughal empire was essentially decentralised and confederate in nature it is still necessary to understand why it was that the empire became less prosperous or less beneficial for those involved. There are numerous explanations for this. The first explanation centres on the Mughal heartland. In the eighteenth century some of the cities on the margins of the empire, cities run by independent princes and those developing around the European factories, saw a rapid rise of population and prosperity. The population of Calcutta, to give an example, was a few thousand in 1710, but 120,000 by 1750, 200,000 by 1780, and 350,000 by 1820. But in the Mughal heartland in north India, the population and prosperity of the region and its major cities steadily declined. One explanation for this is simply over-taxation of the limited resources of agriculture (Habib 1963, 1969). Beyond this, a particular problem was caused by Aurangzeb's increasing use of 'tax farming' in the seventeenth century in order to fund his expansionary plans. Tax farming was practised by the Safavids and Ottomans as well, but not by the Chinese, and one historian, Chris Wickham (1985), has argued that this was possibly one reason why the Chinese empire survived longer and maintained its centralising ethos: that is, because tax revenues were always collected directly by bureaucrats on behalf of the emperor and remitted to the capital. Tax farming could be described as a form of privatisation, or the selling off of state assets, only in this case the asset auctioned off, for a limited period and for a particular territory, was the right to collect taxes. The effect was immediately to generate a huge increase in revenue to the ruler, who no longer had to wait for eight or nine years for money to come in from the taxation of a particular territory. By selling off the revenue collection system he could have a lump sum in advance, which could be employed to equip his armies and feed his troops. The problem, of course, was that once the tax-collecting rights were sold off, those who bought them, in order to make a profit, began to raise far more taxes than formerly had been levied. This led to the impoverishment of the territory that was being tax farmed, and those to whom these concessions were granted became independent and far more prosperous. In fact they became a rival source of finance to the imperial exchequer and very often – once they had exhausted the territory for which they had purchased the farm – they would purchase the tax farm for another territory. This time, though, being more prosperous and holding a number of these farms already, they could afford to strike a harder bargain. Increasingly, then, the deals struck between the emperor and his tax farmers became less and less profitable for the Mughal ruler.

The tax farmers of the Mughal empire were by and large not aristocrats but merchants, and they were only interested in collecting revenue from the peasants. Aristocratic landholders, such as the *jagirdars*, as well as collecting revenue on behalf of the emperor, would usually supply troops for the service of the imperial army, thereby saving the emperor the expense of hiring them, and adding to his military power. The merchants on the other hand were disinclined to become involved in warfare. Some, such as the wealthier *zamindars* (or landlords) of Bengal, preferred to raise their own private armies instead (Calkins 1970). In the long run, then, tax farming became less and less fruitful for the emperor and more and more fruitful for the merchants. An effect of this was to encourage the development of an increasingly prosperous and independent merchant class, as Karen Leonard argues (1979). C.A. Bayly (1983) and André Wink (1986) see this as a very positive development, extending commercialisation of the agrarian economy. From a political point of view, however, the problem was that this independent merchant class was rarely content simply to pay a share of taxes to the Mughal emperor. As they prospered they would seek out alternative avenues for investment. These might be trade with Europeans or other merchants throughout India, or possibly even to lend money (if the interest rate was right) to finance the wars and campaigns of rivals to the Mughals.

The rise of mercantile elites is certainly one reason why rivals of the Mughals became increasingly influential towards the end of the eighteenth century, their resources financing an increasing mercenarisation of warfare (Kolff 1990). Of these rivals to the Mughals the most important was the kingdom of Mysore in south India, and the Marathas – a confederation of Hindu princes – in western India. These two kingdoms became increasingly powerful by borrowing money from merchants, who had in turn drawn tax revenues from the Mughal empire, and hiring mercenary forces (notably in the case of the Marathas) to extend their dominion. Both were also powerful threats to the British until they were crushed at the end of the eighteenth century. Mysore was a military dictatorship, originally an independent kingdom until Hyder Ali, a Muslim general in charge of Mysore's army, deposed the king and set himself up as the ruler of the autonomous territory. Hyder Ali set up a centralised system of taxation and procurement, and a huge standing army that was a powerful rival to the Mughals (Habib 2002). The Marathas were still more interesting. They began as a predatory empire, most formidable when united under the leadership of Balaji Baji Rao I, the Chitpavan Brahmin 'Peshwa' or prime minister of the Maratha king, Shahu, between 1720 and 1740. Initially their system of tax collection was simply to ride en masse to the nearest Mughal village and demand a share of the revenues. This was the so-called Maratha *chauth* (one-quarter), which would be claimed from the Mughal revenue demand on the village. It operated as a sort of protection racket and if it were not paid the village would be burned down. When the Mughal tax collector arrived later to get his share there would often be little left to collect. By such means the Marathas ate into the territory and prosperity of the Mughal dominions, the Maratha chiefs eventually establishing their own dominion and a sophisticated administration in their place. The Marathas first began to pose a serious threat to the Mughals during the mid-seventeenth century, when the great Maratha leader Shivaji Bhonsle twice sacked the Mughal court of Surat in 1664 and 1670 (Pearson 1976; Gordon 1969, 1977, 1993). It has been argued by John Richards (1976, 1993) and others that it was Aurangzeb's failure to deal effectively with this threat that proved to be the empire's most fundamental weakness, enabling Maratha power to grow until ultimately it came to equal that of the Mughals themselves by the latter half of the eighteenth century.

Another problem that faced the Mughals – again a result of over-taxation – was a succession of uprisings amongst the Jats and other peasant communities in the north of India (Alam 1986). *Fitna*, or rebellion, was always a feature of the Mughal system and there was often resistance to tax demands from the ranks of land controllers and revenue collectors. Indeed, it was their duty to strike the best deal they could for their territories, and the final revenue payment, or tribute, paid by *zamindars* to the emperor's provincial governors or regional *deshmukhs* was often not agreed until there had been a show of force (Wink 1986). However, these rebellions of the late seventeenth and eighteenth centuries were quite unlike those that had gone before, as they often came from below and were difficult to contain. A number of uprisings also occurred in tribal areas (Singh 1988); and finally, after Aurangzeb's death, there were successive incursions by the Afghans from the north-west. The Afghans were an even greater danger than the Marathas, and on many occasions their invading armies penetrated deep into the Mughal heartlands in the north of India, culminating in the great defeat of 1739 when the Afghani leader Nadir Shah seized the capital of Delhi itself and carried off the famous Peacock Throne the Mughal emperor had used for important state occasions. The Afghans, as well as the Marathas, were thus amongst the emperor's most powerful enemies in the north and became a major threat to Mughal territorial control.

There are numerous other cultural explanations for Mughal decline. One argument is that the main problem of Aurangzeb was his religious intolerance, paralleled by a development of religious extremism amongst the Muslim aristocracy, which made alliances with rivals to the emperor increasingly difficult to achieve. Earlier Mughal emperors had been demonstrably syncretic, quite happy to do deals with Hindu and tribal kings of one sort or another, accepting their conversion to Islam in many cases and integration into the ranks of the *mansabdars* or nobility. Aurangzeb's period of rule in the mid-seventeenth century, however, had been synonymous with a move towards religious puritanism, which had affected all of his territories, making this sort of political alliance and deal-making more difficult (Sarkar 1932–50; Richards 1976). This was another factor in the development of political opposition to the emperor. A number of Mughal historians (for example, Chandra 1959; Richards 1976), on the other hand, have pointed to the disruptive effects of factionalism and competition over the allocation of *jagirs* (land assignments given in reward for military service) as a result of earlier over-expansion in the ranks of the nobility; M. Athar Ali (1966), on the other hand, has blamed the simultaneous decline of the Ottoman and Safavid empires (from where many of the *mansabdars* were recruited), a decline as much cultural as social and economic in origin. These factors combined to ensure that the emperor's authority was becoming debilitated by the end of the eighteenth century, with a great number of rivals to his political power, and an emerging class of merchant intermediaries. Whilst Chaudhury (1995) and Sen (1998) present a contrary case, emphasising the penetration of the Indian interior by English mercantile capital, it is arguable that it was the Indian merchant intermediaries who played the crucial role by financing the political opponents of the emperor, who in turn funded the growth of a market in mercenary soldiers (*sepoys*) and cavalry willing to fight for the highest bidder. Due to their dominance over sea trade and excellent relationship with the bankers, this ultimately became a force under the monopoly control of the British.

European rivalries, British conquests and the role of Indian merchants

The development of warfare between France and other European powers led increasingly to competition between the French and the British in India. The French Compagnie des Indes was established in 1700, and by 1744 it had become an important trading company in the South of India. On an all-India scale, the wars that ensued between France and Britain were really quite unimportant – far greater battles were being fought between the Mughals and the Marathas, between the kingdom of Mysore and the Mughals, and between the Afghans and the Mughals, and so on. But their significance was that they forced the English East India Company to acquire, for the first time, a standing army to protect its base at Madras, this being close to the French settlement at Pondicherry. New fighting methods were introduced to the subcontinent, some of them even a novelty still in Europe, such as precision firing in ranks, which meant that a European army with quite a small number of muskets could have a devastating effect on opposing forces, including the hitherto invincible Mughal cavalry. The Mughals had cannons, muskets, and war elephants, the same and more equipment than the British, but the adoption of these very different techniques, after a long period in which the massed ranks of the Mughal army had been the predominant fighting force in the subcontinent, gave the Europeans a crucial advantage. Of course, Indians quickly imitated their methods, but in many cases by the time they did so it was too late. It was partly because of this that a great many Indian princes edged into treaties with the British in the eighteenth century, allowing them the loan of British-trained troops: the so-called subsidiary forces treaty system. For a long time the British and French fought against each other through intermediary alliances with Indian princes, and by the time the French had been defeated, at the battle of Wandiwash in 1760, the British were firmly enmeshed in a network of alliances with Indian princes in the south.

From intermittent warfare to formal conquest was a big step, and the story of the British acquisition of Bengal is an interesting and revealing one. The British base at Kalikata was attacked by the Mughal *nawab* of Bengal, Siraj ud Daula, in 1757, leading to the famous and much exaggerated 'Black Hole' incident, in which the number and even gender of the British prisoners who died remains contested. It was in order to restore the British to their base that Robert Clive sent his army to Bengal in that year to do battle with the *nawab*. By rights the governor of Bengal should have won. In any major encounter between the British and a Mughal general, the Mughals at least had numbers on their side. But the fly in the ointment was the Indian merchant elite. Two men in particular, Jagat Seth and Omi Chand, had become powerful bankers and traders in the north of India. They not only funded the Mughals but also numerous other kings and princes, and they traded extensively with the British. They were seriously aggrieved with the *nawab* because he was over-taxing them, and arranged a secret meeting with the British. The army of the *nawab* was subsequently bribed to change sides at the commencement of battle, in exchange for tax concessions from the British. Thus the great battle of Plassey in 1757, which is supposed to mark the start of British dominion in India, was no battle at all. As soon as the armies took to the field, the general in charge of the *nawab*'s army, Mir Jaffar, marched across to the British side and the *nawab* fled the field. When news of the defeat of his governor was heard in Delhi, far from being distressed the Mughal emperor Bahadur Shah I and his counsel were delighted. The effect of efforts to reform and improve revenue collections in the early eighteenth century had been almost counter-productive, and for some time the *nawab* of Bengal, like the *nizam* of Hyderabad to the south, although both nominally Mughal governors, had ceased remitting revenue payments to the imperial capital and had become almost completely independent (Calkins 1970; Leonard 1971). Immediately after the defeat of Siraj-ud-Daula, therefore, the emperor granted the revenue administration of the '24 Parganas' to the East India Company, anticipating an improvement in his receipts. Ultimately the right of the civil administration of the whole of Bengal, the so called *diwani*, was granted to the Company in 1765. Thus, it was entirely with the agreement of the Mughal emperor that the British became the rulers of this eastern half of India, one of the more prosperous of the Imperial provinces; the British, for their part, permitted an approved Mughal nobleman to remain as *nawab* (initially Mir Jaffar), thus nominally upholding the sovereignty of Delhi whilst in practice taking complete control of tax collection and civil administration.

All of this soon proved to be a serious miscalculation, however – both on the part of the emperor and on the part of the Indian merchants who sponsored the British take-over. The Jagat Seths were dismissed from the role of Company bankers in 1772, and rather than being agents of peace and good government, the East India Company proved to be the progenitor of disorder. The style of the East India Company's administration became apparent soon after the take-over: within a month of the victory at Plassey a hundred boats were sent bobbing downstream on the River Hugli, laden with 7.5 million silver rupees seized from the *nawab*'s treasuries. Within six weeks, a further 4 million rupees had been deposited at the Company's Calcutta treasury. On its behalf, Robert Clive, the leader of the British expeditionary force, annexed 900 square miles of territory south of Calcutta and elected himself governor of this territory, with a reward of £234,000 and an annual stipend of £30,000 for his services. These were truly prodigious sums of money in those days, and made Robert Clive one of the wealthiest Englishmen alive, and the first of the so-called 'nabobs' (a corruption of *nawab*), a group of Englishmen who were much resented back home in England for their attempts to use the vast wealth they had accumulated in India to buy political power and social influence. Clive's behaviour was indicative of the manner in which British rule was to continue in subsequent years, as increasing corruption, financial peculation, and misrule culminated in the tragic famine of 1770 in Bengal in which a third of the population died (Marshall 1976, 1987). Initially, however, few were aware of the awesome scale of corruption in the Company's administration in India, and the East India Company directors were only too delighted with their new-found source of income, derived from the land tax revenues of Bengal. The greatest significance of the acquisition, however (and a presage of things to come), was that, where formerly, throughout the seventeenth and eighteenth centuries the Company's ships had to carry boatloads of silver to India to pay for the Indian goods they purchased, the Company could now begin to use some of the £4 million annual revenues of the province of Bengal to finance their trade, as well as to pay for the hire of mercenary troops.

Notwithstanding its rapaciousness, the British take-over of Bengal was a minor event in an Indian subcontinent overshadowed by warfare. For in 1761 another huge Afghan army, led by Ahmad Shah Durrani, once again invaded from the north-west, this time coming into conflict not only with the Mughals but also with the Marathas who by then had acquired control over a great deal of Mughal territory in the north and west of India. The Mughal and Maratha armies allied to oppose the invading forces, and in a prolonged battle at Panipat, just north of Delhi, the two sides fought each other to a standstill, causing the Afghanis eventually to withdraw. The significance of this lay not only in the destruction of the already much-reduced Mughal forces but also in the undermining of the only other major power in the north of India: the Marathas. The battle of Panipat was a turning point in the history of north India, as the success of the invading Afghani armies undermined the sole remaining powers that might oppose the further extension of the East India Company's territorial control. The first casualty of British demands for taxes and tributes in Bengal was the newly appointed *nawab*, the former army commander Mir Jaffar, who having been sucked dry by the British was replaced by another ally, Mir Kasim. Able administrators, such as Seiyyid Mohammad Reza Khan, did their best to manage the transition from Indian to Company rule, but they could do little to mitigate the worst excesses of the Company's officials, and Mir Kasim was soon complaining, as this letter to the British governor reveals:

> And this is the way your gentlemen behave; they make a disturbance all over my country, plunder the people, injure and disgrace my servants . . . Setting up the colours and showing the passes of the Company, they use their utmost

endeavours to oppress the peasants, merchants and other people of the country . . . In every village and in every factory they buy and sell salt, betel-nut, rice, straw, bamboos, fish, gunnies, ginger, sugar, tobacco, opium, and many other things . . . They forcibly take away the goods and commodities of the peasants, merchants etc., for a fourth part of their value, and by ways of violence and oppressions they oblige the peasants to give five rupees for goods which are worth but one rupee, and for the sake of five rupees they bind and disgrace a man who pays a hundred rupees in land-tax; and they allow not any authority to my servants.[6]

Mir Kasim eventually fled to Lucknow where he joined forces with the *nawab* of Awadh, who was at this time *vizier* of the empire and protector of the young Mughal emperor Shah Alam. A perhaps more significant battle than either Plassey and Panipat was then fought at Buxar in south-west Bihar in 1764, when a British force led by Hector Munro faced and defeated the combined armies of the two *nawab*s and what remained of the armies of the Mughal emperor. The British thereby acquired further territories in Awadh, and Bihar, and total control over Bengal, with the young emperor, Shah Alam, who was captured, becoming a pensioner under their control at Allahabad.

These highly fortuitous circumstances gave the East India Company unchallenged influence over the whole of north India at least until 1771, when the emperor was liberated and returned to his throne in Delhi by the army of Madhaji Scindia, a leading Maratha prince. At the same time, Scindia amassed forces that threatened Bombay and other adjacent British territories, leading to the first major direct confrontation between the Marathas and the British, the so-called 'First Maratha War'. Warren Hastings, the recently appointed governor of Bengal, decided to deal with this threat at source by sending a large army in a rearguard manoeuvre to capture Scindia's stronghold at Gwalior. Scindia subsequently capitulated and signed the treaty of Salbei with the British, in 1781, after which he confined his activities primarily to defending the emperor, with limited success, against a series of peasant uprisings led by the Sikhs, Jats, Rajputs, and others in the north. The capital succumbed again to a Rohilla force in 1789, and Emperor Shah Alam was captured and blinded.

East India Company forces defending Madras in the south in the late nineteenth century were often financed by the subsidiary alliance system – under which the British agreed to supply troops to support local rulers, to whom they were allied, in exchange for grants of revenue and tracts of land to pay for their upkeep. This system was a great strain on Indian states allied to the Company, such as Hyderabad and Arcot, which became heavily indebted. Increasingly, these territorial rulers became dependent on loans from the Company, and the support of bankers and financiers. In the case of Arcot, the *nawab* was especially dependent on loans offered by European merchants, to such an extent that when in 1776 Lord Piggot, the governor of Madras, proposed to deprive the *nawab* of Arcot of the territory of Tanjore, fearful creditors of the *nawab*, led by Paul Benfield, worried that they would lose their income, imprisoned the governor until he agreed to rescind the order. This was one of the more striking of the numerous instances of corruption and misrule, which ultimately led to the impeachment and trial of Warren Hastings in 1785. It was in the wake of this incident that a second regulating Act was passed, the East India Company Act of 1784, establishing a Board of Control in London to supervise the activities of the Company. An influential Scot, Henry Dundas, was one of the first members and subsequently became president of the Board of Control from 1793 to 1802, using his position to introduce a great many Scots into the Company's service. He was succeeded by his son, Robert.

The burdens of the subsidiary system were not merely sources of corruption – they caused the collapse of government finances and administration in the Native States that were allies of the British. So serious did their indebtedness become that revenues and supplies owed by territories effectively under British 'control' were often not forthcoming when needed, and garrisons of the Madras army frequently mutinied as a consequence. It was partly because of this that the British suffered a series of defeats at the hands of the highly disciplined and well-trained armies of their main rivals in the south: Haider Ali and his son Tipu Sultan, the rulers of Mysore. It was in order to meet this threat that Lord Richard Wellesley, on his appointment as governor-general in 1797, finally decided to end the subsidiary system in the south-east, and to dismember and take over the kingdoms of Arcot, Trichinopoly and Nellore. He achieved this by claiming that Tipu Sultan had the support of French advisers and mercenaries – for which there was indeed some evidence. In the general atmosphere of hysteria aroused by revolutionary France and Napoleon's recent successful invasion of Egypt, Wellesley was able to persuade the British crown to send government troops from England to reinforce the Company's sepoy mercenaries from England, and, in alliance with substantial forces of the *nizam* of Hyderabad, launched a third and final war with the kingdom of Mysore in 1799, culminating in Tipu's defeat at the battle of Srirangapatnam.

As a result of their contests with the British, the French could be said, indirectly, to have facilitated a further expansion of British control in India. There is no evidence, however, that Richard Wellesley personally shared the contemporary fear of the French, but rather used them, cynically, in order to put into effect a personal desire for aggrandisement and territorial expansion. In this 'imperial vision', Richard Wellesley differed significantly from his predecessors, and by carefully choosing his moment he managed, by the end of the century, to obtain control over all of southern India, as well as much of the north and east. But although Wellesley had a personal imperialist agenda, and was the first governor in India to formulate a coherent imperialist ideology to bolster British rule, the role of Indian merchants and allies of the British should not be forgotten. In the Mysore campaign and elsewhere in India, the consolidation of British rule was often aided financially and politically by Indian merchants. In 1759, for example, the British seized control of Surat, in western India, with the support of the Muslim nobility and local merchants. And on the west coast, the British took over Travancore state, from whence was sourced the bulk of the Company's pepper, with the intention of usurping the powers of the local Hindu princes and putting in place their own puppet ruler who would favour the influential local Moplah merchants with whom the Company traded (Nightingale 1970; Subramaniam, 1996). Indian merchants and commercial interests were thus crucial in the transition from British trade to dominion within the subcontinent.

As rulers, the British were despotic, not unlike the Mughals themselves, and where the subsidiary system failed to undermine native Indian states it was often the repeated demand for the payment of tributes by the East India Company that weakened them, as in the case of the kingdom of Benares (modern Varanasi) in the north of India, which became bankrupt and ultimately fell under British control in 1775. These factors combined to ensure that by the end of the century only the Marathas in the west and the Sikh kingdom of Ranjit Singh, in the north-west, remained to oppose them (Map 3). Neither represented a serious threat to British trade, or to British rule in the north, east, and south of India, but Wellesley was determined that the East India Company should be the paramount power. A massive campaign was therefore launched against the Marathas, soon after the defeat of Tipu Sultan, once again using the pretence that they were allies of the French, and that by defeating them Wellesley could save India from invasion by the armies of Napoleon. His evidence on this occasion however was far less credible, and the Company's directors back in London were worried by the governor-general's escalating military expenditure and the damage to trade resulting from continuous warfare. Wellesley was aided considerably, however, by the difficulties of communication with London: despatches, there and back, often took a year to complete their journey (longer with a little help). The Board of Control thus had little knowledge of his activities until they were almost a *fait accompli*. A large army of Company sepoys was assembled in the Deccan, led by Richard's brother, Colonel Arthur Wellesley, and was marched north to engage in a series of battles against the Maratha princes, themselves divided by conflict between Daulat Rao Scindia and Yeshwant Rao Holkar, the two leading princes. The pretext for intervention lay in an attack by Holkar's armies on Peshwa Baji Rao II near Poona in October 1802, who had soon after signed a treaty with the British at Bassein, and the occupation of territories of the *nizam* of Hyderabad by Ragujhi Bhonsle, the *raja* of Nagpur. A demand was made that the Maratha forces withdraw, and when they failed to do so, Wellesley marched north from Hyderabad in August 1803, defeating Maratha armies at Assaye and Argaon, and capturing the forts of Ahmadnagar, Burhanpur and Gawilgarh. This forced the *raja* of Nagpur to sign the Treaty of Deogaon, by which he agreed to reduce his armies, to commit no further acts of aggression against the Company or its traders, and to transfer large tracts of land, in reparation, to the Company's administration. Simultaneously, General Gerard Lake's army, marching westwards from Bengal, defeated the armies of Scindia and Holkar and took control of the imperial capital at Delhi.

The campaign against the Marathas was seen as a brilliant tactical achievement, a rapid deployment over vast distances enabling a Company force, only 55,000 in number under Arthur Wellesley's command, to defeat a combined

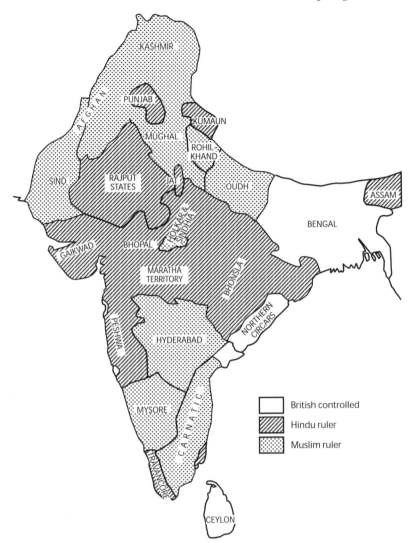

Map 3 India 1785: political control.

Maratha army nearly five times its strength (Cooper 2005). The crucial element in this success was the train of bullocks and bullock carts that supplied Wellesley's army all the way up from the Deccan to Gwalior and throughout the four-month campaign. These bullocks, together with money, food, horses, fodder and ammunition, were entirely supplied by Indian merchants. And it was Indian sepoys, led by British officers, who constituted the great majority of the foot soldiers. In many ways, therefore, the successful campaign against the Marathas at the turn of the century, crucial as it was in the extension of British power and influence, was as much an achievement of Indian mercenaries and merchants. These events, including the final defeat of the Marathas after they had already been undermined by the Afghans, really mark the beginning of British paramountcy in the subcontinent, giving them control over the south of India, over most of Bengal and Bihar, over large parts of western India, and over the capital at Delhi, including a wide swathe of surrounding territory. They still did not control central India, Awadh, Orissa, or the Sikh kingdom. And most of the Maratha princes in fact remained in control of large parts of their territories well into the first half of the nineteenth century. But by 1803 the British had effectively asserted their authority over the subcontinent. As with the acquisition of Bengal, Indian merchants played a crucial part in this feat of arms over the Marathas, and it was largely because of their alliances both with princes and merchants that the East India Company acquired most of their territories in India. It is this that has led some historians to conclude that it was Indians who acquired India for the British empire, rather than the British themselves.

3 Social and economic change in the early nineteenth century and the 'era of reform'

The infatuated Suttee, the murdered female infant, the perishing Pilgrim . . . the sick exposed by the Ganges, and the degraded Slave, present their cry to Britain; and shall not that cry be heard and reiterated from 'Dan to Beersheba' till the Senate and the Throne hear, and feel, and redress their wrongs? . . . May the Father of the fatherless and the Judge of the Widow, even 'God in his holy habitation,' incline those who hold in their hands the destinies of India to regard 'India's Cries to British Humanity.'

(J. Peggs, 1830)[1]

Though it is impossible for a thinking man not to feel the evils of political subjection and dependence on a foreign people, yet . . . we may be reconciled to the present state of things.

(Ram Mohan Roy, 1832)[2]

The second war with the Maratha empire between 1802 and 1803 effectively ended their power, and left the British East India Company with vast new responsibilities to deal with. To begin with, the Company had to develop an administrative structure to cope with the enormous tracts of land, formerly belonging to Mysore, the Marathas and the Mughals, that had fallen to their charge. Maintaining control was a formidable task, since the Company's military campaigns had left much of the country devastated and in a turbulent state. Small armies of defeated and disbanded cavalrymen and soldiers roamed the countryside raiding villages to provide themselves with an income, and there was considerable opposition to attempts by the Company to impose their rule. Opposition also continued amongst the defeated Maratha princes, and in 1818 a final attempt was made by Peshwa Baji Rao II and by Appa Sahib, the *raja* of Nagpur, to throw off British control. The *raja* of Nagpur even managed to incite a general uprising amongst the *adivasis* (or tribals) of the Satpura Hills in central India in his support, although this was eventually put down and Appa Sahib captured and executed. Following this incident further territory, the Narmada valley, was ceded to the Company's control.

In 1845 Governor-General Hardinge used the occasion of a succession dispute to march a large force into the Punjab and seize control of the Sikh kingdom ruled until 1839 by the formidable Ranjit Singh. Complete control of the Sikh kingdom was affected by the end of the second Anglo-Sikh war in 1849. The extent of the territories under the Company's formal control soon after is illustrated in Map 4. The East India Company now needed to stamp its authority upon these newly acquired territories. Since it was primarily a trading organisation, designed for quite different purposes, this required a wholesale reorganisation of the Company itself, one which was overseen by the British parliament in Westminster to which, as a corporation, the Company still remained answerable for the renewal of its charter.

The British government refused direct responsibility for the Indian territories, preferring that the East India Company continued operating as a lucrative chartered trading company, administering the Indian territories on their behalf whilst paying an annual tribute to the British crown for the privilege. In 1813, however,

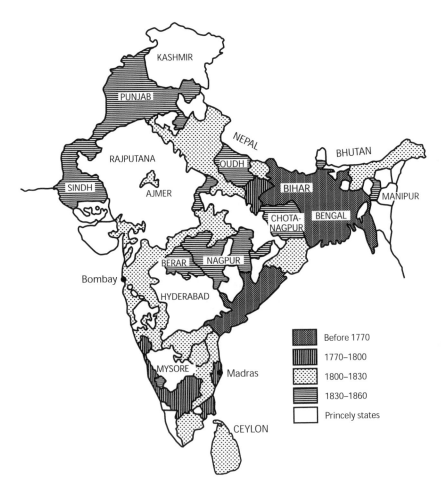

Map 4 The British penetration of India, 1750–1860.

the East India Company's trading monopoly had been revoked. By then space on Company ships was often leased out to private traders and many of the ships were themselves being leased from private merchants. The revocation was therefore something of a non-event, but after 1813 the number of private traders sailing east increased dramatically. In 1833, the Company's trading rights were finally withdrawn entirely by parliament, so diverting the Company's attention altogether into administration. The East India Company thereafter acted as a sort of export bank, policing trade and facilitating the exchange of finance required for private merchants to carry on their business in India. The business of territorial administration was a large and rapidly increasing responsibility, and it was one which the company's bureaucratic organisation was initially incapable of meeting in any satisfactory manner. The East India Company had neither the experience nor the personnel to carry out the task, and corruption was rife. Maladministration in the burgeoning colonial ports and in the recently occupied Mughal cities provoked unrest, with food shortages and rising unemployment leading to riots and looting on a number of occasions. On top of all this, there was a desperate need to increase revenue receipts as the Company was seriously in debt following successive campaigns against the Marathas. The attempt was therefore made to reform the bureaucratic structure of the East India Company, a development most often associated with the governor-generalship of Sir William Bentinck between 1828 and 1835, a period that contemporaries themselves described as an 'era of reform' (Rosselli 1974). Although primarily directed at the Company's administrative structure, the reforms coincided with a time of social and economic upheaval and had a huge and not always intended impact upon Indian society.

Bureaucracy, land, taxation and trade: the policies of 'reform' and their effects

The so-called 'era of reform' has been much misunderstood. What began as an overhaul of the bureaucratic structure of the East India Company was later interpreted by British and imperial historians as a period of change for the benefit of the Indians as much as the British. In practice, administrative reform was entirely undertaken for the convenience of the latter, and Indians only figured in it to the extent that they were needed to help institute a more efficient system of control. In justifying their policies to parliament, however, contemporaries often claimed extravagant benefits, both for the Company and for the wider society. Sir William Bentinck himself was especially inclined to do this, because he was an admirer of and profoundly influenced by Utilitarian thinkers active in Britain at this time. The changes actually instigated under William Bentinck's governor-generalship were in fact limited, the reform of the colonial administration having begun well before and occurring more often out of sheer necessity than from ideological motivations.

It was Warren Hastings who began the process of reforming the East India Company in the 1770s, and Sir Richard Wellesley who made the first attempt to train the Company's servants properly for the business of administration by setting up Fort William College in Calcutta at the end of the eighteenth century – soon after which the Company's directors set up a rival institute – Haileybury College in Oxford – for the same purpose. Until 1800 a great deal of private trading was carried on by Company servants who amassed private fortunes from peculation. After 1800 the Company's directors and governors in India began to take a much tougher line on this. They considerably increased the salaries of the Company's officials, but they insisted thereafter that officials attend only to the Company's business and engage no longer in private trade. Drunkenness, debauchery and general bad behaviour of one sort or another was suppressed, as was the widespread practice of marrying Indian women and taking Indian mistresses. This was the beginning of the social isolation of the British in India: up until 1800 they had been fairly well integrated into Indian society, albeit as a rather unsavoury element. The malpractices of Company officials were blamed in a self-righteous manner on the adoption of 'native practices' and after 1800 a determination was made to make this administration more honest, reliable, streamlined, and 'British'. The old divisions of office between writers, factors and merchants that used to exist in the East India Company were done away with and the administration was given a coherent hierarchy. These ideas of efficiency were a novelty. They were a product first of all of the rise of nationalism in the wake of the Napoleonic Wars, and a virulent strain of Protestant evangelism that began to emerge in Britain at this time (Bayly 1988, 1989). Colonialism, racism, the idea of the British as a chosen people, and other such self-righteous attitudes, all combined relatively rapidly to make this period one of striking contrast to eighteenth-century principles and beliefs. Needless to say they were to have an impact on Indian society as well.

A further reform carried out in the early nineteenth century more directly impacted on Indian society because it concerned the manner in which the Company managed the tax system, and in particular (since this was the states' principal source of income) the way it raised revenues from the peasantry. The Mughal tax system was very flexible – demands were fixed at a level considered reasonable and feasible to collect, but which varied on a year-to-year basis, depending on the quality of the season and the outturn of the harvest. The British tried to increase the tax yields by introducing a contractual system that allowed individuals use of their land subject to an annual payment of tax. The contracts did not strictly confer ownership of this land on Indians, but they did give them the right to continue to use this land in exchange for regular payments of revenue. Whilst the relationship between tax and land control under the Mughals was always subject to negotiation, the system the British tried to introduce was far more rigorous and bureaucratic, and often did not work. The permanent settlement of the revenues of Bengal in 1793 was their first attempt. The Bengal revenue system had already been subject to reform under the later Mughals, when many of the smaller *zamindaris* had been grouped together so as to streamline the collection of revenue. The British adopted this system of *zamindari* divisions and made it permanent, requiring those involved to sign a contract agreeing to pay a fixed amount per year. The effects of this settlement, masterminded by a British aristocrat, Governor-General Lord Cornwallis, can be seen to this day. It created a highly hierarchical social structure: transforming a variable and movable aristocratic class, subject to promotion and transfer and who might move from controlling one territory to another, into one with permanent power and control over specific tracts of land. The untrammelled power given to the *zamindars*, who themselves had little interest in the business of cultivation, created a semi-feudal agrarian situation and consigned cultivators to the status of unprotected tenants, impoverishing the state (Guha 1963). The permanent settlement was unsuccessful in other ways. The initial demands that were set by the British were often excessive, and a number of aristocrats who could not pay them were deprived of their lands in consequence. When they lost their rights, they lost them very often to merchants, who purchased the *zamindari* rights from them, thus encouraging a further commercialisation of the markets (*hats*) of rural Bengal. The scale of the revenue demands made by the East India Company also often meant that the rents levied from the peasantry had to be raised very sharply in the early part of the nineteenth century.

In the south, the British borrowed a revenue system from Tipu Sultan, which depended on collecting tax from individual cultivators – the so-called *ryotwari* system, a *ryot* being a revenue-paying peasant according to the Mughal system. This was widely adopted in the Madras presidency, in the former kingdom of Mysore (modern-day Karnataka) and in the area of modern Tamil Nadu, where it was already in common use. On some occasions, where the British found powerful local land controllers such as the *poligars* on the coast of Madras presidency, they did occasionally undertake permanent *zamindari* settlements. However, more often than not the *ryotwari* system was adopted. Thomas Munro, a lower-middle-class Glaswegian who joined the Company's service in the 1800s (and brother of Hector Munro, who defeated Tipu at Srirangapatnam) was the primary architect of this policy. Munro was a great advocate of peasant rights (perhaps as a consequence of his knowledge of what had happened to the crofters and peasant farmers of Scotland after the union with England) (Stein 1989). It is perhaps no coincidence that in these same areas of southern India, where the *ryotwari* system was instituted, agricultural growth has subsequently been more sustained – especially during the period of the 1970s during the technological revolution in Indian agriculture that has become known as the 'Green Revolution'.[3] In Gujarat and Maharashtra in the west of India, after the defeat of the Maratha empire, the British introduced a similar system. Here the motivation was partly political since by arranging a settlement with individual cultivators they were able to undermine the power of the Maratha princes, all of whom had placed family relatives and other loyalists in positions of direct control over large territories (Perlin 1978). The same policy was followed again in parts of the Punjab after the British annexation in 1840 – especially in the areas later opened up for cultivation by canal irrigation. Significantly, Gujarat and Punjab enjoyed higher rates of economic development in the later colonial period and still higher rates of growth since independence than the states of Bihar and Bengal.

In the north of India, and in the Narmada valley in central India, the British adopted the *malguzari* or *mahalwari* revenue system. A *malguzar* was a village landlord and a *mahal* was a village estate. This intermediary system was aimed neither at the big landlord (*zamindar* or *talukdar*) nor at the peasantry, but rather at the headman of a village, or group of small villages. A semblance of hierarchy was thereby maintained in rural areas whilst tending both to subvert the power of the rural aristocracy and to deny rights to ordinary tenants and cultivators. The prosperity of agriculture in this region over subsequent generations has foundered somewhere between the extremes of poverty seen in Bihar and the prosperity of places such as Gujarat and Punjab.

The British systems of land revenue collection had a number of effects. Access to land was given only to those who cultivated a specific plot recognised by the Company's officials and on which a price had been agreed. This meant the effective loss of rights to any group who were nomadic (for example, pastoralist groups such as the *Gujars*), who grazed their cattle on common lands that gradually disappeared (Pathak 1994; Chakravarty-Kaul 1996). It also resulted in the gradual but effective proletarianisation of all of the *adivasi* or tribal peoples of India who practised shifting forms of cultivation, often in the more hilly and isolated parts of the country. A third effect was to make land a scarce commodity. By surveying the land and minutely dividing up rights to it, the British tied cultivators to particular plots, while any land that was not directly cultivated was reserved for the government's use or auctioned off at a subsequent date. In forest areas the *adivasi* population was often expelled, and the land annexed as government property, so that the timber could be exploited commercially for the construction of ships, etc. Even uncultivated lands within the bounds of settled villages were placed under the control of a *zamindar*, or *malguzar*, or became the property of the state, rather than remaining as common lands or the property of the village community as a whole.

Prior to the nineteenth century India's population density was relatively low (total population numbers being less than 200 million) and scarcity of land was relatively unknown. The real wages of labour were higher and cultivators were valued by *zamindars*, who endeavoured to ensure that they were given no cause to move off and cultivate elsewhere (Mukhia 1985; Washbrook 1993). By claiming for itself all rights to land unoccupied, or thought to be unoccupied, and neatly dividing up the remainder, the East India Company created a situation in which the acquisition of land became increasingly difficult for the labouring classes. One effect of this was to dramatically reduce the real value of wages for labour. Nineteenth-century land revenue settlements that divided up all cultivated land, and restricted access to all forested, 'unoccupied' or uncultivated land meant that an abundant commodity was turned into a scarce resource, and labour surpluses became more commonplace. With this went impoverishment, and instability, to which increased family size and labour migration were often the only resort available to support family incomes (Bates 1994; Bates and Carter 1992). This often became an economic cycle with damaging long-term consequences.

The connection between poverty and population growth is a controversial one.

but it is widely accepted that the new systems of land administration increased immiseration and landlessness, and that they tended to solidify rural hierarchies and render them more rigid (Dirks 1992; Ludden 1985, 1994; Bates 1988, 1992). All of this was often carried on in the name of 'liberating' Indians from former 'feudal' associations – officials believing that in India they found parallels to medieval Europe. The new land revenue settlements were often described as offering a 'gift of proprietary rights' to Indians and the freedom to sell their labour in ways that had never been possible before. But this usually meant merely an invitation to pay more tax, or to lose the family land and starve. In practice the British simply reorganised labour power and redirected it into equally if not more exploitative social and productive arrangements (Prakash 1990). The principal victims were the lower castes, tenant farmers, nomadic groups and, above all, the *adivasis* or tribals who lost their land entirely and all rights to it. Lands where formerly they had hunted, fished and cultivated were now either reserved for logging by the government or auctioned off to Hindu settlers, who then cleared and used it for their own purposes. These policies resulted in accelerated deforestation, and the beginnings of a dramatic reshaping of the Indian landscape and natural environment (Gadgil and Guha 1992). The consequences further included the decline of traditional irrigation systems, as village lands were parcelled up into separate revenue plots (for example, in the Godaveri and Krishna river deltas), and sometimes the sale of these plots to outsiders, making the co-operation required to maintain large-scale irrigation works more difficult to achieve. Over-taxation of irrigated lands also played a part in this decline, and in the Cauvery delta large-scale irrigation works had to be taken over by the British in the 1820s and managed directly (Ludden 1985; Hardiman 1996).

The effects of colonial land policies were gradual, since the early revenue settlements took place over a period of 30 or 40 years, whilst some parts of India such as the Central Provinces did not come within the British jurisdiction until the second part of the nineteenth century. In many cases *adivasis* were rounded up and physically thrown off the land, and were forced to become migrant labourers; sometimes they resorted to arms, and there are numerous instances of uprisings in *adivasi* areas throughout the colonial period – very often over this issue. The most spectacular of the uprisings associated with British land policies was that of the Santhals in Chota Nagpur in Bihar in 1855, described in Ranajit Guha's *Elementary Aspects of Peasant Insurgency* (1983). Guha sets out a particular theory concerning the Santhal insurrection, arguing that they often found common cause with settled peasant cultivators against the Company and its officials (although there is contrary evidence that the Santhal insurrection was often as much directed against Hindu settlers as against the British). There were similar uprisings amongst the Gond *adivasis* living in central India, the Hos in Bihar, and amongst the Bhils in western India. The British even set up special Bhil police corps to put down Bhil uprisings, and the raids from Bhil areas into the adjacent plains, on the grounds that the Bhils were a habitually lawless group requiring a permanent force to deal with them. This was typical of the misunderstandings between Company officials and Indian society at this time (Yang 1985), since the

Bhils believed that they were merely continuing tribute-collecting traditions in dominion territories, an activity always tolerated by former Mughal officials (Skaria 1999).

The East India Company and its officials during the early years of their governance really had very little idea of how Indian society worked, of how people lived, or the basis of their economy, and the Company's attempts to impose some sort of order, primarily for the purposes of taxing it in a more efficient manner, were therefore often highly destructive. Their blunders exacerbated the problems of an already depressed economy. There were other reasons as well, of course. There was a slump in trade at the turn of the century because of the Napoleonic Wars, and soon after the phenomenon of British industrialisation began and British manufacturers started to produce imitations of Indian cotton piece goods, causing the demand for Indian manufactures to fall. Since, initially at least, these manufactured goods were made using raw cotton from the United States there was no concomitant demand for raw cotton from India. In the long run, as these British-made goods were exported in increasing quantities to India, the indigenous Indian cotton handicraft industry was undermined (Charlesworth 1982; Bayly 1983; Habib 1985). Indian taxes began to be used to pay for the goods that were being exported, as well as to pay the salaries of East India Company officials. The boatloads of silver bullion formerly brought to the subcontinent ceased. Deindustrialisation, over-taxation, and deflation of the monetary system together produced one of the longest depressions in Indian history, and where one estimate had put India as having 25 per cent of the world's manufacturing in the mid-eighteenth century, by the mid-nineteenth it had fallen to a mere fraction of this (Bairoch 1982).

The economic outlook in early nineteenth-century India was fortunately not entirely bleak. The reduction of the Company's monopoly in 1813 encouraged Indian enterprise, and some Indian merchants, hard hit in other ways, flourished in the 1820s. For example, Dwarkanath Tagore became a large investor in indigo, setting up plantations in Bengal to meet the demand from European markets. He also championed the anti-slavery cause and was given the freedom of the city of Edinburgh for his services. Unfortunately, the ending of the Company's monopoly caused a flood of private investment into indigo, leading to over-production and a slump in that particular market (Kling 1966). The decade ended in a flurry of bankruptcies. The development of what became known as the two-tier credit system subsequently emerged. Increasingly Indian bankers and merchants, who had been of such importance to the British East India trade in the eighteenth century, were excluded from more profitable enterprises after about 1830, and instead began pouring their money into rural moneylending. This was a growth area due to the recession and pressure of revenue demands, and one of the few markets in which Indian merchants were not subject to discrimination – at least not until later in the nineteenth century when colonial officials began to blame them for the stagnation affecting many parts of the rural economy. A further blow was struck against the Indian bankers in 1835 with the imposition of a uniform currency throughout the Company's territories, resulting in the loss of their money-changing business and mint privileges. This change-over was especially hard for those who had large reserves in local currencies rather than in the Company rupee, which was in scarce supply.

Apart from racial discrimination, government policies were often deliberately biased against Indian merchants. For example, when the construction of the Indian railways began in the 1840s, parliament in London agreed to underwrite any investment made by a British entrepreneur. Indian merchants, however, were not guaranteed the same sort of protection, thereby effectively excluding them. There are many similar examples. However, whilst British demand for Indian manufactured goods declined, the demand for commodities and agricultural produce slowly developed. European firms such as Andrew Yule & Co., and the Raleigh Brothers, began to set up depots in central India for the shipment of raw produce such as wheat and cotton. This would become one of the principal money earners in rural India by the late nineteenth century. Another way of generating money was through the production of opium for export to the East. These exports helped balance the East India Company's trading account with China. The opium plantations were largely set up and run by the East India Company itself in central India, and the smuggling of opium enabled the East India Company to fund the purchase and export of tea, silks and glazed pottery to the UK, much as the taxes paid by Indian peasants financed the export trade from India (Trocki 1999; Furber 1948; Spence 1999). This was to become the essence of India's role in financing the empire later on, her trade surpluses with countries other than Britain counterbalancing British trade deficits elsewhere through the export of vast quantities of agricultural products and raw materials.

Evangelical and Utilitarian influences

Utilitarianism was an influential system of thought in Britain in the early nineteenth century. Developed by Jeremy Bentham, one of its chief exponents was James Mill, author of the highly prejudiced, influential and misunderstood *History of India*, published in 1817. Mill was offered a post with the East India Company (as was his son later on, the more famous James Stuart Mill), becoming examiner of correspondence in 1830 (Majeed 1992). Inevitably Utilitarianism became an influence in the administration of India. The philosophy purported to describe methods for the administration of society in the absence of monarchic rule. In pre-modern times, society had been structured by virtue of divine right and rigid inheritance laws. With the development of a bureaucratic state in the early nineteenth century, the Utilitarians articulated principles of government founded upon 'the greatest good of the greatest number' (Stokes 1959). However, when Utilitarian thinking was applied to India, the greatest good of the greatest number was always directed at Englishmen rather than Indians, so that most of the social and economic policies introduced during this period were profoundly damaging for the latter. Evangelicals, particularly missionaries, also began to arrive in increasing numbers after 1813 when parliament first authorised their activities, and there developed an alliance between the Utilitarians and the evangelicals in India, this having a profound impact. Both groups wished to change the administration of India dramatically – the Utilitarians in order to streamline and 'modernise' it, as they thought; the evangelicals wanting to undermine traditional Hindu practices, which they regarded as heathen, barbaric, and corrupt.

The evangelicals and Utilitarians affected social development in five main areas in the early nineteenth century. The first area of change was the introduction of a system of Western-style education. The second was the implementation of legislation designed to prevent child marriages and to permit widow remarriage (which was customarily forbidden). Legislation was also introduced to ban female infanticide and to police and regulate all those groups believed to practise it. Fourth, attempts were made to ban 'human sacrifice'. And finally attempts were made to ban *sati*, the self-immolation of widows. In most of these areas, the British were chasing red herrings. To begin with there is absolutely no evidence that human sacrifice ever took place in nineteenth-century India. Rumours of human sacrifice abounded, particularly after the British began to react to them and to launch investigations. But the rumours were nearly always purveyed by those who wished to discredit political rivals, so that *zamindars* or *adivasi* chiefs were often to be found alleging that their neighbours practised it. Upon visiting the shrines where these sacrifices supposedly took place, the British never found human bones or any evidence of such activities. However, the allegation of human sacrifice could be used to legitimate the sending of an expeditionary force, and Company officials were always willing to believe such stories whenever it was to their political advantage.[4]

On the matter of female infanticide, undoubtedly there was a large discrepancy between male and female numbers in the population, as there is today. This was probably due largely to neglect, which was, and is, related to the financial costs of marrying female children in a patrilocal system where dowry payments are customary. This made boy children an asset and girl children a burden. The British, however, believed that the killing of female offspring was a specific custom in certain communities.[5] They therefore introduced legislation requiring all births among specified groups to be registered. The parents of Rajput children in north India (who the British considered particularly guilty) had to report to police stations once a year with their children until they reached the age of 11, or else to provide a death certificate demonstrating the cause of death. This was a highly discriminatory policy that cannot be shown to have achieved anything, and British interference in Rajput society – particularly in matters concerning land and property rights – served to exacerbate the problem (Kasturi 2002). As regards the practice of *sati*, some British officials believed that women who took their lives by throwing themselves on the funeral pyres of their husbands were being coerced to do so: a rather different view of *sati* than that which had prevailed before, which reflected the increasingly paternalist attitudes of the time (Major 2006). Initially officers were ordered not to intervene, provided the immolation was voluntary and seen to be done for reasons of personal and religious devotion. Ultimately the practice was banned altogether by an enactment in 1829.

Sati was extremely rare, but, as with infanticide and so-called 'human sacrifice', rumours abounded once it was picked up by evangelical missionaries as an example of the evils of Hinduism. The missionaries printed pamphlets telling of these horrors, which they sold to raise money for their activities abroad, a prominent example being John Peggs, whose wildly imaginative pamphleteering on the subject of the sacrificial victims, whom he alleged were placed under the wheels of the chariot of the god Jagannath during its annual Ratha Yatra (chariot procession) around the temple complex at Puri, is typical of the genre (and brought the word 'juggernaut' into the English language):

> The joy and shouts of the crowd on the first movement of the cars, the creaking sound of the wheels . . . the clatter of hundreds of harsh sounding instruments, and the general appearance of so immense a moving mass of human beings, produce . . . an impressive, astounding, and somewhat picturesque effect, while the novelty of the scene lasts; though *the contemplation cannot fail of exciting the strongest sensations of pain and disgust in the mind of every Christian spectator.*[6]
>
> (Peggs 1830: 251; italics in original)

Having aroused public interest, such issues became an object of concern for colonial officials as well. It should be noted that the treatment of Indians in the matter of suicide was not unique – in England too it was debated at this time whether Church prescriptions against suicides should be enshrined in civil law. If anything, the very rare occurrences of *sati* increased in India after the introduction of legislation to ban it, because of the publicity it had been given (Mani 1985, 1998). This implies that British policy had rather the reverse effect to what was intended, if indeed social welfare was the primary purpose.

The paradoxical effects of the legislation on *sati* have been highlighted by Lata Mani (1985), who argues that these measures were less to do with the reform of Indian society than with the establishment of a discourse and a set of precedents by which Indian custom might be integrated into a newly Anglicised system of law. British-style courts were being introduced at this time, along with a system that combined English common law with Hindu and Muslim jurisprudence, providing a legislative basis for the prosecution of Indians (Singha 1998). For commercial reasons the British law of contract had already been adopted. The controversial area was private law, as a desire to intervene, to 'civilise' the native according to the views of evangelicals, clashed with a concern not to upset local customs for fear of causing political unrest (Washbrook 1981; Derrett 1957, 1968). What most of these debates concerned, therefore, was not the fate of female babies or of widows but the need to develop a model of Indian society and an appropriate set of legal precedents that could be effectively operated by the English courts. To this effect, Lata Mani points out that not one interview was ever conducted with a woman who had attempted to commit *sati*, or was considering it. There were absolutely no formal investigations into the effectiveness of the legislation either. Most of the consultations were conducted by British officials with learned, Brahmin scholars. Their purpose was to ascertain the position of Hindu law on these issues. They eventually banned *sati* after much prevarication, not because they had found some great evil that they decided to extirpate but because they were persuaded by learned *pandits* at Varanasi and scholars such as Ram Mohan Roy that there was nothing in the Vedas that specifically sanctioned the practice, and that it was neither formally approved by Hindu law nor by any other prescription in the Vedas of any sort. Since Hinduism is not a hierarchical or especially scriptural faith the *pandits* of Varanasi, just one of many great pilgrimage centres, had no special authority to rule in such matters. They nonetheless became the legitimation for a great variety of British legislative policies, enhancing thereby north Indian Brahminical influence in the daily life of Hindus, and simultaneously misrepresenting and devaluing indigenous ideas of sovereignty and authority (Raheja 1988; Cohn 1988, 1996).

Similar, well-intentioned but instrumental and self-serving motivations applied in the system of education that was sponsored by the East India Company in the nineteenth century. There were numerous universities and colleges patronised by Hindu and Mughal rulers before the British colonial period. Many of them subsequently fell on hard times, which was one of the reasons why the court of directors issued a minute in 1813 ordering that £10,000 a year should be set apart and applied to 'the revival and improvement of literature and the encouragement of the learned natives of India'. Early colonial administrators and scholars, respected old school orientalists in a 'pre-Saidian' sense (Said 1978), such as Thomas Munro, Mountstuart Elphinstone, James Grant, John Malcolm and William Jones, who admired and wished to learn from Indian culture, actively supported the policy of investing in existing Indian educational institutions. However, after the 1830s, Utilitarians and evangelicals began to take over the direction of educational policy, particularly Thomas Babington Macaulay and Charles Trevelyan. Trevelyan's views on education were clearly directed towards the conversion of Hindus to Anglicanism. The same approach was also adhered to by William Bentinck, the governor-general, who wrote:

> the first and primary object of my heart is the benefit of the Hindus. I know nothing so important to the improvement of their future condition as the establishment of a purer morality whatever their belief, and a more just conception of the will of God. The first step to this better understanding will be dissociation of religious belief and practice from blood and murder. They will then, when no longer under this brutalising excitement, view with more calmness, acknowledged truths.[7]

There was an evident strange synergy between imperialism and cultural superiority and evangelical religious beliefs or fundamentalism. William Wilberforce thought that the main purpose of educational reform would be to enable the British to 'strike our roots into the soil by the gradual introduction and establishment of our own principles and opinions, of our laws, institutions and manners, above all as the source of every other improvement of our religion and our morals'.[8] They were altruistic in the sense that they believed that educating Indians as to the nature of Anglican belief would be a benefit to them. Thomas Babington Macaulay had a rather more ignorant and prejudiced view. He thought that the Indians should be educated in English manners and subjects simply because the latter were superior. In his famous minute on education of 1835, he wrote as follows:

> I have no knowledge of either Sanscrit or Arabic. But I have done what I could to form a correct estimate of their value. I have read translations of the most celebrated Arabic and Sanscrit works. I have conversed both here and at home with men distinguished by their proficiency in the Eastern tongues. I am quite ready to take the oriental learning at the valuation of the orientalists themselves. I have never found one among them who could deny that a single shelf of a good European library was worth the whole native literature of India and Arabia. The intrinsic superiority of Western literature is, indeed, fully admitted by those members of the Committee who support the oriental plan of education. . . . In one point I fully agree with the gentlemen to whose general views I am opposed. I feel with them, that it is impossible for us, with our limited means, to attempt to educate the body of the people. We must at present do our best to form a class who may be interpreters between us and the millions whom we govern; a class of persons, Indian in blood and colour, but English in taste, in opinions and in intellect.[9]

Vernacular education merely 'delayed the natural death of expiring errors' in Macaulay's view. It was therefore a highly elitist and English-oriented system that was proposed and put in its place, and almost every one of those who graduated was immediately drafted into the colonial service to help in the task of administering the empire. Of course, in the long term the policy rather backfired, as this elite was one of the first groups to become critical of the imperial system and to become systematically disloyal at the beginning of the twentieth century. But in the early nineteenth century it was clearly very advantageous for the East India Company to develop a Utilitarian bias in their education policy, one which facilitated the task of governing the vast new territories that had come under their control.

At the same time, a further administrative reform introduced in the early nineteenth century was the establishment of examinations for entry to the civil service. All examinations for elite positions were held in London, so that no Indians could sit for them. Indians could only take part in examinations for lower, subordinate positions in the administration, held in India, and still had to have passed through an elite colonial institution before they could sit for them. One Bengali writer thus characterised the colonial administration of the 1840s as 'despotism tempered by examinations'.

Paradoxical outcomes

In summary, the 'reforms' adopted by the East India Company in the early nineteenth century were not general but specific. They seem to have been largely aimed at the improvement of British administration rather than of India, but in many respects the period was one of unremitting disaster. The land tax policies provoked successive rebellions and uprisings, food shortages, grain riots and, of course, insurrections amongst the *adivasis* in particular. The period furthermore saw a prolonged and continuing economic depression leading to widespread bankruptcy and failures among both Indian merchants and rural landowners. Politically the policies were a failure too. They did not pacify or settle the country-side at all, but rather provoked unrest, and disturbances, culminating, ultimately, in the Great Uprising of 1857. Culturally and socially, the policies adopted by the Company in this period were paradoxical, and often resulted in exactly the opposite of what might have been intended. By introducing a Western education system, the British Westernised a certain elite, but also encouraged a renaissance in Bengal amongst intellectuals who began to apply themselves to the revival of Indian subjects, particularly Bengali literature that flourished in this period (Kopf 1969). Over the vast bulk of the population the combination of the alienating effects of colonial rule, the undermining of traditional religion and authority, and economic depression, was to result in unrest of one sort or another, and reactionary movements of religious revivalism became widespread. Such movements were still more prominent in the later nineteenth century, but many of them began at this time. The Brahmo Samaj was thus formed in Bengal in the late 1820s by Ram Mohan Roy, later to become an all-India movement in the 1860s under the leadership of Keshub Chandra Sen. This elite reformist movement was designed to modernise Hinduism and transform it into a monotheistic cult in order to present some sort of appeal to educated Calcuttans who were turning towards Christianity. In East Bengal there grew up a popular militant revivalist cult, the Fairazi movement, which provoked physical attacks against colonial administrators and bureaucrats, as well as landlords (Metcalf 1982). There was therefore religious revivalism at both the elite and mass levels. An egalitarian strain of Hinduism, Vaishnavism, involving the worship of Vishnu as opposed to Shiva or other gods, also flourished. Vaishnavism became particularly widespread in the early nineteenth century, and this is again partly related to the impact of colonialism. In the early nineteenth century, caste tensions developed as well, arising from preferential treatment accorded by the British to Kayasths and Brahmins, castes known as the '*bhadralok*' in Bengal, both in educational opportunities and employment in the colonial administration. This meant that there was often a growth in conflict and competition between higher and lower castes, particularly in urban areas.

The extent of change should not be exaggerated. There were never more than a few hundred colonial civil servants in India. The Mughal emperor remained the sovereign, albeit nominally, and his image still appeared on the coins minted by the East India Company's treasuries. It may be conjectured that one of the factors that led to the 1857 uprising was precisely this piecemeal gradual 'revolution' introducing administrative reforms in a manner that to most local people was utterly confusing and irrational. Occasionally the British would employ local elites; at other times they would simply undermine and discard them. Occasionally they would defer to Hindu law; at other times they would manipulate it to their own ends. In this way the East India Company seemed to be subverting, undermining and challenging all legitimate forms of authority without putting anything recognisable in its place. This, it might be argued, is one of the longer term effects of this period, and one of the reasons why there was such profound and continuing religious and social unrest, as well as political opposition to colonial rule, despite the best efforts of the Company's administration.

4 Peasant resistance, rebellion and the uprising of 1857

Asked if the people of Oudh [Awadh] were desirous of being placed under British rule, the Jemmadar replied: 'Miserable as we are, of all miseries keep us from that . . . the name of Oude and the honour of our nation would be at an end.'

(Indian Cavalry Officer, 1825)[1]

Bas ki fa'ale mayrid hai aaj,	Today every British soldier
Har silah-shur Englistan ka	Thinks himself an absolute potentate
Ghar se bazaar ko nikalate hue,	Between the house and the bazaar
Zahara hota hai aab insan ka	Terror reigns over the people
Chowk jisko kahain wo maqtal hai,	The City square is an execution ground
Ghar bana hai namunan zindan ka	Home is a ghost of itself
Shahar-e Dilli ka zarra-zarra-e khak,	Delhi's very dust seems to cry out
Tashna-e khun hai har Musalaman ka	For the blood of the Muslims

(Ghalib, 1857)[2]

On land in India as in other parts of the empire, the British had to face continual uprisings of one sort or another, and these were especially commonplace in India in the early nineteenth century. The so-called Pax Britannica in India was thus very much a myth; indeed it was a myth in all parts of the empire and probably only applicable at sea where British naval power was pre-eminent. It is for this reason that one historian has described the events of 1857 as 'unique only in their scale' (Bayly 1988). The uprising of that year began with a mutiny amongst Indian sepoys in regiments of the East India Company's Bengal army based in the plains of north India. It was made worse by the incompetence of those in command, and the fact that no wholly British-recruited regiments were available in north India to restore order. They had been despatched to fight on the north-west frontier in support of the Afghanis against the Persians in their struggle for control of the principality of Herat, under the threat of Russian intervention. The uprising spread outwards from Meerut to become a widespread civil and urban insurrection, affecting all of the towns, villages and cities of north India. The rule of the East India Company was only restored after a bloody nine-month campaign, spearheaded by Sikh troops recruited from the Punjab and reinforcements sent up the Ganges from Calcutta. Unravelling exactly what happened, and why, has been complicated by partisan accounts on both sides. Contemporary and later British historians have sought to minimise the Company's responsibility, whilst Indian historians have tended to depict the events of that year as in some sense an anticipation of the Indian nationalist movement that later on was successfully to challenge colonial rule in the early twentieth century. In both versions of events, the exceptionality of 1857 and its leaders is emphasised, and the struggles of ordinary Indians before, during and after that year have been neglected.

Indian resistance movements in the early nineteenth century

After the final defeat of the Marathas in 1818, the authority of the East India Company in the newly ceded and conquered territories in central and northern India was challenged on many fronts. *Dacoity*, or banditry was endemic, of which the so-called thugs were the most notorious example. The word 'thug' is of Indian origin, *thagi* meaning 'to deceive'. Although terms like it could be found in generic use in previous periods, 'thag' was first used as a specific category by a British district officer named William Sleeman, in application to a variety of groups of marauding bandits in central India in the 1820s. The suppression of the thugs thereafter became part of the great civilising mission of the British in India, along with the abolition of *sati*, infanticide, human sacrifice, and other supposed social evils. Work on these fronts was faithfully reported to the Board of Control in London and the annual *Statement Exhibiting on Moral and Material Progress and Condition of India* from 1859 onwards. Sleeman described 'thuggee' as a religiously inspired criminal conspiracy, the bandits supposedly driven to sacrifice the blood of humans to propitiate the Hindu goddess Kali. They also robbed their victims. Kali was a popular Hindu goddess in eastern India in particular, although shrines dedicated to her can be found in other parts of India, including the city of Nagpur in western central India. If Kali really was enjoining 'thugs' to sacrifice humans to satisfy her blood lust, then a large proportion of the population of eastern India should have been thugs, for Kali was no rarity but simply one of the many incarnations of the god Shiva, worshipped by a great many Hindus.

The thuggee problem was initially 'discovered' in the Narmada valley in central India in the 1820s, in the territories seized by the East India Company from the *rajas* of Nagpur, Bhopal and Indore in 1818. It was alleged to extend into neighbouring Bundelkhand and beyond. The fact that the so-called thugs made a point of targeting off-duty Company sepoys, and shared their booty with local Maratha and Muslim *zamindars* in the Vindhyan hills bordering the Narmada valley, suggests that this was not simply lawlessness but an extension of Maratha-style guerrilla warfare, as practised against the Mughals (Gordon 1969, 1993). It may even have been connected indirectly with the lucrative underground trade in opium produced in the Maratha states of Scindia and Holkar in Malwa and exported to China via Bombay, which the East India Company had long endeavoured to suppress in favour of its own trade and opium sources in Bengal (Farooqui 1998). It was therefore as much a strategic as a criminal threat to the Company's interests. Soon William Sleeman was describing the thugs as not simply a local problem but as an India-wide secret sect, with its own covert signs, language (Ramasi) and rituals (Sleeman 1836):

> While I was in civil charge of the district of Nursingpoor, in the valley of the Nerbudda, in the years 1822, 1823, and 1824, no ordinary robbery or theft could be committed without my becoming acquainted with it . . .; and if any man had then told me that a gang of assassins by profession resided in the village of Kundelee, not four hundred yards from my court, and that the extensive groves of the village of Mundesur, only one stage from me on the road to Saugor and Bhopal, was one of the greatest bhils, or places of murder, in all India; that large gangs from Hindostan and the Dukhun used to rendezvous in these groves . . . and carry on their dreadful trade all along the lines of road that pass by and branch off from them, with the knowledge and connivance of the two landholders by whose ancestors these groves had been planted, I should have thought him a fool or a madman, and yet nothing could have been more true; the bodies of a hundred travellers lie buried in and among the groves of Mundesur, and a gang of assassins lived in and about the village of Kundelee, while I was magistrate of the district, and extended their depredations to the cities of Poona and Hyderabad.[3]

Other local officers were sceptical, but after the subject was taken up by the British press, Sleeman was appointed special agent by the governor-general, heading a 'Thuggee & Dacoity Department' whose brief was to suppress the conspiracy. The word 'thug' entered into the English language, and spawned in Britain an entire genre of superstitious, orientalist, but highly popular adventure writing, such as Meadows Taylor's novel *Confessions of a Thug* (1839), which continues in fashion to the present day (van Woerkens 2002). The importance of this tale of successful local ambition, however, is the very slender evidential base upon which the whole enterprise was launched. Only by granting immunity from prosecution to so-called 'approvers', who accused others to save themselves from a sentence of death, and whose word was deemed by a special Act sufficient in itself to prosecute, was Sleeman able to gather any evidence from witnesses to present to the special jury-less courts set up to handle these cases. Even then the same few 'approvers' had often to be used over and over again. Between 1831 and 1837 no fewer than 3,266 'thugs' were captured, of whom 412 were hanged, 483 gave evidence for the state, and the remainder were transported or imprisoned for life (Figure 3). This apparently solved the problem, as little more was heard of thuggee after Sleeman's transfer to the post of resident at Gwalior in 1843. Nonetheless, the existence of a community of 'thugs' remained an acknowledged fact in the colonial cataloguing of the castes and tribes of central India in 1916

Figure 3 Thugs in Aurangabad jail, 1869 (by A. de Neuville from a photograph by M. Grandier). © M.D. Carter.

(the only source being Sleeman's accounts, which were paraphrased at length), and the 'Thuggee & Dacoity Department' (later to become India's Criminal Investigation Department) continued to pursue bandits of one sort or another until the end of the century.[4]

Lack of information was a common problem for the Indian police force, although opinions differ as to how far the Company succeeded in overcoming it (Bayly 1997). Commencing in the late eighteenth century, the appointment of the local village *daroga*, or constable, and watchmen, was nominally at least taken out of the hands of the *zamindars* or the village community, and brought under the control of the East India Company's district magistrates or collectors (often the same person). A district superintendent and a provincial chief superintendent were appointed so that the police force was transformed, as in Ireland (from where the model was borrowed), into effectively an army of occupation (Chatterji 1981; Arnold 1986). The police enjoyed little co-operation from the local population and were often the last to know if there was trouble brewing and who or what might be responsible for it. The problem of 'thuggee', identified, for what it was worth, by William Sleeman, was thus probably only the tip of an iceberg of banditry, crime and other forms of resistance to the Company's authority.

The thug phenomenon was paralleled by another and more serious law and order problem in the early nineteenth century, which was similar in causation: the *pindaris*. They were bandits who raided whole villages on horseback, principally in the newly ceded territories in central and northern India (Anon. 1818; Ghosh 1966). The *pindaris* were mostly unemployed mercenary cavalrymen who had served in the armies of the Maratha princes and others, before being disbanded in 1818. The threat that they posed was so considerable that an entire sepoy army had to be sent to suppress them.

The thugs and the *pindaris* occupied a great deal of British military manpower, but there were numerous other uprisings in the same period to occupy them, many in *adivasi* or tribal areas. For example, in the 1820s a succession of revolts occurred amongst the Bhil tribes in Gujarat, and amongst the Kol in Bihar between 1829 and 1833. Most serious of all was a revolt by the Santhals in 1855, just two years before the uprising of 1857, following which more than 10,000 tribals were killed in British reprisals in an attempt to pacify the territory (Guha 1983a). Nomadic and 'wandering' communities had good cause to resent the British, by whom they had been systematically persecuted. Thus when Tatya Tope fled south with his army from Kanpur towards the end of 1857 it was not surprising that Gond tribals in central India rose up in support of the rebels. In the early nineteenth century huge areas of grazing lands around Delhi, used by the Gujars, Rangars and Bhattis were cleared and given by the British to Jat peasant farmers to cultivate. These communities were therefore amongst the first to resort to arson and banditry as soon as British control collapsed in 1857. They all had one thing in common, being in one way or another losers in the land revenue settlements of the early nineteenth century. The Gujars and Bhattis lost land because the British did not recognise pastoralists to have proprietary right of access or occupancy. Tribals, who practised shifting forms of cultivation, were also frequently denied rights to the land and expelled from large areas of forest taken over by the government. It can be conjectured that many so-called thugs may have been Gond *adivasis* from the highlands of central India who had been forced out of the forests in which they had traditionally hunted and foraged. From a life of banditry and petty thieving, it was but a small step to join in open rebellion.

Jat and Rajput peasants, being settled cultivators, were more often beneficiaries of the land revenue settlements in the north of India, but they were by no means cohesive communities and some did not benefit at all. Those groups who became involved in insurrection in 1857 did so often as a means of reclaiming land that they thought had been unjustly apportioned to another group through the East India Company's land settlements (Stokes 1978). Others sought to redress minor grievances over taxation, water rates or the loss of smaller plots of land.

Uprisings of more substantial rural elites, as well as of peasants, occurred in the first half of the nineteenth century. The Bundela Rajputs, for example, were relatively prosperous landowners in central India who rebelled in 1842 in reaction to tax increases and oppressive court proceedings that had deprived some of them of land. The mere arrival of a British land survey team, whose task was to measure the fields and decide how much tax should be paid, could provoke a riot, as occurred in Khandesh in 1852. There were also violent outbreaks among the peasantry on the Malabar coast, where Muslim Mappila tenants were almost continuously in revolt against Hindu landlords appointed by the British.

Finally, in urban areas, unrest was often communal, characterised by the rioting of unemployed Muslim artisans against the Hindu moneylenders who were prospering under colonial rule. The replacement of the law officers of the old Mughal cities (such as the *kotwal*, *qazi*, and *mufti*) by brusque colonial officials added further to the prevailing sense of unease. Dissent and unrest were therefore widespread during the early part of the nineteenth century, but the inadequate intelligence of the East India Company meant that the seriousness of this opposition was not appreciated until events overtook them. When the general insurrection occurred in 1857, the company was therefore taken completely by surprise. The sudden collapse of British power merely provided the opportunity for many of these dissenting groups to rise up at the same time. This was what was unique about 1857.

The general causes of insurrection in 1857

In order to ensure the renewal of its charter, the East India Company worked hard to create the impression that the early nineteenth century was a period of slow but progressive improvement for India, but the truth was far removed from this. It was in reality a time of radical experimentation and desperate contingency in the development of a British system of government, which created widespread resentment. Apart from the administrative reforms described in the previous chapters, a host of other petty interventions by the Company's officials, such as the rounding up and incarceration of prostitutes whenever there was an outbreak of venereal disease among the troops, had promoted disaffection (Ballhatchet 1957, 1980). One of the most widespread grievances concerned the increase in land tax, imposed in all of the newly ceded and conquered territories. This might have been bearable at a time of agricultural prosperity, but the early nineteenth century was a period of profound economic depression. British methods of collecting these taxes were also unpopular, involving as they did the introduction of a European system of courts whereby defaulters were arraigned before a magistrate and summarily deprived of their lands for failing to meet revenue payments. Such measures were novel, confusing, and illegitimate in the eyes of many Indians. The courts also greatly increased the powers of the *sahukar* or *bania* moneylenders to whom many were indebted – a further cause of resentment (Hardiman 1996). Most large land controllers, and many smaller ones at this time, had acquired their positions because they were aristocrats or *ulema* (Muslim scholars), the educated elite who ruled the Mughal empire, and had been appointed by the emperor or one of his governors or *deshmukhs*. But in the territories under Company rule, their authority was superseded by lawcourts, presided over by men in black frockcoats and trousers: the British, who did not sit in judgement by right of descent, as aristocrats, or as *kazis* or *pandits*. They occupied posts in court because they had completed an examination in London and had been appointed to the East India Company's Indian civil service. To many Indians this was a strange way to govern a country. Above all, the decisions of the courts were resented because they were final. Tax collection had always been a matter for negotiation under the Mughals:

those who could not pay might be threatened, but ultimately a compromise was often possible. Indian governors and *zamindars* also often made generous gifts of land, so-called *inam* lands, for the maintenance of temples and pilgrimage centres and as pensions to former public servants. But, imbued with Utilitarian ideals, and particularly David Ricardo's theories concerning agricultural rent, the Company's officials were taught that a rental charge imposed on the land, no matter how high, was not likely to undermine agricultural production and that the government's land tax was a form of rent. They did not see the surplus on agricultural production either as a form of subsistence or a reward for enterprise; they saw it as an unearned surplus, of which they could take as much as they pleased (Stokes 1959), whilst the grants of *inam* land were regarded as a drain on the state's resources to be curtailed. For this reason, the British were extremely inflexible in their revenue assessments, and were inclined to suspend privileged landholdings granted by former rulers (Stokes 1978: ch. 2). Their demands for money to recoup the costs of previous decades of war also meant that taxes were often demanded from the rural population for the first time in cash rather than in kind, imposing an additional burden. Taxes were then collected not simply by force but by means of a detailed investigation and close supervision of the resources of the peasant economy, punitive sanctions being imposed for non-payment. Apart from the resulting loss of land, British legal procedures were resented, since they involved being publicly investigated and pilloried by officials in open court. It was an affront to the traditional hierarchy in rural areas, a hierarchy seen by Indians as political and social rather than economic. The British, however, saw agrarian relations in contractual terms. *Zamindars* were expected to pay their dues to the government, and if they did not they lost their position. Furthermore, the success of British district collectors, and their promotion, depended on close accounting and their ability to raise yields. This was an entirely different logic from that of the traditional structure of landholding in India, which was bound up with aristocratic right, and religious and social status (Cohn 1983).

The uprising of 1857 has been characterised as anti-colonial because the changes from which people were suffering in general were those effected by the colonial ruler – the East India Company. The problem was that there were many other causes for rebellion, and not all of those who took up arms were directly fighting against the colonial regime. Many rebels were hoping to restore a pre-colonial social order. They did not know who or what was responsible for the changes going on around them, but what they did want was to revive some form of traditional authority. With the collapse of British military power in north India in that year, others had no alternative but to turn to traditional leaders of one sort or another. Unfortunately, anyone who took to arms, even with the aim of self-defence or to restore some sort of local order, was often regarded as a rebel by the British and ultimately pilloried, tried and executed (Brodkin 1972).

The Indian army mutineers themselves, who signalled the commencement of the wider insurrection, had mixed motives. Some wanted to revive the authority of the ailing Mughal emperor, Bahadur Shah II, and the units of the British army that mutinied at Meerut in May 1857 determined their fate at an early stage by deciding to march on Delhi to reinstall the emperor rather than march, as they might alternatively have done, towards the British seat of power in Calcutta. In doing so, they immediately alienated the large number of Indians who had never recognised the authority of the Mughals, or who, like the Sikhs in the Punjab, had spent many generations struggling against the Mughal empire. They also alienated Hindu rulers who were prospering under the East India Company's rule. Naturally, they did win the support of Mughal aristocrats in the north of India. A further advantage of marching to Delhi was that it gave the rebels a concrete aim, which was greatly needed for the obvious reason that India, at this time, lacked a truly powerful nationalist ethos. Those who took up arms were often fighting for their country against the British, but that country might be Gwalior, Bengal, Awadh, Indore, etc. – it was not in the name of India itself. They were fighting, very often, for the reinstatement of kingdoms, patrimonies, and chiefdoms that had existed in the pre-British period, or for the revival of an empire that covered part of the subcontinent. They were by no means united in struggling for a single political alternative, and this is one of the reasons why the uprising of 1857 was ultimately successfully suppressed by the British. There was no overall strategy; though to say this is something of a truism, since it is absurd to suggest that there could easily have been one.

Unravelling the events of the uprising in 1857

Most of the accounts of 1857 that have survived are unreliable as historical sources. To begin with, it is always the victor's version of events that tends to take precedence, and since the British ultimately overwhelmed the insurrectionists it is the British view that has generally held sway. The uprising was a clear sign that the East India Company had seriously misruled the Indo-Gangetic plain, but they were reluctant to admit this, which is why in many subsequent British accounts 1857 is usually referred to as the 'mutiny'. By this it is implied that the insurrection was simply an act of treason by a group of soldiers that was dealt with appropriately. British descriptions of the 'mutiny' were also typically accompanied by accounts of various barbarities and horrors committed by the Indians as if to justify the violent means by which the restoration of colonial rule was accomplished. But this is not, of course, how Indians regarded the matter, then or now. Neither was the insurrection of that year confined to the ranks of the military; nor were the atrocities committed as one-sided as the British implied.

Reacting against British misrepresentations, many Indian authors, most famously the radical nationalist V.D. Savarkar writing in 1908,[5] have described the events of 1857 as 'the first national war of Indian Independence'. However, this is clearly a misnomer since, as one historian, R.C. Majumdar (1963), has commented, 'on the whole, it is difficult to avoid the conclusion that the so-called First National War of Independence of 1857 is neither first, nor national, nor a war of independence'. More detailed assessments published following the centenary commemoration of 1857 have tended to focus less on the activities of the Bengal sepoys and more on the associated uprisings of the civil population in urban and rural areas. Historians such as S.B Chaudhuri (1955) have thereby furthered the myth that the mutiny of the Bengal army and the rebellion that affected much of northern India during that year was a proto-nationalist and exclusively anti-colonial movement aimed at expelling the British from India. Other authors, such as Eric Stokes (1978), have preferred to argue that the rebels of 1857 were fighting for not one, but a variety of causes and nationalisms.

There remains a problem with source materials, which exacerbates the difficulties of interpretation. The Urdu records of the Lucknow and Delhi courts are preserved in the Allahabad and National Archives, but they are written in *shekastah*, a very difficult form of Persian calligraphy. By contrast, there are extremely voluminous English-language historical records of 1857 that have survived, but they are largely derived from the subsequent attempts made by the British to pacify the country. They are thus part of a project to restore order, rather than a dispassionate, legal investigation into what occurred. Essays by E.I. Brodkin (1972) and Ranajit Guha (1983b) have explained why it is so difficult to deduce what really happened from such sources. A great many of these are the accounts of soldiers who were engaged in pacification exercises, and the trial documents of those they believed, often mistakenly, to be responsible for the uprising. The authors and protagonists were keen to convince themselves that they were in control of the situation and that this was not a popular insurrection. They sought to identify and punish alleged agitators and ringleaders who had misled the supposedly naive masses into insurrection: a more realistic exercise than attempting to punish the population as a whole. The documents are thus filled with fabricated conspiracy theories, and attempts to pin the blame for what had happened on somebody – anybody in fact other than the colonial regime itself.

The 'creation' of a scapegoat often began with the identification of a popular local leader with an anti-British cause. In the district of Bijnor in Rohilkhand it was Mahmud Khan, the Pathan *nawab* of Najibad, who had triumphed over long-standing rivals for power amongst the local Rajputs. Another Pathan, Khan Bahadur Khan, had joined the rebels and held sway over much of the rest of Rohilkhand. Since Nicholas Shakespear, the British magistrate and collector, characterised the Rajputs as loyal (despite evidence to the contrary), the actions of Mahmud Khan, in defeating them and asserting his authority in Bijnor was subsequently defined as rebellious, despite his early statements of support for the British government. Upon hearing news of his condemnation, Mahmud Khan was ultimately forced into the arms of the rebels, but not until the closing months of the uprising, and only after he had saved the lives of several Europeans in his district. His fate was transportation for life, and he died within a few months of commencing his sentence. Local Rajput leader, Sheoraj Singh, by contrast, was rewarded for his loyalty to the British, despite the fact that he had corresponded with the rebels and had claimed to be a true supporter of the rebel leader Khan Bahadur Khan (Brodkin 1972).

So blinkered were contemporaries as to the origins of the uprising, that some alleged it was a plot hatched by Muslims in collaboration with the czar of Russia, as part of an attempt by the Russians to destabilise and take over the subcontinent. Others blamed Nana Sahib, the former *peshwa* or ruler of the Maratha empire, powerless and deprived even of his pension since 1851, alleging that he had organised the entire revolt, together with the *rani* of Jhansi and other disaffected ex-rulers. These theories are extremely improbable. Nana Sahib, for example, although resident near Kanpur at the time, was so much trusted by the British that when the regiments there turned against their officers he was asked to take charge of the Treasury to keep it safe. It was only later that he appears to have joined the rebel forces, probably at the urging of Tatya Tope and others among his retainers. He was vilified for his part in the arrangement of a cease-fire that ended in the massacre of civilians, but there is no evidence that he was responsible. He never had the chance to tell his side of this story: fleeing Kanpur after the final recapture of the city at the end of the year, he disappeared without trace, never stood trial, and was never called upon to explain his actions. The only source available on the events in Kanpur in 1857, from an Indian point of view, is a recent attempt to reconstruct the Kanpur insurrectionists' motives, which, although valuable, remains essentially speculative (Mukherjee 1990).

Grievances of the military

The 19th Native Infantry, stationed at Barrackpore just west of Calcutta, was the first regiment to rebel against its officers, following the now notorious distribution of greased cartridges to be used with newly issued Lee Enfield rifles. These cartridges were greased with fat alleged to be that of cows (revered by Hindus) or of pigs (which was defiling for Muslims), and were believed to be part of an attempt to forcibly convert the sepoys to Christianity. Those involved in the rebellion were arrested and a court of inquiry recommended that the regiment be disbanded. On the day following the initial rebellion – 29 March 1857 – Mangal Pande of the 34th Regiment, which had been barracked alongside the 19th, fired at his commanding officer Sir John Hearsey but was overpowered. He and another sepoy, Ishwari Pande, were tried and executed. The name 'Pande' was thereafter immortalised as the nickname given by the British to the rebel sepoys.[6] After the 34th was also disbanded, rumours about the greased cartridges rapidly spread. Six weeks later, a thousand miles away, a native regiment at Meerut was publicly humiliated for refusing to use the cartridges by being marched in shackles to the jail. The next evening, on Sunday, 10 May, the duty officer at Meerut was shot, and the sepoys rallied around the guns of the regiment, forced open the armoury to seize supplies of the supposed polluting cartridges, and attacked and killed their British officers. The next day they marched to Delhi behind their regimental flag.

Given the unanticipated nature of the military mutiny, and keen to avert blame from themselves, officials made much of the sepoys' objections to the distribution of cartridges for use with the Lee Enfield rifle. However, although the cartridges may have provided a rallying point for a few of the mutineers, it was only one of the issues that concerned them. And interestingly, once they had rebelled, the mutinous regiments showed no compunction at all about using these same rifles and cartridges against the British. The cartridge issue nonetheless underscored the weakness of the military's control over the lower ranks of the Bengal army, highlighting the very small number of British officers, and their poor relationship with the troops. Above all, it symbolised the widespread resentment and distrust of the East India Company's policies. This mistrust revolved, among other things, around a perceived threat to Indian religion. Missionary activities had been permitted in India since 1813, lending credence to the fear that the principal reason why the British were in India was in order to Christianise the population. Such fears had exhibited themselves on previous occasions, as in 1806 when a sepoy regiment at Vellore in the Madras presidency had mutinied after the issue of a new form of leather headgear, also considered polluting.[7] There were other fears of course, but British historiographies have tended to stress the cartridge issue because it could be used to demonstrate the irrationality and fanaticism of the natives and the unreasonableness of their conduct. That they should take up arms over an issue as trivial and superstitious as the greasing of a cartridge, neatly diverted attention from other aspects of the Company's maladministration that provided more contingent and pressing causes for rebellion.

The other concerns of the military were more specific (Stokes 1986). Indian troops were at that time organised into armies based in the three presidencies of Madras, Bombay and Bengal. If these armies fought beyond their frontiers they received an additional allowance. In 1856 the governor-general decided that since the British controlled two-thirds of the subcontinent, these additional allowances were no longer legitimate, and they were removed. The troops of the Bengal army based in Awadh at this time thus immediately received a cut in pay. The General Service Enlistment Act of 1856 also committed the sepoys to sign a declaration that they would be willing to fight overseas if necessary in the service of the East India Company, and this was resented by the majority who had no desire to travel so far. A voyage overseas, it was feared by some, might also entail a loss of caste status because of the inevitable contact with polluting *feringi* or foreigners (although the evidence of migration in other circumstances suggests it could only have been a minority belief). Another cause of resentment was the British policy of garnering recruits from a wide cross-section of the population. Until 1856 a large proportion of soldiers in the Bengal army were Brahmins and Rajputs from the north-west of Bengal. Villagers in this region were becoming accustomed to the income derived from sending recruits to the army. The kingdom of Awadh, independent but allied to the British by treaty since the late eighteenth century, had also become an important source of recruits to the army. The Company offended these groups by stating their intention to recruit more widely across the subcontinent. The sense of grievance had therefore spread to the main army-recruiting villages, and a further discordant note was added to this when the disbanded Meerut mutineers returned home.

The decision by the British to seize control of the kingdom of Awadh had also fostered resentment. Awadh had been a loyal ally of the British. Under the notorious policy of lapse, announced in 1850 by Viceroy Dalhousie, the British stated their intention to seize control of any princely state in which there might be a disputed succession. This they did, rapidly taking over the Nagpur kingdom in

1854 (the largest of all), along with Jhansi, Satara, Udaipur, Balaghat, Sambalpur, Jaitpur, Carnatic and Tanjore. They justified their actions by claiming that 'Indian despotism' was thereby ended, frontiers were consolidated, that it was administratively convenient, and that it was expressly desired by the people themselves (Fisher 1993). In the case of Awadh, they did not trouble to wait for a disputed succession. The British resident (the Company's representative at court) alleged that the *raja* was misruling his country, and this alone was used as a pretext to seize control of the kingdom in 1856 (Fisher 1987; Mukherjee 1984).

Arguably, therefore, it was not the peasants and sepoys who were the rebels in 1857 but the British themselves. In the view of many Muslim political commentators, since the British were merely the revenue collectors of Bengal, they were vastly exceeding their authority, and since the *nawab* of Awadh, Wajid Ali Shah, was the *vizier*, or guardian, of the Mughal empire, the seizure of his kingdom was an attack on Mughal sovereignty itself. Following annexation, the *nawab* was taken to Calcutta along with members of his family, and the British then made matters worse by sending in a high-handed settlement officer, Martin Gubbins, who in the process of fixing the revenue demand dispossessed a great many local aristocrats, known as *talukdars*, from their ancestral estates. These *talukdars*, led by the *raja* of Mahmudabad, were among the first aristocratic leaders to raise arms against the British and were strongly supported by their rural populations.

Other factors played a part in the uprising of 1857. The Sikh regiments of Ranjit Singh, who had been defeated in 1840, had been incorporated into the British army. There were some 15,000 of these troops and they were the first and largest force available to the British to move into the northern plains and retake the areas that had risen in revolt. One of the major failings of the British prior to 1857 was that when they had taken over the kingdom of Awadh they did not recruit the army of the king in a similar manner. They disbanded all 50,000 of the king's troops, effectively dispersing large numbers of aggrieved trained soldiers over the entire region. Once similarly large numbers of men serving in the Bengal army had been alienated the basis was laid for what became a widespread civil as well as military insurrection.

The course of the insurrection

By its nature, the East India Company's rule was a military occupation. The company was staffed by military men holding military titles. Military bases, or cantonments, were positioned so as to overawe the principal towns and cities, and sepoy units were based in all of the princely states, as well as in the coastal trading zones. Because the Company's rule was a military regime, the state itself was imperilled as soon as the military mutinied. As Karl Marx had commented: 'it is evident that the allegiance of the Indian people rests on the fidelity of the native army, in creating which the British rule simultaneously organised the first general centre of resistance . . . (to colonial rule).'[8]

The events at Meerut demonstrated that the cartridge issue, emotive as it may have been, was still merely an excuse for revolt. Many have argued that it had indeed been planned for some time, citing evidence that for months before, lotus flowers and *chapatis* (flat breads) were mysteriously circulating around the villages of north India, it being rumoured that the planned date for insurrection was 31 May. However, Ranajit Guha has put a slightly different twist on these events, arguing that rather than an organised conspiracy this was merely evidence of widespread rural unrest. He traces the exchange of *chapatis* to the traditional technique of disease prevention through transference, a practice in northern India described in detail by William Crooke, which involved 'the symbolic use of a ritually consecrated object or animal to act as the carrier of an epidemic which had broken out in a locality or was about to do so, and push it beyond its boundaries'. Amongst the transmitters that could be used for the transfer of cholera were 'images of the cholera goddess, doles of rice collected from the local residents, filth and sweepings picked up from the affected villages, domestic animals such as goats, buffaloes and fowl, or in the case of an exceptionally cruel custom reported from Punjab, Chamars "branded on the buttocks and turned out of the village" '. The circulating *chapati* was thus a transference sign of this type that acquired new meaning, becoming the predictive sign or omen of an imminent upheaval (Guha 1983: 243–245). Whatever the circumstances, it must have been very obvious to the earliest mutineers that Meerut had to be involved as it was one of the strongest cantonments in the north, but by imprisoning soldiers on 10 May, the British seem to have forced the hands of those involved at Meerut into an early commencement of the revolt. According to eyewitnesses, the Meerut regiments were clearly expected when they arrived at the gates of Delhi, as they were greeted with lotus flowers and *chapatis* and urged to clear Delhi of the British – which they did, slaughtering not only British soldiers and officers but all Christians converts wherever they could be found. Immediately afterwards they sought an audience with the emperor and king of Delhi, Bahadur Shah Zafar II, whom they urged to lead them. To this the frail emperor (he was 82 years of age) reluctantly and hesitatingly agreed.[9] Thereafter, mutinous sepoy regiments steadily flowed into the capital (the ultimate destination of some 100,000 out of the 139,000 who mutinied), and proclamations were circulated calling for Muslim and Hindu to unite in a struggle for *din* (Islamic faith) and *dharma* (Hindu duty), a central characteristic of the revolt (Ray 2003; Dalrymple 2006). Many of these proclamations were written by Mirza Mughal (Zafar's fifth son), who endeavoured to take charge and unite the chaotic rebel force in Delhi. Others were written by outlying *mansabdhars* and supporters of the revolt who endeavoured to rally supplies and troops by invoking the authority and name of the emperor. The following document (known as the Azamgarh proclamation), calling for support and listing the grievances of the rebels, is interesting to read, not least for its clarity of purpose:

> It is well known to all, that in this age the people of Hindustan, both Hindoos and Mahommedans, are being ruined under the tyranny and oppression of the infidel and treacherous English . . .
> Section I – Regarding Zemindars. – It is evident the British government, in

making zemindary settlements, have imposed exorbitant jummas, and have disgraced and ruined several zemindars, by putting up their estates to public auction for arrears of rent, insomuch, that on the institution of a suit by a common *ryot* yet, a maidservant, or a slave, the respectable zemindars are summoned into court arrested, put in jail, and disgraced . . . in the Badshahi government . . . every zamindar will have absolute rule in his own zemindary. The zemindary disputes will be summarily decided according to the Shurrah and the Shasters, without any expense; and zemindars who will assist in the present war with their men and money, shall be excused for ever from paying half the revenue . . .

Section II. – Regarding Merchants. – It is plain that the infidel and treacherous British government have monopolised the trade of all the fine and valuable merchandise, such as indigo, cloth, and other articles of shipping, leaving only the trade of trifles to the people . . . When the Badshahi government is established . . . the trade of every article, without exception both by land and water, shall be open to the native merchants of India, who will have the benefit of the government steam-vessels and steam carriages for the conveyance of their merchandise gratis; and merchants having no capital of their own shall be assisted from the public treasury. It is therefore the duty of every merchant to take part in the war, and aid the Badshahi government with his men and money . . .

Section III. – Regarding Public Servants. – It is not a secret thing, that under the British government, natives employed in the civil and military services, have little respect, low pay, and no manner of influence and all the posts of dignity and emolument in both the departments, are exclusively bestowed upon Englishmen; . . . Natives, whether Hindoos or Mohammedans, who fall fighting against the English, are sure to go to heaven; and those killed fighting for the English, will, doubtless, go to hell, therefore, all the natives in the British service ought to be alive to their religion and interest, and, abjuring their loyalty to the English, side with the Badshahi government and obtain salaries of 200 or 300 rupees per month for the present, and be entitled to high posts in future . . .

All the sepoys and sowars [*sawars*] who have for the sake of their religion, joined in the destruction of the English, and are at present, on any consideration in a state of concealment, either at home or elsewhere, should present themselves to me without the least delay or hesitation . . . Foot soldiers will be paid at the rate of three annas, and sowars [*sawars*] at eight or twelve annas per diem for the present, and afterwards they will be paid double of what they get in the British service . . .

Section IV. – Regarding Artisans. – It is evident that the Europeans, by the introduction of English articles into India, have thrown the weavers, the cotton-dressers, the carpenters, the blacksmiths, and the shoemakers, &c., out of employ, and have engrossed their occupations, so that every description of native artisan has been reduced to beggary. But under the Badshahi government the native artisan will exclusively be employed in the services of the kings, the rajahs, and the rich; and this will no doubt insure their prosperity. Therefore the artisans ought to renounce the English services, and assist the Majahdeens . . . (religious freedom fighters) engage in the war, and thus be entitled both to secular and eternal happiness. Section V. – Regarding Pundits, Fakirs, and other learned persons. – The pundits and fakirs being the guardians of the Hindoo and Mohammedan religions respectively, and the European being the enemies of both the religions . . . the pundits and fakirs are bound to present themselves to me, and take their share in the holy war, otherwise they will stand condemned according to the tenor of the Shurrah and the Shasters; but if they come, they will, when the Badshahi government is well established, receive rent-free lands.[10]

Whilst the mutinous sepoys and a growing number of self-proclaimed volunteer *jihadis* who joined them consolidated their hold on Delhi, preparations went ahead for revolt in Awadh. In the capital Lucknow, the commanding British officer, Sir Henry Lawrence, was warned that a shot would be the signal for the commencement of insurrection on 30 May. The story has it that whilst dining that evening he commented on the inactivity of the supposed mutineers, saying 'your friends are not punctual!', at which point a shot rang out. The next day, 34 miles west of Agra, Indian troops at Bharatpur in eastern Rajasthan revolted, and at Shahjahanpur, in north-central North-Western Provinces the British were attacked whilst attending morning service. At this point the insurrection might still have been contained, but responsibility for its escalation must lie partly in the hands of General James George Neill, commanding the 1st Madras Fusiliers. Upon hearing of the events in Awadh, Neill marched to Varanasi, on what he thought was a pre-emptive mission. As soon as he arrived, he disbanded the local native regiment, lined up the sepoys, and shot them. Upon seeing this, a regiment of Sikhs stationed at Varanasi, normally considered 'loyal', revolted and were also shot. General Neill then embarked upon a general campaign of terrorism, hanging every able-bodied man he could lay his hands on who aroused the least suspicion. News of these atrocities caused two native regiments at Kanpur, hitherto loyal, to revolt, and march to Bithur, where they met up with Nana Sahib, the deposed Maratha *peshwa*, whom they persuaded to lead them to Delhi.

The British garrison at Kanpur was commanded by General Wheeler, who moved his men to the entrenchment surrounding the residency, from where they fired on the 53rd and 56th Native Infantry battalions who had not up until then mutinied, thus immediately prompting them to do so. At this point Nana Sahib's forces turned back to Kanpur and laid siege to the entrenchment. General Neill was ordered by telegraph from Calcutta to move to Allahabad and Kanpur, but he delayed, claiming that he was too busy with operations to 'pacify' the country around Varanasi, which mostly involved burning villages. However, in terror at the prospect of his approach, the 6th Native Infantry at Allahabad mutinied on 6 June, killing their officer and six cadets. Meanwhile, further north, troops under generals Wilson and Barnard attempted to relieve Delhi. Meeting up on 7 June, they managed to regain control of the ridge overlooking Delhi after fierce fighting.

They then clung on to this for the next three and a half months, despite some 22 attacks by rebel forces from Delhi and an outbreak of cholera.

On 8 June, native troops of the formerly independent princely state of Jhansi rebelled and attacked the Europeans in the fort. General Neill reached Allahabad on 11 June, but this was too late for General Wheeler and the residents at Kanpur who surrendered to the forces of Nana Sahib and Tatya Tope in exchange for an offer of safe passage to Calcutta. In the now infamous massacre, as they were embarking on boats on the Ganges on 27 June at Satichaura Ghat (Figure 4), they were set upon by sepoys and city residents, angered (according to Mukherjee [1990]) at news of General Neill's outrages and by rumours that the daughter of Nana Sahib had been captured and burnt alive by the British. When he heard what was happening, Nana Sahib gave orders that the women and children be spared. Seventy British officers in all survived, but they were imprisoned at a house called Bibighar, where they were massacred the next day. The bodies were thrown down a well, where a British memorial was subsequently erected. This was replaced after independence by a statue of Tatya Tope, widely regarded today as a great Indian hero.

At Lucknow, the British retreated to the residency. Foolishly, Sir Henry Lawrence then decided to attack the rebels amassing just outside the city at a small village called Chinhut. There they found themselves outmanoeuvred and outnumbered, and retreated in a panic, blowing up their ammunition dump at Machchi Bhavan on the way back into the residency. The siege of Lucknow continued for many months thereafter. The strength of support for the rebels was due to the

Figure 4 Massacre in the river at Kanpur (from C. Ball, *The History of the Indian Mutiny*, London 1858). © National Library of Scotland.

involvement of the mass of the population of Awadh at an early stage, as revealed in the following proclamation, seized by the British, and which reads like a fiery, populist rendition of the Azamgarh proclamation:

> It has become the bounden duty of all the people, whether women or men, slave girls or slaves, to come forward and put the English to death. The adoption of the following measures will lead to their destruction, viz., all the Moluvees and the Pundits should explain in every village and city the misfortunes which the success of the English will entail on the people and the advantages and spiritual benefit which will accrue from their extirpation. The Kings, Wazeers, Rajahs and Nawabs ought to slay them in the field of battle, the people should not leave their city in consequence of the entrance of the English therein, but on the contrary should shut up their doors and all the people, whether men, women or children . . . ought to put these accursed English to death by firing guns, carbines and pistols, from the terraces, shooting arrows and pelting them with stones, bricks . . . and all other things which may come into their hands. They should stone to death the English in the same manner, as the swallows stoned the Chief of the elephants. The sepoys, the nobles, the shopkeepers, the oil men etc. and all other people of the city, being of one accord, should make a simultaneous attack upon them, some of them should kill them by firing guns . . . and with swords, arrows, daggers . . . some lift them up on spears . . . some should wrestle and with stratagem break the enemy to pieces, some should strike them with cudgels, some slap them, some throw dust in their eyes, some should beat them with shoes . . . In short, no one should spare any efforts, to destroy the enemy and reduce them to the greatest extremities.[11]

The virulence of the language suggests the depth of anti-British feeling known to exist amongst the rural population. Such was the popularity of the revolt in Awadh that whilst the Europeans in the residency died at the rate of ten per day, the rebel forces surrounding them grew in number to more than 10,000.[12]

General Neill delayed advancing from Allahabad, claiming he was too busy 'mopping up', which meant a continuation of his policy of indiscriminate hanging. Soon there was not a single able-bodied man to be found capable of assisting in the transport of military equipment. A force under General Havelock was sent up from Calcutta on 7 July to aid in the relief of Kanpur, arriving too late to be of assistance, although they were able to defeat Nana Sahib's forces in an engagement on 27 July. Soon after this Havelock's forces won a decisive victory at Bithur, forcing Nana Sahib to retreat to Gwalior.

At about this time Bakht Khan, a former gunner from Bareili and a devout Muslim, arrived at Delhi with a large force and treasure and was made commander-in-chief of the rebel forces by the emperor (despite Bakht Khan's disdain for him), displacing Mirza Mughal who was made adjutant-general and therefore effective head of the administration. Bakht Khan did an effective job of rallying the rebel forces and attacking the British on the ridge. On 14 August, however,

John Nicholson finally arrived at Delhi with a large column of troops, consisting of north-west frontier tribesmen and Sikhs from the Punjab. Soon after this, perhaps sensing the danger, renewed proclamations were published in the emperor's name calling for supplies and support from the Delhi hinterland.

The British regain control

On 14 September, Delhi was finally attacked by the reinforcements from the Punjab: the massive Kashmiri gate was partly blown up, and the British rushed in and recaptured the city. On 20 September the last of the Delhi strongholds was taken, and on the 21st William Hodson captured the emperor, who was hiding in Humayun's tomb and surrendered in exchange for the guarantee of his life (Figure 5). The emperor was taken back to the Red Fort, now under British control. The next day Hodson seized from the tomb Mirza Mughal, Khizr Sultan, and Abu Bakr, the three princes who had commanded the Mughal forces in Delhi. Accompanied by an escort of *sawars* (cavalry troopers), he took them out on the road to Delhi, then stopped, stripped the three princes naked and shot them dead at point-blank range with his revolver. For several weeks after its recapture, Delhi resounded to the sounds of gunfire as the British looted and wreaked revenge with a series of horrific executions of mutinous sepoys, hundreds of whom were shot or hanged each day on a gallows especially constructed in Chandni Chowk, or occasionally (in imitation of a Muslim style of execution) blown from the mouths of cannons. Thereafter, in a mirror image of the slaughter when the city was first

Figure 5 Surrender of Bahadur Shah to Captain Hodson (from C. Ball, *The History of the Indian Mutiny*, London 1858). © National Library of Scotland.

captured by the sepoys, able-bodied male civilians were dragged from their houses and killed upon the word of informers, who then shared in the loot of their property. The Urdu poet Ghalib, one of the few notables to survive the ordeal, described the scene in his inimitable fashion in a poem, the opening lines of which are reproduced at the beginning of this chapter. The destruction within the city, which reduced the buildings of the Red Fort alone to one-fifth of their former area, brought to a complete end not only a dynasty but the dominance of Muslim Urdu culture in north India.

On 25 September generals Outram and Havelock reached Lucknow; however, the mutineers had only strategically withdrawn and, soon after, these same British soldiers found themselves trapped within the city walls (described by Maria Germon [1958: ch. v]), forcing the commander-in-chief, Sir Colin Campbell, to set out from Calcutta to relieve them with troops sent from London. He arrived at Lucknow on 17 October, and on the night of the 23rd the besieged Britishers sneaked through the lines of the insurgents to safety. Five days later Nana Sahib's army, led by Tatya Tope, took revenge by engaging and defeating the army of Lieutenant-General Windham and retaking Kanpur. This victory was short-lived, however, as the army of Sir Colin Campbell took the city back again on 6 December, forcing Tatya Tope into retreat. On 21 March 1858, the forces of Colin Campbell finally recaptured Lucknow, the capital of Awadh, engaging in an orgy of looting and plunder, vividly described by *The Times* correspondent W.H. Russell:

> It was one of the strangest and most distressing sights that could be seen; but it was also most exciting . . . Discipline may hold soldiers together till the fight is won; but it assuredly does not exist for a moment after an assault has been delivered, or a storm has taken place . . . Hither and thither, with loud cries, dart European and native soldiery firing at the windows, from which come now and then dropping shots or hisses of a musket ball. At every door there is an eager crowd, smashing the panels with the stocks of their firelocks, or breaking the fastenings by discharges of their weapons . . . Here and there the invaders have forced their way into the long corridors, and you hear the musketry rattling inside; the crash of glass, the shouts and yells of the com-batants, and little jets of smoke curl out of closed lattices. Lying amid the orange-groves are dead and dying sepoys; and the white statues are reddened with blood . . . From the broken portals issue soldiers laden with loot or plunder: shawls, rich tapestry, gold and silver brocade, caskets of jewels, arms and splendid dresses. The men are wild with fury and lust of gold – literally drunk with plunder. Some come out with China vases or mirrors, dash them to pieces on the ground and return to seek more valuable booty. Others are busy gouging out the precious stones from the stems of pipes, from saddle clothes, or the hilts of swords, or butts of pistols and firearms. Some swathe their bodies in stuffs crusted with precious metals and gems; others carry off lumber, brass pots, or vases of jade and China.
>
> (Russell [1858] 1957: 100–101)

After the defeat at Kanpur, Nana Sahib allegedly fled to Nepal while Tatya Tope marched to Kalpi to aid the *rani*, Lakshmi of Jhansi, against the forces of General Walpole. Walpole was defeated, and Tatya continued south. However, on 23 April 1858 General Hugh Rose arrived, and engaged and captured the remainder of the *rani*'s forces at Kopatti Serai. The *rani* led her forces into battle on horseback, was shot and wounded, then rode to Gwalior, where she died. Indefatigable, Tatya Tope marched on through central India, Rajasthan, and Gujarat in an attempt to raise the Marathas in revolt. Only a few Gond chiefs in the highlands of central India agreed to lend support, and he was finally betrayed (by his friend the chief of Narwar) and captured in the forest of Paron. Tope was executed in Shivpuri (formerly Sipri) in present-day Madhya Pradesh in April 1859.

Tatya Tope, whose real name was Ramchandra Pandurang, was one of the more strategically minded, ruthless and efficient of the rebel leaders. Originally just a Maratha gunner, he rose to be the commander-in-chief of the forces led by Nana Sahib. Others were less clear-sighted. The siege of the British residency in Lucknow was prioritised by the rebels because of its royal associations – as the former capital of the kingdom of Awadh – at the expense of advancing on Calcutta, crossing the River Ganges, and cutting one of the means of communication available to the British. This lapse enabled the British to marshal troops in the east and in the western part of India and to retake the northern plains.

The extent of popular support

Although the uprising was confined to the northern part of India, other parts of the country had similar cause to resent British rule. Nonetheless, despite the fact that many Mughal aristocrats had been supplanted by Hindu traders, who had profited from their relationship with the British, the Company's rule had failed to penetrate much towards the village level in *zamindari* areas such as Bihar, where it could even be described as superficial (Yang 1988). There were rulers in other parts of India who had been dispossessed, and local populations with serious grievances. But the fact that the insurrection was confined largely to the Indo-Gangetic plain demonstrates that India was far from being a homogeneous polity at this time. Indians living in Hyderabad thought that yet another war between the Marathas and the British was in progress. Others had little idea of the scale of insurrection, believing it was merely a *zamindari* uprising of the sort that had occurred frequently under the Mughals. Although there are clearly the seeds here of later patriotic nationalism (Bayly 1998), the insurrection was arguably a purely regional affair.

Two areas – Bengal and the Punjab – remained at least superficially loyal despite their proximity to the rebellion's heartland of north India. There was a large British force based in Bengal, and another in the Punjab, which had been recently conquered; British troops were also massed on the borders of Afghanistan. There was thus no practical opportunity for dissent. This also highlights one reason why the collapse of British authority that did take place in 1857 was so sudden: when the Indian regiments rebelled, there was no substantial force of British soldiers under arms anywhere near the region in a position to restore order. It was not until the forces recalled from Afghanistan and the troops in the Punjab and Bengal were assembled, and then joined by reinforcements diverted en route to China, that the insurrectionists could finally be suppressed.

The desire for a restitution of the old system, and for the conjunction once again of civil and moral law, caused many insurrectionists to turn to traditional leaders to achieve this end. To this extent 1857 was a reactionary movement, intended and tending to revive former privileges. So it was that the revolt centred around aristocrats such as Khan Bahadur Khan, the last independent Muslim ruler of Rohilkhand before it was annexed by the British in 1801; whilst in Awadh, the revolt was led by ex-military leaders and focused around the capital, Lucknow. There it was led by Birjis Qadir (a young son of the *nawab* of Awadh who was acclaimed as king on 5 July 1857), Begum Hazrat Mahal the ex-queen mother of the kingdom (who refused to stay with the ex-*nawab* Wajid Ali Shah when the British exiled him to Calcutta the year before), and the *talukdars*.

Subaltern historians have very convincingly demonstrated, using available evidence, that there were many opportunists as well as established local leaders, and numerous individuals who took up arms on their own initiative without waiting for the emperor's appeal, or for feudal aristocrats to tell them what to do. Gautam Bhadra (1985) assesses four localities involved in the uprising and describes the concerns that motivated the insurrectionists. Depicted in detail are characters such as Shah Mal, a Jat resident of the village of Bijraul in the *pargana* of Barout, which had suffered from over-taxation by the British in the months before the uprising. Shah Mal put together a combined force of Jat and Gujar peasants, and attacked and plundered the *tahsil* of Barout and the bazaar at Baghpat. Appointed to the post of *subhadar* (or governor) by the rebel authorities in Delhi, he then set about uniting the territory, instituting a 'hall of justice' in the bungalow of an officer of the irrigation department and assisting in the defence of Delhi against the advancing British by destroying the bridge of boats across the River Yamuna at Baghpat.

Devi Singh was perhaps the quintessential subaltern insurgent, acting entirely on his own without any contact with outsiders. He came from a Jat-dominated region centred around the small rural town of Raya in Mathura district. The land tenure system in the area was *bhaiyachara*, or brotherhood. In other words the village lands were divided up between different families, who paid the land revenue charge jointly. This conflicted with British attempts to distinguish individual peasant holdings in the villages and to estimate the land revenue charge on each of them. Combined with a heavy revenue demand, this brought considerable resentment, misery and indebtedness to the villages, to the benefit of individuals such as Raja Gokul Das, the largest of the Marwari moneylenders in northern central India. Using the powers of the English-style civil courts the moneylenders acquired extensive village lands in lieu of debt. Gokul Das and a number of other moneylenders lived in the town of Raya, and as soon as the *zamindars* and villagers in the locality heard of the king of Delhi's proclamation, they immediately rose up against the moneylenders and attacked the town. Devi Singh, otherwise a man of no distinction, was dressed in yellow, the traditional symbol of royalty, and declared by popular acclaim to be the Jat 'peasant king' of the 14 villages in the locality. Upon entering the town, he proceeded to the school room, where he set up a government upon the English model – thus simultaneously demonstrating the limits of insurgent consciousness at this time (Bhadra 1985: 254). He then set about bringing the *banias*, or moneylenders to trial, interrogating them one by one, seizing their assets, ransacking their property, and destroying their mortgage deeds, surrender bonds and account books. Unfortunately, Devi Singh thought that having driven away the police he had destroyed the British *raj*. When Mark Thornhill, the collector of Muttra arrived in mid-June with a contingent of troops from Kotah, Devi Singh was quickly captured and executed.

Bhadra also details the story of Gonoo, a Kol *adivasi* and cultivator from the Singhbhum district of Chotanagpur, who led the Larkha Kol insurrection in reaction to attempts by the British to interfere with traditional institutions, in particular their attempt to impose new policing demands (such as the prosecution of witchcraft) and land taxes on the community. The arrow of war was circulated, and the insurrection kicked off with a mutiny by the sepoys at Ramgarh. It then escalated into a wholesale Kol insurrection under the leadership of Gonoo and others who forced the *raja* of Porahat to assume the customary role as their head. Gonoo styled himself the 'chief of Singhbhum' and insisted he was merely appointed the local *sardar* by the *raja*. However, according to surviving accounts from the Kols themselves, this was a revolt initiated from below, rather than one instigated at the behest of a feudal master, and the *raja*'s role was purely nominal.

Bhadra's final example is the Maulvi Ahmadullah Shah, an itinerant preacher who advocated *jihad* against the English across north India. In Fyzabad he was imprisoned, but then freed by mutinous sepoys of the irregular cavalry and 22nd Native Infantry who acclaimed him their leader. These he then led to Lucknow, where he joined in the crucial battle of Chinhat, alongside the sepoys and lumpen elements from the city population who took part. Although arousing the jealousy of the Lucknow court, his bravery convinced the troops following him of his invincibility, and contributed greatly to the heroic resistance of Lucknow against the Queen's Regiments of the British in the closing stages of the insurrection (Bhadra 1985: 267).

What all of these rebels shared was a high level of purpose and a common goal. Much as with the insurrectionists in Awadh, they were organised, usually in defence of a territory, as well as through networks of kinship, religion, or political adherence. Caste did not necessarily divide them, they received no instructions from higher authorities, and they were united in their opposition to outside, primarily British, interference. This pattern of organisation was both feasible and commonplace (Guha 1983b; Roy 1995), and was at least as common as the more feudal forms of insurrection in support of local elites, emphasised in the accounts of Stokes (1978) and others.

Counting the cost of war

In times of warfare, acts of brutality are commonly committed on both sides and the 1857 uprising proved no exception. The British practice of executing rebel soldiers and officers by tying them to the mouths of cannons, so that the crowds of onlookers would be spattered with blood and the corpses dispersed over a wide area, was intended to shock. It was furthermore a deliberate offence, because blasting the body to pieces in this manner prevented either cremation or a proper burial. The British also carried out hundreds of arbitrary hangings in northern India as the fighting progressed almost hand to hand through the villages, until they were finally retaken. Marx and Engels wrote extensively at the time about the violence of the mutineers and of the British soldiers, illustrating the latter with extracts from the letters of officers sent home:

> 'We have power of life and death in our hands, and we assure you we spare not'. Another, from the same place: 'Not a day passes by we don't string up from ten to fifteen of them (non-combatants)'. One exulting officer writes: 'Holmes is hanging them by the score, like a brick'. Another in allusion to summary hanging of a large body of the natives: 'Then our fun commenced'. A third: 'We hold court-martials on horseback, and every nigger we meet with, we either string up or shoot'.[13]

By his own account, Frederick Cooper, the deputy commissioner of Amritsar, shot to death no less than 237 captured sepoys at the end of July 1857, a further 45 suffocating in cells – in a grisly re-enactment of Zephaniah Holwell's 'Black Hole' – before he had a chance to execute them. On the Indian side, there was likewise a systematic use of violence, quite apart from incidents such as the massacre in Kanpur at Satichaura Ghat. During his march through central India, Tatya Tope, for his part, ordered that village officials who had collaborated and collected taxes for the British should have their ears and noses cut off as an example to others. In short, this was a time of bloody savagery on both sides because both were desperate to win, and believed violence to be the only language their enemy understood.

The uprising was finally quashed when the governor-general and later the first viceroy, George Canning, amidst howls of protest from the civilians of Calcutta (who petitioned for the removal of 'clemency Canning' as he was called), offered an amnesty to all who gave themselves up after the recapture of Lucknow. This proposal was then published in a General Proclamation made in the name of Queen Victoria in Allahabad on 1 November 1858, which promised to 'respect the rights of Indian Princes as our own'. By promising the non-confiscation of their lands, Canning was able to persuade 14 *talukdars* in Awadh alone to surrender immediately. Despite summary executions continuing thereafter, the amnesty greatly helped in the pacification of the population, all effective opposition coming to an end with the arrest and execution of Tatya Tope early in 1859. The emperor Bahadur Shah was tried for treason at the age of 83, by his concessionaries for trade and the holders of the *diwani* of Bengal (the East India

Company), and was sentenced to transportation. Carried through north India in a bullock cart on his way to Calcutta, he was then exiled to Rangoon where he died and was buried in an unmarked grave in November 1862.

Despite all that has been written on the topic, 1857 will probably remain forever clouded by confusion precisely because it has been used as a political tool both by the British, to justify their actions and their continuing rule in India, despite their unpopularity, and also by the rulers of independent India, who sought to construct a nationalist historiography which downplayed (amongst other things) the centrality of the Delhi court in the events of the insurrection. India, as the nation we know now, was created in the twentieth century, and it would be folly to attempt to trace its origins to the events of a hundred years before. Likewise it would be a mistake uncritically to accept colonial British explanations for the uprising.

The most serious consequence of the uprising was the vacating of the throne in Delhi, which paved the way for the creation of a new British imperium in India. At the same time, however, the uprising helped create a mythology of resistance that became a powerful ideological weapon in the hands of later Nationalists during the freedom struggle of the 1930s and 1940s. This was perhaps to prove to be one of its more important legacies.

5 Zenith of empire
Economic and social conditions in the late nineteenth century

I certainly pity the East India labourer, but at the same time I have a greater feeling for my own family than I have for the East Indian labourer's family; I think it is wrong to sacrifice the comforts of my own family for the sake of the East Indian labourer . . . and I think it is not good legislation to take away our labour and give it to the East Indian because his condition is worse than ours. To raise his condition . . . would make us destitute of employment, and to throw us upon the rest of society to support us by charity, and this I hope will never take place in this country.

(Thomas Cope, silkweaver)[1]

It is, unfortunately a fact, which no well-informed Indian official will ignore, that, in many ways, the sources of national wealth in India have been narrowed under British rule.

(R.C. Dutt)[2]

The 1857 insurrection brought the rule of the East India Company to an end, and in 1858 India was placed formally under the control of the British crown. A secretary of state was given supreme control over Indian affairs, and the governor-general in India was effectively reduced to acting as his agent. This was necessitated, above all else, by the enormous cost of putting down the uprising, some £50 million, much of which was owed by the Company to the British crown, in payment for British troops deployed to restore order. As the Company was wound up, the cost of compensation to the shareholders was added to the India debt, ultimately to be paid by Indian taxpayers. In that same year the Mughal emperor was put on trial by a military court. At his defence it was argued that since he was the emperor of India it was the British who should be considered the rebels and not him. He was nonetheless charged with treason, found guilty and publicly transported in chains to imprisonment in Rangoon, where he died four years later. In 1877 Queen Victoria was appointed empress of India in his place by the British prime minister, Disraeli, the governor-general being renamed her 'viceroy' in India.

In the wake of 1857 the British government was forced to rethink its policies and to moderate those that had caused dissent. A succession of Tenancy Acts, beginning in Bengal and Awadh in 1859, were introduced and then extended to the other provinces. These gave occupancy rights to ordinary cultivators. For some time after 1857 the British also avoided raising agricultural revenues, and when they needed more income they increasingly resorted instead to excise and income taxes. Since over-taxation, the raising of rent and the loss of land had been major issues in 1857, these were clearly sensible measures, and it was not until after the First World War that serious hikes in the land revenue charge were again attempted.

In the wake of 1857 the British also set up a court of wards, which provided that the estates of princes, aristocrats and large landlords could be taken into the care of a court representative in case of bankruptcy. The procedure allowed for the appointment of a manager to run the estate. Once it had returned to solvency and the arrears of debt were cleared, the original owner was reinstated. This was an attempt to appease the landholding elite among the Indian aristocracy and to win their adherence to the status quo (Metcalf 1990).

Amongst other measures aimed at pacifying rural India after 1857, an Arms Act was passed, forbidding the population from carrying weapons without a licence. A Criminal Tribes Act was also introduced in 1871, which placed restrictions on wandering, nomadic groups, many of whom were either newly landless tribals or former pastoralists and traders (such as the Bhanjaras), the indigent poor of the colonial system, some of whom had participated in the uprising of 1857. There were 15 tribes so listed, and another four were added between the implementation of the Act in 1873 and 1895. The oldest males in families of the specified 'criminal tribes and castes' were required under this law to report on a weekly basis to the local police, to inform them of their whereabouts. The purpose was to dissuade them from vagrancy and criminal activities, to which they were regarded as being inherently inclined, as some quite probably were, although the reasons were practical rather than genetic (Nigam 1990). Finally, a Vernacular Press Act was introduced in 1878, which banned the printing of inflammatory or slanderous articles in non-English newspapers (a measure brilliantly circumvented in the Bengali newspaper *Amrita Bazar Patrika*, which immediately commenced publication in English). This curtailment of freedom of speech underlined the fact that the uprising had put a halt for some time to thoughts of involving educated Indians in the government of the empire. Instead a new policy of 'divide and rule' was initiated. Regiments in the Indian army were each recruited from specific communities in the hope that one would always be willing to fire on another, while attempts were also made to conciliate minority communities, each in a different fashion, so as to prevent them from uniting in a common front.

Queen Victoria took her responsibilities as empress very seriously. She is reported to have taken Hindi lessons, and invited the German Indologist Max Müller to her court to give lectures. From 1877 onwards, a series of general assemblies, or *durbars*, were held in India to honour the British monarchs. The first, and most spectacular, was that organised by Lord Lytton in Delhi to celebrate Victoria's inauguration as empress. These were attempts to ingratiate the

British in the eyes of the Indian aristocracy and to shift their traditional allegiances away from the Mughal emperor to the British queen (Ramusack 2004). The princes were further groomed for their role as elite collaborators by programmes of education designed to modernise and westernise them as far possible – an endeavour which was inevitably met with subtle resistance (Bhagavan 2003). The *durbars* were sumptuous if oddly managed events, which aped similar functions held by the Mughals and other Indian rulers, in an attempt to adapt Indian customs and institutions to the service of the very different traditions of British monarchy and British rule. They were intended as part of a systematic structure providing indirect control over the 40 per cent of Indian territory that the independent but treaty-bound Indian princes still ruled. However, the results were somewhat mixed as they bolstered the self-esteem of the British and a handful of Indian acolytes, but proved of marginal importance in terms of solidifying colonial institutions (Cohn 1983). A further effect was that by binding the Indian aristocracy to the patronage of the British crown the powerlessness of Indian *rajas* was underlined and their authority detached from local ritual and social sources (Dirks 1987).

The uprising had placed a check on imperial ambitions, and it led to many of the compromises and inconsistencies of policy that became characteristic of later colonial rule. Thus efforts were made to develop the system and practice of indirect rule, and instead of denouncing Indian rulers as corrupt and despotic, and to use this as an excuse to supplant them, after 1857 the British attempted to prop up the aristocrats and win their allegiance to the British crown. At the same time attempts were made to placate the cultivating classes by tempering tax demands and introducing Tenancy Acts. However, in most respects things remained the same, and if conditions in India improved after 1857, it was largely due to circumstances beyond the control of the British government. Improve they did nonetheless, and as time passed a new, politicised middle class also emerged, which began to raise questions about the rights of Indians, and the powers of the regime that had taken the place of the East India Company's despotism.

Progress in the economy

There was, fortunately for the British *raj*, a period of relatively sustained economic growth from 1860 to 1894, a recovery from the profound depression that had marked the early years of the nineteenth century. There were various reasons for this. First of all, and most importantly, there were a succession of good harvests (a crucial factor even today in the Indian economy). Second, there was a boom in the production of cotton as India was turned slowly into an exporter of raw cotton to the Lancashire mills. There was another source of raw cotton immediately available – the southern United States. However, the eruption of the American Civil War in 1861 cut off this source and English manufacturers were forced to turn to India for their supplies. This gave a tremendous fillip to the cotton-producing areas in western India, Gujarat and Berar, which began to prosper significantly. There was a downturn in prices for a while in the early

1870s, but the opening of the Suez Canal in 1869 increasingly enabled supplies of raw cotton and other products such as wheat, exported from central India, to be shipped cheaply to the European markets. The slow decline of the Indian silver rupee against the gold-based European currencies also helped raw material exports, causing them to become slowly but perceptibly cheaper as the century progressed. Finally, of course, this was the period of railway development in India: from a mere 570 miles of railway in 1857, India had some 4,000 miles of track by 1880.

As for the positive economic developments of the late nineteenth century, the colonial regime can take little credit. The railways were largely constructed with strategic objectives in mind: as a consequence the major cities were linked, and the Gangetic plain where the uprising of 1857 had occurred was criss-crossed with railway track (Kerr 1995). This was to ensure that in the event of another revolt troops could be rapidly brought to the affected region. The railways were not always built with much concern for the impact on the lands through which they passed (Whitcombe 1972), and ownership was largely vested in European hands, British investors being guaranteed a 5 per cent return on their investment by the government of India, a guarantee not extended to Indian investors. Profits thus all went overseas, and when a line made a loss, as was often the case, dividends were paid to investors out of Indian tax revenues. In consequence of the government's strategic priorities, southern India (where there had been no rebellion) was poorly served by the railway, whilst central India had just one line running east–west through an area the size of France (Map 5). Only the areas adjacent to a halt on a railway line could enjoy the benefits of long-distance trade, which is one reason why Indian economic development of the late nineteenth century was characterised above all by its unevenness. Much of the raw cotton that was brought to markets, sold and then shipped onwards to Bombay for export to Europe, had to travel a considerable distance by bullock cart before reaching the nearest railhead. Undeterred, richer peasants and Indian *mahajans*, or middlemen, invested heavily in this form of transport from the early nineteenth century onwards. The railways greatly helped, but the enterprise shown by rural cultivators and by merchants in the *hats* or small-scale rural markets was also crucial for the development of this trade (Guha 1985).

Despite a return of rural prosperity, and a temporary rise in the average real wages of agricultural labour, growth was largely confined to the export zones producing raw materials for the industrial centres of Britain and Europe. And whilst one region prospered, another immediately adjacent to it often might not. The result was the development of a form of internal colonialism, with those regions left out of economic growth becoming themselves suppliers of cheap foodgrains and migrant labour to the developing areas (Bates 1995), a characteristic still more apparent later on in the twentieth century. These areas included places such as the *adivasi*-populated regions of Chhattisgarh in central India and Chota Nagpur in Bihar (Bates 1987; Mohapatra 1985), and arid zones such as the southern Deccan (Banaji 1990). Whilst in Mughal times the cities of north India, as major centres of consumption, had usually led economic growth, in the late

Map 5 Indian railway network, *c.* 1901.

nineteenth century they experienced rising unemployment, and trailed behind the export zones and burgeoning coastal ports. The steady development of the railways in India had facilitated the import of cheap manufactured goods from the UK, especially manufactured cotton goods, which began to flood the Indian market after 1860. This meant unemployment for handloom weavers and artisans in the small towns and cities.

The effects of imports on the urban economy were severe because of the skewed nature of the trading relationship between Britain and India. Although the influence of free traders led to a decline in tariff barriers from the mid-nineteenth century onwards, UK-manufactured cotton always entered the Indian market tax free, whilst Indian tea, cotton and other products entering the UK traditionally had tariffs levied upon them. This obviously had the effect of making it difficult for Indian manufacturers and exporters to compete with the cotton being produced in Britain. On the one occasion when the Indian government proposed introducing a very modest 5 per cent customs duty on British cotton entering India, in 1894, there was a storm of protest from the Lancashire mill industry, and parliament in London insisted that if this customs duty was introduced an equivalent excise duty should be imposed on Indian cotton sold in India (from which UK-manufactured goods would be exempt) so as to prevent Indian manufacturers from undercutting the British (Rothermund 1988). This episode was characteristic of the way in which the colonial economy worked. India was perceived as a market to be exploited for the benefit of the UK manufacturers. Little or no attention was paid to the needs of Indian industrialists or the impact on ordinary workers. It was for this reason that most Indian industrialists and merchants poured their dwindling resources into rural moneylending, in which there continued to be no shortage of demand (Timberg 1978).

As the century progressed, the main manufacturing centre, Calcutta, continued to be dominated by Europeans. The major export from Bengal was jute – a coarse fibre used for making rope and sacking. As global trade and the European economies developed, so did the demand for ropes and sacking. Jute was grown throughout Bengal and manufactured in mills in Calcutta, as well as being shipped to mills in Scotland, most importantly in Dundee – the prosperity of Dundee being founded almost entirely on the Bengal jute trade. Other commodities exported from Bengal included indigo and opium, and the late nineteenth century saw the growth of the tea plantations in Assam and Sri Lanka. Most of these new industries were dominated by Europeans, not necessarily because they had more capital at their disposal but simply because Indians were excluded from investing in them by the exercise of a racial bar (most conspicuous in the case of Assam). It was not until the late nineteenth century that an indigenous cotton industry began in Bombay, an industry that only really took off after the outbreak of the First World War (Gadgil 1942; Bagchi 1972; Ray 1979).

The biggest cash drain on the Indian economy throughout the nineteenth century continued to be the so-called 'home charges' – the payments made to the parliament in London, to civil servants, for the pensions of retired army officers, and so on. These home charges were quite considerable because as a matter of policy the government of India also bought most of its supplies from the UK, which required a constant export of currency by way of payment. When the railways were developed, for example, all of its supplies, including the rails and even some of the sleepers, were brought from Europe, despite the availability of state forests and the abundance of supplies of coal and iron within India itself. This was one of the reasons why despite Marx's prediction that the building of railways would revolutionise India, in fact there was very little knock-on effect from their development on Indian industry (Marx and Engels 1959).

Further expenses were brought about by changes in the composition of the British Indian army. To avoid a repetition of the mutiny, it was decided that the ratio of Indian to British soldiers in the army should be kept at 2 to 1. This meant that many more British soldiers had to be recruited from Britain – up to 65,000 to complement the 135,000 Indian soldiers under arms in 1880. On average, these soldiers cost at least three times as much as an Indian soldier, so the burden placed on the government of India by this policy was very heavy. The fact that money had to be sent back to the UK to pay the soldiers' wages meant a further addition to the 'home charges'. These amounted to £17.3 million by 1901/2, £4.3 million of which was for army expenses, £3 million for interest on the India Debt, £6. million interest on railway debt, £1.9 million being spent on supplies, and £1.3 million on pensions.

The best illustration of the way in which the Indian economy was run in the interests of the British is in the development of Bombay. Bombay was a major port for the shipping of produce throughout the nineteenth century, but it only began to develop a truly large-scale manufacturing base of its own towards the end of the century (Morris 1965; Chandavarkar 1994). One of the reasons i flourished was because it was situated on the coast, as it needed to be if it was to gain access to supplies of cheap coal. India had abundant supplies of coal in Bihar, but they were not well accessed by railway (Simmons 1976). Whenever railways did go near a coalfield it was nevertheless uneconomical to ship the coal to Bombay because of the manner in which freight charges were fixed. Thus, they were set at a low rate for those sending manufacturing goods from overseas, via Bombay into the interior, as well as for those shipping raw cotton for export from the interior to Bombay. But for the shipment of manufactured goods within India or the transportation of coal for the use of manufacturing industries on the Indian coast, the freight charges were very much higher. It was therefore actually cheaper to bring coal all the way from the UK by ship to supply Bombay, rather than bring it the relatively short distance by rail from Bihar (Rothermund 1988: 33). This is a clear example of the way in which the economic management of the country was biased in favour of UK producers and against the interests of Indian industrialists, with inevitable long-term consequences (Dewey 1988). Having said that it would be incorrect to imply that this was entirely a cynical process. One reason for the anti-Indian bias was that the British had little conception of the interests and concerns of Indians, even at this late date. There was no system of democratic representation, the Indian civil servants themselves were very thin on the ground and the Indian population as a whole simply had no voice. It was not until a catastrophe resulted, as in 1857, that the administration became aware of the problems that might exist, let alone the lost opportunities for improvement.

Modern historians have been conspicuously divided in their assessments of the impact of colonial rule on the Indian economy. They have been influenced by neo-classical free-enterprise economics, positivism, cold-war rhetoric or colonial apologetics, and alternatively by anti-colonial or nationalist bias. Several of these positions are entertained in the symposia edited by M.D. Morris (1969) and G. Johnson (1985). Attempts at some sort of 'balance' are made in the studies by Charlesworth (1982) and in Tomlinson (1993), achieved in part by the adoption of a diachronic approach. The principal difficulty is that the arguments of nationalists are often based on essentially counter-factual points of view (i.e. what would have happened if the colonial regime had not existed), whilst their opponents have frequently tried to divorce the study of the economy from the colonial context altogether (e.g. McAlpin 1983). This approach is unconvincing to colonial critics, and at worst can be profoundly ahistorical. Another point of view can be found amongst the ordinary Indians affected by these economic changes, available to us through a variety of sources, and in the writings of contemporary Indian critics, both of which have the advantage of being eye-witness accounts of the events they describe. Spokesmen for Indian economic interests began to make their voices heard for the first time in the late nineteenth century. Foremost amongst them was Dadabai Naoroji, author of *Poverty of India* 1878) and *Poverty and UnBritish Rule in India* ([1878] 1901), who wrote extensively about the 'drain' of wealth from India and became a prominent leader in the early Indian National Congress. Another was William Digby, a sympathetic colonial official, author of *'Prosperous' British India: a revelation from official records* (1901), and, most famously, R.C. Dutt who published *Famines and Land Assessments in India* 1900) and an influential economic history of India in the nineteenth century 1906a, 1906b). These authors argued, for example, that the expenditure on railways was wasteful, not only because of the manner in which they had been constructed, with the supplies for the railways being brought from overseas, but because as far as Indian economic development was concerned what was needed first and foremost was expenditure on canals. If the money had been put into irrigation, they argued, there would have been a dramatic increase in prosperity in rural areas. This would have been a far more useful and profitable investment than the construction of railways, built primarily for strategic reasons, and which sometimes therefore passed through areas that were relatively unpopulated, infertile, and where none of India's mineral resources were to be found.

Even if one disagrees with every element of Naoroji's popular 'drain' theory, one point is clear: further investment in canals certainly might have averted the succession of catastrophic famines and widespread starvation in 1894/5, 1896/7 and 1899/1900, which brought the boom years in agriculture abruptly to a close Bhatia 1967). Harvest failures were provoked by failures of the monsoon rains, but also by a general under-investment and an excessive reliance on the income from cash crops grown on marginal soils in order to boost production (Bates 1988). Investments in canals and irrigation were subsequently embarked upon, especially in western India and the Punjab (Stone 1984), but by then it was too late. The reliance of colonial officials solely on the forces of supply and demand to cope with ecological disaster on such a scale proved wholly inadequate: some 20 million people (according to official estimates) losing their lives in the catastrophe that resulted (Digby 1901; Davis 2001).

The late Victorian famines illustrated the fragility of agriculture and the yawning income inequalities that were emerging in rural areas: the exploitation of cheap, particularly migrant, labour being apparently crucial to the success of commercial agriculture by this period (Bates 1992, 1995). Famine deaths, then as now, were an important symptom of rural poverty (Sen 1982). To a limited extent the government of India recognised its share of responsibility in this disaster, and some of those responsible were reprimanded and transferred (Baker 1993: 199–207). The insights of contemporary critics are thus important, not least because colonial officials listened and even occasionally responded to them. The death toll is nonetheless as clear a condemnation of the imperial system of governance as one can find.

The growth of disaffection among the elite

Naoroji and Dutt were characteristic of the liberal Indian nationalists assuming public roles, who began to make their voices heard from about the 1870s onwards. The initial reaction of the British to the uprising of 1857 had been to exclude Indians entirely from any sort of responsible position in public life, but the sheer sparseness of the British civil servants on the ground meant that more Indians had to be recruited to positions of increasing responsibility within the Indian civil service. Thus growing numbers of Indians began to be trained in the English-language schools and universities set up in the 1830s. By the 1880s, this educational system was turning out a total of 50,000 English graduates a year, a figure that rose to nearly 300,000 by 1887 and to 500,000 by 1907. Compared with the total population these Western-educated Indians represented a tiny minority, but they became an increasingly influential component in Indian social life. The majority came from the upper castes in the presidency towns. For example, 85 per cent of school or university students came from the three castes of Brahmins, Kayasths and Vaidyas and were nearly all from the landlord class collectively known in Bengal as the *bhadralok*, who dominated all of the educational establishments. It would be quite easy to dismiss these as a privileged elite, but many of them were politicised and conscious of their privileged status. In later years many of those who had been English-educated went on to campaign for the extension of education to the ordinary working classes, and even for the ending of upper-caste and upper-class privileges, one of the effects of English education being often the secularisation of these elites.

Although the educated Indian middle classes went on to secure well-paid and influential posts in the English colonial service they were never allowed to rise above a certain level within the hierarchy. The British were determined that the elite positions in the colonial civil service should remain exclusively occupied by white Europeans. A few, from wealthier Indian families, after studying in Indian universities, went on to study abroad at Oxford, Cambridge, London and Edinburgh universities, where they would attempt to add to their educational qualifications. Encounters with racism in England often added to their political consciousness, whilst the experience of travel, and of the highly unequal British society they encountered, added to their self-confidence and their willingness to criticise the colonial regime. It was very rare for any of these Indians to undertake the examinations held in London for elite positions in the Indian civil service. However, one young Bengali Brahmin, Surendranath Bannerjee, with a BA in law at Calcutta University, came to London in 1869 to take part in the annual examination. He scored higher than any of the other British applicants and therefore ought to have been offered a good position as a young recruit. The India Office, however, decided to disqualify him for having lied about his age. The reason he did so was simple: Indians commonly date their age from conception rather than birth. Using his skills as a lawyer, Bannerjee took the matter to court, appealed against exclusion and won the case. The government of India then appointed him as a district magistrate. Within three years, however, he was found guilty of a minor infraction of the regulations and dismissed – this time for good. This was typical of the way in which Indians who exceeded their expected social station were dealt with. For Bannerjee the implications were serious: having been found guilty of a breach of the law he could no longer practise as a lawyer. With few other options left in life, he went on instead to help found Bengal's first nationalist political organisation, the Indian Association, which was set up in July 1876 and which soon supplanted the pro-British and exclusively landlord-dominated Indian League that had been formed a year earlier (Bannerjee 1925; Leonard 1974; Chandra 1971).

Bannerjee was just one among many self-consciously middle-class Bengalis acquiring prominence at this time (Misra 1961). In Bombay on the west coast, political life was dominated by the reactionary *shetya* mercantile aristocracy who controlled, for example, the Bombay Association, founded in 1852 and revived again in 1867. Here, too, a more selfless, educated, liberal middle class was slowly emerging and acquiring a political voice (Johnson 1973). Most were high-caste Chitpavan and Saraswat Brahmins, who dominated positions both in the Maratha and Indian civil service and subsequently in the nationalist movement in Bombay. One of their number was Mahadev Gobind Ranade, who graduated in law and became a subordinate judge in Poona, where he founded the Poona Sarvajanik Sabha or All People's Association in 1870. He went on to become an important social reformer, especially campaigning for the rights of Hindu widows to remarry, and he was one of the guiding hands behind the founding of the Indian National Congress. Perhaps not coincidentally he was denied promotion in the government's legal service for another 25 years. One of his leading disciples was Gopal Krishna Gokhale, who was perhaps the epitome of the moderate national-ists of this period (Nanda 1977; Wolpert 1962). It was Gokhale who first introduced Mahatma Gandhi to Indian politics when he returned from South Africa in 1915. However, although Gokhale was an active social reformer, like many of these politicians he was conservative in his political views. A more militant and vocal group of western Indian nationalists at this time was led by Balwantrao Gangad-har Tilak, or 'Lokamanya' Tilak, as he was called (meaning 'Light of the People'), but theirs was a minority view at this time. Naoroji's views were more main-stream. His book, *Poverty and UnBritish Rule in India*, argued that the British were justly renowned for their sense of justice and fair play and that if only they were more British in their management of the Indian empire, the problems of poverty, injustice and inequality could all be removed. Naoroji and the so-called 'moder-ate' nationalists expected little beyond the reform of British rule in India. It was perhaps not surprising that they should think this way, given the fact that the majority of them were employed by the colonial administration. Naoroji went on to become the first elected Indian in the British parliament, representing the north London constituency of Finsbury in 1892 during the period when he ran the British Committee of the Indian National Congress. Following his return to India he was three times elected president of the Indian National Congress and was regarded by many as the 'father' of Indian nationalism.

Another early nationalist in Bombay was Pherozeshah Mehta, who was also a

Parsi and a Western-educated lawyer. Mehta entered politics following the intro-
duction of the Vernacular Press Act in 1878 by the then viceroy, Lord Lytton.
This Act was an early attempt to silence the political views of the Indian-language
press, which was becoming increasingly captious, especially after Lord Lytton
embarked on a hugely expensive attempt to invade Afghanistan. Soon after, Lord
Lytton lost his post, but this was more to do with the change of government in
London than the attacks of the Indian media and politicians in Bombay and
Calcutta. Like their contemporaries in Allahabad and Madras (Bayly 1975;
Washbrook 1976), these early politicians were essentially reformist, small scale
and regional in outlook. One of the first issues to provoke Indian politicians into
collaborating and developing a more critical stance was the Bill of Criminal
Jurisdiction, introduced by Sir Courtney Ilbert in the imperial legislative council
of 1883, the so-called Ilbert Bill. It was a seemingly innocuous measure, designed
to give Indian magistrates the power to try Europeans living in country districts
for criminal offences, powers they already possessed in the towns and cities, where
it was common for judges to try Europeans as well as Indians whenever they
appeared in the courts. The Bill thus proposed to make it normal for Indian
subordinate judges to circuit outlying rural areas to preside over cases, as they did
in the cities. However, the bill was vigorously opposed by European planters and
settlers, particularly in Bengal, who organised themselves into a European and
Anglo-Indian Defence Association, which vigorously attacked the viceroy for dar-
ing to introduce such an impartial system of justice. Sir Alfred Lyall, governor of
the North-West Provinces, commented that the Assam planters feared the Bill for
no better reason than that it would 'do away with their right of beating niggers'.[3]
The opposition meant that the Bill could only finally be introduced in an emascu-
lated and racist form, whereby Europeans could be tried in a court presided over
by an Indian judge in rural areas only if at least half of the members of the jury
were European or Anglo-Indian.

The Ilbert Bill deeply offended the Indian middle classes precisely because
many of them were lawyers and judges. It called into question whether they were
really worthy and suitably qualified, in the minds of the British, to try court cases,
and whether they might need to have a half-white jury standing over their shoul-
der to ensure they took the 'right' decisions. It was thus both a professional and
racist issue, and it was shortly after this incident that the Indian National Congress
was formed in 1885 at the instigation of Allan Octavian Hume. In the same year,
the conservative Bombay Association was also finally abandoned in favour of a
new, more political, Bombay Presidency Association (with Sir Jamsetji Jijibhai as
president), to give voice to middle-class opinion in the west of India.

A.O. Hume was the son of the radical English reformist Joseph Hume and an
enthusiast for agricultural improvement before retiring from the Indian Civil
Service (ICS), where he had latterly been in charge of the Revenue and Agriculture Department in the administration of the North-West Provinces. He is
regarded by some as the model of an enlightened, liberal colonial, but that would
be a misrepresentation. He had served as a magistrate in Etawah where he had
fought against rebel Indians in 1857, and his main motivation was fear of a

repetition of the incidents of that year. The way to prevent that, he thought, was by further spending on rural development, thus placating rural opinion, and by involving more and more educated Indians in the government of India. It was in order to give educated Indians a mouthpiece, which was so conspicuously absent, that he originally proposed the setting up of an Indian National Union. His campaign had begun a few years earlier, in 1883, when he addressed a circular letter to the graduates of Calcutta University, urging them to 'scorn personal ease and make a resolute struggle to secure greater freedom for themselves and their own affairs'. He set these young students a threefold objective: 'the fusion into one national whole of all the diverse forces and people of the country, the gradual regeneration along moral, spiritual, social and political lines of the nation thus evolved, and the consolidation of the union between England and India by secur-ing a modification of such of its conditions as may be unjust or injurious.'[4] These were the ideas that lay also behind the Indian National Union, which was very much a reformist association.

The Indian National Union quickly turned into something rather different. The first meeting was scheduled to be held in Poona in December 1885, but so many people replied to the invitation and asked to become involved that the venue had to be changed to Bombay where it was held in the Gokuldas Tejpal Boarding School, Sanskrit College and Library. The name was simultaneously changed to the Indian National Congress (INC), and the first session was chaired not by Hume but by a Bengali lawyer and politician, Romesh Chandra Bannerjee (Figure 6). For many years thereafter, Hume remained a guiding hand behind the Congress, partly it is said, because nobody could agree on who else should serve as its secretary, a post he held until his retirement in 1906. The significance of the

Figure 6 The first Indian National Congress, 28 December 1885. © British Library.

early Congress has been undermined by the suggestion that Hume was encouraged to establish it by the viceroy, Lord Dufferin, as a means to somehow placate or control Indian educated public opinion. This is somewhat unlikely, as Dufferin himself, in his private correspondence later on described Hume as an 'idiot', a liar and a 'traducer' of his administration. Although there were several other Englishmen involved in the early Congress, including the English Liberal MP William Wedderburn (who chaired the fifth session), the majority of the delegates were high-caste Hindus, and there were very few Muslim participants. The types of resolutions passed at the Congress's annual meeting were demands for the admission of more Indians into the civil service, the spending of less money on war and for the abolition of the office of the Secretary of State for India in London, which was considered a waste of money and an obstacle to progressive legislation in India. The reformers wanted India to be more autonomous, but did not press for Indians to be involved in the government. None of their demands were likely to inspire the wider mass of the Indian population, nor were they intended to. The Congress was simply a yearly three-day meeting at which an educated elite got together to discuss the concerns of their class. Many of them were extremely privileged individuals. Ranade visited the Simla Congress in 1886 accompanied by 25 servants, and whenever Pherozeshah Mehta travelled he would hire an entire railway saloon for his personal comfort. When Hume suggested that the Congress should recruit peasants by producing a pamphlet translated into 12 regional languages he was snubbed. As soon as it became known that the governor-general disapproved of the measure, the Indian politicians refused to discuss the matter when he proposed it at the Congress in 1891. Mass contacts were thus never on the agenda of the INC, and the tone of their early meetings is well illustrated by Dadabhai Naoroji's presidential address at the second meeting of the Congress in Calcutta in 1886:

> We have assembled to consider questions upon which depend our future, whether glorious or inglorious. It is our good fortune that we are under a rule which makes it possible for us to meet in this manner. [Cheers] It is under the civilizing rule of the Queen and people of England that we meet here together, hindered by none, and are freely allowed to speak our minds without the least fear and without the least hesitation. Such a thing is possible under British rule and British rule only. [Loud cheers] Then I put the question plainly: Is this Congress a nursery for sedition and rebellion against the British Government [cries of "no, no"]; or is it another stone in the foundation of the stability of that Government? [cries of "yes, yes".] There could be but one answer . . . because we are thoroughly sensible of the numberless blessings conferred upon us, of which the very existence of this Congress is a proof in a nutshell. [Cheers].[5]

How a rather more radical type of politician later began to emerge in the subcontinent has a lot to do with religious and social change in the later nineteenth century, a subject discussed in our next chapter.

6 Revivalist and reform movements in the late nineteenth century

Mother, I bow to thee!
Rich with thy hurrying streams, bright with orchard gleams, . . .
Who hath said thou art weak in thy lands
When the sword flash out in the seventy million hands
And seventy million voices roar
Thy dreadful name from shore to shore? . . .
To thee I call Mother and Lord!
Though who savest, arise and save!
To her I cry who ever her foeman drove
Back from plain and Sea
And shook herself free.

(Lyrics of *Bande Mataram*)[1]

O learned pandits wind up the selfish prattle of your hollow wisdom and
Listen to what I have to say.

(16-year-old low-caste girl, Muktabai in Maharashtra)[2]

At its formation in 1885, the Congress Party was simply a gathering of concerned citizens drawn from all over the subcontinent but representing for the most part nobody other than themselves. After Hume's peasant-based proposals were rejected, he published a circular predicting imminent peasant revolution unless Congress and the government began to better represent their interests. This was condemned by the government and repudiated by other members of the Congress. During the late nineteenth century, the only major concession won as a result of Congress campaigning was the 1892 Councils Act, which replaced district boards with councils containing a majority of elected representatives. This proposal, which enfranchised only a very small educated elite, seemed to satisfy the vast majority of the Congress delegates. They were not concerned with further reform beyond the recruitment of more of their numbers into the civil service and the professions.

There were a few exceptions to the generally loyalist character of the early Congress delegates. R.C. Dutt agitated for an improvement in the condition of the peasantry and actually proposed a resolution urging a reduction of peasant rents in a session of Congress in 1899 that he presided over. His proposal was followed by others immediately urging that a limit should also be put on the taxes paid by the *zamindars*. Clearly the interests of the Congress were less with the former than with the latter. The most important failure of the Congress was not only its aloofness from the masses but also its inability to attract the support of Muslims in the north of India, who remained suspicious of the organisation and in particular of the elected councils set up in 1892 on which they feared they were bound to be outnumbered and outvoted. Despite this gloomy scenario, there were glimmers of hope. In 1887 at the Madras session of the Congress there was an unusual popular response to the request for funds. A membership drive was launched at a fee of one and a half annas, and some 8,000 persons contributed.

Along with the Congress there were some individuals who did enjoy mass popular support, men such as Aurobindo Ghosh in Bengal and Tilak in Maharashtra, who were beginning to rally support for a more vigorous and popular brand of nationalism that drew not simply on Western models but on currents of patriotism and idealism within India itself. These individuals were labelled by the British as 'extremists'. The reason for this was simple enough: their mass following was sufficient to make them a threat to the British regime. There were also at this time great strides taken in addressing issues such as women's education by reformers such as Pandita Ramabai, and the emergence of movements attempting to redefine the caste system and the identity of the lower castes and untouchables within South Asia. An unfortunate consequence was the growth of competition and conflict both between high and low castes and between religious groups. The benefit was a great enlargement in Indian civil society, and a growing participation of ordinary middle-class town and city dwellers in a public domain from which they had formerly been excluded (Watt 2004).

The growth of radicalism

Of all of the radical, popular politicians of the late nineteenth century probably the most successful was the western Indian politician Bal Gangadhur 'Lokamanya' Tilak, who was a student of the schoolteacher-cum-Marathi poet Vishnu Hari Chiplunkar, who inspired a whole generation with his poetry and writings celebrating the glories of Shivaji and of the Maratha empire (Wolpert 1962). Under Tilak's influence, the Poona Sarvajanik Sabha, formed by M.G. Ranade, became a highly vocal organisation that attracted a mass following both from the urban and rural populations in the then Bombay presidency (modern Maharashtra). His success, unlike that of other moderates such as Gokhale, was due to the fact that he spoke and wrote mostly in Marathi rather than English, and could thus be understood by greater numbers of people. His principal weapon was a Marathi language newspaper called *Kesari* or 'the Lion' (1881), which he edited; it achieved mass circulation in the towns and cities of the Deccan in western India. He also founded a publishing house, Kitabkhana, and co-founded the Deccan Education Society (1884). Although dubbed an extremist by the British, one of the reasons for Tilak's popularity was in fact his conservatism. For example, in controversies over the 1891 Age of Consent Bill, Tilak firmly opposed raising the age of consent from ten to twelve (which was supported by Gokhale), on the grounds that it represented foreign interference and a challenge to traditional Hindu practices. This was typical of Tilak's tactics of cultural revivalism. He used memories of Shivaji, the great Marathi leader of the seventeenth century, and revived Hindu festivals such as Ganesh Chaturthi) – a celebration of the god of wealth, Ganesh – as platforms for promoting patriotic and nationalist ideals. Amongst other things Tilak established an annual festival to celebrate Shivaji's birthday, and on these occasions would make political speeches in coded language. By extolling the virtues of Shivaji, who had struggled against the Mughals, he implicitly called on Maharashtrians to rise up against the 'new Mughals' in India, the British. It was in fact one of Tilak's followers, in 1897, who carried out the first act of terrorism in the independence movement when he assassinated a British official at the Bombay governor's Jubilee Ball in honour of the Empress Victoria. Shortly after this Tilak was jailed for two years for publishing a seditious article in his newspaper that justified Shivaji's assassination of the Bijapur general Afzal Khan, thereby implicitly condoning this more recent murder.

Being a Marathi speaker and in tune with the culture and ideals of western Indians, Tilak was able to achieve a wide following within a very short space of time, appealing to their myths and prejudices, and he attacked his conservative rivals with both vigour and humour, as in the following speech:

> [T]he venerable leader (Dadabhai Naoroji) who presided over the recent Congress was the first to tell us that the drain (of wealth) from the country was ruining it, and if the drain was to continue, there was some great disaster awaiting us. So terribly convinced was he of this that he went over from here to England and spent twenty-five years of his life trying to convince the English people of the injustice that is being done to us. He worked very hard. He had conversations and interviews with Secretaries of State, with Members of Parliament – and with what result? He has come here at the age of eighty-two to tell us that he is bitterly disappointed. Mr Gokhale, I know, is not disappointed but is prepared to wait another eighty years till he is disappointed like Dr Dadabhai.[3]

The big disadvantage of Tilak and people like him in other parts of India was their very parochialism: the fact that they were entirely concerned with their local societies and the people who spoke the same language as them, a characteristic of identity formation in this period)(Naregal 2002). Needless to say, identifying with leaders such as Shivaji, who had spent much time killing Muslims in the north, made any sort of identification or association between these various movements very difficult to achieve. They all tended to go in their different directions and to undermine any moves towards a transcontinental political consensus. Added to this regional exclusivity was also that of caste. These early and more popular politicians were not only parochial but also often appealed only to certain sections of that local population, particularly the upper castes from which they more often than not derived.

In Bengal there were comparable movements and comparable politicians to those seen in western India. There was also a flourishing of local patriotism and a cultural and religious revival, characterised in the late nineteenth century by an outpouring of patriotic novels and newspapers and associated with the rise of the elite *bhadralok* castes to a position of both cultural and economic ascendancy (Bhattacharya 2002). The most famous novelist in Bengal at this time was Bankim Chatterjee whose novel *Anandmath* became a bestseller. It told of a Hindu uprising against the Mughals in the east of Bengal in the sixteenth century, again another model for political action in the late nineteenth century. It contained the hymn 'Bande Mataram' (Hail to the Motherland) that, set to music by the Nobel prize-winning author Rabindranath Tagore, became an unofficial national anthem. The leading 'extremist' politician at this time was Aurobindo Ghosh. Others played a part: Motilal Ghosh edited the weekly journal *Amrita Bazar Patrika*, which became a mouthpiece for the Communist Party in the 1930s and is a very important source on the politics of Bengal for historians. The problem with these politicians was that they were relatively high caste and therefore never able to reach out to the rural population. In particular, their high-caste Hindu origins meant that, like the Congress politicians, they had very little appeal to Muslims. In the south this problem was if anything more acute. There was a Madras Native Association and later a Madras Mahajana Sabha (or Great People's Society) founded in 1884, but like the Bengali politicians they were only able to forge a limited appeal to a minority of the population. Although more popular than people like Gokhale, they were still largely dominated by Brahmins in Madras and failed to reach out to the larger non-Brahmin population.

The role of Hindu and Muslim revivalism

A serious difficulty was that in both Bengali and western India so-called 'extremist' movements depended heavily on currents of Hindu revivalism, which tended to alienate Muslims. Thus even if they had lower caste origins, they would have had difficulty in reconciling the issues they campaigned on with Muslims. In the north of India this problem was particularly acute due to the growth of the Arya Samaj. Like the Brahmo Samaj established in Bengal in the earlier part of the century (Kopf 1979), the Arya Samaj was a monotheistic reformist sect critical of many aspects of conventional Hinduism, including the worship of idols, casteism, and Brahmin domination, dowry, *purdah*, and the mistreatment of women (Barrier 1967; Jones 1976, 1989). It was founded in Saurashtra in 1875 by Dayananda Saraswati – a wandering *sannyasin* or holy man who spoke only in Hindi and Sanskrit – in order to promote what he considered to be the 'only true and universal faith', as laid out in his *Satyath Prakash*, published the year before (Jordens 1997). Dayananda was probably inspired to establish a fully fledged organisation after a meeting with two leaders of the Brahmo Samaj, Keshub Chandra Sen and Vidyasagar, and his popularity increased as he applied himself to various enterprises aimed at raising the physical, spiritual and social conditions of northern India, and using modern methods of communication and organisation to do so

(Lajpat Rai 1996). In consequence, followers of the sect spread rapidly, and it soon had branches in cities such as Ahmedabad and in the Punjab. Both the Arya and Brahmo Samaj saw the means to advancement as lying in education. Unlike the Brahmo Samaj, however, the Arya Samaj was deeply conservative and aggressive in its claims for superiority over other religions, leading to attempts to make mass conversions of Muslims in north India. The Aryas, unlike other reform movements of the time, blamed the feebleness and errors of Hindus not only on what Dayananda described as a hypocritical and self-serving priesthood (an early target) but also on the effects of foreign rule. They thus came into direct conflict with the colonial regime at an early stage. Quite a number of important Punjabi nationalists, many of whom in later years led the terrorist campaigns in the period up to and including the First World War, belonged to the Arya Samaj. Guru Dutt, Lala Lajpatrai and Lala Munshiram all started off as Arya Samajists but went on to become terrorists, communists or Bolshevists (Gupta and Gupta 2001). More consistently, however, the so-called extremist Punjabi nationalists were deeply and openly communal. Thus an associate of Lalaraj wrote in the newspaper, the *Punjabi*: 'The consciousness must arise in the mind of each Hindu that he is a Hindu and not merely an Indian', and that hence there was a need for the substitution of Hindu Sabhas for the congress committees, of a Hindu press for the Congress press and the organisation of a Hindu defence fund with regular machinery for seeking redress and self-help.[4] The significance of these ideas is that they anticipate in many ways those of the later RSS (Rashtrya Svayamsevak Sangh), which became a powerful Hindu fundamentalist and anti-Muslim political organisation in the 1930s and which is still an influential force in Indian society today (Graham 1990; Pralay 2002). Many Arya Samajists in fact ended up in the ranks of this organisation.

The Arya Samajists not only alienated Muslims but provoked them into introspection and the consideration of the status of their own faith and community within Indian society. Thus it was partly in response to Hindu revivalism that Muslims also began to undergo a period of revival and reform in the later nineteenth century (Hardy 1972; Hasan 1985, 1991; Ahmed 1981). One of the more important Muslim movements grew up centred around the town of Aligarh (home today to the Aligarh Muslim University) (Lelyveld 1978). It was started by a man called Said Ahmed Khan. Hafiz Malik (1980), Khan's biographer, argues that one of the reasons why Khan became involved in this movement was because his was one of the families that suffered particularly in the aftermath of the 1857 uprising. His family were large landowners with a record of loyalty to the British, but they were singled out for punishment after 1857 and lost a great deal of their land. The revivalist and reformist movement that he led was partly a response to this and a product of the sense of remorse and betrayal felt by his community. One of the key issues that concerned the Aligarh movement was therefore the emancipation of Muslims – the desire to re-establish their place in society as it had been prior to the 1860s. The focus for their activities became the Anglo-Muhammadan College founded by Said Khan at Aligarh in 1875, paid for with money given by Muslim landlords in the north of India. Said Khan believed that the emancipation of Indian Muslims would be achieved through social reform and modern education. Extolling the virtues of Western science, he aimed to achieve a Muslim revolution through modernisation. At the same time, he tried to maintain the traditional loyalties of Muslims by claiming that many of the methods and some of the revelations of modern science were to be found in outline form in the Koran. (Western science had in fact derived a great deal from the insights of Muslim scholars and scientists of the pre-Renaissance era.) These ideas about the harmony between Islam and modernity were promulgated by Muslim intellectuals in the north of India, not only through the college at Aligarh but also by the use of a journal and a scientific society that Said Khan founded. Despite his family's suffering after the rebellion of 1857, Said Khan remained throughout his life an admirer of British culture as well as of the authoritarian political system of the British *raj*, which he supported in terms typified by the following comment:

> My friends, I have repeatedly said and say it again that India is like a bride which has got two beautiful and lustrous eyes – Hindus and Mussulmans. If they quarrel against each other that beautiful bride will become ugly and if one destroys the other, she will lose one eye . . . It is, therefore, necessary that for the peace of India and for the progress of everything in India the English Government should remain for many years – in fact forever!
>
> (Sir Said Ahmed Khan)[5]

For such views he was seen as a loyalist by the British, was knighted, and regarded as a representative of the modern Muslim aristocracy they hoped would become a pillar of Anglo-Indian society in north India.

Another reason why the Aligarh movement was encouraged by the British was the less appealing (from a British point of view) alternative role models for Muslims that were developing in the later nineteenth century. Muslim scholars, or *ulema*, connected with the Barelwi 'school', Firanghi Mahal, and later independent seminaries of Nadwat al-ulama in Lucknow and the influential and conservative Dar al-ʿUlum *madrasa* at Deoband in north India, were all working on a revision and updating of the traditional *madrasa* syllabi in order to take into account the changed conditions of modern life, promote unity among Muslims and, implicitly, to provide a viable model for self-government in modern times (Robinson 2001; Metcalf 1982). This was the beginning of a struggle between the modernisers and the *ulema* for the heart and soul of the Muslims of north India, contrasting individual and community identities, which continued right up to Partition (Jalal 2001). One of the scholars at the Deoband *madrasa*, established in 1866, Maulana Muhammad Qasim Nanotvi, played a prominent role in the locality during the uprising of 1857. And one of its students, Mahmud al-Hasan, was later to become known as *shaykh al-hind* (leader of India), forming a government in exile headquartered in Medina in Saudi Arabia with Mahmud al-Hasan as its *amir* (chief), Barkutullah Bhopali as its minister, and Mahraja Pratap Singh as its president. This government in exile began to seek international support against British rule. Unfortunately one of the internal communications between the leaders, written on a silk cloth, fell into the hands of the British in 1916: this *tahrik-e-reshmi rumal* (silk kerchief conspiracy) led to the arrest of more than 200 *ulema*. In 1919, the Jamiat Ulema-e-Hind, a Muslim political organisation based in India, was then started by the *ulema* of this *madrasa*. This organisation, which opposed the two-nation theory of the Muslim League on the grounds that culture, not religion, defines a nation's identity, split in 1937, bringing the militant Jamiat Ulema-e-Islam into existence, which after 1947 found a home in Pakistan.

Parallel to the rise of modernisers, Islamic revivalists and reformers of north India, there was a more general pan-Islamic movement growing in the late nineteenth century, centred on Muslim anxieties about the fate of the Holy Land, given the imminent collapse of the Ottoman empire. The Ottoman sultan was the *Caliph* or protector of Islam, and in particular of the Islamic (and Christian) religious sites in Palestine. In the wake of the Balkan War of 1876 and the Graeco-Turkish War of 1896, there were growing anxieties amongst the Muslims about what would happen to this empire. They feared that the holy sites would fall under the control of either the French or the British. An influential writer on this theme was Sayyid Jamal al-Din al-Afghani, considered the founding father of Islamic modernism and of the pan-Islamic movement, who criticised autocracy and absolute monarchy as well as colonialism and sought to unite both Shiites and Sunnis in the Islamic world (Landau 1990; Hasan 1985). In India his ideas contributed to the development of the so-called Khilafat movement, although its unique strength in India indicated that this movement had yet more powerful indigenous roots (Qureshi 1999). Pan-Islamism was threatening to the British because it criticised British policy towards the Ottoman empire. For this reason, the Aligarh movement was supported by the British regime as a counterweight to the Khilafatists. Since the Khilafat cause was clearly of such concern to Muslims, it was later taken up by Mahatma Gandhi in his attempt to forge an all-India unity, and it became a part of the first national *satyagraha* that Gandhi organised in 1920.

Cow protection and 'communal' conflict

One of the problems that resulted from revivalist movements was growing conflict between Hindus and Muslims, as religious fundamentalism became increasingly prominent on both sides. Along with this there was a steady growth of ill-feeling between the two communities from the 1880s onwards due to a variety of more mundane causes. The word 'communalism' has been coined to describe the use of religion for political ends in the Indian context, which began to become a feature from this time onwards In the 1890s the conflicts between the two communities were confined to two main areas. The first concerned controversy over the use of Urdu or Devanagari scripts in the schools and administration in north India. The two main languages here were Urdu, based partly on Persian and using an Arabic script, and Hindi, based more on Sanskrit and using the Devanagari script. In the spoken form, the two languages have a great deal in common (the term 'Hindustani' being used to describe the combination of both languages commonly spoken); on paper they look entirely different. Urdu and the Persian script was used more by Muslims, while the Devanagri script, and a more 'Sanskritised' version of the language, was preferred by Hindus – increasingly so with the encouragement of polemicists such as Bharatendu Harishchandra (Dalmia 1999). Until the 1830s Persian had been the language of government preferred by both the Mughals and the British who dealt with them, so that most Urdu users could read official documents (Cohn 1984). However, after 1830 the language of government was mostly English. In the 1890s there was a decision to increase the use of vernacular languages in local administration and the issue then arose as to whether Urdu or Hindi should be used, an issue that divided the two communities (King 1983, 1995).

A second focus of conflict between religious communities in north India concerned the sacred cow. The sacred status of the cow arises from the agrarian roots of Hinduism. It is a sin for Hindus to kill cows and to eat cattle flesh. Often as an act of religious devotion Hindus would liberate the cows that they owned and allow them to wander free. In the later nineteenth century, Gorakshini *sabhas* ('cow protection' societies) developed, founded by Hindus in order to look after and care for stray cattle. They also campaigned for the closure of kebab shops. Muslims, not having any particular beliefs about cows, were generally the proprietors of such kebab shops. One of the major activities of municipal councils after the passing of the 1892 Act was to attempt to close down kebab shops by invoking various by-laws on matters of hygiene, and to ban the slaughter of cattle. This was more than a passing problem for Muslims, who commonly sacrificed and ate beef at times of religious festivals. Conflicts over the sacrificing of cattle on the occasion of the festival of Id in 1893 led to the first major large-scale riot between Hindus and Muslims in the cities of north India. These riots eventually spread as far as Bombay and Rangoon.

It is argued by C.A. Bayly (1985) that conflicts between Hindus and Muslims were not a new phenomenon; what was significant about these riots, however, was, first, the speed and extent to which they spread. This was related to the development of communications in the late nineteenth century. There may well have been encounters and troubles before, but their extent had been limited. It was now possible, however, for rumours of atrocities to spread more rapidly, and a response elsewhere was also more likely. But there was more to it than that. The historian Gyan Pandey (1983, 1990) disagrees with other authors who have addressed this topic, such as J.R. McLane (1977) and Francis Robinson (1974), who see the *gaurakshini* (cow protection) agitation as being an entirely urban, elite-led phenomenon. This, argues Pandey, has led them to underestimate the breadth of support in rural areas and the unity of purpose that was expressed in the riots and demonstrations on the issue. Such a unity of purpose had been rarely seen before; it was not confined to the elites, being also shared by Muslim and Hindu masses. In explaining the causes of the riots, Pandey argues that they should not be seen as expressions of 'primordial religious loyalty', as some might argue, but rather as the consequence of a steady escalation of economic conflict in the late nineteenth century, caused by economic stagnation in parts of north India, compounded by the decline of weaving and service communities, many of them Muslim, under the impact of European imports (Pandey 1983).

Economic decline in some parts of north India was contrasted by a rise in prosperity in others, particularly amongst the high-caste peasants and large Hindu landowners, who were supported by the British, leading to social division. There were in fact laws to prevent incitement to religious violence and another issue was the decision reached by the Allahabad High Court in 1886 that the cow was not an object as laid down in the law regarding religious incitement. Hence Muslims who slaughtered cows could not be held guilty under this clause. There then followed a great increase in the incidence of cattle slaughter, the cow protection movement amongst Hindus being partly a response to this. However, a more general phenomenon behind Hindu–Muslim conflict was the desire for an improvement in status on the part of marginal communities. Amongst low-status or economically backward Hindus the means to self-improvement and respectability lay with the development of caste associations and of temperance movements, as well as rallying around the cow. Amongst low-status Muslim communities the desire to raise their position was fulfilled by the reinvention of the tradition of the ritual slaughter of cattle. In this way the conditions for a religious conflict were in fact set by external socio-economic factors, these tendencies being accelerated by rapid changes in the colonial economy of the late nineteenth century.

C.A. Bayly (1988) has argued that many of the later nineteenth-century social and religious movements were not movements of the oppressed, or of the elite *per se*, but of newly prosperous communities striving to assert themselves. In this way, he suggests, religious conflict was a characteristic expression of economic competition and the demand for influence made by a variety of emerging social groups in late nineteenth-century colonial India. Rituals such as protecting the cow were evidently more likely to be indulged in by those who felt they had something to gain from this than by those whose position or status in society was assured. If an element of straightforward competition were to be added – it is sufficient to note here that Hindu landlords and Muslim tenants often found themselves on opposing sides of a class barrier – it becomes evident that the economic causes of this religious conflict were varied and profound and particularly significant given the rapidity of economic change in the decades following 1860.

The increase in communalism in present-day India might be seen to derive from a similar set of circumstances: the 1980s witnessing rapid industrial growth at the same time as there has been an increase of poverty. A high rate of change combined with advanced levels of inequality always engenders social conflict, and Gyan Pandey (1990) has amassed considerable evidence to support the contention that such a process was underway in the late nineteenth century. Amongst Muslims, these desires for self-improvement found an early outlet in countrywide associations such as the National Mahomedan Association, as well as in local societies that encouraged Muslim culture and Western knowledge, and in a plethora of Islamic newspapers and journals. Interestingly, in the case of the Muslims, the development from cultural to political resurgence is seen very clearly in the evolution of the major mouthpiece of the community, the Muslim League. The

Muslim League was founded by a group of delegates attending a meeting of the National Mahomedan Association at Dhaka in 1906. The pretence for forming the League was Viscount Morley's first proposals for political devolution in India. Following a meeting at Simla between the viceroys and elite Muslims, at which the latter successfully pleaded for representation in excess of their numbers as a reward for their loyalty to the empire, the League was formed. Thus, British political initiatives played their part, but it was interesting that the founding meeting of the League actually took place at an educational conference. Here the link between cultural and religious revivalism and later political assertion is graphically self-evident.

Other revivalist and social reform movements

In the late colonial period numerous other religious movements trod the same path as the revivalist and reform trends within upper-caste Hinduism and Islam. One of the most important is the Singh movement, amongst the Sikhs of the Punjab, described by the historians Grewal (1990), McLeod (1976, 1991) and, most vividly, R.G. Fox (1985). The Singh movement began in the 1880s, and culminated in the great *Gurudwara* campaign of 1917 to 1922. Mahatma Gandhi took on the issue of the holy sites of the Sikhs, along with that of Muslims. The *gurudwaras*, or temples of the Sikhs, had been taken over by the British administration, and the campaign sought to restore control of them to the Sikhs. This went on to become one of the important issues raised in the early stage of the nationalist movement. Its origin lay in the desire for self-improvement, and a rise in Sikh status. It began as a movement of core peasants in the canal colonies of the Punjab seeking to gain respectability by the reinvention of the symbols of Sikhism, the so-called five 'K's. At the end of the nineteenth century it was often not possible to distinguish a Sikh from any other north Indian – they looked and dressed similarly. One of the issues taken up was the desire to distinguish themselves; followers of the movement were urged never to cut their hair (*kesh*), to always carry a comb (*kanga*), to always wear breeches (*katch*), to wear a steel bangle (*kara*) and to carry a dagger (*kirpan*). All followers were also required to adopt the patronym of the sixteenth-century founder of Sikhism, guru Gobind Singh (and so successful was the movement that today most Sikhs all still use the name Singh). There are various explanations as to how the movement began. One was that the British themselves gave it great encouragement by their belief that Sikhs were a martial race. They insisted that only Sikhs would be allowed to be recruited into many regiments of the British Indian army, and a British officer could only distinguish a Sikh through the visual symbols, which therefore encouraged others to adopt them. From an early date the Singh Sabha concentrated on religious targets and avoided direct confrontation with the colonial administration. Unlike the Arya Samajists, who organised strikes in the cities of the Punjab and a boycott of government levies for the use of canal water in the Chenab colony in 1907, bringing down upon them the full weight of colonial repression, the Sikhs, by concentrating on social reforms such as the avoidance of alcohol, and the removal of government control over Sikh temples, were able to steadily expand and to gain large numbers of converts, especially in rural areas.

Other movements were found amongst the non-Brahmin, low-caste sections of society (Omvedt 1995; Zelliott 1992), often inspired by missionary education (Battacharya 2002), the improvement in economic conditions, and the increased mobility within this, often labouring, class of society. The most important began in the south and west of India: Ramaswami Naicker in the south, and Jyotirao Phule in the west were the early leaders of two such low-caste movements. In the 1920s, the campaign to liberate India's untouchables went on to become of crucial significance under the leadership of B.R. Ambedkar, the western Indian leader of India's *dalit* or 'untouchable' community, his success forcing Mahatma Gandhi also to focus his attention on their cause and to campaign vigorously on their behalf in the 1930s. Ambedkar was later persuaded that it was impossible to reform Hinduism and converted to Buddhism, taking many untouchables in western India with him, and he went on to play a crucial role as the chair of the committee that drew up India's post-independence constitution. In the late nineteenth century in western India, anti-Brahminism was also a vehicle for the expression of regional patriotism, and particularly for the assertion of Maratha identity (Omvedt 1976; O'Hanlon 1985). In southern India it was a vehicle for regional patriotism too, in this case for the assertion of a Tamil identity (Irschick 1969; Barnett 1976).

Low-caste movements were often predicated upon the interpretation by Phule and others of evidence from the Vedas, and the arguments of British oriental language scholars, such as William Jones, concerning the supposed 'Aryan invasion' of India. If a material invasion had taken place, they argued, then the low castes, and those living in the south of India, the so-called 'Dravidian' peoples who spoke a different language type from those in the north, should be regarded as the original inhabitants, and accorded special privileges, whilst the Brahmins and all northerners should be regarded, like the British, as colonial intruders. From this derived an 'adi-Dravida' consciousness ('adi' meaning 'from earliest times') in the south of India, spawning from 1916 onwards the Justice Party, a loyalist, Madras-based political organisation representing intermediate castes, and in the late 1920s the more radical and low-caste 'self-respect' movement led by 'Periyar' E.V. Ramaswami Naicker (Irschick 1986; Pandian 2007). Finally, from the late 1940s onwards (building upon the following established by Naicker), the Dravida Munnetra Kazagam, a popular party attempting to represent low castes and south Indian Tamils as a whole against the alleged cultural and political hegemony of the north, itself acquired political hegemony in the state. An 'adi-' movement also began amongst the tribals in the 1920s, from whence the term '*adivasi*' (meaning earliest inhabitants) derives. The movement began in Chota Nagpur in Bihar as an attempt to unite the various tribal groups against their common, usually Hindu, oppressors, and has flourished in the years after Independence, the 'Jharkhand' Mukti Morcha (people's march), successfully campaigning for the creation of a separate *adivasi* state in central India (Jharkhand being the title of an ancient *adivasi* kingdom), was its most influential and enduring product.

Both the adi-Dravida and *adivasi* movements were influenced by Christian missionaries, who targeted oppressed groups whom they believed might more easily be converted. Education was their main instrument, and Christian missionary schools became widespread in south India from the late nineteenth century onwards, teaching the English language and inculcating Christian egalitarian ideals in the minds of their pupils. There were only a limited number of conversions to the Christian faith, but their cultural and political influence was nonetheless significant (Bayly 1990), which is one reason why they were banned from Madhya Pradesh, the central India state with the largest tribal population, from the 1950s onwards (Madhya Pradesh 1956). Christian missionary influence also had a profound effect on debates concerning the status of women in colonial India. More often than not, however, their attacks on Hinduism, rather than winning converts, inspired attempts to reform and modernise Hindu faith and society from within. The earliest of the Hindu revivalist and social reform movements was the Brahmo Samaj, founded in the early nineteenth century. Its then leader, Ram Mohan Roy, campaigned famously against *sati* and for the rights of Hindu widows – who were prevented from remarrying until the passage of the Hindu remarriage act of 1856. Even after this Hindu widows were still often considered a burden following the death of their husbands, being without status and expected to live a life of penury and devotion to the service of others, a state of social ostracism savagely criticised by Tarabai Sinde in a pamphlet published in the early 1880s after the trial of a young Brahmin widow for killing her illegitimate child in Surat (O'Hanlon 1994). Many social reformers came to believe in the need for education for women to provide a solution to these and other problems (Forbes 1996). Keshub Chandra Sen, a leader of the Brahmo Samaj, Ishwar Chandra Vidyasagar, and members of the breakaway Sadhran (General) Brahmo Samaj were important late nineteenth-century Bengali advocates of education for women (Shastri 1974). So too was Swami Vivekananda, a disciple of Ramakrishna, who led a more conventional, but hugely influential, revivalist movement centred on education, social reform and the modernisation of Hindu beliefs (Dixit 1975; Sen 1993; Radice 1998). Vivekananda played an important role in defining the newly emergent, modernising Bengali national consciousness. Under Vivekananda's influence worship of the goddess Durga, reverence for the motherland, and a commitment to female education and cautious improvements in the status of women became the hallmark beliefs of the patriotic, middle-class, Hindu, Bengali male.

Social reform issues were taken up by members of the Prarthana Samaj, Bombay's answer to the Brahmo Samaj, founded in the 1860s, and by campaigners such as Kandukuri Virasalingam in the south of India, who persuaded the whole town of Rajamundry to accept the idea of Hindu widow remarriage in the 1890s. M.G. Ranade, in the west of India, was another great advocate of the rights of Hindu widows, whilst the National Social Conference, which he helped to found at the third meeting of the Indian National Congress in 1887, provided a forum particularly for the discussion of women's social issues. Ranade's wife, Ramabhai, herself became a vigorous advocate of education for women, establishing a school for Hindu widows in the late 1880s in Bombay, although she was treated with suspicion for her conversion to Christianity. Meanwhile, in Calcutta the Hindu Mahila Vidyalaya (Hindu Girl's School), the offshoot of a school for women originally founded in 1872 by Keshub Sen and an Englishwoman, Annette Ackroyd, was transformed in 1878 into Bethune College, affiliated to Calcutta University, and in 1883 awarded BAs to the first two women graduates in the British empire.

The modest beginnings of the women's movement in India were often still opposed by social conservatives, such as Lokamanya Tilak. They were also frequently undermined by the conservative attitude of the British courts, as seen in the notorious case of Rukmabai, 'an intelligent and cultured young woman' of 22 who refused to live with Dadaji Bhikaji, to whom she was married when she was 11, a liberty initially upheld by the courts, although she was subsequently ordered to do so by judges of the Appellate Bench in 1887 (Chandra 1998). Her case became a *cause célèbre*, although her plea in a letter to *The Times* did her little good:

> Is it not inhuman that our Hindoo men should have every liberty while women are tied on every hand for ever? If I were to write you all about this system of slavery, it would require months to complete it . . . Oh! but who has the power to venture and interfere in the customs and notions of such a vast multitude except the Government which rules over it? And as long as the government is indifferent to it . . . India's daughters must not expect to be relieved from their present sufferings.[6]

Despite these setbacks, the publicity in such cases still opened the possibility for discussion about improvements in the status of women. They were also important steps towards the involvement of women in public life and the later emergence of women's organisations such as the Ladies Social Conference (founded in 1905) and the All-India Muslim Women's Conference (established in 1915). Later on still, the first national women's organisations were founded, such as the Women's Indian Association (founded by the Irish feminist and theosophist Margaret Cousins in 1915), the National Council of Women in India (an Indian branch of the International Council of Women) and, most importantly of all, the All-India Women's Conference (founded in 1927), which became an influential organisation articulating the concerns of women within the nationalist movement by the 1930s (Forbes 1996; Kumar 1993).

The developments seen at the end of the nineteenth century had tremendous importance for women in Indian society, but it is necessary to be aware of their limitations too: in the longer term, they had the effect of making Hindu revivalism and a reformed, but nonetheless Brahminical, paternalistic and conservative respect for women (of a sort of which Victorian Christian missionaries would have greatly approved), very much the hallmarks of Indian nationalism. Indian women were not encouraged to speak for themselves, which rendered the status of Indian women readily accessible as a subject for communal and patriarchal manipulation (Gupta 2001; Walsh 2004) and an easy target for colonialist propaganda, such as Katherine Mayo's controversial *Mother India* (1927), a rebarbative critique of the Hindu attitude to women squarely targeted at nationalist demands for the right to self-government (Sinha 2006). This situation lay in complete contrast to that in twentieth-century China, for example, where nationalism favoured a complete rejection of traditional religious beliefs, and of missionary influence, in favour of a wholly modern, secular ideology, with woman occupying a radically different place in society, even if one still not quite on equal terms with men. This opened out many more opportunities for Chinese women than their Indian equivalents, who could often only gain influence outside the home by supporting their men-folk, by remaining deferential to their wishes, by being devout and, above all, by conforming to social and religious expectations.

Revivalism, reform and the growth of organised politics

The importance of the late nineteenth-century movements of religious revivalism and social reform have been underestimated in many accounts of early Indian nationalism. All too often, as O'Hanlon has argued, they have suffered a bias towards 'instrumentalism', devoting attention to, for example, the many clearly politically oriented 'caste associations' of this period (Carroll 1977, 1978; Washbrook and Baker 1975) but ignoring cultural and ideological developments whenever they did not involve lobbying of the colonial authorities or activities directly related to the acquisition of political power. It would be a grave mistake to neglect such developments, however, since in the absence of a democratic forum the creation of social and cultural organisations was often the only way in which grievances could be expressed and issues raised concerning the running of the country. The reform movements thus played a crucial role in helping to develop a public consciousness critical of colonial policies and, ultimately, the growth of nationalist rhetoric and of a national consciousness among the middle classes (Chatterjee 1993). For the wider public as well, religious revivalism played a similar role, encouraging the rediscovery of a sense of self-worth and a pride in Indian traditions, sentiments formerly challenged and devalued by the experience of colonial rule (Nandy 1983). Whilst the so-called 'extremist' politicians were often parochial as well as conservative, religious revivalism, both Muslim and Hindu, often crossed provincial boundaries and helped create a climate expectant of change, even one of millenarian hope, that was profoundly useful to later Indian politicians and crucial indeed to the success of the Gandhian Congress. It was these movements, rather than the constitutional initiatives of the British (in 1909, 1918 and 1935), that were to prove most significant in the creation of mass-movement politics in the inter-war years. The issues raised by these late nineteenth-century revivalist and reform movements would prove to be of crucial importance in the nationalist struggle and would continue to haunt Indian politics until the end of the twentieth century and beyond.

7 The Swadeshi and Ghadar movements

What is our name?
The Ghadars.
What is our work?
Ghadar.
Where will the Ghadar break out?
In India . . .
Why should it break out?
Because the people can no longer bear the oppression and tyranny practised under English rule and are ready to fight and die for freedom. . . . Time will come when rifles and blood will take the place of pen and ink.

(*Ghadar*, Nov. 1913)[1]

Hasi hasi porbo fansi
Dekhbe jagatbasi
Ekbar biday de ma
Ghure asi
(Smilingly I will put the noose around my neck, and the world will view it; Mother, send me off, I shall return after the wanderings.)

(Kshudiram Bose attr. 1908)[2]

The rhetoric of late colonial rule was one of 'preparing' Indians for self-government, and the emergence of Indian political parties and of organised opposition to colonial rule has often been described as the outgrowth of British constitutional experiments. These began with the setting up of councils with a purely advisory role in 1909, and the Government of India Acts of 1918 and 1935, which progressively transferred real power into the hands of elected Indian representatives (Seal 1968). This image of managed and orderly devolution, culminating in independence, is to be encountered in British official histories of the period and official collections of archive materials (Mansergh 1970–83). By contrast the research of 'subaltern', socialist and social historians, and others with an interest in the experience of ordinary Indians rather than the elite level of society, provides evidence of continuing and sometimes violent opposition to colonial rule, even after the suppression of the uprising of 1857, and which rapidly escalated after the turn of the century.

Opposition and unrest was often articulated in the form of social, religious and cultural movements, as described in the previous chapter. The late nineteenth century also saw its share of insurrection, beginning in certain Deccan villages in western India in the late 1870s when a downturn in agricultural prices led to disturbances in the villages where Marwari moneylenders, allegedly outsiders, had advanced loans against cotton crops and land used as security (Charlesworth 1972; Hardiman 1992). Such disturbances did not occur in villages where the moneylender was local, but so alarmed officials that legal measures were introduced in 1879 to further improve the security of peasant farmers, and to limit their debt and the possibility of their lands being transferred due to non-payment. There were similar anti-*zamindar* campaigns in east Bengal in response to illegal and excessive exactions of rent, which resulted in the passing of the Bengal Tenancy Act of 1885. Some of the western Indian villages involved in the so-called 'Deccan Riots' were again involved in a boycott on the payment of land revenue demands to the provincial government in the wake of the famine of 1896/7, an agitation encouraged by Tilak and the Poona Sarvajanik Sabha, and an interesting anticipation of later nationalist tactics.

Indebtedness, blamed on 'unscrupulous' Hindu moneylenders (a favourite target of colonial authorities), was held to account for disturbances in *adivasi* (tribal) areas, as elsewhere, in the late nineteenth century, although neglect and exploitation by the Forest Department or British-appointed intermediaries were at least equally responsible. In the *adivasi* areas British conceptions of private property undermined traditional forms of joint ownership, such as the *khuntkatti* tenure in Chota Nagpur. This was combined with renewed restrictions on shifting cultivation enforced by provincial forest departments everywhere after 1867 and reinforced by the Forest Act of 1878, which placed *adivasi* populations under considerable pressure. The principal grievance in Chota Nagpur concerned the exactions of alien landlords and the imposition of *beth begar* (forced labour) (Singh 1983). Local Munda *adivasi* chiefs, known as *sardars*, turned to rural missionaries and to the courts for assistance and in an attempt to find redress for their grievances – with no success. The missionary-educated son of a local sharecropper, Birsa, then stepped forward claiming to have seen a vision of a supreme god and to be a prophet with miraculous powers. Thousands flocked to hear him preach, and after a period in jail he returned to the forest in 1898–9, urging his followers (which by then included many former Christian Mundas) to kill all landlords, Christians and government officials. Promising that the guns and bullets of all enemies would turn to water, the insurrection began on Christmas eve 1899 with the burning of Christian churches over a wide area in the districts of Ranchi and Singhbum, and went on to include direct attacks on the police themselves. The insurrection was finally suppressed in January 1900, and 350 Mundas were put on trial, of whom 44 were transported for life to the Andaman islands and three were hanged. Soon after, the government introduced the Chota Nagpur

Tenancy Act of 1908 to attempt to preserve *adivasi* lands against outsiders. Such protection was not available elsewhere, but, nervous of popular insurrection, local enactments of this sort were made in many *adivasi* areas, and indeed in any locality, such as the Punjab, or western India, where peasant unrest threatened towards the end of the nineteenth century (Barrier 1966). This does not suggest a government in command, but one that was merely reacting to circumstances.

In the Godavari Agency, in the north of modern Andhra Pradesh (another hot-bed of unrest), an insurrection led by Koya and Konda Dora hill chiefs in the 'Rampa' country in 1879 was one of many provoked by attempts to raise taxes on timber and grazing. It required the deployment of no less than six regiments of Madras infantry to suppress it (Arnold 1982). Similar insurrections with similar causes were seen in the tribal kingdom of Bastar in central India in 1910 and in the Bhil country in southern Rajasthan, where a revivalist and temperance movement spilled over into open insurrection and demands for the creation of a Bhil *raj* in 1913. Many of these movements had a millenarian element, a belief in the imminence of a golden age. Thus one Konda Dora leader in 1900 armed his followers with bamboos, which he convinced them would turn by magic into guns, while their enemies' weapons would turn to water. A similar element of millen-arianism was to be seen in the uprisings of poor Muslim 'Moplah' leaseholding tenants (*kanamdars*) against the rack-renting practices of British-backed Hindu *jenmi* landlords in southern Malabar in the 1880s and 1890s. After attacking temples and landlord property, they would hurl themselves into the face of police bullets in the conviction that as martyrs they would go straight to heaven. Hindu tenants in the region were often similarly aggrieved, but their protests here, as elsewhere, more often took the simpler form of social banditry. Not until later did peasant unrest here take on a predominantly communal form, although the anger of tenant farmers, the element of religious revivalism, and the coincidence of class and religious divisions made this an imminent threat (Panikkar 1989).

Details of many more rural insurrections in the late nineteenth century and the early twentieth have been collected by historians, all of which, like those above, could be described as anti-colonial in nature if not always a direct harbinger of later nationalist campaigns amongst the peasantry (Hardiman 1992; Singh 1982). In addition, there was sufficient evidence of the emergence of class-consciousness among the urban working classes of Calcutta and Bombay to cause anxiety among European employers and factory owners and the colonial authorities, not to mention a variety of other forms of passive and non-violent forms of resistance either directly to colonial rule or at least to the policies instigated by colonial administrators (Haynes and Prakash 1991). In the light of this evidence, the British constitutional initiatives of the early twentieth century appear more like a strategy of containment, and an effort to 'divide and rule', rather than a serious effort to involve Indians in the management of the country.

Until the very end, the British government appears to have made skilful use of constitutional manoeuvrings to avert decolonisation rather than prepare for it. By contrast, the policies of the very last viceroy to be appointed in the reign of Queen Victoria, Lord Curzon, seem almost to have been designed to stimulate

Indian politicians into action and to imperil the security of the imperial system rather than stabilise it. Lord Curzon's actions during his brief reign as viceroy led directly to the eruption of the so-called 'Swadeshi' campaign, the very first large-scale popular anti-colonial movement since 1857, instigated by his government's decision to partition the province of Bengal. The Swadeshi campaign also saw the first eruption of organised urban terrorism directed against the colonial regime both in Calcutta and western India. Later on, the Ghadarite conspiracy brought organised terrorism to the Punjab and northern India as well.

The peasant insurrections mentioned above, combined with Swadeshi and the emergence of terrorism, were all highly significant, in that they took place long before Mahatma Gandhi emerged on the political scene, yet anticipated many of the strategies, tactics and features of the Congress Party's campaigns in the inter-war year. Combined with other signs of unrest, they were also the most probable cause of the British government's later policies of limited devolution and the greater involvement of 'moderate' Indian politicians in the business of empire.

The partition of Bengal and the Swadeshi campaign, 1905–11

The Indian National Congress was, in its early days, an extremely moderate annual meeting of mostly Hindu politicians, and it was the Hindu characteristics of the early Congress that alienated some Muslims. This attitude was typified by Sir Said Ahmed Khan who wrote: 'is it supposed that the different castes and creeds living in India belong to one nation or can become one nation and their aims and aspirations be the same? I think it is quite impossible, and when it is impossible there can be no such thing as a National Congress.'[3] Although an exaggerated description of the early Congress (which contained quite a few Parsis and Muslims), this view was characteristic of prevailing attitudes at the turn of the twentieth century. The growth of Muslim and Hindu revivalism and of many other sects and associations meant that the development of an anti-colonial consciousness was being dispersed in different directions. It was not until 1905 that an issue arose which for the first time brought some of these different movements together. It was the arrival in India of the new viceroy, Lord Curzon, in 1899, that began this process. Lord Curzon's character has been summed up by a doggerel poem penned by fellow students at Balliol College, Oxford, where he studied:

> My name is George Nathaniel Curzon
> I am a most superior person
> My cheek is pink, my hair is sleek
> And I dine at Blenheim once a week.

Curzon came from a privileged academic background and was an intolerant right-wing imperialist convinced of England's civilising mission (Dilks 1970, Goradia 1997; Gilmour 1994). He was the last viceroy to make a serious attempt to add to the territories under the control of the British. He wished, for example, to extend the authority of the British in the Persian Gulf, and when thwarted in this attempt he established consulates and naval bases as strongholds instead. He wished to take over the rule of Afghanistan as well, but was prevented from doing so by London. He did, however, send an expeditionary force into Tibet, which had to turn back before it got very far following advice from London. Curzon next established a separate government in the North-West Frontier Province and fortified this region as a bulwark against an imagined Russian threat. Elsewhere he made great efforts to improve, streamline and strengthen the administration, but is most particularly remembered for his unrepentant hostility towards educated Indians and to the Indian National Congress, which he described in 1900 as an 'organisation teetering to its fall', a demise he hoped to hasten. Characteristic of the trend in policies he sought to pursue was Curzon's decision to reduce the number of elected Indian representatives on the Calcutta City Corporation in 1899, setting back the first faltering steps in democratic representation. In 1904, concerned by the increasing radicalism of university students, he also increased the number of officials and reduced the number of elected Indians in the Senate of Calcutta University. Such measures, though, had exactly the opposite effect from what he intended. Rather than silencing the criticism of the British regime by Bengali intellectuals, Lord Curzon's policies irritated and angered them. But his biggest blunder was the decision to partition the province of Bengal in 1905.

The division of Bengal into eastern and western provinces was based supposedly on administrative convenience: Bengal included Bihar at this time and was one of the largest provisional governments in India. This would not have been so problematic if it had not been for the development in the later part of the nineteenth century of a growing sense of Bengali nationalism. Much as Tilak was encouraging Maratha nationalism in western India, so the Bengali renaissance, and the activities of politicians such as Aurobindo Ghosh and Rabindranath Tagore, was encouraging the growth of Bengali nationalism. Curzon's move was thus opposed primarily for reasons of nationalism, it being seen as an attempt to divide the Bengalis, and particularly to divide the educated elite in Calcutta from its immediate rural hinterland in east Bengal. As if that was not enough, the dividing line suggested largely distinguished the Muslim areas of east Bengal from the Hindu areas of west Bengal, and suspicions immediately arose that this was not only an attempt to undermine Bengali nationalism and to inhibit the political development of the region, but was also an attempt to set Muslims against Hindus by creating separate administrative areas for the regions in which they were each in a majority (Map 6). The evidence for this exists in a number of memos written by government officials. Herbert Hope Risley was a temporary home secretary at the time this measure was introduced, and summed up the government's intentions in two notes written in February and December 1904. 'Bengal united is a power; Bengal divided will pull several different ways. That is perfectly true and is one of the great merits of the scheme. It is not altogether easy to reply in a despatch which is sure to be published without disclosing the fact that in this scheme as in the amalgamation of Berar to the Central Provinces, one of our main objectives is to split up and thereby reconsolidate opponents to our rule'.[4]

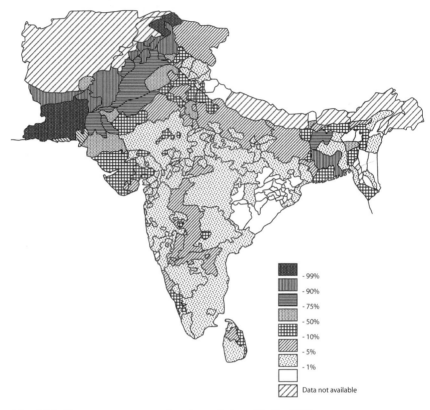

Map 6 Muslims as a percentage of total population of India, 1931 census.

In the case of Berar, Marathi speakers were amalgamated to a Hindi-speaking region, when the province was ceded to the British by the *nizam* of Hyderabad in 1904, as an attempt to inhibit the growth of Marathi nationalism. At the time, Curzon said in one note: 'We have heard quite enough of Shivaji as it is.' Regarding Bengal, a similar sentiment clearly existed. Curzon himself wrote: 'The best guarantee of the political advantage of our proposal is its dislike by the Congress Party'.[5]

Other factors in the resentment at the partitioning of Bengal were rooted in religious and cultural revivalism. The religious aspects of revivalism in eastern India are characterised in the following of Swami Vivekananda (1863–1902), the chief disciple of the similarly influential Pandit Ramakrishna Paramahamsa (1836–86) of Calcutta's Kalighat temple. Vivekananda achieved worldwide fame after attending the 1893 World Parliament of Religions in Chicago, after which he founded the Sri Ramakrishna Math and Mission, one of the largest monastic orders in India. Vivekananda articulated a philosophy of Hinduism (Advaita Vedanta) that maintained the unity of God, the harmony of all religions, the indivisibility of the self (*atman*) from the whole (*Brahman*), that all individuals are divine, and that the freedom of the one could not therefore be achieved without the freedom of all. He rejected ritual, emphasised the duty of service, particularly for the poor, and argued, most significantly, for the political and social consequences of his philosophy. This played an important part in the modernising of Bengali nationalism of the period (Raychaudhuri 1988; Radice 1998; Basu 2002). Another factor that encouraged resistance to Curzon's proposal was the defeat of British troops during the early stages of the Boer War and the victory of the Japanese over the Russians in the war of 1904–05. All of these factors came together to provoke Indian popular opinion in Bengal (Sarkar 1984). The consequence was a tremendous wave of opposition to the partition proposal, which rapidly spilled over from the columns of newspapers into demonstrations in the streets. It was a time of great political awakening, and even rural areas were affected – as depicted famously in Rabindranath's novel *Ghare-Baire* (Home and the World), which nonetheless critiqued the militancy of less scrupulous elements involved in the campaign. Very conveniently, before this demonstration reached its peak, Curzon resigned, ostensibly after a dispute over the control of the army with the commander-in-chief, and late hero of Khartoum, Lord Kitchener. So Curzon left the scene with his political proposals intact, popular unrest swelling, and the administration in the charge of a less-than-subtle military man. Kitchener's response to the street demonstrations was of course to send in the army. He approved the banning of all demonstrations and even backed a prohibition introduced by the lieutenant-governor of east Bengal (Bampfyld Fuller) on the singing of the patriotic hymn 'Bande Mataram', which had become popular at this time. Inevitably, this had the reverse effect of what was intended, encouraging further opposition and widespread support in other Indian cities. Thus the conservative Bombay politician, G.K. Gokhale, spoke as follows at the twenty-first meeting of the Indian National Congress in 1905:

> A cruel wrong has been inflicted on our Bengali brethren and the whole country has been stirred to its deepest depths in sorrow and resentment as has never been the case before. The scheme of partition concocted in the dark and carried out in the face of the fiercest opposition that any government has encountered in the last half century, will always stand as a complete illustration of the present system of bureaucratic rule, its utter contempt for public opinion, its arrogant pretension to superior wisdom, its reckless disregard for the most cherished feeling of the people, the mockery of an appeal to its sense of justice, and its cool preference of service (administrative) interests to those of the government.[6]

After the banning of demonstrations and the shutting down of printing presses in Bengal in order to suppress the agitation, the tactic increasingly resorted to was one of boycotts: hence the name ascribed to the campaign, *swadeshi*, meaning 'of one's own country'. (The Swadeshi movement that arose in Bengal after 1905 was a campaign to persuade ordinary Indians to give up purchasing foreign goods and to boycott the British government.) These policies were not only pursued in

Bengal but were advocated by politicians in other parts of India. In western India, Lokamanya Tilak was a particularly vocal advocate of this form of boycott, and his exposition of its principles in 1907 is clearly similar to the ideas articulated by Gandhi in the 1920s:

> We are not armed and there is no necessity for arms either. We have a stronger weapon, a political weapon, in boycott. We have perceived one fact that the whole of this administration which is carried on by a handful of Englishmen, is carried on with our assistance. We are all subordinate servants. This whole government is carried on with our assistance and they try to keep us in ignorance of our power of co-operation between ourselves. The point is to have the entire control in our hands. I want to have the key of my house and not merely one stranger turned out of it. Self government is our goal, we want a control over our administrative machinery. We don't want to become clerks and remain clerks. This is boycott and this is what we mean when we say boycott is a political weapon. We shall not give them assistance to collect revenue and keep peace. We shall not assist them in fighting beyond the frontiers or outside India with Indian blood and money. We shall not assist them in carrying on the administration of justice. We shall have our own courts, and when the time comes, we shall not pay taxes. Can you do that by your united efforts? If you can you are free from tomorrow.[7]

In Bengal itself there were a number of local politicians involved in organising the Swadeshi movement. Surendranath Banerjee, Bipin Chandra Paul, Motilal Ghosh (editor of the influential newspaper *Amrita Bazar Patrika*), Rabindranath Tagore, and the most prominent of them all, Aurobindo Ghosh. So effective was the campaign of boycott that there was a marked decline in the volume of imported goods received into Bengal between 1905 and 1947. The Swadeshi workers encouraged people to buy Indian goods; in fact there was even a group of Calcutta businessmen who put their money together to set up a cotton mill, a few miles up river from Calcutta, called the Swami Lakshmi mill, in order to create an alternative Indian supply of machine-made cotton thread. In order to try and persuade shops not to sell foreign goods *samitis*, or volunteer groups, were established to patrol the streets and to try and close down any merchants who were displaying imported goods. Government repression, however, drove many of these *samitis* underground. And it was because of this repression that what began as peaceable boycott turned into terrorism. These activities were encouraged by Aurobindo Ghosh who disparaged the peaceable activities of most Bengali intellectuals, urging a resort to arms instead. As a result a conspicuous rise in terrorist activity took place between 1907 and 1908. There were two wings of revolutionary terrorism: Anushilan (which was overtly Hindu and right wing) and the smaller Jugantar (which was secular, internationalist, and left wing): most revolutionary cells were affiliated to one or the other. Their activities finally attracted international attention when a terrorist cell set up by Ghosh succeeded in killing two British civilians in April of 1908 as they were returning from a ball held by the viceroy at his residence in Alipore. The terrorists' target had actually been Douglas Kingsford, a Calcutta magistrate and later Muzaffarpur district judge, who had punished a great many Swadeshi agitators. But Khudiram Bose and his associate Prafulla Chaki threw the bomb into the wrong carriage by mistake and instead blew up a Mrs and Miss Kennedy (the wife and daughter of barrister Pringle Kennedy), causing widespread public outrage. Chittaranjan Das led the successful defence of Aurobindo Ghosh, who was implicated in the famous Alipore bomb trial along with 49 others, but Khudiram Bose was tried and subsequently executed. His accomplice, Prafulla Chaki, never faced trial, instead committing suicide when cornered by police. Aurobindo came out of the trial with a newly discovered sense of spriritualism, but the major political consequence was yet more vigorous repression by the colonial regime.

In other parts of the country protest activities continued apace despite the repression in Calcutta. In every case, however, they ran into difficulties. In the Punjab, the Swadeshi movement became mixed up with Hindu fundamentalism under the influence of the Arya Samajists and this lent a radical character to the demonstrations of the Swadeshi supporters. Lala Lajpat Rai was one of the Samajists who rallied to the Swadeshi cause in Punjab. It was he who helped to organise a boycott against canal water rates in the Chenab canal colony in 1907, an act that provoked an immediate reprisal on the part of the British who locked up many of the Arya *samajists* involved and deported Lajpat Rai. This is one of the reasons why after 1907 the *samajists* concentrated their activities largely on urban areas and ceased to organise in the rural areas of the Punjab, leaving the field open to the growth and further extension of the Sikh revivalist Singh movement (Fox 1985). In the south of India, most political support for Swadeshi was articulated in Madras. Here various initiatives were undertaken: a Swadeshi steam navigation company was set up to compete with British ships ferrying passengers from Tuticorin to Colombo in Sri Lanka, and there were strikes organised by the mill workers against the partition policy. In every instance those involved were rounded up, arrested and deported. In Bombay, industrialists and conservative congressmen initially reacted lukewarmly to the idea of Swadeshi, but the followers of Tilak in particular organised demonstrations in which foreign cloth was burned and liquor shops were picketed. The idea of giving up eating meat, smoking and drinking alcohol is a common feature in Hindu revivalist movements and it was brought into the boycott campaign in Bombay. It was effective, since it was not only a way of asserting the values of devout Hinduism but also a means of attacking the colonial government, which licensed and imposed heavy excise duties on the manufacture of alcohol. This again was to be a tactic Gandhi would use after 1920. Tilak himself toured the countryside campaigning for a programme of national education to do away with the tyranny of Western learning. This campaign was particularly successful among the factory workers of Bombay who mostly came from the Ratnagiri district, as did Tilak himself (Wolpert 1962; Cashman 1974). In 1908, however, Tilak published an article in his newspaper *Kesari*, describing the activities of the Bengali terrorists.

As a result he was put on trial for sedition and sentenced to six years' transportation. Interestingly, as soon as the sentence was announced, the cotton workers went on strike for six days, one day for each year of the sentence. He was placed in prison in Rangoon where he remained until 1912 when he returned to help organise home rule leagues. After Tilak's transportation, as in Bengal, government repression provoked violence, and there were a number of deaths in police firings on rioting crowds. In 1909 the uncovering of a revolutionary organisation, the Abhinava Bharat, and the subsequent assassination of a magistrate in Nasik, outside Bombay, provoked redoubled repression by the colonial government.

One might have expected all the activities of the Swadeshi activists to arouse a flicker of interest on the part of the Indian National Congress – at the very least a discussion of the issue of partition. This was not the case. In the December 1905 session of Congress, soon after the partition policy was announced, the matter was not even raised. Instead, a resolution was passed welcoming the coming visit of the Prince of Wales to India. At the Surat session in 1906, however, an attempt was made by radicals from Bengal to put the issue of partition on the agenda, proposing three resolutions for discussion by the Congress. The chairman, a loyal pro-Britisher, suggested an adjournment instead. A shoe was then hurled at him, and the meeting broke up in uproar (Johnson 1973). At a subsequent meeting of the Congress held in Allahabad in 1908, conservatives passed a resolution stressing that the Congress's methods were to be strictly constitutional and banning the sending to Congress of delegates from organisations of less than three years' standing. In this manner they purposefully excluded any political organisation that had been founded in the wake of the partition of Bengal, effectively keeping out all of the radical groups. Thus, the Congress was intimidated and backed away from political discussion of the partition issue as the repression of the British in Bengal increasingly began to bite.

Constitutional reform, the Ghadarite conspiracy and other opposition movements, 1909–17

By 1909 a great many of the leading Bengali Swadeshi activists had been either imprisoned or deported. The government accordingly decided to seize the political initiative. This was typical of British colonial policy after 1905. The next 40 years of colonial rule would be characterised by periods of agitation, then repression and then constitutional reform, in an attempt to seduce those moderates who had not yet been imprisoned to give up their campaigns and once again co-operate with the regime. In 1909 the first measure of constitutional reform was introduced by the liberal secretary of state John Morley, and the viceroy, the Earl of Minto. Known as the Morley–Minto reforms, the Indian Councils Act of 1909 set up provincial councils and an imperial legislative council with elected representatives, a special number of seats being reserved for the Muslim community, a concession agreed to at a meeting between the viceroy and representatives of the newly formed Muslim League in 1906. The element of democracy in these elections was insignificant, and the measure saw for the first time the introduction of the concept of separate representation. It was thus a clear articulation of the tactic of divide and rule on the part of the government, which was to be built upon in later constitutional reforms.

The Morley–Minto measures were disappointing from a democratic nationalist point of view, since only in Bengal were elected representatives in a majority on the proposed councils. In all the other provincial councils, the elected representatives were outnumbered by official nominees. There was also an income qualification for voting, with only around 1 per cent of the population being allowed to vote. Furthermore, the government had the right to ban anyone from standing for election who was thought to be an 'extremist'. At the all-India level in Calcutta, an imperial legislative council was set up, but only 27 of the 60 members of that council were elected, eight of them Muslim. Despite its feebleness, there were enough conservative-minded congressmen to respond to this proposal with enthusiasm.

In 1911 the government made a further major concession to nationalist opinion. This was to wind up the largely Muslim province of east Bengal – a reversal of policy announced at the Delhi *durbar* of George V at his personal request. This move, like the decision to set up the separate province in the first instance, was undertaken without consultation, thus upsetting many Muslims who had recently been seduced into alliance with the government and had taken the idea of a Muslim-dominated East Bengal to their hearts. In conceding to the major demand of the Swadeshi activists, the government gave with one hand while taking with the other, deciding simultaneously to remove the seat of the imperial government from Calcutta to Delhi, thereby distancing themselves from the area of the country in which they had encountered the most aggressive criticisms of government policies. The measure, announced in 1911, was actually put into effect in 1915. The entire imperial government was then shifted to Delhi where it was housed in spectacular new buildings. It was hoped that these measures combined would finally bring an end to political agitation, but in this the government was to be disappointed. Underground terrorism continued unabated. In fact a new form of terrorism arose: the ironically named Ghadar movement (*ghadar* being an Urdu word for treason or mutiny as well as insurrection), founded by expatriate revolutionaries living in San Francisco, Seattle and Vancouver (Puri 1983; Gupta and Gupta 2001). They published a weekly journal called *Ghadar*, which was circulated throughout India as well as amongst the expatriate community in the United States. Many of the expatriates were Sikhs (like the Gujaratis, a highly migratory community), and the journal had a particularly wide following in the Punjab where some attempted to put its ideas into practice. Meanwhile, in London a revolutionary group led by V.D. Savarkar from Nasik, where the magistrate Jackson had been murdered, assassinated an India Office official, Curzon-Wylie, in July 1909. At Stuttgart in Germany, Madam Bhikhaji Cama, a Parsi revolutionary and former private secretary to Dadabhai Naoroji, unfurled an Indian 'national flag' at the International Socialist Conference in 1907. Later, in Paris, she published a magazine called *Bande Mataram*, which was circulated amongst the expatriate community in Europe, advocating freedom and independence for India. On 23 December 1912 the Bengali revolutionary Rash Behari Bose organised an assassination attempt on Viceroy Hardinge as he entered Delhi in an official procession. A bomb ripped through the crowd and the viceroy narrowly escaped. Bose's accomplice, 17-year-old Basanta Kumar Biswas, who actually threw the bomb, was less fortunate, being arrested, tried (along with others of the so-called Delhi–Lahore conspiracy) and eventually hanged in 1915. Following the outbreak of war, terrorist activity in India increased still further, with 19 political murders between 1914 and 1915 and 32 in the year 1915 to 1916.

With the outbreak of war in Europe, more than sixty Ghadar supporters in the USA decided that the time was ripe for revolution in India. They sold their property and bought tickets to return to India, recruiting further supporters and attempting to smuggle arms en route via Korea, Canton and Singapore. Their aim was to set up revolutionary cells in north-west India and the Punjab and from there to commence a nationwide revolution. Unfortunately, they bought their boat tickets rather visibily en masse and were accompanied on their journey by several British spies. The inevitable consequence was that hundreds were arrested before they could even land on Indian soil, and their attempted gun-running was unsuccessful. Some did manage to slip past the police, however, and make their way to the Punjab, where there were a number of incidents, including attacks on army arsenals. An attempt was made to enlist the Germans in the supply of arms, but shipments were seized at Indian ports upon arrival. Generally, the colonial administration acted effectively to suppress the Ghadar movement, and any possible insurrection was nipped in the bud. One of the means used was the passing of the Defence of India Act in 1915, which enabled persons to be held for indefinite periods of time and for revolutionaries to be tried by special courts without resort to a jury. As a result of this Act there were 46 executions and 64 life sentences given to revolutionaries in Bengal and the Punjab, effectively crushing the Ghadar movement. Of those involved in the assassination attempt on Lord Hardinge, four were eventually hanged, whilst Rash Behari Bose, after a brief involvement with Sachin Sanyal and the Hindustan Republican Association (Sanyal being transported for life) and an attempt to encourage mutiny in various units of the Indian army, fled to Japan in May 1915. Thirty years later he was to re-emerge amongst the early organisers of the Indian Independence League and of the Indian National Army before the leadership passed to Subhas Chandra Bose.

After the passing of the 1915 Defence of India Act, violent political activity effectively came to an end. The only political initiative taken during the First World War was the setting up of the Home Rule leagues, which later on helped Gandhi to organise his first political initiatives in 1919 (Owen 1968). Home Rule leagues were the Indian equivalent of the Fabian Society; they were essentially debating societies. Tilak and his followers set up a number of them in Bombay and western India. In the south of India, Annie Besant, the radical theosophist, was involved in the setting up of leagues in the major towns and cities at the same time. The leagues published pamphlets and established lending libraries where political treatises could be read. Despite their moderate nature, they soon ran into trouble. Tilak's league sold 47,000 pamphlets in 1916, its first year, and by 1917 Besant's Home Rule league had 27,000 members. In the same year both Tilak and Besant were imprisoned under the Defence of India Act, as it was considered that their activities threatened to become subversive. Despite their quietism, however, the Home Rule leagues were important because they involved a more middle-class section of society, including traders and industrialists in politics for the first time, as well as introducing a new constituency of younger people to political activity (including men like Jawaharlal Nehru).

The only continual agitation of the First World War period was confined to Muslim activists. The Turkish or Ottoman empire sided with the Germans and this fuelled the Khilafat movement, established by those concerned about British policy towards Muslim holy lands in the Middle East. The Khilafat movement only took off towards the end of the war, but there was a shift in stance of the Muslim politicians at the time, particularly in Turkey, where a group of younger nationalists (known as the 'Young Turks') began to assume influence. There were a number of religious issues in India itself that also aroused the resentment of Muslims at this time, such as the refusal of the government to allow a Muslim university to be set up in Aligarh alongside the secular Anglo-Mahomedan college, riots in 1913 over the demolition of a mosque in Nellore and of a bath-house connected to a mosque in Kanpur. The winding up of the province of east Bengal had also offended many Muslim politicians. But the most important element in their politicisation was the involvement of Turkey in the war on the side of Germany. A number of younger radical Muslim politicians such as Maulana Muhammad Ali Jauhar and Maulana Shaukat Ali (commonly known as the Ali brothers), M.A. Ansari and Zafar Ali Khan became prominent within the Muslim League. Wazir Hasan, a supporter of the Young Turks, also became secretary of the League. Hasan helped push through a resolution stating colonial self-government to be the League's ultimate aim and this helped to lead to a growing convergence of interests between Muslims in the League and those remaining in the Indian National Congress, culminating in the joint meeting of committees of the Muslim League and the Congress in Bombay in 1915. There then followed another meeting in Lucknow in December 1916, at which the famous Lucknow Pact was signed whereby the Congress formally accepted the idea of separate representation for India's Muslims in the Imperial and British councils established by the British, and a distribution of seats between the League and Congress was agreed. Shortly before this a joint petition was sent to the British viceroy by 19 Indian, non-official members of the Imperial Council calling for elected majorities in the councils and dominion status for India. Amongst the organisers of the Lucknow meeting was Muhammad Ali Jinnah, who would later assume outright leadership of the League. The Lucknow meeting was perhaps the most significant event of the war. The Home Rule leagues were useful to Gandhi in organising later political meetings, particularly the Rowlatt *satyagraha* of 1919, but the Lucknow Congress was significant as it was the first occasion that so many prominent members of the Muslim League had sat in the same conference hall as prominent Hindu politicians. Although large-scale riots between Hindus and Muslims in Bihar in October of 1917 (the origins of which are unclear) did not necessarily bode well for the future of this alliance among the elites, the groundwork laid in Lucknow was to be crucial to the launching of a national movement by Gandhi in the years after 1918.

8 Aftermath of the First World War and M.K. Gandhi's rise to power

I do believe that when there is only a choice between cowardice and violence I would advise violence . . . Hence it was that I took part in the Boer War, the so-called Zulu War and the late War. Hence also do I advocate training in arms for those who believe in the method of violence. I would rather have India resort to arms in order to defend her honour than that she should in a cowardly manner become or remain a helpless witness to her dishonour. But I believe that non-violence is infinitely superior to violence, forgiveness is more manly than punishment. Forgiveness adorns a soldier. But abstinence is forgiveness only when there is power to punish; it is meaningless when it pretends to proceed from a helpless creature.

(Gandhi 1920)[1]

The First World War began with continuing incidents of political terrorism, but by the end of 1916 terrorism had been largely brought to an end and all political agitation stamped out by means of the repressive Defence of Indian Ordinances. The only political activities that continued were the peaceful meetings and discussions undertaken by the Home Rule leagues in the major cities of southern, western and northern India, and even their leaders, Tilak and Annie Besant, had been imprisoned by the end of 1918. Thus the First World War began with lingering discontent following the Swadeshi campaign against the partition of Bengal and ended with wholescale political suppression. In many respects, however, the First World War transformed the nature of Indian politics, initially by changing the nature of Indian society as a whole. The demand for wartime goods encouraged the growth of industry in India in quite an extraordinary manner. Whereas before British policy had tended to be neglectful of Indian industry, in wartime the British government suddenly became extremely keen to encourage Indian manufacturing, particularly if it produced goods that might aid the war effort. So the textile industry, especially in Bombay, and the munitions industries received a fillip. The beginning of a trade union movement simultaneously began to take place. The cause was not merely high employment but also the rapid inflation that struck immediately after the end of the First World War, leading to discontent among the workforce and widespread strike action in many of the newly emergent industries.

During the war the Indian army was expanded hugely until it numbered some 1.2 million men, thousands being sent to fight in Egypt, France and Mesopotamia. Many of them returned to India with a new and somewhat critical view of the European imperialists. The expense of this new army was enormous. It led to a 300 per cent increase in defence spending, and customs, excise, income and land taxes all had to be raised in order to meet the costs of India's contribution to the war, particularly in temporarily settled areas such as Gujarat. Basic commodities also became more expensive and food riots erupted in several cities in 1918 and 1919 as grain prices rose sharply. The Punjab in particular was disturbed in the wake of the Ghadar disturbances in the early years of the war, and as a consequence spent several years immediately after 1914 under martial law.

By causing distress and rapid economic change the First World War encouraged dissent. At the same time the British government in London, realising that in order to pay the costs of war it needed to raise taxes, solicited the support of 'moderate' Indian politicians in order to achieve this. A few also felt the need to reward some of the many Indians who had loyally supported the war effort. The issue of constitutional reform thus returned to the political agenda. The outcome, and hoped-for solution, of these problems was the Montagu–Chelmsford Report of 1918, so called because it was drawn up by the secretary of state, Lord Montagu and the viceroy, Lord Chelmsford. This led to the introduction of a new Government of India Act, passed in 1919, superseding the Morley–Minto reforms of 1909. The purpose of the reforms introduced was described by Lord Montagu in the House of Commons as 'the gradual development of self-governing institutions with a view to the progressive realisation of responsible government of India as an integral part of the British Empire'. This new policy was an important step. It marked above all a shift in rhetoric and in the legitimating ideology of colonial rule. Before 1857, it was argued that Britain was in India to bring the benefits of free trade and civilisation and to save the Indians from anarchy and despotism; after 1857 they were there to maintain good government and to suppress savagery (witnessed in the events of that year); after 1918 the British presence was justified by a new mission to 'educate' Indians in order to prepare them for self-government. To contemporary Indians this might have seemed rather odd, since the days of Indian self-government were not so remote, and as recently as 1911 G.K. Gokhale had moved a bill proposing compulsory and universal primary education before the Imperial Council, only to have it rejected by the British official majority, the reason being, as the Bombay governor confided in a private letter to the viceroy, that the 'power to stir up discontent would be immensely increased if every cultivator could read'.[2] As a concession to nationalist opinion, however, the Montagu–Chelmsford Act was clearly a big step forward, and the benefits of the new measures were more important than the delusory preamble that preceded it.

The 1919 Government of India Act set up a Council of State and an Imperial Legislative Assembly elected by the wealthiest 1.5 million of India's 300 million population. The most important element in the Montagu–Chelmsford reforms was the introduction of the idea of diarchy, or dual rule. The principle of diarchy, as stated in the Government of India Act, was that all of the key strategic subjects such as foreign policy, defence, and taxation were to be administered centrally, while the less important subjects such as education, economic development, and so on, were all to be made the sole responsibility of the provincial governments. At the centre, in Delhi, the Imperial Legislative Assembly was to have merely an advisory capacity, and its elected Indian members therefore no power whatsoever, but at the provincial level, even though executive power would remain in the hands of British officials, elections were to be held for assemblies that would have legislative powers (i.e. they could pass bills that the executive then had to act upon). Those taxes that were most controversial, such as the land tax, were then cleverly allocated to pay for the activities of provincial governments. Thus the British would appropriate the excise and income taxes that were easiest to raise for their own uses (primarily military and strategic), leaving the others to be collected by provincial governments, therefore allowing them to spend money on worthwhile projects only if they raised unpopular and antiquated taxes. This was obviously something of a Trojan horse by way of constitutional devolution. It was also a very mediocre experiment in democracy as the provincial electorate, even after expansion, numbered only 5.5 million; women were entirely excluded from the franchise, despite unanimous support from the Indian National Congress for the proposal that they should be included and personal representations made in London to the joint select committee on reform by prominent women activists such as Sarojini Naidu (Forbes 1996: ch. 4). Unfortunately, the committee preferred the advice of the Southborough Franchise Committee, who toured India and successfully argued that 'Indian custom and tradition' was opposed to female franchise (this despite the fact that many women already sat on municipal councils).[3] Furthermore, the government, despite the fact that it gave the provincial legislatures the chance to commit taxes raised to specific projects, still retained the right to ban candidates regarded as extreme, whilst the governors of the provinces could veto any Acts passed by the provincial assemblies of which they did not approve. Beyond that, the provincial assemblies were packed with official representatives and nominees of one sort or another, making it hard for the elected Indians to achieve a majority. The 1919 Act was thus hardly a radical step, but it was a crucial element in the British attempt to extend their control over India, and to increase its tax revenues without having to deal with the criticism that would inevitably result from this. In other words, they tried to seduce Indian collaborators, as in the past, into doing the unpopular and most difficult business for them.

Another important aspect of the Montagu–Chelmsford reforms was the introduction of special seats for Muslim and non-Brahmin categories, typically 30 per cent of the seats being reserved in this fashion. They believed that this was necessary in order to protect these minorities from the neglect of their interests by the majority; but even if it were not so, it tended to become the case as the creation of reserved seats divided Indian politicians and discouraged members of the legislative assemblies from representing anything other than their own particular section. In short, it encouraged communalism and perpetuated a policy of divide and rule. Thus, while some historians, notably Anil Seal (1968), have argued that the Montagu–Chelmsford reforms were important in forcing Indian politicians to adopt more modern Western-style political tactics, others have emphasised the cynical and undemocratic aspects of the exercise, which left working-class, tribal and peasant groups almost wholly unrepresented. This 'subaltern' view, from the bottom up, of this stage of Indian history has some weight to it, not least because many aspects of political life after 1919 have their roots in developments going on before the First World War. They were not therefore a response to post-war political reforms. However, from a British point of view the reforms were obviously a tremendous success because they clearly seduced a great many conservative politicians into once again co-operating with the British regime.

Amongst those political movements that began before and continued after the First World War, was the Khilafat agitation. This arose from Muslim concerns about the security of the holy places of Islam and became more acute during the First World War when the Ottoman empire sided with Germany and was defeated. It was because of concern over the Khilafat issue that the younger, radical members of the Muslim League took control of the organisation and held a series of joint meetings with the Indian National Congress in 1915 and 1916. A unity of purpose was already developing, therefore, well before Khilafat became one of the key issues Mahatma Gandhi was to employ when he began to organise campaigns against the British in 1919 and 1920. As with so many of Gandhi's strategies the issue had been anticipated by previous politicians. Nonetheless, Gandhi did show a unique capacity to somehow unite diverse politicians and diverse issues, even if they had been articulated prior to his arrival on the scene.

Mahatma Gandhi

There are a variety of excellent biographical accounts of the life of Mohandas Karamchand Gandhi (later known as the 'Mahatma' or 'Great Soul') (Brown 1989; Copley 1987; Dalton 1993; Nanda 1996; Gandhi 1995), various published selections from his voluminous writings (e.g. Mukherjee 1993), as well as analyses of his political and religious thought (Parekh 1989; Chatterjee 1984; Bondurant 1958; Chatterjee 1983). Gandhi was not, as some might assume from his later peasant style of dress, a man of lowly origins. He was a Bania, from a wealthy merchant caste and family. His father was chief minister of the princely state of Rajkot in Gujarat, and pictures of Gandhi from his youth depict him attired in Western clothes, as was common with men of his background and class. He was educated in English and studied law in London before returning to India to study Indian law and to practice in Bombay. So he began his life, like that of many others who were later on to be leading Indian politicians, originating from a wealthy background, pursuing Western education and a career in law. As a lawyer, however, Gandhi was not very successful. He did well in his examinations but performed badly in public, whilst finding it hard to retain interest in the proceedings of the High Court in Bombay (where, by his own account, he slept much of the time). Moving on to work alongside his brother in Rajkot as a legal adviser to the prince of Porbander, amongst others, he coped badly with the intrigue surrounding the English court, and after a few months an argument with a British official further sapped his confidence (Gandhi 1923: chs 27–30). He therefore felt obliged to take a job in 1893 with a Muslim firm, Dada Abdulla & Co., in Natal in South Africa (Figure 7). Here he was to enjoy rather more success and to undergo perhaps the most defining experiences of his life. It was because he worked for a Muslim firm that, unlike many other Hindu politicians of his time, Gandhi rapidly became aware of Muslim grievances and concerns. South Africa also had a large Indian population of indentured labourers, as well as merchants, and in South Africa Gandhi came into contact with both of these sections of society (Swan 1985). After experiencing South African racism, personally and in his work, Gandhi started to take an interest in political issues. In particular, as a lawyer Gandhi began to assume the role of defending Indians who had fallen foul of South Africa's pass laws. These laws originated in a keen desire of the government to find employment for white Boers in the wake of the Boer War, and in order to achieve this they attempted to end Indian immigration and encouraged repatriation. A means of doing this was to introduce restrictions on immigration, a poll tax on ex-indentured labourers at a prohibitive level of £3 per head, the de-recognition of non-Christian Hindu marriages in the case of new entrants, and a system of compulsory registration and passes that restricted the movements of Indian immigrants in the Transvaal. This was followed by an

Figure 7 Mahatma Gandhi as a barrister in Johannesburg, South Africa, 1893. © *The Hindu.*

extortionate £25 annual tax proposed in Natal on indentured workers who had served out their term but who chose neither to renew their contract of indenture nor to return to India (Huttenback 1971). A series of agitations were initiated by Indians over these issues, and Gandhi graduated to become one of the principal organisers. Amongst other achievements, he and his followers eventually managed to get the Natal tax removed altogether, and this was to prove a formative experience for him.

By organising strikes and campaigns in South Africa Gandhi first began to develop what were later to become his characteristic tactics of *hartal* (strike action), *satyagraha* (the use of passive resistance as a weapon) and the voluntary courting of arrest. Through his actions he began to acquire an international reputation, his name becoming known in India through expatriate connections. Despite developing a flair for meticulous organisation, the South Africa experience also demonstrated some of the weaknesses of Gandhi, such as his paternalism and his readiness to agree to compromises on his own authority (for example, without consulting with his supporters). Thus on one occasion he called off an agitation after receiving a verbal promise from the South African prime minister, Jan Smuts, that the compulsory registration of Indians would be suspended. When news of this broke, he was beaten up by one of his supporters. He did not learn a lesson from that, however, and demonstrated this weakness on later occasions, to the grief of many Indian politicians.

South Africa was not only crucial for the development of Gandhi's political tactics and knowledge, it was during this time that he became completely vegetarian and celibate (a decision sealed with a vow in 1906) (Gandhi 1923: ch. 109), and began wearing simple, traditional Indian rather than Western clothes – a step of great symbolic significance and soon imitated by other nationalists (Tarlo 1996). Gandhi also became converted to a revivalist, highly eclectic form of Vaishnavism and set up meditative centres, or *ashrams* (the Phoenix Settlement and Tolstoy farm), which conveniently served at the same time as temporary shelters for the families of imprisoned supporters. Indian forms of devotion commonly refer either to Shiva (the creator/destroyer) or Vishnu (the preserver of the world), and their many incarnations. Shiva worship is most popular in the east of India; Vishnu worship is more popular in the west and in rural areas. Followers of Vishnu (Vaishnavites) tend to be more pacifistic and do not carry out animal sacrifices of any sort. Gandhi came from Gujarat in western India where Vaishnavism was common, and his philosophy exhibited key characteristics of this sect, although he evolved his own rather quirky version of it. What was significant was the emphasis which he placed on certain aspects of Vaishnavism, particularly the element of non-violence, or *ahimsa*, which he reified both in his personal life and in his political campaigning. It was a philosophy that had tremendous practical relevance, whether in South Africa or India, and indeed wherever those demonstrating were vastly outgunned by the colonial military machine (yet there might be a Western liberal conscience somewhere to be poked).

In common with other Hindus, Gandhi believed that the search for *satya* (truth) through *swaraj* (self-rule) was the most important goal of human life. However, since no one could ever be sure of having attained the goal of ultimate truth, the use of violence to enforce one's own imperfect understanding of it was sinful. It was this idea that led Gandhi to argue that *ahimsa* (non-violence) was relevant to political agitation. But he also drew inspiration from the philosophy of the contemporary American writer Ralph Waldo Emerson, an advocate of pacifism, and the Russian author Tolstoy, who practised a communitarian life (as Gandhi did at the Tolstoy farm) and non-violence. Gandhi explained his use of *ahimsa* in the pursuit of truth as the application of truth-force or *satyagraha*, a word he concocted by combining Hindi and Gujarati expressions. He coined this word to describe the power that would be given to ordinary Indians if they adopted non-violent tactics in political agitations. In many ways the tactic was extremely pragmatic; not only did it present the agitators in any confrontation with the colonial regime with a measure by which to judge their conduct, it also meant that by espousing this philosophy he could keep the actions of large numbers of ordinary people involved in an agitation within controllable limits. Many might disagree with his ideas about *ahimsa*, but as an exigent political tactic, and as a philosophy, it could be used to restrain those who had the opportunity to resort to violence. Above all, the *satyagraha* method appealed to those sections of society which provided his most prominent supporters, both in South Africa and India – the businessmen and wealthy peasant classes.

Another element of Gandhi's philosophy was *sarvodhaya* or social uplift through education and self-help. He believed that the best means of achieving this was by the restoration of a traditional Indian lifestyle, as outlined in his romantic, idealist manifesto *Hind Swaraj*, written and published in 1909, which condemned all things modern and Western influences in particular. The idea of boycotting foreign manufactures stemmed from this, and he encouraged the wearing of *khadi* (home-spun cloth) to restore employment to India's hand-loom weavers. He believed that everybody should practise the spinning of cotton at home using a spinning wheel, both as a meditative exercise and as a contribution to India's self-sufficiency. He had a simple idea of economics, which hailed a mythical golden era of India's past and presumed that self-sufficiency would enable India to do away with factories and industry and free the country of dependence on European-manufactured goods. The idea at least was appealing to the desperately poor, and in the short term it was a useful tactic. But it offered no practical economic policy for the government of India following independence, and although this was to be initially one of the most appealing elements in his political programme, in the long term it proved to be one of its biggest disadvantages.

Despite the novelty of his political philosophy, in his early career Gandhi was not an anti-colonialist but in essence a reformist. Like others in pre-First World War India, he did not desire or envisage an immediate end to the British empire, but wished to see a great many colonial policies ameliorated. In many ways, in fact, Gandhi started out even as a loyalist. He organised an ambulance service that served in the Boer War and during the Bambata rebellion of the Zulus in 1906, and assisted in recruiting Indian soldiers in 1914 for service on the Western

Front. For these efforts he was awarded the Kaiser-i-Hind medal (in 1915), the Zulu War medal, and the Boer War medal by the British – all of which he was eventually to return in 1920. Following his return to India in 1915, however, Gandhi began to take an interest in the political activities of ordinary Indians. This, added to his previous experience of inter-caste and inter-religious political organisation in South Africa, set him apart from other middle-class Indian politicians. The INC at this time was still dominated by moderate constitutionalists, often of high-caste, elite backgrounds, but from the beginning of his return to India Gandhi distanced himself from them, and expressed instead an interest in a variety of issues, soon becoming involved in local, peasant-based agitations. Accounts of this period have described Gandhi building up a 'network' of local politicians, sometimes described as 'sub-contractors' to help in creating a political movement: men such as Sardar Patel, Mahadev Desai and Rajendra Prasad in Gujarat and Bihar respectively (Brown 1972). But this would be a somewhat cynical and abstract political scientific interpretation.

The problem with many studies of political Indian nationalism is that they have often benefited too much from hindsight, failing to appreciate quite how daunting and difficult a task it was to unite a subcontinent the size of India into one nation and one nationalist movement. They therefore commonly employ inappropriate analytical tools (Hardiman 1982). An important detail to recollect about these early agitations, and often crucial to the success of political interventions by nationalist politicians, was that all of them had a profoundly millenarian aspect, rooted in part in the religious revivalism of the late nineteenth century. An article by Shahid Amin on Gorakhpur describes very well the aspirations that abounded in the countryside, the power of rumour, and how those aspirations came to focus symbolically on Gandhi (Amin 1984). Gandhi's ultimate achievement was to mould these aspirations into a political movement, something he achieved by conflating the Hindu ideal of *swaraj* (self-rule) with the concept of home rule and independence from colonial rule, rendering a political end (independent nationhood) into a spiritual aim as well. Evoking at the same time an imagined golden past, he made the idea of India as a nation, free from foreign influence, both meaningful and desirable to ordinary Indians. Gandhi would not have obtained the support that he needed to do this, however, if he had not first established a reputation – not merely as a spiritual leader but also as a successful advocate of Indian interests in conflicts with the colonial authorities. Gandhi's first opportunity to do this was when he became involved in an agitation going on amongst the indigo cultivators in Champaran in north-west Bihar in 1917.

The early *satyagrahas*

Millenarianism was the product not only of religious enthusiasm but also of material distress. In the Champaran agitation this was shown by the belief held by many (according to police reports) that Gandhi had been sent by the viceroy or the king to overrule all the local officials or planters. One peasant compared Gandhi to Baba Ramchandran, a local peasant activist, and said that the tenants would not fear the *rakshas* (devils) or planters now that Gandhi was here. Nobody had much idea who he was or what he stood for, but they knew he was an outsider and hoped he would somehow help them. He arrived, however, not at the request of local lawyers (the backbone of the Congress in Bihar), but simply through the intervention of a local, rich, peasant-cum-moneylender, Rajkumar Shukla, who had heard of him, and went to Lucknow to ask for his support in an agitation that he and other better-off peasants had organised with the support of local Hindu traders. They were agitating against the *tinkathia* system, according to which European planters, holding *tinkathia* licences from local *zamindars*, forced peasants to cultivate indigo on part of their land in exchange for payment at well-below market prices. As market prices fell with the introduction of chemical dyes from the early 1900s onwards, the planters recouped their losses by increasing rents and cutting the payments to the peasants for their indigo, unless they paid a substantial sum in order to be relieved from the obligation to grow it. This created enormous distress, and in 1917 a strike broke out amongst the indigo growers (one of many), who refused to hand over their crops or pay their rents. Gandhi's intervention and representation of the peasants' concerns led to the setting up of an official inquiry, and eventually the abolition of the *tinkathia* system; but his impact was essentially limited. The agitation had been ongoing for some time when he arrived, and after he left there were only three village workers remaining active in Champaran by the spring of 1918 who continued to espouse his methods (Pouchepadass 1974, 1999).

Gandhi's involvement in Kheda district, Gujarat, was more successful, and this district went on to became a hotbed of support. One of the reasons for this was that the peasant community there was relatively homogeneous, mostly belonging to the landowning Kunbi-Patidar caste, known as 'Patels'. Gandhi himself was Gujarati, and since Gujaratis (especially traders) were to be found in significant numbers amongst those who had migrated to South Africa, Gandhi's activities there were well known in local circles. The main issue that concerned the Patidars of Kheda was the moves being made by the government to raise land taxes to meet the costs of war. The agitation against a proposed revision of the land tax had already begun, including a boycott, when Gandhi arrived on the scene in March 1918. Many of the poorer peasants had commenced paying it, being fearful of government fines and the loss of their land. This was the first full-scale peasant *satyagraha* in which Gandhi was involved, and once again it was only partially successful. The agitation was called off after the granting of a few minor concessions by the colonial regime. Gandhi himself said: 'the end was far from making me feel happy. The Kheda peasants had not fully understood the meaning of satyagraha.'[4] Hardiman's account of the movement (1981) demonstrates how the peasants by and large organised themselves by their own means, through the use of local marriage circles (or *gols*). Some historians have further claimed that this, like other early *satyagrahas*, was merely a movement of self-assertion by rich peasants rather than being genuinely anti-colonial, or a response to economic distress (Epstein 1988; Dhanagare 1987: ch. 4). Hardly surprising then that Gandhi was not satisfied by the outcome: there had been no religious-style conversion as he had hoped. Initially at least, Gandhian tactics had been employed as a mere tool. However, the Kheda peasants did become firm and unequivocal supporters of the nationalist cause in later years, and the publicity Gandhi gained here contributed greatly to the snowball effect by which his reputation was established.

The third local *satyagraha* in which Gandhi became involved in 1918 was an industrial dispute – a strike by the Ahmedabad millworkers, also in Gujarat. It was here that Gandhi first used the technique of the hunger strike, which he put into practice as an alternative to violent picketing. The millworkers were on strike because their pay had been cut by 50 per cent. Their wages had risen rapidly during the war, boosted by bonuses paid to persuade them to continue working despite an outbreak of cholera, but following the war's end, and a collapse in demand, the employers cut back wages. Gandhi involved himself in an attempt to restore some of the original increase, but was compromised by the fact that he himself was friendly with some of the mill owners. In fact he had recently set up an *ashram* in Ahmedabad for which he had received generous contributions from industrialists involved in the dispute, the family of Sarabhai Ambalal in particular, with whom he was on close terms. For this reason the striking workers were suspicious of him, and the strike was a somewhat unsatisfactory example of Gandhian tactics. The mill owners were eventually persuaded to concede a wage increase, and raised them again by 30 per cent after Gandhi threatened to refuse food until his death. It was perhaps only for reasons of personal acquaintance that the employers responded sympathetically, but for whatever reason, Gandhi's personal intervention did have an effect and was given widespread publicity. In the long run, Gandhi's involvement in the strike therefore enormously enhanced his reputation and popularity, and in Ahmedabad itself a textile workers' association was set up to organise arbitration along Gandhian principles in all future disputes (Patel 1987). Gandhi had hoped for mass conversion to his religious ideals, but once more was disappointed, and he never again involved himself with industrial disputes, feeling frankly mystified and out of his depth in such contexts. He and other Gandhians thus snubbed invitations to take part in meetings of the All India Trades Union Congress that was set up in the 1930s, which was one reason why that organisation ultimately fell under the influence of the communists.

The Rowlatt *satyagraha* and Jallianwalla Bagh massacre

Importantly, apart from the above-mentioned local agitations in 1917 and 1918, Gandhi took no part at all in the constitutional developments organised by the British. He was completely uninterested in the Montagu–Chelmsford reforms, attended few of the INC meetings and took no interest in other aspects of Indian politics apart from appealing for the release of the Ali brothers and Annie Besant. The situation, however, was transformed in 1919 by the introduction of the Rowlatt Act, so called because it embodied the recommendations of the sedition committee of 1918 chaired by Lord Justice Rowlatt. This Act, rushed through the imperial legislative council despite the unanimous opposition of Indian members, made wartime courts and imprisonment without trial permanent features of

India's peacetime constitution. The measure was introduced by the British partly as a response to their fear of the rising tide of Bolshevism in the Soviet Union. It also reflected their desire to hold on to the grip they had established over Indian politics during the war. The Act was, however, bewildering to even the most sympathetic Indian politicians, being introduced in peacetime, without consultation, and with no major sign of dissent on the horizon, and at the same time as the government was proposing to introduce constitutional reform. The Rowlatt Act was therefore itself the cause of widespread opposition, and brought Gandhi into the fray. He attended several meetings of congressmen at which the issue was discussed, and when asked what he thought should be done about it proposed the tactic of *satyagraha*, beginning with the courting of arrest by the public sale of banned tracts. Moderate Indian politicians with little experience of organising campaigns were grateful for this suggestion, and also accepted his proposal that there should be *hartals* or general strikes throughout India, which were observed on 30 March and 6 April 1919. The response to this call was somewhat patchy, since the Congress at this stage did not have any sort of national organisation, but the Home Rule leagues and the Muslim Khilafat organisations helped organise public demonstrations, and the strike action was effective in Bombay, Delhi, Lahore and many north Indian cities, particularly those that had been most affected by post-war inflation and food shortages, and those cities with large Muslim populations and where the Khilafat movement was strong.

The Punjab was already under martial rule because of the Ghadar revolutionary outbreaks of 1914 to 1917, and with the commencement of the Rowlatt *satyagraha* in 1917 there was a revival of violent protest emanating from Lahore. In other parts of India, street demonstrations, boycotts of imported goods and the courting of arrest by the sale of banned political tracts took place. But in the Punjab there were street disturbances of a more serious nature. In Amritsar riots broke out, and a number of Europeans were physically attacked. In response, British officials in the Punjab imposed a curfew and embarked on severe and sometimes bizarre punishments, undertaking public floggings and (a novel tactic) the aerial bombardment of villages: army Sopwith Camel aircraft flying low over rural areas and the pilots lobbing bombs over the side at random. State terrorism can thus be said to have been employed in an attempt to restore order in the Punjab. This repression finally culminated in the Jallianwallah Bagh massacre of 13 April 1919. An order prohibiting all meetings and gatherings had been issued the day before, but 13 April marked the Baisakhi festival, a particularly important occasion in the Sikh religious calendar, for which reason a large number of people had poured into the city from the surrounding villages, few of whom had heard about the order. A market was taking place in the Jallianwallah Bagh, a square enclosed on three sides, and local leaders had announced that a meeting was to be held at 4.30 to discuss the Rowlatt Bill and recent police firings. The square was thus packed when General Dyer, the officer in charge of martial rule in Amritsar, marched in a platoon of gurkhas who lined up in front of the only exit. He ordered the crowd to disperse, which they could not do because there was nowhere for them to go, and a minute later ordered his soldiers to open fire.

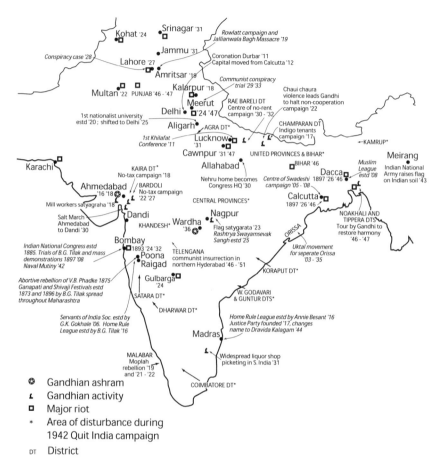

Map 7 Key events of the independence struggle.

Figures of 379 killed and 1,200 wounded were a conservative estimate of the casualties. General Dyer's written report read as follows:

> I fired and continued to fire until the crowd dispersed, and I considered this the least amount of firing which would produce the necessary moral and widespread effect it was my duty to produce if I was to justify my action. If more troops had been at hand, the casualties would have been greater in proportion. It was no longer a question of merely dispersing the crowd, but one of producing a sufficient moral effect from a military point of view, not only on those present but more specifically throughout the Punjab. There could be no question of undue severity.[5]

The subsequent curfew and martial rule imposed on Amritsar was extremely oppressive. For example, in a street where a missionary, Marcella Sherwood, had been attacked during the Amritsar riot General Dyer gave an order that any Indian passing down the street had to crawl on their stomachs. Throughout the Punjab, the massacre was followed by widespread floggings and arbitrary punishments.

When martial rule was finally lifted in June 1919, news of the military atrocities leaked out, provoking a riot in Ahmedabad, a two-day strike in Bombay and strikes in Calcutta. Indian politicians were shocked and Gandhi called off the Rowlatt *satyagraha*, stating that it had been a 'Himalayan blunder'. This phrase has been somewhat misunderstood. Colonial officials at the time claimed that it proved that even the organisers had confessed the *satyagraha* campaign to be inappropriate and unjustified. What Gandhi was probably expressing was his sense of personal responsibility for having launched the *satyagraha* without preparing the population, and those who joined it, for the sort of violence meted out by the colonial regime. He did not think that the act of protest itself was wrong. The government in India was, understandably, ashamed of the actions of General Dyer, who was suspended. An inquiry, the Hunter Committee, was then set up to look into the incident. However, the inquiry, typically, concerned itself solely with the issue of whether or not there had been a conspiracy to subvert colonial rule, the supposition being that if this had been the case the action might have been justified. The Hunter Report concluded that there had probably not been a conspiracy and therefore implied that Dyer's retribution had been excessive, but without actually saying so. Dyer was relieved of his command and sent back to the United Kingdom, where parliament accepted the Hunter Report; but in the House of Lords a motion was passed approving of his conduct and stating that he had been treated unjustly. The *Morning Post* launched a fund for Dyer, whom they described as 'the man who saved India', and raised the then considerable sum of £26,000 as a gift towards his retirement.

The effects of all of this were important: Indians were shocked by the British response, and Gandhi himself following the events of 1919 became a lot more wary about the manner in which he launched mass agitations. Significantly, Gandhi also became convinced of the impossibility of ever negotiating with the British. Until 1919 he had been essentially a reformist politician; after 1919 he and many other moderate Indian politicians changed their views. 'Shaken' by the British and Indian governments' complete disregard of the Indian Khilafat campaign, as seen in the terms of the peace treaty ultimately imposed upon the Ottoman empire in 1920, Gandhi was yet more disturbed by the conclusion of the official inquiry into the Jallianwalla Bagh massacre. Writing in his newspaper *Young India*, he described the Hunter Commission Report as 'page after page of thinly disguised official whitewash' and stated: 'the Hunter Report has taken away all my faith even in the good intentions of the British ministry and the Viceregal Council . . . If the British Constitution survives this shock, it will be due to some inherent vitality in it. Those who are at the helm, at the present moment, have left no stone unturned to smash that Constitution to pieces.'[6] Mahadev Desai, his personal secretary, characterised his conversion in the following terms:

Reluctantly and almost painfully, Gandhi was driven to the conviction that the system of government which he had been trying to mend needed to be ended. In December 1919 he had advised the Indian National Congress to make a success of the new instalment of reforms granted by the British Government and thus prepare for a fuller measure of responsibility. In September 1920 he declared that reformed councils and governorships for Indians were 'subtle methods of emasculation'.[7]

In a moving letter to the viceroy (on display at the Tagore Museum in Shanti Niketan in Bengal), the Nobel prize-winning Bengali author Rabindranath Tagore resigned his knighthood. Shortly after, Gandhi too returned all of the medals he had been awarded for his services during wartime and became involved in a entirely new programme of organised and outright opposition to colonial rule.

9 Non-co-operation and civil disobedience, 1920–39

The prime movers of these movements do not in their hearts desire that the agricultural labourers should get real relief. They seek only their own ends. Then how will the poor be benefited? They will be benefited in the long run because despite the determined efforts of these false leaders to the contrary, this movement will gradually cause the oppressed to awaken. And when they begin to understand the reality of what is happening and who is at the root of their sorrows and sufferings, their dishonour, disgrace, hunger and disease, and when they also understand how to eradicate them, then their goals are certain to be realized.

(Swami Sahajanand Saraswati, Central Jail Hazaribagh, 1941)[1]

The difficulties of poor peasants of Lohara zamindari is [*sic*] well known to all. Though we have been fighting since long but all was in vain . . . Even being with the Congress we are crushed . . . Congress leaders gave hopes that the matter was under consideration with the Prime Minister but nothing has yet come out. What is the use of having a house of gold built after one's death? Congress people said that the Lohara zamindari affair is equal to an elephant but one should remember that a small insect can kill an elephant . . . The tendency of the Congress leaders is that they sympathise with the tenants when they have their own interest, otherwise they don't care for any grievance.

(Sarju Prasad, pleader, Kusumkasa, Chhattisgarh, 1938)[2]

The non-co-operation campaign, 1920–2

It was soon after 1919 that Gandhi gained the support of the majority of Indian political leaders, and won their acceptance for his plan for a joint, all-India campaign of non-co-operation, the first major nationwide campaign in support of the idea of independence. The campaign was launched at Allahabad in June 1920, where Gandhi played a key role as a mediator between Hindu and Muslim politicians, and managed to forge a united front among leaders of such diverse movements as the Khilafatists, the Home Rule leagues, the Congress and the Sikh Akali Dal. His capacity to do so was a great testimony to his skills as a political negotiator, his ability to temper rivalries and to secure trust among members of the highly fissiparous Indian political elite. Gandhi's self-effacement, and the fact that he regarded his own purpose as primarily spiritual, partly explains this achievement, but equally important was his by now well-established reputation as an organiser, his growing popular following, and his previous and well-publicised success in negotiating with the British.

The Muslims were among the most important supporters of the non-co-operation campaign, the Khilafatists being already mobilised over the fate of the Holy Lands in the Middle East, a fate to be determined by the Treaty of Sevres, published in May 1920. This treaty divided up the Ottoman empire, turning Palestine into a British protectorate and Syria into a French one, thus confirming all the worst fears of the Khilafatists that Ottoman rule over the Muslim holy places was to be ended. Gandhi involved the Sikh politicians of the Akali Dal in the campaign because they had an agitation actively under way as well, which was attempting to wrest control of the Sikh *gurudwaras* (temples) from the British administration. Gandhi was crucially dependent on these groups, and the Home Rule leagues, to help organise demonstrations because Congress itself was still nothing more than a three-day annual conference. However, following a special session of the Congress in Calcutta in September 1920, which accepted Gandhi's programme of non-co-operation to redress the Punjab and Khilafat wrongs, it was also agreed that there should be complete reorganisation of the Congress itself. Under Gandhi's management the Congress was then transformed into a mass political party with a regular membership paying annual subscriptions, together with a hierarchy of village, *taluka*, district and town committees, as well as provincial committees and a 15-member working committee set up as its executive head. So although Gandhi was dependent on the support of a variety of groups for the launching of the non-co-operation campaign, 1920 was crucially important in the longer term as it saw the transformation of the Indian National Congress itself into a mass political party.

The principal tactic of the 1920 non-co-operation movement was a boycott of the civil services, the police and the army, and a campaign for the non-payment of taxes, which is how it derived its name. The issues that were its focus were a concatenation of the various concerns of the parties involved, the primary target being what Gandhi called the three wrongs – the wrong of the massacre in the Punjab, the Khilafat wrong and the wrong of colonial rule. According to the terms of a resolution at the Nagpur Congress in December, Gandhi also called for *swaraj* in a new wider sense of the word – not merely in the Hindu philosophical sense of self-rule but in terms of independence, or home rule for India. In an article in *Young India*, Gandhi promised *swaraj* within a year, and there began a campaign supported by a broad cross-section of society throughout the length and breadth of India. It commenced with the resignation of congressmen from the newly elected provincial councils, followed by widespread street demonstrations (Figure 8). Unlike the Rowlatt campaign, which was largely urban-based, this movement was also supported by a number of *adivasi* and peasant groups, *adivasis* in the Kumaon division of United Provinces (UP) burning down thousands

Figure 8 A non-co-operation demonstration in Bombay, 1922 (from *Asia* magazine, New York, July 1922). © M.D. Carter.

of acres of reserved forest in protest against the government's forest regulations (Guha 1989), and peasants in the north of India organising themselves into Kisan Sabhas (cultivators' societies) to agitate for their own concerns – some of which went on to affiliate to the Congress (Pandey [1978] 2002). In rural areas Gandhi urged economic revival through means of the spinning wheel and the wearing of *khadi* or country cloth, a call taken up by many. The campaign, however, drew heavily on instruments already deployed effectively in the earlier Swadeshi campaign in Bengal, including the boycott of foreign cloth and techniques favoured by Hindu revivalist groups, such as the picketing of liquor shops. This hit the revenues of the colonial regime, which lost the tax income from liquor sales, and also served as a Sanskritising activity for participants: an opportunity to enhance their religious status. In order to court arrest in great numbers, the Congress organised public meetings, which were banned, and the jails were soon flooded with volunteers. Amongst the richer peasants of Kheda in Gujarat there was also a revival of previous anti-revenue campaigns with the boycott of the government land tax (Hardiman 1981).

Despite its promising beginnings, after a year the non-co-operation movement began to degenerate into violence. In Bombay, Muslims in particular took to arms after the gaoling – for the second time – of the Ali brothers, leaders of the Khilafat movement. And in the south-west of India, although the Congress was barely active there (perhaps indeed because of the lack of formal political organisation), there was an uprising amongst the Moplahs of Malabar, a Muslim community, which this time, unlike on previous occasions, became overtly communal. Hindus were predominantly the landlords and moneylenders of the Malabar region and the principal target of this insurrection, and although they were unconnected, the coincidence of this movement with non-co-operation brought discredit to the latter. In Assam, tea plantation workers took the opportunity of the non-co-operation movement to air their grievances too and staged a walk out, and in Bengal large numbers of industrial workers went on strike. In UP in the north of India, the Kisan Sabhas started by demonstrating peaceably in support of non-co-operation. In a major popular upsurge, the peasants of Awadh in the 'Eka' movement, as it was known, and elsewhere, then began putting landlords on trial for illegal rent exactions and other crimes against the peasantry, threatening to introduce a class dimension to what was intended by Gandhi and others to be a purely anti-colonial movement. This was to be a recurrent problem in the north of India, and was especially alarming to the Congress in UP where the landlord element had a powerful influence within the party and were among its major backers. Congressmen in UP therefore frantically attempted to discourage peasant activism and refused to allow many Kisan Sabhas from affiliating to the Congress for fear of radicalising the movement (Pandey 1982, and [1978] 2002).

The increase in violence finally culminated on 15 February 1922 with the burning alive of 23 policemen by peasants at Chauri Chaura in Gorakhpur. This incident followed the beating up of a local Congress volunteer by the police, after which the police fired upon picketers (killing three) who had been protesting in a local bazaar against liquor sales and high food prices. The crowd chased the policemen back into the police station, surrounding it and setting it on fire, and clubbing to death anyone who escaped. Horrific as the incident was, it was not without provocation, and it paled in comparison to the violence being meted out by the colonial army and police elsewhere. Nonetheless, as news of Chauri Chaura broke, Gandhi decided to call off the non-co-operation campaign without consulting any of his co-organisers or supporters, to whom these events had many very different meanings (Amin 1995).[3] This decision was in many ways a crucial turning point in Indian politics. Inevitably, nearly all of India's politicians, especially the younger generation, were profoundly angered by his actions. Jawaharlal Nehru, one of Gandhi's most loyal supporters, describes in his autobiography (written a decade later) his frustration at the time:

> Must we train the 300 and odd millions of Indians in the theory and practice of non-violence before we could go forward? For the National Congress as a whole, the non-violent method was not and could not be a religion; it could only be a policy and method promising certain results. And by those results, it would have to be finally judged.[4]

Gandhi can be said to have seriously miscalculated by his action, and especially in announcing his decision publicly without prior consultation. It had the effect of seriously alienating all those elites that he had so carefully courted and persuaded to take part. And following his suspension of the agitation, Gandhi was immediately arrested and imprisoned by the British (he was released again early in 1924), who moved quickly to suppress all remaining symptoms of political dissent. The effects of Gandhi's action can thus be said to have been little short of cata-strophic. The newly created Congress Party began to collapse; the membership declined rapidly and members began to drift into the ranks of loyalist political organisations, such as the Justice Party in Madras, or to join the ranks of more militant communal organisations. Although some Gandhi loyalists stated their intention to continue non-co-operation and to eschew the Montagu–Chelmsford reforms, others, led by C.R. Das and Motilal Nehru, split away to form the Swaraj Party, declaring their intention to put up candidates in elections to the provincial assemblies.

Significantly, co-operation with the Muslim League ended after 1922 and was never successfully revived, the Muslim League being never again involved in any Congress campaign. As the Muslims began to go their own way, the 1920s also saw the growth of Hindu revivalist associations such as the Hindu Mahasabha (or Hindu 'great society') – first founded in the Punjab in 1915 and forefather to the Jan Sangh (founded 1951) (Graham 1990). The Mahasabha won many Congress members into its ranks under the moderate leadership of Pandit Madan Mohan Malaviya, and contested the latter's position in elections in north India in 1926. It became a powerful force within the Congress in later years and was a crucial obstacle to subsequent Muslim collaboration. In this manner the British tactic of granting devolution by stages seems to have succeeded in dividing Indian politicians, and when the provincial elections were held in 1926, large numbers of them were persuaded to give up non-co-operation and collaborate again with the colonial regime. These British tactics, and the corresponding threat to Indian unity, were apparent throughout the 1920s and 1930s (Moore 1974). Two other important phenomena seen in the 1920s, after the collapse of non-co-operation, were, first, the rise of the trade union movement with the creation of an All-India Trades Union Congress, founded in October 1920, of which both Jawaharlal Nehru and Subhas Chandra Bose later served as president; second was the advance of the non-Brahmin movement, particularly in western India under the leadership of B.R. Ambedkar (Keer [1954] 1981; Jaffrelot 2001; Omvedt 2004). Finally came the emergence of the Indian Communist Party. Gandhi himself devoted his efforts to setting up the All-India Spinners Association, having failed to persuade Congress to adopt a spinning qualification for membership (of 2,000 yards per annum), and he declared 1926 to be his 'year of silence'. The events of the 1920s were thus momentous, and Gandhi's actions after the Chauri Chaura incident for a time spelt the end of his influence over Indian politics, at least until 1927.

The Simon Commission and revival of Congress

The proposal in 1927 that an all-white Commission was to visit India under the chairmanship of Sir John Simon to enquire into the possibilities for further reform was, finally, the occasion for the beginning of a slow revival in the Indian National Congress, a renewal marked also by a *satyagraha* against the land tax launched in Bardoli in Gujarat under the leadership of 'Sardar' Vallabbhai Patel (Desai 1957; Dhanagare 1987; Shah 1974). The Indians were to be excluded from the Simon Commission, because, according to Lord Birkenhead, the secretary of state, they were quite incapable of agreeing on a workable political framework. This was sufficiently offensive to goad many moderate politicians and members of the Swaraj and Justice parties to join with Gandhi and members of the Muslim League in a series of all-party conferences held in 1928. These conferences were organised to thrash out a new united front to deal with the Simon Commission. The attempt was thus made to reunite the coalition that Gandhi had pulled apart in 1922. Unfortunately it ended in disaster, mainly because of the activities of the Hindu Mahasabha, which adopted an aggressive stance and refused to accept participation by the Muslim League unless the latter accepted an end to the separate representation of Muslims first introduced by the Morley–Minto reforms of 1909 (and agreed to by Congress in 1916). Mohammed Ali Jinnah tried desperately to compromise with militant Hindu leaders, for example, accepting the notion that reserved seats for Muslims might be abolished in the provincial legislatures if only they could still be retained at the centre. Even this was not acceptable to Hindu militants, and it was quite obvious that they and others were determined not to accept the participation of the Muslim League on anything other than their own terms. Their pretext was the ending of colonial policies of divide and rule, but their solution was merely to deprive Muslims of any special representation or guarantees of any sort, which was hardly a compromise with which they were likely to agree. Therefore, in December 1928 the League finally left the all-party conference, an outcome that Jinnah described as 'the parting of the ways', and there was very little co-operation between the League and the Congress after this date. It is important to underscore the efforts Jinnah made to effect compromise at this time, as he is often unfairly described in later years as the chief architect of partition.

The Akali Dal stood aloof from subsequent meetings, as did the Muslim League, primarily because they had achieved much of what they had set out to do by 1924 – namely, Sikh control of the *gurudwaras*. B.R. Ambedkar, leader of western India's movement of untouchables (or *'dalits'* as they were later known), also stood aloof, so in many ways the all-party conferences could be described as failures, although they were successful in giving a voice in Indian politics for the first time to a new, younger generation of more radical politicians. Two individuals rose to prominence in Congress at this time: Subhas Chandra Bose and Jawaharlal Nehru (Leonard 1990; Toye 1959: Gopal 1975; Ali 1985). Both had roots in the urban politics of Bengal and north India, Bose succeeding to the leadership of the Bengal Congress after C.R. Das's untimely death in 1925, and Jawaharlal Nehru, a lawyer and former Allahabad city councillor, following in the footsteps of his father Motilal into leadership of the UP Congress around the same time. They distinguished themselves from other politicians by their relatively young age and by their socialist credentials, being both actively involved in the trade union movement and enjoying a wide following on the left of the Congress Party. This was quite important because in the 1920s industrial activism was becoming a major feature of Indian political life. A succession of strikes after 1924 were organised by the communists who became increasingly active both in industrial disputes and in the north Indian Kisan Sabhas. There were thus strikes on the railways, as well as the famous Bombay millworkers' strike of 1928. Gandhi, with his limited economic understanding and opposition to modernity, had little time for trade union activism. He seems to have realised, however, that his loyal follower, Jawaharlal Nehru, could be used as a cat's-paw to control these active leftist movements, and in 1929, to everyone's surprise, he proposed the election of Jawaharlal as president of the INC (Figure 9). This might be described as the first part of Gandhi's strategy to contain left-wing activism and thereby re-establish and maintain Congress unity.

In 1929 numerous other strikes took place: there was an anti-feudal uprising in Rajasthan, as well as movements of unrest in some of the more remote *adivasi* areas (Baker 1984; Sarkar 1985). There was also a general strike of the Bengal jute workers, and the government organised what came to be called the Meerut conspiracy trials in which they succeeded in convicting and subsequently imprisoning a number of prominent (and it might be added, wholly innocent) trade union leaders for allegedly 'Bolshevik' activities. Bhagat Singh and comrades of the Hindustan Socialist Republican Army (HSRA) were also put on trial for revolutionary activities. This followed a series of bomb explosions in the Punjab, an attempt to blow up the train of the viceroy, Lord Irwin, the throwing of bombs in the Punjab Legislative Assembly, and (soon after the start of civil disobedience)

Figure 9 Jawaharlal Nehru, after election as Congress president, is taken in procession to the opening of the Congress session at Faizpur in Maharashtra, 1929. The chariot is pulled by six bullocks. © *The Hindu.*

the assassination of the district magistrate, Saunders – in revenge for the death of the Punjab leader Lajpat Rai from injuries received in a police *lathi* charge. For a while before his execution Bhagat Singh, the HSRA and its youth wing, the Navijavan (Naujawan) Bharat Sabha, acquired a popularity that even rivalled Gandhi's (Gupta and Gupta 2001) – but all this while the Congress did nothing. The trials, the release of political prisoners, the widespread industrial unrest, all might have been incorporated into Congress agitation after 1920, but they were not. Gandhi stood assiduously aloof from these widespread symptoms of activism amongst the poor and industrial workers, saying, in 1929: 'I know well enough how to lead into civil disobedience a people prepared to embark upon it on my own terms, but I see no such sign on the horizon.'[5] Instead, he urged congressmen to rebuild their organisation and Jawaharlal Nehru was assigned this charge as his principal responsibility. Gandhi wrote of him: 'Nehru is undoubtedly an extremist, thinking far ahead of his surroundings, but he is humble and practical enough not to force the pace to breaking point. Steam becomes a mighty power only when it allows itself to be imprisoned. Even so have the youth of the country of their own free will to allow their inexhaustible energy to be imprisoned and set free in strictly measured and required quantities.'[6] Thus Gandhi set Nehru to rebuilding the party, not to campaigning, a task in which he conspicuously succeeded, increasing the membership from 56,000 in 1929 to 6.5 million after an energetic recruiting drive lasting only six months.

The civil disobedience campaign, 1930–2

With the party revived, the Congress leadership felt that the time was right to pick a confrontation with the colonial government. The viceroy, Lord Irwin, on the advice of the Simon Commission, stated in the vaguest possible terms in October 1929 that dominion status was the 'natural issue' of the Indian constitutional process, and promised a Round Table Conference involving Indian representatives once the Simon Report had been published. The Congress retorted that it was not interested in the Simon Report, and was in no mood to listen to the deliberations of an exclusively British committee. Congress came up instead with its own proposals that the British should accept the principle of dominion status immediately and that the proposed talks should then concentrate solely on the details. They also suggested that the Congress should be given a majority status at the proposed conference on constitutional reform, to revenge the debacle of the Simon Commission, and amongst a series of other demands asked that an amnesty be given to all political prisoners, and for the removal of restrictions on public meetings. Following a meeting of Gandhi with the viceroy these proposals were inevitably rejected; the Congress then adopted a resolution demanding *purna swaraj*, or complete independence. The actual details of how *purna swaraj* was going to be achieved were left to Gandhi to decide, placing him once more in a unique position of authority and leadership.

The Mahatma came up with a number of tactics. First of all he called on Congress legislators to resign, which many did, and for a boycott of the assembly elections due in September. Muslim League members, of course, ignored this. Gandhi then declared that 26 January 1930 was to be 'independence day' when independence pledges were to be taken at numerous meetings throughout the country, pledges that denounced the British for ruining India economically, politically, culturally and spiritually, and asserting that it was a crime against man and God to submit any longer to British rule. The pledge also called for civil disobedience. Ignoring a general strike, then taking place on the railways and allowed to collapse, Gandhi then announced that the central platform of the civil disobedience campaign was to be the non-payment of taxes on salt (the abolition of which was one of the demands presented to Lord Irwin). This issue initially bewildered many Congress leaders, including Nehru, who had proposed an anti-*zamindar* rent campaign. Boycotting the salt tax was in fact a brilliant choice of target, both tactically and symbolically. Salt was something abundantly available that anyone could make, as well as being crucial to life itself (especially in the Indian climate). Yet as with liquor, the British had introduced a series of excises whereby salt could only be manufactured under licence, obtained at auction. This was manifestly exploitative and unjust. Boycotting the tax was something that everybody could easily do simply by making or distributing salt themselves. It had the merit furthermore of a material appeal to the peasants who paid the tax, whilst having no socially divisive implications, unlike the railway strike, or the proposed agitation against *zamindars*. Sumit Sarkar, the Delhi University historian, has thus written: 'Salt offered, like khadi, the chance of paltry but psychologically important extra income for peasants through self-help and – like khadi, once again – offered, to urban adherents, the possibility of a symbolic identification with mass suffering' (Sarkar 1983: 286).

Gandhi launched the salt campaign in Gujarat by organising a demonstration in March 1930 that proceeded from the Sabarmati *ashram* in Ahmedabad down to the coast at Dandi in Surat district, accompanied by a large band of volunteers (Figure 10). As the march progressed, thousands joined it, until they reached the coast where they bathed, prayed and then picked up dried salt at the beach, symbolically, therefore, breaking the law. Soon after, all the Congress leaders were arrested by the British and there then began an all-out nationwide campaign of civil disobedience. As in 1922, this included the boycotting of liquor shops, as well as the breaking of the salt laws and the burning of foreign cloth. Gandhi was arrested before he could undertake a raid he had planned on a salt works near Surat. Despite this, his followers carried on without him, and further arrests followed. The campaign was then widened to include the boycotting of forest laws, banks and insurance companies, and the government reacted by introducing emergency legislation that made it possible for the police to detain people at will without any charges being laid, and by attempting to ban political activity throughout the country, using violence and terror tactics wherever necessary.

Part of the significance of the civil disobedience movement is that it involved many poor and marginal social groups, in substantial numbers, who had never previously joined in the nationalist struggle. Although a number of rich peasant groups had joined the movement, the Khilafat and non-co-operation campaigns

Figure 10 Gandhi during the 20-day salt march, Ahmedabad to Dandi, Maharashtra, where he refined salt in defiance of British law (from *Asia* magazine, New York, August 1930). © M.D. Carter.

of 1920, like the Rowlatt *satyagraha* of 1919, were still predominantly urban affairs. By contrast, in 1930, although the Congress did not mobilise support in the princely states (which covered one-third of the country), and although political activity in areas such as Malabar was discouraged by the leadership because of previous incidents of communal violence, Congress volunteers ventured for the first time into many more isolated rural areas in the British-run districts. This included *adivasi* regions where agitations were sometimes already going on for quite different reasons, as with the Devi movement in Gujarat, which Congress activists from Bardoli district attempted to incorporate into their own highly successful no-revenue *satyagraha* campaign. Congress volunteers attempted to draw these communities into the nationalist movement, even if Congressmen themselves might be classed amongst the *adivasis'* exploiters, as with the Parsi moneylenders in this instance (Hardiman 1981, 1984 1987; Dhanagare 1987: ch. 4). Elsewhere, even though the Muslim League was not involved, large numbers of Muslims joined in the Congress's civil disobedience campaign, especially in the North-West Frontier Province under the leadership of Abdul Ghaffar Khan, as well as, of course, in north India.

Another new departure in the 1930 civil disobedience movement was the involvement of significant numbers of women. A step forward had been taken already in many of the provincial assemblies, all of which had voted by 1930 (under a permissive clause in the 1919 Act) to extend the franchise to a small number of eligible women and to permit them to stand for election. Gandhi himself viewed the franchise as a secondary issue, but ever since his first *satyagraha* over the Rowlatt Bill in 1919 he had urged women to take part, as many did, exhorting them to follow the example of the ancient heroines of the Vedas: Sita, Damayanti and Draupadi. This religious and Sanskritising element in Gandhi's rhetoric made nationalism an eminently respectable cause for women to support. Towards the end of the 1920s he further warmed to this mythological theme, comparing the British to the demon king Ravana who had abducted Sita, and calling upon women and men to help restore the righteous rule of Lord Ram (*Collected Works of Mahatma Gandhi* [CWMG], vol. 22: 18).

As early as February 1920, in his letters from a tour through the Punjab, Gandhi had noted approvingly the growing numbers of women turning out to hear him speak (CWMG, vol. 22: 402–403), and when there was a wave of support following the arrest of the wife of C.R. Das's son and other 'respectable' women selling *khadi* on the streets of Calcutta, Gandhi realised that involving women was an effective way of shaming men into taking part in nationalist activities. From 1930 onwards, Gandhi gave women a still more prominent role, and although he would not let them join the salt march in Gujarat, in speeches he exhorted them to support the freedom struggle, describing them (somewhat patronisingly) as ideally suited to constructive work such as spinning and picketing, and thousands of Gujarati women attended rallies held along the route of the march from Sabarmati *ashram* to Dandi on the coast (Kishwar 1986; Kumar 1993). In Bombay considerable initiative was shown by individual women and 'respectable' women's groups during the civil disobedience movement, such as the Desh Sevika Sangha, who were in the forefront of activists breaking the salt laws on Chowpatty beach. Equivalent organisations, the Mahila Rastriya Sangha and the Nari Satyagraha Samiti were active in Calcutta also, the former, set up by Latika Ghosh at the instigation of Subhas Chandra Bose, even trained and marched in uniform alongside the men in the procession to inaugurate the annual Calcutta Congress meetings. Perhaps the highlight of women's participation was the nomination of Sarojini Naidu (Figure 11) in May 1930 to lead the raid on the Dharasana salt works. She was imprisoned for this, but her role inspired many hundreds of women to take part in street demonstrations, and to join pickets attempting to persuade shopkeepers to trade only in *swadeshi* goods. The ideal of an independent India presented, in the eyes of many women, new opportunities for social reform, but in Calcutta the romance of revolution was a part of the appeal too, and women featured prominently in a number of violent incidents, including the assassination of the Comilla magistrate Stevens by two schoolgirls, Santi and Suniti Chaudhuri, in December 1931, and the attempted shooting of the Bengal governor, Jackson. Gandhi's motives may thus have been mixed, and his vision of (Hindu) Indian womanhood conservative and reactionary (Forbes 1988). Nonetheless his personal efforts to involve women, and dependence upon them, established a precedent in Indian public life that was to have a lasting influence, and it led to the involvement of women in politics in a variety of ways in numbers never seen before; sometimes in neither a 'respectable' nor predictable fashion.

Figure 11 M.K. Gandhi and Sarojini Naidu on the eve of the salt march, 1930. © *The Hindu.*

Unfortunately, although the civil disobedience campaign had begun in a highly disciplined manner, the fatal flaw was the impact of the Great Depression. Huge numbers of Indians found that their cotton products suddenly had no market, and there was a rapid increase in unemployment. As the 1930s progressed and distressed bankers began to call in their loans, there followed a collapse of the all-important credit system in rural areas, evinced by huge distress sales of gold, primarily jewellery (the last resort of any family) (Rothermund 1992; Bose 1982, 1986; Markovits 1985). This began to bite towards the end of 1930 and in 1931, with large crowds of unemployed landless labourers roaming the countryside in search of relief, many more of them heading towards the cities, where they swelled the slums and the ranks of street-dwellers and urban destitute. The decline of British trade, and later on the introduction of imperial preference schemes to help prop up the economies of the British empire, did give a fillip to some sections of Indian industry – especially since most Indians could no longer afford imported goods. For the first time ever the government of India was allowed a limited measure of fiscal autonomy in the 1930s, and they were even permitted to introduce a small 5 per cent increase in the excise on imported cotton goods in February 1931 without imposing equivalent cost penalties on Indian manufacturers. In one important respect, though, London retained control of the Indian economy – although sterling was taken off the gold standard in

1931, the exchange rate of the Indian rupee remained pegged against it at the artificially high rate of 1 shilling 6 pence per rupee. The reason for doing so was to maintain the value of the 'home charges' being paid by the government of India, which still amounted to some 15 per cent of the UK's invisible earnings. But doing this, at a time when all other world currencies were competitively devaluing against each other, rendered Indian manufactured exports uncompetitive in the world market, halving their value, and damaging her export industries (Chatterji 1992). India's role was thus clearly still seen as being to help Britain cope with the stresses of depression, regardless of the costs to herself.

Increasingly the civil disobedience campaign began to suck in those worst affected by the depression: the landless labourers, industrial workers, *adivasis* and others, and as it did so it became increasingly radical. Their motivations being more desperate, they were also more often inclined to violence. In Bengal there was a revival of terrorist activity, including a raid on the headquarters of the Writers' Building in Calcutta, an armed attack on the European Chittagong Club led by Pritilata Waddedar, a lady schoolteacher in the town, and an attack on an armoury in Chittagong (in the name of 'Gandhiji Raj'), both by members of Surya Sen's Indian Revolutionary Army (Chandra 1981; Heehs 1993; Gupta and Gupta 2001). In Lahore there was street violence and bomb explosions, and for a while the British completely lost control of Peshawar in the North-West Frontier Province, where local Muslim troops joined in the popular insurrection, and of the city of Sholapur in Bombay presidency. Violent demonstrations by millworkers were seen in Madras too, especially following the arrest of the Madras Congress leader Rajagopalachari and a number of volunteers (including many women) involved in the 1931 salt march to Vedaranyam (Arnold 1977; Baker 1976). *Adivasis* united with poor peasants in parts of central India in large-scale breaches of the Forest Law, involving not only the burning of reserved forests but illegal grazing, foraging and tree felling (Baker 1984). Unlike in 1922, however, Gandhi did not immediately call off the civil disobedience campaign. He allowed it to continue despite a rising toll of deaths, and despite even the emergence in Bengal of communalism and communal violence, which has been described in detail by Sugata Bose (1982, 1986) and Suranjan Das (1993). Bose ascribes a great deal of the communal tension at this time to the rise of class conflict resulting from the collapse of the rural credit system, a point in which Das concurs, although chauvinist and openly communal propaganda sustained by militant Hindu groups since the 1920s had a part to play too (Chatterji 1994; Gould 2002).

Eventually Gandhi was pressured into calling off the agitation in March 1931, following requests from influential Congress members, notably the elite landlords and, finally, from industrialists and businessmen such as G.D. Birla, Purshottam Thakurdas and J.D. Tata, who had joined the nationalist movement in large numbers after 1929, especially after Gandhi began signalling support for them by evolving his idea of the princes and industrialists as 'trustees' of the nation's wealth. Thereafter they had played a large part in funding the activities of the Congress Party and could not be ignored (Markovits 1985; Mukherjee 2002). Such individuals were fearful of pressures from below, and the industrialists had succeeded in winning some concessions of late from the British in negotiations over imperial trade. They were thus now more inclined towards negotiation and compromise. In consequence, Lord Irwin, the viceroy, proposed a truce, released Gandhi from jail, and invited him to a second gathering of the Round Table Conference that had been discussing Indian reform in London, which this time he accepted, backtracking at the same time on his earlier insistence that congressmen should be in a majority at these talks. Most left-wing congressmen, including Nehru, were bitterly opposed to this cessation of the agitation, and to the pact that Gandhi made with Irwin, according to which the British conceded little. The peasants of Kheda in Gujarat, who had sacrificed their liberty and their land in the struggle, were especially disappointed, and the outcome of the London talks was to justify their pessimism fully. As Gandhi made his way to London in August there was a change of government owing to the gathering financial crisis, and the Tory-dominated national government, which took over from the Labour Party, had no interest in making concessions. The talks therefore made little progress (from a nationalist point of view). Gandhi himself was the only INC representative, and Sarojini Naidu the only delegate sent by the Indian women's groups. The other delegates, Indian princes (carefully nurtured by the British as an alternative political voice since the 1920s), representatives of the Indian Liberal Party, and members and representatives of 'minority groups', including women, were all chosen by the British. Realising the inevitability of disaster, Gandhi sensibly distanced himself from the talks, using the opportunity instead to court international publicity, and particularly the attention of the American media, by embarking on a tour of east London slums and the cotton milling towns of Lancashire, where he was photographed meeting with unemployed millworkers and expressing sympathy for their plight. When Gandhi returned to India in December, empty handed, he called for a revival of civil disobedience in January 1932. However, the British had taken advantage of the interlude to reinforce their troops in India, and they were able to put in place an effective campaign of repression from the beginning of 1932 onwards; this effectively crushed the movement by the end of the year, some 120,000 being arrested between January 1932 and March 1933, compared with 92,000 in 1930 to 1931.

Aftermath of civil disobedience, and the provincial elections of 1937

With no agreement from the Congress forthcoming, the British government announced its own ideas for a division of seats between different communities in August 1932. Under this so-called 'communal award', the reservation of separate seats for Muslims was confirmed and a separate electorate for *dalits* was proposed as well. Gandhi insisted that the *dalits* – otherwise untouchables, or *harijans* (children of god) as Gandhi preferred to call them – were an indissoluble part of the Hindu community and should be treated as such, and he went on a hunger strike in protest against these proposals. In September 1932 a compromise was reached between Gandhi, Ambedkar (the *dalit* leader) and the British, in the form of the so-called Poona Pact, under which reserved seats were allocated to the so-called 'depressed' classes within the Hindu constituency. Ambedkar was deeply disillusioned by this experience and was later to condemn Gandhi's insistence on this compromise as a betrayal of the *dalit* cause.[7] This was the last serious negotiation with Congress leaders before the publication of the final White Paper on Indian constitutional reform in 1933, which ultimately became the Government of India Act in 1935 – later to become one of the main pillars of independent India's constitution. According to this Act, an increase in the number of voters to one in six adults was proposed, including women (a proposal agreed to by congressmen without consulting with women's groups), but the disproportionate representation of Muslims by separate reserved seats remained – a tactic of 'divide and rule', by this time firmly entrenched. Most Indian politicians criticised the final Act as offering little if any advance on the concessions of the Act of 1919, which was indeed the case, except in two major instances: an increase in the size of the provincial electorate from 6.5 to 30 million, and the replacement of diarchy by responsible government in the provinces. At the same time, though, the British still retained the right to disallow 'dangerous', 'extremist' candidates, and the governors could still refuse to give assent to bills passed by the assemblies. Ultimately, if they wished, they could suspend the assemblies – and the powers of elected Indian ministers – and assume direct control whenever they chose. The British also retained direct control over the so-called 'scheduled areas', predominantly *adivasi* districts, considered too backward to exercise a vote, and which were represented instead by British officials. These officials sat in the provisional assemblies, as did a number of British-appointed representatives for a variety of other sectional interests, thus limiting the nationalist majority. The central legislature meanwhile contained members nominated by the princely states occupying some 30 to 40 per cent of the seats, with similar effect.

After the Poona Pact, Gandhi paid little attention to either the White Paper or the resulting Government of India Act, which finally implemented the constitutional reforms, turning his attention instead to the cause of the *dalits*. Their pitiful condition was described in the contemporary novel *Untouchable* by Mulk Raj Anand, on which Gandhi himself offered editorial comments. It was at this time that Gandhi launched his so-called '*harijan* campaign' setting up a weekly journal (the *harijan*) and an All-India Anti-Untouchability League, and campaigning (unsuccessfully) for legislation compelling temples to admit the *harijans*. These activities occupied him for much of the period between 1932 to 1934. His reasons for concentrating on this issue are complex. The campaign could be interpreted as another brilliant tactical move by Gandhi, an attempt to incorporate and control those elements that had proved to be most unruly during the civil disobedience movement. It was also probably, in part, a response to the growing success of other leaders such as Ambedkar in organising the *dalit* community, and was an effort by Gandhi to prove to Ambedkar and others, as he had claimed at Poona, that there was a home for *dalits* within the Hindu fold. However, the campaign was considered by many elite congressmen as a distraction from the real business of the independence struggle, and the fact that it was a campaign to raise the status of the lower castes within Hindu society meant that it aroused considerable antagonism amongst high-caste groups within the Congress. The rallies that Gandhi held to win public support on the temple entry issue – the idea of throwing open Hindu temples to *dalits* (who were formerly banned) – were thus poorly attended, and there was even an assassination attempt made upon Gandhi's life in Poona in June 1934 when a bomb was thrown at his car. Important as this movement may have been for Gandhi and the *dalits*, for the Congress it was unhelpful, and in the years after 1932 dissension broke out once again within the party ranks. Left-wing trade unionism experienced a resurgence, a general strike being organised in Bombay in 1934, and the Kisan Sabhas (peasant associations) were revived as well, the socialist peasant leader Swami Sahajanand Saraswat recruiting large numbers to the Kisan Sabha in Bihar, a Kisan Sabha being later founded also in Bengal. In May 1934 the Congress Socialist Party was formed from a splinter group of leftists within the Congress Party. This group enjoyed close links with the All-India Kisan Sabha, formed the following year, and the Communist Party became increasingly influential over both organisations by the late 1930s, despite a government ban on the party introduced in July 1934 (Rasul 1989; Joshi and Joshi 1992). This advance in the membership and influence of the Communist Party of India was assisted by a shift again in Comintern policy, which after the 7th Comintern Congress in 1935 once more enjoined Communist parties in the colonial world to co-operate with bourgeois national movements (a policy formerly suspended after a leftward shift at the 6th Comintern Congress in the late 1920s). This more realistic Comintern policy was partly due to awareness of the growing threat from Fascism in Europe.

As on previous occasions when Congress activism and unity declined, the British government took the initiative and proposed the holding of elections in 1937 under the terms of the new 1935 Government of India Act. For the first time rich peasants were eligible to vote, the franchise being extended to 11.5 per cent of the total population, a deliberate attempt to seduce those elements that had been active in the *satyagrahas* but which had been most moderate; to some extent it was successful. As with earlier reforms, large numbers were persuaded to co-operate, and elections were held that resulted in the formation of Congress ministries in all but a handful of provinces. However, due to the voters being drawn from the upper sections of the peasantry and other elites, the character of the representatives elected to form these legislatures was conservative. Furthermore, although the elections were democratic, they were fought according to the British system of 'first past the post', so that inevitably – despite their high numbers of votes – neither the Communists nor the Muslim League performed as well as they might have done.

Since a large proportion of the new electorate was illiterate, a system of colour coding was used and the slogan 'vote for Gandhi and the yellow box' carried all before it. Overall, the Congress won 711 out of 1,585 seats, including 26 of the 58 reserved seats for Muslims that it contested, mostly in the North-West Frontier Province, and the Muslim League had to rest content with only about a quarter of the 424 Muslim seats won by non-congressmen. The ministries that were formed were composed almost entirely of congressmen and their close allies, with the exception of Bengal (where the Muslim League led a coalition government under Premier Fazl-ul-Huq), Punjab (where the National Unionist Party led by Sir Sikander Hyat Khan won a clear majority), Assam (where Congress was the largest party but a majority coalition of Muslim parties assumed power), and Sindh (where the Sindh United Party led a coalition government). In the North-West Frontier Province the Congress had less seats than the Muslim League, but enjoyed a commanding position since the League was divided. Even in Madras, where the anti-Brahmin Justice Party had dominated since 1922, the Congress – led by the veteran Rajagopalachari – won a clear majority with 159 seats against the Justice Party's 21. For many, this confirmed their worst fears about the nature of democracy under colonial rule and the Westminster system of representation. It was expected that a nationalistic party such as Congress might feel the need to make some sort of concession and to at least draft in some members of other political parties into the ministries, particularly in UP where a Muslim League candidate had contested almost every constituency. This, however, the Congress refused to do, a decision for which the later Congress president Maulana Azad held Nehru at least partly responsible (Azad 1988: 170). And not only did the ministries refuse to have anything to do with the League, in addition they posted the Congress flag, as if it were the national flag, on all government buildings, including schools. The Muslim League was deeply offended by such policies, and the duration of these ministries was therefore marred not only by their conservative characteristics but also by profound sectarian conflict.

Under the electoral systems introduced by the British, it seemed to many as if the majority elite had taken over and that the minorities and the powerless had been excluded. This was a view with which even the moderate socialist congressman Jawaharlal Nehru concurred. He described the Congress ministries of 1937 to 1939 as 'tending to become counter-revolutionary' and 'merely carrying on the traditions (with minor variations) of the previous governments'.[8] There is plenty of evidence to support this view. For example, the Congress ministry of Maharashtra introduced a Trades Disputes Act that imposed compulsory arbitration, six-month jail sentences for those involved in illegal strikes, and compulsory registration of trade unions – a measure that the British governor described as 'admirable' and one clearly motivated by the fact that some of the most influential congressmen in the west of India by this date were Bombay mill owners. At the same time, it is important to recognise the achievements of these ministries, not least in that they gave Indians a real taste of power and a sense that they might eventually succeed in assuming full control of their own affairs.

The Congress manifesto of 1937 had promised radical land reform and immediately the elections were over Kisan Sabhas demonstrated outside the provincial assembly buildings in Bihar and elsewhere to hold the party to this pledge. Revolutionary measures were never likely, given the predominance of landlords amongst the elected members, but radical proposals to abolish or at least severely curtail the *zamindari* system were adopted (though never put into action) in Madras and Orissa. Elsewhere there were bold attempts to provide security to tenants and to cut the burdens of tax and rent upon the poorer peasantry. In UP the Tenancy Act of 1939 gave all statutory tenants in Awadh and Agra full hereditary rights in their holdings, and loopholes enabling landlords to prevent the accrual of such rights were curtailed. Rents were fixed at a rate to be determined by special officers at a level that did not exceed one-fifth of the value of the produce, tenants could no longer be imprisoned for non-payment of rent, and a limit was placed on the amount of land that could be seized in the execution of a decree for default. Finally, all rent payments were to be receipted on an official form (failure to do so being an imprisonable offence) and the rights of grove-holders were made heritable. In Bihar, more radically, all increases in rents after 1911 were abolished (amounting to a reduction of around 25 per cent), and interest rates on arrears of rent were cut by half. Share-cropping was abolished and tenants given the right instead to pay their rents in cash, sale of entire holdings in payment of arrears was made illegal, and in the case of so-called 'occupancy tenants' it was made altogether impossible for a landlord to eject the tenant from his holding. In the Central Provinces, Bombay Province, Orissa and the North-West Frontier Province similar though less radical measures to assist the peasantry were introduced. In the Central Provinces the rents of tenants on less than five acres were reduced, and here and in other provinces far-reaching Moneylenders, Debt Conciliation, and Debt Relief Acts were introduced that fixed interest rates and provided for the registration of moneylenders and the limitation or cancellation of debts by means of official arbitration. Other measures included the provision of additional famine relief funds, better marketing facilities, and in Bombay the establishment of 1,500 village *panchayats*, funded out of local taxation (Coupland 1944: 137–158).

Most state governments – apart from Bombay – found they could not afford the imposition of prohibition within three years, as demanded of them by the Congress high command, but legislation banning discrimination against *dalits*, or untouchables, and the opening of temples to them was passed, notably in Madras – although Ambedkar insisted that little effort was made to implement the legislation – and serious but underfunded efforts were made to introduce the Wardha Plan of 'basic education' proposed by Gandhi, which involved training in practical handicrafts for primary schoolchildren. This did not dramatically increase the numbers attending school, but there was considerable discussion of new ideas in education, and a successful campaign to raise adult literacy levels was launched, most notably in the Central Provinces. Adult literacy training, however, was dependent entirely on voluntary efforts, and the shortage of funds restricted the number of night schools that could be established.

Whilst Nehru expressed his disillusion with the Congress ministries, he devoted his efforts instead to establishing agreement on the management of the Indian economy after independence. A National Planning Committee was established by Congress in December 1938, with Nehru in the chair, to formulate a scheme for the development of heavy, medium and cottage industries. It met five times before Nehru was imprisoned in 1941 and passed a series of resolutions insisting on the need for the socialisation of agriculture, the state ownership of key industries, the promotion of cottage industries (in deference to Gandhi), and the protection of large-scale private Indian industry against foreign competition. This latter point was underlined in 1944 in the notorious 'Bombay Plan' whereby Nehru pledged Congress to uphold the interests of leading industrialists, as 'trustees' of the nation's wealth, in exchange for their continuing support (Mukherjee 2002).

Gandhi himself took no part in politics in the late 1930s. His *harijan* campaign having been ignored by Congress, after 1934 he devoted himself largely to private reflection: he played no part in the Congress's abortive Muslim mass contacts campaign in 1935 and played little heed either to the growing evidence of activism amongst *kisans* and within the princely states, where Praja Mandals (States Peoples Conferences) – first mooted at the Nagpur Congress in 1920 – and the Communist-influenced States Peoples Movement were developing a parallel campaign to that led by the Congress within the British territories (Copland 2002; Vaikuntham 2004). For the Congress ministries, however, life soon became difficult. The suffering arising from continuing economic depression was causing increasingly militant popular discontent, most conspicuously in Bihar, where Swami Sahajanand inspired the *kisan* to refuse payment of rents, to seize crops, and to loot the property of landlords, moneylenders and merchants. *Kisan* volunteers marched around the countryside with red flags, urging others to do the same, the provincial revenues of Bihar and UP were severely affected, and in Lucknow a procession of 50,000 *kisans* invaded Lucknow, only to disperse after hearing an address from the Congress chief minister. Apart from the *kisan* movement, there was serious labour discontent in the cities, beginning with a strike of the textile workers in Ahmedabad in November 1937 and culminating in a general strike, organised by the Communist Party, the Bombay Branch of the Trades Union Congress, and Ambdekar's Independent Labour Party in protest against the Congress government's trades disputes bill, affecting the whole of Bombay presidency on 7 November 1938 (Chatterji 1999). There was considerable talk of revolutionary action and a general strike of the cotton mills in Kanpur in May 1938, and unrest amongst the student population, with a crowd of students attacking a police outpost near Aligarh University in January 1939. This was all part of what could be described as a developing struggle for hegemony within the nationalist movement between the bourgeois and landed elites and the working-class and peasant masses, under petit bourgeois leadership, who had joined the movement since 1930 (Joshi and Joshi 1992), and there was widespread criticism amongst Indian leftists:

> The dominant moderate leadership in effective control of the Congress machinery and of the Ministries was in practice developing an increasing co-operation with imperialism . . . (and) acting more and more openly in the interests of the upper class landlords and industrialists, and was showing an increasingly marked hostility to all militant expression of forms of mass struggle.[9]

Most seriously, there was growing communal strife: beginning with a riot at Jubbulpore in the Central Provinces in the first months of the Congress administration. There were disturbances in several places in UP and Bihar in July and August 1938, and progressively worse disturbances throughout India from the beginning of 1939, most seriously around the Muslim festival of Mohurram and the Hindu festival of Holi. In the Central Provinces a prominent congressman was murdered in broad daylight by Muslims in Berar. A particular threat was posed by the Khaksar Muslim militia movement in the Punjab, led by Inayatullah Khan Mashriqi. This movement of social service volunteers who drilled, wore khaki uniforms, and armed themselves with spades, attempted to intervene in conflicts between the Sunnis and Shias in Lucknow, were banned from doing so, and in the closing months of 1939 launched an invasion of the United Provinces, in groups of 300–500, in defiance of the ban. Numerous arrests resulted. This was grist to the mill of militant Hindu organisations, like the Rashtriya Svayam-sevak Sangh (RSS), which was founded in Nagpur in 1925 by Keshav Baliram Hegdewar as an instrument of Hindu cultural revitalisation and led by Madhav Sadasgiv Golwarkar from 1940 till 1973 (Anderson and Damle 1987; Kanungo 2002). The RSS drilled in a similarly provocative fashion and engaged in martial activities to prepare the youth of India to 'defend the Hindu nation'. Overall, between the beginning of October 1937 and the end of September 1939, there were 57 serious riots in the Congress provinces resulting in 1,700 casualties, more than 130 of them fatal.[10] An entirely new dimension was that Muslim League politicians, excluded from power, took the lead in many demonstrations and directed the anger of the crowds against the Congress provincial governments. An alliance was thus emerging between elite and popular Muslim discontent.

To deal with popular unrest, the Congress – once a subversive organisation itself – found that it had to use the hated colonial police force, powers of detention, and powers to ban meetings and publications in order to maintain order. When they came to office Congress ministries released all of the political prisoners from jail, only now to find themselves locking many of them up again. Initially there was hesitation, until in October 1937 Gandhi came firmly down on the side of the right wing, declaring that 'civil liberty is not criminal liberty' and arguing that it was not against the principal of *ahimsa* for the provincial governments to incarcerate those inciting violence.[11] After this the ministries exercised their powers with renewed vigour, albeit with continuing anxiety. It is thus said that by 1939 many in the Congress were looking for an excuse to retire from office, an excuse readily afforded by Lord Linlithgow's decision, without consultation, to involve India in the war with Germany. At this point Gandhi himself once again began to take a renewed interest in Congress Party politics. His candidate for the party presidency having been defeated by the leftists in favour of the Bengali leader Subhas Chandra Bose, Gandhi manipulated Bose into an impossible position, and forced him to resign by persuading Congress to pass a motion keeping the existing Gandhians in their positions on the Central Working Committee: a wily manoeuvre by the now-ageing politician, which proved that he could still command influence within the party (Bose 1995). With Gandhi's influence restored, and the issue of the war with Germany before them, the scene was then set, after a lull of more than half a decade, for another confrontation between the Congress and the British.

10 Quit India and partition, 1939–47

When France declared war on Germany in 1939 and the campaign began, there was but one cry which rose from the lips of German soldiers – 'To Paris, To Paris! . . . Comrades! My soldiers! Let your battle-cry be – 'To Delhi, To Delhi!'. How many of us will individually survive this war of freedom, I do not know. But I do know this, that we shall ultimately win and our task will not end until our surviving heroes hold the victory-parade on another grave-yard of the British empire – the Lal Kila or Red Fortress of ancient Delhi . . . May God now bless our army and grant us victory in the coming fight, INQUILAB ZINDABAD!, AZAD HIND ZINDABAD! (LONG LIVE REVOLUTION, LONG LIVE FREE INDIA).

(S.C. Bose, speech to INA troops)[1]

The Japs are advancing and so [we] will be helped . . . This is the time to show something to the white skins.

(Letter from Vindbasani Singh, Hajipur, to Ramgati Singh, on the distribution of arms to underground resistance groups in Bihar, 1943)[2]

Frustrated, and beset by popular discontent, by 1939 the Congress ministries were looking for an excuse to retire from office. This was very conveniently afforded by Viceroy Linlithgow who declared war on Germany in September 1939 on behalf of India without consulting the provincial ministries or a single Indian leader. Not surprisingly, in response, all of the Congress provincial ministries resigned. Since war was underway, the British reaction was to pass a new Defence of India Ordinance restricting civil liberties, and the government in New Delhi took over control of all provincial subjects. This was a great relief to British officials in India, many of whom had found the period of the Congress ministries (from 1937 to 1939) extremely disturbing. Having recovered power in the provinces, they immediately set about reversing many of the more radical changes in the administration that had been introduced in the intervening two years. This policy was strongly supported by Winston Churchill who declared in November 1942: 'I have not become the King's first Minister in order to preside over the liquidation of the British Empire.'[3] Unsurprisingly, Churchill was deeply reactionary in his attitudes towards the colonies, Secretary of State Amery commenting to Lord Wavell, prophetically, that Churchill knew as much about the Indian problem as George III had known about the American colonies (Wavell 1973: 21). Unfortunately, Labour leaders in the British wartime government, such as Attlee and Cripps, were not able to moderate this attitude. In consequence, although Viceroy Linlithgow was allowed to make vague offers to consult Indian politicians about further constitutional reform once the war was over, he was not permitted to make any substantive concessions beyond that.

Congress politicians were thoroughly disgruntled. Gandhi wanted India to have no part in the war, and even went so far as to urge Poland, Britain and France to adopt tactics of non-violent resistance. Meanwhile, Congress insisted that if it were to support the British war effort, Indians should at the very least be drafted into the wartime government so that Indian opinions could be heard. Churchill allowed no such concessions and as a consequence the Congress called for a renewal of civil disobedience on the issue of freedom of speech – the right of Indians to speak out against the conduct of the war. This campaign was initiated by Gandhi in October 1940, but was singularly low key and the issue itself unlikely to inspire mass participation. Under the Defence of India Ordinances many were arrested, but by the autumn of 1941 the movement had largely petered out after several key Congress leaders, including Nehru, had been thrown into jail.

Two years after the resignation of the Congress ministries, the prospects for the national movement in India were more than somewhat depressing. Subhas Chandra Bose gave up the idea of political agitation altogether: he was under house arrest in 1941, but fled from Calcutta to Afghanistan and on to Germany where he signed a pact with Hitler and briefly helped organise a small army – the Free India Legion – comprising about 3,000 Indian prisoners of war captured in North Africa.[4] Bose was then smuggled by submarine to Japan where with Japanese support he went on to assume leadership of the by then 40,000 strong Indian National Army (Azad Hind Fauj) formed by Captain Mohan Singh (an Indian officer who had defected to the Japanese in Malaya) with the help of Rash Behari Bose, an Indian revolutionary exiled in Japan who had established the Indian Independence League, a forerunner of Bose's provisional government of Azad Hind. The army was recruited from the ranks of captured Indian soldiers, along with Indian volunteers from the British plantation colonies in South-East Asia which had been seized by the Japanese army. For many, the INA was an attractive alternative to the possibility of being forced to labour on the Siam–Burma railway. Others undoubtedly joined out of sheer patriotic enthusiasm. The Japanese did not trust the INA, regarding it more as a propaganda tool than anything else, as did Hitler the Free India Legion. However, Bose became a hero for his efforts, being supreme commander of the only Indian army that actually fought against the British, as it did briefly on the Indian frontier in Burma between 1942 and 1944, until their capitulation following an engagement on the outskirts of Mandalay. Bose himself was never captured, dying in an air crash in Taiwan while attempting to make his escape from the advancing British forces in 1945 (Toye 1959; Leonard 1990; Fay 1993).

Within India itself, many of those arrested in 1941 were released again and dissent continued, albeit in a somewhat muffled form. Gandhi in particular continued to speak out against the war, although both the Muslim League and the Communist Party declared their intention to support the war effort, at least until Fascism was defeated. In talks with Churchill in December, following their first meeting and the publication of the Atlantic Charter in August 1941, the American president, Roosevelt, made it clear that American support for the British in the war required that further attempts be made to devolve political power in India: America was willing to help the British in the fight against Germany and Japan but would not assist in the restoration and entrenchment of the British empire. In order to placate American public opinion, Churchill, against his inclinations, agreed to send a British delegation to India in 1942, led by Sir Stafford Cripps, a member of the cabinet, in order to engage in further discussions about constitutional reform.

Stafford Cripps went to India intending to draw up a draft declaration of dominion status for India after the war, for which he hoped to gain the support of Congress politicians. Unfortunately, the Cripps mission failed. The essence of his proposals was that India should become a federated republic. Most Indian politicians were happy with this arrangement, but Churchill, afraid that there might be an agreement that would commit the British to withdraw after the war, engaged in some cunning intelligence. He sought to find out the one point on which Congress officials were most insistent, and that was Indian representation in the wartime government of India. Churchill then sent a telegram to Cripps informing him that the one concession he should not make was any form of Indian participation in the government. Inevitably, the mission then failed; Churchill was delighted; American public opinion was placated; and the British government in India could return to the business of war without any further worries about democracy.

The collapse of the Cripps mission was followed by renewed repression, and as 1942 progressed conditions within India worsened. There were food shortages, rising prices and a famine in Bengal. One causal factor was the destruction by the British army of bridges and boats on the rivers of east Bengal, to impede a Japanese invasion, before the onset of the monsoon in 1942. The lack of boats meant that harvested produce could not get to market. On top of this, the Japanese capture of Burma meant that eastern India could no longer obtain supplies of Burmese rice, on which it had formerly relied. This was made worse by government purchasing of food grain to supply the army, which remained Viceroy Linlithgow's first priority even as shortages became increasingly apparent. Food hoarding began to occur, prices rose, and rationing had to be introduced, beginning in Calcutta, but then extended to all the major Indian cities. The army and police began forcibly to requisition the grain of merchants and rich peasants to supply the ration system, yet still the government did not move to provide any rural relief. Ultimately a famine situation developed in Bengal, where somewhere between 1.5 and 3 million had died of starvation and related disease by the end of 1943 (Greenough 1982; Sen 1981).[5] The situation only came under control when

Lord Wavell (commander-in-chief of the Indian army) instigated large-scale relief works soon after taking over as viceroy in October 1943. Living conditions were further exacerbated by a general rise in prices of all commodities. The government of India, in an attempt to pay for wartime supplies had printed more money, and the amount of notes in circulation was doubled in the space of five years, causing rapid inflation (Kamtekar 2002). This particularly affected basic commodities such as food grains and kerosene, and the repressive measures imposed by the British, including the forcible requisition of food grain surpluses in rural villages in an attempt to meet the food shortages, encouraged a steady rise in mass politicisation and discontent. Japanese successes in Burma and South-East Asia, and the return of large numbers of refugees and wounded soldiers from the Burmese front, led to widespread rumours of a Japanese invasion and anticipation of the collapse of British power.

Everywhere the power of rumour was evident, both reflecting and promoting unrest. Rumours acted as a form of resistance as well as expressing a form of subaltern knowledge and understanding of the political struggles within which they found themselves. In the tribal areas of the Central Provinces, for example, there were rumours that the blood of Gonds was being used to restore the injured limbs of British soldiers, and that the signatures of Gonds were being obtained by deception on recruitment papers.[6] Another rumour said that 'the king emperor owing to bombing had to seek shelter in a latrine'[7] and had then come to Jabalpur for his safety, whilst in speeches (reported straight-faced by F.K. Khan, district commissioner Betul) wandering *satyagrahis* were reported to be saying that the English people were red-faced monkeys, that Mr Churchill was an ass, and that policemen would have to polish the shoes of congressmen in future. At Bahmni in Mandla on 2 May 1941, Bhaiyalal Misra was telling people that the government had issued forged notes and coins, as they were running away tomorrow. Rather more poignantly, at a meeting in Lakhanadon in Chhindwara district on 6 May 1941, Ram Prasad Kalar of Khawasa said that the government had 'deliberately opened only very few relief works in the Raipur district, which was hit by famine, so that the people would be compelled by sheer starvation to join the army'.[8] By 1942 these rumours were added to because of the anticipation of a Japanese invasion and growing anxiety about food shortages. Thus in Jabalpur a rumour circulated that owing to food shortages the government was going to order a general evacuation of the city by 20 March, and there were stories circulating that the Japanese planned to land at Vizagapatnam and then march to Raipur, Jabalpur and Nagpur. In Raipur on 15 March 1942 it was rumoured that wheat would be difficult to obtain and should be stored, and that a 'black-out' would commence every night from the 25th. On top of this there was resentment at the abandonment of Indian migrants and soldiers in South-East Asia when the British fled the Japanese advance. Many of these migrants and soldiers came from east UP and Bihar, districts adjacent to the famine-struck province of Bengal. Unsurprisingly, these were among the districts where the strongest support for the Congress Party's Quit India campaign was found.

Popular unrest, the deteriorating war situation, and the refusal of the British to countenance any involvement of the Congress in government during wartime, persuaded Gandhi to decide upon a more militant line. He drew up a resolution demanding that the British 'Quit India' and proposing negotiations with the Japanese. This first draft of the Quit India resolution was rejected in a meeting of the All-India Congress Committee (AICC) on 27 April, but, undeterred, Gandhi gave a speech the next month calling on Britain to '[l]eave India to God. If that is too much, then leave her to anarchy.'[9] On 14 July the AICC adopted a resolution proposing a programme of civil disobedience if the British did not concede to their demands. At a meeting of the All-India Congress Committee in Bombay on 8 August 1942 a revised 'Quit India' resolution (modified by Jawaharlal Nehru) was finally adopted demanding that the British let go of her hold on India for the sake of India's safety and for the cause of world peace, and calling for mass struggle on the widest possible scale. The very next day, the British, who had an informer at the meeting, arrested all of the major leaders of Congress, leaving behind, unqualified and unaltered, this announcement of a new campaign. Gandhi's last words before his arrest in a speech given at the Gowalia water tank *maidan* were as follows: 'Here is a *mantra*, a short one that I give you. You may print it on your hearts and let every breath of yours give expression to it. The *mantra* is do or die. We shall either free India or die in the attempt. Every true Congressman or woman will join the struggle with an inflexible determination not to remain alive to see the country in bondage and slavery.'[10] There were no other instructions from Gandhi, who in dawn raids the very next day was locked up along with other key Congress leaders and rendered temporarily incommunicado. News soon got out about the arrests (more than a thousand in the subsequent week), as well as reports of the committee's call for a mass struggle. Later that same day, on 9 August, a group of congressmen still at large – Maulana Azad, Sadiiq Ali, Dhayabhai Patel, Pyarelal Nair, Ram Manohar Lohia, Achyut Patwardhan and Sucheta Kripalani – met in Bombay to draw up a programme of action: the so-called Twelve-point Programme, consisting of a call for strikes, salt-making, and non-co-operation. This was copied and circulated by typewriter and by hand; but for most Congress supporters there was little or no guidance available and they were left to their own initiative. There then followed what Linlithgow privately described as 'by far the most serious rebellion since that of 1857, the gravity and extent of which we have so far concealed from the world for reasons of military security'.[11]

Quit India was the last of the three great nationwide anti-colonial nationalist *satyagraha* campaigns instigated by Gandhi – the civil disobedience campaign preceding it in the 1930–32 period and the non-co-operation campaign from 1920 to 1922 (the Rowlatt *satyagraha* [1919] is not included, as it was essentially a reformist movement, calling for the restoration of civil liberties, which did not specifically demand a British withdrawal). Whilst non-co-operation was urban-based, and supported mostly only by richer peasant groups in the countryside (especially in Gujarat), the civil disobedience campaign was far more widespread, involved many more poor peasants, and was radicalised by the impact of the depression. Quit India was the most radical and violent of them all, and was conspicuously supported by the poor and labouring classes, who were the most hard hit by wartime inflation and food shortages. Although there was crippling strike action in nearly every major city, beginning in Bombay and continuing for three and half months in the cotton mills of Ahmedabad, in most urban areas British control was too tight for Congress activism to last very long. Since the campaign commenced in August, many landowning peasants (including the formerly radical Patidars of Kheda district) were busily engaged in agricultural operations – at least during daylight hours – trying to harvest the best possible crop at a time of pressing grain shortages. In rural areas, though, conditions were sufficiently desperate, and the huge numbers of rural poor sufficiently politicised, for mass insurrection to take place.

The Quit India movement had two phases: an initial mass movement from August until September, followed by a longer, quasi-guerrilla insurgency. In the cities, strike action continued from 9–14 August in Bombay, and in Calcutta from 10–17 August. There were strikes in Kanpur, Lucknow and Nagpur and violent clashes with striking millworkers in Delhi. In Patna the police almost completely lost control over the city for two days after clashes in front of the secretariat on 11 August. Thereafter those activists who had not been arrested, including militant groups of students, spread out from the cities to join the insurrection in rural areas. Mass participation was inspired by inflammatory

Figure 12 Calcutta Women's Quit India march, 1942. © Mahatma Gandhi Research and Media Service.

Figure 13 Women joining the march, Calcutta 1942. © Mahatma Gandhi Research and Media Service.

underground publications, such as the *Bombay Province Bulletin*, *Free India*, *War of Independence Bulletin*, *Do or Die Newssheet*, *Free State of India Gazette* and the *Congress Gazette*, which flourished after the official Congress leadership had been imprisoned and their offices, assets and printing presses seized. There was also widespread distribution of handbills; one of the earliest, an appeal to students distributed in Bombay on 9 August, read as follows:

> This is our final struggle for freedom . . . Let us put up that resistance which will dislocate the entire machinery of the government. The students else-where in India have done the same thing. The student community of Bombay shall not lag behind . . . Therefore, students, students, the back-bone of Indian aspirations, should fight and FIGHT until India is FREE. No 'power on earth is going to give freedom to India, we shall have to snatch it from our imperialist foe.' DOWN WITH IMPERIALISM.[12]

Apart from the impact of food shortages and returning refugees, Bihar and eastern UP were the areas where the Kisan Sabhas were most strongly organised in the 1930s. By the 1940s most had fallen under the control of Congress socialists rather than the Communist Party, and they therefore fully backed the Quit India campaign (Damodaran 1992b). Bihar and eastern UP thus saw by far the strong-est support for Quit India, with attacks on rail lines, roads and bridges by peasants and militant students, rendering the capital Patna completely inaccessible, except by air, for several days. More than three-quarters of the police stations in central and northern Bihar were attacked or had to be evacuated. And in Ballia district in UP, all ten police stations were captured and a 'national government' briefly established under the leadership of Chitu Pandey (Mitra, in Pandey 1988). Elsewhere eyewitness accounts describe a crowd of 5,000 attacking the police *thana* at Azamgarh, armed with sickles, spades and anything else they could lay their hands on. All in all, some 16 districts were seriously affected and it was several weeks before the British had restored control by a truly massive use of troops and armed police. Even after the suppression of the initial uprising, attacks by politically motivated groups, or 'Azad Dastas' as they were called, continued well into 1943, the monthly incidence of *dacoit* crime in June 1943 being 310 in Bhagalpur district in Bihar, against a previous monthly average of around 50. The targets were commonly food stores, in response to the near famine conditions, but included raids on post offices, post bags, government treasuries and ammunition depots. The attacks were accompanied by prison breaks by members of the Congress Socialist Party and renewed acts of sabotage against telegraph and telephone wires. Interestingly, cries such as 'Gandhiji ki jai!' were heard from one group of *dacoits* whilst in the process of the very un-Gandhian and violent looting of a *zamindar*'s house in the Santhal Parganas. In Darbhanga, a crowd of 500 attacked the local *zamindar*'s *kutcheri* (office), led by Congress Socialist Party (CSP) leader Suraj Narayan Singh, and was only driven off after armed police opened fire, killing two. Suraj Narayan Singh had received training in Nepal before beginning his operations, which included terrorising police informers and sending threatening letters to the police, and he was in regular contact with the CSP activists in Bombay such as Achyut Patwardhan and Aurna Asaf Ali. He also allied with the leaders of conventional *dacoit* groups in Bihar, such as Mahendra Gope, in a successful attempt to turn their looting towards the nationalist cause, and he received numerous donations from Marwaris and other local businessmen, thereby demonstrating the breadth of his support (Damodaran 1992a, 1992b).

Elsewhere, in the Banka subdivision of Bhagalpur, it was reported that as many as 50 villages were giving food and money to support one of the more active gangs, led by Siaram Singh. It appears that Jayaprakash ('J.P.') Narayan was the mastermind behind many of these attacks. One of the early founders of the Congress Socialist Party in 1934 (which later split from Congress in 1952), he had been prominent in the August 1942 disturbances only to be jailed in Hanumannagar prison in Nepal. From here he escaped in November 1942 after 50 underground Congress activists broke into the jail to release him. Along with Rammanohar Lohia he then established a parallel government on the Nepal border from where he directed operations until 1944. Jayaprakash Narayan went on to become a prominent campaigner against corruption and for the rights of peasants, leading the Bihar movement in the mid-1970s that helped bring down the government of Indira Gandhi (Bhattacharjea 2004). Militant peasant activism has been a prominent feature of political life in Bihar ever since.

Stephen Henningham's (1983) study of Quit India suggests that there was a high level of elite as well as popular – including *adivasi* – involvement in Quit India in Bihar and eastern UP, which he characterised therefore as a 'dual revolt'.

Elsewhere though it was more unequivocally a subaltern effort and the frequency with which 'national governments' were established in the localities underlined the revolutionary purpose behind the uprising. Apart from eastern UP and Bihar, the other main centres were in the impoverished district of Midnapur in Bengal, Orissa, and in the desperately poor districts of southern Maharashtra and northern Karnatak (Mathur 1979). In Gujarat a parallel government was briefly operated for three months in the Jambusar *taluk* in Broach district with the aid of a local bandit, Megzi, as described by Hardiman in Pandey (1988). Far more successful was the *prati sarkar* or parallel government established in Satara district in southern Maharashtra, led by Nana Patil. Here the movement was linked to the non-Brahmin *bahiajan samaj* movement, and its activities included running people's courts and a constructive programme along Gandhian lines (including enforcement of prohibition), as well as active guerrilla warfare that continued from mid-1943 until as late as 1945–6. In a few cases mortgaged land taken by rural moneylenders was returned to poor peasants and the harassment of village women by landlords was punished (Shinde 1990; Omvedt 1995; Pandey 1988). Elsewhere in the Karnatak, 'dislocation' activities organised by the Congress Socialist Party included 1,600 attacks on telegraph lines and raids on 26 railway stations and 32 post offices. And in Orissa, 35 were killed in a mass attack on the Eram-Basudevpur police station on 28 September, following the spread of rumours that *swaraj* would be won within a week and that under a Swaraj government no taxes would be paid and the paddy of the rich would be available to the poor. Cuttack was another centre of activity, and the tribal population of Koraput launched forest *satyagrahas*, attacks on *thanas* (police stations), and a no-rent movement in the Jeypore *zamindari* (Sarkar 1983: 401–403).

The Quit India uprising in Midnapur district in Bihar was less violent, but better organised, more Gandhian and sustained longer than most, only winding up in September 1944 upon Gandhi's request. Support was concentrated in the Tamluk and Contai subdivisions, where meetings were held and Gandhian volunteers circulated from early August onwards. A particular emphasis was placed on the constructive programme, and the achievements of the Congress were described in a weekly newsletter, *Biplabi* ('the Revolutionary'), probably edited by Prahlad Kumar Pramanik and circulated between September 1942 and late August 1944 in the Tamluk subdivision. The role of the paper was to keep up support for underground anti-government activity in the wake of the suppression of the overt public campaign in support of Quit India. From January 1943 onwards it declared itself to be the 'Mouthpiece of the Tamluk National Government' (Jatiya Sarkar). In the wake of a devastating cyclone, which hit the district in October 1942, it carried news of relief efforts by Congress volunteers, as well as denouncing the brutality and 'beastliness' of British police officers and the artificial nature of the developing food shortage – which was to turn into a full-blown famine. The Jatiya Sarkar organised an armed *vidyut vahini* (guerrilla army), set up arbitration courts, gave grants to schools, organised relief, and endeavoured to tax and redistribute grain from wealthy farmers and merchants to the landless and the starving. The most spectacular achievement of the underground movement was a simultaneous attack by crowds of 5,000 to 10,000 on four of the six police *thanas* in Tamluk subdivision on 29 September. One *thana* was actually seized, but elsewhere police firing killed a total of 44 peasants. Soon after, though, most of the full-time revolutionaries were driven into hiding. Publication of *Biplabi* nonetheless continued. Criticism focused particularly on the habit of the local police of burning down the houses of Congress volunteers and the alleged raping of village women by British soldiers and Indian sepoys (generally identified as Muslims) – of which numerous incidents were recorded in *Biplabi* (Chakrabarty 2002). In such terms the metaphor of the 'rape of Mother India', described for so long in nationalist publications, acquired a new and vivid reality that, even in terms of Gandhi's thinking on *ahimsa* (non-violence), justified a violent response. Even if some of these reports were exaggerated 'it is difficult not to believe that terror was official policy'. One police *daroga* achieved particular notoriety, being widely referred to as *ghar-pora*, or 'house-burner' Nalini Raha (Greenough 1983: 369–370). The recording of the names of police officials involved in such atrocities clearly implied that the Jatiya Sarkar anticipated that the day would come when they would be held to account for their crimes. Even the otherwise loyal Fazlul Huq administration in Bengal was sufficiently impressed by the litany of accusations to propose a judicial investigation early in 1943, although this idea was quashed by the governor, Sir John Herbert.

As conditions worsened in Midnapur district, as they did over the entire province of Bengal, *Biplabi* went on to carry gruelling accounts of famine deaths, suicides, the sale of children, and outmigrations, along with exhortations to support the Congress as the only possible recourse: 'Inhabitants of Tamluk! If die you must, then why condemn yourself to a slow death made painful by pangs of hunger? Instead, let us submerge this devilish administration' (Greenough 1983: 376). In this fashion, Gandhi's famous last words before his arrest, to 'Do or Die', came to be widely interpreted as 'Do and Die'. Quit India was thus by far the most popular, radical, and violent of the anti-colonial campaigns. However, for many years the events between August 1942 and early 1943 remained veiled in obscurity; and little was written about it in depth until more than forty years later when secret documents became available and subaltern and other historians began to consider the topic (Mathur 1979; Chopra 1986; Pandey 1988).

The reasons why the history of Quit India has been neglected are due to the fact, to begin with, that neither the Congress leadership, the Communist Party leadership, nor the Rashtriya Swayamsevak Sangh (RSS), the Hindu Mahasabha or Muslim League organisations as a whole, played a central role in the movement in 1942: demonstrating the fact that genuine mass activism in the Indian national struggle was often to be seen in inverse proportion to the efforts made by political elites to organise political campaigns – campaigns that invariably were more conservative in form. This point has been particularly emphasised in Gyan Pandey's work on Uttar Pradesh where differences between the Congress elite and the masses were often conspicuous. Interestingly, in 1942 even some left-wing congressmen such as Jawaharlal Nehru, normally a staunch supporter of Gandhi, had doubts about the Quit India strategy (hence the redrafting of Gandhi's Quit

India resolution), since they were inclined to support the British for the moment in the struggle against Fascism. The Muslim League leadership took no part in Quit India as the party's policy was to support the British during the war, whilst the Communist leadership refused to sanction any agitation between 1939 to 1945 that might counteract the struggle against Fascism, which they believed to be primordial – thereby doubtless losing some popular support. The Hindu Mahasabha, under the militant leadership of V.D. Savarkar and B.S. Munje, also refused to back the campaign (Mathur 1996; Gondhalekar and Bhattacharya 1999). At the same time, all of the Congress leaders, at a national and provincial level, were imprisoned, gave no orders and took no part in the movement: this is clearly apparent, despite the best efforts of the British (in order to justify their repression) to find evidence that the Congress leadership had pro-Axis sympathies and had planned a violent insurrection (Tottenham 1942).

Quit India was therefore very much a movement of the subaltern classes. No political leader or party could directly take credit for it, and therefore few national leaders have discussed it in detail in their memoirs. The Gandhians least of all wished to draw attention to an uprising that was so very un-Gandhian in its form and content. The British on the other hand were unwilling to report events that constituted the surest proof that the Indian independence movement was a mass campaign founded on profound discontent, especially since British over-reaction and repression itself appears to have provoked much of the violence. News of these events had to be kept quiet above all during wartime, when it might have seriously undermined morale at home in the UK. Both British colonialist and Indian nationalist accounts have therefore paid slight attention to the actual events of 1942: despite the fact that the Quit India struggle possibly had more impact on the British imperial machine than any previous *satyagraha*, demonstrated more activism at a grass-roots level than any other anti-colonial campaign, and played an important part in the British decision eventually to leave India at the end of the war.

The reasons why Quit India had such an impact, and aroused fear and anxiety in the minds of so many British in India, are more than amply demonstrated by the statistics. To begin with, 57 army battalions had to be mobilised to restore order, and by the end of 1943 some 100,000 people had been arrested, 1,000 killed in firings and 3,000 injured according to official figures. Furthermore, terrorism was not incidental, but central to the uprising: in total 208 police outposts were attacked and destroyed, 332 railway stations were wrecked, and 945 post offices were burnt to the ground according to official statistics. Thousands of miles of telegraph wires were put out of action and 664 bomb explosions took place, whilst 63 policemen died in the struggle and a further 216 defected – mostly in Bihar (Tottenham 1942). The response was equally vigorous: in reprisal raids by the British, martial law was imposed, and whole villages were razed to the ground by the army or machine-gunned from the air – although there were no official numbers published of the resulting injuries and fatalities.

A notable feature of the agitation was the frequency with which allegations of excessive use of force, and in particular of the mistreatment of women, were levelled at the British soldiers stationed in India and at the Indian police and sepoys who aided in suppression of the uprising. This undoubtedly reflected a reality of British repression, but also betokened that the liberation of India from colonial rule had become synonymous with the defence of Indian tradition and the purity of Indian womanhood. The most infamous incidents occurred at Chimur and Ashti in Chandrapur district in the Central Provinces, where Indian police who had arrested local Congress leaders and fired upon demonstrating crowds were in turn murdered by villagers. In the former case, allegations of the abuse of village women were used to justify the violent retaliation of the villagers against the police action, and leading Congressmen rallied to the defence of the accused (Dev Das Gandhi 1944). Gandhi himself wrote and spoke in their defence, with eventual success, the sentence of death passed on those involved being commuted to life imprisonment in August 1945. This was all in stark contrast to Congress's response to the Chauri Chaura incident 20 years earlier, which at the time was widely condemned, even though the British at one point had threatened to hang as many as 179 villagers in response, and despite the all-too-evident provocation by the Police.

Throughout August and September 1942 Congress offices were closed, assets seized, and the repression culminated in the imprisonment of even the most local Congress politicians, effectively shattering the party's organisation by the end of the year. Most of these congressmen then remained in jail until the end of the war. This had a number of important effects. First, it meant that at the close of the Second World War the Congress Party was debilitated, and even after the release of most of its leaders from prison in 1945 there was no prospect of further political campaigns for many years to come under Congress auspices. Despite their lack of participation (at least officially) in Quit India, the Communists nonetheless benefited from the lack of competition, being allowed to build up its membership and organisation rapidly after 1942 when it was legalised in reward for support given to the war effort, the party's active membership rising from 4,000 in 1942, to 53,000 in 1946, and to over 100,000 by 1948. The debility of Congress also left the way open for the rapid growth of the Muslim League, and after 1942 vigorous efforts were made by the British to build up the League as the only constitutional party, representative of Indians, upon which they could rely. This official support took a number of forms. To begin with, following the imprisonment of Congress leaders in many parts of north India, Muslim politicians were enabled to set up administrations in Sindh, Bengal and the North-West Frontier Province (NWFP). Thus from a Congress predominance in provincial government between 1937 to 1939, by 1944 wholly bogus Muslim ministries were in place in five major north Indian provinces – a complete reversal of political fortunes. Support was also received in the form of financial subsidies, indirectly given by the placing of official advertisements in the newly founded Muslim League newspaper *Dawn*. By these and other means the growth of the League was encouraged, until by the end of the Second World War in 1945 the Muslim League, although at best representing less than 20 per cent of the population, had become easily as powerful a political organisation as the Congress Party itself.

The partition of India

The concept of Pakistan and the reasons behind partition are shrouded in controversy. The history that is studied is nearly always the history of the victors and their version of events, and one of the major reasons why the events of partition have been misrepresented is that two key Indian politicians of the time died within 12 months of partition and never wrote their memoirs. Muhammad Ali Jinnah died of tuberculosis in 1948, and Gandhi was assassinated in the same year. Gandhi was always opposed to partition, whilst Jinnah led the Muslim League towards the separation of India and has always been blamed for it; but neither of these two key players have been able to leave a considered record of these crucial events. On the Congress side, however, Nehru played a prominent role in the negotiations and controlled India for the next 15 years, and the version of events between 1942 to 1945 that has been largely accepted is that disseminated by him and by the last viceroy, Lord Mountbatten, who were both voluminous memoirists, and have dozens of biographies written about them.

The British and Congress version of events together give an impression of a tortuous but orderly debate eventually leading to the decision to partition India, a decision to which they were both opposed but which was forced upon them because of the intractability of the man portrayed as the evil genius behind it all – Muhammad Ali Jinnah, the leader of the Muslim League.

It is difficult to accept that Jinnah played an entirely negative role during the partition when one considers his immense popularity amongst Muslims at this time (Ahmed 1997), and recent historical research has tended to shift the balance of interpretation substantially. Ayesha Jalal (1985) has thus argued, basing her reasoning in part on new evidence available from CIA and British files released under the 30-, 40- and 50-year rules banning access to official documents, that Jinnah himself never wanted partition and only used it as a bargaining tool in order to obtain a greater share of power for Muslims at the centre of a united India. Jalal instead pins the blame for partition rather more on Nehru, suggesting that it was he who pressed the point to its conclusion because he refused ever to consider seriously the possibility of sharing real power in a government with Muslim League politicians. The British too take their share of the blame. She has described their part in partition as 'an ignominious scuttle enabling the British to extricate themselves from the awkward responsibility of presiding over India's communal madness' (Jalal 1985: 293). The unexpurgated diaries of Maulana Azad, the Muslim president of the Congress Party, who might otherwise be relied upon to have a sympathetic view of the Congress leadership, were finally published in 1988 following a long court battle, and they reveal a not dissimilar perspective from that of Jalal. Maulana Azad depicts Nehru as overreaching himself, as greedy for power and reluctant to compromise. A famous passage reads as follows:

> Sixteen August 1946 was a black day . . . The turn that events had taken made it almost impossible to expect a peaceful solution by agreement between Congress and the Muslim League. This was one of the greatest

tragedies of Indian history and I have to say with the deepest regret that a large part of the responsibility for this development rests with Jawaharlal. His unfortunate statement that the Congress would be free to modify the Cabinet Mission Plan re-opened the whole question of political and communal settlement . . . Jawaharlal is one my dearest friends . . . I have nevertheless to say with regret that this was not the first time that he did immense harm to the national cause. He had committed an almost equal blunder in 1937 when the first elections were held under the Government of India Act . . . If the League's offer of co-operation [in the U.P. government] had been accepted, the Muslim League party would for all practical purposes merge with Congress. Jawaharlal's action [rejecting the terms of this offer] gave the Muslim League in UP a new lease of life . . . Mr Jinnah took full advantage of the situation and started an offensive which ultimately led to Pakistan.

(Azad 1988: 170–171)

Another explanation, articulated by a few historians (Kamtekar 1988; Aiyar 1995), may be termed the 'crisis of the state' theory of partition. This has been little discussed so far in print but could be described as drawing its inspiration in part from subalternist critiques of Indian historiography, which have lambasted the idea that partition was simply the outcome of an elite political contest or a triumph of religious communalism over the ideals of secular nationalism, pointing out the artificiality of the binary opposition between the two (Pandey 1994). In particular, the 'crisis of the state' theory criticises the simplicity of conventional explanations of partition, which concern themselves with 'blaming' events either on the manipulation of Congress politicians or the Muslim League, or on wheelings and dealings of the British. Such positions are absurd, it is argued, because in the period after the Second World War leading up to partition, none of these elites really had the power or ability to deliver on any of their policies. The British empire was in a debilitated state, the army had been demobilised, and by 1946 large numbers of civil servants had resigned or had taken early retirement. This crisis in the Indian civil service (ICS) had been developing since the 1930s, but reached its peak immediately after the war when the shortage of qualified personnel combined with the all-too-evident unreliability of the ICS as a career both for old and new recruits (Brown 1994: ch. 3). There were police strikes, a naval mutiny and widespread disaffection. The British state in India was crumbling and, it was widely recognised, could not hope to retain control if an insurrection on anything approaching the scale of Quit India was to be repeated. The Congress Party was also disordered and chaotic and the Muslim League, after Jinnah's Day of Direct Action on 16 August 1946, had lost control of its followers. Widespread civil disturbance and rioting then ensued until 1947. That this theory has still not been widely circulated in print is an indication that the whole issue of partition still dominates strained relations between India and Pakistan, and it is not really possible at present for commentators, even those on the left, to articulate a view that suggests that partition might not have been the fault of either Jinnah or the British – that what happened was not a division of the spoils but a fracturing of the state in 1947. The facts are all known, but the conclusion is never articulated, so keen are we always to envision ourselves as masters of our destiny. It remains, nonetheless, a highly plausible explanation.

The growth of communalism and the demand for Pakistan

The history of partition begins at various points depending on one's appraisal of what is important. Supporters of the 'Cambridge School' approach, emphasising the role of political factions, would argue that it begins *c.* 1943–4. Others place an emphasis on the adoption of the resolution calling for the formation of a separate state of Pakistan by the Muslim League in 1940. The term 'Pakistan' itself was invented in 1933 by a group of Punjabi Muslim students at Cambridge University. The derivation of the word is interesting as it is coined from the initial letters of the provinces claimed for Pakistan: Punjab, Afghan, Kashmir, Sindh and Baluchistan provinces. Although it has also been claimed to mean 'the land of the pure', this was not in fact its origin. Nonetheless, the idea of setting up a separate state was arguably never taken very seriously by most Muslim League politicians. The party's recent history included a joint pact agreed between the Muslim League and Congress in 1915, the Muslim League had co-operated in the agitation of 1920–2, and Jinnah and others had tried to forge a united front with Congress in response to the Simon Commission in 1928–9. It was not because of intransigent communalism that the League took no part in the subsequent civil disobedience campaign, but because it had been excluded by fundamentalist Hindus. Thus in the early 1930s, the League was not lacking in inclination to co-operate with Congress.

The real parting of the ways, many have argued, began with the defensive anti-Muslim agitations of high-caste Hindu *bhadralok* elites in Bengal in the 1920s, fearful of their declining control given the numerical preponderance of Muslims in the province, economic rivalry, and divisions within the Bengali Congress (Datta 1999). Subhas Chandra Bose was one of the few Bengali politicians to perceive this danger and to endeavour to reach out and bolster Muslim support for the Congress. Most, however, did not perceive this need until too late. Other historians have argued that Hindu–Muslim rivalry did not become a serious problem until much later, during the civil disobedience period itself and after (Chatterji 1994). Sugata Bose has stressed the role that the Great Depression played in exacerbating communal conflict, since religious and economic divides – particularly in Bengal – were often coterminous (Bose 1986). Bose argues that there was always a certain degree of conflict between landlords, moneylenders and peasants, but that rural society was given considerable cohesion by the existence of the credit system. Even during the Kishoreganj food riots of 1930 this cohesion persisted (Bose 1982). With the onset of the Great Depression, however, this collapsed, as did many traditional ties of dependency between rural elites and the masses. Conflict that had been covert thus became overt. As labourers were sacked or loans called in, new conflicts arose and the desperate Muslim peasantry of east Bengal came gradually to anticipate the economic benefits that might derive from political autonomy (Hashmi 1992).

At a popular level, serious disputes begin to emerge between Hindus and Muslims in the early 1930s, particularly in the east of the country. At the elite level, however, many Muslim League leaders were still willing to co-operate with congressmen. Conflict here did not really break out until 1937–9 when the Muslim League seized power in Bengal but were excluded from the Congress-dominated provincial governments in the United and Central Provinces. The Congress also adopted a number of what were perceived as communal symbols – flying the Congress flag over public buildings, for example. Very quickly the disaffected, disenfranchised Muslims vented their sense of frustration and anger through actions such as attacks on temples. In the 1940s the Muslim League went still further in a separate direction when it was decided to co-operate with the British wartime government, whilst Congress politicians resigned from the ministries. The destruction of Congress's political organisation during the war left an open field to the League to recruit more followers. The League was directly encouraged and subsidised by the British because of Muslims' perceived loyalty. Thus by 1945 the Muslim League was both a more important organisation and one whose stance was directly opposed to that of Congress, and deliberately trying to poach Muslim supporters from the Congress. The Muslim League did this without invoking Pakistan. A resolution urging the creation of a separate state was passed by the League at a Lucknow meeting in 1940, but this was only one of a number of policies under review.

The origins of partition could be taken back still further. Developing communal conflict in north India in the 1890s and the cow-protection movement might be seen as the starting points. British politicians of the time generally took the view that there had always been conflict between Muslims and Hindus, which was why separate representation was necessary for the former. It was a self-serving strategy disguised as liberalism. The British sought to divide and rule, to create a separate system of representation for different castes and creeds, so making it difficult for them to unite on a common strategy. The British justified this under the guise of offering protection for minorities. This was a reasonable policy, provided evidence of discrimination was forthcoming. This was not always easy to find. Gyan Pandey (1983) has commented on the construction of communalism through the cow-protection movements of the 1890s. There is an ongoing debate as to the nature and extent of communal conflict under British rule. Francis Robinson and Paul Brass take opposing points of view on this issue (see Taylor and Yapp 1979). C.A. Bayly, in an article on communal violence in eighteenth-century India, argues that much evidence exists of Hindu–Muslim conflict at this time (1985). Most Indian nationalists would disagree, describing communalism as very much a response to colonialism. This argument has been given renewed force with the emergence of the powerful political ideology of Hindutva ('Hinduness') in the present day, a word coined by Vinayak Damodar Savarkar (later president of the Hindu Mahasabha) in his 1923 pamphlet *Hindutva: Who is a Hindu?*, with the resurgence of legal disputes (and open conflict) over a mosque in

Ayodhya (birthplace of Ram) that began in the 1930s, and a continuing crisis of identity amongst India's Muslims that can be traced back more than a hundred years (Gopal 1991; Hasan 1997).

Although it was tied to colonial developments, and indeed the term itself was a colonial invention, most historians agree that by 1945 'communalism' was beginning to acquire a momentum of its own. This was true both at mass and elite levels. By this time, Jinnah had reluctantly come to the conclusion that his role was to speak out on behalf of Muslims and Muslims alone against the Congress Party. Likewise, by 1945 a great many Hindu and Muslim congressmen were highly suspicious of the League. Towards the end of the war, however, an immediate British withdrawal from India did not seem likely. Jinnah was consolidating his position, whilst Gandhi made the mistake, following the death of Kasturba and his release from prison due to declining health in May 1944, of meeting with Jinnah, publicly giving the impression that they were leaders of equal stature of the two main Indian communities. Gandhi proposed a demarcation and grouping of Muslim areas that would then be offered a plebiscite to determine whether they wished to remain a part of India following independence, or to separate and join a looser federation, still sharing common services such as defence and communication. This idea was rejected out of hand by Jinnah as a 'shadow, and a husk, a maimed, mutilated and moth-eaten Pakistan'. Following the release of the remaining Congress leaders in June 1945, the viceroy, Lord Wavell, arranged a meeting in Simla where he proposed an executive council made up of half 'Caste Hindus' and half Muslim representatives (Figures 14 and 15). Jinnah insisted that the Muslims should all be members of the League; but the Congress resisted being reduced to the status of a 'Hindu' party – not least of all since the Congress president, Maulana Azad, was himself a Muslim. The talks therefore came to nothing.

At the end of the war there was no serious proposal on the table for further constitutional reforms. However, the ball began to roll in the direction of British withdrawal with the victory of a Labour Party administration in elections held in July 1945 in Britain. The change in government was not solely responsible for a change in policy, but it was responsible for a sudden recognition of realities. Everyone in the wartime government knew that with the end of the war and demobilisation of the British army, Britain would not be able to hang on to the Indian empire. But Churchill himself was resolutely opposed to the idea of negotiation. With the election of a Labour government the determination was made to grasp realities. Wavell, the viceroy at the time, noted in his diary that many of the Labour leaders such as the Labour foreign secretary, Aneurin Bevan, were in reality imperialists, who like everyone else hedged the topic of India, but like everyone else had no alternatives to suggest (Wavell 1973; Gupta 1975).

The collapse of the state

Rapid post-war inflation, continuing food shortages, unemployment and disaffection in the armed services and police as a result of demobilisation and cuts in pay,

Figure 14 Jawaharlal Nehru and Sardar Vallabhai Patel at Simla, 1946. © *The Hindu.*

played an important part in the events leading up to partition. The Indian army was particularly aggrieved because, unlike British troops who were sent home, proposals were made to send them to assist the French in Vietnam. The Indian soldiers had no desire to take part in further colonial adventures. In the Indian navy there was a mutiny in February 1946, which began with a hunger strike in protest at the quality of food and racist remarks directed at seamen by their officers. This soon spread to all 22 ships in the harbour at Bombay and to barracks on shore. The demands of the naval mutineers expanded to include calls for equal pay for white and Indian sailors, and a call for the release of all political prisoners. This mutiny was not suppressed until various other naval bases along the coast had joined in, extending as far as Karachi and Madras. In Bombay the Communist Party organised a general strike in support of the mutineers, which only ended after 228 civilians were killed and more than a thousand were injured in police and army actions. Sardar Patel, the Congress peasant leader, helped to persuade the mutinous naval ratings to surrender, although he did nothing afterwards to prevent the victimisation of the ringleaders. Patel commented: 'discipline in the army cannot be tampered with, we will want an army even in free India'. Disaffection was the spirit of the times. Amongst other examples one may cite demonstrations held in Calcutta and other Indian cities in protest at a crass British proposal in November 1945 to put on trial at the Red Fort in Old Delhi

Figure 15 Govind Ballabh Pant (ex-UP chief minister) and Mohammad Ali Jinnah in conversation, *c.* 1946. © *The Hindu.*

(symbol of Mughal power) three captured members of Bose's Indian National Army (INA): a Hindu, a Sikh, and a Muslim, who were charged with the sweeping offence of 'waging war against the king'. Leading congressmen, Jawaharlal Nehru, Bhulabhai Desai and Tej Bahadur Sapru offered to represent the INA soldiers at the trial and a major confrontation threatened, causing the British eventually to abandon the idea, to withdraw charges against them, and to announce that henceforth only those guilty of murder or violent treatment of fellow prisoners of war would be charged. This still did not prevent further demonstrations, and a student and Communist-led general strike paralysed Calcutta on 12 February 1946 in protest against the imprisonment for seven years of Abdul Rashid of the INA.

In all these agitations, Congress stood very much aloof, being in no position at this time to organise or support widespread disaffection. It was partly for this reason that Congress was willing to go along with proposals made for a move towards constitutional reform by the British. An election to be held early in 1946 to set up new imperial and provincial assemblies was mooted. Previously, Congress had always argued for an election to be held on the basis of universal suffrage. In its weakened state, it accepted the British proposal. With Nehru as a star orator, the Congress Party did well, winning majorities in all of the provincial assemblies except Bengal, Punjab and Sindh. In the Punjab, the Unionists, an organisation of Muslim loyalists, came to power and the Muslim League won in

Bengal. The Communist Party gained many votes and won some seats, but not enough in a first-past-the-post system. Only 1 per cent of the population had been allowed to vote in the central elections and 10 per cent in the provincial elections. This was a far cry from the universal suffrage demanded by Congress. If Congress had stood firm and ensured the extension of the franchise, it would probably have been in a far better position to negotiate with the British and might have succeeded in marginalising the League, but the course of events proved otherwise.

In the March to June period, 1946, a three-man Cabinet mission was sent out to India, being led by Stafford Cripps once again. The visit took place against a background of police strikes, postal strikes and threats of an all-India rail strike. But rather than take a lead in these negotiations, Congress embroiled itself in the minutiae of negotiations. Eventually the cabinet mission came out with a proposal for a three-tier federation, with a weak centre controlling only foreign affairs, defence and communications. While electing the constituent assembly the provincial assemblies would be grouped into three sections: section A for the Hindu-majority provinces, sections B and C for the Muslim-majority provinces of the north-west and north-east. Each section would have the power to set up intermediate-level executives and legislative assemblies of their own, thus allowing the Muslim League the possibility of dominating the government of the Muslim majority, yet remaining within a superficially still-united India. It fell short of Pakistan, but it was the nearest alternative to have been suggested and Jinnah accepted the proposal on behalf of the League on 6 June, with the Congress following soon after on 24 June. This apparent break, however, soon came undone. Both parties had rather different ideas on how the grouping of provincial assemblies would be done. Jinnah wanted grouping to be compulsory and envisaged a short-lived transition to quasi-autonomy for the Muslim-majority areas. The Congress envisaged grouping being an optional process, anticipating that the Congress stronghold in the North-West Frontier Province, led by 'the frontier Gandhi', Khan Abdul Ghaffar Khan, and probably Assam as well, would remain aloof. At a press conference Nehru explained that in the view of Congress there need not be grouping at all. This placed Jinnah in an impossible position: having given up the idea of a strong and entirely separate state of Pakistan, it now seemed possible the League would win nothing at all for its supporters, and Jinnah withdrew his earlier agreement to the cabinet mission plan.

Efforts to form an interim government foundered at the same time as the cabinet mission plan. This was upon Jinnah's insistence that there should be equal numbers of Muslim League and Congress ministers, forcing Viceroy Wavell to press ahead to form a government entirely composed of officials. Naturally, this lacked credibility and within a few weeks he was urging the Congress to participate (to which they eventually assented at the beginning of September) in the hope that they might be able to forestall threatened strikes in the railway and postal services. Meanwhile, Jinnah rallied his supporters and called for a 'day of action', scheduled for 16 August 1946, in order to press again the demand for Pakistan. It was a somewhat desperate gamble: his bluff having been called and having effectively given up the demand for a separate state once already.

something dramatic needed to be done to put the League and its demands back at the centre of negotiations. At the same time, Jinnah had no clear idea as to how the 'day of action' might proceed since the Muslim League's organisational abilities on the ground were comparatively limited. This was to prove a fatal flaw, since what was envisaged as a day of demonstrations and strikes soon degenerated into anarchy and violence on a scale that Jinnah could not possibly have imagined.

The worst violence on 16 August occurred in Bengal where the Muslim League was in power. Evidence has come to light suggesting that League members on the city council were in cahoots with Muslim criminal gangs who were given carte blanche to loot and pillage Calcutta's Hindu merchants. This provoked a response from those affected and the situation degenerated into an orgy of looting, murder and mayhem with gangs of hired *goondas* on both sides playing a leading role. The suspicions of official connivance are underlined by the fact that the city council did not call in the army to bring order to the streets until at least 24 hours later. By 19 August, 4,000 had been killed and 10,000 injured in what became known as the 'Great Calcutta Killing'. Rioting then spread to the famine-ravaged rural areas of Bengal. Those politically organised districts involved in Quit India stood notably aloof, but elsewhere an uncontrolled mixture of class and communal conflict erupted with attacks by Muslim tenants on Hindu landlords and other elites in the Noakhali and Tippera districts in east Bengal. There were 300 deaths, and millions of rupees worth of property was looted or destroyed. This was followed by an uprising of Hindu peasants against Muslims on a far larger scale in Bihar on 25 October, which ended in some 7,000 deaths, and the slaughter of approximately 1,000 Muslim villagers by Hindu pilgrims in Garhmukteswar in UP.

A few right-wing congressmen naively defended Hindus involved in violence, believing it to be defensive and therefore by some twisted logic legitimate. The interim government, however, struggled desperately and unsuccessfully to contain the situation. That they could not was largely due to the demobilisation of the army and the disordered state of the police. British colonial officials, looking to depart, were moreover unwilling to act at the behest of Indian politicians to risk their lives in crowd control measures.

At the same time as civil war erupted in parts of northern India, a major uprising occurred in the princely state of Hyderabad, where the Congress Party rarely had much political influence and still lacked it in this period. The Telengana movement in north-western Hyderabad affected at its height some 3,000 villages spread over 16,000 square miles with a population of 3 million. In villages controlled by the Communist Party, *vetti* (forced labour) and bonded labour was abolished, unjustly seized land was restored and steps taken to redistribute wastelands to the poor. This was an organised peasant insurrection with an agenda and an army. What started as a revolt against Nawab Mir Osman Ali Khan, *nizam* of Hyderabad, led to an effective declaration of independence in the Telugu-speaking region north of the country. In response, Kasim Razvi, leader of the Majlis Ittehadul Muslimeen (a Hyderabad political party), called for the creation of a separate Muslim state in Hyderabad and the Deccan, and helped raise an army of armed Muslim volunteers – the Razakars – who rampaged through the country alongside the *nizam*'s police in an effort to terrorise the population into submission. According to the *Sundarlal Report*, later commissioned by the government of India, the worst sufferers were the districts of Osmanabad, Gulburga, Bidar and Nanded, in which the number of people killed was probably more than 18,000, whilst at least 5,000 lost their lives in the four districts of Aurangabad, Bir, Nalgunda and Medak. However, neither the *nizam* nor the British could suppress the uprising. It was not until the Communist Party was declared illegal and the army of independent India marched into Hyderabad in 1951 that the movement was eventually crushed.

In the state of Hyderabad as a whole, at least 27,000 to 40,000 people lost their lives during the Telengana uprising, but, with a few exceptions (Moore 1966; Dhanagare 1987; Thirumalai 2003), most of the available narratives of these events mainly derive from those directly involved in the insurrection (Reddy 1984; Sundarayya 1972; Lalita *et al.* 1989). This is due to the government of India refusing permission to any subsequent professional archival research due to its communal aspects. It represents nonetheless the largest Communist-led peasant insurrection in Asia outside China and Vietnam. No doubt, the British, the Congress and the Muslim League were brought by this uprising to the realisation that unless they reached some kind of agreement about the division of spoils there would be no power left to transfer.

Another movement, which began as a sharecroppers' (*bargadars*) dispute in northern Bengal and took on the character of an uprising, was the Tebhaga (two-thirds) agitation. This was a movement to claim back the crops landlords had expropriated by taking half of the produce or even more in lieu of rent (a practice condemned by the Floud Commission report on the land revenue system in Bengal, published in 1940). Spearheaded by the Bengal Kisan Sabha, it was a campaign to lower rural land rents that involved poor peasants, tribals and Muslims (Custers 1987; Cooper 1988). It too involved the Communists and became increasingly radical. In many other princely states, such as Travancore in south-west India (see Map 8), uprisings occurred as peasants sought to contest the aspirations of local princes to independent status once the British had left (Jeffrey 1977–8; Ouwerkerk 1994; Vaikuntham 2004). In the Punnaprea–Vayalar districts of Travancore, unarmed demonstrations by the Communists and trade unions were fuelled by food scarcities and met with brutal suppression by the state police, some 800 deaths resulting. These radical movements, together with growing communal violence in the provinces destined to be partitioned, presented the interim government with a situation it was helpless to control.

In desperation, to try and restore order, members of the Muslim League were drafted into the interim government, where they merely served to be a disruptive influence. Liaquat Ali Khan was put in charge of finance and refused to release funds required by Congress ministers, whilst Abdur Rab Nishtar as the minister for Posts and Air proceeded to bug the phones of every Congress minister – even that of the viceroy himself. The Muslim League refused to take part in any

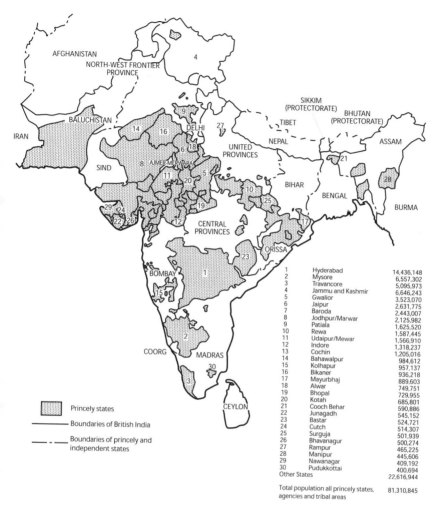

1	Hyderabad	14,436,148
2	Mysore	6,557,302
3	Travancore	5,095,973
4	Jammu and Kashmir	6,646,243
5	Gwalior	3,523,070
6	Jaipur	2,631,775
7	Baroda	2,443,007
8	Jodhpur/Marwar	2,125,982
9	Patiala	1,625,520
10	Rewa	1,587,445
11	Udaipur/Mewar	1,566,910
12	Indore	1,318,237
13	Cochin	1,205,016
14	Bahawalpur	984,612
15	Kolhapur	957,137
16	Bikaner	936,218
17	Mayurbhaj	889,603
18	Alwar	749,751
19	Bhopal	729,955
20	Kotah	685,801
21	Cooch Behar	590,886
22	Junagadh	545,152
23	Bastar	524,721
24	Cutch	514,307
25	Surguja	501,939
26	Bhavanagur	500,274
27	Rampur	465,225
28	Manipur	445,606
29	Nawanagar	409,192
30	Pudukkottai	400,694
	Other States	22,616,944

Total population all princely states, agencies and tribal areas	81,310,845

Legend:
- ▨ Princely states
- —— Boundaries of British India
- —·—· Boundaries of princely and independent states

Map 8 British India and princely states, 1947.

constituent assembly meetings, and the interim government, far from controlling the chaos, was itself fast becoming a causal factor. By February 1947 the Congress was demanding that the Muslim League ministers should resign. This crisis led the British prime minister, Clement Attlee, to declare to the House of Commons on 20 February 1947 that a deadline of June 1948 was to be set for the transfer of power. In order to effect this he recommended that Lord Mountbatten be appointed as viceroy to oversee the transfer.

Mountbatten was probably the most vain and publicity-seeking member of the Royal Family to have occupied government office in the twentieth century. Many Indian commentators believe that his appointment was dominated above all by the desire of the British government to save face, and it was for this reason that he pushed Indian politicians so precipitously towards the partition of India (Roy 1990). It was not without some hesitation however. Abandoning the cabinet mission proposals, Mountbatten's initial 'Balkan' plan envisaged the transfer of power to separate provinces and princely states, the various units thus formed then being given the choice of joining India or Pakistan, or remaining separate. The result would have been the complete fragmentation of the Indian subcontinent, and the proposal was rejected out of hand by Nehru when Mountbatten suggested it. The idea of partition as the only possible solution was already circulating by this time. The novel idea was then proposed by V.P. Menon of an immediate grant of dominion status, thereby obviating the need for any constituent assembly, with the provinces of Bengal and Punjab being divided and power being transferred immediately to two sovereign governments. Nehru immediately agreed to this in January 1947, with Jinnah reluctantly following.

All the while, it is arguable, the subaltern factor was the main issue forcing the hand of the British. They were desperate to get out and to hand over power to a respectable successor before events overtook them. The moral and physical incapacity of the British *raj* by the end of 1946, and the failure of Nehru and Jinnah to agree on any alternative, led to the solution of partition. Whether this intransigence may be laid at Nehru's or Jinnah's door, or whether indeed all players were relatively powerless in the face of the state's collapse, will remain a subject of continuing debate.

Once the decision was made to divide up India, the Pakistan that was offered to the League was not so different from the 'moth-eaten and truncated Pakistan' Jinnah had rejected more than two and a half years earlier. He only got a part of what he had demanded: a chunk of the Punjab, North-West Frontier Province, Sindh and Baluchistan and eastern Bengal. He did not get a corridor connecting the two areas and after partition there were still more Muslims living in the north of India, some 90 million, than were living in Pakistan. Thus Jinnah obtained much less than his demand for a separate state for all Indian Muslims. It was an unsatisfactory compromise that nonetheless allowed the Congress Party to establish a government over a united territory in which there was no League representation, over which Jawaharlal Nehru and the other Congress leaders were to assume sole authority. During the last two months of British rule, Sir Cyril Radcliffe, a British lawyer who knew next to nothing about Indian geography, was drafted in to draw the boundary line between India and Pakistan, at times dividing villages and lands or canals from their human settlements: a farcical yet cruel affair, later parodied in the poem 'Partition' by W.H. Auden:

> Unbiased at least he was when he arrived on his mission,
> Having never set eyes on the land he was called to partition . . .
> The maps at his disposal were out of date
> And the Census Returns almost certainly incorrect . . .
> But in seven weeks it was done, the frontiers decided,
> A continent for better or worse divided.

As soon as the new frontiers were published, communal violence on an unprecedented scale was unleashed as people scrambled to get from one side of the border to the other. In the Punjab, Sikhs – many of them recently returned from war or decommissioned from military service – organised themselves into armed bands, known as *jathas*, and took the law into their own hands, clearing out the Muslims in order to make way for their western cousins (Aiyar 1995). Those Muslims who did not wish to move were slaughtered. The Sikhs migrating from the west were then set upon by Muslims before they could make their way across the border. Looting and murder was inspired not by religious emotion or aggressive chauvinism but pure greed for *zar* (wealth) and *zamin* (land). Gender 'eroded the barriers that religion had been forced to create',[13] with some of the most nightmarish violence being perpetuated by men of all three communities as they delighted in their momentary sense of power over vulnerable women (Major 1998). Although central in so many individual and community experiences of partition, the suffering of women was silenced in the subsequent nationalist narratives of these events, and even further perpetuated in the forced 'repatriations' of kidnappees (without reference to their wishes) in later peace negotiations between the two states (Menon and Bhasin 1998). Only many years later are their experiences assuming a central place in historiography and beginning to be told (Pandey 1994, 2001; Menon and Bhasin 1997; Butalia 1998). Around a million people were killed in fighting in the border areas in Punjab and to a lesser extent in Bengal. In total some 6 million Muslims left India and around 4.5 million Sikhs fled the areas designated for the new state of Pakistan. Refugee camps overflowed (Figure 16). A large population of Sikhs fled to Delhi after the partition, where they have remained ever since, and in west Bengal (where there was not so much exchange of population) some 800,000 people were still living in camps in 1958 that had initially only been set up as a temporary measure (Chatterji 2001).

A lonely figure in the midst of all the violence of partition was Mahatma Gandhi. In the final years of the British *raj* Gandhi had disassociated himself almost completely from the political negotiations, one of his last desperate proposals being a united India with Jinnah as prime minister rather than accept the tragedy of partition. Thereafter, he devoted himself to footslogging from village to village, preaching peace as violence raged all around him. In both Delhi and Calcutta he was able to bring violence temporarily to a halt by embarking on a fast until death, and he continued to oppose partition until the very end, talking of his determination to visit Pakistan and accepting an invitation to speak at a Muslim shrine in Delhi only a few days before his assassination on 13 January 1948 at the hands of a Hindu fanatic, a member of the Hindu Mahasabha and RSS and the editor of two Hindu nationalist newspapers (*Agrani* and *Hindu Rashtra*) published in Poona. Some would argue that Gandhi himself had furthered the Hinduisation of the Congress, which in turn gave the Muslim League a weapon with which to divide the Indian nation. Gandhi, in this view, was thus a symbol of the zealotry that he had helped to arouse and which he was on his own helpless to combat. This is uncharitable, since during the last ten years of

Figure 16 Refugees camping near the India–Pakistan border. © Sunil Janah 1947.

his life he took no part in negotiations and resolutely opposed them. Nonetheless, in his tragic death Gandhi can be said to have played a part in the final shaping of democratic, secular India. Since it was a Hindu, not a Muslim, who ended his life, in the horrified hush that followed the fans of communalism were suddenly stilled.

11 Pakistan and Bangladesh, post-1947

Cheeji mangde bal ayane	Little kids ask for sweets
Munh wich panday dekh siyanay	Grown ups see them put (sweets) in their mouths
Radio uttun suno qawwali	Hear *qawwali* on radio [say]
Allah rakha panjtan wali	God save all and bless the five [Muhammad, Fatimah, Ali, Hussain and Hasan]
Jidhar dekho cigaret paan	Wherever you look are cigarette and *paan*
Zinda bad o'Pakistan	Long live o'Pakistan
Charas afeem thay thekay khullay	Licensed shops of opium are open
Piyo khao lutto bullay	Eat, drink and make merry
Paani paa diyo apne chulhay	Pour water upon your stoves
Saun jao le ke utte jullay	Pull the sheet over you and sleep
Jaga jaga te chhole naan	Everywhere are *chhole naan*
Zinda bad o'Pakistan	Zinda bad o'Pakistan
[. . .]	[. . .]
Saday mulak de naujawan	The youth of our country
Bhangi charsi te bhalwan	Are drug addicts and stupid
Fashion hay inhan de jaan	Fashion is their life
Geet hijar de ganday jan	They sing songs of missing love
Mitte role de apne shaan	Grind their grace to dust
Zinda bad o'Pakistan	Long live o'Pakistan

(Ustad Daman)[1]

Ethnic and political dilemmas of independent Pakistan

The political history of Pakistan post-1947 is complex and confusing. A major characteristic is instability, with a succession of political leaders taking power, often lasting no more than a few months in office. This marks a contrast with India, which in terms of its political leadership was blessed with considerable continuity throughout the 1940s, 1950s and 1960s. The distinction may be related to a number of factors. First, Pakistan was divided into two parts: east and west.

Clearly, with these areas separated by hundreds of miles it was always likely to be a difficult nation to manage. Second, apart from having a shared religious tradition in Islam, the two halves were culturally very dissimilar. In the east, Bengal was the mother tongue, and Muslims there had arguably many more cultural affinities with their Bengali Hindu neighbours than with other Pakistanis. In west Pakistan, the numerous ethnic communities of Sindhis, Baluchis, Punjabis, Pathans and Mohajirs (the refugees from the east) did not have a shared culture, nor even a common language in Urdu, there being marked variations in dialect with many speaking local languages such as Pukhtun instead. Third, whilst in India politicians had for the most part simply moved into the vacuum of governance created by the British departure, in Pakistan there was no fully fledged centralised administrative structure in place. Individual regions of Pakistan such as Punjab and Sindh had local state governments, but this was an inadequate basis for the running of an entirely new nation. Quite apart from the lack of a bureaucratic structure, even the most basic equipment and accommodation in which to house the newly created central government was absent. At one point it was said that the entire Ministry of the Interior had amongst all its officials the use of only a single typewriter.

In Pakistan the entire apparatus of civilian government had to be created from scratch, and in this enterprise the new state inherited some serious disadvantages. Although it was bequeathed 30 per cent of the defence forces of undivided India this was barely sufficient since Pakistan inherited India's longest and strategically most problematic borders. At the same time 90 per cent of the subcontinent's industry and taxable income base remained in India, including the largest cities of Delhi, Bombay and Calcutta. The economy of Pakistan, both east and west, with the sole exception of the then small port city of Karachi, was entirely agricultural and that agriculture was largely controlled by powerful feudal elites who paid little by way of income or land tax. Furthermore, at the division of India, Pakistan did not get its due share of the central government's financial reserves. At the moment of their withdrawal, the British government struck a deal whereby the vast amount of debt – some £1,000 million – owed to the Indian government for their contributions to the war effort between 1939 and 1945 was written off (Kamtekar 2002). Control of the colonial government of India's financial reserves was then passed to the newly independent governments in proportion to their populations, without regard to their obligations or geographical area. Thus Pakistan, with 23 per cent of the undivided land mass, inherited only 17.5 per cent of the former government's financial assets. With an opening cash balance of only Rs 200 million, this left Pakistan with severe difficulties in meeting its military expenditure, which alone totalled Rs 35–50 million per month, quite apart from finding sufficient funds for the construction of central government buildings in the capital, initially established at Karachi. Neither were there any funds left over to carry on development work at a provincial level. In consequence, the provincial governments in India enjoyed revenues per capita nearly half as much again as their Pakistan counterparts in the early 1950s (Jalal 1995: 22–23).

A fourth major difference between the two nations lay in the fact that India had struggled to gain independence over a period of 40 years, allowing large numbers of people the time not only to accept the leadership of the Congress Party but to forge a common national identity. The process was by no means complete, but in Pakistan it had less than a decade in which to get underway. The Muslim League began to enjoy the support of a majority of the subcontinent's Muslim population only relatively late on in the independence struggle. Many Muslims had supported the Congress, such as those in the North-West Frontier Province, or had voted for other Muslim parties such as the Punjabi Unionists, right up until the 1940s. Indeed in Punjab, the League was a latecomer on the political scene (Talbot 1988). The Muslim League's strongest support from the beginning of the century had always been amongst the landowning elite of northern India, an area that was never included within the boundaries of the 'moth-eaten' state of Pakistan finally accepted by Jinnah. By contrast, the majority gained by the Muslim League in Bengal in 1946 was a slim one, and the League was soon to be challenged for representation of Bengali Muslims. Thus, support for the Muslim League within Pakistan was fractured, and in Punjab, Bengal and Sindh was an innovation following on from a relatively short period of participation in government (i.e. during the Second World War) or otherwise generated out of the fear of communal conflict in the months leading up to partition. The League's *raison d'être* had been to represent Muslim interests in the subcontinent, but it had been an advocate of a separate state of Pakistan for fewer than eight years prior to independence. At partition, furthermore, a large number of its grass-roots supporters had been left behind in India (Map 9).

There was no doubting the popularity of the Muslim League, nor the jubilation amongst Pakistanis at the achievement of independence. But after partition had been effected, the League often found itself with difficulties in maintaining the momentum of popular support, especially in areas where it lacked an efficient local party organisation. The Congress Party in India, by contrast, was able to rebuild much of its local party organisation, shattered during the war years when the party had been banned, and by 1948–9 was assuming once again a thoroughgoing control of the Indian political scene.

The Muslim League was held together in the months leading up to partition largely by the formidable talent, personality and efforts of Muhammad Ali Jinnah. The great misfortune of the League was that within a year of partition, Jinnah, already a sick man in 1946, was to die from tuberculosis, leaving no obvious successor. Thus, after 1948, Pakistan not only lacked an efficient democratic structure but found itself politically adrift. Major disagreements soon emerged over the direction the country's future should take. On the one hand, the 'Mohajirs' – post-1947 migrants to Pakistan – were typical products of the late nineteenth-century Aligarh movement in north India. Highly educated, they envisaged a future for Pakistan as a modern, secular society. Jinnah himself may be included in their number despite studying at the Sindh *madrasa*, and later in London. Ranged against them were the feudal elites of western Pakistan and the theocracy, both suspicious of change, with the latter harbouring an ambition to establish a strictly Islamic state. It was not surprising that there should be

Map 9 Pakistan: principal cities and provinces, 2006.

sharp disagreements as to the constitutional form that the new state should adopt. And this was without the politicians even beginning to accommodate the demands of east Pakistan, which quickly came to resent the concentration of political power in the west. Arguably it was this factor above all else that inhibited political developments. The Muslim League did not fear elections *per se*, so much as the radical shift in power from the western to the more populous eastern half of the country that would inevitably result from the establishment of fully fledged, self-regulating, participatory political institutions. It was the reluctance of the Mohajir–Punjabi bureaucratic elite to give up their control until a solution to this problem could be found that fatally stymied Pakistan's political development.

A committee was set up to frame a secular body of laws and to deliberate proposals for the establishment of a constitution, but its first report – a highly commendable secularist, liberal-democratic set of proposals, presented to the Pakistan Constituent Assembly in March 1949 – had to be withdrawn after little more than a year owing to fierce opposition. Soon after, in October 1951, Jinnah's successor, Liaquat Ali Khan, was assassinated. Political life in Pakistan thereafter began to degenerate into factionalism as rival elites vied for political influence in the absence of an elected assembly. The political struggles of these and later years are satirised in Salman Rushdie's novel *Shame*:

> The newness of those days felt pretty unstable; it was a rootless sort of thing. All over the city (which was the capital then) builders were cheating on the cement in the foundations of new houses, people – and not only Prime Ministers – got shot from time to time, throats got themselves slit in gullies, bandits became billionaires, but all this was expected. History was old and rusted, it was a machine nobody had plugged in for thousands of years, and now all of a sudden it was being asked for maximum output. Nobody was surprised that there were accidents.[2]

Nonetheless, it is important to avoid the impression that political instability in Pakistan was a consequence of the personal failings of the individuals involved. As Jalal (1995) points out, the problems of Pakistan were above all structural, and it is doubtful that even Nehru, with all his political skills, might have fared any better in overcoming the burdens and resolving the conflicting expectations of the Pakistani state.

The responsibility for Liaquat Ali Khan's assassination remains a mystery. M.J. Akbar (1996) quotes a rumour to the effect that he was killed, like Mahatma Gandhi, by a religious zealot of his own faith. Others have pointed to the fact that Khan was killed in Rawalpindi, the headquarters of the army, which even at this early stage, it is suggested, was plotting to take over the government. Whoever was responsible, Liaquat Ali Khan's successor was chosen not by election but by the governor-general, Khwaja Nazimuddin, who appointed *himself* as prime minister. Gulam Mohammad, a Punjabi bureaucrat, was then appointed by Nazimuddin as governor-general. Writing about these developments, M.J. Akbar, a-not-unbiased source, has commented:

> It is important to understand that the only time power has changed hands in Pakistan on the strength of the popular will has been when the humiliated army handed over the government to Zulfikar Ali Bhutto in 1971 ... Otherwise every shift of authority has been a drawing room decision made by whichever was the most powerful section of the ruling elite ... There was no system or political ideology governing the acquisition, and therefore the exercise, of power. It was open house for schemers.[3]

However, scheming was arguably a rational response to the manifold difficulties faced by the emergent state, as Pakistan was beset not only with factionalism, but with ethnic and religious conflict.

Religious discord in post-independence Pakistan was apparent in a campaign organised by Maulana Maudoodi, leader of Jamaat-e-Islami (an Islamic political organisation), and joined by disgruntled right-wing elements in the League, which railed against the proposals for a secular constitution and called for the expulsion from the country of the Ahmadiyya sect of Muslims. The sect included several prominent members of the government itself, such as the foreign minister Zafrullah Khan. The campaign, which continued until the 1980s, flourishing in particular under the rule of General Zia, led to violent demonstrations in the streets of Lahore, and the first involvement of the military, in March 1953.

Ethnic conflict became conspicuous soon after the migration of Muslims at the time of Partition. It required little mobilisation. Those fleeing India settled largely in the city of Karachi and the surrounding province of Sindh, and were given the name 'Mohajirs'. This was a loaded term in Islamic history, which evoked the escape or exile of the Prophet Muhammad from Mecca to Medina. Unlike the Indian term for the Sikhs and Hindus who fled from Pakistan, *sharanarthi* (refugees), which was not a privileging title and was quickly disclaimed, the term 'Mohajir' had a tinge of virtue about it that ensured its perpetuation. As the so-called Mohajirs increased their control over urban trade and employment, owing in part to the capital they brought with them and their greater privileges in education, conflict soon developed between them and the resident, largely rural, Sindhi population, fuelled by economic competition, as well as cultural and linguistic differences.

Another major conflict arose from the fact that western Pakistan was dominated by Punjabis, who controlled the military, and who tended increasingly to share economic and political power with the Mohajirs. In the absence of democratic institutions this Mohajir–Punjabi dominance of the bureaucracy became institutionalised, and aroused deep resentment amongst the Sindhis to the south and the Baluchis and Pathans resident in the north-eastern and western parts of Pakistan, who had been denied the same opportunities for advancement. Many communities in the north-west in particular had a long history of fighting for their independence from British control, an independence they were not willing to give up to anyone else (Ahmed 1986; Barthorp 2002). In the eastern half of the country, ethnic Bengalis were even less willing to accept domination by the Punjabi–Mohajir west Pakistani elite. The Awami Muslim League was formed in Dhaka soon after partition to represent Bengali Pakistani interests, and it soon found itself contesting the domination of the west Pakistani elite. The first major conflict was over language, after Urdu was proposed as the national language by the Basic Principles Committee of the constituent assembly. This created a furore, and several lives were lost as Bengalis took to the streets in language riots in 1952. Eventually, in 1956, the Bengali language was accorded equal status in the constitution, but by then the seeds of mistrust had been sown, and the Bengalis, along with other regional ethnic groups, began to mobilise to demand far greater provincial autonomy (Rahman 2003).

Pakistan experienced its first coup soon after the language and religious riots of 1953. It was a coup from above, led by the governor-general, Gulam Muhammad (with the full knowledge and backing of US diplomats it is alleged), who in April 1953 declared martial law in Lahore and replaced the ex-governor-general and then prime minister, Khwaja Nazimuddin, with a more pliant politician of his choice. This was the first step in the rapid disintegration of political life in west

Pakistan. In the east, the Awami League, after dropping the word 'Muslim' from its name, pursued a successful campaign to win power in provincial elections held in March 1954, forming an alliance with the Krishak Sramik (peasants and workers) Party led by Fazlul Haq. Together, they swept the board, the Muslim League winning just ten seats. Soon, however, disputes arose between the partners after the governor-general, Gulam Muhammad, used the vaguest of pretexts to sack the Haq government. Notoriously, fighting broke out and furniture was thrown in the provincial assembly, killing the deputy speaker. Soon after, the governor-general arbitrarily dismissed the entire Constituent Assembly in October 1954.

In 1956, Gulam Muhammad retired due to ill health, and his successor, President Iskander Mirza, an ex-army major-general, appointed a Bengali, Chaudhury Mohammad Ali, who managed to put into law Pakistan's first constitution. However, the political in-fighting continued unabated, the civil service in particular being reluctant to see power transferred to an eastern-dominated legislature if the scheduled elections were to take place. Ali was soon replaced by three other PMs in rapid succession, until finally in 1958 Mirza abrogated the short-lived constitution and asked General Ayub Khan (commander of Pakistan's armed forces since 1951) to take charge, inaugurating Pakistan's first military government. Thereafter Ayub Khan deposed the president himself – who was exiled to London – and became the sole dictator of Pakistan.

The Ayub Khan era

One reason for the military take-over in 1958 was that the army had remained, after independence, one of the few functioning centres of power within Pakistani society. Pakistan was lacking in many of the essential elements of civil society – a constitution, political system, free press and the necessary checks and balances on the abuse of power. In the absence of any agreement on these elements, the military stood out as the only disciplined and organised institution within society. This theory has been developed by Hamza Alavi (1973), who argues that the phenomenon of weak civilian government giving way to military dictatorship is a common feature in post-colonial societies, which can readily be explained by the difficulties encountered in incorporating the disproportionately large armies often left behind by the former colonial powers. Newly independent societies commonly found themselves burdened with strategic problems not of their making, and equipped with an oversized military machine, intended partly for internal control. Such armies were disproportionate to the economic resources of the country, whilst simultaneously lacking any developed system of democratic control. Pakistan is a good example of such a 'top-heavy state', and as the financial pressures began to pinch, intervention in politics became a means of self-preservation for those in charge of the ex-colonial military machine. To this we should add the baleful influence of the two superpowers, the USA and Russia during the cold war era, one party or the other often being involved in regime change in developing countries (the USA in the case of Pakistan) as it suited their strategic interests (Aijazuddin 2003; Kux 2001).

By 1959 Pakistan had gone through six different presidents and eight or more prime ministers. Ayub Khan's rule was more long-lived: he was to remain sole dictator for the next ten years. Justifying his take-over, he later wrote in his auto-biography, *Friends, Not Masters*: 'Whatever institutions we had inherited at the time of independence, or had set up since then, were crumbling one by one . . . Everyone had joined the political vaudeville. There was no organ of administration which was not pressed into service to promote individual political interests.'⁴ Ayub was perhaps one of the sincerest of Pakistan's military dictators, making determined if heavy-handed attempts to solve some of Pakistan's fundamental economic and political problems. One of his first steps was to shift the capital from Karachi to Rawalpindi, pending the construction of a new purpose-built capital at Islamabad, inaugurated in 1966 as part of an attempt to modernise the country. There followed efforts to liberalise the economy and to institute land reforms, although most of these progressed no further than the planning stage and achieved little measurable benefit (La Porte 1976). Ayub also further progressed Pakistan's policy of alignment with the West, begun initially with a series of military alliances in the late 1950s when Pakistan joined SEATO (the Southeast Asia Treaty Organisation) and CENTO (Central Treaty Organisation: an alliance of Britain, Turkey and Iraq). In the 1960s, under Ayub, Pakistan drew ever closer to the United States, from which it gained both economic and military aid, and an ally capable of countering India's links with the Soviet Union and its influence within the Non-Aligned Movement. This was nevertheless achieved at some cost, since links with the US alienated potential friends within the Islamic world, particularly Egypt, which under Nasser's influence had adopted an anti-Western, or at least a non-aligned, stance in common with many other newly independent nations.

Ayub Khan imposed strict censorship of the press and organised a token system of representation called 'basic democracy', in which vetted candidates, elected per 1,000 of the population, were asked to confirm Ayub in power. This they duly did by an overwhelming majority in 1960. A fresh constitution was then introduced in 1962, giving the 'elected' president a viceregal-style authority over the affairs of government at both a national and provincial level. Ayub subsequently rewarded himself with the title of field-marshal for his efforts – an example later followed by General Zia, who reportedly acquired every military medal of honour, including those normally given posthumously. However, Ayub's authoritarian rule could do little more than disguise the growing discontent at the burgeoning inequalities both between regions and within society as a whole in the 1960s. This was particularly noticeable in the disparities between income and government expenditure in the eastern and western halves of the country. Thus it was revealed that 66 per cent of industry, 97 per cent of insurance and 80 per cent of banking was controlled by just 22 families, all of them based in west Pakistan, whilst the disparity in per capita income between east and west, which was 30 per cent at the inauguration of Ayub's reign, had risen to 45 per cent by the end of it (Noman 1988: 35–42). There was a minor boom in wheat production experienced by a handful of landlords and rich peasants in the Punjab, following the introduction of new, high-yielding varieties of wheat grain, but expenditure on education in Pakistan remained the lowest in Asia, and despite growth in the sector the wages of industrial workers in the west of the country fell by 12 per cent between 1954 and 1967. The fourth five-year plan tacitly recognised that although an elite had benefited, real wages had fallen overall by a third in the 1960s. These problems created a general climate of discontent. In east Pakistan this discontent was mobilised behind the Awami League, led by Sheikh Mujibur Rahman.

The secession of Bangladesh

Under the rule of General Ayub Khan, east Pakistan had become by 1967 virtually a colony of the western half of the country, administered largely by Urdu-speaking bureaucrats from Punjab, and kept under martial control by Sandhurst and Pentagon-trained Muhajir, Pathan, Baluchi, and Punjabi colonels. Despite having the largest population and the greatest poverty, and earning the majority of Pakistan's foreign exchange through the export of jute, east Pakistanis (or 'Bingos' as they were contemptuously referred to in the military) nonetheless received less development funding from the government than the west. Unemployment was rampant in east Pakistan, leading to unrest amongst both workers and students (Umar 2004). The solution to these manifold problems, argued Mujibur Rahman, was a far greater degree of autonomy for the eastern half of the country, with a separate parliament, separate currency, separate fiscal policy, and its own militia, with the appointment of Bengali-speaking officials to run it – the government in Islamabad being allowed authority in little more than foreign policy and defence. This six-point plan, agreed by the Awami League in 1966 against a background of demonstrations and riots, was unacceptable to Ayub Khan's military regime, but repressive measures, including the arrest of Mujibur Rahman and other leaders for secessionism (the Agartala Conspiracy Case), merely incited further unrest. Sheikh Mujib thereafter spent almost three years in jail, from May 1966 to January 1969, until a wave of popular demonstrations spearheaded by the Sarbadaliya Chhatra Sangram Parishad (All Parties Student Resistance Council, or SCSP) forced Ayub Khan to suspend the conspiracy case against him and 34 others. Soon after, the SCSP held a huge rally to honour Sheikh Mujib, at Ramna racecourse in Dhaka, with Tofael Ahmed, an SCSP leader, presiding. Tofael Ahmed proposed that Sheikh Mujib should be adorned with the nationalist title, Bangabandhu – a proposal that met with a rousing endorsement from the crowd and cries of 'Joy Bangla', which became a rallying cry for the movement.

In west Pakistan it was Zulfikar Ali Bhutto's Pakistani People's Party that benefited most from unrest, culminating in demonstrations and a general strike, organised by students and labour unions, which brought Karachi, the main industrial city, grinding to a halt in March 1969. Ayub might have survived this, were it not for the perception amongst the military, reinforced with accusations from Bhutto, that he had given away too much during peace negotiations with India at Tashkent in Russia in 1965. These talks had followed a pre-emptive strike by the Pakistani army into Indian territory in the Rann of Kutch that year, which had led to an all-out war and an attempt to capture parts of Kashmir. The army had gained nothing from it, but the popular perception was that it was the political leadership of the country that was at fault. Opposition to the military regime obliged Ayub to announce the holding of parliamentary elections in February 1969, and continuing protests in March eventually forced him to move aside in favour of General Yahya Khan (Gauhar 1993).

The Yahya Khan interregnum was brief. In accordance with his predecessor's promise, elections – postponed for two months owing to major floods – were eventually held in December 1970:

> The elections . . . were not . . . straightforward. As how could they be, in that country divided into two Wings a thousand miles apart, that fantastic bird of a place, two Wings without a body, sundered by the land mass of its greatest foe, joined by nothing but God . . . O confusion of people who have lived too long under military rule, who have forgotten the simplest things about democracy! Large numbers of men and women were swept away by the oceans of bewilderment, unable to locate ballot-boxes or even ballots . . . Others, stronger swimmers in those seas succeeded in expressing their preferences twelve or thirteen times. Popular front workers, distressed by the general lack of electoral decorum, made heroic efforts to save the day. Those few urban constituencies making returns incompatible with the West-Wing wide polling pattern were visited at night by groups of enthusiastic party members, who helped the returning officers to make a recount . . . Outside the errant polling stations large numbers of democrats assembled, many holding burning brands above their heads in the hope of shedding new light on the count. Dawn light flamed in the streets, while the crowds chanted loudly, rhythmically, spurring on the returning officers in their labours.[5]

Rushdie is doubtless exaggerating, but nonetheless – despite the best efforts of their rivals – the elections resulted in an overwhelming victory in the east for Sheikh Mujibur Rahman's Awami League, which won all but two of the National Assembly seats for east Pakistan. Meanwhile, in the west the Pakistan People's Party won a majority of 81 seats out of 148. No major party won seats in both halves of the country. The first task of the new National Assembly was to agree on a constitution with which to run the country, which presented a dilemma. Having the largest number of seats, the Awami League was in a position to impose its demands for greater autonomy for the eastern half of the country, which would have amounted to the transformation of Pakistan into a confederation. Yahya Khan thought he had an agreement with Mujibur to tone down these demands, but Bhutto, perhaps fearful of an erosion of his powerbase in the west (where Baluchistan also threatened secession), allied himself with hawkish elements in the army, who were convinced that a compromise was impossible. In the absence of an agreement between Bhutto and Mujibur on the shape of the constitution, Bhutto called for a postponement of the Assembly just two days before the scheduled date for its inaugural session. Reluctantly Yahya Khan agreed, and preparations were made for a military clamp-down instead. As might easily have been anticipated, a popular uprising in the eastern half of the country then ensued. News of cancellation of the National Assembly inaugural session sparked popular uprisings in Dhaka and in Chittagong, and thousands assembled outside the Purbani Hotel, in Dhaka, where the Awami League Council was meeting, to demand that Sheikh Mujib immediately declare independent national sovereignty. Student leaders formed an apex action committee, the Shawadhin Bangla Kendriya Chhatra Sangram Parishad (SBKCSP), on 2 March and 4 March national *hartals* (strikes) erupted, and SBKCSP leaders organised massive public meetings at which independence was solemnly declared in an *ishtehar* (declaration), which began: 'Joy Bangla: Proclamation of independence. Independence for Bangladesh is hereby declared. It is now an independent and sovereign country . . . The name of this territory of 54,506 (obsquare) miles is Bangla Desh.' Simultaneously, the population was enjoined to form resistance cells in every village, town and city, and activists sang the song 'Amar Sonar Bangla' as their new national anthem.

Sheikh Mujibur Rahman, the prime-minister-in-waiting of Pakistan and the leader of a popular insurrection, struggled valiantly to press his preferred federal solution, but to no avail as he and other elected politicians were overwhelmed by the popular demand for independence and, above all, the initiative of student organisations (Samaddara 2002; Ludden 2003). The Pakistani army perhaps hoped for direct backing from China or the United States to restore control, but this did not transpire. On 25 March 1971 the Pakistani army expelled all foreign journalists and launched a terror campaign calculated to intimidate the east Pakistanis into submission. On 26 March (the day later officially chosen as independence day) Sheikh Mujibur, anticipating arrest, allegedly sent a message to East Pakistan Radio, declaring independence and urging citizens to take up arms for their freedom. The day after, Major Ziaur Rahman of the East Bengal Regiment broadcast a message on Sheikh Mujibur's behalf, appealing for international recognition and support. There followed nine months of bloody repression and civil war, until the intervention of a liberation army of east Pakistani rebels, known as the *mukti bahini*, equipped and aided by the Indian military. After a brief but violent 12-day war, Dhaka fell on 16 December 1971, the Pakistani army surrendered, and east Pakistan was reborn as the independent state of 'Bangladesh' (meaning 'Bengal nation'), with Sheikh Mujibur Rahman as its first president (Sisson and Rose 1990; Khan 1999).

Zulfikar Ali Bhutto

The secession of the eastern half of the country was perceived as the third major failure of the Pakistani military after its brief and quixotic war with India in 1965 and its inability to take Kashmir in 1949. Discredited by these failures, there was no question of the resumption of military rule in the western half of the country. Instead, Yahya Khan resigned, and the army reluctantly handed over power to a civilian government led by Zulfikar Ali Bhutto (Figure 17) in December 1971 (Choudhury 1974). Four months of civilian martial law followed, with Bhutto as

Figure 17 President Zulfikar Ali Bhutto of Pakistan speaking during a 1973 visit to Britain.
© Hulton-Deutsch Collection/CORBIS.

chief martial law administrator, whilst a national assembly was formed on the basis of the 1970 election results in west Pakistan. The Assembly then ratified a new interim constitution, introduced in April 1972, under which Bhutto became prime minister of a civilian government. The regime that followed has been characterised as one of authoritarian populism. Zulfikar Ali Bhutto was not a democrat by instinct, coming from a feudal family background in Sindh and having indeed served as foreign minister under Ayub Khan. Furthermore, the Pakistan People's Party was ethnically relatively exclusive, being predominantly Sindhi and Punjabi, which helped to explain the insecurities of Bhutto's government. Despite the separation of the eastern half of the country, problems of ethnic conflict continued – in particular a separatist movement in the impoverished though oil-rich province of Baluchistan, which was ruthlessly suppressed after the dismissal of the provincial government in 1973 (Harrison 1981). Bhutto consolidated his power by reducing the size of the bureaucracy, and to keep the military out of politics he established a separate paramilitary unit, the Federal Security Force, which was used to quell public disturbances and to intimidate opposition politicians (Burki 1980). At the same time, he endeavoured to appease the armed forces by maintaining military spending at a high level, and to control it by appointing as his chief of staff a relatively junior officer, Zia-ul-Haq, whom he regarded as personally loyal.

In terms of foreign policy Bhutto achieved a major success by signing a deal with India, following negotiations with Indira Gandhi at Simla in August 1973, under which Pakistan was given back its prisoners of war and some territory captured by India in 1971, without having to sign a no-war pact (offered by Mrs

Gandhi), or even to recognise the new nation of Bangladesh (Pakistan did not in fact do so until the following year). Pakistan's independence was further asserted by leaving the Commonwealth and SEATO, forging closer strategic links with China, and by making new friends in the Middle East. In addition, Bhutto pressed ahead with a programme to develop Pakistan's nuclear capabilities by establishing a plutonium reprocessing plant and a nuclear power station with Libyan and Saudi money and French help. Pressure from President Carter's government in the US caused the help from France to be withdrawn, but not before Pakistan had significantly increased its capacity to build a uranium bomb, and had acquired most of the materials and equipment needed to do so.

On the economic front, Bhutto embarked upon a programme of nationalisation, intended to redress the inequalities that had burgeoned during the Ayub Khan era, and to curb the power of the Mohajir trading class, the large industrial families who had profited at the relative expense of the working class and peasantry, and the Sindhi landholding elite – key supporters of the Pakistan People's Party (PPP). The task of redressing inequality was greatly helped with the development of employment opportunities for migrant Pakistani workers in the Gulf, especially after 1973 when oil price rises brought an influx of capital to the region. In order to generate employment and improve the infrastructure of the economy the Bhutto government spent heavily on large-scale capital projects (accumulating foreign debt and fuelling inflation in the process), and a further programme of modest land reforms was initiated. The impact of these measures in terms of redistribution and the general standard of living was limited, but the fact that Bhutto appeared to take inequality and poverty seriously, coining the slogan of 'Islamic Socialism' to characterise the aims of his government, earned him considerable popularity. This popularity was Bhutto's greatest asset. Since it was combined, however, with a centralisation of power (Bhutto spoke of establishing a one-party state and a presidential form of government), and alliances with conservative landed elites in Punjab and Sindh, it also inhibited the development of effective democratic and consultative institutions. This proved to be the PPP's weakness, as the energy and popularity of one man could only carry the party so far.

It has been suggested that it was a desire to perpetuate his rule through constitutional reform (requiring a two-thirds majority) that caused so many irregularities to arise in the general elections held in 1977. Much has been made of the personality faults of Bhutto, or Quaid-I-Awam ('Great Leader') as he liked to be called, including his megalomania, dictatorial instincts, and unstable character (Wolpert 1993). In-fighting within the PPP between Punjabi and Sindhi elites, and the sudden and unexpected unity of the opposition in the Pakistan National Alliance (PNA), was another important factor weakening the party's position. Bhutto probably miscalculated the scale of this opposition, precisely because of his effectiveness in using censorship and intimidation to inhibit and suppress the activities of opposition groups prior to the election campaign, most notably in Baluchistan. Significant too was the loss of support from small town traders, many of them Mohajirs, hard hit by new labour regulations. The peasantry and the working class had suffered as well from the rapid rise in prices that followed the OPEC oil hike in 1973. Their enthusiasm for Bhutto was undiminished by this, but support for his party was not.

Despite the decline in its popularity, the PPP still apparently 'won' 155 out of 200 seats in the March 1977 elections, and over 58 per cent of the vote, leading the PNA, the opposition alliance, to complain of widespread poll rigging. Allegations were made that in some constituencies more votes were in fact declared for the PPP than there were registered electors, and demonstrations organised by the PNA erupted on the streets, accompanied by violence, leading to the declaration of martial law by Bhutto in the cities of Lahore and Hyderabad. As the demonstrations continued, a series of meetings between Bhutto and the opposition leaders failed to achieve any compromise. Eventually an impatient army decided to intervene on 5 July 1977.

Mohammad Waseem has argued that the ineffectiveness of the PPP as a party machine and an overdependence on landed elites for support were Bhutto's principal liabilities (Waseem 1994a: ch. 5). To this one might add an over-reliance on his personal popularity, and bullying tactics, using either party workers, the FSF or the army (to their intense dislike), in order to get his way. The absence of an organised power base meant that at a crucial moment support from the bureaucracy and the middle classes was lacking when faced with public disorder and a renewed challenge by the military for political control. At the same moment, Bhutto's government was abandoned by its former patrons in the USA (Raza 1997). The term 'Bonapartist' has been used to characterise Bhutto's regime (a phrase he himself used to describe the 'fat and flabby generals' in the military), and Bhutto's eventual demise has been more often compared to that of Juan Peron in Peru than that of the Chilean leader Salvador Allende. There are interesting parallels too with the problems and dilemmas of Indira Gandhi's government in neighbouring India in the same period (see Chapter 13).

Zia-ul-Haq and the return of military rule

The military regime that supplanted Bhutto was led by General Zia-ul-Haq, the army chief of staff. Zia assumed the office of chief martial law administrator and soon after, in September 1978, the office of president (Figure 18). Where Bhutto was glamorous and quick-witted, Zia-ul-Haq was plodding and conservative. Undoubtedly a pious man, Zia could nonetheless be both ruthless and reactionary, and, unlike his predecessor, he was to enjoy the full support of the US government, which took a renewed interest in Pakistan following the Soviet Union's invasion of neighbouring Afghanistan in 1979 (Kakar 1995; Kux 2001). Upon seizing power Zia announced that martial rule was to last for only a 90-day period, pending fresh elections, and whilst both PNA and PPP leaders were arrested, they were released again three weeks later to begin preparations. The constitution was not abrogated, as in 1958 and 1969, and a schedule for polling was announced by the chief election commissioner on 2 August. A few days later, however, the chief martial law administrator announced that he would be willing to postpone the elections if

Figure 18 Pakistani president Zia-ul-Haq arrives in Kuwait for an Islamic Summit in 1987. © Peter Turnley/CORBIS.

the political parties wished it, that presidential rule was in keeping with Islamic principles, that an Islamic ideology council would be constituted to guide decision-making, that flour-milling and husking enterprises were to be denationalised, and that military servicemen were to be immune from civilian prosecution.

From the very beginning therefore, Zia attempted to set right the perceived errors of the previous administration that had rendered it unpopular with the trading classes. At the same time he wished to legitimise his rule with reference to Islam, to maintain apparently normal constitutional and judicial process, and yet to place the military itself above the law. By his pronouncements, Zia-ul-Haq revealed his key personal dilemma. If judicial norms were to be maintained there was a risk that once civilian rule was restored Zia might himself be arrested and prosecuted. Bhutto was the man most likely to do this, since his enduring popularity meant that he was most likely to win any fresh elections, albeit by a smaller margin, an outcome that was completely unacceptable to the PNA opposition. On 3 September therefore, Bhutto was re-arrested and an inquiry launched into the assets of PPP politicians with a view to debarring them from the polls. The chief justice released Bhutto on bail, but he was then rearrested again under the martial law regulations, and the chief justice replaced. At the same time a new oath of loyalty, which avoided any mention of upholding the constitution, was introduced in the Supreme Court.

On 1 October, Zia, as chief martial law administrator, announced the postponement of elections, a decision that was upheld by the Supreme Court whilst discussing a writ of habeas corpus introduced by Begum Nusrat Bhutto demanding the release of her husband. The learned judges agreed that whilst the 1973 constitution and legal system remained in force, it was legitimate for the CMLA and president to take control and enforce whatever regulations he chose – even to amend the constitution – since he had the best interests of the country at heart. Bhutto therefore remained in prison and soon afterwards was placed on trial for conspiracy to murder.

The prosecution of Bhutto had very little to do with justice and everything to do with General Zia's instincts for self-preservation. Bhutto's case was tried by a special bench, without a jury, and his lawyers were given little opportunity to defend their client, while the government and even the chief justice himself, who sat on the bench, gave regular, prejudicial briefings to the press on the progress of the case. After six months Bhutto was found guilty and given an unusually harsh sentence for the crime of conspiracy: death. When the news broke there were demonstrations on the streets, particularly in Sindh, which were halted by the army by force. PPP supporters were arrested and punished with the lash for their participation. An appeal to the Supreme Court was lost by a narrow margin (three out of seven judges dissenting). Bhutto's wife and daughter, who were under house arrest, were allowed to visit him in jail, and the following day, 4 April 1979, Bhutto was hanged. He was buried without any of his relatives being permitted to attend.

Bhutto was no saint, but to many his treatment was a clear-cut case of judicial murder. What is peculiar is how the military regime felt the need to maintain an air of legality in its proceedings. The elections promised within 90 days were deferred, and deferred again, and not eventually fulfilled for a further 90 months. Continuing demonstrations caused the PPP to be banned, and a government of military personnel was created, accompanied by a scattering of PNA civilian politicians. Zia also created a nominated 350-member consultative assembly, the Majlis-i-Shura, which was largely ignored. In December 1984 a referendum was finally held in which people were asked to say 'yes' or 'no' to the continuation of Zia's 'Islamic' presidency. No other candidates for the post were offered. Campaigns against the poll were declared illegal, and few bothered to vote (most of those who did voted 'yes'). This gave President Zia, for the first time, a semblance of a popular mandate for the continuation of his rule. National Assembly elections were then held, on a non-party basis, in February 1985. During the elections, public meetings, processions and public address systems were banned, which rather limited opportunities to discuss the issues, the main beneficiaries being members of the feudal landholders and new industrial elite who won seats in the 217-member Assembly. Zia was sworn in as elected president at the first Assembly, appointing Mohammad Khan Junejo as his prime minister. Martial law was then lifted, but not before a variety of special powers had been passed, including the notorious eighth amendment to the constitution, which gave the president the authority to dismiss the prime minister at any time (regardless of his or her support in the Assembly), as well as the right to appoint provincial governors and the chief of the armed forces.

The suspension of martial law

With the lifting of martial law in 1985, Bhutto's Oxford and Harvard-educated daughter, Benazir, was able to return from exile and to re-enter politics, and the PPP became active once again on the streets, in alliance with other parties of the 'Movement for the Restoration of Democracy' (MRD). However, the Muslim League had already emerged, with Junejo's support, as the dominant party in Pakistani politics. Furthermore, the PPP had problems of its own, with conflicts between Benazir's younger supporters and the old guard of the party, centred around the Sindhi landlord Ghulam Mustafa Jatoi, who created his own breakaway party, a difficulty to be repeated in later years in relations between Benazir and her uncle, Mumtaz Bhutto. Doubtless more than a hint of chauvinism, and reluctance to accept the leadership of a mere woman (no matter how distinguished her father), played a part in this. However, the biggest problems faced by Pakistan and its politicians in the late 1980s arose from continuing internal territorial and ethnic conflict, and the spillover from the civil war in neighbouring Afghanistan (Kakar 1995; Rubin 2002; Ewans 2002). The ethnic problems of Pakistan assumed a more serious scale than ever before, partly because of the breakaway of the eastern half of the country in 1971. Rather than quell divisions within the west, it established a precedent for others to follow. It also led to a revised and more exclusive definition of Pakistani identity as that of the four cultures of the Indus valley (Ahsan 1997). Unfortunately this left little room for the Mohajir migrants, now under the leadership of the Mohajir Qaumi Mahaz (MQM) founded by Altaf Hussain and others in 1984, who began to develop not only political, but territorial claims of their own and had become an increasingly popular movement, especially amongst bored and disaffected youth (Verkaaik 2004). This was notable in Sindh, and in the city of Karachi, where the largest numbers of Mohajirs had settled. It posed at the very least a perceived threat to ordinary Sindhis as well as to the Sindhi elite, who felt excluded and disempowered under the Punjabi-dominated Zia regime. Through his policy of Islamicisation, Zia had hoped to maintain the legitimacy and respectability of his control over government, but although popular with a minority it proved no solution to these burgeoning ethnic divisions.

In foreign policy terms, the conflict from 1984 onwards in Afghanistan between insurgent tribal groups – the *mujahidin* – and the communist government of President Najibullah, backed by Russian troops, had the effect of bringing Pakistan into a much closer strategic alliance with the United States, thus ending its diplomatic isolation. Whilst US president Jimmy Carter's government had supplied money and covert support via the ISI (Pakistan's Inter-Service Intelligence), with Ronald Reagan's accession to the presidency the Americans completely re-equipped the Pakistani army and used the country as a staging post to equip the Afghani rebels, with the aim of providing them with sufficient firepower to win the war (Kux 2001; Coll 2004; Weaver 2003). Paradoxically, while still ostra-cised by the Commonwealth and many others, due to the undemocratic nature of its regime, Pakistan was to receive more overseas aid in this period in the form of arms and cash than at any other time in its history. To pay for supplies, some of the *mujahidin* themselves became major exporters of narcotics and captured weapons to Pakistan, and from there overseas, including to the USA, which was thereby recompensed for its efforts in an unwelcome fashion. A side effect was the creation of major social problems within Pakistan itself. By 1993 the Human Rights Commission of Pakistan estimated that one in every sixteen Pakistani males was an addict, and throughout the 1980s and 1990s the 'Kalashnikov culture' saw increasing use of weapons in the execution of crimes such as kid-napping and in conflicts between rival groups. Afghani refugees – totalling some 3 million – flooded into Pakistan. The eventual defeat of the Russians, their withdrawal from Afghanistan in 1989, followed soon after by the end of the cold war and the collapse of Russian communism, was a major achievement in US foreign policy, in which Pakistan played a part. Nonetheless, the civil war in Afghanistan carried on, as did US and Russian arms supplies, and Pakistan con-tinued to back the *mujahidin*, and later on the Taliban, in the hope of establishing a sympathetic client regime in Kabul.

In respect of internal affairs in the late 1980s, Pakistan achieved little more than notoriety, and there was increasing civil unrest, particularly in Karachi, where violence occurred between Pukhtun migrants (made wealthy by the war in Afghanistan) and the Mohajirs, and between Mohajirs and Sindhis, including supporters of the MQM and the PPP. This was eventually the pretext used for the dismissal of Junejo's government, which proved that although decision-making was theoretically in the hands of the elected parliament, the government in Islamabad would survive only if it pursued policies approved of by the president. Islamicisation was one of those policies, and amongst other things there was growing international criticism of attempts by the government to make a bowd-lerised version of Shariat law the keystone of the Pakistani legal system. This led to the introduction of qazi courts at local level, the appointment of *ulema* to a Shariat court at federal level, as well as a range of laws and judgments that exacerbated rivalries between state-sponsored Sunni and Shia versions of Islamic jurisprudence, as well as impinging upon the rights of women (Mumtaz and Shaheed 1987). Most notoriously an Islamic penal code that authorised punish-ment by amputation was introduced, and stoning and flogging for crimes such as theft, adultery and rape. The impact of these laws was limited by stricter rules of evidence, introduced by presidential order in 1984, which made conviction only feasible if the perpetrator confessed, or if the crime was witnessed by no less than two adult Muslim males (four in the case of sexual crimes), or twice that number of female witnesses. A consequence was that perpetrators often escaped, while in one notorious case a blind servant girl was punished with 15 lashes for adultery after becoming pregnant following multiple rape, while her assailants avoided punishment altogether (Weiss 1985).

Apart from civil unrest, another reason for Junejo's dismissal in May 1988 was his attempt to investigate a huge explosion at a munitions dump in Ojhri controlled by the increasingly powerful ISI, the Pakistani military intelligence service. The cause of the explosion was unknown, but rumour spoke of officers trading on the black market with imported American weapons, whilst the official report uncovered extensive evidence of maladministration. The ISI claimed that Indian spies were responsible. Either way, the blast covered up the evidence, and for good measure the ISI blew up an Indian arsenal at Jabalpur in central India to ensure that the incident was interpreted as an Indo-Pakistani dispute, even if it had not been so originally. Zia removed the prime minister, ostensibly in order to protect the ISI, and having done so assumed the premiership himself. Announcing a renewed round of Islamicisation measures, Zia went on to declare that fresh elections were to be held in November. Given past experience, there was little confidence that this promise would be fulfilled. However, whilst bankers struggled with the implementation of measures such as the abolition of interest, a new crisis hit the government in August 1988 when President Zia was killed in the crash of a Hercules military aircraft. This occurred just minutes after the plane's take-off from an army base where Zia had been watching the new American M1 Abrams tank being put through its paces.

Either sabotage or equipment failure, or a combination of the two, caused the crash of the presidential plane, but those responsible, if any, have never been identified. Since the American ambassador and the chief of the US military mission in Pakistan were killed, the CIA is an unlikely suspect. There were doubtless many others who thought that the time had come for Zia to retire from government. For once, the army decided not to intervene, but instead followed the constitution in asking the chairman of the Senate, Ghulam Ishaq Khan, to assume the office of acting president. In an address to the nation, it was confirmed that elections would go ahead as scheduled. Interestingly, soon after, the Lahore High Court ruled that Zia's suspension of the elected assemblies in May was illegal, and the Supreme Court decreed that the holding of 'party-less' elections was against the spirit of democracy. Accordingly, when elections took place in November they did so in an unprecedented climate of freedom, albeit one that bred some foreboding. It was a climate in which the principles of democratic civilian government had been thoroughly undermined by sectarianism, spawned by more than a decade of bigoted, corrupt and centralised military rule.

Democracy reprised: Benazir Bhutto and Nawaz Sharif

It is not unusual in Pakistan for the general public and the intelligentsia to approach the army chief and ask him to save the nation. In all crises, everyone sees Pakistan's army as the country's saviour. Whenever governments have malfunctioned (as has frequently occurred), whenever there has been a tussle between the president and the prime minister (especially during the 1990s), all roads lead to the general headquarters of the army.

(General/President Pervez Musharraf, 2006)[6]

The victor in the November 1988 elections was the recently married Benazir Bhutto at the head of the Pakistan People's Party, which won 92 out of 207 National Assembly seats. Optimism about the future of civilian rule in Pakistan was soon blunted, however, by the dismissal of that government by the president using the notorious eighth amendment to the constitution only 20 months later (Akhund 2000). The cause of this was undoubtedly the reluctance of the military and all-powerful intelligence services fully to hand over control to an elected civilian administration, especially one dominated by Sindhis. Allegations of attempted theft also led to the imprisonment of Mrs Bhutto's husband, Asif Ali Zardari. A combination of anti-PPP political parties, known as the Islamic Democratic Alliance, led by the Punjabi businessman turned Muslim League politician Nawaz Sharif, was cobbled together to supplant the PPP and received backing from the military, who hoped it would prove to be more pliable. They were disappointed, and despite its Punjabi power base it too was dismissed by the president in 1993 as soon as it began to show signs of independence.

Both Benazir Bhutto's administration and that of Nawaz Sharif were terminated on the grounds of corruption. In Benazir's case the activities of her husband Asif Ali Zardari, or 'Mr 10 per cent' as he was known, lent substance to these charges. However, it was the increasingly turbulent state of Sindh, Benazir's arrest of MQM leaders, the violence of her Sindhi supporters and the police (seen in incidents such as the Pucca Qila massacre of May 1990), and Benazir's resistance to demands that the army should be allowed to impose martial law in Sindh to restore order, that ultimately persuaded the military to effect her removal. Both premiers were also victims of a social and political system riven by vendetta. Locally, the electoral process was dominated by feudal elites, and by rivalries, as in colonial times, between opposing *biraderis* (kinship groups) and Sufi *pirs*. Political rhetoric had become extreme, the judicial system corrupt, and patronage the sole means by which government business could be carried on. Furthermore, the military insisted that the government could not interfere with defence spending, and that the army would have the final say in matters of foreign policy. It seemed that if a government was to have any autonomy at all this could only be accomplished by cunning, bribery, and occasional *force majeure*.

Following a brief period under a caretaker administration, Nawaz Sharif came to power after fresh elections in October 1990, at the head of the Islami Jamhoori Ittehad (Islamic Democratic Alliance), a nine-party coalition led by his faction of the Muslim League and including the Jamaat-i-Islami. Since Pakistan 'benefits' from the Westminster-style 'first-past-the-post' system, it required only a small shift in their favour, given the low turnout of 45 per cent, combined with a modicum of vote rigging (alleged by the PPP and some international observers) for them to win a total of 105 seats in the National Assembly. Sharif embarked upon a limited programme of liberalisation of the economy and other reforms, but his efforts were restricted by the cessation of American aid due to the continuation of Pakistan's nuclear development programme. His own government was also seriously divided over a continuing programme of Islamicisation, particularly a Shariat Act, which some saw as highly flawed, and Pakistan's continuing participation in the Gulf War in support of the Americans. Despite populist measures such as a minimum wage (practically unenforceable) and a programme of cheap loans for the self-employed (the so-called 'yellow taxi scheme'), the government's popularity was damaged by oil price rises of 40 per cent and growing unemployment. Matters did not improve when trade sanctions were imposed by the US in January 1993 following Pakistan's purchase of M-11 missiles from China. Rivalry between the government and the PPP became increasingly acrimonious, as government supporters attempted to demolish the PPP's power base in Sindh. One of many innocent victims was a close friend of Benazir Bhutto who was gang raped, allegedly by supporters of the government, possibly even Pakistani Central Intelligence Agency operatives. At the same time Benazir herself undertook secret negotiations with the president offering her support in his candidacy for a second term as president, something to which the prime minister refused to commit himself.

Sharif's coalition with Muslim religious parties finally fell apart. At odds with both the army chief of staff and President Ghulam Ishaq Khan, not only over the issue of a second term but also concerning the control of Punjab, Nawaz Sharif's administration was finally dismissed by the president in April 1993. On this occasion the fates were on Sharif's side, as an appeal to the Supreme Court overturned the president's decision. The army then stepped in to force both of them out of office, establishing a caretaker administration led by the former World Bank economist Moeen Qureshi, and a new president, Farooq Leghari. Almost immediately, and with the backing of the army, an agricultural income tax was introduced (soon to be suspended), subsidies cut, and publicity given to the corruption of the banking system and the vast number of loan defaulters among the ruling elite, involving a total of some Rs 62 billion – much of it apparently salted away overseas.

Fresh elections in October 1993 ushered in a second PPP government, led by Benazir Bhutto (Waseem 1994b). Internal conflicts within the PPP, however, marred Benazir Bhutto's second term to an even greater degree than her first, both her mother and brother, Mir Murtaza Bhutto, leading factions against her. Vigorous extra-parliamentary opposition from the Islamic Democratic Alliance amongst its core supporters in Punjab further weakened her hold on political power. In response, growing numbers of opposition politicians and activists, particularly members of the MQM in Karachi, were murdered in confrontations between police and gangs. A state of virtual anarchy prevailed in the city, with the death-toll from shootings of MQM and PPP supporters in the autumn of 1995 running at more than a hundred a month. Publicity was given to the Bhutto family's acquisition of significant assets overseas, including a country house with an estate and a stable full of Arabian horses in southern England. At the same time the government's foreign reserves dwindled to the point where there was only sufficient cash to pay for three weeks of imports, and an appeal for assistance had to be made to the International Monetary Fund. When Murtaza Bhutto was killed in a confrontation with police, accusations were levelled by Benazir against the president.[7] A tussle for power also emerged once again over control of the all-important province of Punjab, these factors together prompting the president to bring her government to an end in November 1996. Her husband Asif Ali Zardari was arrested for a second time and imprisoned for complicity in several murder cases, including that of Murtaza Bhutto (he was not to be released until the end of 2004 in a probable deal with President/General Musharraf), and Benazir herself became a fugitive from justice, retreating to her estates abroad.

With the demise of Bhutto's second term, Nawaz Sharif returned again, this time with widespread support, having won a considerable majority in elections held in February 1997. With an even lower turnout than before, this victory was undoubtedly assisted by vote rigging (some perpetrated by the ISI), but also by the publication of the Supreme Court's ringing condemnation of Benazir Bhutto's government only four days before polling commenced. One of Sharif's first acts upon taking office was to reform the constitution, removing the notorious eighth amendment by which his first term in office had been terminated. To many this seemed, at last, to signal the transition of the Pakistani political system towards a state of greater maturity. However, although the constitution was modified Sharif's government was neither able to reform nor control the military. This was partly because in many areas he depended upon it, owing to the deterioration of the civilian administration.

Whilst diplomatically Nawaz Sharif did his best to improve relations with a newly elected anti-Pakistani Bharatiya Janata Party (BJP) government in India, meeting with the Indian prime minister at Lahore, the military was unsupportive. When India tested a second nuclear device in May 1998 (the first had been in 1974), the Pakistan government had little choice but to make an immediate response with test explosions of its own. The economy already wavering, it then had to bear the brunt, far more costly for Pakistan than India, of US-led sanctions in response. By the late 1990s the economy was so much in hock to the IMF and foreign banks that the country's debt amounted to some US $500 for every man, woman and child. Whilst Sharif attempted to recover from this parlous state by the raising of sales taxes, the military launched an adventurous campaign in Kashmir in March 1999, infiltrating Indian positions and attempting to grab strategic territory in the Kargil region. When President Clinton intervened, and Sharif ordered his troops to withdraw, he was seen to be exercising an influence in strategic and foreign policy issues that the army considered its own preserve.

Sharif had attempted to strengthen his position by placing sympathetic individuals in key positions in the bureaucracy and judiciary, with whom he was engaged in a fierce and damaging struggle for much of his term of office. When he then sought to do the same with the military, and replace the army chief of staff, it was decided that he had gone too far. The economic difficulties of his government had already made it unpopular, and with little opposition the army moved in on 11 October 1999 and arrested Sharif and his family; General Pervez Musharraf, the chief of staff, and the man who had organised the Kargil offensive, took over as chief martial law administrator. This action Musharraf (2006) later justified as a 'counter-coup' against the 'coup' attempted by the prime minister in trying to concentrate all power in his hands. This was something that prime ministers in Pakistan are clearly not supposed to do and was too urgent a matter to wait for something so strange as a democratic election to resolve. Musharraf's first broadcast to the nation was a masterly piece of public relations. Casting aside the be-medalled uniform of previous military dictators, Musharraf was photographed relaxing with his wife and family. There was, however, no mention of fresh elections. Although the US ambassador declared that this was a man with whom the US could 'do business' – doubtless thinking primarily of strategic issues such as drug control, Afghanistan, and Indo–Pakistan relations – Pakistan's membership of the Commonwealth was once more suspended. The position of Pakistan's new dictator remained uncertain. Although there was clearly widespread public support for the drive against corruption that he promised, no one knew where political evolution would take the country next.

The war in Afghanistan and 9/11

The position of General Musharraf was transformed by his decision to side with the Americans following the fateful attack by Al-Qaeda on the Pentagon and on the Twin Towers in New York on 11 September 2001. In order to avert any possible autonomy movement among the Pushtuns, amongst other reasons, Pakistan was keen to secure a sympathetic ally across the border and from the very start had backed the take-over of Afghanistan by the Taliban: a youthful political movement of Islamic fundamentalists that grew up in the country's south-east, around Kandahar. Arms, training and even military support was provided during Benazir Bhutto's first government, and thereafter. Saudi-funded *madrasas* in Pakistan were important recruiting grounds for fighters in both Afghanistan and in Indian-controlled Kashmir (often the same people), and the Pakistan Intelligence Services and the Pakistani army were awash with enthusiastic supporters of both insurgencies (Rashid 2001; Margolis 2001; Abbas 2004). With the Taliban taking over the bulk of Afghanistan, it seemed that Pakistan's strategic interests were secure. Indeed, Pakistan was one of the few countries in the world formally to recognise the Taliban as the government of Afghanistan. It was thus a source of intense embarrassment to find America's number 1 enemy now being sheltered by this same regime. General Musharraf's decision to aid the American campaign against the Taliban and Al-Qaeda was almost a volte-face from policies he had pursued before, and doubtlessly hugely unpopular with Islamicists within his own regime as well as the country at large. However, by doing so, and placing his country on what ultimately proved to be the winning side, he not only secured enormously renewed economic and military support for his country from the Americans but also ensured the future of his own regime.

As the American campaign to unseat the Taliban and to capture Osama Bin Laden and other members of Al-Qaeda progressed, the prospects of free elections in Pakistan and a return to civilian rule were disappearing into the remote future. Instead, what Pakistan got was a variety of manoeuvres designed to give a semblance of legitimacy to Musharraf's regime, without in practice witnessing any loosening of military authority. To begin with a controversial referendum was held in April 2002 to approve Musharraf's adoption of the title of president for five years, and a national security council was established as the final authority in issues of national importance, in which the military were to enjoy a dominant role. At the insistence of the Supreme Court an election of sorts was then held in October 2002, subject to restrictions on public meetings and the eligibility of candidates. During the campaign, Benazir Bhutto, the leader of the PPP, was refused permission to return to Pakistan under threat of prosecution, and the former prime minister, Nawaz Sharif, was liberated from prison only on condition that he be exiled to Saudi Arabia and make no attempt to return. Inevitably the lead was taken by the PML-Q, a faction of the former Pakistani Muslim League, known to opponents as 'the king's party' owing to its vociferous, reciprocated support for the government. Despite a low turnout and allegations of vote rigging, a coalition of Islamicist parties, the MMA, achieved substantial public support – to the alarm of the Americans – notably in the north-western province where Pushtun supporters of the Taliban had taken refuge. Soon afterwards Zafarullah Khan of the PML-Q was appointed prime minister (he famously described Musharraf as his 'boss'), and the resulting parliament was asked to accept as a part of the constitution the legal changes Musharraf had made, known as the Legal Framework Order. This was only reluctantly agreed to by the Islamicist parties on condition that he step down from the position of army chief of staff. In June 2004 Musharraf accepted his prime minister's resignation, it is believed owing to disagreements on policy, and in November 2004 then reneged on his promise and had parliament approve his continuation in the role of army chief of staff. Although this earned the wrath of opposition politicians, Musharraf continued to enjoy the support of the West due to his active role in the 'war against terror'. Even the Commonwealth, which had formerly suspended Pakistan, allowed its readmission in May 2004.

Despite its negative consequences for democracy, Pakistan's close involvement in the international war against terrorism has had one important effect of enormous long-term consequence for its citizens – of forcing the regime to give up its sponsorship of 'liberation fighters' in Indian-controlled Kashmir and to seek a rapprochement with its powerful neighbour. Prior to September 11, relations with India were extremely poor, as one might have expected given the previous histories of the leaders of both countries at the time. An all-time low was reached in December 2001 following an attack on the Indian parliament by Kashmiri extremists who the Indian government claimed were backed by Pakistan. A massive Indian troop buildup followed in border areas, to which Pakistan responded in kind. Quite rightly, the Americans saw this as a serious distraction from the war against the Taliban and Al-Qaeda and insisted, with threats and bribes, that both sides come to terms. Negotiations subsequently commenced and ironically, thanks to Osama Bin Laden, a final resolution of the Indo-Pakistan conflict appears now to be in sight for the first time in the history of the two countries since independence. The results of this may prove economically and politically profound, as well as transforming the lives of ordinary civilians on both sides of the border as a consequence of the revival of trade and communications between the two countries. A doubt remains as to whether a truly independent civilian government can ever be established in Pakistan. Immediately after his fall from power, commentators suggested that by removing the eighth amendment Nawaz Sharif engineered his own demise, ensuring that nothing short of an old-style military coup could supplant him. However, there are three other venerable institutions by which a corrupt government, and certainly its premier, can be removed: by a vote of confidence in parliament, by legal prosecution, or by means of a general election. None of these options has ever been used to unseat a government in Pakistan. The country has endured military rule for more than thirty of the years that have passed since independence, and the heavy hand of the military has controlled the office of both president and prime minister on most other occasions. Constitutions can take a country only so far. Custom and precedent are also important in the functioning of a democratic polity. Both the legal system and civil society in Pakistan have been undermined and corrupted by successive regimes and Pakistan has become a country in which military despotism, poverty and religious extremism are customarily intertwined and the links all too easily traced (Haqqani 2005). Even were this not so, it is doubtful there is now anyone alive within Pakistan with relevant experience of how a democratic regime should function, or what one might reasonably expect from such a government. To govern in Pakistan is to act with forthright and military precision. The toleration of opposition, the possibility of debate and disagreement, and the trusting of the electorate rather than self-appointed bureaucrats and military elites, to make key political decisions concerning the country's future, are customs that are simply not ingrained in Pakistani society. Whether these values will ever develop, perhaps as a by-product of peace with India, is a matter for speculation. Meanwhile, the price continues to be paid by ordinary people, as weak public institutions have enabled a few to prosper at the expense of the many, and desperately needed economic and social reforms continue to be neglected. Without them, life in Pakistan will remain insecure, and the war against 'terrorism', in all its forms, will only be half won.

East Pakistan/Bangladesh post-1971

Bangladesh came to independence amidst a wave of popular support, spearheaded by student organisations and passionate assertions of Bengali nationalism. Like India, Bangladesh adopted a secular constitution soon after the birth of the new state, but there the similarities ended. In many respects the country soon began to suffer the same symptoms of political instability associated with its borders and minorities, as had west Pakistan (Van Schendel 2005). These included serious problems of democratic secessionism in the Chittagong hill tracts to the north, provoked by and inherited from the former regime, which had ridden roughshod over the relative autonomy formerly enjoyed by the region in colonial times. Conspicuously, Bangladesh's new constitution lacked any reference to the rights of multilingual national minorities, and an armed movement sponsored by the Jana Samhati Samiti (formed in 1972 to represent the Chittagong tracts) has fought an underground campaign to win recognition ever since, a conflict that has at times degenerated into civil war between rival factions, further adding to the plight of this region. Hundreds of Shanti Bahini (armed opposition group) members have been captured or killed and thousands of hill people have become refugees deep in the forests or in neighbouring India. The Shanti Bahini was formally dissolved after an unpopular accord between the JSS and the Awami League in 1997, which failed to put a check on Bengali settlement and to resolve land disputes, but the struggle for regional autonomy by the Chakmas and the Marmas and other subaltern groups continues (Mohsin 2003; Majumdar 2003; Chakma 2002).

Beyond the problem of its borders, the difficulties faced by Bangladesh in 1971 included the legacy of chaos and destruction following the independence war itself, and the culture of violence and extremism that it enjoined. It is estimated that as many as a million Bangladeshi civilians may have died in the fighting and as a result of the associated chaos and dislocation (Mascarenhas 1986). These difficulties were piled on top of the economic problems already inherited in the years immediately following partition. Bengal's main industrial city and principal port, Calcutta, having been joined with India in 1947, the most serious difficulty faced by east Bengal was its woeful lack of industrialisation. A consequence was that the country was completely dependent on its annual rice harvest in order to feed itself. This was precarious at best, as almost the entire country is deltaic and below sea level, and therefore highly susceptible to flooding both from the sea and from the Ganges and Brahmaputra rivers and their tributaries as they flow through the state.

Poorly administered and deprived of development finance, Bangladesh had furthermore to bear the burden of years of political disorder, which had culminated in the civil war of 1971. Arms abounded, and the government had difficulty in finding qualified staff to fill the positions formerly occupied by fleeing west Pakistan personnel. This was a problem in the military as well as in the civil service. At the commencement of the civil war, Bangladesh had been devastated by floods following a catastrophic cyclone that claimed some 500,000 lives and rendered millions homeless. This, plus the mayhem wrought by the Pakistani army, meant that there were terrible shortages of almost everything. In such a context Mujibur Rahman made several mistakes, most particularly in his dealings with the military. One of these was to establish a personal praetorian guard that swore allegiance to him and had special privileges, including priority access to supplies (Maniruzzaman 1980).

Prior to the elections held in 1973 Muslim political parties were banned, but this made little difference. Despite the presence of a number of socialist parties, the Awami League was overwhelmingly popular and swept all before it. However, soon after the elections, economic problems closed in. Embarking on a widespread programme of nationalisation before the government was fully on its feet did not help, but in 1974 the country was devastated yet again by floods, followed by famine (Alamgir 1980; Hartman and Boyce 1979). His government clearly unable to cope, Mujibur Rahman declared a state of emergency. Having nationalised the newspapers in order to curb criticism, he then amended the constitution to give Bangladesh a presidential system, and to make himself president for the next five years. At the same time Mujibur persuaded the National Assembly to approve the creation of a one-party system. A new party, the Bangladesh Krishak Sramik Awami League was set up under his leadership, and those opposition parties which did not join it were banned.

Whether true or not, the perception grew in the Bangladeshi military that Mujibur was more interested in self-aggrandisement than anything else. It was also becoming clear that he lacked the personal capacity to solve the country's problems. Yet having been declared president for at least the next five years, a group of young army majors, sacked from the army by Mujibur the previous year, decided that there was only one way to be rid of him. On 15 August 1975, Mujibur, his wife and sons were murdered in an early morning raid on his private residence. Only two daughters survived, one of them Sheikh Hasina Wajid.

A conservative Awami League member of the cabinet, Mushtaque Ahmed, was appointed to replace Mujibur Rahman as president by the coup leaders. Elections were announced, and a hero of the war of independence, Major Zia-ur Rahman, was appointed as army chief of staff. In early November, however, a further coup – this time engineered by conservative officers loyal to Mujibur Rahman, led by Brigadier Khalid Musharraf – rocked Bangladesh. Zia-ur Rahman was placed under house arrest, and the president persuaded to appoint himself as army chief of staff. Twenty-four hours later another coup was instigated by soldiers loyal to Zia-ur Rahman from the cantonment in the capital, Dhaka, who were members of the socialist Jatityo Samajtantrik Dal (JSD). Musharraf was killed in an exchange of gunfire a few days later.

Chief Justice Sayem became president, but Zia-ur Rahman soon emerged as the principal figure in the government, and whilst elections were postponed, Zia-ur spent the next few years carrying out administrative reforms, and travelling the length and breadth of the country whilst he reinvented himself, with some success, as a popular leader. Elections were still scheduled by the president for 1977, but as the date approached the army began to get cold feet, and a further suspension was announced. President Sayem then resigned, and Zia-ur ('Zia') Rahman took his place in April 1977. Presenting a radical reform manifesto to the public, a snap referendum was held, seeking popular approval: 88.5 per cent voted 'yes' (although there was no alternative on offer). Five months later yet another coup was attempted by air force personnel at the Dhaka cantonment, who attacked Zia-ur Rahman's residence. Although Zia survived this, and the rebels were put down, the government was shaken. Nevertheless, in a full-scale presidential election in April 1978 Zia was once again confirmed in office with an overwhelming popular mandate, this time in the face of a rival candidate.

Relations with India did not prosper. Where Mujibur Rahman had been understandably pro-Indian, the supporters of the JSD and of Zia-ur Rahman were not. There was also an ongoing dispute, which would not go away, over the utilisation of irrigation waters from the Ganges after the construction of a barrage by the Indians upstream at Farakka in the late 1960s (Crow 1995), and arguments over Bangladesh's borders through which refugees continuously leaked into neighbouring Indian districts of Assam and west Bengal. Nonetheless, garnering substantial foreign aid, which kept the army happy, and the population (or most of it) fed, the next few years were a successful time for Bangladesh, which began slowly on the path of economic recovery (Sobhan 1984). There were also a number of popular reforms instigated, such as a network of *gram sarkars* (village governments) set up to help plan and implement developmental objectives. However, in May 1981 President Zia was assassinated in a coup attempt led by the army commander at Chittagong. The chief of staff, Major-General Ershad, and most of the army, remained loyal, and the perpetrators were all executed in the aftermath. The vice-president, the ageing and uncharismatic Abdus Sattar, then stepped forward to take the president's place. In elections held in November Sattar won 65 per cent of the vote, confirming him in office. However, Sattar was a former judge, not a military man, and the exclusion of the army from key posts in the cabinet raised the ire of the military who, through Ershad, demanded a greater role in government. When this was not forthcoming, Ershad himself assumed the role of chief martial law administrator – ushering in almost a decade of authoritarian military rule – at the same time replacing the president with his own appointee, Abul Fazal Choowdhury, a former Supreme Court justice.

The parallels with Pakistan are uncanny, and in some respects share similar origins. However, Zia-ur Rahman had laid the basis for a proper democratic administration, perhaps better than any yet seen in west Pakistan, and the retreat into all-out military rule in 1981 was a seriously retrograde step. General Ershad justified his actions by saying that the country was in a state of economic crisis and racked by corruption. Whilst in many respects true, Ershad himself offered no obvious or immediate cure and had no popular mandate, nor even the united backing of the military. Nonetheless, Ershad set about consolidating his rule, abolishing the *gram sarkars* and making the subdistrict (*upazilla*) the basic unit of local government. He also set up his own political party, the Jana Dal ('People's Party'), and announced that elections were to be held immediately after a new constitution based on Shariat law had been introduced. By wrapping himself in the colours of Islam he hoped to lend legitimacy to his rule, a tactic that would later be repeated by others (Ahmed, Rafiuddin 1990; Riaz 2004). And by assuming the office of president in November 1984, Ershad clearly intended to follow Zia-ur Rahman's footsteps and turn himself into a popular civilian ruler. Whilst political rallies remained banned, political parties were allowed to function again. In no time at all, however, opposition spilled over into a general strike and street demonstrations against the government, inspired by Begum Khaleda Zia, Zia-ur Rahman's widow, and Hasina Wajid, Mujibur Rahman's daughter and leader of the Awami League. Both were arrested, and the planned elections never took place.

In 1975 General Ershad sought a democratic basis for his regime by holding a referendum, which approved his presidency but was entirely lacking in credibility. In 1986 Ershad renamed his political party the Jatiya Dal ('National Party') and announced elections, boycotted by all but Sheikh Hasina's Awami League. The Jatiya Dal won a small majority, but when Ershad proposed that the new parliament should pass an indemnity bill, legalising all actions taken under the martial law regime, the BNP walked out. The bill was then passed unopposed. With a semblance of civilian government in place, General Ershad next attempted to transform himself into a civilian president by resigning his position as chief of army staff and holding an election in October 1986. Once again the election was boycotted by most of the opposition parties and Ershad won. This did little to secure his position, however, as the opposition parties campaigned for fresh elections, their demonstrations being joined by trade unionists opposed to the programme of privatisations foisted on the government by the IMF and World Bank. After prolonged demonstrations in Dhaka, Ershad finally gave in and announced a poll in March 1988. Once more, however, the opposition boycotted the poll on the grounds that it would not be free and fair.

The absence of any credibility in the electoral process would probably have brought down the Ershad regime much sooner, were it not for the the the lack of co-operation – even outright hostility – between Sheikh Hasina's Awami League and Begum Zia-ur Rahman's BNP. In 1990, however, the student wings of the two main opposition parties united in violent street demonstrations against the government. Events mirrored those in the Philippines in 1986, when a 'people's revolt' led by Corazon Aquino had brought down the dictatorship of Ferdinand Marcos. When demonstrations continued despite the declaration of a state of emergency, the army told Ershad that it was no longer willing to back him, and Ershad was forced to resign. Within a few days he and his wife were placed under arrest. Despite this, when elections were held in 1991 Ershad contested five seats from jail and won all of them, as he did again, whilst still in prison, in 1996.

Despite widespread support for the Awami League, it was a forward-looking government of the BNP (Bangladesh Nationalist Party), led by Begum Khaleda Zia, widow of President Zia-ur Rahman, that won the elections in 1991. A crisis that occurred within weeks of the new government's taking office when Bangladesh was hit by a major cyclone, with floods covering nearly two-thirds of the country, was dealt with effectively. Constitutional reform then became a major concern, with the government abolishing the elected *upazilla* councils (considered a legacy of the Ershad era) and a debate emerging as to how best to do away with many of the powers of the president and restore Bangladesh to something resembling parliamentary democracy. The constitution was eventually changed to render the position of president ceremonial and give primary executive power to the prime minister. However, co-operation between the BNP government and the Awami League opposition did not last for long. There were major demonstrations by Muslims in Dhaka protesting against the destruction of the Babri mosque at Ayodhya in India in 1991, and after the BNP seized a former Awami League stronghold in a by-election, allegations of irregularities began to surface once again. The Awami League boycotted elections held in February 1996, which were then restaged in June 1996 when it won a clear victory, with Sheikh Hasina Wajid being elected as prime minister. The following year General Ershad was released from prison, and old scores were settled in 1998 when 15 former army officers were sentenced to death for involvement in the assassination of President Mujib in 1975. By then the opposition had begun a concerted campaign of strikes against the government, but political discord was curtailed when unusually heavy and lengthy monsoon rains brought floods to nearly two-thirds of the country. The effects, although severe, were fortunately nowhere near as disastrous as the floods of 1970, as the country has instituted increasingly effective emergency evacuation measures and has constructed cyclone shelters across the country in order to limit the loss of life.

Bangladesh today is still one of the poorest countries in the world, with an annual average income per capita of less than US $200. It also has one of the lowest literacy rates, most children under the age of 15 being unable to read or write. Although the land is highly fertile, the typical farmer holds on average only 2.2 acres, and Bangladesh is chronically unable to feed itself, being heavily dependent on food aid from the developed world. As such, the country was for a long time pilloried as a 'basket case' – in the arrogant parlance of many Western observers. Nonetheless it is in Bangladesh that some of the most innovative development schemes in recent years have been unfolding. Successful 'alternative' or 'intermediate' technologies have been developed here (Kramsjo *et al.* 1992), and the Grameen Bank has pioneered the provision of 'micro-credit' to small-scale farmers (Wahid 1983; Bornstein 1997) with such success that the model is now being adopted amongst poor communities lacking access to credit all over the world, including depressed inner-city areas in the UK. A flourishing women's movement has campaigned for educational and political rights with considerable success (Haque 2002) and is backed by the activities of numerous non-governmental organisations; it has worked tirelessly to fill the gaps in state welfare provision. Remittances from Bangladeshis overseas have also helped considerably to reduce levels of dependency in some of the most vulnerable agricultural regions, such as the district of Sylhet (Gardner 1995). Despite the ongoing insurgency problem amongst the indigenous peoples of the Chittagong hills, the general level of violence and instability in Bangladeshi political life subsided in the closing years of the twentieth century.

A major blot in Bangladeshi public life has been a groundswell of anti-Hindu feeling in reaction to events in neighbouring countries. This culminated in the persecution and flight of the feminist novelist Taslima Nasrin in the mid-1990s following publication of her novel *Lajja* (Shame), which tells the tale of a fictional Hindu family in Bangladesh made to suffer atrocities at the hands of Muslim fundamentalists – a dangerous phenomenon in a country in which 15 per cent, or some 19 million of its population, are Hindu. It has also become apparent that the conflict between Sheikh Hasina's Awami League and Khaleda Zia's BNP is more personal than ideological, and that the opposition parties are reluctant to see any parliament serve its full term, uniting periodically in campaigns of street demonstrations aimed at forcing early elections. The ferocity of this conflict is intimately linked to corruption, which renders all public appointments a lucrative source of kick-back and illegal income. According to Transparency International

(2004) Bangladesh is second only to Haiti in terms of the lack of public confidence in the honesty of its officials and politicians. Nonetheless, in July 2001 the Awami League became the second government to stand fast and serve its full term, although the election resulted in a landslide victory for the four-party alliance led by the opposing Bangladeshi Nationalist Party. This brought Begum Khaleda Zia once again to power, this time in a dubious alliance with the staunchly Islamicist Jamaat-i-Islami and a spate of vengeful measures to assert the authority of the new regime. These measures included the repeal of a law that guaranteed lifelong security to former prime minister Sheikh Hasina, and a conflict with President Chowdhury over his reluctance to visit the shrine of the BNP founder Zia-ur Rahman (on constitutional grounds), which led to his resignation. In response there were no less than 21 general strikes called in 2004 as part of an opposition campaign to oust the government, whilst 'fundamentalists' were held responsible for the harassment of journalists and a succession of bomb attacks in towns north of Dhaka. The bombings culminated in 459 synchronised explosions in all but one of the country's administrative districts on 17 August 2005 – widely interpreted as a public demonstration of the strength of militant underground Islamic organisations. This continuing lawlessness, the rise of Islamic militancy with possible links to Al-Qaeda,[8] violent political opposition and the constant threat of military intervention – once again realised before elections could be held in January 2007 – make it hard to be optimistic. Nevertheless, there appear reasons to believe that Bangladesh may be beginning to establish a more equitable pattern of government than it has experienced in the recent past and is learning better how to cope with the violent natural catastrophes to which the country is prone. These, plus the conspicuous resourcefulness of its people, may together form the foundation of greater security and stability to come.

12 The Nehruvian era

I see no way of ending the poverty, the vast unemployment, the degradation and subjection of Indian people except through socialism . . . That means ending of private property except in a restricted sense and the replacement of the present profit system by a higher idea of co-operative service. It means ultimately a change in our instincts, habits and desires. In short it means a new civilisation radically different from the present capitalist order.

(Nehru 1936)[1]

There is of course no question of doing away with private capital, though it has to be controlled in the interests of the people.

(Nehru 1949)[2]

I was in class nine at that time . . . Each member of the family had to work very hard for the sake of a few paise. I never had all the textbooks. I had to get by through borrowing from friends. It was the same story with clothes. I wore whatever I could get. And I ate whatever I was given . . . What a cruel society we live in, where hard labour has no value. There is a conspiracy to keep us in perpetual poverty . . . Why is it a crime to ask to be paid for one's labours? Those who keep singing the glories of democracy use the government machinery to quell the blood flowing in our veins. As though we were not citizens of this country. They have suppressed the weak and helpless for thousands of years, just in this manner. No one will ever know how many talents their deception and treachery have wiped out.

(Omprakash Valmiki)[3]

In Pakistan, failure to agree on a constitution stultified political development and the army stepped forward to take a leading role in the management of the country. India, by contrast, moved very quickly to agreement on a constitution following independence, and the army has remained for the most part under political control – a rare phenomenon when comparisons are made with other developing countries, and even many countries in the so-called developed world. However, the transition to democracy in India was by no means easy, not least because within two months of achieving independence India found itself at war with Pakistan.

Kashmir

The occasion for the dispute was Pakistan's 'invasion' of the princely state of Kashmir in October 1947. This occurred after a similar 'invasion' by India of the princely state of Junagadh, which was followed in mid-1948 by an invasion of the princely state of Hyderabad. These latter two states had prevaricated over whether to join Pakistan or India in the run-up to the partition of British-run territories in the subcontinent (Copland 1997). In both Junagadh and Hyderabad, although the populations were largely Hindu, the rulers were Muslim and they were thus reluctant to join India, even though both states were surrounded by Indian territory. Hyderabad was given a year to make up its mind before the Indian army marched in. The ruler of Junagadh actually elected to join Pakistan in August 1947, but then suffered an economic blockade before being taken over by a 'liberation army' of Hindus in the state, sponsored by India.

The case of Kashmir was similar, but different, since although its *maharaja*, Hari Singh, was a Hindu, three-quarters of its population were Muslim. And it lay exactly between India and Pakistan. Hari Singh ruled with the support of an elite of educated Brahmins and Jammu-based Dogra Rajputs until 1932, when a Muslim religious leader, Sheikh Muhammad Abdullah, known as 'the lion of Kashmir', organised the all-Jammu and Kashmir Muslim conference, later named the all-Jammu and Kashmir conference, which won a number of reluctant concessions towards democracy from the *maharaja*. Despite this Kashmir remained essentially a Hindu, non-Kashmiri, Jammu-based autocracy up until 1947. Hari Singh, a Dogra Rajput himself, hoped that Kashmir would remain independent. However, an uprising of Muslim tenants against their Hindu Dogra Rajput landlords in the province of Poonch, in the south-west of the country, was assisted by Pakistanis from across the border, leading Hari Singh to fear a full-scale Pakistani invasion. He therefore turned to Delhi for help, sending his envoy to request military assistance. With the assistance of Sheikh Abdullah he succeeded in persuading the Indian prime minister (Nehru's family were themselves descended from Kashmiri Brahmins), but on condition that Kashmir join the Indian Union (Mahajan 1963: 265). Ostensibly therefore, Indian intervention had the support not only of the *maharaja*, but of the majority Muslim political party within the state, whilst the Hindu Dogra elite remained distant, if not suspicious of these developments, fearful that it would undermine their power base (Puri 1993: 5).

In late 1947, Lord Mountbatten, the former viceroy, was still governor-general of India and both the British and Pakistani armies were largely officered by British soldiers. When Hari Singh formally acceded to India therefore, Mountbatten insisted that troops could be deployed in support of the *maharaja* only if the accession was subsequently confirmed by a referendum. To this both Hari Singh and Nehru gave their assent, and Indian troops were air-lifted to Kashmir. In response, the dying Mohammed Ali Jinnah, now governor-general in Pakistan, attempted to order in his troops, only to have this move blocked by his supreme commander – Field Marshal Auchinleck. Therefore, although Pakistan never formally declared war, Pakistani irregular soldiers, and Pathan tribesmen, assisted by the Pakistan government, crossed the border from the west and continued to fight in Kashmir until a ceasefire was arranged by the United Nations in January 1949. A condition of the ceasefire agreement was that a referendum should be held to determine the fate of the state once normality was restored. But since the Pakistanis refused to withdraw, such conditions have never prevailed from the Indian point of view. The result was the effective partitioning of Kashmir – the western side joining Pakistan, and the eastern side joining India, with another bite taken out of the north by China. Both India and Pakistan have allowed a considerable measure of autonomy, at least at first, to their sections of Kashmir, but a referendum to determine the fate of the territory as a whole has never been held.

The war in Kashmir marked the beginning of an animosity between India and Pakistan, which has continued ever since. Two subsequent wars have been fought between India and Pakistan: in 1965 in Kashmir, along the border, and in the Rann of Kutch; and in 1971 during the civil war in east Pakistan. On both occasions the Pakistani army, equipped by the United States, has achieved successes in the early stages of the fighting, but has then been overwhelmed by the numerically superior forces of the Indians. Apart from these three full-scale wars, there have been numerous minor confrontations between India and Pakistan – usually in the first instance in response to internal difficulties within the two countries rather than any infringement of the ceasefire line. The Pakistani army in particular has made frequent use of the apparent 'threat' from India as an excuse for perpetuating military rule and the restriction of civil liberties at home.

Within India, an effect of conflict with Pakistan in the short and longer term was to seriously worsen Hindu–Muslim relations, already embittered in the wake of partition. In 1948 the situation became quite serious as millions of Hindu refugees from Punjab, Sindh, the North-West Frontier Province and Baluchistan poured into the capital at Delhi, sparking an increase in anti-Muslim feeling. Leading the persecution of Muslims in India were a number of chauvinistic Hindu organisations, the most widespread being the Rashtriya Svayamsevak Sangh ('National Self-service Society' – also known simply as the RSS), a sister organisation to the Hindu Mahasabha, the Hindu patriotic party founded in the 1920s. It was a member of the Hindu Mahasabha, Naturam Godse, who was responsible for the assassination of Mahatma Gandhi in January 1948, shortly after which the organisation was banned.

News of Gandhi's assassination was met with fearful anticipation. If his assassin had been a Muslim, communal violence would almost certainly have erupted. Within 48 hours, however, it was known that his killer was a Hindu fanatic, and this almost certainly helped to restrain the impact of Hindu extremism. Nonetheless the war with Pakistan and the banning of the Hindu Mahasabha led to rioting in a few major cities, such as Poona and Nagpur, where the RSS offices were ransacked by Congress supporters. Both the RSS and Mahasabha were temporarily banned by the government, and the Mahasabha was so discredited that it subsequently had to reinvent itself as the Bharatya Jan Sangh at the initiative of the Bengali Hindu leader Shyamaprasad Mukherji.

The outbreak of urban riots helped give the secularists in the government, in particular Jawaharlal Nehru himself, the upper hand, and in reaction to the threat of further disturbances the Indian constituent assembly speedily moved to ratify a constitution in January 1950 that was purely secular in tone, emphasising justice, equality, liberty and fraternity.[4] This constitution ambitiously gave the right to vote, for the first time, to the entire adult population of the country – some 173 million people. A close follower of Gandhi, Rajendra Prasad, was appointed president, and full-scale elections were held little more than 18 months later in the winter of 1951 – a mammoth and bold undertaking, especially in view of the fact that 80 per cent of the population at the time were still largely illiterate.

The 1951 elections were a tremendous success for the Congress Party. Nehru, as the party's star public speaker, travelled the length and breadth of the country, and when all the votes were counted Congress had won a huge majority of 362 out of 489 seats in the Lok Sabha ('assembly of the people'), and majorities in all of the newly formed state assemblies. The newly elected government then reappointed Nehru as prime minister, a post he was to hold for the next 13 years.

Social and economic change under Nehru's premiership

India was the first and largest country in either Africa or Asia to achieve independence from colonial rule, and soon afterwards embarked on the greatest experiment in representative democracy the world has ever seen. Since Jawaharlal Nehru was India's leader for the first 17 years of its independence, and in many ways the principal architect of this transformation, his premiership has attracted considerable attention. With few exceptions (Zachariah 2003), accounts of his life and work have tended to be uncritical and excessively adulatory (Khilnani 1997; Mukerjee 1992; Akbar 1988) or otherwise constrained by the terms of access to the Nehru family papers (Brown 1999).[5] For many of his contemporaries Nehru represented a dedicated socialist, determined to do the best for his country. Educated in an English public school, Harrow, and at Cambridge University, he was apparently at ease with both the English and the anglicised, as well as with members of the Indian business elite. Latterly he has been greatly admired by the Westernised liberal intelligentsia, nostalgic for the days (arguably less democratic) when Hindu fundamentalism was held in check, and more 'civilised' standards pertained in Indian politics and public life. However, even the more objective and comprehensive study of Jawaharlal Nehru's life, by Sarvepalli Gopal, can in retrospect now seem to be at times too kind to his subject.[6]

Credit for India's effective transition to democracy, to begin with, lies for the most part with the Constituent Assembly presided over by Rajendra Prasad, and the committee charged by the Assembly with the task of drawing up the constitution under which the first elections were held. In this constitutional drafting committee, Nehru's influence was limited to the appointment of the chair, Dr B.R. Ambedkar, a leader of the untouchables in the western state of Maharashtra and a critic of Gandhi during the days of the independence struggle, who helped to give the constitution a distinctly radical edge. One of the constitution's most important features was the banning of untouchability and of religious discrimination in any form, a measure the government backed up by introducing the Untouchability (Offences) Act of 1955, which provided specific penalties for discrimination.

In addition to outlawing caste discrimination, the government introduced a policy of positive discrimination that reserved special places in government service and in the universities for members of the so-called 'scheduled castes and tribes' (including the former untouchable communities), ironically, and perhaps ominously, employing the same definition of these scheduled communities as that used in the notorious Government of India Act of 1935. At the same time the status of women was significantly improved, beginning with the vote. Subsequent Acts gave Hindu women the right to marry outside their own caste, as well as to divorce their husbands, and the minimum age of marriage was raised to 18 in the case of males and from 12 to 15 in the case of females. Under the Hindu Succession Act of 1956 female children were also given rights of inheritance equal to those of male children.

The various anti-discrimination measures enacted had together a revolutionary impact on Indian society – although not unequivocally, as later became apparent. Thus, despite the system of reservation, and their constitutional status as equals, the former untouchables, or *dalits* (the 'oppressed') as activists now call them, remained severely under-represented in politics as in all walks of life beyond those menial occupations that were the traditional preserve of the community. Despite changes in the legal position of women, it was still also a long time before Indian women began to be aware of their new-found rights, and in many cases these have made little difference to their actual status. Where it has, migrancy and a rise in economic inequality have in many cases had the opposite effect – making their position very much worse, as was shockingly revealed in the *Report on the Status of Women in India* prepared to coincide with the first international women's year, organised by the UN in 1975 (CSWI 1975). The combination of prejudice and impoverishment has been particularly harsh on Muslim women (Hasan and Menon 2004). Moving away from kith and kin in the countryside in search of work has made women an easy target for exploitation, whilst the increasing commercialisation of marriage and so-called 'dowry deaths' have gone hand in hand in many Indian cities. Nonetheless, in the 1950s – at least initially – the policy of positive discrimination or 'reservation' in favour of the lower castes had a positive impact, and created a real sense (however illusory) amongst the elite that they had lived up to their promises to Indian women and to the mass of downtrodden lower castes, whose position they had avowed to improve in the days of the independence struggle.

An advantage of the new Congress government's leftist social policies was that it won considerable support from the poorer sections of Indian society, thus leaving the communists with little opportunity to make headway at the Congress Party's expense. Many within the Communist Party of India (CPI) indeed took a sympathetic attitude to Nehru, despite the CPI being the principal party in opposition, whilst Nehru's leftist stance on social policies kept many socialists within the ranks of the Congress.

More controversial than his social policies were Nehru's attempts to modernise India economically. Being an avowed socialist, Nehru had long been convinced that the most successful way to advance the country would be to adopt a system of centralised planning, comparable to that applied in the Soviet Union. Accordingly, in 1950, Nehru established and chaired a national planning commission, created to provide the 'most effective and balanced utilisation of the country's resources', and in April 1951 India's first Five-year Plan was announced. In this initial plan some US $3.7 billion of public funds was expended, though much of it went on simple repairs to India's pre-war consumer industries, on power generation, and on communications. It was not until the second Five-year Plan was introduced, in 1956, that a serious strategy for industrial expansion was established. The commission that put together this plan was chaired by the world-famous statistician and economist P.C. Mahalanobis, and it became known thereafter as 'the Mahalanobis plan'.[7] This second Five-year Plan not only directed considerable public funds towards industrial investment but attempted to channel private funds in what they considered the right direction by setting up a complex system of licensing, subsidies and import controls.

To some extent, the Mahalanobis strategy was successful: iron production leapt from 4 million tons in 1956 to almost 11 million tons in 1961, coal production jumped from 38 to 54 million tons, and electricity generation doubled. However, the direction of this development was not as radical as one might expect. Despite his leftist rhetoric, Nehru had opted for a 'socialistic' rather than a 'socialist' strategy in the Industrial Policy Resolution of 1956 and encouraged the growth of a 'mixed economy', which allowed just as much growth, if not more, in the private as in the state sector. The Gandhian idea that the capitalist classes might be allowed to continue to enjoy their power as 'trustees' of the national wealth remained very influential, as indeed did their role within the Congress Party. Nehru wrote to the secretary of the Planning Commission: 'It should be our endeavour to effect enormous transformation without challenging the existing order.'[8] In reality, much of the private sector growth was highly monopolistic in nature, as India's fledgling bourgeois enterprises were protected from foreign competition by extensive tariffs and other barriers to imports.

The importance of the private sector in the Indian government's economic strategy is clearly demonstrated by the following statistics, in *crores* of rupees at current prices: public expenditure 55 (first Five-year Plan), 938 (second Five-year Plan); private expenditure 283 (first Five-year Plan), 850 (second Five-year Plan).[9] In consequence, according to one estimate about nine-tenths of the total domestic product still came from the private sector at the close of the third Five-year Plan period while the public sector's share had increased by only 4 per cent in the 15 years since India's independence (Chaudhuri 1975: 161). This is a far smaller share for state enterprise than in most developed Western European countries, less than in neighbouring countries such as South Korea, and a small achievement for an avowedly 'socialist' state. The figures are somewhat deceptive, of course, since the vast bulk of India's 'private' economy at this time still consisted of peasant agriculture; rather, what is disturbing is not so much the low proportion of state expenditure to the whole but the relatively minor changes in those proportions, despite the government's greatly vaunted efforts towards the creation of a fully 'developmental' state (Chibber 2004).

In terms of the relative contribution to National Income a similar story is to be seen: the private sector's contribution ranged between 90 per cent in 1950/1 and 85 per cent in 1960/1, while the public sector's ratio increased from 7.4 per cent in 1950/1 to only 10.7 per cent in 1960/1. The reason for this lack of change is that while the state-run enterprises worked hard to expand and to build up the industrial infrastructure so neglected in the colonial period, the top business houses worked equally hard to tighten their grip on the sectors and regions within the economy where they were already predominant. According to Mahalanobis there were 20 such key business houses, 75 according to the Monopolies Inquiry Commission Report of 1965 (Bagchi 1982), and together they remained a commanding force within the economy, discouraging competitors and smaller scale private enterprise in the process.

The explanation for the power of Indian private business monopolies is not too hard to find, since from the mid-1930s onwards India's indigenous business elite had slowly acquired a dominant voice in the affairs of the Indian National

Figure 19 'The Forgotten Master': Nehru redrawing the map of India with Gandhi forgotten (*Punch* magazine, August 1951). © M.D. Carter.

Congress. Nehru and other Congress leaders went along with this, partly due to a rightward shift in the Congress after 1935, partly out of a concern for national unity, partly because the Congress Party needed their financial support, and partly due to a somewhat distorted application of Gandhi's *swadeshi* idealism: the perceived need to support Indian enterprise against that of the British and other 'imperialists'. By lending support to the Congress Party, India's business elite were able to ensure that their interests were protected. Their support for *swadeshi* idealism, although self-interested, was often undoubtedly sincere, and a great many British enterprises sold out to Indian businesses. But whilst hiding behind import barriers, India's industrialists often went on to choose new allies, and did not hesitate to co-operate with foreign companies if there was profit to be made in doing so. As a consequence, whilst the volume of direct foreign investment rose from Rs 2,176 million in 1948 to Rs 6,185 million in 1964, the share of foreign companies in the gross profits of the Indian corporate sector also increased from 29.8 per cent in 1959/60 to 33.3 per cent in 1962/3 (Chandra 1977; Shirokov 1973).

In sum, therefore, the economic policies of the Nehruvian era fell far short of the progressive claims made for them. Nehru himself confessed his awareness of this situation, but did nothing to address the problem. This was at least partly due to a three to one majority for the conservatives, led by Vallabhai Patel (till his death in 1950), in the Congress Central Working Committee. However, Nehru's own commitment to socialism clearly waned in his later years (Gopal 1979–84, 3: 119). As far as he and others were concerned national security and production were critical priorities. Distributive justice was mistakenly regarded as conflicting with the ambition for rapid industrialisation, and was therefore forced to take a back seat. Not only did this have detrimental effects for Indians as a whole – the poverty gap widening as a consequence in the first two decades after independence – it was also bad for the economy, since poverty and overpopulation stultified enterprise and inhibited the growth of an internal market for industrial goods.

The fatal effects of the Nehru government's faint-heartedness and bias in favour of the status quo was tragically to be seen in the failure of its programme of land reform. Reform of the landholding and tenurial system was vital if India was to address the multiple problems of rural poverty that had become endemic since the early 1930s. As in the present (Jeffery and Jeffery 1997), a lack of educational opportunities and the expectation of high infant mortality – the main consequences of poverty – meant that disadvantaged villagers in rural India continued to have larger families. In the absence of income and savings only family members could provide economic security to the elderly. This was not a relationship that even female education could break, as those at the bottom of the rural hierarchy in social and economic terms were rarely allowed the chance to make use of it, including access to the means of birth control. As death rates fell throughout the twentieth century a further vicious cycle began to develop: poverty was leading to larger families, causing landholdings to become highly subdivided. The rural population was soon increasing at a rate faster than agricultural growth could accommodate. In 1951, after partition, India's population stood at some 350 million, of whom 295 million lived in the countryside, and average life expectancy was a mere 32 years. Thereafter in the 1950s this total grew at an annual rate of between 5 and 6 million. Despite a growth in food production from 52 million tons to 65 million tons, by the end of the first Five-year Plan agriculture could barely keep up. For the poorer sections of the population standards of living remained completely static, and serious food deficits occurred in 1951, 1952 and 1953. In the long term, further improvements in life expectancy made the pressure on land even worse.

Short of a sudden technological revolution, only land reform could break the vicious cycle of rural impoverishment and population growth, a fact of which the Planning Commission was keenly aware. With this in mind a delegation was sent to China to observe the working of the Chinese system of communes, and shortly after recommended a programme of land reform to be adopted in accordance with local conditions by each of the state governments. Accordingly, land reform Acts were passed by all of the state assemblies, abolishing the big *zamindars* and the numerous petty landlords (in theory at least), and transferring ownership of all tenant lands into the hands of the cultivators themselves. In addition, ceilings were set on all landholdings, and any land in excess of this ceiling was supposed to be handed over to the government for redistribution to the landless and poor peasants. Unfortunately the Planning Commission could only recommend, it could not direct. In deference to the need for unity, Nehru's government never gave the Planning Commission the teeth it needed to make these separate enactments of the state governments effective, and since the Congress at state level, even more so than at the centre, was funded and controlled by members of the business and landholding classes, in most instances the legislation put in place was so full of loopholes as to be easily subverted. What little land was redistributed proved to be hopelessly infertile and of the worst sort, and in many cases the power of local landlords made it impossible even to begin to enact the legislation.

A similar fate befell the co-operative movement. Rather than have the state take over all the land and establish peasant communes – the practice in China and the Soviet Union – the government of India, in accordance with its philosophy, chose the less radical (and less costly) path of encouraging the setting up of agricultural co-operatives. This was hardly original, as the British had done the same thing between the wars, partly through a mistaken attempt to win the allegiance of the richer peasantry. In most cases, however, the rural co-operatives that were established, notably in Madhya Pradesh in central India, proved to be a sham. There was extensive misappropriation of funds, and most of them eventually had to be closed down.[10]

Equally unsuccessful was the programme of community development and rural extension. This ambitious, well-intentioned, but grossly under-funded project was intended to tap the energy of India's newly educated youth by sending them out into the more backward areas in the role of 'village-level workers' with the intention that they should teach the villagers new techniques of co-operative management, health care, irrigation, and agricultural improvement, etc. The results of this in practical terms were, however, meagre by comparison with the tremendous enthusiasm with which the planning was undertaken. As with so many other schemes for economic and social reform, the community development programme was defeated by the sheer scale of poverty in post-colonial rural India and by the opposition of aristocratic privilege and feudal prejudice (Herring 1983).

In consequence, the next great initiative for development 'from the bottom up' – the scheme of *panchayati raj* – introduced in 1959, was embarked upon more cautiously. *Panchayati raj* aimed at the development of self-governing institutions at the village level, in imitation of the *panchayat* ('council of elders') that was to be found in the villages of ancient India – though in this scheme, unlike in ancient India, the *panchayat* was supposed to be elected. Unfortunately, political parties were banned from taking part, which might have offered some leverage against the power of local landlords and rich peasants. Mindful as they were of previous failures and concerned to hold on to powers of patronage (useful in the run-up to an election), state-level politicians were furthermore reluctant to grant more than minor juridical responsibilities to these village institutions, which remained essentially powerless in practice. Within a few years most villages did not even bother to hold elections and *panchayats* remained largely under the control of richer peasants within the village.

It was partly the failure of official programmes of land reform, community development and *panchayati raj* that encouraged a flourishing of 'unofficial' campaigns in the 1950s to deal with poverty and backwardness in rural India. One of the most famous was the *bhoodan* movement, started by Vinoba Bhave, one of Gandhi's foremost disciples, in Andhra Pradesh in southern India in the late 1940s. Initially the campaign was launched to try and wean support away from the communists who were leading a peasant revolt in the Telengana region at the time. Bhave's tactic was to ask wealthy landowners to adopt him as if he were their fifth son and then voluntarily to give him gifts of land (*bhoodan*) amounting to a fifth of their property. This land he then redistributed to the landless poor.

The *bhoodan* movement soon spread to other parts of India, millions of acres were redistributed, Vinoba Bhave was revered almost as a saint, and he became an international celebrity. Nonetheless, it later came to be recognised that the land donated was commonly unwanted land of low fertility, the movement only touched the tip of the iceberg of rural deprivation, and it did little to compensate for the overall failures of government policy. Communists continued already established movements for land reform and peasant rights, but their activities were for the most part confined to northern Bengal, Tripura, the Telengena region of Hyderabad, Kerala, eastern UP and the Begusarai region in Bihar.

Political problems of the Nehruvian regime

The difficulty with government programmes of redistribution was not merely the scale of the problem, but also the lack of political will. An attempt to deal with this was launched in 1963 by Nehru and Kamraj Nadar, the influential leader of the Congress in Tamil Nadu and Congress Party president. The so-called 'Kamraj plan' called upon Congress politicians to resign from office and devote themselves to grass-roots work in the rural areas. Intended as a means to revive the flagging spirits of the party, and also to rally local-level support for its initiatives, it was interpreted by many as simply an attempt to undermine already established and influential Congress politicians such as Morarji Desai. Desai – a potential successor to Nehru favoured by the Congress right-wing – and his supporters alleged that the policy was an attempt to clear away possible contenders to the succession of the prime minister's daughter, Indira Gandhi. The initiative therefore was quietly ignored by the majority of cabinet members and state-level politicians.

The struggle with right-wing elements constantly marred Jawaharlal Nehru's premiership, undoing many of his government's best initiatives. Its origins lay in the rightward shift of the Congress post-1936, and the strong continuities that existed with the pre-existing colonial regime in consequence of the peaceful transition to independent rule. The colonial government was a system of command and control, the bulk of expenditure going on the military, police and related infrastructure, with limited resources devoted to education and to development. At the time of independence, the bureaucracy that ran this machine was little changed, unaccustomed to administering democracy, and preferring – for the most part – to maintain the status quo.[11] When radical changes were attempted, they not only met resistance within the bureaucracy but were all too often contradicted by right-wing elements within the Congress Party itself. This party–state conflict was one faced in many post-colonial societies. In India, it came to a head in August 1950 when P.D. Tandon won the post of party president, despite Nehru's opposition. Like the first post-independence party president, Kripalani, he began to insist that governmental policy decisions be approved by the Congress Central Working Committee. At a time of political turbulence in east Pakistan, with Hindu refugees fleeing across the border into India, Nehru saw this as a very real threat, particularly in the light of Tandon's known association with the right-wing and allegedly also with anti-Muslim elements in the party. Nehru dealt with this challenge by threatening to resign (the first of several occasions), forcing Tandon to step down from the party leadership. Nehru then allowed himself to be proposed and elected as party president in September 1951, thereby uniting the leadership of the party and government. Subsequent holders of the office of president, elected only with Nehru's approval, were all second line congressmen, or otherwise the prime minister's own daughter (elected in 1959), none of whom were likely to attempt to assert their authority. The conflict was thus resolved, but at a cost: centralisation, personalisation of Nehruvian rule, and the complete subordination of the office of the Congress Party president

The nascent authoritarianism of the prime ministerial office in the early 1950s, justified on the grounds of preserving unity, was compounded by the appointment of subservient governors in each of the states, the Westminster-style 'first-past-the-post' electoral system adopted at independence, and the disunity of the opposition parties. This created the illusion that the government remained popular and united behind the Congress Party, which continued to gain 60–80 per cent of the seats in parliament, even though it rarely actually achieved more than 45 per cent of the popular vote. When the opposition did break through to electoral success, this was greeted with considerable alarm, as if it were a subversion of the natural order of government, summarised in Nehru's 1952 electoral slogan: 'The Congress is the country and the country is the Congress.'

Nehru's centralising instincts were most conspicuously held in check, however, during disputes over the language of government (King 1997). In the years before 1947 the Congress Central Working Committee had passed a resolution that Hindi, not English, should be the language of government following independence. A sensible nationalist position, it nonetheless immediately met with opposition when the attempt was made to implement it. Opposition was fiercest in the south of India, where English rather than Hindi was the common medium of expression between middle-class Tamil, Malayalam, Telugu and Kannada speakers. The Hindi national language policy was regarded as another attempt by the Aryan/Mughal north of the country to lord it over the Dravidian south, and there were calls for Tamil to be given equal status (Ramaswamy 1997). Reluctantly Nehru agreed to the appointment of a commission, which recommended the redrawing of state boundaries in 1956 so that the states corresponded to linguistic and cultural unities, enabling government to be carried on in the predominant local language in each region whilst at the centre all government documents were to be produced in both Hindi and English, and translated into relevant regional languages when being communicated to each state. For the linguistic nationalists (of which Gandhi had been one), who thought that India ought to unite behind a single language, this was a major climb-down. In the process, however, several demands for the creation of separate states were rejected out of hand by Nehru – amongst them the demand for a Sikh, Gurumukhi-speaking state in the Punjab, a Gujarati state, and a central Indian state for *adivasis* or tribals. All of these claims would resurface later.

Despite the concessions made on language and the reorganisation of states (which were arguably much to his credit), Nehru nonetheless ordered the imposition of 'president's rule' – invoking a clause (article 356) in the constitution that allowed central rule in any of the states at times of national emergency or of a breakdown in law and order – no less than five times between 1952 and 1964. In practice, the occasion was usually afforded by the need to dislodge a non-Congress government or to offset the failure in attempts at a merger between Congress and non-Congress groups – Andhra Pradesh in 1954, Kerala in 1956 and Orissa in 1961. The most controversial imposition of president's rule arose when the election of India's first Communist state government in Kerala in 1957, under the leadership of E.M.S. Namboodiripad (Figure 20), appeared to signal a rise in discontent with the Congress regime as well as marking a significant step forward for the Communist movement in India. In order to unseat the Communist government, a blatantly communalist tactic was adopted by the Keralan Congress, which united with Muslim political groups and Christian religious bodies as well as various Hindu caste organisations in opposition to plans to introduce a secular system of secondary education within the state. This led to

Figure 20 E.M.S. Namboodiripad leading a procession of Communist Party workers after his ministry was dismissed, Kerala, August 1959. © *The Hindu*.

street demonstrations and riots, in which Congress workers participated. This then became the pretext to impose president's rule and to suspend the elected government (thereby discrediting it) in July 1959, on the grounds that they could not maintain law and order.

Indira Gandhi, the Congress president in 1959, headed a delegation sent to Kerala to negotiate the formation of a Congress-led coalition to replace the CPI. In subsequent elections in Kerala the Communist Party of India increased its share of the vote, but the Congress alliance with the Muslim league meant that it was able to obtain a majority in the state assembly and retain control of the state government. Many worried that this ruthless use of central power undermined the federal nature of the Indian constitution, not to mention its democratic principles, and united far more responsibility and power in the office of prime minister than was healthy in a country as diverse and large as India. Eventually, indeed, the high-handed and undemocratic dismissal of the CPI government in Kerala in 1959 was to become the norm in the Congress government's behaviour towards recalcitrant state governments under the control of opposition parties – particularly under the later government of Mrs Gandhi, who carried the arbitrary use of presidential authority (wielded by her nominees) to its furthest limits.

Foreign policy

By contrast with is domestic policy, far greater success and international plaudits were achieved by the Nehru government in matters of foreign policy, for which, as with the Planning Commission and the party presidency, responsibility fell directly on Nehru. Whilst Pakistan aligned itself with the United States, Nehru determined instead upon a policy of non-alignment with both east and west. His approach was partly due to the fact that despite being on friendly terms with the United States, India shared a border with China and was on Russia's doorstep. Nehru felt that the risk of joining the American camp in the cold war era was simply too great. This view was confirmed after Nehru's visit to the United States in 1949 when, beyond sending a few army medical units, he refused a request from the Americans for support for their intervention in Korea. The American president, Harry Truman, was reportedly furious, but Nehru's decision was founded upon a very realistic assessment – not only of India's strategic position but also of the country's future development.

To sum up, the Congress Party was clearly a bourgeois party, India's economy capitalistic, and the government's development strategy was highly centralised, involving considerable regulation, and the creation of a very large public sector. Indian banks and industry were inward looking and were encouraged by a protectionist system that excluded foreign competition. India had no great need for international trade at this time, and given the weakness of its currency was not in any case in a position to trade with the United States. More importantly still, the Congress Party's main backers, the wealthy Tata, Birla and Dalmia industrial families, did not want to have to deal with either American or British competition. India's foreign policy was thus in many ways a reflection of its domestic policy. But as an initiative in international affairs it was strikingly original, and attracted immediate support both from President Nasser in Egypt, who was trying to escape from the grip of British imperialism, and from President Tito in Yugoslavia, who was attempting to resist pressures from the neighbouring Soviet Union, and from President Sukarno of Indonesia, who had just gained independence from Dutch imperialism. After a visit to Cairo in 1954, the Indonesian city of Bandung was chosen as the first meeting place of the three leaders the following year, joined by representatives from China and Vietnam. Following the principles agreed at that conference, the non-aligned movement was officially created, with an initial membership of 25 countries, at a summit in Belgrade in 1961 (Shukul 1994). The movement now has some 113 member countries (IINS 1997).

Chinese participation in the non-aligned movement followed a visit by the Chinese premier Chou En-lai to New Delhi in June 1954 and a return visit by Nehru to Peking in October 1954. When Chou En-lai visited he was greeted with cries of 'chini-hindi bhai bhai' ('Chinese and Indians are brothers'), but Chou En-lai later recalled that Nehru was one of the most arrogant men he had ever met – a bad omen for the future. At the time there was no sign of animosity between the two and a Sino-Indian peaceful co-existence pact, known as 'Panch-sheel' (five principles of peaceful co-existence), which recognised China's occupation of Tibet, was readily agreed upon between the two nations. On his visit to Peking, Nehru himself had raised the issue of the Sino-Indian border with Chou En-lai, expressing surprise that certain parts of Indian territory were marked as Chinese on Chinese maps. These fears were dismissed by Chou, with the comment that the maps were pre-Revolutionary and had not been updated.

The relationship between India and China quickly soured as a result of growing pressure from the two superpowers: the USA and Soviet Union. Following the Bandung conference, the USA became more suspicious of India and began to back SEATO (the Southeast Asia Treaty Organisation), which was a defensive alliance of the Philippines, Thailand, Pakistan, Britain, France, New Zealand and Australia. Ignoring this, Nehru visited the USSR in 1955, and in 1956 backed Egypt against Britain during the crisis over the Suez canal. Mindful of its alliance with the West, Pakistan on this occasion backed the British. Nehru was later to back Algeria in its liberation struggle against France. His anti-Western stance attracted considerable attention, and courted a probable intervention in Indian affairs by the CIA.

India's problems with China were to be aggravated by the growing distrust between the Chinese and the Soviet Union. Although the West tried to use the Chinese take-over of Tibet as a pretext to attempt to weaken Mao Tse-tung's regime, it was the ideological and border disputes with the Soviet Union that made China nervous about its frontiers; and it was, it is believed, largely to threaten Russia with a display of Chinese military power that an invasion of northern India was launched in 1962 (Maxwell 1970). The disputed area was a totally uninhabited and uninhabitable part of the northern, eastern territory of Ladakh, which had been the subject of negotiations between the Chinese and Indians since 1959. Perhaps believing that the Chinese would never invade, Nehru allowed the dispute to become increasingly vituperative. He was also influenced by inaccurate advice from his defence minister, Krishna Menon, who informed him that the Chinese were in no position and would not dare launch an attack, since the Indian army was in a full state of readiness and preparation. This was, perhaps, one of Nehru's biggest mistakes since, after a few minor border skirmishes, China suddenly embarked, without warning, on an all-out attack in October 1962, completely overrunning nearly all of the North-East Frontier Agency and Ladakh, forcing the Indian army into a chaotic retreat.

After a few weeks of fighting, the Chinese called for a ceasefire and withdrew – virtually to their pre-war position. The exercise was thus probably a simple display of force. Chou En-lai seemed to confirm this when shortly after he told a group of visiting Pakistani army officers that he had never intended to invade India: '[I]f we had really wanted to conquer India', he is reported to have said, ' all we would need to do is march half our population to the top of the Himalayas, and with their backs turned to their own country, they would all piss at the same time. The result would be floods in India for at least a year.'[12]

Conclusion

The war with China was perhaps the greatest disappointment of Nehru's career. His greatest successes were largely confined to the area of industrial development, in which India had made notable advances by the middle of the 1960s. In the period 1961 to 1966 a large chunk of foreign aid input into the third Five-year Plan helped to catapult India into the position of the world's seventh most industrial nation. This foreign aid was obtained partly because of Nehru's policy of non-alignment, which enabled India to survive the cold war without seriously alienating either the Soviet Union or the USA. In the 1960s, India was thus able to draw upon both East and West for help in its programme of industrial development.

If not always successful in practice, Nehru nonetheless remained until the end of his career a master of political rhetoric – and this alone was sufficient to enable the Congress Party to win majorities in subsequent general elections, retaining control not only at the centre but in the majority of provincial elections as well. The Congress defeat in Kerala was perhaps the first sign of the rot that was beginning to beset the party. It also made the CPI, for the first time, a national political force, increasing its strength in the national parliament from 16 to 29 members, and with just under 10 per cent of the total number of votes cast. The electoral defeat of the Congress also gave a great fillip to regional and workers' and peasants' movements elsewhere in India, encouraged by the 1956 states reorganisation.

As Nehru's period in office came to an end, all seemed to augur well for the future of the Congress Party. Apart from the country's ignominious defeat at the hands of the Chinese, India had managed effectively to overawe Pakistan in 1949, and the country's foreign policy in general seemed to be going well. The Congress Party as a whole retained some semblance of unity, and none of the later discord was at this stage apparent. India's economic strategy, particularly her import-substituting industrial policy, seemed in general to be a success. However, the party's experience in Kerala, the food shortages of the early 1950s, and the collapse of the Indian army in 1962, all indicated that there were unsolved problems remaining to be dealt with by the administration – one which, at the same time, was rapidly using up the unqualified popular support Congress possessed post-independence. There were also significant tensions developing within the party at the time of Nehru's death in May 1964, which were soon to become only too apparent.

13 Indira Gandhi

Progress, poverty and authoritarian rule

'You cannot sweep clean without making the new broom dirty.'
'I see,' said Maneck. The bizarre aphorisms were starting to grate on him.
[. . .]

'All we wanted was a ration card, Mr. Facilitator. And the fellow wanted our manhood in exchange! What kind of choice is that, between food and manhood?'
    'Ah, he wanted the F.P.C. . . . You see, since the Emergency started, there's a new rule in the department – every office has to encourage people to get sterilized. If he doesn't fill his quota, no promotion for him. What to do, poor fellow, he is also trapped, no?'
    'But it's not fair to us!'
    'That's why I am here, no? Just pick the names you want on the ration, up to a maximum of six, and whatever address you like. Cost is only two hundred rupees . . .'
    'But we don't have so much money.'
    The Facilitator said they could come back when they did, he would still be here. 'While there is government, there will be work for me.'

(Rohinton Mistry, *A Fine Balance*)[1]

The major event in Indian politics in the decade and a half following Nehru's death was the emergency from 1975 to 1977 when the democratic constitution was suspended and India became, briefly, a dictatorship under Mrs Gandhi. How did this come about? At first sight, India's constitution seemed to be flourishing, but the writing was on the wall from the manner of Nehru's succession. The obvious candidate to succeed Nehru at his death was Morarji Desai, a revered older congressman, who had worked with Gandhi, helping to lead the non-co-operation *satyagraha* in 1922 and widely regarded as the most distinguished Gandhian within Congress. However, Desai did not acquire the premiership because his candidacy was blocked by Kamraj Nadar, a close friend of Nehru's, chairman of the Tamil Nadu Congress and president of the party. Kamraj had been accustomed to running Nehru's kitchen cabinet and had considerable influence over Congress policy. Upon Nehru's death, Kamraj manoeuvred to provide himself and various other influential Congress chief ministers with the final say as to the next premier. Kamraj thought that their interests would be best served by the election of a manipulable individual. The man who was actually appointed to succeed was Lal Bahadur Shastri, a mild-mannered, hitherto undistinguished, member of Congress. The choice of Shastri was subsequently approved by the party's Central Working Committee, and then presented as a *fait accompli* and duly ratified by the parliamentary party. Shastri's election set the pattern for the creation of subsequent leaders. India's constitution provided for elected representatives of the majority party in the Lok Sabha to elect the post of premier, which was how Nehru had acquired the position. This should have occurred again in 1964, but Kamraj and his cohorts decided that Shastri was the only viable candidate and no election was held. This was the manner in which all subsequent accessions to the premiership took place. Party politics was already beginning to undermine the democratic conventions of India's constitution.

Immediately following Shastri's appointment as the Indian prime minister, Pakistan seized the opportunity to declare war, seeing in the accession of a weak-willed leader a chance for military advantage. Under Ayub Khan, Pakistan had become a close ally of the United States, and had acquired considerable arms and ammunitions. His army and air force, newly armed with American weapons, were eager to try them out. Accordingly Pakistan launched an invasion of Kutch.[2] Fighting continued for several months, extending also to Kashmir. In response, India launched strikes across the border into the interior of Pakistan. Fortunately a US embargo on arms supplies to both countries prevented a continuation of hostilities. The Soviet premier, Kosygin, called Shastri and Ayub Khan to a meeting at Tashkent where an agreement for normalisation of relations was signed. Immediately afterwards, Shastri died at Tashkent of a heart attack (some say he was poisoned). This threw India into political chaos. Within 18 months of Nehru's death they had to find a second successor. A dispute broke out between the right-wing group around Morarji Desai and the young Indira Priyadarshini Gandhi, who was supported by the left. Mrs Gandhi had been considered briefly in 1964 as a possible successor to her father – she had after all become very influential in politics after the death of her husband Feroze in 1960, and she had served as Congress Party president during the closing years of Nehru's rule. However, she was rejected as too young. Two years later, Indira Gandhi was the only candidate around whom Kamraj's faction could rally. They thought she would be preferable to Desai, being considered the candidate who was more likely to be tractable (Brecher 1966).

Following Indira Gandhi's accession to the premiership, Kamraj briefly enjoyed considerable influence over the government of India. In 1966 growing food shortages plagued the country. Nehru's policies of promoting industrial development had left few funds available for agricultural innovation or reform to feed India's burgeoning population, which by the mid-1960s had grown to some 475 million. Food grain reserves were low and it only required one bad harvest to bring the rural economy to a state of crisis. This is exactly what happened in 1966. The previous year's harvest had totalled 88 million tons; in 1966 it was

76 million tons. This may seem an insignificant difference, but it is important to remember that famines in the Third World are rarely caused by an absolute shortage of grain: instead food shortages lead to price rises and a rise in unemployment among landless labourers as farmers cut back their workforce. It is the lack of purchasing power amongst the poor that causes starvation. In a free market system the only way to cope with this is to import and distribute large quantities of food grain as quickly as possible, both to feed the starving and in order to depress prices to levels that the poor can afford. Much of the machinery for this system of government purchasing and distribution was put in place by the British during the Second World War, but this time it was vastly extended, with private sales of grain even being banned by law for a time in 1966/7 (as it was again in 1973). In 1966 substantial amounts of international food relief were made available to India, mostly from the United States where Public Law 480 provided for Midwestern farmers to supply stocks of grain for Third World countries. India was able to overcome the crisis, but it signalled that something was seriously wrong with the way the country's economy was developing and forced the government into a rapid and dramatic rethinking of its development policies.

Partly because of the food grain shortages, India was forced to borrow money from the World Bank, which therefore acquired a voice in Indian economic policy. The American Ford Foundation also offered its services as an adviser on food policy and published an influential report condemning India's industrialisation strategy, insisting that India had to face up to the fact that it was a poor country, and that it should rethink its agricultural policy. Social economists like Daniel Thorner suggested that this smacked of a conspiracy by Western multinational capitalism to perpetuate India's backwardness, and there was considerable opposition to any change in economic policy. There was no doubt, however, that some change was necessary, and from the point of view of ordinary Indians the provision of affordable food grain was more important, at least in the short term, than the ideological purity of the means chosen to provide it. The effect of the innovations introduced by Indira Gandhi's government from 1967 onwards subsequently became known as the 'Green Revolution' (Frankel 1971; Byres and Crow 1983; Bayliss-Smith and Wanmali 1984). In essence the new policy involved a switch in priorities from investment in heavy industry to investment in agriculture. Under the new policy the government distributed free fertiliser and insecticides, and new, high-yielding varieties of food grain to peasant farmers. More was spent on irrigation; sugar and food grains were purchased by government and redistributed at a subsidised rate in order to promote growth in the agricultural economy whilst ensuring good prices for consumers. The problem was the choice of grain. The high-yielding grain introduced was wheat and those able to take advantage of the new seed grains, and therefore those entitled to the government irrigation and fertiliser subsidies, were all rich peasant farmers in the wheat-growing areas. The Punjab and adjacent areas were therefore the main beneficiaries of this policy, and Punjab soon became the principal wheat supplier of the country. Rice farmers in the poorer states of eastern India were not really helped under the Green Revolution. Thus, although the spectre of food shortage was removed, this was achieved by assisting the more prosperous farmers, who suddenly became very much richer, thereby exacerbating inequality in Indian agriculture (Byres 1981; Glaeser 1987). These farmers went on to become a powerful political lobby, resisting the redistribution of agricultural resources or any extension in agricultural income tax that might reduce the government's fiscal debt. In this respect, it was something of a mixed blessing.

Despite its promise, the benefits of the Green Revolution were not experienced fully by producers and consumers until well into the 1970s. In the late 1960s there remained anxiety over the economy and resentment against American interference; strikes and food riots broke out in the major cities and a communal dispute arose between Sikhs and Hindi speakers in the Punjab. The widespread discontent produced a disastrous result for the Congress Party in the 1967 election, which saw a dramatic fall in its share of the vote to 40 per cent. However, because of the first-past-the-post system it was just able to cling onto power with a majority of seats in the Lok Sabha. In subsequent state elections, though, Congress lost out in a big way. In both Kerala and Bengal, a newly formed Communist Party, the CPI (Marxist), came to power, and in six other major states Congress lost power to opposition groups. There was much disquiet within the Congress, and Kamraj and others in the higher echelons of the party considered replacing Indira with Morarji Desai. As a first step, Desai was given the post of finance minister and was also made deputy prime minister. In order to fight back, Mrs Gandhi decided to adopt an increasingly leftist stance in her policy pronouncements. This was popular with the electorate and served to marginalise Desai and the old guard within Congress. At the Bangalore session of the Congress in July 1969 she presented economic policies comprising land reforms, restriction of monopolies, nationalisation of banks and other radical measures, despite the personal opposition of Desai, which the party was forced to go along with. Desai was then sacked. Indira next attempted to undermine the control of the Kamraj syndicate by putting forward her own candidate for the presidential elections of 1969. The head of state is elected every five years. In 1969 the official Congress Party candidate was Sanjiva Reddy, but Indira put forward her own nominee, V.V. Giri. The latter won following a free vote in parliament, causing consternation in the party. Soon after, Mrs Gandhi was expelled from the Congress Party by the old guard at a meeting of the Central Working Committee. However, a 'requisition meeting' of 207 out of 269 Congress MPs backed Mrs Gandhi and formed a new party, called the Congress (R), later to become the Congress (I) following a post-emergency split.

The split of the Congress Party in 1969 might be viewed as an achievement for Mrs Gandhi, the rump Congress (O) Party of 65 MPs soon fading into obscurity. The defeat of the old guard also brought about a distinct leftward shift of the party. However, it marked the end of internal Congress Party democracy. The subsequent serious decline of Indian democracy, it has been argued, dates from these events. Because Congress was the single largest party in India, this centralisation of authority and control by Mrs Gandhi had grave implications for the political system of the country as a whole. She herself, furthermore, became almost paranoid in her management of the government, refusing to allow anyone to occupy a position of responsibility who might be deemed a future threat. As time passed she was obliged to surround herself with yes-men and incompetents, which increasingly began to tell on the fortunes of the party. At the time, however, Mrs Gandhi's triumph over the old guard was popular. Her loss of the rump transformed Congress into a minority party, but she continued to rule with the support of the Communists, the DMK and the Akali Dal. In order to maintain the support of the left wing she radicalised her policies, proposing renewed land reform ceilings on personal income and profit, and the nationalisation of all banks. She fought India's fifth general election in 1971 under the slogan '*garibi hatao*' (eliminate poverty). This resulted in the restoration of a handsome Congress (I) majority in the Lok Sabha, where they won 342 seats out of 518, as well as in a majority of Vidhan Sabha or state assemblies.

By the early 1970s Mrs Gandhi had begun to reap the rewards of the Green Revolution: although population growth was continuing, food grain production reached 100 million tons by 1968/9. War strengthened her position as well, contributing to her success at the polls. The causes of the 1971 conflict with Pakistan were complex. In 1970 a cyclone caused severe flooding in east Pakistan. Elections followed, with the Awami League accusing west Pakistan of ignoring the plight of the eastern half of the country. When the Awami League won a majority, the president refused to acknowledge the result and a general uprising in the east ensued (events are described in more detail in Chapter 11). In an attempt to suppress this, the Pakistani army embarked on a wholesale campaign of suppression and slaughter of Bengali civilians supportive of the nationalist Awami League. By the end of summer 1971 as many as 300,000 civilians in east Pakistan were thought to have lost their lives as a result of military action. The result was an exodus of some 8 million refugees into India, swelling the tide of those already displaced by floods. India was obliged to spend huge sums of money to feed and house these refugees, and a motion in the Indian parliament was passed urging the government to offer assistance to the east Pakistani rebels.

At the same time as the civil war erupted in Pakistan, so-called 'Naxalites' – a movement of ultra-leftists, which began in 1969 in the Naxalbari region of Darjeeling district – threatened armed revolt in the Communist-run state of west Bengal (Ray 1988; Franda 1971). The uprising, led by the newly formed militant CPI (Marxist-Leninist), threatened the position of the ruling CPI (M) and led to open warfare between supporters of the two parties throughout Bengal, including on the streets of Calcutta itself (Mitra 1997). Mrs Gandhi took advantage of this situation to declare a state of emergency, and introduced martial rule in the whole border area, including the entire state of west Bengal. She then armed Bangladeshi refugees, under cover of emergency regulations, creating a *mukti bahini* (liberation force) who were sent across the border to help liberate east Bengal from Pakistani rule. America's closeness to Pakistan and the rapprochements of both America and Pakistan with China had caused India by this time to draw closer to the Soviet Union, signing an Indo-Soviet 'Treaty of Peace, Friendship and Cooperation' early in 1971. The USA therefore envisaged Indian activities as a strategic threat and the American Seventh Fleet was sent into the Bay of Bengal in a threatening gesture in an effort to deter them. Soon after, Pakistan declared war on India, launching pre-emptive strikes on Indian airfields on 3 December and causing the Indian army to join directly in the fighting. The USA put a motion to the Security Council (vetoed by the USSR) and then successfully to the General Assembly, demanding a ceasefire and a withdrawal of all troops. The Pakistani army attacked in the west in an attempt to distract the Indian army, but after 12 days of fighting the 93,000 Pakistani army in the east surrendered to a combined force of Indian soldiers and *mukti bahini* on 16 December. Before the UN Security Council could reconvene to discuss the matter further, east Pakistan had become the newly independent state of Bangladesh.

In the light of the events of 1971 Indira Gandhi came to be seen as a forceful ruler, having both curbed Naxalite excesses and defeated Pakistani forces in the east and west. In 1972, the results of the state elections confirmed the resulting surge in her popularity. Two years later in May 1974, India conducted its first test explosion of an atomic bomb (code-named 'Smiling Buddha') in the desert of Rajasthan. The country's status as a dominant regional power was assured (Damodaran and Bajpai 1990). Soon after, however, the popularity of the Indian government dramatically declined, and the sweet taste of victory turned sour. The cause was the world economic crisis of 1973, triggered by the decision of the Organisation of Petroleum-Exporting Countries (OPEC) to restrict the supply and quadruple the price of oil. Petrol rationing was introduced in most European countries and the United States. Western countries would learn to live with higher oil prices, but the consequences for the Third World were far more severe. India, as a heavy importer of oil for transport and for cooking, suffered dramatically. Household budgets rose as the price of kerosene quadrupled. Thousands, almost overnight, were forced below the poverty line. The proportion of the Indian population eking out a living on the equivalent of 10 pence a day jumped to 40 per cent. Although the class of rich peasants continued to prosper from selling their food grains to the government, the poor found their living standards back to the levels of the 1950s.

Another important factor that began to eat away at Indian public life was increasing corruption within the body politic. Indira Gandhi's leftist strategy after 1971 meant that big business and landowners began to suffer from corporation and profit taxes. A huge increase in the black economy resulted, a covert level of transactions that by the late 1980s was believed to account for a third of all economic activity. It became increasingly profitable to bribe tax-collection officials to turn a blind eye. Big business ceased to contribute to the Congress and began to fund opposition parties instead. Congress itself increasingly had to resort to covert and corrupt means of raising electioneering funds. In this way corruption became like a cancer, affecting all parts of Indian government and society. From 1971 top-slicing of government contracts, to benefit the ruling party, became the norm, and *baksheesh* a national institution. Few were surprised when Sanjay Gandhi, Indira's son, was made managing director of a new government-sponsored car production unit, and that five years after its establishment, at a cost of millions of rupees, the Maruti Udyog plant had still not produced a single vehicle. Although now a successful and expanding enterprise, it is widely believed to have been at the time nothing but a front for the raising of party funds. As corruption spread to the judicial system, police force and petty officials, it began to impact upon the lives of ordinary people, making a mockery of India's supposed socialist path to progress. As a result, within a few years of Mrs Gandhi's election victories she found herself in serious difficulty.

The increasing ossification of the bureaucratic planning and licensing regime, coupled with tax rises and the weight placed on the system by the measures enshrined in the Green Revolution, had, by the early 1970s, produced an archaic and underfunded government service, the inefficiency of which was underscored by the appointment of growing numbers of ill-qualified junior officials as a sop to win electoral advantage. The global oil crisis of 1973, which resulted from price hikes inspired by the Organisation of Petroleum Exporting Countries (OPEC), dealt a further crushing blow to the Indian economy. Discontent with Congress, coupled with increased funding flowing into opposition parties from businessmen estranged by its left-wing policies, led to a number of virulent protest movements. The most important of these was the 'JP' movement, named after its leader the popular socialist politician and hero of the Quit India movement, Jayaprakash Narayan. He had a strong following in Bihar, which had lost out during the Green Revolution. In the western state of Gujarat, Morarji Desai also began to recruit supporters from amongst the more prosperous peasants and business elites and became chief minister of the state. Many former Congressmen joined opposition ranks. A number of right-wing movements also flourished, among them Anand Marg, the Rashtriya Loktartrick Dal (National People's Party), and the Swatantra: parties that eventually came together to form the Janata Morcha (People's Front), under the leadership of Morarji Desai and J.P. Narayan. There was a certain circularity in this process as the more the opposition flourished, the greater the likelihood that Congress would resort to corrupt practices to maintain its funding, and the more corruption there was, the greater the gains of the opposition.

Indira Gandhi had suffered quite an extraordinary reversal of fortune by 1974. Her authority was challenged by a national railway strike, to which she reacted aggressively by calling in the army. An unsuccessful assassination attempt against A.N. Ray, the chief justice, took place. The minister of railways, L.N. Mishra, was also blown up in a train carriage and killed (although rumours persisted that both attacks were initiated within the prime minister's office). In the same year Mrs Gandhi was prosecuted and convicted in the Allahabad High Court on two of 52 charges of fraud relating to her election to the north Indian seat of Rae Bareli in 1971. She should have resigned, and an opposition rally was organised in Delhi in June in which calls were made for her to stand down. J.P. Narayan addressed the crowd, calling for a nationwide campaign of *satyagraha*, including the army and police, if she refused to go.

Mrs Gandhi knew that short-term attempts to alleviate inflation were impracticable and regarded the opposition to her as illegitimate. Rather than resign, she persuaded the president, Fakhruddin Ali Ahmed, to institute a state of emergency, including the suspension of civil rights, the curbing of the press and a curfew in all major cities. The pretext was the growing chaos caused by worsening economic conditions, and the threat to law and order posed by the opposition's call for a *satyagraha* against the government. She also suggested that some opposition parties were being funded by the CIA. In the short term her motivation seems simply to have been to hold onto power. Even before the emergency was declared, she ordered the arrest of opposition politicians, soon followed by that of so-called subversive students, lecturers, lawyers and journalists. By August 1975 there were believed to be some 10,000 to 50,000 in jail without trial. Opposition parties were banned, and to legitimate her actions Mrs Gandhi announced a 20-point programme to bring down prices; to abolish rural debt, tax evasion, smuggling and bonded labour; and (in the hope of winning back student support) to provide subsidies for books, stationery and canteen food in India's universities. All strike activity was banned, which appealed to many businessmen, and to top it all Mrs Gandhi announced a meeting of the Lok Sabha attended by those MPs not in jail, at which a vote of support for the emergency was proposed and voted in her favour. A new amendment to the constitution was also passed exonerating Mrs Gandhi from all legal charges pending against her and which might be brought against her while she remained prime minister. Were this not bizarre enough, the 26th amendment also declared itself to be unamendable. In Bangladesh, Mujibur Rahman had suspended future elections and made himself president for life, whilst Pakistan had long given up any pretensions to democracy. Across South Asia therefore, it seemed as if communal and political tensions, accompanied by economic distress, had made democratic government untenable.

A month after Mrs Gandhi's declaration of emergency, Mujibur Rahman was shot dead in an army coup in Bangladesh, which may have perhaps led Mrs Gandhi to doubt the wisdom of her actions. It has been suggested that she was leaned on by the army to restore democracy, or alternatively that she had actually begun to believe her own propaganda and to imagine that she could still command the popular vote once the emergency was ended. Whatever the reasons, in January 1977 she suddenly announced elections for the coming March. This short notice gave opposition parties, whose leaders had just been released from prison, very little time to organise. Presumably she thought this would guarantee the Congress a victory; but she did not count on Jagjivan Ram, an avuncular leader of the *dalit* community from Bihar, who had played a part in Gandhi's *harijan* movement of the 1930s, became president of the All-India Depressed Classes League (formed in 1935), and took part in the Quit India uprising in Bihar. He was the only former 'untouchable' in Mrs Gandhi's cabinet. As soon as elections were announced, he resigned and joined the opposition. But this was only one of the more notable cases amongst a mass desertion of Congress supporters that ensued at all levels. The result was a crushing defeat of Mrs Gandhi's government by the Janata Party, which won 295 out of 542 seats. The Congress won just 154 seats.

Leniency about corruption in the police and civil service is not so commonly extended to politicians in India. When prime ministers are found to be guilty of misdemeanours, the population is generally outraged. This may be a legacy of Mahatma Gandhi's time in Indian politics: the belief that the leader should be of saintly virtue. By that measure, Mrs Gandhi was found to be clearly deficient. Her resounding defeat by the opposition alliance is one of the most significant election reversals of modern Indian history. Other explanations for her fall take account of the considerable abuses of power during the emergency period, strikingly demonstrated in Sanjay Gandhi's massive and illegal programme of slum clearance, undertaken to beautify Delhi and which resulted in thousands being made homeless (Selbourne 1977; Nayar 1977; Dhar 2000; Tarlo 2001). A further crucial factor was the government's programme of compulsory sterilisation. This scheme was again put into the hands of Sanjay Gandhi who recruited members of the Youth Congress to impose the policy. Initially, sterilisations were offered in exchange for money, but as quotas were raised less savoury tactics were used. Eventually, pressure was even brought to bear on police officers, teachers and other government officials to participate in the programme. As a result of the resentment generated, public discussion and advocacy of population control by the government became impossible for several years; and subsequently there has been an unhealthy enthusiasm for the sterilisation of women as a means of birth control (Jeffery and Jeffery 2006). This is perhaps one of the sadder legacies of Mrs Gandhi's years of authoritarian rule.

The Janata government that succeeded Mrs Gandhi's Congress in 1977 proved to be no better, being both incompetent and riven by factionalism. The parties of the ruling coalition were thus unable to co-operate in the business of running the country. The new prime minister, the octogenarian Morarji Desai, proved to be a supine and spineless politician. He was soon saddled with the sobriquet 'Peanuts' Desai because of his habit of subsisting on a diet of nuts and a pint of his own urine. Within a few months he was faced with the defection of a succession of cabinet ministers: first Charan Singh, then George Fernandez and finally Raj Narayan, all key members of the government. In an attempt to meet extravagant election promises, within two years the Janata coalition had used up all food grain and foreign currency reserves. With the relaxation of regulations, there was an upsurge in smuggling and tax evasion. Retail prices once again began to rise, and the government was seen to be mismanaging the Indian economy.

After a few unsuccessful attempts to imprison Mrs Gandhi on corruption charges, she was re-elected to the Lok Sabha in a by-election. A few months later, Morarji Desai resigned. He was succeeded briefly by Charan Singh, who, unable to form a government, was also forced to resign (Byres 1988). New elections were held in 1980. To no one's surprise, after two years of misrule, Mrs Gandhi was returned to power at the head of a newly formed Congress (I) with a huge majority.[3] Despite this electoral success, the style of her subsequent government was significantly marked by her period of exile, and she continued to be influenced by the events of 1969 when the Congress Party had tried to marginalise her. She was also severely shaken by the death of her youngest son, and chosen successor, Sanjay, who crashed his private plane whilst performing acrobatics over the capital, in breach of all air traffic regulations, in the summer of 1980. The

Figure 21 Indira Gandhi addressing a rally at the Boat Club in New Delhi, August 1978. © *The Hindu.*

rumour that this was no accident continued to circulate around New Delhi for several years after. Unsurprisingly, Mrs Gandhi remained somewhat paranoid, but she became also increasingly cautious, preferring to divide and rule in secret rather than in public. She began to pander far less to the minorities as she felt they had betrayed her in 1977, and to court conservative Hindu opinion in the hope of restoring her popularity in the traditional Congress strongholds in the north. From this date onwards she also began to depend upon the support of her other son, Rajiv, a pilot with Indian airlines, who reluctantly entered politics (of which he had no experience), against the wishes of his Italian wife Sonia, whom he had met whilst studying for two years at Cambridge University. He was given the responsibility of managing preparations for the Asian Games in New Delhi in 1982 in order to boost his public profile. Soon after, he was elected to parliament in his brother's former seat at Amethi and in 1983 was appointed general secretary of the Congress Party.

Publicly, India seemed restored to a new state of prosperity and unity. Mrs Gandhi's hard work and ruthless management of government rapidly lifted the country's finances and economy, and by 1983 India had achieved an industrial growth rate in excess of 7 per cent. The country's first communications satellites were launched, providing nationwide colour television for the first time (albeit government run). As prosperity returned to India, however, the government continued to ignore problems of inequality. It became increasingly apparent that despite the politicians' socialist rhetoric, the country was moving in a markedly capitalist direction. Regional, communal and secessionist movements were aroused by the politics of envy that growing inequalities inevitably engendered. The central government's response to these regionalist threats was crucial. Whereas

Nehru had been willing to negotiate and compromise with regional politicians, Mrs Gandhi's paranoia precluded this. She acted quickly to remove successful local politicians from the seat of their power by a policy of judicious promotions to honorific posts. Since 1980 the lack of internal democracy in Congress had meant that local politicians could not promote issues within the party, and Mrs Gandhi had little time for opposition representatives. Not surprisingly, dissent often took a militant turn. There were separatist stirrings in the south of India, and a sons-of-the-soil movement erupted into violence in Assam after 1983 when the centre attempted to hold assembly elections, practically by force, and to install a Congress (I) government. However, the most serious problem arose in the Punjab. Mrs Gandhi had herself played a large part in the growth of Sikh discontent, firstly because she refused in any way to negotiate with moderates, and because she had turned a blind eye to support being funnelled to one of its militant wings, led by Sant Bhindranwale during the 1975 to 1977 period, as part of an attempt to subvert the Sikh Akali Dal, then part of the Janata national coalition as well as in control of the state government. After her return to power, Bhindranwale's faction grew in strength, eventually turning to terrorism. It was this group, and her military actions against them within the precincts of the Golden Temple of the Sikhs in Amritsar, that eventually led to her assassination by two of her personal bodyguards in October 1984.

14 Local patriotism and centre–state relations

The ones who wave the red flag and make peasant movement have also said not a word about the minimum wage. Though they're Comni they are true Indians, and they know that if you give minimum wage the big farmers will be enraged. And you cannot do a peasant movement if you anger the rich farmers . . . Hey, why do you think no one does anything for the untouchables and the adivasi? Because they love 'em. And even so . . . in Bihar, Andhra and Uttar Pradesh the harijan is tortured. I love the outcastes and tribals of Bihar more than my life. But I am a realist . . . Trying to implement the law at this time, shall I throw the untouchables and adivasis of my Bihar into the tiger's jaws? How can that be?

(Mahasweta Devi, *Chotti Munda and His Arrow*)[1]

The Indian State has become a cauldron of bickerings, thanks to coalitions, where nobody has any control over anybody. It is time to take on the Indian State and liberate Tamil Nadu.

('Pulavar' Kaliyaperumal, August 2000)[2]

Whenever Tamils put forward the demand for self-determination, it is suppressed under the guise of Indian nationalism.

(Veerappan, south Indian *dacoit* (bandit), 18 November 2000)[3]

The dilemmas of Indian federalism

Ethnic, communal, and regional conflicts assumed increasing frequency and importance in the last two decades of the twentieth century, nearly all of them expressing a profound degree of alienation and subaltern discontent. The phenomenon became sufficiently pronounced for people to talk of a 'crisis of Indian democracy' and of India's 'ungovernability' (Kohli 1990). In truth, the seeds of many of these conflicts had been sown from the very inception of the nation. To begin with, there is the first-past-the-post electoral system, which means that despite India's considerable size and diversity a majority in parliament could only be achieved by a single large party alone or in an unequal combination with one or two others. Multi-party coalition governments were, until the end of the twentieth century, a rarity and invariably short-lived. Between 1951 and 1991 the ruling party never enjoyed the support of more than 48 per cent of the popular vote and in five elections (1952, 1961, 1971, 1977, 1980) won 45 per cent or less. In 1967, the Congress even won a majority with a mere 40.8 per cent of the popular vote (Brass 1994: 76). Since at least 40 per cent of those eligible did not vote, this is less than one-third of the total electorate voting in favour of the majority party. This would not have mattered so much had power at the centre been limited, and the ruling party possessed of an effective system of internal democracy – as in some post-colonial one-party states such as Tanzania. Unfortunately, although matters of health, education and rural development were delegated to the state governments, the centre in the Indian constitution held unusual powers, modelled upon its colonial predecessors, in matters of internal security and economic management. It also, importantly, had the power to suspend state governments – a power increasingly to be abused – and to intervene directly in matters of law and order (as in the French system) by use of a central reserve police force. Ironically, in other matters where more central power might have been desirable, such as the ability to redistribute resources from richer to poorer states, or to modify land rights, central control was singularly weak (Sathyamurthy 1985; Mukarji and Balveer 1992).

A consequence of the electoral system was that it was very easy for a party that was unrepresentative of the country as a whole to assume control in New Delhi, for it to abuse that position, and to remain deaf to protests and complaints, even from its own supporters. Such was the case after the ending of Congress Party internal democracy in 1969, and still more pronouncedly after Mrs Gandhi's return to power in 1980. A further problem was the untrammelled growth of inequality, both between regions and within communities (Bardhan 1998; Desai 1975). India was well and truly on the path towards an American-style capitalist system of development even by the mid-1970s. L.K. Jha, once economic adviser to Indira Gandhi, favourably compared inequality and growth in India to that in the USA, concluding that India was on 'the right path'. This sat very awkwardly with the socialist rhetoric of successive governments and the rampant poverty all too apparent in many rural areas, most particularly in states such as Bihar where agrarian relations remained barely changed since the days of *zamindari* control (Bardhan and Srinivasan 1988). At the same time, the government's licence-permit British *raj* made it extremely difficult for new entrepreneurs to establish themselves whilst old monopolies flourished. The inevitable consequences of the resulting poverty trap in many rural areas were population growth (as family labour was one of the few assets that could easily be acquired) and migration.

The destinations for migrants were those states, such as the Punjab, that had flourished under the Green Revolution, and by the late 1970s some 275,000 Bihari labourers were migrating a distance of 1,800 kilometres each year to the Punjab to harvest the produce of rich capitalist farmers: a figure that must have increased several times since.[4] Tamil Nadu, Gujarat, and Maharashtra also flourished under the Green Revolution. The development of canal irrigation in former drought zones in the late colonial period, and after, combined with the limited scale of land reform and protectionist measures to encourage the rise of a powerful class of rich peasant farmers cultivating cash crops such as sugar-cane, ground nuts and cotton, who made use of their political clout wherever possible to ensure continuing favourable treatment from the government (Rudolph and Rudolph 1984; Brass 1994; Bardhan 1998; Vanaik 1990; Byres and Crow 1983). This class formed the backbone of support for the Congress Party in Maharashtra.

Elsewhere in the Punjab, western UP and Haryana, the state immediately adjoining New Delhi, the Congress enjoyed similar support until the government began to cut the costly levels of subsidy given to rich farmers, at which point they shifted their support to non-Congress opposition groups who were promising debt relief and a more traditional policy of *swadeshi*, or support for home producers.

As the heavy industries protected by the state began to suffer increasing losses in the 1980s, some had to be closed down, losing support for Congress in many of the older northern cities (Rothermund 1996). Meanwhile, new technology industries began to flourish from the early 1980s onwards in Bombay and Bangalore, in Karnataka, and subsequently in New Delhi as planning regulations were liberalised. The recruits to these industries came mainly from the educated middle classes: the lucky recipients of one of the world's most advanced higher education systems, a system originally established to serve the needs of the colonial government. By the 1980s Indian universities were turning out as many engineers, doctors and scientists as the USA and USSR. Many went abroad in search of work – leading to the growth of a huge and prosperous community of NRIs (non-resident Indians) – or found employment within the new growth centres of the Indian economy, especially following the loosening of the government planning regime from the late 1980s onwards. None of this affected the mass of the rural poor, who migrated in millions to the major urban centres in an often futile search for work. For this class there was little hope of advancement, as levels of literacy and education at primary and secondary levels remained seriously underfunded (Sen 1985; Drèze and Sen 1995). For members of the most backward castes there were of course places reserved in government service, universities and technical colleges – but no system of grant aid or government scholarship, so only the better off amongst them were able to take advantage of such opportunities. This was social engineering on the cheap: it did not work, and merely generated resentment amongst higher caste students, who were refused appointments and places at university even though they were at least as well qualified (Galanter 1984; Weiner and Katzenstein 1981; Karlekar 1992).

Whilst old caste divisions had been much undermined by the end of the twentieth century, the majority of enterprises, both urban and rural, remained family-run affairs (Béteille 1991b). A completely free market in labour has been slow to develop, restricting access of the poor and underprivileged, whether they be low castes, Muslims, *adivasis*, or women. The resulting disaffection, in a climate of extreme inequality, was for some as much a matter of frustrated expectations as absolute penury, and India became a society divided between the politics of the affluent and the partial politicisation of the subaltern masses (Sathyamurthy 1996). At election times when these interests converged, corrupt or inefficient governments could be quickly thrown out. At other times the public was merely offered a choice between populist sops, and religious and nationalist sloganeering, none of which addressed their fundamental grievances (Vanaik 1997).

Regional parties and movements

It is arguable that Indian unity and the secular consensus in Indian politics of the 1950s and 1960s was nothing but a temporary aberration, achievable in part only because of the monopoly on political power enjoyed by the Westernised Indian elite. Since then there has been a return to the status quo ante, and the more fissiparous regional style of politics found in thoroughgoing federal states of the sort, some believe, that India should have been in the first place. It has indeed been strongly argued that central power should be curbed, and a separation effected between legislature and executive, as in the US; there were indeed proposals by A.R. Antulay, the Congress chief minister of Maharashtra, for an American-style presidency in the early 1980s – although the motive in this case was the desire to perpetuate Congress rule by enhancing the personal authority of Mrs Gandhi.

Ironically, the Congress Party itself first began to undermine the secular consensus that had served it so well in an attempt to win electoral advantage. Beginning in 1959 with the introduction of the president's rule in Kerala to placate the Muslim League, Christian religious organisations and even some Hindu caste groups, the resort to communalist tactics by Congress politicians became ever more frequent, particularly under Mrs Gandhi, as one by one opposition parties in the regions, more in touch with the electorate, threatened its hold on power. In Tamil Nadu (see Map 11, p. 315), E.V. Ramaswami Naicker was amongst the founders of the Dravida Kazhagam (DK) movement at Salem in 1944, whilst C.N. Annadurai formed the breakaway Dravida Munnetra Kazhagam (DMK) in 1949. Together they laid the foundation for constitutional regional movements in the 1950s with a pro-Dravidian, pro-Tamil stance, combined with an anti-Hindi campaign and the championing of backward caste issues (Washbrook 1989). Latterly, control of the Tamil Nadu government has alternated between two subsequent incarnations: the Marumalarchi Dravida Munnetra Kazhagam (MDMK), led by M. Karunanidhi, and the All-India Anna DMK (AIADMK), founded by film star M.G. Ramachandran, who was succeeded as leader following his death in 1988 by his Brahmin mistress Jayalalitha Jayaram. Despite the hypocrisy and factionalism of these parties, the Congress in Tamil Nadu has been completely marginalised and has preserved an influence in Tamil politics only by means of successive electoral alliances – won at the cost of generous central government subsidies, which have funded schemes such as a free school meals programme.

In Andhra Pradesh, the populist Telugu Desam Party, under the leadership of former film star N.T. Rama Rao (hero of *Shri Venkateshwara Mahatyam*, where he played the deity of the Tirupati temple), effectively supplanted the Congress in 1982 for the first time since independence. One of the party's successful tactics has been to promote son-of-the-soil programmes, such as Janambhoomi, which seeks to develop villages with a can-do, self-help philosophy. Latterly the party has been led by N. Chandrababu Naidu, a champion of high-tech industrial growth centred in the capital, Hyderabad. In Kerala, Congress rule was intermittently replaced by the CPI (M) led by E.M.S. Namboodiripad, while since 1977 west Bengal has been continuously under CPI (M) control, led chiefly by Jyoti Basu, and by Buddhadeb Bhattacharya since 2000. In Bengal, the CPI (M)'s support in rural areas has been cemented by a thoroughgoing and effective programme of land reform (operation Barga) and by rural education. The only effective competition came from the populist Trinamul Congress led by Mamata Bannerjee from the late 1990s, which managed to win control of the Kolkata Municipal Corporation in 2000 only to lose it again in 2005, along with half of the eight seats the party held in the state assembly the following year (Nossiter 1982, 1988; Harris 1993; Mallick 1992, 1994; Kohli 1987, 1989).

The Shiv Sena, or army of Shivaji (the seventeenth-century Maratha hero), a militant Hindu and Maratha nationalist party, was founded in Bombay in 1966 by Bal Thackeray, a self-confessed admirer of Adolf Hitler. In the 1980s the Shiv Sena's uncompromising stand on immigration and employment (jobs for 'sons of the soil' first) found favour with disenchanted lower middle-class Hindus in the poorer suburbs, and it assumed power in the city of Bombay in 1985, and in the entire state of Maharashtra in the mid-1990s, only to lose it again to the Congress in 2004 after a decade of bomb explosions, riots and communal confrontations (Katzenstein 1979; Gupta 1982; Hansen 1996, 1999, 2001; Purandare 1999). In Haryana, a peasant party, the Lok Dal, led by Devi Lal and latterly his son Om Prakash Chautala, assumed power in 1987 with the promise of a moratorium on all agricultural debts. Control of the populous state of Bihar passed, from the mid-1990s onwards, into the hands of the Rashtriya Janata Dal (RJD) led by the controversial yet highly skilful Laloo Prasad Yadav (Thakur 2000). Like the Samajwadi Party in UP of Mulayam Singh Yadav, the RJD is a low-caste political organisation that split away from the Janata Party after 1980 (Hasan 1998). In Karnataka, a state that had formerly prospered under the rule of one of India's most enlightened and forward-looking princely rulers, the Janata Party (a fraction of the Janata government that ruled India between 1977 and 1980) assumed control of the state from 1982 to 1989 under the leadership of Rama Krishna Hegde. The party then split, but since 1994 has been reincarnated as the Janata Dal Party under H.D. Deve Gowda. In Orissa, the Janata Dal, led by Biju Patnaik, took power from the Congress between 1989 and 1994. Patnaik's son, heading a new party called Biju Janatadal (controversially in alliance with the BJP), swept back into office in 1999. In the Punjab, the Congress was effectively supplanted by the Akali Dal, the Sikh political organisation founded at the beginning of the twentieth century to win back control of Sikh temples from the British. It has been the mainstream political party of the Sikhs ever since.

In Gujarat and Uttar Pradesh, and Madhya Pradesh too to a lesser extent, the Congress Party has been progressively supplanted since 1986. Uttar Pradesh is the most extreme example: in the general election of 1984 Congress won 83 out of 85 seats, with 50 per cent of the total vote; five years later the party won only 15 seats, with 32 per cent of the vote; and in 1991 the Congress vote slipped further to 18 per cent when it won only five seats. This was a serious setback for the Congress, because Uttar Pradesh, with its minority low-caste and Muslim 'vote banks', had traditionally been the backbone of the party's support. The parties benefiting included the Janata Dal and its offshoots, such as Mulayam Singh Yadav's Samajwadi Party, the former winning 54 seats and 36 per cent of the vote in 1989. More recently the Bharatiya Janata Party (BJP) has taken seats from Congress. In 1991 the BJP became the largest party for the first time with 51 seats and 33 per cent of the vote. Whereas the Janata Dal and the Samajwadi Party draw their major strength from the backward castes, the BJP has been strongest among the upper castes of the towns, although it has sought to make inroads into the low-caste vote by allying with the *dalit* Bahujan Samaj Party (BSP), a failed strategy after the BSP spectacularly swept to power with an overall majority under the leadership of Mayawati in the 2007 state elections.

The BJP is effectively the political arm of the Rashtriya Swayamsevak Sangh (RSS) or National Self-Service Society – a right-wing, all-male Hindu nationalist association founded in 1925 explicitly to work for the achievement of a Hindu Rashtra or nation. UP has India's largest Muslim population, and the BJP's success here is explicitly related to the rise in anti-Muslim feeling and communal conflicts in north Indian politics since the early 1990s. It is seen as a party of the Hindi-Hindu north and has failed to win a following in more southerly Indian states where there is stiff resistance from the Dravidian movement in Tamil Nadu and regional parties such as the CPI (M) in Kerala. It has, however, made inroads in some areas with significant Muslim populations where communal relations are strained, such as Hyderabad, Coimbatore and Bangalore cities. Previous incarnations of the BJP were the Hindu Mahasabha (outlawed following Mahatma Gandhi's assassination in 1948) and the Jan Sangh, which disbanded itself in 1977 to form the Janata Party (in combination with the Congress (O), Bharatiya Lok Dal and Socialist parties).

Militant and indigenous peoples movements

To a greater or lesser extent most of India's regional political parties have followed a constitutional path to political power, but others, frustrated by the first-past-the-post system, profound inequalities, exploitation, and severe environmental degradation, have adopted a more militant and even violent approach, with pockets of Naxalite guerrilla activity flourishing in remote, disaffected, often tribal parts of the country (Calman 1985; Duyker 1987; Singh 1985). Mrs Gandhi must take the blame to some extent for these developments, since her personalised and authoritarian style of rule, considering any threat to Congress hegemony as treasonable and secessionist, forced those with grievances into just such a stance. Some secessionist movements have, however, been deliberately encouraged by the parties in power in an effort to discredit and undermine regional opponents. For example, the separatist movement in Darjeeling in the early 1980s – the so-called

Gorkhaland agitation, led by Subhash Ghising – was taken very seriously by the Congress central government but speedily brought to an end by the CPI (M) in Bengal, who offered Gissing and some of his key followers posts in a newly formed regional autonomy council (Samanta 1996; Subba 1992; Akbar 1988).

A more significant sons-of-the-soil movement has flourished in Assam, where the main political parties have alternately allied and conflicted with the small-scale but violent United Liberation Front of Assam (ULFA). This Maoist group was launched in opposition to the flow of migrants into the state, which commenced in the 1940s with the notorious Land Settlement Bill of 1941 introduced by the then Muslim League state government, and which prompted mass immigration of Bengalis, particularly Muslims, from Bangladesh. The ULFA itself emerged from the All-Assam Students Union (AASU) agitation launched in 1979 (Weiner 1988; Baruah 1999, 2005). Symbolically, the ULFA was founded at the Rang Ghar pavilion of the Ahom kings located in the Sibsagar district of Upper Assam. The AASU agitation kept Assam in a state of ferment until 1985 when an accord signed with Rajiv Gandhi led to elections that brought the more moderate yet politically important Ahom Gana Parishad (AGP) to power – also founded by former AASU activists. Subsequently, however, ULFA elements infiltrated the AGP state administration and became increasingly active, obliging New Delhi to introduce president's rule – the suspension of the state government and resumption of central control – and send in the army in 1990. The 1991 elections were only won by the Congress after covertly promising to release all ULFA activists from jail, thereby undoing the efforts of the army and police. Inevitably the armed struggle soon recommenced with renewed vigour. In state elections in the late 1990s the Ahom Gana Parishad returned to power, but extremist violence continues, allegedly backed in part by the Pakistani Inter-Services Intelligence (ISI) agency, and still claims up to 400 lives each year. The power of the terrorists and their links with established politicians was clearly illustrated in 1999 when an AGP Lok Sabha candidate was killed after allegedly attending a clandestine meeting with ULFA representatives in an effort to win backing for his campaign.

In neighbouring Tripura there has been a similar insurgency to that seen in Assam, the root cause of which can be traced to Bengali Hindu migration from erstwhile east Pakistan, which has transformed the largely tribal state into a predominantly Bengali-speaking region (Harihar 1999). Close observation, however, reveals a similar interweaving of insurgent activities and electoral politics to that seen in Assam. It is thus alleged that murders have been committed by the Tripura National Volunteers (TNV) activists before the 1988 assembly election at the behest of the Congress (I). Similarly, a massacre committed by the All-Tripura Tribal Force (ATTF) activists on the eve of the 1993 election is believed to have helped the CPI (M)-led Left Front to make a comeback to power in the state.

Amongst the most extreme secessionist movements in the north-east of India are those in the tribal areas of Nagaland and Mizoram, where since the 1950s a movement of the Naga people led by Angami Zapu Phizo of the Naga National Council until his death in 1992, and the Mizo peoples, championed by Laldenga of the Mizo National Front (MNF), have refused to reconcile themselves to rule from the centre (Singh 1982: vol. I, ch.9; Nag 1999). The two organisations have engaged in successive campaigns of guerrilla warfare, first against the British and then the Indian governments, with backing since the 1960s from China, Pakistan and Myanmar. The tragic consequence has been 20 years of dislocation, misery and military oppression for their populations. The Mizos eventually achieved peace under an accord – signed between Laldenga and Rajiv Gandhi in 1986 – that made Mizoram a full Indian state. Following this, considerable success has been achieved in rebuilding the prosperity of the state.

A similar outcome to that experienced by the Mizo National Front has been seen in the case of the Jharkhand Party, a Santhal-dominated political party founded in 1950 to campaign for a separate tribal state in eastern-central India (Devalle 1992; Sengupta 1982; Corbridge 1988). The party grew out of the Adivasi Mahasabha, co-founded in 1939 by Jaipal Singh. It fizzled out in the late 1960s (after Singh became a minister in the central government), but was revived again after 1973 when the Jharkhand Mukti Morcha (JMM) was founded under the leadership of Shibu Soren. It was most active in the Chota Nagpur region of Bihar, where several JMM MPs were regularly elected with as many as 32 representatives in the state assembly. When in power, the Congress blew both hot and cold on their ambitions, according to how much they needed to win their support in parliament. Although the JMM never went so far as to demand secession or to engage in sustained guerrilla operations, their demands were sometimes unfairly branded as 'secessionist' by the central government (an illegal cause according to India's Anti-Secession Act) as an excuse to ignore them. However, the JMM's determination to follow a largely constitutional path eventually achieved success when, after they polled more than any other party in the region in the elections in 1999, the central government, with the agreement of the state government in Bihar, passed a bill establishing a new tribal state in place of the existing Jharkhand Area Autonomous Council (JAAC), established in 1990, for the tribal peoples in the southern part of Bihar. The new state, with a total of 18 districts, and a population of about 30 million of whom just under 30 per cent are *adivasi*, came into effect on 15 November 2000. It also inherits enormous natural resources, including 40 per cent of India's coal and copper reserves, with Bihar losing some 63 per cent of its revenues as a consequence. It remains, nevertheless, but a truncated version of the original Jharkhand demanded, since it excludes eight neighbouring districts of west Bengal, Orissa and Madhya Pradesh that were a part of the campaign. Shibu Soren failed to become chief minister of the new tribal state due to factionalism within the Jharkhand movement and pending bribery charges. The first chief minister appointed was therefore, ironically, a member of the BJP, the party then in power in the central government; the BJP have continued to dominate the state government ever since.

A similar movement to that of the Jharkhandis arose in neighbouring Chhattisgarh in eastern Madhya Pradesh. Although the Chhattisgarh Mukti Morcha is far smaller in scale and less ambitious than the JMM, it is still predominantly an *adivasi* movement. Despite the small scale of this agitation, a new autonomous state was nonetheless announced by the BJP government here, as well as in

Jharkhand, and another – Uttaranchal – carved out of the Kumaon and Garwahal hill districts of Uttar Pradesh, where formerly the Chipko ('tree-hugging') environmental movement, the most recent in a long line of local agitations, had achieved a popular following and international recognition (Gadgil and Guha 1994; Guha 1989; Weber 1985; Mawdsley 1997). A later demand by upper caste Hindus for a separate state in the region, called 'Uttarkhand', which was supported by the BJP as a way of undermining Mulayam Singh Yadav's RJD state government in Uttar Pradesh, was the imminent cause of the concession once the BJP came to power.[5] All three new states were approved by parliament and came into existence at the same time in late 2000. In all three states, those who had campaigned for their creation were marginalised in the subsequent state governments, which is perhaps one reason why anti-state 'Naxalite' guerrilla activity has continued and even escalated in recent years in these states. They are known as 'Naxalites', after the district of Naxalbari in west Bengal where they staged an uprising in 1967. Split into various armed factions, including the People's War Group and the Maoist Communist Centre, these two merged and formed the CPI (Maoist) Party in September 2004. Together they have as many as 9,000 to 10,000 armed fighters and 40,000 full-time supporters, spread across forested areas in the states of Bihar, Chhattisgarh, and Andhra Pradesh. In the region of Dantewada district, a part of the former princely *adivasi* state of Bastar – a region with a long history of resistance to outside interference (Sundar 1997; Anderson 1988) – pitched battles between Naxalites and the police in 2005 and 2006 left as many as 350 dead and 50,000 refugees. A local militia the Salwa Judum has been armed by the government to fight against the Naxalites in the forests, using questionable methods such as the ransacking of villages known to sustain them. Inevitably this has added to rather than diminished support for the insurgency.[6]

A movement for greater autonomy even arose in 1996 in the tiny former state of Coorg – a part 'C' state under the constitution between January 1952 to 1 November 1956. Thereafter, it was amalgamated into the neighbouring Kannada state of Mysore (now Karnataka), as carved out by the States Reorganisation Commission (Fazal Ali Commission) and ratified by the States Reorganisation Act, 1956. Since then there has been a movement to revive the state and the hill culture of the region by the Kodagu Rajya Mukti Morcha, who have called for the creation of a 'separate ethnic state of Kodagu'. The KRMM is confessedly inspired by the Jharkhand movement, and is obviously very much a consequence of the spirit of decentralisation that has arisen since the decline of Congress hegemony.

Of all the secessionist and anti-state movements that India has suffered in recent decades, the largest and strategically the most significant have been in Kashmir and the Punjab. The Kashmir issue is of course regarded as an international affair by Pakistan (as described in Chapters 11 and 12). There is no doubt, however, that at the time of its accession to India a significant section within Kashmiri society had supported the move, not least of all the All Jammu and Kashmir Muslim National Conference (Kashmir's leading political party), led by Sheikh

Mohammad Abdullah, who had always rejected Jinnah's 'two-nation' theory. Kashmir had been promised special status guaranteeing it far greater autonomy than other states within the Indian Union (Shankar 1996). At the time, it seemed a practical and fair arrangement. Therefore there was nothing inevitable about the falling out between India and Kashmir, nor the emergence of an entirely separatist movement and identity, *Kashmiriyat*, within the region. By 1953, though, Sheikh Abdullah and Jawaharlal Nehru, formerly close friends and allies, had become political foes and the bonds of union that had been forged in conflict began to fall apart (Zutshi 2003; Alebar 2002).

In the early 1950s Abdullah made an attempt to implement land reforms in Kashmir that would undermine the position of the predominantly Hindu landed aristocracy. The Hindu-dominated Jammu region was subordinated to Kashmiri rulers in Srinagar in this period – all of which contributed to discontent among Hindus in the region. An agreement was made in New Delhi between Nehru and Abdullah guaranteeing autonomy for three different regions in the state, but this was rejected by the Hindu nationalist parties, the Jan Sangh and Hindu Mahasabha, who launched a movement for the full accession of the state to India. The death of a Jan Sangh leader in Srinagar gaol gave the campaign renewed force in the Indian media, and Nehru succumbed to the pressure by arresting Abdullah. From then onwards Kashmir was governed without a proper democratic government, completely undermining, some would argue, the terms of its accession (Lamb 1991). The relationship between Kashmir and India improved slightly when an accord was signed by National Conference representative Mahammed Afzal Beg and the Indian government representative G. Parthasarthy in November 1974, immediately prior to Mrs Gandhi's declaration of the emergency, which offered the perfect excuse not to implement its terms. The situation deteriorated rapidly after July 1984 when the government of Farooq Abdullah (Sheikh Abdullah's son) was dismissed by the state governor under Mrs Gandhi's instructions, despite his National Conference Party having a majority in the state legislative assembly. This arbitrary dismissal by the central government convinced most Kashmiris that even if they chose to accede to India they would not be allowed to elect their government freely. Despite later backing for Farooq Abdullah from the central government, in exchange for reciprocal support for Congress in the Lok Sabha, Kashmiris never felt comfortable with Indian rule thereafter, and Farooq Abdullah came to be regarded as a mere political pawn. The discrediting of the National Conference as a political force then allowed various secessionary groups, principally the Kashmiri Liberation Front (KLF), to take its place (Wirsing 1994; Hewitt 1997).

Whilst some militant groups have been pro-Pakistani, the KLF is sympathetic neither to the Pakistani nor Indian governments. Its aim is a greater say for Kashmiris in Kashmir affairs, and it has fought a stubborn guerrilla campaign since 1989 in an effort to drive the Indian army out of the state (Engineer 1991; Bhattacharjea 1994). Between 1989 and the middle of 1999 the insurgency claimed the lives of more than 25,000 people, with some estimates as high as 60,000. Bombs, grenades, landmines, rifle and machine-gun fire have been targeted at passenger buses, passenger trains, the Indian police and military, and Hindu minorities. Violent retaliation by the Indian police and military against the Muslim population has ensued. The insurgency was obviously assisted with arms and money from across the border in Pakistan, which seriously aggravated Indo–Pakistan relations. Border clashes between Indian and Pakistani troops became common as the insurgency progressed, and in 1990 the two countries were very close to war. In 1995 alone there were nearly 2,000 exchanges of fire across the 'line of control' established in 1949 and 1971 between the two countries (Ganguly 2002; Schofield 2002). Officially the Kashmiri *intifada* had been tamed by the late 1990s, but only at the cost of an enormous and continuing Indian army presence, the flight of most Hindus from the state, and frequent if disparate acts of kidnapping and terrorism (Marwah 1995).

The conflict in Punjab, effectively over by the mid-1990s, was for a time far more serious than that in Kashmir and the associated terrorist campaign extended as far as the capital New Delhi, claiming the life of Prime Minister Indira Gandhi. It was also one of the most paradoxical of secessionist campaigns, since it arose in a prosperous state without any apparent provocation. Its roots nonetheless are profound, reaching back into the colonial period. It also reveals, perhaps more strikingly than any other such movement, the dilemmas of democracy and federalism within the Indian union, and the developing crisis associated with the decline of Congress hegemony. It is therefore deserving of special consideration, including a short digression into the pre-colonial and colonial history of Punjab.

The Punjab crisis

Prime Minister Indira Gandhi was assassinated on 31 October 1984 by two Sikh members of her bodyguard whilst crossing the compound of her New Delhi residence. Since the army's attack on the Golden Temple and the final suppression of the militant Sikh campaign for independence for a brief interval, she and her family had received numerous death threats, but she had refused a suggestion that Sikh members of her bodyguard be removed, convinced as she was of their loyalty. This conviction proved to be misplaced when two of them, Beant Singh, a sub-inspector of police, and constable Satwant Singh, shot her at close range.

Quite why many Sikhs had developed such an extraordinary animosity towards Mrs Gandhi and her family personally is difficult to understand, if not to describe. It is therefore worth considering in some detail. As with all great political movements there is no single explanation but a concatenation of causes. The obvious origins of Sikh animosity lay in the invasion of the Holy Temple in Amritsar by the army at Mrs Gandhi's orders in 1984. At the same time, Sikh animosity towards Mrs Gandhi and her government may be perceived as merely the most recent expression of a centuries-old conflict between the Sikh community and the government in Delhi. Punjab, the home of the Sikhs, in the very north-west of India, was a legendary marcher territory. Every invading army entering India had to traverse the Khyber Pass, and march through Punjab and Rajasthan, on the way to the heartland of the Indo-Gangetic plain of north India. Whoever held these regions stood to gain tremendously from the trade that passed from India to the Middle East. This was a crucial area, a site of great prosperity, but also one of great conflict, and the Sikh religion evolved very much in response to this long history of warfare and insecurity (see Chapter 1).

It was the tenth and last of the gurus, Gobind Singh, who transformed the Sikh *Khalsa* ('army of the faithful') into a formidable fighting force in the late seventeenth century, effectively organising and training this army as well as giving it a powerful ideological impetus. Following his death, the Sikh kingdom went from strength to strength under a succession of rulers, and as the Mughal Empire declined so the Sikhs consolidated their hold on the Punjab. The last Sikh king, Ranjit Singh, built himself an impressive empire in the north-west of India in the eighteenth century. So forbidding was his army that the kingdom was left largely untouched by the British until ten years after Ranjit Singh's death, when they took advantage of disputes within the ruling family to step in and annex the Punjab in 1842. Having done so, they recruited most of Ranjit Singh's soldiers into the British army and gave them generous rates of pay. For many years afterwards, and most outstandingly during the uprising in 1857, the Sikhs maintained their militaristic traditions, established under the last of the Gurus, and under the kings that followed them, and became a loyal mainstay of the British army in India.

British encouragement of the Sikhs and of Sikh militarism began to backfire at the end of the nineteenth century, as has been described in *Lions of the Punjab* (Fox 1985). Increasingly obsessed with notions of caste specialisation, the British went so far as to refuse to recruit people to the army in north-west India unless they were Sikhs, and considered true Sikhs to be only those who bore the five symbols of the faith. They furthermore often refused to accept that anyone who was not called Singh was a Sikh, thereby unwittingly encouraging the entrenchment of a militant and exclusive Sikhism. Religious revivalism was further spawned by the pressures of Westernisation, and of economic change and the organisation of rival Hindu and Muslim revivalist movements, such as the Arya Samaj and Tabliq movement, at this time.

During the Indian independence movement, and particularly following the Jallianwalla Bagh massacre, the Sikhs began to turn against the British. Their anger focused in particular on the issue of the *gurudwaras* (Sikh temples), which since the early nineteenth century had been under British administration. The extent of British influence may be gauged by the fact that the high priests of the Golden Temple actually congratulated General Dyer following the Jallianwalla Bagh massacre, commending his determination to maintain law and order. The Sikh challenge to this authority was mounted when the Akali Dal political party was formed, together with the Shiromani Gurudwara Parbandhak Committee (SGPC), set up for the purpose of wresting administration of the Sikh temples from the British. The Sikhs took part in Gandhi's non-co-operation movement in 1920, winning control of the Golden Temple in that year, and of all of the temples in the Punjab by 1925. These concessions were prompted by British disinclination to alienate a key element in their army. However, the movement had been highly militant: both violent and non-violent tactics were used during the course of the campaign, and, with their own religious and political agenda, Sikhs rapidly outgrew Gandhian leadership. They set their own targets and, achieving most of their stated aims by 1925, were far less prominent in later political campaigns.

During the Second World War the Sikhs supported the British, and continued to do so until the imminent withdrawal of the British from India became apparent, at which point the Akali Dal, in reaction to Jinnah's demand for an independent Pakistan, also raised a demand for a separate Sikh state. This demand was never taken seriously, and they (and others) were sidelined in the negotiations leading up to the partition of India in 1947. After partition, the Sikhs were left with a sense of grievance against both the Pakistani and Indian governments. They felt left out of negotiations despite having borne the brunt of communal fighting during the process of partition itself. In the years following independence anxieties and instabilities within the Sikh community increased. Partition occasioned a great upheaval in landholdings: although many Sikhs gained land from Muslims, a great many others lost out, the consequences of which can still be seen today in the wide dispersal of Sikhs. The huge refugee population created by partition settled chiefly in the cities, which is why there are so many Sikhs in Delhi for example.

Economic and social change also impacted upon the Sikh community and its traditions. Class divisions were exacerbated, threatening the religious egalitarian ideal of Sikhism, while traditional Sikh culture was confronted by a tide of jeans, pop songs, Coca-Cola and all the other symbols of modernity. Many traditionalists felt that this was undermining the faith. The Punjab was particularly prone to economic change, since it had become a prosperous part of the country by the 1960s. At the same time Sikhs worried about the fact that they were such a small minority. Overall, the Sikhs, who numbered 11 million, accounted for only 2 per cent of the Indian population, and even in the Punjab itself where 80 per cent of them lived, they were barely a majority. Even within the Punjab, the majority of the population was Hindu, and there was a continual fear of discrimination and – perhaps more importantly – of the Sikh religion being absorbed, as others had been before, into the broad pantheistic mass of Hinduism (Wallace 1986).

Aware of these dangers, soon after independence a number of Sikh leaders began pressuring the government to make concessions to the community – in particular, the creation of a separate state within the Indian Union. Tara Singh warned the government in the 1950s: 'if you are true nationalists then for the sake of the nation you must let the Sikhs live honourably. You will err in attempting to extinguish in the name of nationalism the distinctive entity of the Sikhs. We value our honour and if we have no separate existence we shall have nothing to be proud of.'[7] Tara Singh regarded Nehru as a Hindu chauvinist and other Congress politicians as still more threatening. This was not, perhaps, without some justice. In other parts of the country, Hindus, Muslims and Sikhs lived together quite equably, but the Punjab had a history of terrorism and violence. A number of Hindu political organisations such as the Jan Sangh continued to target the Punjab, as they had done in the 1920s and 1930s. The Sikhs certainly had much to fear from the activities of such organisations, as well as the continuing influence of the Arya Samaj in the area (Kapur 1986; O'Connell 1988).

Another reason why the Sikhs had cause for anxiety was the 1956 reorganisation of states. After independence India inherited the administrative divisions bequeathed by the British, which were largely determined by convenience. In 1953 a committee recommended the reorganisation of states along linguistic lines. Significantly, the claims of the Sikhs for a separate Punjabi state – a state where Punjabi was spoken and the Gurumukhi script was written – were rejected on the grounds that Punjabi was not a sufficiently distinctive language. Nehru was further convinced that the demand was secessionist. Rejection led to one of the first violent confrontations between the Sikhs and the government, with demonstrations in the streets of Amritsar. After 1960 the demand was revived, with 132 members of the SGPC taking an oath to sacrifice their body, soul and property to achieve a separate Sikh state. Tara Singh, the Akali Dal leader at this time, began a fast to the death in support of this campaign. He gave it up after 43 days, and was subsequently considered disgraced. His successor, Sant Fateh Singh, repeated the demand with rather greater success, though this was more to do with the war with Pakistan in 1965, when Sikh units in the army, and civilians, were in the forefront of the fighting that pushed the Pakistani army back. As a consequence, Mrs Gandhi decided to reward the Sikhs by acceding to the Akali Dal demand for a separate Sikh-majority state. She set up two new states: Himachal Pradesh in the north and Haryana in the east. What had been greater Punjab was now divided into three, with a new smaller Punjab in which the Sikhs would be a majority. Even here, Sikhs still amounted to only 56 per cent of the population, but they would have more of a chance to bring their own policies and religious beliefs into practice in matters of local government (Saberwal 1986; Brass 1988).

Interestingly, immediately after the concession on statehood was made, Sikh agitation switched from the issue of a separate state to focus on the modern city of Chandigarh. Built as the capital of old Punjab after 1949, it was very close to the border with Haryana, and was initially proposed to be part of that state. However, the Akali Dal wanted Chandigarh in the Punjab, and this became, immediately after 1965, the new campaign issue of the Sikhs. In support of this demand, Sant Fateh Singh threatened to set fire to himself in an elaborate, escape-proof ritual if the demand was not met. Intimidated by this, Mrs Gandhi again gave in but failed to implement the agreement to transfer Chandigarh. This became characteristic of her dealings with the Sikhs. She would wait too long before making a concession – for fear of encouraging opposition – so that by the time she did, new demands would already have been formulated. Mrs Gandhi also frequently reneged on previous agreements, which led the Sikhs to make bigger and bigger demands on the grounds that they needed to pitch their demands high in order to have a hope of gaining anything. Thus a relationship of profound distrust between even moderate Sikh politicians and the Congress government developed.

Another key figure in the subsequent deterioration of relations between the central government and Punjabi politicians was the then Congress chief minister in the Punjab (later president), Giani Zail Singh. Zail Singh had considerable influence over Indian politics from the mid-1960s until the mid-1980s. A power-hungry politician, willing to do anything to advance his political career, he increased his popular support amongst Sikhs by feting religious leaders, especially at times of religious festivals. It is he, many claim, who helped to ensure the prominence of religion on the political agenda of the Punjab. Until then controversy had mostly centred on the boundaries of the state, and its language and capital. Zail Singh began to encourage a new sense of religious pride and to associate it with his political campaign. Partly in order to compete with him, the Akali Dal began, from the late 1960s, to graft religious issues onto its political agenda simply to gain votes (Wallace 1990). The Dal set up a committee of eminent Sikhs and charged them with 'redrawing the aims and objectives of the Sikh community to give a more vigorous lead for their achievement because of the anti-Sikh policies of the Congress government'.[8] The proposals of this committee were adopted by the Akali Dal at a meeting held at the Anandpur Sahib in 1973 ('Sahib' being a term of deference used to refer to the gospels of the Sikh faith and its temples).

The Anandpur resolution was crucial because of its wide-ranging demands, and much of the Sikh agitation over the next 15 years would centre around it. The demands included restricting the power of the central government in the Punjab to defence, foreign policy and communications, thus leaving the state government free to set whatever laws, taxes and tariff barriers it wanted. This would have given the Punjab greater autonomy than any other state in India. It was particularly unlikely in view of the fact that the Punjab was on the border with Pakistan. This meant that the central government could not afford to concede too much autonomy to the region. Second, under the policies of the Green Revolution, the large, prosperous farmers of the Punjab had become even more prosperous and the region had become the granary of India, making it strategic not only militarily but as the main source of India's food supply.

Not surprisingly, given the importance of Punjabi agriculture, the Jat peasant farmers of the Punjab were the main supporters of the Akali Dal, particularly of the militant proposals of the Anandpur resolution. Sikh farmers were becoming anxious that the advantages and subsidies they had been given in the early 1960s might soon be withdrawn. It had always been intended that the Green Revolution subsidies should be temporary. Thus the Anandpur resolution insisted that there should be no changes in agricultural subsidies without approval; nor in agricultural prices, which were above world market levels. Mrs Gandhi's socialist policies further worried the Sikh farmers. In 1972 she embarked on renewed land reforms that threatened the many large-sized Punjabi farms. The government was also threatening to reinforce the laws on inheritance. In 1966 women had been given rights of inheritance equal to those of male heirs, but in the Punjab, as in other states, this law had been largely ignored. The Sikhs, like Gujarati Patidar farmers, practised primogeniture (i.e. the land passed to the eldest son). This was one reason why the farms had remained relatively large and why they were able to apply Green Revolution technology so effectively. Discrimination against female and younger male heirs was crucial to the prosperity of the Punjab's agricultural economy, as they saw it, as well as to male patriarchy, and proposed changes to the law of inheritance rights were seen as a threat to their livelihood as well as to their way of life (Leaf 1985). Added to this were anxieties about the profitability and sustainability of wheat farming itself as many farmers had assumed debts whilst adopting the new technology, and, whilst enjoying an immediate increase in output, quickly found themselves committed to unending inputs of fertiliser and insecticides in the face of static or even diminishing yields and a less certain market (Shiva 1989).

Another issue dealt with by the Anandpur resolution was industrialisation. The Punjab's position close to the border meant that heavy industries, such as iron and steel works, were not located in the state. However, the Green Revolution had entailed a rapid increase in secondary industrial output, particularly in processing industries associated with agriculture. Coca-Cola and Pepsi-Cola, for example, had both situated their factories in the Punjab in the 1960s because of the availability of supplies for the production of their carbonated beverages. The problem of primogeniture now raised its head again because of the large demand for employment amongst second and third sons in Punjabi families. The lack of government investment in local industry was resented, perhaps irrationally. Where employment was not readily available, second and third sons would often pursue a career in education or the army – the Punjab enjoying one of the highest literacy rates in the country. Universities locally were churning out graduates, who at times of recession had nowhere to go. Students were an important constituency in militant Sikh campaigns.

A third resolution made at Anandpur was for change in army recruitment policies. After the 1960s, the government announced that it intended future appointments to army positions to be non-discriminatory in terms of ethnicity. The intention was to create a more ethnically heterogeneous army. The separate Sikh regiment in the army, instituted by the British, was also to be phased out. The Anandpur resolution also tackled the issue of irrigation waters. In the 1970s proposals had been made to develop canal irrigation in this region. The three major rivers flowing through the Punjab, tributaries of the River Indus, were proposed to be dammed in order to divert water supply to irrigation canals in Haryana. With Haryana no longer part of the state, the Punjabis wished to reserve these waters for their exclusive use.

One of the most interesting things about the Anandpur resolution was that from 1973 until the end of the emergency in 1977, the Akali Dal campaigned vigorously on the issues raised in the resolution. In 1977 the Akali Dal became part of the Janata coalition that ruled India until 1980, yet not one of these issues was ever resolved by the Akali Dal whilst it was in power. In fact they spent little time talking about the Anandpur resolution after 1977, which suggests that these issues had simply been seen as sticks with which to beat the Congress whilst in opposition. As soon as they gained influence, they allowed these issues to go onto the backburner. Mrs Gandhi, however, took the Anandpur resolution very seriously and was particularly incensed by the activities of the Akali Dal during the period from 1977 to 1980 when she was in opposition. It has been suggested that she actively encouraged the establishment of a militant force within the Sikh community. The policy was said to have been invented by Zail Singh and was almost certainly supported by her son, Sanjay, who devoted most of his efforts at this time to getting his mother back into power.

The main purpose in supporting Sikh militancy was to undermine and divide the Akali Dal, then under the leadership of three key characters: Badal, Longowal and Tora. Prakash Singh Badal was a farmer and politician, Harchand Singh Longowal was a religious leader, and Gurcharan Singh Tora a long-established politician who rose to become president of the SGPC (Shiromani Gurdwara Parbandhak Committee), the body in charge of controlling *gurdwaras* (Sikh temples). Zail Singh's and the Gandhis' main purpose in encouraging the rise of Jarnail Singh, otherwise known as 'Bhindranwale', was to threaten this dominant coalition. Born into a Jat peasant family, Jarnail Singh studied at a school for Sikh missionaries, founded by a famous Sikh martyr. The head of this school having died in a road accident (he refused to have his hair cut to enable surgery on his head injury), Jarnail Singh was appointed to take his place, adopting the name of Bhindranwale after a neighbouring village. He was still at this stage a missionary and a teacher, and in no way a significant figure, although he had figured on a list of 20 candidates drawn up by Zail Singh as possible leaders for a breakaway faction which the Congress Party was looking to support. One of the vehicles of this militant campaign was a political party called the Dal Khalsa, or Land of the Pure. Supporters of Bhindranwale, although not Bhindranwale himself, were invited to an inaugural meeting of the Dal Khalsa, held in New Delhi in 1978 at the Aroma Hotel. A bill for entertainment at that meeting, some 600 rupees, was paid for by Zail Singh although neither he nor any Congressmen attended. It was at this meeting that the demand for Khalistan, a separate Sikh state, was first raised. There is also evidence that Bhindranwale and Mrs Gandhi knew each other. In the 1980 election campaign that returned Mrs Gandhi to power, it is said that Bhindranwale appeared on an election platform alongside Mrs Gandhi. He certainly appeared on election platforms with Zail Singh and the president of the Punjab Congress, B.R.L. Bhatia (Tully and Jacob 1985).

After Mrs Gandhi's re-election in 1980, Zail Singh was rewarded for his efforts with the post of home minister. This might have been the end of the affair, Bhindranwale having served his purpose. However, Mrs Gandhi, wary as ever, was concerned about Zail Singh, and at the same time as promoting him ensured that Darbara Singh, a rival, was appointed to the chief ministership of the Punjab. It is likely, therefore, that after 1984 it was not Mrs Gandhi but Zail Singh himself who continued to support Bhindranwale. This took a variety of forms: money in the form of cash donations was given, and more significantly by using his position as home minister on more than one occasion to protect Bhindranwale from arrest, despite the increasingly violent activities in which the latter and his followers were involved. His motives in doing so were complex, but undoubtedly arose in part from the proxy influence it gave him over Punjabi politics.

Like other militant religious leaders, Bhindranwale saw himself as a campaigner against heresy. He was opposed to a Sikh sect called the Nirankaris, with which he and his followers first clashed in 1978. Several people were killed, and afterwards Bhindranwale approached a group of amateur politicians who claimed proximity to Sanjay Gandhi. Through connections in the All-India Sikh Students' Federation, they assisted him in setting up his own candidates against the Akali Dal in the Shiromani Gurudwara Parbandhak Committee elections of 1979. He was badly defeated, but began to attract attention when in 1980 some of his followers assassinated the leader of the Nirankari sect. As their notoriety increased they assassinated other critics of their movement, including newspaper proprietors and politicians. It was in 1981 that the first major intervention by Zail Singh occurred. An order had gone out to arrest Bhindranwale for questioning following the shooting of the editor of a Punjabi newspaper, and it is believed that Zail Singh telephoned Bhajan Lal, the Congress chief minister of Haryana and ordered him to obstruct the arrest. The chief minister accordingly sent an official car to pick up Bhindranwale and drive him across the state border to ensure that the Haryana police couldn't reach him. In celebration of his escape Bhindranwale then drove through Delhi with a busload of armed followers, and only allowed himself to be arrested after a gun battle with the police. Zail Singh made sure that he was released within a few days, allowing him to renew his campaign. The extent to which Mrs Gandhi was aware of this is debatable. But with the aid of Zail Singh's covert support, Bhindranwale's movement became increasingly unruly. The fact that government did not take any positive action against him led many to believe him invulnerable, increasing his popular support. Finally, the Akali Dal itself decided to change tactics, sensing that if they did not support the new Sikh militancy their own influence would be eroded. From within the Golden Temple the Akali Dal started a *dharmayudh morcha* (religious fight), appointing the mild-mannered Sant Harchand Singh Longowal as their leader. Bhindranwale, however, hijacked the movement by announcing that it would not end until all the demands in the Anandpur Sahib resolution were met.

One of the strongest elements of support for Bhindranwale's movement came from the All-India Sikh Students' Federation. They formed the shock troops of Bhindranwale's campaign, throwing bombs and knifing opponents. It was they above all who were responsible for the use of communal tactics to sponsor demands for a separate Sikh state (Mahmood 1997). It was also members of the Federation who began the tactic of machine-gunning pedestrians from the backs of motorcycles, planting bombs on buses, and embarking on random killings of policemen. Much of this activity took place in Delhi itself. Sikh *gurudwaras* there became bases from which terrorist activities were organised. Mrs Gandhi may have been unwilling to move against these temples because many of them had been supporters of the Congress Party in Delhi and were crucial in mobilising the Sikh vote at election times.

To the delight of Zail Singh, who by now had been appointed president in a vain attempt to appease Sikh opinion, Mrs Gandhi was eventually forced by the escalating violence to suspend the Congress government in the Punjab, run by his rival Darbara Singh, and to impose president's rule. From this date onwards the police were given *carte blanche* to deal with the situation, and both sides – the police and Bhindranwale's supporters – commenced on a path of confrontation that was to lead to an orgy of revenge killings. The battle was eventually won by Bhindranwale, who so intimidated the Punjab police that after a few months they dared not arrest a single one of his supporters or to countermand his orders. Bhindranwale himself set up a sort of court in the Golden Temple complex, where he listened to disputes and complaints and ordered the punishment of offenders or critics throughout the length and breadth of the Punjab. To deal with this situation the central government finally drafted in the central reserve police (a paramilitary force) from outside the Punjab. Fearing arrest, Bhindranwale took refuge in the Akal Takht, one of the holiest of the buildings in the Golden Temple complex, where the sacred scripture of the Sikhs was kept.

The escalation of violence soon led to a Hindu reaction: a Hindu defence committee was formed, and anti-Sikh demonstrations took place in the capital. Serious consideration began to be given to calling in the military. Even at this late stage it is believed that the Punjab Congress president was still in touch with Bhindranwale. Mrs Gandhi, however, lost patience as victims of the killings began to include senior policemen, journalists and Congress politicians. Bhindranwale commenced fortifying the Golden Temple, and after the failure of a last-ditch attempt at negotiations Mrs Gandhi ordered the central reserve police to surround the Golden Temple – something they had previously been prevented from doing.

At 8.30 p.m. on the night of 2 June 1983, Mrs Gandhi appeared on television to appeal to the Akali leaders to call off their agitation and to accept the terms of the settlement she had offered, arguing that:

> the reality that has emerged is not the adequacy or otherwise of the terms of the settlement offered by the government . . . but the fact that the agitation is now in the hands of a few who have scant regard for the unity and integrity of our country or concern for communal peace and harmony or the continued economic progress of the Punjab . . . (T)o all sections of Punjabis I appeal – don't shed blood, shed hatred.[9]

Shortly afterwards, All-India Radio announced that the army had been called in and martial law imposed on the Punjab. Four days later, on 6 June, the army attacked the Golden Temple. Time was of the essence because of fears of a general uprising among the Sikhs in the surrounding countryside in reaction. The total number of casualties as a result of the attack will never be known for sure, though it is understood that the list included many Sikh pilgrims, men, women and children, who were visiting the temple at the time. The death-toll was increased as a result of the army's poor intelligence – they had insufficient knowledge of the extent and placement of fortifications – and their decision to launch a full-frontal assault as the quickest way to seize control of the complex. At the onset of the assault the army was instructed to avoid direct fire on the Akal Takht or other sacred buildings, but eventually tanks were used, causing large parts of the ornately decorated Akal Takht to be demolished. The desperate battle resulted in the deaths of some 83 soldiers (nearly one in three were killed or injured).

Many innocent civilians and SGPC employees were killed in the assault and some 250 injured. Eyewitness accounts of what happened include the following by Bhan Singh, the then SGPC secretary:

> I saw about thirty-five or thirty-six Sikhs lined up with their hands raised above their heads. And the major was about to order them to be shot. When I asked him for medical help, he got into a rage, tore my turban off my head, and ordered his men to shoot me. I turned back and fled . . . Sardar Karnail Singh Nag, who had followed me, also narrated what he had seen, as well as the killing of thirty-five to thirty-six young Sikhs by cannon fire. All of them were villagers.[10]

Bhindranwale himself was killed, together with 493 of his armed supporters, within the temple complex; another 200 of his followers escaped. The victims were cremated *en masse*, and it has been estimated that the total number of deaths may have been as high as 1,600. In reaction to the assault, several Sikh units in the army, stationed elsewhere in India, mutinied. Zail Singh himself contemplated resignation.

In the aftermath of the Golden Temple incident, the army in the Punjab embarked on a wave of arrests and killings (so-called 'encounters') of suspected Bhindranwale supporters throughout the Punjab, using brutal interrogation techniques on those captured. This campaign of suppression, code-named 'Operation Woodrose', was to some extent counterproductive as it incensed even moderate Sikhs, who in many cases became targets themselves (Pettigrew 1995). A government report published subsequently to justify the assault further outraged moderate Sikhs by branding the whole of the Akali Dal as a separatist organisation. This then was the background to Mrs Gandhi's assassination (Hardgrave 1984; Jeffrey 1986).

Concluding their description of these events Mark Tully and Satish Jacob (1985) wrote:

> Zail Singh [supported] Bhindranwale . . . because he thought he could . . . use him to bring about the downfall of his political rival, the Punjab chief minister. Mrs. Gandhi apparently wanted him released [when he was arrested] so that she could maintain her hold over Delhi's Sikhs. By surrendering justice to petty political gains the government itself created the ogre who was to dominate the last years of Mrs. Gandhi's life and to shadow her until her death.[11]

Damning as this judgement is, it needs to be placed within the wider context of India's structural political and economic problems, since the violent disturbances in the Punjab were totemic and merely mirrored, in an extreme form, the alienation and discontent that many Indians have come to feel, both rich and poor, throughout the length and breadth of the country (Basu and Kohli 1998). Mrs Gandhi herself justified her actions, as did her father before her, as necessary in the pursuit of unity. That unity, however, has been increasingly difficult to maintain in the decades since independence. The explanation for this is complex, but it undoubtedly lies partly in the persistence of extreme income inequalities, combined with the increasingly fissiparous impact of globalisation on the Indian economy (Bardhan 1998; Bhagwati 1993; Rothermund 1996; Saez 2002). It also lies to a considerable degree in the type of unity conceived: one very largely built upon the centralist, European nationalist (and colonial) political and consti-tutional models of the nineteenth century (Brass 1991; Bates and Basu 2005). It is in part the recognition of this failure, and the search for alternatives, that has led to the resurgence of the politics of religion along with that of region towards the end of the twentieth century, an issue which will be described in greater detail in the next chapter.

15 Rajiv Gandhi and the demise of the Congress system

People stood on their rooftops watching our houses burning, just as they do when observing the Republic Day Parade.

(Sikh victim of riots in Gurgaon, November 1984)[1]

'After the riots began, Khushal and others in our area had volunteered to protect our *basti* (hutment cluster) from outsiders. When they heard the trouble around the masjid, all of them ran up to see what was going on.' A police bullet hit 20-year-old Khushal in the chest. 'The police were firing without even looking at where their bullets were going.'

(Kaushalya Samsherpasi on the December 1992 Bombay riots)[2]

'After the attack, my neighbours helped me escape, by putting a bindi on my forehead, and escorted me to a safe place along with my husband, Qasim Ali.' When she returned home, Marzina discovered that her chawl room had been occupied by a Hindu family. 'I managed to get them out after a great deal of difficulty, but when I did so, I sold the room and moved to a Muslim colony. People protected me once, but I can't help thinking what if they had not? What if they do not help me the next time?'

(Marzina, former domestic worker in Indira Nagar colony, Jogeshwari, Bombay, December 1992)[3]

At 9.20 a.m. on 31 October 1984 India's prime minister Indira Gandhi was shot by two of her security guards in the garden of her home at No. 1, Safdarjung Road in New Delhi. Two Sikh bodyguards pumped 16 bullets into her whilst she was crossing a leafy pathway from her residence to an adjacent bungalow, used as an office and guest house, for an interview with actor-director Peter Ustinov. According to the original police FIR (First Information Report) the two assailants were arrested, but Beant Singh was shortly after shot dead by other guards (the cause of many later conspiracy theories), Satwant Singh was shot too, but survived, and went on to be tried and executed. Sonia Gandhi was inside the main house at the time and rushed out, but there was nothing she could do to help her mother-in-law. Indira Gandhi was taken to the All-India Medical Hospital, accompanied by Sonia, where she underwent an emergency operation to remove the bullets, but the 66-year-old prime minister was confirmed dead an hour and a half later. Large crowds gathered anxiously outside to await news, but her death was not officially announced until Rajiv Gandhi, who had been rushed to her bedside, had agreed, informally, to take over the government.

Mrs Gandhi's assassination was immediately followed by anti-Sikh riots in New Delhi – events that have never been properly investigated. There is considerable evidence that these riots were orchestrated by and involved Congress Party supporters (Van Dyke 1996). Amongst them, H.K.L. Bhagat, the MP for the trans-Yamuna colonies and information minister, was accused of organising the bussing of supporters to attack Sikhs and loot shops and houses in the prosperous defence colony sector of the city (People's Union 1984). His residence was sensibly fortified against the possibility of Sikh reprisals. Some 1,200 Sikhs were killed in New Delhi and 2,717 in India overall. Around 50,000 Sikhs fled to the Punjab from the capital and a similar number took refuge in special camps (Das 1990). In a manner reminiscent of the time of partition, Sikhs on trains coming from the Punjab were attacked and the service had to be suspended. Official connivance is suggested by the fact that, despite blood on the streets and a pall of smoke hanging over the city, it was only on the occasion of Mrs Gandhi's funeral three days later that the army acted to impose some semblance of order, a curfew imposed on the evening of 1 November being widely ignored (Kothari and Sethi 1985; Chakravarti and Haksar 1987). When quizzed about these events three weeks later, Rajiv Gandhi rather cavalierly remarked: 'For some days, people thought that India was shaking. But there are always tremors when a great tree falls.'[4]

Delhi remained in a state of tension for some time and an official inquiry was not finally announced until August 1985 – five months after the riots had taken place. In evidence to the later Nanavati Commission, former prime minister I.K. Gujral said: 'From what I had seen and heard, it appeared to me that the riots were organised, particularly so when many persons had participated in them and they were spread throughout the city . . . there was no effort to arrest those people who were looting and burning the properties of the Sikhs, nor anybody trying to control the riots.'[5] Despite this, no officer has been disciplined and none of the major ringleaders have been convicted.

It was not only Mrs Gandhi's naivety in allowing Sikh bodyguards to remain at their posts that led to her death; lax security was also a factor. This was demonstrated a few weeks later when a spy-ring was uncovered within the prime minister's office. Junior members of her staff had been photocopying documents and selling them to foreign embassies, and Mrs Gandhi's personal secretary, R.K. Dhawan, was implicated. Since Dhawan was also responsible for security, it has been suggested that he was bribed or otherwise involved in the assassination, and inevitably he had to be sacked. Dhawan was characteristic of the men with whom Mrs Gandhi surrounded herself during the last years of her premiership: sycophantic and often corrupt and incompetent.

Rajiv Gandhi himself soon succumbed to the same weaknesses as his mother. Like her, he was elected to the post of prime minister by the Congress Central

Working Committee upon the recommendation of a small coterie, an inner circle of congressmen, without reference to parliament, who were then asked to approve the *fait accompli*. Shortly after taking over, he surrounded himself with old friends, many graduates of the Doon School where he had studied as a boy. Falling prey to the same paranoia that had affected his mother, he was soon deserted by them. For some time after his mother's death, however, the 40-year-old Rajiv was riding high on a wave of sympathy votes. In the December 1984 general election he obtained a huge majority of 415 out of 542 seats (the BJP winning just two seats). He was initially touted as the Mr Clean who would do away with old corruptions and inefficiencies in government, and for a while his supporters, and he himself, seemed to believe he could do no wrong.

Rajiv Gandhi's main achievement following his accession to power was the signing of an agreement with moderate leaders of the Sikh Akali Dal in the Punjab, and the restoration of democratic government in that troubled state. Whilst she was still alive, Mrs Gandhi had given back control of the Golden Temple to the SGPC, the Sikh *gurudwara* management committee, after the completion of repairs by the Public Works Department at a cost of some 30–40 million rupees. She did this only reluctantly as it had been her hope to amend the Gurudwara Temples Bill of 1925 and deprive the SGPC, and indirectly the Akali Dal, of a good part of their income. Her hand was forced by the excommunication of President Zail Singh, and the threat of renewed militancy. By contrast, Rajiv Gandhi determined from the outset to pacify Sikh militancy, and released moderate Sikh leaders from prison soon after his election. This was despite some appalling acts of terrorist violence by militants, including a device set off at a children's birthday party and an explosion of 20 bombs in New Delhi and another 18 in other cities of north India on 10 and 11 May 1985. Rajiv invited the most moderate of the Akali Dal leaders, Harchand Singh Longowal, to New Delhi, and commenced negotiations personally, with the help of Arjun Singh (a wily former chief minister of Madhya Pradesh, then governor of the Punjab) and close friend Arun Singh. He thereby circumvented the network of police, army and state-level politicians who had often hampered Mrs Gandhi's attempts at intercession. Within 48 hours agreement was achieved, although Longowal was assassinated soon after. President's rule was brought to an end, but the Punjab remained a centre of disaffection, held in check mainly by means of a ruthless 'bullet for bullet' police operation engineered by chief officer Julius Ribeiro and his successor K.P.S. Gill. This eventually paid dividends since within a few years there were no more militants or their supporters alive to carry on the conflict, and by the early 1990s a semblance of normality had been restored. Rajiv Gandhi also agreed terms with separatists in Assam and Mizoram. In both these disputes, using the same tactics, with a small negotiating team, he reached accords that, although subsequently eroded, remain among the most positive legacies of his government.

With the assassination of Longowal, the political deal Rajiv had put together in the Punjab seemed in peril, but moderate Sikhs successfully contested a state election held in 1985. The agreement included measures designed to deal with a river water dispute, to foster the Punjabi language, and to ensure that army promotions would be made on merit. A commission was set up to transfer two Hindu majority towns to Haryana in return for Chandigarh, this being ear-marked to be capital of the Sikh state. It was not long, however, before Rajiv Gandhi began to renege on these promises. Chandigarh was not transferred to the Punjab as promised because of growing dissension within his party and the rapid increase in opposition to his government. In 1987 he switched to an anti-Sikh stance in an attempt to win votes in upcoming state elections in neighbouring Haryana. Rajiv Gandhi's growing anxieties about electoral support also led him to intervene disastrously as broker between the warring Tamil and Sinhala com-munities in Sri Lanka in 1986. Both were catastrophic policies. The intervention in Sri Lanka discredited his government because the Tamil Tigers were not con-sulted in the negotiations. The resulting peace agreement therefore had to be imposed by force in Tamil areas, and huge casualties for the Indian peacekeeping force resulted (Bullion 1995). Moreover, Rajiv's tough policy against the Sikhs did not prevent him from losing the Haryana election, while at the same time en-couraging the revival of Sikh militancy in the Punjab. Rajiv then used the revival of political violence in the Punjab as an excuse to suspend the state government and reintroduce president's rule, but the tactic was seen for what it was – a craven attempt to appease Hindu voters, and it meant that he had left himself no line of retreat without appearing weak and vacillating. Having removed power from moderates, he once again had to resort to violence to control Sikh militancy. Like his mother, he had back-pedalled on promised reforms as a result of excessive caution and political uncertainty.

Rajiv Gandhi's cabinet began with an untainted and reformist reputation due to the inclusion of individuals such as V.P. Singh, the former chief minister of Uttar Pradesh, famed for his anti-corruption stance, who was made minister of finance, and Sam Petroda, a successful businessman, placed in charge of Telecommunications. It also included close family relative Arun Nehru, and Arun Singh, a former school friend. Rajiv Gandhi quickly proposed a number of reforms to demonstrate his intended style of government. He began with an anti-defection amendment to the constitution (the 52nd), to prevent members of parliament crossing the floor in exchange for bribes. The amendment required members to resign their seats and recontest them if they changed parties, unless a third of party members did so, in which case it was considered a split. This made little difference to smaller parties in which the one-third quota was easily achieved, but it probably played a significant part in helping to usher in the era of coalition and minority governments that came to dominate the Indian parliament from the 1990s onwards. Rajiv also legalised political contributions from business and trade unions, reversing the policy instigated by his mother in the early 1970s in order to prevent funds from flowing to her rivals. By these two measures he hoped to render backdoor dealing and corruption less prominent. He also pro-posed to reintroduce elections within the Congress Party. Collectively, the changes promised a drastic reform of political life, although the last of them soon fell foul of political circumstances and was never put into practice. It was not in fact until after the Congress government of Narasimha Rao came to power in 1991 that elections within the Congress Party were to a limited extent restored, beginning with the Central Working Committee.

Rajiv Gandhi's slide into insecurity commenced with public attacks on him by President Zail Singh, who was resentful of his exclusion from decision-making under the new regime. Sensing that Rajiv was a weaker man who could be bullied, Zail Singh also encouraged those plotting behind the scenes to replace the prime minister. The problem was not eventually resolved until a new president, R. Venkataraman, was appointed in 1987.

Rajiv's next major problem arose from his failure to give appropriate support to the anti-corruption and liberalisation policies of his finance minister, V.P. Singh. V.P. Singh proposed a major cutting back on the licensing system, which acted as a barrier to private enterprise and foreign investment (Kochanek 1986; Lucas and Papanek 1988; Rosen 1992). This, however, posed problems for large Indian monopolies, which had hitherto been protected from competition. As licensing and import controls were dismantled, these influential groups began covertly to lobby against the policy and to fund opposition parties. Rajiv Gandhi did have a defence against this. His liberalisation policies advantaged some supporters, such as the fast-growing Reliance Industries Corporation led by the influential Dhirubhai Ambani and his two sons Anil and Mukesh. Their major petro-chemicals division manufactured textiles using artificial fibres, for which they depended on the import of certain chemicals subject to import duties. Their major competitors used natural fibres or locally produced artificial fibres. Rajiv allegedly promised to lower the duties on artificial fibres in return for their support. Given advance notice of his intent, Reliance was able then to undercut its competitors and generously donated to Congress Party coffers by way of thanks. However, other textile manufacturers began to support the opposition *en masse*, so the Congress did not benefit in the long run.

V.P. Singh's bold initiative to cut income taxes by 20 per cent was another policy that proved controversial. Initially the scheme achieved great success, persuading many wealthy individuals who had previously evaded taxes to start paying them. A scheme of 'bearer bonds' was also announced to enable undeclared income, including monies smuggled abroad, to be brought back into the country in exchange for government debt, with no questions being asked. These bonds could subsequently be sold, thereby converting illicit or 'black money' into licit funds that were then widely invested. It was a wise policy, and these measures led not only to a rise in government income but also to considerable acceleration in trade and modernisation in the industrial sector. There was also a wave of inward investment, notably from Japan. However, in order to make the policy work, V.P. Singh had to step up the prosecution of tax evaders to encourage people to resume proper declaration of their incomes. A number of well-publicised raids was carried out against prominent individuals. Unfortunately, one of those raided was Amitabh Bachchan, a well-known actor and friend of Rajiv Gandhi. Even the Ambani brothers were targeted. The Indian elite was made thoroughly anxious by such manoeuvres and responded either by putting pressure on Congress and the prime minister, or by switching their support to the opposition. Eventually,

Rajiv Gandhi bowed to their demands and, rather than back his finance minister, transferred him to the defence portfolio in January 1987.

Following the hasty transfer of V.P. Singh, members of the cabinet were brought to the sudden realisation that the reforms they had been putting their heads on the line for might not be supported by their own prime minister, and there was an upsurge of criticism and discontent both from the opposition and from within Congress (Gupta 1989). From 1987 onwards reputable politicians began to desert the government, causing Rajiv to abandon his proposals for the reintroduction of internal Congress Party elections. The opposition Bharatiya Janata Party and Shiv Sena became not only increasingly strident but also effective against the Congress in several municipal and state elections. In Bombay there was a rise in gangsterism in the city's politics, the resulting tensions led to communal riots in 1984, and in 1985 the Shiv Sena ousted the Congress from control of the Bombay City Council. Senior congressmen soon began to distrust Rajiv and to talk about replacing him, and congressmen and opposition leaders had meetings with the president about this.[6] Following the Congress defeat in the Haryana state election of 1987 – which was won by the Lok Dal, a Jat peasant party led by Devi Lal – a covert meeting of 220 of the 445 Congress MPs took place to discuss whether Rajiv Gandhi should be replaced as premier by V.P. Singh. Rajiv Gandhi intercepted the waverers, persuading them to remain at his side; but his troubles were not at an end.

The Bhopal gas disaster of December 1984 was a tremendous human tragedy and yet another of the issues haunting Rajiv Gandhi from the very beginning of his administration onwards. More than 3,000 people died and 50,000 people were injured following a poisonous gas leak from the Union Carbide fertiliser factory. It was the worst industrial disaster ever seen anywhere in the world, but rather than allow a mushrooming of private litigation, much of it in the hands of American law firms, the government decided to take over the responsibility for prosecuting Union Carbide. The problem was that this was botched, with the government finally getting less, in 1988, than the original out-of-court offer made by Union Carbide in 1985. Distribution of relief and subsequent payments were also mismanaged, with very little getting through to the survivors, many of whom died before receiving any payment (Shrivastava 1987; Lapierre and Moro 2001).

In 1986/7 a serious drought afflicted large parts of India, and the resulting shortfall in food supply encouraged inflation and made the life of ordinary Indians increasingly difficult. Government overspending made the situation worse, as expenditure on telecommunications, space and weaponry spiralled. The increase in military spending was related to the decline of the Soviet Union and the need felt by the Indian government to begin severing its links with, and dependence on, Moscow and to start sourcing arms from a variety of Western suppliers instead. In a first step towards improving its relations with India, America supplied Cray supercomputers, ostensibly for weather forecasting, but probably also used for nuclear calculations – which greatly alarmed the Pakistanis. The Indian government also bought frigates from France, submarines from Sweden, and a second-hand aircraft carrier from Britain.

Sensing its strategic advantage and the weakness of the premier, in 1986 the Indian army decided to try out some of its new weapons by organising large-scale manoeuvres involving some 200,000 troops on the Pakistani border, the so-called Operation Brass Tacks. So incautiously was this undertaken – the army marched with a full supply of ammunition in tow and precariously close to the border – that some have regarded it as an attempt by hawks within the Indian military to provoke a war with Pakistan, without the consent of the Indian prime minister. Certainly within Pakistan there was a sense that war was imminent (Arif 2001). Keen to maintain good relations with America (which was concerned above all by the Russian presence in Afghanistan), Zia-ul-Haq of Pakistan had taken a leading role in the formation of SAARC – the South Asian Association for Regional Co-operation – a forum established in 1985 in order to alleviate tensions between neighbouring nations. Fortunately Zia took a pacifistic stance on the Brass Tacks issue, which helped to circumvent India's act of perceived aggression.

Among the new weaponry acquired in 1986 were long-range howitzers, bought from the Bofors Corporation of Sweden at a cost of US $100 million. Having arrived at the defence ministry, V.P. Singh, continung his crusade against corruption, began investigating defence contracts for fraud. Immediately he uncovered erroneous calculations in the Bofors case, which revealed that more than US $2 million had gone astray (Statesman 1989). Doubting the independence of the Indian CBI and wishing to gather evidence in secret, he employed the services of an American detective agency, the Fairfax Corporation, who traced the money to various destinations. Some clearly went to Win Chada, the American-based businessman who negotiated the contract, but it was alleged that some had also gone through the Swiss bank account of Amitabh Bachchan, and also (as was revealed much later), through the accounts of the Hinduja brothers – all friends of the Gandhi family and then backers of the Congress Party. The suspicion was that kickbacks had been demanded for this and other defence contracts, which were then deposited in Swiss bank accounts or siphoned back to India for the benefit of the Congress Party or influential persons unknown. It was a major scandal to discover that well-known individuals were in possession of Swiss bank accounts, which were strictly illegal, and worse still to learn that they had been involved in the laundering of commission charges. About this time charges against Win Chadah, who had been targeted for tax evasion, were withdrawn, hinting at government involvement. It was at this point, in April 1987, that the prime minister demanded the resignation of V.P. Singh from his post as defence minister. The fact that his most principled and admired political collaborator had been forced out of office simply because he had discovered corruption close to the centre of government, sounded the death-knell for Rajiv Gandhi himself. Soon after, Amitabh Bachchan, by this time a Congress member of parliament, was forced by the clamour of protest to resign his seat – despite his close connections to the premier.

By 1987, having lost the Haryana state election, and with other elections forthcoming, Rajiv Gandhi began to panic. He had failed to win the support of Hindus in Haryana and had alienated the Sikhs, but one of the traditional Congress constituencies still left in the north was that of the Muslims. In 1985, a branch of the Indian Supreme Court ruled that a 75-year-old Muslim woman from Indore, Shah Bano, was entitled to maintenance for life from her husband under a section of the Indian Criminal Code that entitled destitute, deserted, or divorced women to receive support from able husbands. Shah Bano's husband had previously divorced her, but refused to pay her maintenance beyond the period of *iddah* (i.e. three months' waiting period after divorce before which she cannot remarry). The court ruling went beyond the usual judgments, speaking in favour of enacting common personal laws for all religious communities instead of the existing laws that differentiated between religious communities. Hindu communalists upheld the court's judgment and stressed the need for a common civil code, whilst many Muslims regarded the judgment as an affront to Shariah law and began a campaign, involving mass street demonstrations, in favour of a bill to exempt them from the relevant criminal law. In a desperate attempt to win support from Muslim voters, and, despite resistance from feminists and progressive Muslims, Rajiv Gandhi bowed to pressure and in 1986 introduced a law exempting Muslim women from existing maintenance laws. There were clearly precedents for this, but the action was seen as a sop to Muslim fundamentalist opinion and was fiercely contested. Subsequently Rajiv's new law was undermined by court rulings, which made one-off payments on a scale that was equivalent to maintenance for life. The result was that Rajiv lost the support of Hindu fundamentalists, as well as that of many Muslims, owing to his failure to implement the new law effectively (Engineer 1987; Pathak and Rajan 1989; Hasan 1989; Chhachhi 1991). He also succeeded in arousing the antagonism of the numerous grass-roots movements for women's rights, which were becoming increasingly well organised and politically active by this time (Forbes 1996). Finally, the government's capitulation contributed to a rise in communal sentiment by making it clear that organised pressure campaigns could force the government to back down from a secularist position.

As if this were not enough, in 1988 Rajiv made a further blunder by reinstating R.K. Dhawan, the discredited personal secretary of Mrs Gandhi, in his government. The Thakur Commission of Inquiry into Mrs Gandhi's assassination had not entirely exonerated Dhawan, but if Rajiv now ousted Dhawan he would be seen as having made the error of reappointing him, while if allowed to remain in office a suspicion would be raised in the public mind as to why he was shielding an alleged conspirator in the murder of his own mother. Foolishly, Rajiv kept Dhawan on, probably because he was desperate by this stage to fill vacant posts in the government as his former friends deserted him. As Bhabani Sen Gupta has argued (1989), Rajiv Gandhi had mistakenly interpreted his landslide victory in 1984 as a personal achievement rather than the sympathy vote it was, and he had seriously underestimated the long-term decline in the Congress Party's grass-roots organisation and support and ability therefore to dominate every election – the so-called 'Congress system' (Morris-Jones 1971) – which began, as many commentators have pointed out, even as far back as the later years of Nehru's regime. His remedies were piecemeal, opportunistic, and unsuccessful. Increasingly he was forced to fall back on his mother's tactics and former cronies in the endeavour to hold on to power.

It did not help the government's position when Arun Shourie, editor of the *Indian Express*, began to run a series of revelations in his paper concerning the Bofors affair, along with other scandals. These scandals concerned, for example, Satish Sharma, a friend from Rajiv's time as a pilot, who found the means to build a swimming pool in his back garden lined with Italian tiles. Rajiv took a luxury Christmas holiday in the Lakshwadeep islands at this moment, apparently confirming the popular impression that he was a bourgeois prime minister out of touch with the problems of the Indian masses (Nugent 1990).

By contrast, Rajiv's former defence minister V.P. Singh went from strength to strength. Following his resignation, he formed a small party, the Janata Morcha, which became the focus of opposition to the government. In July 1988 V.P. Singh contested a by-election in Amitabh Bhachan's former constituency of Allahabad and won it by a large majority over the Congress candidate Sunil Shastri. In February 1989 the Congress was also defeated in state elections in Tamil Nadu by the DMK (Dravida Munnetra Kazhagham), in alliance with the Janata Morcha. Elsewhere, Congress rapidly began to fall apart: its chief minister in Bihar was challenged by dissidents, whilst the Congress chief minister in Madhya Pradesh, Arjun Singh, was forced to resign over the infamous Chaurhat lottery case – charges that he had once embezzled funds from a lottery set up to benefit orphaned children. In May 1989 the elected Janata government in Karnataka was dismissed by the prime minister in a desperate move to promote Congress influence within the state. Violence in Kashmir simultaneously increased, led by the Kashmir Liberation Front and the centrist Muslim United Front, with the beginning of the 'Quit Kashmir' movement (Engineer 1991).

Having lost control of most state assemblies and with defeat in the general election looming, Rajiv Gandhi initiated perhaps the most original policy of his government: a proposal to revive the long-faded power of village councils (*panchayats*) as the foundation of local self-government. The Constitution (64th Amendment) Bill, introduced in April–May 1989, proposed to make the empowerment of *panchayats* a legally binding feature of the constitution, with supervised elections and proper financial resources. This was widely seen as an attempt to appeal over the heads of the regional political parties to the peasant masses and therefore unsurprisingly failed to win the necessary two-thirds majority for a constitutional amendment in parliament, even though several opposition groups had previously advocated such a measure. The proposal won considerable support, but it was not enough to save the government. In August 1989 a report by the auditor-general condemned the government over its handling of the Bofors contract, and there were calls for the resignation of the Congress government, with 73 opposition MPs marching out *en masse* from the Lok Sabha. The Janata, Lok Dal and Janata Morcha (the 'Janata Dal') then joined with the Telugu Desam and DMK to form the National Front in order to fight the upcoming general election, with the BJP and CPI (M) separately promising support from outside the coalition in the event of victory. This unprecedented level of opposition unity spelt doom for the Congress.

The rise of Hindu fundamentalism and the 1989 defeat of Congress

The problems of the Congress Party gave a major fillip to opposition parties, and particularly to Hindu fundamentalist organisations, which were able to make much political capital from the Shah Bano case in particular. Another issue that afforded great opportunities for fundamentalist propaganda was the *sati* (ritual suicide) of Roop Kanwar, a 17-year-old convent-educated Rajput widow, married for only six months, who immolated herself on the funeral pyre of her husband in the village of Deorala in Rajasthan in 4 September 1987. Later more than a million and a half villagers collected in Deorala for a religious ceremony on the fourteenth day after Roop Kanwar's death – defying prohibitory orders and waving pro-*sati* slogans, despite a new law banning glorification of the practice (Jain *et al.* 1987; Qadeer and Hasan 1987). This incident shocked the nation, and activists in the women's movement condemned the revival of what many had thought an extinct and barbaric practice, banned during the colonial period. For others, it was used as an opportunity to celebrate 'traditional' Hindu values, or 'Hindutva', against the 'pseudo-secularism' (i.e. religious intolerance) of the Congress Party.[7] Roop Kanwar was allegedly drugged by her relatives and they, along with the presiding priest and others attending, were arrested and wrongly charged with murder rather than complicity in suicide. For this reason, plus the 'lack of evidence' and the wilful inaction of the state government, they were later acquitted by a court ruling in 1996, which described *sati* as a 'social practice'.[8] According to Radha Kumar, 'almost all the major center to right wing political parties sent representatives to the site, not to enquire what had happened, but to stake their own claim to "tradition," and via this to the Rajput vote'.[9]

The beginnings of the Kashmir insurgency presented a further opportunity for propagandists on the Hindu right. However, the most important issue upon which they began to garner support arose from an ongoing campaign to erect a Hindu temple – the Ramjanambhoomi temple – on the supposed site of the birthplace of Ram, hero of the Ramayana epic, at Ayodhya, Uttar Pradesh, in the north of India (Van der Veer 1987). A temple had allegedly once stood on the site but had been demolished, and a mosque, the Babri Masjid, had been built on the spot in Mughal times. A Hindu organisation, the Vishwa Hindu Parishad (VHP), or World Hindu Council, an offshoot of the RSS, had for some time been running a campaign to demolish the mosque and rebuild the temple (Katju 2003). Their campaign coincided with a growth of Hindu revivalism (Van der Veer 1984), indirectly encouraged by the Congress government that, amongst other things, unprecedentedly approved the televising of a religious epic, the Ramayana, on Doordarshan (the government TV channel), commencing in January 1987, in an attempt to win sympathy from Hindu voters (Rajagopal 2001).[10] Lord Ram's birthplace was frequently mentioned in the serial, which attracted unprecedented audiences.

The conflict over the Ayodhya site was an old one, dating back to the 1850s and reviving again in the 1920s, since when the Masjid had been kept under government control (Elst 1990; Thapar 1989; Gopal *et al.* 1991). In 1984 the controversy resurfaced, and by 1987 had assumed serious proportions. At this point the Bharatiya Janata Party increasingly began to use the conflict as a weapon against Rajiv Gandhi. In 1988 the dispute escalated when the VHP obtained an order in the Allahabad High Court that ruled the shutting of the Masjid by the government to be illegal.[11] The controversy was further fuelled by the Congress, who adopted a contradictory stance, sometimes seeming to favour the Hindu fundamentalists and at other times the Muslims. Other perceived communalist stances of Congress included their backing of Muslim fundamentalists in the Shah Bano case, and the blatant use of Arun Govil, star of the TV serialisation of the Ramayana, to campaign for Congress during the Allahabad by-election in 1988 in an effort to win Hindu votes.

In consequence of the growing tensions, between January and September 1989 some 336 were killed in communal violence in the north of India. The situation reached a climax from September 1989 onwards as thousands of holy bricks (*ramshilas*) were consecrated in *pujas* (Hindu religious ceremonies) all over the country and were sent north to arrive in Ayodhya by 9 November, the date set by the VHP for commencing construction of the temple. In this campaign they were strongly supported by both the RSS and the BJP. The Congress government dragged its feet over the affair: they refused to allow demolition of the mosque, but at the same time allowed the 'foundation stone' of the new temple to be laid, adjacent to the Babri Masjid, and granted government land in Ayodhya for storing the consecrated bricks. This caused many Muslim voters to desert the Congress – the party they had traditionally seen, along with other minorities, as the best guardian of their interests.

The general election was finally held in November 1989. Congress, with 415 seats at the start of the election, was left with only 197 at its close. The Janata Dal won 142, the BJP 86, the Left Front (an alliance of the CPI and CPI [M]) 52, AIADMK 11, and the Kashmiri National Conference 3. The Janata Dal then formed a government (in retrospect inherently unstable), supported on the outside by the BJP and the Left Front. At an extraordinary meeting of the Janata Dal parliamentary board, Devi Lal from Haryana was proposed as PM, and then promptly stood down in favour of V.P. Singh, who was elected unanimously.

These events marked the end of the last majority government in post-independence Indian history and the dawn of a new era of minority and coalition governments, in which the influence of regional parties and minority groups was to come to the fore in a way never seen before. Seen by some as a source of instability and an unmitigated disaster, this long-term trend has come to be regarded by many commentators as a 'second democratic revolution'.

The Janata Dal in power, 1989–91

The new Janata Dal coalition government suffered an inauspicious start when in December the daughter of the newly appointed home minister, Mufti Muhammad Sayeed, a Kashmiri (India's first Muslim home minister) was abducted by members of the Kashmiri Liberation Front (KLF) as part of their campaign to liberate Kashmir from Indian rule. His daughter was only returned after the release of Abdul Hamid Sheikh and four other imprisoned KLF leaders.

V.P. Singh's first act as prime minister was to visit the Punjab, where militants were by now beginning to rally to the leadership of Simranjit Singh Mann – a former Indian police service officer, said to have advised Bindranwale on the fortification of the Golden Temple, and who had recently been released from prison and elected president of the Sikh Akali Dal. Singh created a good impression by making this visit, but no new accord was forthcoming – partly due the lack of a leader with the same broad support as that previously enjoyed by Harchand Singh Longowal during Rajiv Gandhi's period in office. An all-party meeting held in March also tried to resolve the Kashmir problem. V.P. Singh and Rajiv Gandhi together paid a visit to Srinagar – but without success, and the province was to remain under martial law and in a permanent state of unrest for most of the decade.

V.P. Singh had never been on good terms with Devi Lal, the leader of the Lok Dal Party in Haryana and now deputy prime minister. But the ruling coalition really began to fall apart when Om Prakash Chautala, prospective chief minister for Haryana and Devi Lal's son, was found guilty of malpractice during his election to the seat of Meham – following which V.P. Singh ordered his expulsion from the Janata Dal. In response, Devi Lal resigned from the post of deputy prime minister; but this was not accepted. He then showed his anger by ejecting Ajit Singh, the former Janata Party leader and a close supporter of V.P. Singh, from his post as secretary to the Janata Dal Parliamentary Board. V.P. Singh still refused to backtrack over the expulsion of Om Prakash Chautala, and after further threats from Devi Lal, finally called his bluff by accepting his resignation. In response Devi Lal mobilised his supporters in Haryana and organised a rally of peasants in protest at the government in New Delhi.

As relations within the government deteriorated, the communal situation took a turn for the worse as the BJP, led by the soft-spoken hardliner Lal Krishan Advani, swung more strongly in support of the Vishwa Hindu Parishad (VHP). An alliance was mooted with Devi Lal, the BJP thereby signalling its ambition to become the dominant party in the government. In August 1990, in a radical move, V.P. Singh suddenly announced an increase to 27 per cent in the reserved places in the universities and in central government administration for the so-called backward classes. He based his decision on recommendations by the 1980 Mandal Commission on caste discrimination. This commission had been ordered by Indira Gandhi, but its recommendations never implemented. The move was seen by many as a crude attempt to try to outmanoeuvre both Lal and Advani by winning over lower caste support, but V.P. Singh had in fact previously implemented the recommendations in Uttar Pradesh when he was its chief minister and 81 of 144 MPs supporting the government were backward caste members of the Janata Dal. The decision (although perhaps not the timing) was therefore more than anything an act of principle (Engineer 1991; Burman 1992; Karlekar 1992). In practice the proposals would have proved of little benefit to *dalits*, since few were in a position to take up the places on offer, for which reason they did not pose much of a threat to the upper castes. However, V.P. Singh had clearly miscalculated as the implementation of the recommendations caused widespread unrest (as Mrs Gandhi had feared they would) amongst the increasingly desperate, unemployed, educated youth of north India, leading to a wave of student protests in towns and cities. Grotesquely, these demonstrations culminated in the self-immolation of more than a hundred young men and women in protest at the generosity being shown to the oppressed and backward class of lower castes and tribes (Omvedt 1990).

Despite the protests V.P. Singh clearly had won support amongst some sections of rural society, and in response the BJP felt it had no alternative but to escalate its involvement in the Ram Jamabhoomi controversy. This sat well with the party's clearly articulated anti-Muslim prejudices (Basu *et al.* 1993). Theatrically, Advani announced his intention to embark on a march to Ayodhya, riding in a gold-painted chariot (*rath*) mounted on the back of a truck, supposedly representing the chariot used by the god Ram in his battles with the demon-king Ravana. The so-called 'Ram Rath Yatra' began from the Somnath temple complex in Gujarat on 25 September 1990, Pandit Deendayal Upadhyaya's birth anniversary, and was supposed to culminate at Ayodhya on 30 October after traversing 10,000 km. Amidst mounting tension, on 23 October as the *rath* entered the state of Bihar with its large Muslim population, the Janata Dal chief minister, with the prime minister's agreement, felt obliged to put a stop to it, and arrested Advani to avert the threat of communal conflagration. This led to the immediate withdrawal of BJP support for the government. Rioting followed in several cities in north India, curfews were imposed, and in November 1990 V.P. Singh's government was brought down after just 11 months in power by a vote of no-confidence in parliament. The ambitious Chandra Shekhar (famous for his imprisonment during the days of Mrs Gandhi's emergency) took over as caretaker prime minister with, ironically, Congress support.

An important factor in rising communal tensions and political instability in 1991 was large government spending deficits, high prices and growing unemployment, a legacy of Rajiv Gandhi's period in government (Vanaik 1997; Van der Veer 1987). The economic situation was aggravated by the Iraqi invasion of Kuwait from where much of India's oil imports had been secured at a discount. India now had to source its oil on the international market resulting in an immediate rise in the price of petrol and kerosene (used for domestic cooking). This further fuelled inflation and added considerably to the burdens upon ordinary households. During the Gulf War India stood by the *détente* with the USA that had been agreed in 1988, and prime minister Chandra Shekhar allowed US ships to refuel at Bombay, despite considerable opposition and criticism from within the country. In return India received little help, apart from a loan from the International Monetary Fund, granted on less than generous terms at the end of 1991 in order to cope with the spiralling deficits on India's balance of payments and a collapse in the value of the Indian rupee (Jalan 1991; Jain 1992; Vaidyanathan 1995).

Regardless of the government's difficulties, Rajiv Gandhi could not resist making further demands of the prime minister who now depended on Congress support, and after being forced into dismissing the Tamil Nadu state government in January 1991 against his will – allegedly for supporting Tamil Tiger terrorism in Sri Lanka – Chandra Shekhar finally hit back and resigned from office four months after becoming prime minister, forcing another general election only two years after the last. For this debacle the country at large held the Congress at fault. It was a development that Rajiv Gandhi intended to avert until he had had time to rebuild Congress support. It seems likely that he had hoped to remain a minority party in government, quietly sewing the seeds of disorder until public discontent rebounded to the benefit of his party. It was certainly true that the Indian public yearned for a stronger, more stable government, and when voting began on 20 May 1991, Congress initially performed better than expected. Sadly, one of the errors of Rajiv Gandhi's previous administration then caught up with him. Amongst supporters of the campaign for an independent Tamil homeland in the north of Sri Lanka there was still profound resentment at his government's intervention in that country in 1985. At a crowded election rally in Sriperumbudur, Tamil Nadu, on the third of five days of voting, a woman stepped towards Rajiv Gandhi, ostensibly to greet him, before exploding a bomb strapped to her body, killing the former prime minister and numerous innocent bystanders.

By the time of his death Rajiv Gandhi had learned the hard way the dangers of populist politics and the importance of genuine grass-roots campaigning of the sort in which he was engaged at the time of his visit to Madras. In his early career Rajiv Gandhi was frequently naïve, but amongst the sincerest political leaders seen in India since independence; his tragic death denied India the opportunity he would otherwise have had to put right his mistakes. The consequence of this suicide attack by a Tamil militant (and hardly the result intended by the Tigers), was a final surge in support for Rajiv's party in the south of India, and the restoration of a leaderless Congress to power in parliament.

Congress minority government, 1991–6

Congress returned to power with 232 seats out of 543: 40 seats short of an overall majority, but still the largest party. The BJP also emerged stronger with 120 seats, on the strength of their campaign to build the Ram temple at Ayodhya, but failed to put together a coalition sufficient to win control. Nostalgia for the days of Nehru and Indira prompted an immediate offer of the Congress Party leadership to Sonia Gandhi, Rajiv's widow, who wisely turned it down. Narasimha Rao, a Congress leader from Andhra Pradesh, was elected party leader by the Congress Central Working Committee ahead of two other main contenders – Arjun Singh from Madhya Pradesh, and Sharad Pawar, the Congress leader in Maharashtra.

Rao pledged to carry on the liberalising policies of Rajiv; indeed he had little choice: India's foreign exchange reserves were at a record low and the country was forced to take on renewed loans from the IMF in order to avoid defaulting on international debts. Help from the IMF, however, was conditional on an accelerated programme of major economic reforms. This was clearly pressing, since between 1986 and 1991 state-owned enterprises had made 39 per cent of gross investment but generated only 14 per cent of GDP. In tackling these problems, the liberalising budget introduced in February 1992 by finance minister Manmohan Singh exceeded most expectations. Measures included the denationalisation of banks (first nationalised by Indira Gandhi), a move towards the partial convertibility of the Indian rupee (the intention being to make it fully convertible within two to three years), a 5 per cent cut in excise and custom tariffs (which gave a boost to trade), the abolition of wealth tax on income from shareholding (in order to encourage investment), and the lowering of statutory liquidity ratios for bank deposits (in order to boost the funds available for private borrowing and thereby ease the pain of the transition towards a more open and less regulated economy). These measures were reinforced in later budgets, and by 1995 average tariffs had fallen to 25 per cent from 87 per cent in 1990, whilst foreign investment rose from US $300 million in 1992/3 to US $2 billion in 1995/6 (Bhagwati 1993; Cassen and Joshi 1995; Ahluwalia and Little 1998).

At a meeting of the Congress Party, held in Tirupati in April 1992, another of Rajiv Gandhi's ambitions was fulfilled when elections were held for key party posts for the first time since 1969. Regional power bosses were weakened by this move, but Narasimha Rao remained prime minister after securing places for most of his protégés (including Muslim representatives after he threatened resignation) on the Congress Central Working Committee and the District Committees. By pursuing policies of liberalisation, however, the Congress was in effect doing away with its *raison d'être*. Since independence it had cast itself as a socialist party whose aim, however imperfectly executed, was to defend the poor and minorities. By trumpeting their success in doing away with government controls, closing loss-making state enterprises, and even cutting subsidies for the public food distribution system – an important resource for the urban poor – Congress politicians, and particularly the finance minister, won international plaudits. They also advertised the fact that their main concern was now the business community, and that they were willing to abandon the means to redistribute income and welfare measures to ameliorate the social impact of economic change. The popularity of the government steadily fell, while, as Indira and Rajiv had both discovered to their cost, many indigenous monopoly capitalists continued to fund opposition groups promising an 'India first' *swadeshi* policy (Rothermund 1996; Linnemann and Rao 1996).

The opposition was led by the Bharatiya Janata Party, which continued to support the campaign to build a Hindu temple at Ayodhya (Hansen and Jaffrelot 1998; Basu *et al.* 1993). In December 1992 militant groups led by the VHP and the Bajrang Dal, another offshoot of the RSS, marched on the 400-year-old Babri Masjid at Ayodhya. Uttar Pradesh was this time under the control of a BJP-led coalition, which mysteriously failed to reinforce the state police on guard at the site, who were quickly overwhelmed. The mosque was demolished. Riots broke out in all the major Muslim cities in the north of India, leaving some 1,600 dead (Mukhopadhyay 1994). In response the central government suspended the BJP-led governments in Uttar Pradesh, Rajasthan, Himachal Pradesh, Madhya Pradesh and Delhi. This, of course, was tantamount to shutting the stable door after the horse had bolted. It also banned the RSS, Bajrang Dal and several Muslim organisations such as Jamaat-i-Islami, seized cassette tapes of provocative speeches by BJP leaders and proscribed inflammatory literature.

Some of the worst communal violence was seen in the cities of Ahmedabad, Surat and Bombay where, with the tacit encouragement of politicians in the ruling Shiv Sena, Muslim slums were raided by Hindu gangs, some of them directed by slum landlords who stood to gain from the destruction and the subsequent opportunities for property development (Vanaik 1997). The Justice B.N. Srikrishna Commission on the Mumbai riots reported:

> There is no doubt that the Shiv Sena and Shiv Sainiks took the lead in organising attacks on Muslims and their properties under the guidance of several leaders of the Shiv Sena from the level of Shakha Pramukh to the Shiv Sena Pramukh Bal Thackeray who, like a veteran General, commanded his loyal Shiv Sainiks to retaliate by organised attacks against Muslims.[12]

Around 150,000 Bombay residents fled to the countryside, while 100,000 more moved into refugee camps. According to (conservative) official statistics, 784 people died, and around 5,000 were injured, 70 per cent of them Muslim. In Surat, Muslim women were allegedly gang-raped and videos made of the acts of aggression. These were then said to have been distributed by Hindu extremists in order to incite further violence. Whether true or not, such anxious rumours were indicative of the appalling state of communal relations and the environment of fear and disorder. Worse was to come. On Friday, 12 March 1993 a Muslim section of the Bombay underworld linked to the smuggling gang of Dawood Ibrahim (which had relocated to Dubai and subsequently Karachi) set off a series of 15 massive explosions by way of revenge. The explosions rocked the length and breadth of Bombay, killing 317 people, injuring more than 1,200, and gutting the Stock Exchange, the Air India building, the passport office and three 5-star hotels near the airport. Dawood Ibrahim has since been designated a supporter of international terrorism by the USA. A reward equivalent to US $32,000 was posted by the Indian government for information leading to the capture and conviction of the bombers, and the Shiv Sena administration vowed to deport Muslims in the city 'back to' Bangladesh, an arbitrary threat to which they ultimately subjected several hundred as part of a provocative programme of slum clearances several years later. In July 2000, with a change in state government, Bal Thackeray, the Shiv Sena leader, was finally obliged to appear in court to account for his role in inciting the 1992 anti-Muslim riots, but he was acquitted due to the seven-year time lapse since the offence was committed.

In November 1993 state elections were held. The Bharatiya Janata Party gained New Delhi and Rajasthan, but Congress was restored to power in a number of states – a warning to the BJP that it needed to be more cautious in its advocacy of militant anti-Muslim causes. Congress itself was not regarded as entirely blameless in the Ayodhya debacle, this being particularly evident in Muslim Uttar Pradesh where there was no revival of Congress support. Instead, in an important departure, the low-caste Samajwadi Party, led by Mulayam Singh Yadav, came to power in the state in alliance with the Bahujan Samaj (BSP) or 'Common People's Party', a *dalit* political party supported by poor, low-caste farmers and Muslim voters. This was the first time a political organisation run by and for *dalits* had achieved political power of any sort and was a powerful indication of popular, subaltern discontent with the politicking and indifference of all the major parties.

The BSP, led by Kanshi Ram and Mayawati, first contested elections in 1984 without success. The party increased its share of the vote in 1991, and again in 1993 after allying briefly with the Samajwadi Party (with Mulayam Singh Yadav, leader of the other backward castes in the state, as chief minister) and by campaigning aggressively with slogans such as 'Tilak, Taraju, Talwar. Maaro Unko Joote Char' (which rudely advocates that Brahmins, Banias and Rajputs should all be beaten four times with a shoe – a classically demeaning punishment due to the ritual impurity of leather). In 1995 the BSP formed an unlikely but strategically skilful alliance with the BJP (from which they were ideologically poles apart); this gained Mayawati the office of chief minister – the first time a *dalit* or untouchable politician had occupied this post in any state assembly. Her success was greeted with rapturous approval and galvanised lower caste voters throughout the north of India (Hasan 1998; Jaffrelot 1999).

After the violence at Ayodhya it is difficult to imagine that the fortunes of the BJP could revive within just two years. The explanation lies in the continuing malaise and corruption of the Congress Party. Conspicuously no longer the friend of the Indian poor, as it continued to champion liberalisation, Congress turned its attention to the increasingly powerful middle class. To win their support, economic reforms had to be seen to work and the material benefits, at least to the middle classes, needed to be transparent. To achieve this junior ministers in the Treasury and Finance departments turned a blind eye whilst public money was siphoned off from government securities transactions and used in stock market speculations in order to inflate share prices artificially. Harshad Mehta, an important broker at the Bombay stock exchange, was found guilty of creaming some US $1.2 billion in securities from the state-owned Maruti car company in 1992. Stock prices were dramatically inflated, but when 'the scam' was uncovered India's financial market collapsed – stocks plummeted by more than a quarter, and thousands of investors lost out. More than forty were eventually arrested for their involvement, and two ministers and many senior officials in the Rao administration were forced to resign. The impact on the party's middle-class supporters was naturally negative.

The following year an acute sugar shortage developed in India. In normal circumstances imports would have been allowed to close the gap, but instead sugar prices soared, leading to speculation that the scarcity had been engineered to allow the millowners to profit. These were then allegedly shared with Congress Party officials – either personally, or in order to fund electioneering. In another incident, a police raid on the house of a minister responsible for privatising the telephone system uncovered a mattress stuffed with bank notes. One possible explanation lay with the minority status of the government and the need to bribe MPs in the Lok Sabha to ensure its support. The most infamous bribe was that offered to MPs of the Jharkhand Mukti Morcha in exchange for their votes, but there were doubtless many others. Some Congress Party members may simply have been concerned to make hay while the sun still shone, aware of the party's sinking standing in the opinion polls. After leaving office, no fewer than 16 ministers in the Rao administration were to face corruption charges.

The worst scandal of all was uncovered in January 1996 when a police investigation of *hawala* dealer S.K. Jain uncovered two ledgers detailing transactions totalling US $17 million allegedly paid in bribes to 115 people, each recorded by their initials. These were later revealed to be those of top-ranking individuals in Indian politics. *Hawala* trading had been popular for decades. It was a means of illegally exchanging foreign currency above official rates. A paperless transaction, and therefore usually entirely covert, it was used to move untaxed or 'black' money out of the country for investment abroad and back into the hands of friends and relatives. More notoriously it is alleged to have been used to move funds by terrorist groups such as Al-Qaeda. There is evidence that at least US $4 billion is transacted annually in this fashion, but the likely figure is very much higher. The payment of bribes to individual politicians in India was undoubtedly intended to enable *hawala* dealers to carry on their trade without fear of prosecution and may indicate the involvement of politicians in the business themselves. The police revelations caused an immediate furore, and obliged three members of Narasimha Rao's government to resign, as well as a leader of the BJP. Unofficial reports suggested that the prime minister himself was under suspicion, although he remained in office until elections were held in 1996.

Congress defeat, 1996

Indian public opinion generally reacts strongly to tales of corruption amongst politicians, despite the frequency of their exposure. Inevitably, therefore, and for all its successes in promulgating many urgently needed economic reforms and finally bringing peace to the Punjab, the most scam-prone Congress government since independence plunged to its worst-ever defeat, winning only 140 seats in the 1996 Lok Sabha election. Narasimha Rao resigned soon after. Sonia Gandhi was again asked to assume the leadership, but she refused and it was octogenarian former party treasurer, Sitaram Kesri, who was elected to replace Rao. Bribery charges were shortly afterwards brought against Rao, who was eventually convicted of corruption, although he died in 2004 (aged 83) before he could serve any part of his sentence.

The 1996 election produced a badly fragmented parliament, since neither the Congress nor the BJP held any great appeal for the voters. Congress won a total of 161 seats and was therefore the largest party, but was well short of an overall majority. The BJP formed a 12-day minority government under Prime Minister

Atal Bihari Vajpayee, which quickly lost power having failed to secure support from any of the minor regional parties. The BJP's involvement in the destruction of the Babri Masjid had irrevocably marked it as a communal party that numerous politicians refused to support in government – not least because many had Muslim constituents. In its place a coalition of secular regional parties, the so-called United Front, led by Janata, assumed power, supported from the outside by the CPI (M) and Congress parties.

The new government was headed by H.D. Deve Gowda, the Janata Dal leader from Karnataka. The United Front engendered considerable optimism and popular support, offering what seemed a realistic alternative to the extremism of the BJP and the corruption of Congress rule. Initially it was effective enough, governing with sage advice behind the scenes from former Janata Dal prime minister V.P. Singh. However, Deve Gowda failed to develop good relations with the Congress Party, who soon demanded that he be replaced, claiming that the coalition was pursuing policies 'detrimental to the interests of the Indian people'. Another Janata Dal leader, Inder Kumar Gujral, took over in March 1997 and was generally regarded as a successful PM, particularly in addressing the insurgency problem in Kashmir and in cultivating a good working relationship with Nawaz Sharif, then prime minister of Pakistan. Unfortunately, Sitaram Kesri was not content to allow the government untrammelled authority. Described by *The Times of India* as an 'old man in a hurry', he provoked a second crisis after prepublication reports of the Jain Commission of Inquiry suggested indirect links between the Tamil terrorists who assassinated Rajiv Gandhi and a partner in the ruling coalition – the DMK. On the strength of these leaks, Kesri demanded the removal of the DMK from government. When Gujral refused, the Congress tabled a vote of no confidence. For all his bluster, it soon became apparent that Kesri could not assemble sufficient support to form a new government himself. The president therefore suspended parliament and India was forced once again to the polls within 18 months.

Immediately prior to the February 1998 election the Congress published a formal apology to India's Muslims for having failed to do more to avert the destruction of the Babri Masjid in 1992. This did the party little good, as it was still widely criticised for having forced an unnecessary election. For its part in this debacle the Congress suffered another hammering early in 1998, gaining only 141 seats, whilst the BJP, after many years of struggle, finally emerged with sufficient seats (182) to stand a realistic chance of forming a government. It could do so only with the help of a variety of minor political parties, but, with the failure of the United Front experiment, most felt that there was no alternative. They were confronted with the choice of either joining the BJP in government, or remaining outside with the increasingly maverick and quixotic Congress. The CPI and the CPI (M) both refused to have any truck with a party associated so consistently with communal politics. Nonetheless, the Telugu Desam, the AIADMK, and other regional opposition parties decided to throw in their lot with the BJP, enabling it to form what could be described as the first avowedly non-secular[13] government India had seen since independence.

16 Colonial and post-colonial Sri Lanka

The dilemmas of national identity

My mother always told me this was not our country . . . How often, I don't remember. But regularly enough for the thought to register. I was born here, I would usually counter. You were born here. How can this not be our country? This is their country, she would respond, tryingly. Don't make a noise about it. We should be glad the Sinhalese are tolerating us.

(Qadri Ismail, May 2002)[1]

I am not worried about the opinion of the Tamil people . . . now we cannot think of them, not about their lives or their opinion . . . Really if I starve the Tamils out, the Sinhala people will be happy.

(President J.R. Jayawardene, July 1983)[2]

War is always here and from every house there is someone who has gone to the war and died. Before this fighting started we didn't have so much violence and when someone died we cried. But now everyone is used to it and it has to stop.

(Ananda Jayatileke, Polgahawella village, Sri Lanka, 21 December 1999)[3]

The population of Sri Lanka is three-quarters Sinhalese, principally followers of the reformed sect of Therevada Buddhism, combined with elements of local, magical animist beliefs (Ames 1964; Gombrich 1991). Otherwise the island is ethnically highly diverse, including Malays (migrants from Malaysia), Veddahs (a tribal group), Moors (descendants of Arab traders), Burghers (who trace their descent from former Dutch colonists), 'Jaffna' Hindu Tamils and Muslim migrants of ancient origin, more recent Hindu Tamil migrants, brought in by the British, and both Catholic and Protestant Christians found within the Sinhalese Tamil and Burgher groups.

Before the entire island came under British rule in 1815, the coastal areas of Sri Lanka (or Ceylon as it was then known) had been ruled by the Portuguese and the Dutch, and had for many years been an important staging post in the Indian Ocean trade. The British East India Company took control of the island from the Dutch in 1796, during the French Revolution. The island was formally ceded by the treaty of Amiens in 1802. Whilst taking on Dutch commitments to protect the autonomy of the highland kingdom on Kandy, the British soon breached this agreement and took over Kandy in 1815, thus bringing the entire island under their rule. The Kandyans reacted with a popular rebellion in 1818 and further abortive rebellions in 1843 and 1848. After their suppression, the administration of the island was radically restructured: a separate administration was installed, English was made the language of government and schools, and (unlike in India) restrictions on European landownership were lifted. Encouragement was given to the cultivation of cinnamon, pepper, sugar-cane, cotton and coffee. The selling of crown lands stimulated the expansion of coffee production on plantations in the highlands, with the assistance of growing numbers of migrant labourers brought from the south of India after the 1840s (Peebles 2001). Following an attack of coffee leaf disease in the 1870s, the production of tea and rubber expanded, leading to further labour immigration into the highlands. The plains and the coastal areas to the south, however, remained devoted to subsistence agriculture, and for the most part were unaffected by these changes.

The origins of the island's inhabitants did not become an important issue until colonial administrators – inspired by the works of British and German scholars, including Max Mueller and Wilhelm Geiger – began to devise hierarchical classifications of various groups according to the historical period in which they are supposed to have settled on the island. It was the British who defined the descendants of the Dutch colonists as 'Burghers' and labelled other groups as Muslims, Tamils, Low Country Sinhalese and Kandyans. The 'Tamil' and 'Muslim' denotation was somewhat arbitrary, since many Muslims were also Tamils. Likewise, the categories of Kandyan Sinhalese and Low Country Sinhalese simply referred to those living in the hills in the territory of the former Kandyan kingdom, who were regarded as culturally more sophisticated yet traditional, and the coastal Sinhalese, mostly farmers, who were regarded as more 'backward'.

Even after centuries of colonial rule, Sri Lankans had not become used to the idea of being a subject people, and in reaction to aggressive Christian missionary activity, both Buddhist and Hindu revivalist movements began to develop in the late nineteenth century. In the north, Arumugam Navalar led a Hindu renaissance in the 1860s and 1870s, whilst in the south in the early 1900s Anagarika Dharmapala and Walisinha Harischandra led a campaign to protect places of Buddhist worship. They were also leaders of a temperance movement, which asserted the values of a modernised Buddhist faith, commonly referred to as 'Protestant Buddhism'. A symptom of this religious revivalism was the growth of lay meditation centres, which not only enabled some of Sri Lanka's 15,000 to 20,000 Buddhist monks (*bhikkus*) to engage with a wider population but became important religious centres in their own right, transforming the nature of Sri Lankan Buddhism in the process (Gombrich and Obeyesekere 1988). As well as being a reaction to colonialism, such movements were also a means of self-assertion by the emergent Sri Lankan middle classes. At about the same time archaeological discoveries unearthed evidence of powerful ancient kingdoms, of indigenous and external origin, the existence of which had hitherto been doubted. This fuelled a reassessment of the island's history and the identity of its inhabitants (Spencer 1990b). The Aryan theory of Indo-European origins, promulgated by various British scholars, presented a further challenge. In pre-colonial Sri Lanka the notion of Arya existed, but Aryan was a status obtained through the performance of meritorious acts. British physical anthropologists, by contrast, believed it to be a racial category, enabling the differentiation of the South Asian population into discrete racial groups. A key moment in Sri Lanka, Nira Wickramasinghe (1995, 2001, 2005) suggests, was the translation of the *Mahavamsa* epic into Sinhalese in the early twentieth century by W. Geiger. This enthused the Sinhalese literati of the time who linked colonial racial classifications with the tale of the landing of King Vijaya on the island in the sixth century BC, thus providing the myth of a common, superior, Aryan origin for the Sinhalese people (Dharmadasa 1992; Kemper 1991). This was far more appealing than depicting them as the descendants of the hordes of the demon-king Ravana (as depicted in the Ramayana), or any of the other popular mythic theories of origin that abounded at the time. The Vijayan myth captured people's imagination and became the kernel of Sinhalese nationalism. At the same time the identity of migrants was defined as everything 'un-Vijayan' by Buddhist revivalists and Sinhalese nationalists such as Anagarika Dharmapala, who were attempting to build community consciousness in the early decades of the twentieth century. Arguably, this negative way of defining Sinhalese nationalism first bore fruit in race riots, which grew out of a conflict between Sinhalese and Moorish traders in Kandy in 1915 (Kannangara 1984; Roberts 1994: 201). Subsequently, the 1920s saw the emergence of a symbiotic relationship between Sinhalese politicians and the *bhikku*. Thus, the trade union leader and politician A.E. Goonesinha enjoyed the support of radical monks Boose Dhammarakhita and Udakandawela Siri Saranankara, who contributed to Goonesinha's political journal and addressed strike meetings. The pioneer labour leader (who counted Ranasinghe Premadasa amongst his protégés) slowly turned into a communal politician in order to protect his political fief. Under the strains of the great depression in the 1930s, this then led to violent encounters between unemployed Sinhalese and groups of migrant workers in Colombo and other industrial centres (Jayawardena 1980). It also added considerable significance to early attempts by the British to devise a constitution for the island, based upon their system of racial classification.

The British believed that the island's various ethnic groups had quite distinct cultures and forms of social organisation, and that the constitution ought therefore to be unitary and secular but rigged in such a way as to prevent the majority Sinhalese from overwhelming any of the minority communities. The first scheme was announced in 1909. Demands for the abandonment of communal representation were rejected, and officials were in the majority, but there were elected representatives introduced for the Europeans, the Burghers, and 'educated' Ceylonese (including Sinhalese, Tamils and Muslims). It was a highly elitist constitution, and for a long time remained so, the qualifications to vote being a pass in a Senior Cambridge Board English Examination, masculinity, and an income of Rs 1,500 per annum. In 1921, however, the franchise was greatly widened by allowing a pass in a vernacular examination to count, although the ethnic distinctions remained. No rights at all were given to the Veddahs – an ancient tribal community in the island. As with their equivalents in India at the same time, they were considered too backward to merit much consideration, a neglect they still suffer to this day.

The initial British attempts at constitutional reform were, needless to say, insufficient to satisfy an increasingly articulate and educated Ceylonese public opinion. Rapid economic growth during the First World War, as well as British attempts to suppress dissent by arresting prominent Sinhalese politicians, helped to foster the development of a national consciousness, and in 1919 Sinhalese and Tamil organisations came together to form the Ceylon National Congress. The Congress soon drafted proposals for further constitutional reforms, demanding an elected majority in the legislature, control of the budget, and at least partial responsibility for the executive arm of government. In response to these demands, the Donoughmore Commission promised further major reforms in 1928. Sri Lanka was relatively prosperous, however, and the middle classes were educated and reasonably egalitarian. This presented a problem. According to the thinking of officials in South Asia, as elsewhere at the time, the franchise should be a privilege, the granting of which would earn the loyalty of colonial subjects if it was to serve any purpose (Bates 2001). Donoughmore therefore proposed the abandonment of communal representation and the introduction of a universal adult franchise. At the same time he ruled out the idea of a bill of rights in favour of specific clauses protecting minority communities, and recommended that the right to vote should be restricted to those who could meet a test of residence for more than five years, and who affirmed a willingness to settle permanently on the island. The issue of the various migrant origins of Sri Lanka's population thus suddenly became a crucial part of the definition of civic rights. Wickramasinghe (2001) argues that a sharp boundary was created between the Sinhalese and more recent immigrants to the island – particularly the Tamil workers on the colonial tea plantations in the highlands. Middle-class Sinhalese nationalists demanded further restrictions, including the retention of a specific literacy test for those who could not prove they had five years of residence (thereby excluding most Indian workers). These were adopted in the final form of the constitution in 1931, together with a clause allowing the vote to anyone who met a property qualification, thus enfranchising every European and the richest Indians. More positively, attempts to restrict the franchise of women were given up (women in India by contrast did not get the vote until more than twenty years later). However, in most respects, the Donoughmore constitution was a divisive affair, extending the suffrage according to simplistic concepts of class and ethnicity.

Unsurprisingly, anti-immigrant rhetoric (the principal target being 'the Malayalees' – migrants from the south-west of India) and violence were a feature in the run-up to the 1936 council elections, although the colonial government did its best to keep the situation in check. Thereafter, class and ethnicity – more than religion, the key feature in Indian constitutional arrangements in the 1930s – became increasingly the points of fracture in Sri Lankan public life. Still more significantly, as Wickramasinghe (2001, 2005) argues, anti-immigration legislation

Map 10 Sri Lanka: principal towns, cities and provinces.

came to be regarded by many as the sensible and legitimate way to deal with economic difficulties, and Sri Lanka introduced stringent restrictions on immigration during the depression years, long before such measures were even thought of elsewhere. This process of exclusion became yet more virulent in the decades following independence.

The colonial experience increased the likelihood of ethnic conflict for a number of other reasons. The British selected the Tamils as collaborators, and preferred them to carry on administrative work, the Sinhalese in the south being less often favoured with government positions. This encouraged the growth of anti-Tamil feeling after independence, much as the use of Brahmin collaborators by the British helped to encourage anti-Brahmin feeling in India. A further problem was that, unlike India, Sri Lanka experienced no long-drawn-out national struggle that might have helped to define the character of the post-colonial nation. After Lord Soulbury implemented the constitutional arrangements for self-government, elections were held in 1947, and the British then simply left the following year, having already cut their ties with India. The 1947 elections thus took place in a vacuum. There was little in the way of established political organisations, and although the middle classes involved themselves in the political process, and radical monks backed a number of leftist parties, for the rural majority the political process was largely meaningless.

The major political party that existed at independence was the United National Party (UNP) formed by D.S. Senanayake in 1946. Inevitably, the dilemmas of nationhood, which had been debated over 50 or 60 years in India, soon came to the boil in Sri Lanka. The process was particularly fraught because of the gulf between the educated middle classes (7 per cent) and the unpoliticised mass of the population, and was compounded by economic stresses in the wake of the Second World War. During the war itself Sri Lanka had profited greatly from its exports, particularly of rubber, but falling prices in the post-war period, combined with rapid population growth, eroded the country's prosperity and generated social and political tensions. The United National Party, led by D.S. Senanayake (succeeded in 1952 by his son), formed the first government of Sri Lanka in 1947 and attempted to address the issue of national identity. At the top of the agenda was the rewriting of the Soulbury constitution. Because the UNP was dominated by Sinhalese, they decided to restrict the franchise to residents with three generations of paternal ancestors resident on the island. The problem with this was that a large section of the island's population was of recent arrival. Distinct from the Sinhalese and Ceylon Tamils who had arrived in ancient times, the nineteenth- and twentieth-century immigrant Tamil plantation workers were targeted by this policy. Large numbers of plantation Tamils were called upon to claim citizenship, but the registration of births had never been compulsory, and in the absence of birth certificates many were unable to do so, 900,000 eventually being disenfranchised. The intervention of an Oxford-educated politician and son of an Anglican Christian, S.W.R.D. Bandaranaike, turned this policy into a nationalist issue (Manor 1989). Bandaranaike argued that if the rights of the Tamil population could be distinguished by their length of residence, then Tamils as a whole ought also to be distinguished from the Sinhalese, whom he and others viewed as the more ancient inhabitants. He converted to Buddhism, and in 1951 he and his leftist group of supporters split away from the UNP to found the Sri Lanka Freedom Party (SLFP), which in the 1956 elections campaigned on the issue of Sinhalese representation.

The main focus of Bandaranaike's agitation was that there should be a single language of government – Sinhalese. This appealed particularly to the vernacular-speaking middle class of schoolteachers, shopkeepers, *ayurveda* doctors and monks – whose support was actively solicited. Inevitably, the Tamils, who up until then had been uneasy but divided, closed ranks on this issue. The two main Tamil parties, the Tamil Congress and the Tamil Federal Party (TFP), decided to unite in order to oppose Bandaranaike, and formed the Tamil United Front to represent their joint interests in the election. They were not successful: Bandaranaike's SLFP was elected in alliance with various smaller Sinhalese parties, and introduced the Official Languages Act of 1956, which made Sinhala, the language of the Sinhalese majority, the sole official language on the island. This led to strikes and demonstrations by Tamils in the north of the country and clashes with Sinhalese in the streets. The government declared an emergency, at India's insistence, in May 1958, during which some 10,000 Tamils living in the south of the country were shifted to the relatively safer Tamil-majority areas around Jaffna in the north. Unfortunately this further entrenched regional concentrations of the different ethnic groups.

In 1958, the Tamil Language (Special Provisions) Act was passed to allow for the 'reasonable' use of Tamil in education, public service exams, and in the administration of Tamil majority areas in the northern and eastern provinces. Regulations for its enforcement were not immediately compiled, and ultimately the Act was never implemented, but the concession was too much for some, and in 1959 Premier Bandaranaike was assassinated by a fanatical Buddhist monk at the instigation of Mapitigam Buddharakkitha (high priest of Kelaniya temple), one of the SLFP's most important founding members, who felt his support had been betrayed (Tambiah 1992). The premier's wife, Sirimavo Bandaranaike, was then appointed to the Senate and made premier and leader of the SLFP. She won the general election in 1960 (Figure 22) – becoming the first-ever elected female prime minister in the world – and retained control until the next elections took place in 1965. Mrs Bandaranaike was widely approved of in the West because she ruled within a socialist coalition and introduced a number of important welfare reforms, as well as nationalising industries and private schools, making education free to all, from kindergarten through to university level. The consequence was that Sri Lanka was able to build upon its reputation for the best health and educational systems and the highest level of literacy in South Asia, and seemed on course to join those countries in South-East Asia that were beginning to experience rapid advances in economic wealth. The dependence of her government on coalition partners meant, however, that Mrs Bandaranaike's political position was vulnerable, and the Tamil Language Act in particular remained unimplemented.

Figure 22 Sirimavo Bandaranaike, prime minister of Ceylon, following her election in 1960
– the first woman head of govement in modern history. © Bettmann/CORBIS.

In 1965 the elections produced a hung parliament. Neither the SLFP and its
allies nor the UNP won a majority, and the Tamil Federal Party, with 14 seats, held
the balance of power. The UNP was by this time under the leadership of Dudley
Senanayake, who had taken over following the death of his father, D.S. Senanayake, in 1952. The TFP foolishly decided to enter into an alliance with the UNP, on
the understanding that a compromise settlement of the language dispute would be
brokered in favour of the Tamil language, and regions. Rioting, led by Buddhist
monks – who have often been at the forefront of political agitation in Sri Lanka –
immediately broke out, and amid a resurgence of Sinhalese militancy, a far-left
extremist Sinhalese party, the Janatha Vimukthi Peramuna (JVP), was formed. The
JVP attracted adherents among students, the unemployed and low castes, and was
founded in 1967 by Rohana Wijeweera, the son of a businessman from the seaport
of Tangalla. Wijeweera had studied medicine in Moscow (though without complet-
ing the course), and later became a Maoist and an influential figure in the Communist Party of Sri Lanka. In consequence of the violence, the SLFP–Tamil pact
was never introduced, and following elections in 1970 Mrs Bandaranaike again
returned to power – this time in alliance with the Communist Party and the LSSP
(a Trotskyist group) – promising to defend the 'rights' of the majority Sinhalese.
The JVP supported Mrs Bandaranaike in the election, but pressured the government to address the needs of the proletariat whilst simultaneously amassing arms.
When Wijeweera was arrested, the JVP launched an insurrection in the south.
Within two weeks the army had regained control, and the JVP was proscribed,
but an estimated 10,000 of the country's youth lost their lives in the insurgency.

Mrs Bandaranaike commenced her second term in office by extending nationalisation to encompass a large part of the wholesale and distribution trades,

agency houses, and foreign-owned plantations, and by initiating a programme of land reform. After consulting her astrologer, she moved in May 1972 to introduce a new constitution. The name 'Ceylon' was dropped in favour of 'Sri Lanka' (meaning 'Resplendent Island'), ties with the British crown were severed and the Westminster-style bicameral parliament (the old Soulbury constitution) was abandoned. Sri Lanka instead became a socialist republic with executive power concentrated in the hands of a prime minister answerable to a single National State Assembly. Sinhalese was enshrined as the country's official language and no concession was made in favour of the Tamils' demands for a federal structure. Ominously, section 29 of the original 1948 constitution, which barred discrimination and guaranteed equal status to all religious groups, was revoked. Instead governments were enjoined by the constitution to foster and protect the majority religion, Buddhism. Although the constitution allowed parliament to pass an enactment (as it eventually did in 1978) allowing Tamil to be used in the courts of the north and eastern provinces, and for other concessions to be made in accordance with the Tamil Language Act of 1966, all such concessions were to be subordinate to constitutional provisions.

The year before the 1972 constitution was passed, a system of district quotas in regard to appointment of university places was introduced, similar to the positive discrimination legislation employed in India, but in this case weighted against the minority Tamil community. The rationale was that the colonial education system had always advantaged the predominantly urban Tamils, and to redress this imbalance, discrimination was now put in place and extended to the judiciary, the civil service and other public sector posts. This was but an official enactment of a discriminatory policy that had been going on for some time. Already, Tamils had been excluded from government service in the south, and by 1975 only 5 per cent of government posts were still held by Tamils. At the same time, the number of Tamil students in the science-based disciplines fell from 35 per cent in 1970 to 19 per cent. After 1975, no more Tamils were recruited at all into the civil service. There thus developed a large reserve of educated and unemployed Tamil youths, and an even greater pool of Tamils, who had expected, but now were no longer able, to go to university. Tamils had always placed a high value on education; restricting university places was a great insult to them, and the loss of opportunity for employment in the public service drove many young Tamils to join the Tamil Tigers, formed in 1972. In 1976 the Tamil Tigers renamed itself the Liberation Tigers of Tamil Eelam[4] (LTTE) and was reorganised into a highly disciplined fighting force, led by Vellupillai Prabhakaran. Prabhakaran, like many of his followers, is alleged to wear a cyanide pellet around his neck to be swallowed in the event of capture, and is said to be personally responsible for the assassination of the mayor of Jaffna in 1975, one of the first acts of terrorism committed in the Tamil cause.

Initially the LTTE co-operated with the Tamil United Front and organised a convention that denounced the 1972 constitution and called for a separate state of Tamil Eelam. This convention was supported by many TUF delegates, who renamed their party the Tamil United Liberation Front (TULF). In the general election of 1977, the TULF won all seats in the north, but did less well in the east where Tamils and Sinhalese resided together. There, the UNP obtained the highest number of votes on the strength of a virulently anti-Tamil campaign. In the south, discontent at growing corruption within the newly state-owned industries, inflation in the wake of OPEC's oil price rises, and rising unemployment, led to a rout of the SLFP. Once again the UNP took control of the government, this time under the leadership of J.R. Jayawardene, a barrister who had been second-ranking leader under D.S. Senanayake and his son, Dudley, who had died in 1973. UNP supporters celebrated the election victory by attacking the offices of Mrs Bandaranaike's party, and soon after Mrs Bandaranaike herself was banned from the National Assembly for abuses of power while in office. For many, these developments marked the end point of efforts to politically integrate the island, as well as an end to political harmony for some time to come (Manor 1976).

The Jayawardene government terminated the SLFP's programme of nationalisation, and attempted to revive the private sector and attract foreign investment. In 1978 it also introduced a new constitution, renaming the country the Democratic Socialist Republic of Sri Lanka, and making the presidency an elected post (for six years) with executive powers on similar lines to that of the French model of government, with the prime minister becoming merely an appointee of the president. Sinhala and Tamil were both recognised as national languages, but Sinhala was affirmed as the official language of administration. In elections held the same year Jayawardene was elected as the first president under the new constitution, and the UNP's Ramasinghe Premadasa became prime minister.

In reaction to Jayawardene's constitutional reforms, Tamil groups, the strongest of which was the LTTE, stepped up their insurgency in the north and east of the country, establishing training camps in the jungle, and targeting the police and institutions of the central government. In an effort to maintain peace, the Sri Lankan army was enlarged and deployed in growing numbers. However, it was as yet still an inexperienced and poorly equipped force, and when a UNP candidate and a policeman were killed during a district council election in the north in 1981, the Sri Lankan army ran amok in the city of Jaffna. Civilians were attacked, the offices of a Tamil newspaper were set alight and the famous Jaffna Public Library, with its valuable collection of books and manuscripts, was burned to the ground. This assault at the very heart of the community united both plantation and Ceylon Tamils in support of the Tamil Tigers. The UNP government's response was to escalate its opposition to the guerrillas in the north. It began to embark on a campaign of state terrorism aimed at driving Tamils out of the Sinhalese-dominated eastern zone, whilst the LTTE attempted a counter-programme of terrorism aimed at the Sinhalese. Both the army and the LTTE thereby contributed to the regionalisation of communities. The government's systematic targeting of Tamil civilians and business interests culminated in an anti-Tamil slaughter launched in Colombo on 24 July 1983. Effectively a pogrom, the Colombo massacre was undoubtedly undertaken with official connivance. There had been the minor provocation of the ambush of an army convoy the preceding day, which aroused public anger, but police and civil servants were seen accompanying bands of soldiers holding aloft electoral rolls in order to pinpoint Tamil homes and businesses. As further proof of official involvement, there was simultaneously a brutal slaughter of 52 Tamil political prisoners held in the maximum security prison at Welikade in Colombo. The bodies were reportedly stacked in front of a statue of Gautama Buddha in the main prison yard, as if it were a form of sacrifice. No official explanation was offered as to how this might happen in a maximum security institution. The violence in Colombo and the surrounding area lasted for a week, at the end of which time 18,000 Tamil homes and 5,000 business premises had been devastated; 150,000 Tamils were driven into refugee camps and 3,000 were killed. While this was going on, the UNP president, J.R. Jayawardene, turned a blind eye to the atrocities. His government followed up the riots with a 6th amendment to the constitution in August 1983, which banned from parliament any politician who advocated secession, effectively disenfranchising the Tamil population's chosen representatives and making a political solution to the troubles virtually impossible.

It is arguable that until 1977 the Tamil–Sinhala dispute might have been resolved peacefully. Up to this point it was still the constitution that was the point of argument, and political rights within it. However, by the end of the decade, Tamil terrorism and government retaliation had escalated, and the pogrom of 1983 finally set the seal on what became a revenge-seeking frenzy. Tamils launched a guerrilla war, seeking to achieve the complete secession of the north and north-eastern parts of the country and the creation of a separate homeland for the Tamils: Tamil Eelam. At one time there were as many as five guerrilla groups active in the north. Meantime, the government found itself increasingly unable to maintain control, and tourism and foreign investment began to slip away, while the economy ground to a halt under a barrage of terrorist assaults. Many militant Tamil groups not only targeted the UNP and Sinhalese businessmen, the army and police, but also the official TULF. Partly as a result of this, the TULF shifted its headquarters from Jaffna to Madras. Some guerrilla groups even trained in the Tamil Nadu countryside. The embarrassment caused by the presence of terrorists on Indian soil was tempered by an anxiety not to offend Indian Tamils, and Mrs Gandhi's government reluctantly became involved in the dispute, brokering an all-party conference in Delhi in 1984. Initially, Jayawardene was reluctant to make any kind of political settlement with the Tamils, but the heavy casualties suffered by his army persuaded him to agree to a ceasefire, signed at Temphu in Bhutan. Despite this, a resolution of the political dispute proved impossible. The LTTE refused every concession offered until eventually the government of India hounded the Tigers out of Madras. Back in Jaffna, the LTTE set up what was to become a virtually separate administration for that part of the island. Having regrouped its forces, the Sri Lankan army gave up the ceasefire, launching an economic blockade of the Jaffna peninsula and an all-out military offensive in 1985 that very nearly succeeded in crushing the Tigers. At the last moment, as the army threatened to overrun the peninsula, the Indian government stepped in, flying a squadron of bombers over the north and forcing the Sri Lankan army to back off. If there was to be a solution, India wanted to be part of it. Jayawardene was forced to sign a pact with the Indian government under Rajiv Gandhi by which it effectively yielded to most of the Tamil demands. Rajiv Gandhi's incompetence then became telling. He failed to consult with Tamil leaders, who were unhappy with some of the details. The agreement also obliged the Indian government to back up the Sri Lankan government in the implementation of the accord. An Indian peacekeeping force was assembled to police the ceasefire and to persuade the Tigers to lay down their arms. Some bogus ceremonies were instituted at which Tigers gave in their weapons. Within a short time, however, fighting broke out between the Tigers and the Indian army as the former failed to agree to the proposed settlement. What resulted was in some ways an even more bitter conflict than had been fought with the Sri Lankan army. The Tigers made sure of a united command by eliminating rival guerrilla groups, and pitched fighting raged throughout northern Sri Lanka in which huge casualties were suffered by the peacekeeping force. Indian forces were expanded from an initial 3,000 troops to more than 70,000, and the Indian peacekeeping force (IPKF) launched a major assault that succeeded in taking Jaffna in late October 1987. The IPKF lost 700 of the 2,500 force that led the final assault, but the rump of the Tigers was forced to retreat into the hills.

District council elections held in 1988 were disrupted by skirmishes with the Tigers in the north and the newly resurgent JVP in the south. The JVP opposed Jayawardene's policy, and an offshoot of the JVP, the Patriotic Liberation Organisation (Deshapremi Janatha Viyaparaya – DJV), launched a bombing campaign against the cabinet, killing several ministers. In addition, the group organised a campaign of intimidation against the ruling party, killing numerous members of parliament between July and November. General strikes and street demonstrations were held in protest against the Indo-Sri Lankan agreement and in the presidential election of December 1988 Bandaranaike was tipped to win, despite her former reputation for corruption. Sensibly, Jayawardene announced his retirement and allowed Ramasinghe Premadasa to run as the UNP's candidate in his place. Premadasa was untainted by the 1983 pogrom and had a better chance of making peace with the JVP. This was enough to win him the election. After succeeding to office in January 1989 he managed to persuade the Tigers to agree to a ceasefire, which enabled him to concentrate his efforts on the JVP guerrillas in the south, whom he successfully suppressed. Meanwhile the Tigers had re-armed (some say with the help of weapons handed over by Premadasa's go-betweens in the army) and renewed their insurrection. The presence of the peacekeeping force in the north was now widely perceived to be a source of instability, so unpopular was it. The Indians had privately admitted to wanting to withdraw in talks with Jayawardene, and began to pull out in 1989.

Under Premadasa's leadership, the UNP retained its majority in the parliamentary elections of February 1989, and the last Indian troops finally departed in March 1990. However, the period of relative peace that followed was short-lived. In 1991 and 1992 a series of major battles was fought between the army and the LTTE, and in early 1993 the country was rocked by two assassinations. Lalith Athulathmudali, who had founded the opposition Democratic United Liberation

Front in 1991, was shot and killed during a political rally on 23 April. A week later, during the annual May Day parade, President Premadasa was assassinated by a suicide bomber, alleged to be a member of the LTTE. The Sri Lankan parliament reacted by immediately electing UNP member Dingiri Banda Wijetunge, and former prime minister, to serve as president until the next general election. Meanwhile, the LTTE took advantage of the political turmoil and in November 1993 managed to seize control of a government military base at Pooneryn, about 32 km (20 miles) south-east of Jaffna. Government forces managed to drive the rebels back, but the fighting was some of the fiercest seen between the Sri Lankan government and Tamil insurgents. According to government estimates, 1,200 people were either missing or killed in this action alone, adding to the total of some 60,000 people who have lost their lives in the conflict between 1983 and 1998.

In national parliamentary elections held in August 1994, the People's Alliance, comprised of the Sri Lankan Freedom Party, the Communist Party, the Lanka Sama Samaja Party (LSSP), the Ceylon Workers Congress and various Tamil groups, defeated the UNP. Chandrika Bandaranaike Kumaratunga, the daughter of former prime minister Sirimavo Bandaranaike, became prime minister. As well as being intelligent, energetic and well educated, and from one of Sri Lanka's principal families, her husband had acquired a reputation as a popular actor before becoming the golden boy of Sri Lankan politics (leading his own party, the Sri Lanka Mahajana Party) prior to his assassination in 1989. Chandrika Kumaratunga was thus well placed to secure widespread support, and in presidential elections held that year in November pledged to bring peace to the island through negotiation. She won a landslide victory over the UNP's candidate, Srima Dissanayake, to become Sri Lanka's first female president. The UNP's original candidate, Gamini Dissanayake, had been killed during an election rally in October. As president, Kumaratunga appointed her mother, Sirimavo Bandaranaike, prime minister in November 1994, and her uncle as defence minister, creating an unprecedented monopoly for the Bandaranaike family in government.

One of Chandrika Kumaratunga's campaign pledges had been to convert the presidency into a largely ceremonial position. Many believed that the reason she appointed her mother to the premiership was so that they could easily switch positions if this promise was carried through. The necessary arrangements were not made immediately; however, an agreement for a ceasefire between the LTTE and the government – another campaign ambition – was achieved in January 1995. Both sides released prisoners in an attempt at reconciliation. What constituted the longest ceasefire in the history of the conflict – 14 weeks – ended when the LTTE sank two government gunboats in the port of Trincomalee. In response Sri Lankan troops launched a new offensive, with the assistance of intelligence on Tamil shipments supplied by the Indian military and training and arms supplied by various overseas governments. At the end of 1995, after a two-month siege, the government succeeded in recapturing the city of Jaffna, and by the following year had gained control of the entire peninsula, though not before the Tigers had persuaded much of the population to depart with them into the forest, leaving

Jaffna a ghost town. The following year the Tigers gained their revenge when a lorry full of explosives driven by a Tiger smashed into the heart of Colombo's financial district, wrecking banks and buildings, killing 87 people, and injuring more than a thousand.

A safe road from Jaffna to the south could not be kept open by the army, which had to be continuously supplied by sea and air. Nonetheless, despite the expense and the casualties involved in holding on to the Tamil capital, Mrs Kumaratunga's coalition government kept up the military pressure, whilst forging ahead with a plan to devolve power to the regions. This was placed before parliament in October 1997, but foundered on the need for an amendment to the constitution, which the SLFP-led People's Alliance coalition government lacked the majority to achieve without support from the opposition. This was not forthcoming, and the Tigers also rejected the proposals. Shortly afterwards, on 25 January 1998, the week before the celebration of 50 years of independence was due to take place, another suicide bomber drove a lorry filled with explosives into the temple containing the Buddha's tooth in Kandy, demolishing part of it and killing 16 people. The temple is Sri Lanka's holiest Buddhist shrine and was to have received a visit from Britain's Prince Charles as part of the nation's fiftieth birthday festivities. After the bombing, the celebrations were hurriedly switched to Colombo, which was surrounded with a ring of steel.

The bombing of Kandy so outraged Sri Lanka's Buddhists that Mrs Kumaratunga was forced formally to outlaw the Tigers. This could only worsen relations between the government and LTTE, and subsequent attempts to restore local democracy in Jaffna were abortive, with only 16 per cent of the population turning out to vote in local elections held at the end of January 1998, the first for 16 years. The LTTE continued to demand complete independence for the Tamil minority, and fighting between the government and the rebels carried on unabated. In December 1999 Kumaratunga won a second term as president, once again vowing to end the nation's 16-year civil war. She secured 51 per cent of the vote, amidst claims of voter intimidation and ballot rigging, only just above the minimum 50 per cent required to take office. Her main opponent, Ranil Wickramasinghe of the UNP, won approximately 43 per cent of the vote.

Kumaratunga had called the election in October 1999, at short notice and 11 months earlier than scheduled, in the hope of reviving popular support for her presidency. Violence during elections has become habitual and widespread in Sri Lanka, and 1999 was no exception. The Colombo-based Centre for Monitoring Election Violence logged more than 1,000 instances of election-related aggressions, mostly in rural areas, in the two months leading up to the polls. The culmination came just three days before the 21 December election, when Kumaratunga herself was wounded in a suicide bomb attack by a suspected Tamil Tiger. The bomb went off just as she was leaving the stage at an election rally, killing 23 people – including the most senior policeman in the country, T.N. Da Silva – and wounding more than 100, along with three government ministers. The bombing seemed to reinforce popular support for Mrs Kumaratunga, who was injured in the eye and narrowly escaped with her life, whilst her opponent was uninjured when a second bomb exploded at a gathering of the UNP in Ja-Ela, a Colombo suburb (at which he appeared only briefly). Nonetheless, Kumaratunga had hardly achieved the resounding vote of support she had hoped for.

During her swearing-in ceremony as president, with her eye still bandaged, Mrs Kumaratunga called on the LTTE to enter new peace negotiations with the government. She also invited the leader of the UNP opposition, Wickramasinghe, to support her government's efforts to end the war by introducing greater autonomy for the Tamil regions in the north and north-east. At first sight, this appeared to be little different from previous rhetoric on the issue; however, in February 2000, in a dramatic breakthrough, Norway publicly offered to act as an intermediary in a new peace initiative. This announcement came after careful preparatory meetings with Velupillai Prabhakaran, the founder of the LTTE, and with the government, both of whom agreed to the proposal.

Partly on the strength of the positive moves towards talks, President Kumaratunga's People's Alliance (incorporating the SLFP) became the largest party in parliament (although still short of an overall majority) in the general elections that followed in October 2000. Although the LTTE had by then succeeded in recapturing the strategic Elephant Pass in the north of the island, pressure on the LTTE had begun to rack up, beginning with new anti-terrorism laws in the United Kingdom that promised to halt the flow of funds from one of the more important Tamil communities abroad.

The progress towards peace was by no means easy. In July 2001 President Kumaratunga was forced to suspend parliament for two months to save her minority government from defeat in a no-confidence vote, and in July 2001, the eighteenth anniversary of the 1983 Tamil pogrom, a spectacular suicide attack by

Figure 23 Tamil civilians meeting in support of Tamil Tiger leader V. Prabhakaran.
   © C.Orjuela.

the Tamil Tigers on the international airport resulted in 14 deaths. After a no-confidence motion was tabled, which threatened to defeat the minority government in parliament, President Kumaratunga was then forced to call a fresh general election in December. This election was narrowly won by the United National Party, whose leader Ranil Wickramasinghe was sworn in as the head of a new cabinet.

With the president coming from one party and the prime minister coming from another, conflict was inevitable, but compromise with the LTTE was made a top priority by the Wickramasinghe government. At the same time a new urgency was given to the peace process by the fallout from the 11 September terrorist attack on New York. This threatened to include the LTTE as a target in the American-sponsored global war on terrorism, and thus spurred them on towards the negotiating table. The result, in February 2002, was a permanent ceasefire agreement signed by the government and Tamil Tiger rebels, paving the way for talks aimed at a final end to the long-running conflict.

The 2002 ceasefire initiative was sponsored by Norway and was accompanied by the first-ever public meetings between international journalists and the LTTE leader Velupillai Prabhakaran. The signs were therefore promising, and between March and May 2002, as government forces began a partial withdrawal from the north of the country, a decommissioning of weapons began. The road linking the Jaffna peninsula with the rest of Sri Lanka was reopened after a gap of 12 years and passenger flights to Jaffna resumed.

A key demand conceded was that the government should lift its ban on membership of the LTTE. The first round of talks began in Thailand, accompanied by an exchange of prisoners. Crucially, like the IRA in Northern Ireland, the LTTE formally abandoned their demand for a separate state in exchange for a 'power-sharing' arrangement, agreed at further meetings held in December 2002 in Norway. A central problem, though, was that the LTTE conception of the modalities of 'power-sharing' (outlined in their proposal for an interim self-government authority) was to allow the Tamils almost complete autonomy in the mainly Tamil-speaking areas of the north and east, which hardly amounted to power-sharing at all.

The talks continued in February 2003 at the Norwegian embassy in Berlin; however, there was growing unease with the process on all sides. To begin with, the LTTE continued to carry arms illegally outside of Tamil-controlled areas, and there seemed to be no end to their 'recruitment' (abduction) of child soldiers in the east of the country, as if in preparation for further war. Furthermore, there were criticisms of the bi-polar methodology of the Norwegian-sponsored peace talks, which focused on just the two main protagonists. Other minorities, notably the Sri Lankan Muslims, were completely left out. There was also no involvement of Tamil spokesmen other than members of the LTTE from the north. When these concerns were raised and talks advanced to consideration of the conditions for holding free and fair elections, the Tamil Tigers suspended their participation in the peace talks, claiming that they were being marginalised.

In monsoon rains in the summer of 2003, Sri Lanka suffered its worst-ever floods (the horrors of the December 2004 tsunami being yet to come), causing more than 200 deaths and leaving 4,000 people homeless. Amidst growing dissent over the peace process President Kumaratunga dismissed three government ministers and briefly suspended parliament, claiming that there were too many concessions being made to the LTTE. Thereafter, the peace negotiations were put on hold, as a power struggle erupted between the party of the prime minister, the UNP, and that of the president, the SLFP. This dissent within the government was mirrored by dissent amongst the Tamils, as one of the LTTE commanders, Karuna, split away and went underground with his supporters, vowing to renew the armed struggle. In the run-up to new elections the LTTE then began eliminating – as it had done before – all critics and rivals to its influence in the north and east of the country, determined that the party it was backing, the Tamil National Alliance (TNA), should sweep the polls. The candidates of the Tamil United Liberation Front (TULF), the Eelam People's Democratic Party (EPDP), the Eelam People's Revolutionary Liberation Front (EPRLF) (V), and the Democratic People's Liberation Front (DPLF) were thus singled out and subjected to violent harassment and assault.

To President Kumaratunga's delight, the elections in April 2004 gave her newly formed United People's Freedom Alliance (UPFA) 105 out of 225 parliamentary seats: well short of an overall majority but sufficient to justify her swearing in as prime minister one of her supporters, Mahinda Rajapaksa, a devout Buddhist and described in the media as a hawk. Presidential elections followed in November 2005 at which Mahinda Rajapaksa was elected as president (Figure 24). To retain control of parliament, however, Rajapaksa's United People's Freedom Alliance (with the SLFP as its largest member) was forced to include the militant, Marxist, nationalist Janatha Vimukthi Peramuna (JVP) – responsible for the violent anti-Indian insurgency of 1987–9 – which has given a distinctly anti-Tamil bias to the government.

At the same time as an apparently new hard line emerged within the Sri Lanka government, the eastern faction of the LTTE, led by Vinayagamurthi Muralitharan (alias Karuna), seized control of several Tamil areas in the east of the country with the tacit co-operation of the Sri Lankan army. This served to heighten anxieties within the ranks of the LTTE, and a suicide bomb in Colombo in July 2004, the first such incident since 2001, signalled a deterioration in the peace process. This was followed by a suicide attack on a Sri Lankan navy gunboat and the killing of nearly a hundred soldiers between November and December 2005. Unsuccessful attempts were made to preserve the peace by a renewed round of talks between the LTTE and the Sri Lankan government, mediated by the Norwegians again. Since July 2006, however, Prabhakaran's faction of the Tigers appears to have embarked upon a renewed campaign (which some are calling Eelam War IV) to reassert their authority over the eastern half of the country and to regain control of the Jaffna peninsula, with fighting breaking out on several fronts and casualties amongst soldiers and civilians once again mounting.

Since, in their view, the Tigers have been betrayed so often in the past, they continue to react violently to the smallest perceived threat to their position, as was apparent in the aftermath of the horrific tsunami of 26 December 2004, which

Figure 24 Newly elected Sri Lankan president Mahinda Rajapaksa in Colombo, November 2005. © *The Hindu.*

claimed the lives of some 31,000 Sri Lankans. The relief effort quickly became politicised, with the Tigers objecting to army soldiers being involved in relief efforts in the north and the Sri Lankan government deterring Kofi Annan, the UN secretary-general, from visiting the area. Rather like Jinnah in India in 1947, the Tigers appear to be of the view that any concession weakens their position – perhaps in part due to the fact that a majority of the Tamil population live outside of the one-third of the island being claimed as the Tamil homeland. There are many other similarities between the conflict in Sri Lanka and the frictions seen in India at the time of partition, as well as the various regional movements that have plagued India, most particularly the separatist movement in Punjab in the 1980s. Unsurprisingly, the instability of her southern neighbour has also seriously involved India herself on more than one occasion.

The problems of Sri Lanka have very clear economic and political origins, which have been articulated in the form of political and armed conflict on the island since its independence. The solutions to this violence have more often than not tended to exacerbate divisions and have been as debilitating as the divisions themselves. Since Sri Lanka achieved independence from Britain in 1948 the country has been under emergency rule for more than half of the entire period. President Chandrika Kumaratunga was forced to admit, during the official fiftieth-year independence celebrations on 4 February 1998, that Sri Lanka had so far effectively failed to build a nation.[5] As in the Punjab (see Chapter 14), conflict in Sri Lanka has a communal or religious aspect, but this has not always been at the forefront of agitation.[6] In some ways this contrasts with Hindu–Muslim conflict, which is widespread, intermittent but endemic in north India. The language of political conflict used by Sikhs in the Punjab, and by Tamils and Sinhalese in Sri Lanka, has more often revolved around the ballot box and administrative problems, although the resort to arms and communal hatred have inevitably ensued, as disputes have become embittered and entrenched. Ethnic or separatist, rather than communal, conflict might therefore be a better description of the situation in Sri Lanka, as well as in Indian Punjab in the 1980s, since the main issues in both have concerned the sharing of economic power and political control, the resolution for which is seen to lie in division of the country. The many Tamils who have no interest in either, live comfortably with their neighbours and keep away from the fighting. Those who are involved continue to receive support in terms of money and arms from wealthy Tamils living abroad, which has made them more than a match for the Sri Lankan army, even though that army also receives help from overseas and more than a third of the government's annual budget in Sri Lanka. The end result is that prosperous and affluent regions, with considerable promise, have been devastated by violence. Apart from the 65,000 deaths between 1983 and 2003, nearly 1 million out of a population of 16 million have been rendered refugees by the conflict. The scars from this will take a long time to heal, even once it has ended. In the case of Sri Lanka, although the fallout from 9/11 has taken its toll on overseas support for the LTTE, the two sides appear to be still quite evenly matched, making the progress towards peace a long-term process indeed.

17 Neo-nationalism and the challenge of democracy

The police . . . said that a Hindu mob attacked a Muslim mob . . . I am not a 'mob,' I am a woman who was gang-raped by three men. How can I hope for justice when they don't even register my complaint properly? To my surprise, the police said I cannot file an FIR [first Information Report]. They said an FIR already existed for that day's events.

(Sultana Feroz Sheikh, Gujarat, June 2002)[1]

Every time we find a box or a toy that is lying around, we panic and call the police.

(Hanif, ice cream vendor, Bombay, August 2003)[2]

This is the work of the Devil. These people have no cause, no religion, no God.

(Mohammad Afzal, a Zaveri shopkeeper, Bombay)[3]

The mid-term elections of 1998 had brought the Bharatiya Janata Party (BJP) fully into power for the first time in a minority coalition called the National Democratic Alliance (NDA), formed under the premiership of the BJP's Atal Bihari Vajpayee (Figure 25).[4] During the course of the election the BJP tried hard to raise its vote in the south of India, with limited success, and some 50 were killed in bomb explosions during a visit to the city of Coimbatore by L.K. Advani, the party's firebrand deputy leader. Coimbatore is one of the few southern cities outside Kerala and Andhra Pradesh that has a significant Muslim population. It was believed the bombs were set by Muslim extremists, although there was evidence of provocation.

If Advani could arouse resentment for his role in the Ayodhya dispute, Vajpayee for many represented the 'acceptable face' of Hindu nationalism and he was a popular choice as leader of the National Democratic Alliance coalition government. Nonetheless, within a few months the new prime minister demonstrated an unexpected ruthlessness. Right from the start his government was constrained by its coalition partners from putting into effect some of the more radical elements in its manifesto and rhetoric, such as the banning of cow slaughter, the abolition of article 370 in the constitution (which provides for a special status to the state of

Figure 25 A.B. Vajpayee and former Pakistani prime minister Benazir Bhutto in New Delhi, December 2003. © *The Hindu.*

Jammu and Kashmir unlike any other state of the Union), and the removal of other privileges afforded recognised minorities such as the legal recognition of Muslim marriages under Shari'ah law and the freedom to run their own educational institutions, recognised under articles 29 and 30 of the constitution (Chandhoke 1995; Austin 1999). Instead, it ruled according to a national agenda for governance, agreed with its coalition partners soon after the election, which confined itself to relatively limited ambitions such as the restoration of food subsidies and encouragement of *swadeshi* (home-produced) goods, and which obliged the government to adhere to judicial rulings in the matter of the Ayodhya dispute. In these circumstances it was difficult for the BJP to make its mark, except in areas of foreign policy. Defence therefore became a major priority for the government.

Nuclear India

A plan was soon hatched to conduct a nuclear test, India's first since 1974, with the aim of enhancing India's international status as well as her defensive posture *vis-à-vis* Pakistan, which was itself known to have developed a nuclear capability, along with medium-range ballistic missiles, with assistance from China (Abraham 1998; Kapur 2003). The plan for the nuclear test, it is believed, was known only to the defence minister, the once-respected socialist leader George Fernandes; the prime minister; the scientists involved in the project (led by A.P.J. Abdul Kalam) and, significantly, the leader of the RSS – the Hindu nationalist extra-parliamentary organisation that marshalled support for the BJP in the country at large. Not one of the BJP's coalition partners was informed prior to what is believed to have been a series of three successive test explosions totalling some 43 kilotons, carried out at Pokhran in the Rajasthani desert, close to the Pakistan border, on 11 May 1998.[5]

India's test explosion was followed less than three weeks later by 'retaliatory' tests totalling approximately 15 kilotons over two days by Pakistan in the Chagai Hills in Baluchistan. The repercussions of both were serious. Within India there was near hysterical approval for India's shattering of the 'nuclear club of five's' hegemony on nuclear weaponry. However, India's relations with China, which had greatly improved in the 1990s with the signing of two major peace and tranquillity agreements in 1991 and 1996, suffered a severe setback. Likewise relations were seriously affected with the US (apparently completely taken by surprise by the tests), which saw itself as the guardian of the Nuclear Non-Proliferation Treaty (NNPT) and the more recent Comprehensive Test Ban Treaty (CTBT) (which India and Pakistan had hitherto refused to sign). Trade sanctions were therefore imposed on both countries. These sanctions were especially damaging to the Pakistani economy.

The Indian and Pakistani tests were not only a severe set-back to hopes of global nuclear disarmament but they also seriously worsened relations between the two countries. South Asia was soon widely regarded as the region in which nuclear conflict was most likely to occur. The Indian government insisted that their test was for entirely 'peaceful' purposes, although a variety of explanations were subsequently offered for it as a defence against China and/or Pakistan. It was further argued that the NNPT and CTBT were a sham, since significant exceptions were made for countries such as Israel. The demand that other countries should not develop nuclear weaponry was not being simultaneously accompanied, it was argued, by sufficient steps towards disarmament by the nuclear powers themselves. This was persuasive reasoning, but in reality the sole purpose of the tests was most probably simply to bolster the BJP's standing in the eyes of the public and to please the anti-Muslim sentiments of their principal supporters.

Despite the NDA government's apparent military and foreign policy successes, it nonetheless lost its majority after just 13 months in power when a key regional ally, the All-India Anna Dravida Munnetra Kazhagam (AIADMK), led by former Tamil Nadu chief minister J. Jayalalitha, decided to withdraw support. The AIADMK had been an unhappy partner from the start. It was said that Jayalalitha only joined the coalition in the first place in order to fend off corruption charges levelled against her during the time when she was chief minister in Tamil Nadu and in the hope of bringing down the DMK government, which had supplanted the AIADMK in the state. When the prime minister failed to do much to her liking on either front, Jayalalitha withdrew her party's support.

Sonia Gandhi and Congress

Following the blundering of Sitaram Kesri's leadership, the Congress had decided by this time to adopt Sonia Gandhi as its new leader. Although she had taken part in campaigning in 1996, she had previously refused any position of responsibility.

She had nonetheless remained a behind-the-scenes adviser to party leaders over cups of tea at the Gandhi residence at number 10 Janpath, and had played an active role in their appointment (Chatterjee 1998). Indian newspapers had described her as 'sphinx-like'. Her reasons for agreeing to be nominated and elected as party leader now, and not before, were said to be due to her awareness of the political ambitions of her children, Priyanka and Rahul (who entered parliament in 2004), the divided and enfeebled state of the party, and the continuing progress of inquiries into the Bofors scandal, which threatened once more to embroil her family. Sonia herself did not win a seat in the Lok Sabha until 1999, so the party initially found itself, following her election in April 1998, with an Italian-born leader, bearing the Gandhi family name, but having no formal political constituency. This dilemma was resolved by Rajesh Pilot taking on the leadership of the party in parliament, whilst Sonia Gandhi chaired the Central Working Committee and led the party outside.

The Congress Party was partially revived by Sonia Gandhi's leadership, but her role was bitterly resented by some (largely middle-class politicians), who considered a foreign-born leader to be an electoral liability. Sharad Pawar, the ambitious Congress leader in Maharashtra in western India, was foremost amongst these critics, and having failed to win the party leadership himself, split away to form a rebel group: the Congress Nationalist Party. To some extent these critics were right, as Sonia Gandhi's origins were stridently employed in BJP propaganda, although with mixed results. Personal attacks on the widow of a former prime minister did not seem to many a particularly gracious tactic.

Elections need not have been held after the withdrawal of the AIADMK from the ruling coalition, but a vote of confidence was forced by the Congress in the mistaken belief that they could form a government to replace it. Late 1998 had seen a serious onion shortage (a staple in Indian cooking), which despite the nuclear test had damaged the government's popularity. Arjun Singh, Sonia Gandhi's main adviser at this time, believed he could assemble a sufficient number of supporters in the Lok Sabha. He calculated wrongly: Mulayam Singh Yadav's Samajwadi Party deciding against backing a Sonia-led government. Unexpectedly, therefore, India was forced once more to the polls before the BJP-led government had served even half its term.

Elections and renewed Indo-Pakistan conflict

Elections were announced soon after the government's defeat in a vote of confidence in April 1999 (by just one vote), and it had become apparent that the Congress was not able to form an alternative government. They were due to be held in September. Now no longer the ruling party, but simply an interim government, the BJP was forbidden by the constitution from pursuing any new domestic initiatives, being required merely to oversee the transition. An exception was permitted in matters of foreign and defence policy. Fortuitously, in the same month as the government's defeat in the Lok Sabha, Agni-II, an intermediate-range ballistic missile that had been under development for some years, was successfully launched from a test site on the Orissa coast. Defence minister George Fernandes announced that 'we have reached the point of operationalisation of *Agni* as a weapon system',[6] and the prime minister declared in a public statement: '[E]ver since you elected my Government in March last year. I have been working with one single aim, with one single purpose: to make India strong and self-confident in every sphere of development and defence . . . *Agni* is a symbol of that resurgent India which is able to say: "Yes, we will stand on our own feet." '[7] This was not entirely true, since exports and the value of the rupee against the dollar had been declining and the government's own estimate was that post-Pokhran sanctions had cost the economy some US $6 billion.

Seventy-two hours after India's test of the Agni II missile, Pakistan again came out with a matching response by testing a version of their own intermediate weapon, Ghauri, with a range of 2,000 km and the ability to carry a 1,000 kg payload consisting of either a nuclear warhead or conventional weapons. On 15 April Pakistan then test-fired the medium-range (600 km) Shaheen (Hatf-IV) surface-to-surface missile, also reportedly capable of carrying a nuclear payload, whilst simultaneously announcing the conclusion 'for now' of 'the series of flight tests'.

The tensions that resulted strengthened popular support for the Vajpayee government. Luck then once more favoured the BJP-led NDA coalition when the Pakistani military decided to launch a push into Indian territory in Kashmir. Between January and May 1999 some 300 to 600 Islamic militants (including Kashmiri rebels, Afghan mercenaries, and Pakistani army regulars) invaded the Kargil heights area of Kashmir, providing a strategic advantage for Pakistan in ongoing battles on Siachen glacier (India Kargil Review Committee 2000). It was the first forcible occupation of enemy territory since the two countries' 1971 war. The initiative came from the then Pakistani chief of staff, General Musharraf, perhaps concerned by the conciliatory noises Prime Minister Nawaz Sharif had been making towards India before and after the Pokhran test. The Pakistani assault had also to some extent been provoked by India, which had moved 20,000 additional troops into Kashmir during the preceding year. The invasion was not detected by India until 6 May, and on 25 May Pakistani forces shot down an Indian jet (another crashed). There then followed from late May to late July some eleven weeks of fierce combat between thousands of Indian troops and separatist guerrillas in Kargil and Batalik, with over a thousand dead on both sides; at the same time, Pakistani and Indian troops exchanged artillery fire across the line of control. On several occasions India deployed bombers against Pakistani positions – which was unprecedented in such relatively low-level conflicts and something the Pakistanis had not counted on. Eventually on 4 July, following intense international pressure, Pakistani prime minister Nawaz Sharif and US president Bill Clinton signed an accord in Washington in which Pakistan agreed to withdraw, whilst President Clinton agreed to take a 'personal interest' in the Kashmir dispute. Despite this the Pakistani army, smarting from its perceived humiliation at the hands of the civilian authorities, continued to engage Indian troops in battles and attacked Indian army camps along the line of control throughout the month of August. In retaliation, India shot down a Pakistani navy reconnaissance plane.

The sustained violence in Kashmir provided the perfect background to an election from the NDA government's point of view, which seemed to be patriotically defending the nation against an unprovoked foreign assault – regardless of the fact that it had played a part in escalating the conflict in the first place (Rai 2001). During the Indian elections between 5 September through to 3 October Kashmiri rebels stepped up their attacks, assassinating two Indian politicians in the process. The total death-toll in Kashmir from political violence during the elections was at least 91, and India moved 60 new army battalions into Kashmir, adding to the sense that full-scale war was imminent. The result was a significant increase in the popular vote for the NDA coalition, the BJP and its supporters winning a total of 298 seats, against a total for the Congress and her allies of only 135.

Soon after the BJP/NDA victory in India's general election, a military coup in Pakistan, led by General Musharraf, brought to an end the civilian rule the country had enjoyed for the previous ten years. For India, this was hardly good news since it was Musharraf who had launched the Kargil campaign in the first place. However, Indo–Pakistan relations, and the future course of the NDA government, were soon to be irrevocably transformed by the attack on the Twin Towers in New York in September 2001.

Figure 26 A.B. Vajpayee and Shiv Sena leader Bal Thakeray (second right) at an election rally in Mumbai. Other Sena leaders (from left) are Manohar Joshi and Uddhav Thakeray. © *The Hindu.*

The war on terror

Following a visit from the US president Bill Clinton, relations between India and Pakistan improved sufficiently for a meeting to be held in July 2001 between the Indian prime minister Vajpayee and Pakistani president Pervez Musharraf – the first summit between the two neighbours in more than two years. However, the meeting ended after unscheduled press briefings by Musharraf had embarrassed his Indian hosts, while President Clinton's replacement by George Bush as US president left a vacuum in previous international efforts to force the two parties to a solution. However, immediately following the 11 September attack on the Twin Towers, America turned to India and, above all, to Pakistan, for support in the war against terror and lifted the sanctions it had imposed against the two countries after they had staged nuclear tests in 1998. Although Pakistan quickly offered the Americans backing in their war against the Taliban (Pakistan's former allies in neighbouring Afghanistan, who were harbouring Al-Qaeda terrorists), relations between India and Pakistan did not improve; rather, they worsened. Instead of being the pariah of the international community, Pakistan's military dictator was suddenly transformed into America's closest ally, with generous offers of military support, and this caused intense anxiety in India, which had itself been drawing closer to the US in an endeavour to promote its economic and strategic interests (Talbot 2004). As a result, in October 2001 India fired on Pakistani military posts in some of the heaviest fighting along the line of control in Kashmir for almost a year. Relations then went from bad to worse when a suicide squad attacked the Indian parliament in New Delhi, killing several police, in December 2001. A suicide bomb went off, the vice-president Krishan Kant came face to face with one of the gunmen, and was saved only by the intervention of a parliamentary official who was himself shot, and hundreds of rounds of ammunition were expended over the course of an hour before the five gunmen involved were finally overwhelmed and killed. Blame immediately fell on the Kashmiri militant groups backed by Pakistan: Lashkar-e-Toyeba and the more recently formed Jaish-e-Mohammad (Army of Mohammad), which two months earlier had admitted responsibility for a similar attack on the Kashmiri State Assembly in Srinagar that had resulted in 29 deaths. India and Pakistan massed troops on their common border amid mounting fears of war, and India imposed sanctions against Pakistan to force it to take action against the militants. Pakistan retaliated with similar sanctions, but nonetheless banned the two groups in January under American pressure.

In January 2002 India successfully test-fired another Agni ballistic missile, capable of carrying a nuclear payload. There then followed, in February 2002, the worst communal bloodshed for a decade after Muslims at Godhra station in Gujarat allegedly set fire to a train carrying Hindu *karsevaks* (volunteers) returning from a pilgrimage to Ayodhya. The riots were transparently encouraged by officials of the BJP state government, led by Narendra Modi, and between 1,000 and 2,000 Muslims died in subsequent revenge killings by Hindu rioters. The 58 *karsevaks* who died on the train were members of the Vishwa Hindu Parishad and

Bajrang Dal – pseudo-religious groups committed to building the Ram temple in Ayodhya and restoring true Hindu rule in India. The train caught fire (the flames may have originated inside according to a later report) shortly after an alleged attempt to kidnap a young Muslim girl and an assault on a Muslim tea seller at Godhra station by the *karsevaks*, who were reportedly chanting 'mandir ki nirmaan karo, Babar ki aulad ko bahar karo' ('Build the temple and throw out the Muslims').[8] Without waiting for a police inquiry into what had happened, VHP Bajrang Dal and, allegedly, khaki-clad RSS supporters burned down a Muslim *basti* (neighbourhood) and a mosque near the railway at Godhra, and shortly afterwards assaults on Muslims erupted in the state capital Ahmedabad and in towns and villages across Gujarat. The situation was undoubtedly made worse by high unemployment resulting from the recent closure of several loss-making, government-owned cotton mills in Ahmedabad, where Muslim shops and enterprises were particularly targeted, as well as the houses of Muslims, which were often burnt to the ground with their inhabitants still inside. One eyewitness, Khalid Noor Muhammad Sheikh, described his experience of the violence:

> The attackers wore underclothes that were white, with brown scarves tied around their necks. They had swords, hockey sticks, pipes, diesel, petrol, acid, and so many things to attack us with . . . We tried to save ourselves and battle it out from 9:30 a.m. to 5:30 p.m. Eventually we got tired, but people continued to throw pipes and swords and stones at us. And then at around 5:30 or 6:00 they surrounded all the people, including women and children from two to ten years of age. They encircled them and burnt them alive. There were also many rapes.[9]

Whilst all this went on the police stood by and in some cases, it is alleged, even encouraged those engaged in the assaults. Not until the worst of the violence had passed did paramilitary forces attempt to restore order, and the relief provided to more than 70,000 homeless Muslims in camps on the outskirts of Ahmedabad was entirely inadequate. In the State Assembly, the chief minister Narendra Modi promised 2 *lakhs* of rupees in compensation to the families of the 58 Godhra victims, but not even half that amount was offered to the victims of the communal riots. Journalists attempting to cover the violence were harassed by state officials and the police. In an interview Modi was later to explain what happened, with the famous dictum 'Every action has an equal and opposite reaction'.[10]

Initially, the response of the Indian government and public was pure shock, and many anticipated the resignation of the Gujarat chief minister or at least a public distancing of the administration from the Hindu militant groups widely held to blame for the widespread nature of the violence. However, following a meeting of BJP and the RSS, and other members of the Sangh Parivar in Goa, the prime minister finally came out firmly in support of the state government, and the deputy prime minister said: 'If you see any virtue in me, I have imbibed it from the Rashtriya Swayamsevak Sangh (RSS) – its discipline, patriotism and commitment to integrity of public life. It is absurd to ask me to de-link from the RSS.'[11] In the minds of many the BJP thereby demonstrated its unwillingness and inability to hold in check the extremist forces, which many had hoped they would restrain if elected to power.

The events in Gujarat were condemned by the Pakistani government and, making matters still worse, more than 30 people were killed in a raid on an Indian army camp in Kashmir in May 2002, which India blamed on Pakistani-based rebels. The moderate Kashmiri separatist leader Abdul Gani Lone, who had been engaging in talks with the Indian government, was also shot dead in Srinagar by suspected Islamist militants. At this point the American government was still distracted by the war against the Taliban in Afghanistan, but when Pakistan test-fired three medium-range surface-to-surface Ghauri missiles, capable of carrying nuclear warheads, it was realised that worsening relations between India and Pakistan were becoming a serious distraction from the global war against terror. Urgent efforts were therefore made to mollify both sides. There were no sanctions, but tremendous pressure was put on India in particular by the issuing of government advisories in June by Britain, the US, Australia and several other countries, warning their citizens to keep away from the subcontinent due to the threat of war. Since India was courting international investment this was perceived to be a disaster and both sides stepped back soon after from their position of confrontation.

As if the situation on the Indo-Pakistan border was not bad enough, a successful Maoist insurgency in the previously peaceful country of Nepal caused renewed anxiety about India's northern borders. King Gyanendra ascended the throne in June 2001 after Crown Prince Dipendra allegedly committed suicide (although this account is widely disbelieved in Nepal) after gunning down his parents King Birendra and Queen Aishwarya and seven other royals, following a drunken argument over his plans for marriage. In the summer of 2002 King Gyanendra dismissed a popular elected government, ruling subsequently through a succession of appointed prime ministers. By taking effective control over the government the king hoped to consolidate his rule, but only made matters worse with the Maoist insurgents driving back government troops and taking control of most of the countryside, government support being increasingly confined to the capital, Kathmandu. The king travelled several times to New Delhi, and India – facing a Maoist movement of its own in Jharkhand – offered support in the form of advisers and weapons. Simultaneously talks were opened with China in order to settle disputes over adjacent border areas, resulting in a *de facto* agreement in June over the status of Tibet and Sikkim, which opened their borders to trade. However, the king's decision to dismiss even his appointed ministers, to impose complete censorship, detention without trial, and direct executive control in a 'royal coup' in January 2005, did not augur well for future stability in the region, nor indeed for the future of the monarchy itself. Whilst the Maoists advanced, blocking communications across the country, massive popular demonstrations erupted on the streets of the capital, Kathmandu, eventually forcing the king to stand down in April 2006 and restore power to the elected House of Representatives.

Soon after, parliament permanently deprived the king of all his constitutional political powers, including control of the army.

Whilst remaining America's most important ally in the war against Al-Qaeda, General Musharraf of Pakistan was uniquely vulnerable to American pressure due to the weakness of the Pakistani economy and his dependence on American military and financial support. Once committed to the war on terror, Musharraf became a target for Islamic extremists as well, and given the fact that he himself had seized power by force of arms there was a risk that he might be removed by the same means. For this reason, as the Americans put more and more pressure on Pakistan to resolve their differences with India, this could not be resisted for long. In order to increase this pressure the Americans revealed that the architect of Pakistan's missile programme, Dr Abdul Qadeer Khan, had been passing on nuclear secrets to some of America's enemies – including Libya, Iran and possibly also North Korea (from where missile technology had been obtained). In fact, this had probably been known for some time, but the willingness of George Bush's administration to embarrass the Pakistani government in this fashion was a measure of their seriousness.

Given A.Q. Khan's popularity and importance he could be required to do no more than offer a public apology for his actions, but the cards were clearly on the table and Pakistan was forced ineluctably towards negotiating with India. Seizing the opportunity, Indian prime minister Atul Behari Vajpayee made a speech in Kashmir in April 2003 offering 'the hand of friendship' to Pakistan. This was a calculated move, intended not only to pressurise the Pakistanis but also to win favour with the centre-ground of Indian public opinion, clearly sickened by the ongoing threat of war and communal conflagration that the BJP had allowed to occur in Gujarat. The offer remained on the table, despite simultaneous bomb blasts in August in Bombay, interpreted as an act of revenge for the Gujarat killings and widely believed to have been assisted by the Pakistani secret services. India announced the resumption of a bus service between Delhi and Lahore, diplomatic links were renewed, and in October 2003 India unveiled a series of proposals aimed at improving relations and making progress on the Kashmir dispute. Therefore, in November, Pakistan reluctantly declared a ceasefire in Kashmir, immediately matched by India.

In December 2003 India and Pakistan agreed to resume direct air links, which had been terminated two years before, and in a meeting of the South Asian Association for Regional Co-operation (SAARC) in Islamabad, Prime Minister Vajpayee and General Musharraf arranged to convene for more than a hour of talks. Shortly after, a series of talks were commenced between Indian and Pakistani officials, the strategy being to focus on minor issues first before approaching the most serious points dividing them. Simultaneously, the Indian government commenced talks with representatives of the more moderate Kashmiri separatist groups and in March a historic cricket match was held between Indian and Pakistani teams, the first since 1989. India won the cricket match, but the BJP-led National Democratic Alliance was not so fortunate in the general elections subsequently held in India in May 2004.

The return of the Indian National Congress

The defeat of the BJP-led NDA coalition in May 2004, despite Prime Minister Vajpayee's tremendous personal popularity, came as a great surprise to most commentators. Struggling for explanations, many attributed the NDA's defeat to the violence in Gujarat in 2002, resentment at its policy of continuing economic liberalisation, or to a simple 'anti-incumbency' factor. However, none of these explanations told the whole story.

As expected, the BJP indeed lost votes in the Gujarat elections, its tally of seats falling from 20 to 14 and the number of Congress seats doubling to 12, but it still managed to hold on to a majority of seats from the state in the Lok Sabha. Elsewhere, along the western side and in parts of central India, in the states of Punjab, Kerala, Chhattisgarh, Madhya Pradesh and Kerala, the National Democratic Alliance actually acquitted itself quite well. Only in seven or eight out of the 18 major states in the Indian Union was there a clear anti-incumbency vote, and from this the NDA gained in Maharashtra, Karnataka, Uttaranchal and Punjab. In other states, incumbency proved rather an asset than a burden in Rajasthan, Madhya Pradesh and Chhattisgarh, in all of which the NDA increased its share of seats. The election of 2004 has thus been characterised as a concatenation of 28 separate state elections rather than a single national swing – as used formerly to characterise Indian elections. If so, this is a reflection of the major transformation in Indian politics that has ensued since 1991 with the collapse of the Congress system. The end of Congress hegemony allowed smaller and regional political parties to come suddenly to the fore, as well as opening up new opportunities for subaltern, marginalised groups to make their voices heard in the electoral process (Chandra 2004). A key example of this was the emergence of the Bahujan Samaj in Uttar Pradesh, a *dalit* party led by *dalits* but drawing support also from a broader constituency of Muslims and other backward castes (OBCs). This was sometimes characterised as the rise of *goonda* politics by middle-class elites, but it was symptomatic of a dramatic democratisation of the political process and the articulation of a hitherto silent subaltern voice (Jaffrelot 1999; Pai 2002).[12]

Although the collapse of the Congress system generated what has been dubbed 'a second democratic wave' in Indian politics, the Indian political system – as an inevitable consequence of the first-past-the-post system – soon coalesced in the late 1990s into two monolithic camps: the Congress (UPA)[13] and BJP (NDA)[14] coalitions, which became increasingly indistinguishable on key issues such as the economy. The process began with 'Mandalisation' after 1991 – the political system becoming increasingly divided on lines of caste, class and community following the introduction of the Mandal reforms on caste reservation. According to Yogendra Yadav (2004), the process ended in the core support of the Congress Party and its allies in the United Progressive Alliance deriving largely from an extended but poorly organised constituency of the poor, *dalits*, OBCs, Christians, Muslims, and women – where the Congress had a 2.9 per cent advantage over the BJP. The core constituency of the BJP, and to a lesser extent also its NDA allies, on the other hand, came to be drawn largely from a well-organised and highly motivated constituency of urban, upper caste Hindu voters, supplemented with sporadic 'issue-based' support from other groups.

In the 1990s the issues of Mandal, Mandir and Market (the three 'M's) galvanised popular engagement in Indian politics as never before. The core support of the BJP arose not only from upper caste elites who stood to benefit from its pro-Hindu and conservative policies but also from popular support on the Ayodhya Mandir issue and the perception that they alone had the power to control the forces of communalism they had helped to arouse. The riots of 2002 in Gujarat widely confounded the latter belief and probably contributed to a significant decline in support for the NDA in 2004 among its urban middle-class constituents. Thus in 1999, the NDA won 51 of the 74 predominantly urban constituencies, but only 21 in 2004, the Congress and its allies pushing their total from 16 to 35.

On the economic front the issues were not so clear. If discontent amongst the rural poor were a cause of the NDA's defeat in 2004 they might have been expected to have lost a great many votes within this section, but this was not so. And although the UPA still won more votes overall amongst the *adivasis*, the BJP managed a significant increase in their support within this section as a result of the grass-roots campaigning, religious conversion, and educational programmes of its extra-parliamentary Hindutva allies (hence, notably, the victories in Chhattisgarh and Jharkhand).

According to Yadav (2004), although the BJP and its allies did not lose significant votes amongst its rural supporters, it did fail to increase them to the degree that would have been necessary to counter the attacks of secularist critics and the wavering of its support in small towns and urban centres. Although the economy was in good shape, growth was almost entirely confined to new, high-tech and urban-based export industries. The party's slogan of 'India Shining' thus held no appeal for the mass of the population in rural areas, which had seen little or no improvement in their economic condition and standard of living. At the same time, there was no single vital issue, such as the Ayodhya Mandir, to revitalise the party's urban base. The Congress, by contrast, ran a very skilful campaign that concentrated on marginal seats and a careful choice of allies. The Congress thus contested 39 fewer seats, 414 as compared with 453 in 1999, leaving those uncontested seats to its allies in the UPA, in the assumption that they had a better chance of winning – as proved to be the case.

Overall, the Congress won a smaller proportion of the voting total than in the previous election, but in the seats it contested it registered a 1.3 percentage swing in its favour. Its allies, though, did very much bettter, their seats increasing from 23 in 1999 to 77 in 204, their overall vote share moving up from 5.7 to 10.1 per cent. The victory of the UPA over the NDA was thus due largely to the fresh support brought to the Congress by its choice of allies, giving them 222 seats with a combined vote share of 36.5 per cent. This was hardly a ringing endorsement by the electorate, but nonetheless it marked a significant defeat for the NDA, whose vote share fell from 40.8 per cent to 35.9 per cent, and total number of seats from

182 to 138. Although the BJP held on to power in a number of populous states, such as Rajasthan, and made impressive gains in Karnataka, the Indian National Congress emerged as the largest party in the Lok Sabha. In alliance with the DMK in Tamil Nadu, and with support from the Communist Party of India (Marxist) in Bengal, a Congress-led 'United Progressive Alliance' (UPA) was thus able to form a majority in parliament and to assume control of the central government.

The wholly unanticipated outcome of this election marked in some way an end to the process of democratisation begun in the 1990s. The Congress Party itself had always been a coalition of sorts, but now it was forced to share power as part of an even broader coalition in order to achieve office. It could no longer alone 'rule the roost' as in the days of Indira Gandhi. The BJP was forced into a more moderate position by the assumption of office and had its more radical policies diluted still further by the demands of its coalition partners. The radical, mould-breaking, low-caste and regional parties were then forced to choose between one or other of these alliances. The Indian electorate was therefore offered a very limited choice between two amorphous political groupings, not dissimilar to that seen in the political system of the United States of America.

In 2004 a weak mandate was given to Sonia Gandhi's Congress and coalition partners, who collectively draw most of their support from the poor of India; it is therefore assumed that tackling poverty will be amongst their priorities. At the same time the UPA will need to move quickly to consolidate its new-found support in India's urban areas if it is to avert the possibility of a right-wing revival and the return of the BJP. This will involve, not least of all, a root-and-branch modernisation of the Congress Party itself.[15]

In a state of shock after the election, the BJP latched upon the only target they could find: the fact that the Congress Party was led by Italian-born Sonia Gandhi (Figure 27). Declaring that it would be an affront to national pride if India were ruled by a 'foreigner', they threatened to boycott parliament if she was appointed prime minister – to the considerable confusion of a majority of public opinion, which never doubted she would be entitled to assume this role. Sonia Gandhi was by now an Indian citizen, and as marriage customs in India are patrilocal women are assumed to share the caste and status of the men they marry. Some speculated that Sonia's son, Rahul, who had been elected to parliament in the old family constituency of Amethi in north India, might be an alternative. However, Rahul (born June 1970) was too young and inexperienced. Rather than endure a confrontation over this issue, Sonia Gandhi wisely stepped aside and nominated as prime minister Manmohan Singh, the widely respected former finance minister in the last Congress government, where he had pioneered the liberalisation of the Indian economy. Although elderly, he was a selfless and honest politician from an academic background, and Sonia's proposal was met with immediate acclaim (from the business community in particular). Sonia Gandhi herself retained the chairmanship of the Congress Party's Central Working Committee, a position of enormous influence but which still left some division between party and government – an arguably healthy development.

Figure 27 Congress president Sonia Gandhi at an election meeting in Guntur, April 2004, next to a picture of her late husband Rajiv. © *The Hindu.*

Figure 28 Pervez Musharraf and Manmohan Singh saluting and waving at an Indo-Pakistan cricket match, April 2005. © *The Hindu.*

Having been elected to bring peace and stability, and in anticipation that he might do something to tackle India's endemic poverty, Manmohan Singh's government found itself in something of a dilemma. The Indian government is committed to free-market economics, and it was Manmohan Singh who did most to promote the programme of liberalisation in the early 1990s that has so greatly encouraged growth in the urban, service and high-tech industrial sectors. This did not fit well with socialism. Soon after assuming power, however, the new government boldly announced a national rural employment guarantee scheme, based upon a programme pioneered in Maharashtra in the 1980s, providing 100 days of work each year to one person from any household officially classified as impoverished. Since it inherited a budget deficit amounting to 10 per cent of GDP and public debt amounting to over 80 per cent, it remains to be seen whether the scheme will be either effective or affordable. The inadequacy of educational provision is still to be tackled; nonetheless, the scheme might at least enable more poor households to afford to send their children to school.

An immediate priority of the UPA government was the announcement of its intention to press ahead with the rapprochement with Pakistan, initiated under the previous government, and India has accordingly begun to withdraw troops from Kashmir whilst continuing with talks. Meetings were held between Indian and Pakistani foreign ministers in New Delhi, and General Musharraf and the Indian prime minister met in New York whilst attending a United Nations General Assembly in September 2004. In 2005, in a continuation of confidence-building measures, it was agreed that a bus service would be resumed linking the eastern (Indian-controlled) and western (Pakistani-controlled) halves of Kashmir. Clearly, public opinion on both sides is tired of confrontation, and both the national and international climates are more in favour of agreement of rapprochement than they ever have been before – although the obstacles are still substantial (Paul 2005; Ganguly 2002).

How successfully the Indian government can address the other challenges it faces depends in part on progress in improving relations with Pakistan. It is speculated that the 'peace dividend' resulting from agreement could save the two countries as much as US $2 billion per year each in defence expenditure, whilst adding two or more percentage points to economic growth. This could go a long way on both sides of the border towards fulfilling the dissatisfaction with economic conditions justifiably present amongst large swathes of their populations. Such dissatisfaction has limited outlets at the polls and shown itself in various forms of religious and political extremism. In the past there has been an unhealthy association between electoral politics and the constant threat of war, but with the fracturing of democratic politics on both sides of the border, and in the context of an international campaign against terrorism, this is a very much less comforting equation. Although both sides have never previously allowed an opportunity to go unmissed and powerful obstacles remain in the way, the prospect of an advance on all three fronts – strategic and political stability and economic progress – is therefore very enticing.

18 South Asia in the new millennium

I have voted since the first election in 1952 . . . I felt excited, but not as much as I was when zamindari was abolished. That was the most important thing in my life. Having the vote is better than having rajas! With democracy you can change governments, but with rajas there is just dynasty and dictatorship. But even then we have not gained much from the vote.

(Ram Dass, c. 1997)[1]

In Pakistan, Abdul Qadeer Khan was hailed as a hero of Islam and as Mohsin-e-Pakistan – the country's greatest benefactor – for his role in shepherding Pakistan's nuclear programme until the successful explosion of a nuclear device in 1998. Five years later he was being denounced as a terrorist accomplice and worse for his role in supplying nuclear technology to North Korea, Libya and Iran, whilst supplying himself with a luxury holiday home in the Mediterranean and other perks. In India, the popular retired scientist and architect of India's missile programme, A.P.J. Abdul Kalam, was similarly acclaimed and elected as president in July 2002. Nonetheless, a survey of public opinion conducted by the *Hindu* newspaper (October 1998) on 'Pokhran II and what it has done for India' showed that the desired impact on public opinion had been achieved only to a limited extent by India's nuclear tests. Of the 482 respondents 44 per cent recalled 'joy' as their 'immediate reaction' to the tests, but 41 per cent reported 'worry' as theirs. Significantly, only 25 per cent of the people surveyed believed that India's renewed status as a nuclear power would help economic development, and only 38 per cent felt that India should go on to develop a range of deployable nuclear weapons. Seventy per cent of the respondents felt that Pokhran-II would lead to a substantial increase in defence expenditure. At the same time, when asked about national priorities, 41 per cent stated population control to be the nation's top priority, whilst despite the events of the preceding six months only 21 per cent of the sample considered 'national security' as the most important issue. Poverty elimination emerged as the most preferred national goal for 31 per cent of the respondents. This suggests that once the initial enthusiasm had passed, further reflection caused many to doubt the NDA government's conducting of nuclear tests, along with some of its other priorities. This proved to be the case in the elections of 2004.

On other fronts there was no doubting the inconsistency within the policies of both the Congress-led United Progressive Alliance (UPA) and the BJP-led National Democratic Alliance (NDA) governments in India as in public they both extolled the virtue in preferring *swadeshi* (home-grown) goods, at the same time as they oversaw, in the years from 1991 to 2005, the continuing progress of economic liberalisation and globalisation, accompanied by a rapid increase in part-time working (Jenkins 1999). It was also hard to conceal the inconsistency in the celebration of 'traditional Hindu values' by right-wing politicians at the very moment when India fell prey to the worldwide epidemic of the human immuno-deficiency virus, AIDS. Thus by 2003 India found itself amongst the countries with the highest infection rates with more than 5 million infected with HIV/AIDS, a situation not helped by the complacency of politicians.[2] It was also impossible to hide the conflict between significantly increased defence expenditures and the fact that India and Pakistan shared between them some of the lowest average literacy rates in the world, with women and backward castes and tribes particularly badly affected. It is true that Indian literacy is measured by a standard higher than in some other countries (the reading standard of a literate 12-year-old), but the woeful standard of India's primary and secondary education system was – and continues to be – all too apparent, while that in Pakistan is even worse. The Indian constitution provides for free education for children from age 6 through 14, but only about half of those aged 10 or over continue studying. Meanwhile India's 8,000 universities and colleges (with 200,000 students in Delhi alone), some of them of world-class standard, churn out more than 3 million graduates each year, mainly derived from, and benefiting, the urban middle classes.

Statistics are a poor reflection of reality, but we can illustrate some broad themes concerning economic, social and cultural change using quantitative data, which are otherwise hard to reveal. These statistics mostly relate to India, but since India contains the largest population it is a good general indicator of the problems and opportunities facing the subcontinent as a whole. Amongst these indicators, the most striking are those relating to population and wealth. Thus by the beginning of the twenty-first century, overall economic growth of 6–7 per cent and industrial growth at an average of 8 per cent had caused India's capital, New Delhi, to triple in size over the preceding two decades, whilst India's middle class swelled to some 200 million – almost as large as the combined middle classes of Europe. The software industry was booming, and the southern city of Bangalore, wired end to end with optical cable, had become the fastest-growing city in Asia. Due to the advanced education of India's middle-class elite, internet-based enterprises flourished, and IT experts from India were poached by multinational companies from abroad. Azim Premji, majority owner of one Bangalore-based software and IT consulting company, WIPRO, was cited as being among the 50 richest men in the world, according to the US-based *Forbes* magazine between 2000 and 2003, whilst the owners of outsourcing companies such as HCL Technologies and INFOSYS were expanding their businesses rapidly. The widespread use of English was a particular advantage enjoyed by Indian business in

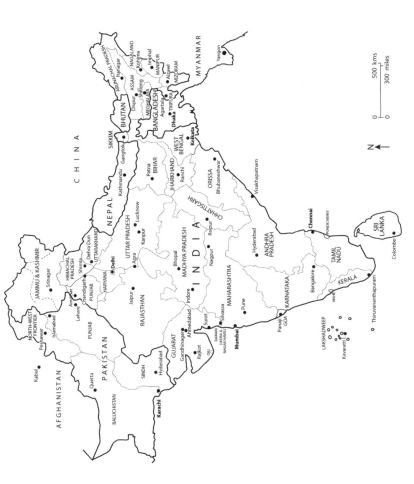

Map 11 Contemporary South Asia: nations, states and principal cities, 2006.

a global trading environment. It was ironic, therefore, that a priority of the BJP/NDA government had been an increase in the teaching of the ancient Indian language, Sanskrit, in Indian universities, and the relabelling of all the government offices in New Delhi in Sanskrit. This was one policy for which enthusiasm quickly evaporated after the return to power of the Congress.

Whilst in power the BJP had continued the policy of encouraging inward investment initiated by Congress in the early 1990s, with considerable success, it was widely accepted that the activities of the party had encouraged a significant increase in religious zealotry and extremism. Increasingly, this was directed not only against Muslims in the north but against Christian and other religious minorities in southern and eastern states, where the Muslim population was far smaller and Hindu fundamentalism had hitherto not been such a force. Minority rights, freedom of religion, equal citizenship, and even the lives of minorities seemed to be under threat almost everywhere (Chandhoke 1999). One of the most publicised examples, internationally, was the murder of Graham Staines, an Australian-born Christian missionary, and his two sons when their car was set alight in the eastern Indian state of Orissa in January 1999. The murderer was Dara Singh who, along with his gang, was responsible for a number of attacks on religious minorities in the tribal district of Mayurbhanj, including the killing of a Muslim trader and a Christian priest the year before. Two weeks later two Christian teenagers in Orissa were killed.

Dara Singh's arrest in February 2000 was met with widespread relief, but less welcome was the promulgation of an Orissa state government order at the end of November 1999 prohibiting conversions without the prior permission of the local police and district magistrate. Initially Dara Singh was sentenced to death and 11 gang members awarded life sentences, but in May 2005 the Orissa High Court commuted Dara Singh's sentence to life imprisonment and ordered the release of his co-conspirators. This seemed to signal what many have suspected – that a pervasive official prejudice, and even permissiveness, lay behind the violent communal incidents that were erupting with increasing frequency. In May 2000, at least 30 people were injured in a bomb explosion during a Christian religious meeting in Machlipatnam town in the southern state of Andhra Pradesh. Meanwhile, in Gujarat state an order by the BJP-led state government lifted a ban on government employees being members of the Hindu nationalist Rashtriya Svayamsevak Sangh (RSS), and a Freedom of Religion Bill was proposed that forbade the conversion of a person from one religion to another 'by use of force or allurement or by fraudulent means', with a maximum penalty of three years' imprisonment and a fine. This was just the beginning of Gujarat's plunge into religious extremism and civil disorder.

Not only Hindu–Muslim rivalry, but a variety of other forms of religious intolerance emerged as a continuing threat to the stability of Indian society and, indirectly, India's relations with her neighbours, in the late 1990s. Neo-nationalists, found increasingly in all walks of life, for the most part argued that this was all for the good, or at least understandable – a complacency that proved shockingly apparent with the resurgence of Islamic terrorism in 2002 and the eruption of anti-Muslim riots in Gujarat, which killed more than a thousand and injured nearly three times that number in the following year. Many came to realise that the BJP rode a dangerous tiger of communalism, xenophobia and intolerance, which was perhaps not a phenomenon of genuine patriotism and religious sentiment but a more profound symptom of widespread and desperate economic distress resulting from corruption and the growing disparity between income distribution and population growth. In elections in the late 1990s India's poor had turned to the BJP for salvation from this fate, but their response was mostly just anti-Muslim rhetoric.

The biggest change of all has been seen in the field of population growth. In the 1930s, mortality from famine, malnutrition and infectious diseases was so high that in India average life expectancy was only 32 years. At independence, still over one-third of children died before they reached their first birthday. By May 2000, however, India's population had achieved a total of 1 billion people, accounting for one-sixth of the world's population. At 733 people per square mile the country was a hundred times more densely populated than the United States, and since it was still growing at 2 per cent there were 18 million more mouths to feed each year. Overall, the population was likely to exceed that of China by 2035. The bulk of this population (nearly three-quarters) still lived in rural areas, where the rapid economic growth of the past decade and a half, confined largely to the cities, has passed them by.

In rural areas contraceptive advice and health care services are limited. Nearly all women aged 15–19 are already married and some 60 per cent of women aged 17–19 are mothers. On average, each Indian woman has now between 3.1 and 2.73 children, according to figures for the period 2001 to 2005 and 2006 estimates.[3] This is an extraordinary reduction on the figure of 5.9 in the 1960s; but this average disguises large regional variations, and in poorer areas of rural north India both infant mortality and fertility rates are significantly higher than elsewhere in the country.[4] To feed this population on a land mass one-third the size of the United States was a miracle in itself, and indicative of the extraordinary economic growth India has achieved since independence. Nonetheless, that wealth has become perhaps more unequally divided than in any other society in the world, India being home to nearly a third of the world's poorest poor, with some 350 million living at or below a poverty line defined as a monthly income of less than US $25 and therefore insufficient to provide the intake of enough calories to maintain a healthy diet. Some 20 per cent of the population in 2000 still had no access to clean water, which contributed to extremely high levels of infant mortality (72 deaths per 1,000 births).

Of the Indian population, 34.7 per cent live on less than a dollar a day (at 1983 purchasing parity rates), according to the UNDP's 2004 *Human Development Report*, which averages statistics for the period 1990 to 2002. The problems of poverty in India are thus comparable, but in terms of absolute (total) numbers far worse than in Nepal, Bangladesh, and Pakistan where some 37.7 per cent, 36 per cent, and 13.4 per cent, respectively, of the population falls into the same income category. All four countries come out worse than Sri Lanka where only 6.5 per cent fall into this category. In terms of sheer numbers, India's problems are daunting, yet a better idea of them may be derived from other indicators. Thus in terms of life expectancy at birth, Indians in 2002 could expect to live for 63.9 years, compared with 72.6 years in Sri Lanka, 61.4 years in Bangladesh, 61 years in Pakistan and 59.9 years in Nepal. Although a huge improvement on previous decades, these figures still fall well short of the standards clearly attainable, as shown by the Sri Lankan example, or those prevailing elsewhere in South-East Asia.

The exceptionally poor position of the Nepalese in these rankings of prosperity and health probably goes a long way towards explaining the success of the Maoist insurgency that has raged through Nepal, finally ending the monarchy's grip on power after mass demonstrations in the capital in April 2006. The same reason undoubtedly explains the similar rise of 'Naxalite' guerrilla insurgency in a wide and impoverished, predominantly *adivasi*, belt across central India, with whom the Maoists in Nepal have fraternal links.[5] Many of these discrepancies in life expectancy can be explained in terms of health facilities and expenditure. In terms of literacy, Sri Lanka clearly tops the South Asian league table, and this has obviously made a large difference – but there are other factors too, such as housing, employment (or lack thereof) and the environment, which profoundly affect standards of living and life expectancy.

Whilst the area of 'open forest' has increased, India's dense forest cover fell from 14.1 per cent (1972–5) to 11 per cent (1981–3), and has probably fallen very much lower since. Due to deforestation (most importantly), urbanisation, and over-consumption for irrigation purposes, water tables have also been falling at a rate of 1–3 metres per year almost everywhere in the country. This desperate shortage of water has led to one of the most important subaltern movements of recent decades: the Narmada Bachao Andolan (Save the Narmada Movement – NBA). This was a non-governmental organisation that mobilised *adivasis*, farmers, environmentalists and human rights activists against the Sardar Sarovar dam, the largest of a series of 30 dams being built across the River Narmada in central India. The purpose of the dams is to irrigate arid areas such as Kutch and Saurashtra in the state of Gujarat, but in the process they will inundate many thousands of hectares of land, including forests, currently occupied by impoverished *adivasi* (tribal) people in the state of Madhya Pradesh (Drèze *et al.* 1997). The NBA fought first to prevent the dam from being constructed, which led to the withdrawal of World Bank finance, and then for the proposed height of the Sardar Sarovar dam to be lowered. Subsequently, as construction of the dam has progressed, the campaign has aimed at ensuring that those rendered homeless by the dam are given the full rehabilitation support promised by the government. The NBA campaign tactics have involved demonstrations and hunger strikes, and skilful use of the media. In the process, critical attention has been brought to bear upon the priorities and imperatives of state and central government 'development' policies, as well as upon those who claim to speak for the otherwise voiceless and dispossessed (Baviskar 1995). Prominent supporters have included Medha Patkar, a former postgraduate of the Tata Institute of Social Sciences, who left her studies to found the movement; the revered social and moral leader, Baba

Amte, who left his leprosy mission near Warora in 1990 to join the struggle; and the author Arundhati Roy, whose book *The Cost of Living* (1999) later helped bring widespread international attention to the cause. Medha Patkar won numerous awards for her advocacy and went on to form the National Alliance of People's Movements (NAPM) to campaign against globalisation and corporatisation in India.

Environmental degradation as a consequence of unregulated growth is not only a problem in rural areas but in the cities too. By the end of the twentieth century, for example, Delhi had become the fourth most polluted metropolis in the world, as some 3 million vehicles clog its streets. Each day, on average, five people die in road traffic accidents in the capital and some 1,430 tons of exhaust fumes are released into the air. One report suggested that the daily inhalation of these fumes by the city's citizens was equivalent to the consumption of some 20 cigarettes. Endeavours to improve this desperate situation only surfaced following an initiative by the Supreme Court, which, in response to a public interest petition raised by the Centre for Science and the Environment (an independent research and lobbying group), forced the entire bus fleet of Delhi Municipal Corporation, taxis and auto-rickshaws to switch from petrol to low-emission compressed natural gas for fuel in April 2002, marking a significant improvement in the quality of life of many Delhi-ites.

Although they gained the vote in 1950 and account for more than 9 per cent of parliamentary seats, women in India are in many ways still second-class citizens and bear the brunt of persistent poverty and inequality. Thus at the beginning of the twenty-first century only 46.4 per cent of Indian women were literate (as compared to 69 per cent of men), and only 38 per cent of women were enrolled in secondary school. This compares starkly with India's rapidly growing neighbour, China, where adult female literacy rates are 87 per cent.[6] Worst of all, 540 out of every 100,000 women still die in childbirth. Women do the majority of household work and the majority of work in the fields as well (at least in rice-growing areas). Yet girl children are considered a burden and the persistence of customs such as dowry, the lack of medical care given to girl children, and even outright instances of female infanticide, has caused the ratio between the sexes in India to become grossly skewed, there being some 93.5 females for every 100 males in the population in 1981 (compared with 97.2/100 in 1901), and 93.3 per 100 according to the 2001 census. Whilst this is a modest improvement on the figures for 1991, and the census is possibly flawed by the practice of *purdah* – which forbids married women from being seen in public – the ratio of women amongst those aged 0–6 has worsened from 945 to 927 since 1991, boding ill for the future.[7] Even as adults, women are often expected to sacrifice themselves for the benefit of their families and to go without. Thus in November 1999 a World Bank report, *Wasting Away: The Crisis of Malnutrition in India*, said that as many as half of all children under 4 were malnourished and that 60 per cent of women were anaemic.

Perhaps one of the most appalling reflections of the second-class status of women in India (linked also to consumerism) was the rise of the phenomenon of 'bride-burning' – the murder by fire of women so that greedy husbands can remarry and win another dowry. Fire is used, since this leaves no trace of a murder weapon and it can easily be written off as a domestic accident, since kerosene is used in cooking. This phenomenon arose, largely in urban areas, due to the improvement in communications and an increase in long-distance marriage migration. Whilst a symptom of growing prosperity, such migrations deprive women of the protection of family and friends and render them far more vulnerable. So frequently did such deaths occur in the capital, Delhi, in the 1980s, that a special law was introduced by the municipal corporation obliging the police to treat every death by fire of a woman at home as a murder case until evidence to the contrary was uncovered. This helped curb the phenomenon, but other forms of abuse such as acid attacks and (especially in Pakistan) so-called 'honour killings' of women alleged to have brought shame upon their families, and the increasing involvement of women as targets in communal conflicts, are an ongoing cause for concern (Sen 2001; Jayawardena and de Alwis 1996). These modern social problems have been the major concern of a large number of women's organisations that are now highly active in the urban areas of northern India (Kumar 1993; Kishwar and Vanita 1996; Forbes 1996).

In Pakistan there was a big leap forward in the representation of women in the national parliament in the elections organised by General Musharraf in 2002, but this has not been matched by changes at other levels of government, or by an increase in the very low level of involvement of women in senior management (9 per cent) and in technical and professional occupations. At the same time, a Women's Protection Bill, which amongst other things proposed to repeal the controversial Hudood law (introduced by Zia-ul-Haq) that failed to distinguish between rape and adultery, was narrowly passed in November 2006 by the Pakistani National Assembly after several failed attempts. In India, a means to advance the status of women was proposed in the so-called Women's Bill in 1999, which provided for a 33 per cent reservation for women in parliament and state assemblies. The measure arose partly because the BJP had made a point (at least superficially) of recruiting women to its cause, partly in order to counteract the all-too-obvious all-male bias of supporting organisations such as the RSS (Jeffrey and Basu 1998). However, notwithstanding the fiery oratory of politicians like Sadhvi Rithambara and Uma Bharati, the Women's Bill was defeated due to a lack of support within the ruling coalition. The only compensation (but an important one) is that within rural areas, the regulations governing the functioning of village *panchayats* typically require a minimum 33 per cent representation for women. This, along with the development of the women's movement in India, still offers considerable grounds for optimism (Hust 2004).

In Indian states such as Kerala, where land reform is combined with high levels of literacy, particularly among females, the birth rate has dramatically fallen, and the prognosis for more generalised prosperity is good. The same can be said for Sri Lanka, where general literacy rates are in excess of 90 per cent. In backward northern regions such as Bihar and eastern UP, however, the prospects for poverty alleviation and a more egalitarian agrarian structure are almost non-existent. It is scarcely surprising, therefore, that it is in these states that some of the most extreme examples of inter-caste and Hindu–Muslim communal conflict are to be found.

India thus remains a startling mix of old and new, a mix that can be explained largely in terms of the lack of commitment to growth with equity and the self-serving myopia of urban elites. There is nothing mystical or quaint about it. India has rich deposits of coal, petroleum production is rapidly increasing, and it is one of the world's top producers of iron and steel, with huge mills operating in Bhilai, Bokaro, Durgapur and Raurkela. In April 2001, a high-powered rocket launch propelled India into the ranks of the select club of countries able to fire big satellites deep into space. It has the largest film industry in the world in terms of the number of films made each year, ironically dominated by Muslim actors and directors, which are wildly popular with largely Hindu, male, cinema-going audiences within India as well as enjoying a large overseas market via satellite, tape and DVD. And India now has the fourth largest car industry in Asia, producing more than 700,000 passenger vehicles each year, the leading company in 2002 – Suzuki-Maruti – producing some 1.7 million vehicles worldwide and ranking as the thirteenth largest manufacturer. At the same time, 70 per cent of the population are dependent on agriculture for their livelihoods, with half of India's farms being less than 2.5 acres (1 hectare) in area, and only a few larger than 25 acres (10 hectares). Millions of Indians, both adults and children, work at home or in small-scale plants engaged in simple hand-loom weaving and artisanal crafts and play no part at all in the global market revolution.

On the positive side, the annual growth rate of the Indian software industry has been 60 per cent between 1992 and 1999, and the industry today employs 160,000 professionals with a turnover of US $4 billion in 1998/9 (of which 2.6 billion was exported), most of it concentrated in the southern states of Karnataka, Andhra Pradesh and Tamil Nadu.[8] Strikingly, India graduates 70,000 computer professionals every year (in addition to the graduates from the prestigious Indian institutes of technology), and many Indian software firms have earned the Carnegie Mellon Software Engineering Institute's capability maturity model certification, with five of them having reached level five. Only nine firms worldwide have achieved this status. In rural areas, however, qualified practising physicians are few and far between, and medical facilities are almost non-existent, with overcrowded government hospitals being accessible only in the major towns and cities, where patients have to pay for their food, and medicines too (unless they are completely impoverished). There is no national scheme of health or unemployment insurance (although the Congress-led United Progressive Alliance government was working in 2005 to introduce the latter), and less than 60 per cent of children study as far as grade five.

While as much as 12 per cent of public expenditure in India goes on education, this expenditure is skewed towards the cities and is inadequate to the country's needs, given the youthfulness of its population and decades of underinvestment. Thus, when in 1987 Rajiv Gandhi proposed 'Operation Blackboard', a plan to equip every village school with a blackboard and a roof, the scheme was abandoned as it was considered too costly. In 1995 a similar centrally sponsored drive to supply midday meals in every primary school foundered on the lassitude of many state governments. Only Tamil Nadu had any length of experience of school meal provision (since the 1950s), and many thought that provision of primary school midday meals throughout the entire country was impossible. However, a huge leap forward occurred in November 2001 when the Supreme Court ruled in a 'right to food' case that every state government must provide cooked school meals to all primary schoolchildren. This judicial initiative was followed by local-level activism in 2002. The Supreme Court ruling was copied and distributed, demonstrations held, and children lined the streets with empty plates in a symbolic protest in Bangalore. By 2006 coverage was almost universal – a small step, but a sign of what could be done.

Profound inequalities, and the fragility of life for most people, make it very much harder for rural dwellers to cope when struck by the periodic natural disasters that blight the subcontinent. Enduring a climate of extremes, and being a major earthquake zone, the Indian subcontinent has more than its fair share of both. Orissa has thus been devastated twice by cyclones recently, in 1999 and again in 2001, whilst a massive earthquake-induced tsunami in late December 2004 demonstrated the vulnerability of coastal communities in the Indian Ocean region. On this occasion the south-eastern coastline of India, the Andaman islands, and two-thirds of the coastline in Sri Lanka were devastated without warning with the loss of more than 45,000 lives. Particularly affected were fishing communities and coastal fishermen using small boats. These could not hope to withstand waves that rose to 3 or even 6 metres in height. Perhaps the worst legacy of poverty, though, is poor housing, which not only affects health in the long term but can turn a serious earthquake into a far greater catastrophe. Such an earthquake occurred in Latur and Osmanabad districts in Maharashtra in 1993, when 7,600 died and tens of thousands were rendered homeless as their poorly made dwellings collapsed. Likewise, in January 2001, an 8.5 magnitude earthquake, centred on Bhuj in north-west Gujarat, killed close to 20,000 and left 600,000 homeless. Most disastrous of all, the October 2005 earthquake in Kashmir left a trail of death on both sides of the Indo-Pakistan border, killing 1,400 in India and more than 73,000 in Pakistan.

Throughout the subcontinent, conspicuous inequalities are compounded by the limited development, for the most part, of a politics of class, which might demand that they be addressed. And whilst the politics of ethnicity and cultural and religious nationalism offer a source of pride, which can do something to hold divided nations together, it does nothing to resolve the twisted political priorities of the elite – such a major part of the problem in the first place. Many have argued that this is nothing more than a colonial legacy. Clearly both colonialism and *goonda* politics are characterised by the habitual abuse of power, and it could be argued that over the generations Indians and Pakistanis have become inured to such excesses. This still does not entirely explain why in the general elections held in India in 1999 some 1,000 of the candidates were alleged to have committed crimes ranging from murder, theft and rape through to banditry and extortion, the states worst affected being Uttar Pradesh, Bihar, Maharashtra and Madhya Pradesh. The reason surely lies partly in the willingness of the political elite to protect their own kind. A renewed spirit of judicial activism during the past decade, inspired by judges P.N. Bhagwati, Krishna Iyer, A.M. Ahmadi and J.S. Verma in the Supreme Court of India, new rules on public access to the court and public interest litigation (typified by the 2002 ruling on traffic pollution in New Delhi), may suggest a remedy to this situation. However, it remains the case that prominent regional leaders such as Laloo Prasad Yadav, former chief minister in Bihar and minister for railways in the UPA government, and Jayalalitha, former chief minister in Tamil Nadu and member of the NDA government, are still at large despite corruption charges being brought against them. In Jayalalitha's case, she was found guilty – a judgment overturned in 2003 due to lack of evidence, although the Supreme Court told her she should atone by 'answering her conscience' and returning land acquired by dubious means, which she did. If such big fish can escape so easily it is no wonder that a blind eye is turned to the smaller scale incidents of kidnapping and extortion carried on in pursuit of electoral success.[9] It is also the case that although the Supreme Court is able to exercise considerable influence, due to the elites' reliance upon it for their own legitimation, this is in itself a somewhat unsatisfactory – arguably undemocratic – phenomenon, and such independence is not often seen in India's lower courts (Moog 1998; Roy 2002; Sathe 2002).

The BJP came to power in India for the second time in 1999, partly on the back of a claim that it would put an end once and for all to corruption in the higher echelons of government. For many the filming in March 2001 of the BJP Party president receiving bribes in an office within the defence ministry from Tehelka.com journalists, masquerading as arms contractors, persuaded them that little had in fact changed. The incident brought to mind an earlier visit by Congress Party activists to a *jhuggi* (slum) at the southern foot of Arera Hill in Bhopal. According to Kaliram, a resident (as explained to the author), they offered saris to the ladies and bottles of liquor to the men, which were gratefully received. When asked if this changed anyone's mind as to who they would be voting for, he replied firmly, with a grin: 'Haan – hum BJP ko apna mat denge' ('Yes – we will vote for the BJP!'). Perhaps the greatest asset of all that India possesses in the face of precarious leadership is this healthy scepticism amongst its electorate, an electorate that continues to exercise power on a scale unparalleled anywhere else in the world and which obviously needs to be treated with caution.

A further cause for optimism lay in the successful prosecution in October 2000 of former prime minister Narasimha Rao, found guilty of bribing Jharkhand Mukti Morcha MPs to vote with the Congress during his time in office in the early 1990s. Although Rao subsequently won an appeal shortly before his death, the case was significant as it was the first time such a senior politician had been prosecuted and the law permitted to complete its course. In August 2005 a report by Supreme Court judge G.T. Nanavati on the 1984 anti-Sikh riots (the ninth such report – this one commissioned under the NDA administration) led to the resignation of Jagdish Tytler from the cabinet and the resignation of Sajjan Kumar as chairman of the state-run Delhi Rural Development Board. A similar exercise was undertaken after the elections in 2004 concerning the 1991 destruction of the Babri Masjid in Ayodhya, with the arraignment of several BJP politicians for their alleged involvement. Arguably a highly politicised process, this nonetheless keeps alive the possibility of politicians being held to account for their misdeeds in a fashion rarely seen elsewhere even in the developed world.

A phenomenon related to judicial activism, and one of the subcontinent's largest and most powerful democratic assets, is its newspaper industries, entirely privately owned, which (for the most part) freely criticise their respective governments. India has about 4,453 daily newspapers, published in a variety of languages. Of these, 402 are national dailies and the major English-language newspapers – including *The Times of India, Indian Express, Statesman*, and the *Hindu* – all wield considerable political influence. The same can be said for Pakistan where some 303 daily newspapers, including popular dailies such as the *Daily Jang*, still challenge the government's version of events. Bangladesh has some 25 national daily newspapers that are largely free of government control, although press freedom in Bangladesh has been increasingly under threat since 2003. Nonetheless, it could be said that corruption alone is not the problem, that inequality is the cause of corruption as much as the other way around, and that freedom of speech alone can do little to counter it. Arguably, therefore, a new spirit of morality and democracy in public life can only emerge on the shoulders of a more generalised prosperity. If so, in economic terms, the countries of South Asia have a huge advantage within the newly emerging global markets since they are home to the second largest pool of English-speaking manpower in the world, as well as having relatively transparent and effective laws of contract (at least compared to those in China). To seize this advantage and to make the most of it, India and her neighbours must first address the deficiencies of markets closer to home, such as the market for child labour.

India has the dubious distinction of being the nation with the largest number of child labourers in the world. The official figure for child labourers is 13 million, but according to a 1996 report (quoting ILO and UNICEF as sources), the actual number in India could be anywhere between 14 million and 100 million children, working in industries such as fire-cracker making, diamond polishing, glass, brassware, carpet weaving, bangle making, lock making, and mica cutting, as well as a large number of domestic servants and prostitutes too. In Pakistan, the situation is even worse, child labour having assumed almost epidemic proportions. In total, there are estimated to be some 15 million child labourers in Pakistan. In areas such as Tharparkar, 60–70 per cent of all children of 15–17 years work, whilst figures of 20–25 per cent are normal in most cities. Of 20 million bonded labourers in Pakistan, according to the International Labour Organisation (ILO), 7.5 million are children, and more than 19,000 boys from the region, ranging in age from 2 to 11 years old, have been trafficked as camel jockeys to the Middle East – a trade that can cost them their lives. Some 40,000 children from Bangladesh are alleged to be involved in prostitution in Pakistan.[10] The causes of this phenomenon lie in the already stressed inadequacies of the education system, and the lack of employment opportunities for adult members of the household – a vicious circle, since it is not seriously possible for the countries of South Asia to address problems of low pay and adult unemployment, whilst child employment and similar violations of human rights on such a scale persist.[11] The interests of the subaltern mass of the population and the long-term interests of business communities arguably coincide on this point, which must be addressed if the citizens of independent India, Pakistan, Bangladesh and Sri Lanka are to enjoy a future as prosperous and/or harmonious as other industrialising nations in South-East and East Asia.

Finally, and above all, the future of the nations of South Asia must lie in closer regional co-operation economically, politically and strategically, leading ultimately to the establishment of a common market and common policies on a range of issues from the environment through to communications and even defence. This can only be achieved through the resolution of outstanding conflicts and a recognition of the long-term benefits to be won. This is hard to achieve in an environment where the needs of survival and short-term political advantage dominate. A promising beginning was made with the establishment of the South Asian Association for Regional Co-operation (SAARC) in 1985, which, despite slow beginnings, has nonetheless proved its worth by acting as a platform for crisis-resolving initiatives, most recently serving as a facilitator in the rapprochement between India and Pakistan. Given the faltering pace with which regional co-operation is developing in other parts of the world, including central Asia, South-East Asia and South America, an opportunity therefore still exists for the countries of South Asia to steal a march on their competitors.

In a liberalising, globalising world order, the economic advantages are considerable for those with the political will and determination to make use of them on their own terms. In this respect, the release of a flood of popular Indian films such as *Veer Zaara* (an Indo-Pakistan love story) and *Main Hoon Na* (which casts an Indian nationalist extremist in the role of the villain attempting to undermine an Indo-Pakistan peace initiative), along with the enthusiastic media coverage of the faltering rapprochements between India and Pakistan and between the Tamil minority and the Sinhalese government in Sri Lanka, suggests that the popular will for change is present on a scale that has never been seen before. Seen alongside moves towards a reform of the UN Security Council, with possible membership for India, progress in the war against terrorism in South Asia, an invitation to Pakistan to join the ASEAN-sponsored Asian Regional Forum, and the 2005 nuclear rapprochement between India and the USA (which saw the lifting of American sanctions on the supply of peaceful nuclear technology to India), the subcontinent appears to be advancing not only towards a reconfiguration of internal strategic alliances but of its standing and importance in international affairs. Whatever one thinks of these developments, they are all indications of the important role the subcontinent is set to play at the beginning of a century in which the legacies of European colonialism are perhaps fully, and finally, consigned to the past.

Glossary

Note on transliteration: as elsewhere in the book diacritical marks have been omitted, but the simplest English spellings have been used that phonetically approximate to the pronunciations in use in recent times. Exceptions are terms that came to be commonly known in a particular form (e.g. *madrasa* instead of *madrassah*).

adivasis Modern word for 'tribals'; Hindi equivalent of 'aborigine'.

ahimsa Non-violence.

Ahmadi Minority sect of Islam. Ahmadiyya Muslims are followers of Mirza Ghulam Ahmad who claimed to be the returned Messiah and Mahdi. The sect split into two after his death in Lahore in 1908.

amir Chief, leader.

anna Unit of currency (outdated); there were 16 annas in a rupee. Following decimalisation the anna was abolished, but 8 annas has continued in use as a colloquial term indicating half a rupee (50 *pice*) and 4 annas a quarter of a rupee (25 *pice*).

Arya Samaj Reformist Hindu movement founded in Mumbai (Bombay) in 1875 by Swami Dayanand Saraswati.

ashram A Hindu spiritual retreat.

atman The indivisible self (or soul).

ayurveda Traditional Indian medicine.

bagh A town square.

baksheesh A bribe, tip or gratuity.

bania/n Moneylender, grain dealer, intermediary trader (also *baniya*, *baniah*, *bunya*). The name of a tree applied by the Portugese to the merchants who met and traded under it.

bargadar A share-cropping peasant cultivator (Bengal).

basti A cluster of huts, or *katchi abadi* ('simple neighbourhood') in Urdu.

begum Muslim lady of very high rank.

beth begar Forced labour.

bhadralok Educated, upper classes of Bengal.

bhaiband Brotherhood, grouping of heads of families in a locality.

bhaiyachara System of family or 'brotherly' landholding.

bhakti Devotional worship.

bhang   Pulp or infusion of marijuana.

Bharat   Term for India.

bhikku   Buddhist monk.

bhoodan   Gift of land.

bigha/beegah   Unit of land equivalent to 2,468 square metres or 0.6 acres in Maharashtra; 2,529 square metres or 0.63 acres in north India; 1,338 square metres or 0.33 acres in Bengal; 6,771.41 square metres or 1.6 acres in Nepal.

bindi   Forehead decoration worn by Hindu women and men. It symbolises the opening of the spiritual third eye. Similar to but different from the *tilaka*, or *tilak*, applied to the forehead after worship.

biraderi   Kinship group.

Brahma   Hindu god of creation, husband of Sarasvati (goddess of knowledge). Typically represented with four heads and four arms.

brahmadeya   Village gifted to a Brahmin group.

Brahmin   Member of priestly caste (also *Brahman*).

Brahmo Samaj   Reformist Hindu movement founded in 1828 by Raja Ram Mohan Roy in Calcutta.

Caliph/Khalifah   Temporal and spiritual leader and protector of the community of Islam. Literally means the successor to Muhammad. Applied for many generations to the sultan of the Ottoman empire.

chapati   Unleavened flat bread.

chauth   Revenue demand in the Maratha empire; literally one-quarter.

chawl   Tenement.

chhole naan   Chick-peas served with unleavened, layered, whole-wheat bread or *naan*. A cheap and fast food.

chowkidar   Watchman.

crore   Amount, equivalent to 10 million.

dacoit   Bandit.

dacoity   Banditry.

dalit   Term for untouchable and scheduled castes, meaning 'the oppressed'.

daroga   Native police constable.

deshmukh   Sub-regional or district governor (Mughal India).

deshpande   District accountant (Mughal India).

dharmayudh morcha   Religious fight.

dharma   Religious duty (Hindu); each caste has its own *dharma*.

diku   Outsider (Jharkhand).

din   Faith (Muslim).

diwan   Prime minister in a pre-colonial or colonial Indian princely state.

diwani   Power of civil administration (in eighteenth-century Bengal).

Dravidians   Inhabitants of south India, speakers of 'Dravidian' languages.

durbar   General assembly, or celebratory gathering.

feringi   Foreigner, derived from the Portugese *farangi* (frank), meaning European.

fitna   Rebellion (against Mughal rule).

gana   Clan.

Ganesha/Ganapati   Hindu god: the son of Shiva and Parvati, born with an elephant's head. Also known as Ganapati.

Ganesh Chaturthi   Celebration of Ganesha's birthday. Festival revived by the western Indian politician Balgangadhar Tilak.

gaurakshini   Cow protection (movement).

ghadar/ghadr   Terrorist movement, derived from the Urdu word for revolution.

gol   Local marriage circle.

goonda   Henchman, gang member, 'hooligan'.

gram sarkar   Village government.

Gujars   Ancient Indian Community whose members include both Hindus and Muslims.

guna   Cosmological quality.

gunnies   Cloth/fibre sacks (Indian English).

gurudwara   Temple of the Sikhs.

haj   Pilgrimage to Mecca.

harijan   Children of god; Gandhian term for untouchables.

hartal   Strike action.

hat   Agricultural market.

hawala   'Providing a code' (in Hindi) also known as *hundi* – an informal method of money transfer, commonly mediated via a network of (e.g. Marwari or Sindhi) merchants of the same kin group.

Hindutva   'Hinduness' – word coined by Vinayak Damodar Savarkar in 1923 pamphlet *Hindutva: Who is a Hindu?*

hundi   See *hawala*.

iddah   Three months' waiting period before remarriage after divorce (Muslim).

inam   Land gifted in exchange for services or for religious purposes.

intifada   Uprising inspired by religious ideals.

Jagannath   Hindu god worshipped at a famous temple in Puri, Orissa. As at most Hindu shrines the image of the god is transported in a *ratha yatra* (chariot procession) during a purification ceremony and festival each year.

jagir/dar   Land given in reward for military service/the landholders.

jana   The People.

Jati   Caste cluster, subcaste; subdivision of the *varna* system.

jatha   Gang; armed band.

jatiya sarkar   National government.

jehad/jihad   Muslim holy war.

jemadar   Sepoy lieutenant.

jenmi   Leaseholding landlord (Kerala).

jhuggi   Slum.

jizya   A tax on non-Muslims.

jumma   Tithe, rent.

kaliyuga   Age of chaos and evil.

kanamdar   Leaseholding tenant (Kerala).

karma   Spiritual fate.

karsevak Hindu volunteer.

kashmiriyat Separatist movement in Kashmir.

Kayastha or ***Kayasth*** A scribe/administrator; an Indian caste.

khadi Homespun cotton cloth.

Khalistan Call for/name given to a separate Sikh state.

khalsa Sikh for 'pure'; name given to the army of the faithful founded by the Sikh guru Gobind Singh.

Khilafat/Caliphate The succession of the *Caliph* (Arabic)/*Khalif* (Persian).

khuntkatti Land tenure system (in Chota Nagpur).

kisan Peasant.

kotwal Law officer (Mughal era).

Kshatriya Member of the Hindu warrior and ruler *varna*.

kulkarni Village accountant.

kutcheri Administrative/government office, court house.

lakh Amount equivalent to 100,000; 10 *lakhs* is one million.

Lakshmi Hindu goddess of wealth, consort of Vishnu.

Lal Qila Red Fort.

lathi Baton or stick used like a truncheon.

Lok Sabha Lower house of Indian parliament; literally 'assembly of the people'.

madrasa Islamic school.

Mahabharata 'The Great Epic of the Bharata Dynasty', ancient Sanskrit Hindu religious text written between 1400 and 3100 BCE and transmitted orally through successive generations.

mahajan Banker, moneylender, merchant, *rentier* landowner; literally 'great' or 'big' people.

mahal/wari Village estate/landlord-based system of revenue settlement. A Mahal can also be a palace.

maharaja Great king.

mahasabha An association; literally 'great society'.

Mahommedan Term for Muslim (used in colonial times).

maidan A park (urban area), or plain (rural north India).

malguzar/i Village landlord/landholding.

mansabhdar Mughal noble.

mantra Holy words, magical incantation.

Marwari Member of the merchant caste from Marwar, western India.

masjid Mosque.

Mohajir Migrant to Pakistan, post-partition.

moksha Union with the supreme divine power (*nirvana* in Buddhism).

moulvi/maulvi Muslim religious leader, priest.

mufti Law officer (Mughal era).

mujahidin Holy warriors (fighters in the name of Islam).

mukti bahini Freedom force or liberation army (Bengali).

nabob A wealthy or powerful merchant in India, usually English; English colloquialism derived from *nawab*.

nadu   Ancient south Indian territorial community.

nawab   Provincial governor or viceroy (in Mughal times).

Naxalite   Militant left group in favour of armed insurrection.

nizam   Abbreviation of *nizam ul mulk*, meaning 'governor of the kingdom' (Mughal); special title given to the governor of the Hyderabad Province in the Mughal empire.

nurwa   Term for 'brotherhood' in Gujarat.

paan   Mouth-freshening snack.

panchayat   Traditional village council, group of councillors (usually five 'panch' in number).

pandit   A Brahmin priest.

pargana   Regional administrative area (Mughal) equivalent to a district in modern India.

Parishad   Pertaining to an assembly; person present at an assembly.

Parvati   Hindu goddess, consort of Shiva; otherwise known as Durga or Kali.

patel   Village headman.

patidar   Joint village landlord, community of joint village landlords (Gujarat); a caste.

periyanadu   Supra-village territorial unit in ancient south India.

peshwa   Hereditary rulers of the Maratha empire from 1713 to 1818, equivalent to a *diwan* or prime minister.

pice/paisa (pl. **paise**)   Unit of currency: there were 4 paise and 12 pies in each anna and 64 paise in each rupee up until the 1950s; after decimalisation there were 100 paise to the rupee, and the anna and pie were abandoned.

pindaris   Irregular horsemen (including many Rohillas) who accompanied Maratta armies in central India during the eighteenth century. Remunerated by plunder, their extirpation was the cause of the third Anglo-Maratta war of 1818.

pir   Sufi master.

poligar   Landlord (Madras presidency).

praja   Subject people.

puja   Hindu worship.

Puranas   Post-Vedic religious text.

purdah   Veiling, separation or seclusion of women from the gaze of men.

purna swaraj   Full or complete independence (Gandhi).

qawwali   Ecstatic Sufi devotional music.

qazi   Islamic judiciary, law officer (Mughal era); also *kazi*.

Quaid-i-Awam   'Great Leader'.

raj   Rule, sovereign government; Anglo-Indian term for the British rule of India.

raja   Ruler or king.

raksha   Devil.

Ramayana   Life history of the god-king Ram recorded by Valmiki *c.* 300 BCE; Sanskrit epic; rewritings include the *Ramacharit Manas* by Tulsidas (*c.* 1574 CE), and the *Kambaramayanam* by Kamban in Tamil.

ramshila Holy brick.

rani Female ruler.

rath Chariot.

Razakars Army of armed Muslim volunteers.

rupee Unit of currency: since decimalisation in India (1957) and Pakistan (1961) it has been worth 100 new *paise* or *pice* (sing. *paisa*).

ryot Revenue-paying peasant.

ryotwari Peasant-based landholding system.

sabha Council.

sahukar Moneylender.

samaj Society or congress.

samsara The cycle of rebirth.

samiti Volunteer group, committee.

sangha Monastic order.

sannyasin Holy man.

sardar Local chief or foreman.

sarkar Government.

sarvodhaya Social uplift through education and self-help.

sati Act of female immolation on funeral pyre of husband; women performing same.

sattva Clarity; white (*sattvika*).

satya Truth.

satyagraha Truth-force; word coined by Gandhi to describe non-violent protest.

sawar Rider or cavalry trooper.

sepoy Native Indian professional soldier, derived from the Persian/Urdu *sipahi* or soldier.

sharanarthi Refugees (from partition).

Shariah/t Islamic jurisprudence.

shaykh Leader (*shaykh al-hind* – leader of India).

shetya Mercantile aristocracy.

Shia Sect of Islam. Believe that the Prophet Muhammad appointed his son-in-law Ali ibn Abi Talib as his successor; the cause of civil war following Muhammad's death.

Shiva Main god of Hinduism along with Vishnu and Brahma. Equivalent to Rudra in the Rig-Veda. God of destruction. Devotees are known as Shivaites.

shuddhi Purification, also refers to the rituals of 'reverting' someone to Hinduism from another religion, invented by the Arya Samaj.

Shudra Member of the peasant or labouring *varna*.

subha Mughal province.

subhadar Regional governor.

Sufism Mystical form of Islam found in the north-west and in the Punjab.

Sunni Largest sect of Islam. Believe that Abu Bakr, the Prophet Muhammad's close friend and father-in-law, was appointed as the rightful first *Caliph*.

suttee See *sati*.

swadeshi Political campaign for home rule. Literally means 'of one's own country'.

swaraj Self-rule.

tahsil Regional administrative area.

talukdar Landholding/landholder; a *taluk* or *taluqa* is also a subdivision of a district and a *taluqdar* can be the title of the official in charge of the same, subordinate to a district commissioner/magistrate or collector.

tapasya Hindu ascetic exercises.

thag/i Term used to describe a band of violent robbers in nineteenth-century India (from which the English word 'thug' is derived).

thana Police station.

thug/gee See *thagi*.

tinkathia The 3/20 *katha* system, a sharehold rent common in indigo-growing areas. The tenant was obliged to use three *kathas* out of twenty (= 1 acre) for indigo cultivation and to give this produce to the landlord in lieu of rent.

ulema/ulama Scholars and teachers of Islam and Islamic law (also known as 'mullahs').

upanayanam Thread ceremony, associated with the 'twice-born' Brahmins.

upazilla Subdistrict; local administrative unit.

Vaishya A member of the third of the four Hindu *varna*, comprising merchants, artisans and landowners.

varna Social ranking system, of which major social divisions are the Brahmin (priestly castes), Kshatriya (warrior castes), Vaishya (artisanal and agricultural castes), and Shudra (labourer castes).

Vedic From the Vedas – religious text, comprising the Rig-Veda, the *Brahmanas* and *Upanishad*.

vetti Forced labour.

videshi Foreigner.

vidyut vahini Guerrilla (literally 'lightning') army.

Vishnu Hindu God, known as 'the Preserver'. Earthly incarnations include Krishna and Rama. Followers are known as Vaishnavites.

vizier/wazir Regent or senior adviser to the Mughal emperor.

zamin/dar/i Landed property; land or estate held by a *zamindar*; the office or tenure of a *zamindar*; landlord-based system of revenue collection.

zar Wealth.

Notes

1 History, society and culture of the Indian subcontinent

1 Jawaharlal Nehru, *Discovery of India* (New Delhi: Oxford University Press, 1990), p. 56. First published in 1946, the *Discovery of India* was written during Nehru's imprisonment (1942–6) in Ahmednagar Fort. The ambitious, syncretic, liberal vision of this text helped shape the idea of India in the minds of several generations of post-independence South Asians.

2 T. Raychaudhuri, 'Indian Politics as Animal Politics', *Historical Journal* 22, 3 (1979), pp. 747–763 at p. 763. Throughout his career at Oxford University during the 1970s to 1980s, Tapan Raychaudhuri defended the humanistic possibilities of the History discipline and the political responsibilities of the historian amidst the then fashionable tide of developmental and structuralist critiques of Indian society and history. Like several of the best historians of this era he was 'post-foundationalist' (Prakash 1994) well before the concept was invented.

3 'Post-orientalist' refers to the theories of the political and literary critic Edward Said in his influential books *Orientalism* (1978) and *Culture and Imperialism* (1993). 'Post-modernist' refers to the theories of Jean Baudrillard, Frederick Jameson, Ernest Mandel *et al.* On 'post-colonialism' see Bart Moore-Gilbert (1998).

4 One of the most trenchant recent articulations of the colonialism as transformation thesis is that of Sudipta Sen (1998, 2002).

5 The problematics of articulating subaltern views in the medium of contemporary historical scholarship are succinctly addressed by Spivak (1988), whilst the negative political effects of an entirely discursive approach to subaltern positions that denies class and material relations are described in Washbrook and O'Hanlon (1992), reprinted in Chaturvedi (1999).

6 A contribution to the continuity versus change argument, which posits a 'dialogical' approach as a possible solution, has been suggested by D.A. Washbrook (1999). For a range of alternative, empirically rooted perspectives see Bates (2006).

7 BCE = Before Common Era. The 'Common Era', as the name implies, is the calendar in most common use, which begins in the first year of the Christian calendar, or Anno Domini 0.

8 There is considerable controversy in contemporary India over the different versions of the Ramayana and India's mythic tradition – usually for socio-political ends. Thus a furore over school textbooks from 2002 to 2004 saw the then ruling Bharatiya Janata Party trying to force adoption of a version that describes Ram and other gods as real historic characters rather than mythic figures. At stake was the treatment of minorities, women and the very nature of Hinduism in the present day (see Thapar [1993]).

2 The decline of Mughal India and rise of European dominion

1 J. Horton Ryley (ed.), *Ralph Fitch: England's Pioneer to India and Burma* (London: Haklyut Society, 1899), p. xviii.
2 William Foster (ed.), *Early Travels in India 1583–1619* (Oxford University Press, 1921), p. 296. The magnificence of the Mughal court at this time is brilliantly captured in the 1960 Indian cinema classic *Mughal-e-Azam* (director K. Asik), re-released in colour in 2004.
3 Paul Bairoch, *The Economic Development of the Third World since 1900* (Berkeley: University of California Press, 1975).
4 T.B. Macaulay, 'Lord Clive, January 1840', in *Critical and Historical Essays*, vol. 1 (London, 1846).
5 The concept of the 'segmentary state' was adapted by Burton Stein to explain the powerful ritual and religious role of the king compared with his limited instrumental (economic and political) authority in the pre-modern Chola empire of southern India. Modern interpretations of kingship in north India have been influenced by this idea whilst arguing that the contestation and negotiation of power was here often more intense, giving the centre even less fixity. Notwithstanding the influence of Persian-derived administrative traditions, elements of the same argument may be applied to the later Mughal empire, which was not a purely centralised system but has been described rather as a 'patrimonial-bureaucratic' regime. See Stein (1980: esp. 264–285, 1990); Peabody (2003); Richards (1993: ch. 3); and Blake (1979).
6 Philip Woodruff, *The Men Who Ruled India* (London: Cape, 1953), vol. 1, p. 106.

3 Social and economic change in the early nineteenth century and the 'era of reform'

1 J. Peggs, *India's Cries to British Humanity: An Historical Account of Suttee, Infanticide, Ghat Murders and Slavery in India*, 2nd edn (London: Seely & Son, 1830), pp. v–vi.
2 J.K. Majumdar (ed.), *Indian Speeches and Documents on British Rule, 1821–1918* (Calcutta: Longmans, 1937), p. 48. Ram Mohan Roy often had complimentary things to say about British rule, but his qualifications to these remarks are commonly overlooked.
3 A statistical demonstration of the links between British land tenure reforms and long-term economic development trends is available in Abhijit Banerjee and Lakshmi Iyer, *History, Institutions and Economic Performance: The Legacy of Colonial Land Tenure in India* (World Bank discussion paper, 2002).
4 *Narrative by Major General John Campbell of his Operations in the Hill Tracts of Orissa for the suppression of human sacrifices and female infanticide* (London: Hurst & Blackett, 1864). See also Bates (2006), ch. 3; also Padel (1995).
5 W.R. Moore, *Report on Female Infanticide: Selections from the Records of Government, NW Provinces* (London, 1859); Parliamentary Paper House of Commons 1843, XXXV (613) 183 Infanticide: Correspondence, 1834–42. The suppression of rites and practices associated with witchcraft was another *cause célèbre* at this time – see Skaria (1997).
6 Peggs (1830: 251); italics in original.
7 Minute on the Suppression of Sati by Lord Bentinck, Governor-General of India, 8 November 1829, from R. Muir (ed.), *The Making of British India 1756–1858* (Karachi: Oxford University Press, 1969 [1st pub. 1915]), p. 295.
8 Stokes (1959: 35).
9 T.B. Macaulay, 'Minute on Education, 2 February 1835', IOR: V/27/860/1, pp. 107, 115. Paul Bairoch, 'International industrialization levels from 1750–1980', *Journal of European Economic History* 11 (1982), pp. 269–333.

4 Peasant resistance, rebellion and the uprising of 1857

1 Conversation between Captain Lockitt and a junior cavalry officer reported to Bishop Heber during his journey through the kingdom of Awadh in 1825. Bishop Heber,

Narrative of a Journey through the Upper Provinces of India from Calcutta to Bombay 1824–25 . . . (London: J. Murray, 1849), vol. 1, p. 225.

2 Epistle from Ghalib to Alauddin Khan Alai, a scion of the Loharu *nawab* family who was also a disciple of Ghalib and a cousin of his wife. Ghalib, *Diwan-e-Ghalib* (Dilli: Ghalib Academy, 1997), pp. 301–302. Mirza Asadullah Baig Khan (1796–1869), pen-name Ghalib, was a renowned classical Urdu and Persian poet and through his *ghazals* (poetic recitations) and letters is probably the most influential author in Urdu. He resided and survived in Delhi throughout the siege of the city in 1857.

3 William Sleeman, *Ramaseena, or A vocabulary of the peculiar language used by the Thugs / with an introduction and appendix, descriptive of the system pursued by that fraternity and of the measures which have been adopted by the supreme government of India for its suppression* (Calcutta: G.H. Huttmann, Military Orphan Press, 1836), introduction. Also Bundle file of Collected Correspondence of William Sleeman, Central Provinces Central Record Office, Nagpur Secretariat, Nagpur.

4 R.V. Russell and Rai Bahadur Hira Lal, *The Castes and Tribes of the Central Provinces of India* (Nagpur: Government Press, 1916). After serving as resident at Gwalior until 1849, Sleeman then became resident at Awadh until his retirement due to ill health in 1854 and death in 1856. At Awadh, his critical reports on the administration of the state were to play a role in Dalhousie's subsequent decision to annex the state.

5 Vinayak Damodar (commonly Veer) Savarkar's *The Indian War of Independence, 1857* was originally written in Marathi, published in 1908, and immediately banned by the British. The author, having taken part in terrorist conspiracies in London and Nasik, was later sentenced to transporation to the Andaman islands (where he wrote about the concept of Hindutva or 'Hinduness'). He returned following a personal amnesty and was president of the Hindu Mahasabha for seven years in the 1930s and 1940s. Savarkar's *Indian War of Independence* was finally published (in English) and distributed for the first time in 1947.

6 This name Pandey was in turn inherited by an English children's toy – a stuffed doll wearing pyjama pants – known as 'Andy Pandey'.

7 Maya Gupta, 'The Vellore Mutiny', in M. and A.K. Gupta (eds), *Defying Death: Struggles Against Imperialism and Feudalism* (New Delhi: Tulika Press, 2001), pp. 18–38.

8 Karl Marx in the *New York Daily Tribune*, 1857, reprinted in Karl Marx and Friedrich Engels, *The First Indian War of Independence* (Moscow: Progress Publishers, 1959), p. 36. Marx went further, stating his belief that the wars in Persia, India and China were connected events.

9 The scenes in Delhi, and particularly the role of the Mughal court during the course of the mutiny, are brilliantly evoked in William Dalrymple's *The Last Mughal* (Harmondsworth: Penguin: 2006). Chapter 5 describes Bahadur Shah Zafar's reluctant acquiescence to the demands of his effective captors – the sepoy mutineers.

10 This proclamation was published in English in the *Delhi Gazette* on 29 September 1857, according to Charles Ball, *History of the Indian Mutiny* (London: Printing and Publishing Company, 1859), vol. 2, pp. 630–632. Rudrangshu Mukherjee, though, has argued that its author was neither Bahadur Shah Zafar nor Mirza Mughal, but the emperor's grandson, Firoz Shah, who fought in Awadh and Lucknow where this was probably first circulated. See Mukherjee (1976).

11 Proclamation enclosed with a translation of a pamphlet entitled Fateh Islam: For. Dept. Political Proc., 30 Dec. 1859, Suppl. No. 1135–1139; cited in Mukherjee (1984), p. 148.

12 This and many other aspects of the siege are effectively parodied in J.G. Farrell's comic historical novel *The Siege of Krishnapur* (London, 1978). A detailed blow-by-blow account of the uprising is available in P.J.O. Taylor (1997).

13 Karl Marx, *New York Daily Tribune*, 4 September 1857, from Marx and Engels (1959).

5 Zenith of empire: economic and social conditions in the late nineteenth century

1 Evidence of Thomas Cope, a silk-weaver from Macclesfield, to the Select Committee, 1840. House of Commons Select Committee Report on East India Produce, *PP* 1840, vol. 8, pp. 272–275.
2 R.C. Dutt, *The Economic History of India Under Early British Rule*, 7th edn (London: Routledge, 1950), p. ii.
3 These views were recorded in the diary of W.S. Blunt, 10 January 1884. W.S. Blunt, *India Under Ripon: A Private Diary* (London: Fisher Unwin, 1977), p. 265.
4 William Wedderburn, *Allan Octavian Hume, C.B., Father of the Indian National Congress, 1829 to 1912* (London 1913).
5 IOL. SW 63: *Report of the 2nd Meeting of the Indian National Congress* (Calcutta, December 1886), p. 52; also to be found in C.L. Parekh, *Essays, Speeches, Addresses and Writing . . . of the Hon'ble Dadabhai Naoroji* (Bombay: Caxton, 1887), pp. 332–333. The whole text is reproduced in S. Hay (ed.), *Sources of India Tradition* (New York: Columbia University Press, 1988), vol. 2, pp. 93–94.

6 Revivalist and reform movements in the late nineteenth century

1 'Bande Mataram' lyrics translated by Shri Aurobindo. The song was composed by the Bengali author Bankim Chandra Chatterjee and first appeared in his book *Anandamath*, published in 1882. 'Bande Mataram' became a patriotic hymn across India during the freedom movement and was banned by the British during the Swadeshi campaign. Although a candidate for the national anthem of India, 'Bande Mataram' was eventually overtaken by 'Jana Gana Mana', on the grounds that Muslims felt offended by its depiction of the nation as Durga – a Hindu goddess – thus equating the nation with the Hindu conception of *shakti* (divine feminine dynamic force), and by the song's origin as part of *Anandamath*, a novel concerning a Hindu peasant uprising against Mughal rule.
2 'The words of a 13-year-old low-caste girl who studied in Jyotiba Phule's school in Maharashtra' from 'On the Grief of the Mangs', in *Women Writing in India: 600 BC to the Present Day*, editors Susie Tharu and K. Lalitha (Delhi: Feminist Press at the City University of New York and Oxford University Press, 1991), vol. 1, p. 216.
3 Bal Gangadhar Tilak, a leading extremist, attacking Dadabhai Naoroji and Gopal Krishna Gokhale, two 'moderate' members of the Indian National Congress, January 1907. From *Tilak: His Writings and Speeches*, 3rd edn (Madras: Ganesh, 1922), pp. 55–57, cited in S. Hay (ed.), *Sources of Indian Tradition*, 2nd edn (New York: Columbia, 1988), vol. 2, p. 144.
4 Quoted in S. Sarkar, *Modern India 1885–1947* (New Delhi: Macmillan, 1983), p. 75.
5 Shan Muhammad (ed.), *Writings and Speeches of Sir Syed Ahmed Khan* (Bombay: Nachiketa, 1972), pp. 159–160. Said Ahmed Khan was considered a model citizen by the British who strongly supported his ambitions to modernise Muslims and thereby recover their status and position in society.
6 Letter by 25-year-old Rukumbhai, published in *The Times* of London, 9 April 1887 (see Chandra (1998: 216)).

7 The Swadeshi and Ghadar movements

1 First issue of *Ghadar*, weekly paper of the Ghadar (or Ghadr) Party, 1 November 1913, from M. and A.K. Gupta (eds), *Defying Death: Struggles Against Imperialism and Feudalism* (New Delhi: Tulika Press, 2001), p. 66. Although crushed in India after 1919 and with its (mostly Sikh) supporters forced into exile in Canada and the United States, the revolutionary Ghadar Party continued to enjoy scattered support in parts of South-East Asia and helped Indian army deserters from the British army in Mesopotamia in the First

World War. After the entry of America into the war, eight Ghadarites in California were prosecuted in the so-called Hindu-German conspiracy trials.

2 Street-singer's account of Kshudiram Bose's final words on the gallows on 11 August 1908. From M. and A.K. Gupta, *Defying Death*, p. 42. Kshudiram joined Jugantar, a party of revolutionary activists, in his early teens and was involved in several bomb blasts before his involvement in a bungled attempt to assassinate Calcutta magistrate Douglas Kingsford. Kshudiram was just 19 when he was executed.

3 Sir Said Ahmed Khan to A.O. Hume from Ram Gopal, *Indian Muslims: A Political Study (1858–1947)* (Bombay, 1959), p. 67.

4 S. Sarkar, *The Swadeshi Movement in Bengal* (New Delhi: People's Publishing House, 1973), p. 17.

5 Ibid., p. 16.

6 Gopal Krishna Gokhale's presidential address at the Benares Congress (1905), from 'Documents on Indian Liberalism: Speeches and Writings of Surendra Nath Banerjea, Dadabhai Naoroji, and Gopal Krishna Gokhale', in K.P. Karunakaran (ed.), *Modern Indian Political Tradition* (New Delhi: Allied Publishers, 1962), pp. 31–122.

7 Bal Gangadhar Tilak (1856–1920): Address to the Indian National Congress, 1907, reprinted in William T. de Bary *et al.*, *Sources of Indian Tradition* (New York: Columbia University Press, 1958), pp. 719–723.

8 Aftermath of the First World War and M.K. Gandhi's rise to power

1 Gandhi, 'The Doctrine of the Sword', *Young India*, Ahmedabad, 11–8–1920, p. 3 from M.K. Gandhi, *Collected Works*, 18: 132–133. This quote illustrates the subtlety that lay behind Gandhi's principle of non-violence that could permit violent action when no other honourable course was available.

2 B.R. Nanda, *Gokhale: The Indian Moderates and the British Raj* (London: Allen & Unwin, 1974; reprint New Delhi: Oxford University Press, 1974), p. 392.

3 The Government of India Act 1919 allowed provincial legislatures to grant votes to women if they wished, and eventually most Indian provinces gave women the vote between 1921 and 1930, although the numbers eligible remained very small, ranging from 2.5 per cent to 8.5 per cent. This increased to 16 per cent (the general adult franchise) under the Government of India Act of 1935.

4 M.K. Gandhi, *An Autobiography or The Story of My Experiments With Truth* (London: Jonathan Cape, 1972), p. 366. (Original edition 1929, reprinted in English in a single volume by Mahadev Desai in 1940.)

5 Penderell Moon, *The British Conquest and Dominion of India* (London: Duckworth, 1989), p. 944. Also Tim Coates, *The Amritsar Massacre: General Dyer in the Punjab 1919* (London: Stationery Office, 2000).

6 Mahadev Desai, *Day-to-Day with Gandhi* (Varanasi: Sarva Seva Sangh Prakashan, 1968–72), vol. II, pp. 164, 179.

7 Ibid., p. 180.

9 Non-co-operation and civil disobedience, 1920–39

1 Walter Hauser (ed.), *Sahajanand on Agricultural Labour and the Rural Poor* (New Delhi: Manohar, 1994), p. 4. Swami Sahajanand Saraswati was born of a poor Brahmin family in UP. He became a monk of the Dandin Sanyasi order at the age of 18 but later developed into a devout yet severe critic of conventional Hinduism. From 1914 to 1920 he served as a political worker and in 1921 participated in the non-co-operation movement. He was arrested and sentenced to 13 months' imprisonment. Thereafter he established an *ashram* at Bihta, near Patna, and threw himself into political work on behalf of the peasantry, founding the Bihar Provincial Sabha in 1929. He fell out with Gandhi over the issue of *zamindari* exactions from the peasantry in the wake of the 1934 Bihar earthquake and joined with the Congress socialists to form the All-India

Kisan Sabha in 1936, over which he presided as president. He died in 1950 before he could see the abolition of *zamindari* in Bihar.

2 Madhya Pradesh Record Office Bhopal: Central Provinces Political and Military Dept. (confidential), file no. 25, 1939: 'Revival of the Agitation in Dondilohara zamindari and decision of govt. not to take any action against him for the present.' Report on a meeting of around 2,000 in Kusumkasa, 11 December 1938. This was one episode in a lengthy agitation against regulations restricting grazing and foraging in government forests in Chhattisgarh. Sarju Prasad was a local lawyer who took it upon himself to represent the grievances of the peasants and suffered several terms in jail for his efforts under both British and Congress administrations.

3 On 20 April 1923 the Allahabad high court imposed death sentences on 19, and various goal terms from life imprisonment to two years to 113 of the 172 accused in the Chauri Chaura incident. Unlike in 1942 at Chimur and Ashti, or in 1946 at the Indian National Army trials, there was no rush of congressmen to the support of those involved. Gandhi condemned the volunteers as criminals and urged them to give themselves up, but later nationalist historians have hailed them as freedom fighters. Curiously a martyrs' memorial has even been erected on the site of the police station where the 23 policemen were killed by non-co-operation volunteers.

4 J. Nehru, *An Autobiography: With Musings on Recent Events in India* (London, 1936).

5 M.K. Gandhi, 'Bitter as poison', originally published in *Navajivan*, 11 August 1929, in *Collected Works of Mahatma Gandhi* (CWMG) (Government of India, Information and Broadcasting Ministry, 2001), vol. 46, p. 377.

6 M.K. Gandhi, 'Youth on trial', *Young India*, 3 October 1929, in *CWMG*, vol. 47 (1985).

7 Ambedkar's condemnation of Gandhi and the Poona Pact is to be found in the 1945 pamplet *What Congress and Gandhi Have Done to the Untouchables* (Ambedkar, 1979–95, vol. 9 [1990]).

8 J. Nehru to Govind Ballabh Pant, 25 November 1925, in J. Nehru, *A Bunch of Old Letters* (New Delhi, 1958; Oxford: Oxford University Press, 1988), p. 263.

9 Dutt ([1940] 1979: 228).

10 Coupland (1944: 131).

11 *Harijan*, 23 October 1937.

10 Quit India and partition, 1939–47

1 S.C. Bose, *On to Delhi: Speeches and Writings*, edited by Narayana Menon (1st Indian edn) (Poona: R.J. Deshmukh, 1946), pp. 54–58. This speech was made on 5 July 1943 at Singapore to 13,000 volunteers of the Indian National Army the day after S.C. Bose had taken over the role of president of the Indian Independence League (the political front of the INA) from Rash Behari Bose.

2 Cited in Vinita Damodaran, 'Azad Dastas and Dacoit Gangs: The Congress and Underground Activity in Bihar, 1942–44', *Modern Asian Studies* 26, 3 (July 1992), pp. 436–437. The heroic and violent activities of the militant underground resistance that fought in the name of Congress in 1942 are rarely discussed in detail in conventional nationalist histories of the period.

3 Prime Minister Winston Churchill's speech at the Mansion House, London, 10 November 1942, as reported in the *New York Times* on 11 November.

4 Three thousand signed up for the Free India League, which became leaderless when S.C. Bose left Germany for Japan. They subsequently served in France under Himmler's Waffen SS. The story of the Free India League was recounted by three German officers who defected towards the end of the war, the records of which were considered so sensitive that they are closed until 2021. In 2004 a BBC documentary team was allowed access to the records for the first time.

5 During the Bengal famine the worst affected, as usual, were the landless agriculural labourers. A survey of five villages in Faridpur, Tippera and Noakhali, quoted by

Amartya Sen (1981), revealing the death of more than 40 per cent by 1944 against an aggregate mortality of 15 per cent. In 1943 also, some 600,000 tenants in Bengal lost their land and still more lost their stocks of cattle.

6 C.M. Trivedi to R.J.J. Hill, DC Chindwara, 23 May 1941. CP and Berar Political and Military (Confidential) Case Files, 1941–298, 'Intimation to M. Gandhi regarding anti-govt. and anti-war rumors spread by satyagrahis . . .'

7 Ibid.

8 Ibid.

9 'My appeal to the British', by M.K. Gandhi, *Harijan*, 24 May 1942 (in *Collected Works*, vol. 82, p. 294).

10 M.K. Gandhi, *Collected Works*, vols. 1–100 (Publications Division, Ministry of Information and Broadcasting, Government of India, 1956–94), vol. 76, appendix 10, p. 461.

11 Telegram from Linlithgow to Churchill, in P.N.S. Mansergh (ed.), *The Transfer of Power*, vol. II (1971), p. 853.

12 Chopra (1989: 317–318, no. 68).

13 Ayesha Jalal, 'Nation, Reason and Religion: the Punjab's role in the Partition of India', *Economic and Political Weekly*, xxxiii, 12 (August 1998).

11 Pakistan and Bangladesh, post-1947

1 From Ustad Daman, *Daman di Moti* (Lahore: Ferozsons, 1997), p. 82. A young Congress supporter before partition, called 'The Poet of Freedom' by Jawaharlal Nehru, Ustad Daman (his real name was Chiragh Deen) wrote Sufi poetry and poems railing against British rule. Hugely admired by the more internationally famous poet Faiz Ahmed Faiz, Ustad Daman chose to settle in Pakistan after independence where he continued to observe acutely the travails of everyday life. He kept no record of his poems until his death in 1984. What is available to us today is due to the effort and memory of his admirers.

2 Rushdie (1984: 82).

3 Akbar (1996: 41–2).

4 Khan (1967: 42).

5 Rushdie (1984: 178).

6 Pervez Musharraf, *In the Line of Fire: a memoir* (London: Simon & Schuster, 2006), p. 137.

7 Murtaza Bhutto's violent career as a terrorist and would-be assassin of Zia-ul-Haq following the execution of his father is sensationally related in Raja Anwar, *The Terrorist Prince: the life and death of Murtaza Bhutto* (New York: Vanguard, 1988).

8 Selig S. Harrison, 'A New Hub for Terrorism?: in Bangladesh, an Islamic movement with Al-Qaeda ties is on the rise', *Washington Post*, 2 August 2006. This article perhaps underestimates Bangladeshi nationalism and the commitment of Bangladeshi politicians to their own causes.

12 The Nehruvian era

1 Nehru's speech at the Lucknow Congress of April 1936, cited in Narahari Kaviraj, *Gandhi–Nehru through Marxist Eyes* (Calcutta: Manisha, 1988), p. 70. Three years later the little known Jawaharlal, son of Motilal Nehru, was elected president of the Indian National Congress at the instigation of Mahatma Gandhi. Some say his role was as a cat's-paw to control the more radical elements on the left of the party.

2 S. Gopal (ed.), *Jawaharlal Nehru: Selected Works*, 2nd series (Oxford: Oxford University Press, 1992), vol. XI, pp. 310–314. By the end of the Second World War the concept of 'trusteeship' had already firmly replaced that of class war in the socialist rhetoric of the Congress as plans were laid for a mixed economic system.

3 Omprakash Valmiki, *Joothan: an untouchable's life*, translated by Arun Prabha Mukherjee (New York: Columbia University Press, 2003), pp. 39–40, 45. Stories of progress in the first 20 years following Indian independence rarely look below per capita statistics to

the experiences of the oppressed and landless poor where there was often little change.

4 The distinguishing characteristics of Indian secularism have been a subject of academic debate, as well as coming under considerable criticism in recent years in India (see Bhargawa 1998 and Madan 1987).

5 The most thorough and comprehensive study of Nehru's life was by Sarvepalli Gopal (1975–84), but even this can be seen in retrospect, as more and more of the Nehruvian legacy has been rejected, as somewhat dated and excessively sympathetic. A whole genre of adulatory writing about Nehru's life flourished during the halcyon days of the regime of his daughter, Indira Gandhi, as part of an effort to perpetuate the Nehru–Gandhi dynasty. M.J. Akbar's study (1988) belongs to this era. Nehru has, though, always found a sympathetic following amongst British socialist intellectuals and left-leaning, middle-class Indians living abroad, for many of whom Nehru's liberal, Westernised world-view tends to reflect their own education and experience.

6 See the critique of Gopal in Partha Chatterjee, *A Possible India* (Delhi: Oxford University Press, 1998).

7 For a biography of this remarkable man see Sunil Khilnani, *The Idea of India* (London: Penguin, 1988), pp. 82–88.

8 Nehru, *Selected Works*, vol. IX, pp. 373–374.

9 Source: Chaudhuri (1975), p. 160; quote in S. Das (2000).

10 A report published in the mid-1960s, *Co-operative Credit in Raipur District (Factors Contributing to Heavy Overdues)*, by C. Muthiah of the Agro-Economic Research Centre for Madhya Pradesh (Gwalior 1966), was the final nail in the coffin of the co-operative movement in Madhya Pradesh. So damning were its conclusions that for a considerable time it was suppressed.

11 Between 1949 and 1950 the Congress government in Delhi used some 12,000 armed police personnel to curb the Telengana peasant upsurge; as many as 800 recorded deaths resulted directly from police actions in the first decade of independence; the police expenditure of the Indian government increased from Rs 9 million in 1951/2 to Rs 800 million in 1970/1; and the army assisted civil authorities to restore order on a total of 476 occasions between 1947 and 1970 and 350 times between 1980 and 1983 (Shepperdson and Simmons 1988, p. 16).

12 Quoted in Tariq Ali (1991), p. 107.

13 Indira Gandhi: progress, poverty and authoritarian rule

1 Rohinton Mistry, *A Fine Balance* (London: Faber & Faber, 1996), pp. 432, 204. In Mistry's evocative novel Indira Gandhi's emergency and forced sterilisation campaign serve as a background to the heroic tale of four ordinary people struggling to survive: an impoverished student, an itinerant tailor and his nephew (fleeing from caste discrimination in his village), all of them boarders and eventually friends in the apartment of Dina Dalal, a fortyish widowed seamstress.

2 Needless to say, this version of events is contested in many Pakistani accounts. For example, Pervez Musharraf in his memoir *In the Line of Fire* (London: Simon & Schuster, 2006), p. 45, recalls his own award for gallantry, and states: 'India attacked Pakistan on all fronts and strafed a passenger train, killing many civilians . . . but Pakistan gave India a fright and a bloody nose to go with it. There was no strategic gain on either side. Still, Pakistan certainly achieved a tactical victory in the sense that we conquered more territory, inflicted more casualties, took more prisoners, and almost blew the Indian Air Force out of the sky.'

3 The Congress split following the emergency, a breakaway faction being led by regional bosses Sharad Pawar (Maharastra), Devraj Urs (Karnataka) and A.K. Anthony (Kerala). Mrs Gandhi's Congress (I) – for Indira – was formed out of the remaining group of Gandhi loyalists. The breakaway faction later rejoined the party.

14 Local patriotism and centre–state relations

1 Mahasweta Devi, *Chotti Munda and His Arrow*, translated from Bengali by, Gayatri Chakravorty Spivak (Oxford: Blackwell Publishers, 2003), p. 246. Born in Dhaka in 1926, but settling in India after partition, Mahasweta Devi is an activist, whose elegant Bengali prose is dedicated to the struggle of tribal people in Bihar, Madhya Pradesh and Chhattisgarh, which she describes as the inspiration for all of her stories. *Chotti Munda* tells of the experience of living as a tribal or *adivasi* in one part of central India from the years of late colonial rule up until the time of unrest in the 1970s.
2 'Pulavar' Kaliyaperumal, former schoolteacher-turned People's War Group (PWG) leader. Chennai, 18 August 2000: *Indian Express*, as reported on the website of the 'Tamil Nadu Liberation Front' at www.dalitstan.org/tamil/
3 From the reported statement of the notorious Tamil bandit Veerappan, who allied briefly with Tamil militant Maran and the Tamil Nadu Liberation Army cause in November 2000, following his release of kidnapped popular Kannada actor, Rajkumar. Veerappan's demands for Rajkumar's release had included the freeing of TNLA prisoners, that compensation should be paid to Tamil victims of the 1991 riots in Karnataka over the River Cauvery waters issue, that Karnataka should make Tamil an additional language of administration, that steps should be taken to unveil the statue of Tamil saint-poet Tiruvalluvar in Bangalore, that the minimum procurement price for green tea leaves in the Nilgiris should be fixed at Rs 15 a kg, and that the minimum wage for coffee and tea estate workers in Tamil Nadu and Karnataka should be fixed at Rs 150 a day. It is said that he desired to enter politics like the famous Rajasthani 'bandit queen' Phoolan Devi. Veerappan was eventually killed in a police 'encounter' in 2004 after 20 years of evading capture.
4 M. Dingwaney and U. Patnaik (eds), *Chains of Servitude: Bondage and Slavery in India* (Madras: Sangam Books, 1985).
5 The name of Uttaranchal state was changed to Uttarakhand by the Congress Party after it came to power in 2004.
6 *The Economist*, 19–25 August 2006, p. 56: 'India's Naxalites: a spectre haunting India'.
7 Mark Tully and Satish Jacob, *Amritsar: Mrs Gandhi's last battle* (Calcutta: Rupa, 1985), p. 38.
8 Ibid., p. 45.
9 Ibid., pp. 142–143.
10 Ibid., p. 170
11 Ibid., p. 71.

15 Rajiv Gandhi and the demise of the Congress system

1 Quoted in *'Who are the Guilty?' Report of a Joint Inquiry into the Causes and Impact of the Riots in Delhi from 31 October to 10 November* by the People's Union for Democratic Rights and the People's Union for Civil Liberties, 1984. The anti-Sikh riots followed the assassination of Indira Gandhi and raged for nearly four days, with little apparent effort made by the authorities to control them. There have since been no less than ten commissions of inquiry, which highlighted the culpability of three leading Delhi Congress politicians.
2 'Riot victims: living down the trauma', *Frontline* 15, 18, 29 August to 11 September 1998.
3 Ibid. The rioting in Bombay in December 1992 followed the destruction of the Babri Mosque in Ayodhya by Hindu groups. There then followed, in March 1993, a series of bomb blasts in the city set by militant Muslim groups after which there were further anti-Muslim riots in retaliation.
4 Rajiv Gandhi in address at the Delhi Boat Club three weeks after his mother's assassination (*New York Times*, 20 November 1984).

5　I.K. Gujral, former Indian prime minister, in evidence to the Nanavati Commission, reported in the *Hindu*, Wednesday, 16 January 2002.

6　*India Today*, 15 April 1998.

7　The international vice-president of the VHP, Acharya Giriraj Kishore, initially reacted to the Roop Kanwar case by saying that 'Hindu dharma has no space for sati', but later defended the practice, saying: 'There is nothing wrong if any woman who cannot bear the separation from her husband opts to join him in his funeral pyre' and that the revival of *sati* would not be out of tune with the VHP's ideology of establishing Hindu Rashtra (DH News Service, Ahmedabad, 8 February 2000).

8　A defence of *sati* as a 'cultural tradition' has also been made by a handful of leftist academics, such as Ashish Nandy (2005) and Madhu Kishwar, editor of the women's journal *Manushi*. See Patel and Kumar (1988) and Gandhi (1988).

9　Radha Kumar, quoted in Nikki R. Keddie, 'The New Religious Politics and Women Worldwide: A Comparative Study [Part 2 of 3]', *Journal of Women's History* 10, 4: 11–34, at 16 (winter 1999).

10　TV transmissions that employed a satellite to simultaneously cover the whole nation only commenced in 1981. As a state monopoly in the first instance, it was consistently used to promote pro-government coverage, which could sometimes work to the government's discredit when the reality and news reporting diverged too greatly. In the 1990s the service was opened up to competition. See also V. Farmer, in Ludden (1996).

11　*India Today*, 31 October 1989, p. 17.

12　*Justice B.N. Srikrishna Commission Report on the Bombay 1992–93 Riots*, vol. 1, ch. II, 1.27 (ii) Causes of January 1993 rioting (Bombay: Sabrang Communications & Publishing Pvt Ltd [www.sabrang.com], 2001).

13　See Bhargava (1998) for various definitions of secularism. The BJP defined itself as 'secular' by accusing its predecessors of 'bogus secularism' in consequence of their deliberate bias in favour (others would say defence) of Muslims and other minorities versus the Hindu majority. The BJP's stance was one in support of 'majoritarianism' (i.e. Hindu rule).

16　Colonial and post-colonial Sri Lanka: the dilemmas of national identity

1　Qadri Ismail, 'Minor Matters: Living in Another Country', *Lines*, May 2002 (online magazine: http://www.lines-magazine.org). Qadri Ismail is Assistant Professor in the English Department at the University of Minnesota, Minneapolis, USA.

2　As quoted in the *Daily Telegraph* (London), 11 July 1983. The Christian son of a judge of the Ceylon Supreme Court, Jayawardene descended from a south Indian family but converted to Buddhism in his youth. Initially a member of the Ceylon National Congress, he joined D.S. Senanayake's United National Party soon after its formation in 1946 and became finance minister in the island's first cabinet. Always more willing than Dudley Senanayake to play the ethnic card in order to counter rising support for Bandaranaike's Sri Lanka Freedom Party, he backed the Sinhala-only Official Languages Act of 1956 and succeeded Senanayake as UNP leader after the latter's death in 1973.

3　Reported in The *Guardian* newspaper, 22 December 1999. During the last local elections in Sri Lanka, Ananda Jayatileke, who runs a small business in the village of Polgahawella, in the North-Western Province about 45 miles north-east of Colombo, did not get a chance to vote. A gang of political thugs snatched his family's voting cards and voted in his place. So on December 21st, he said, 'My wife, daughter and I came as early as possible to ensure we could vote.' 'Now we are safe because we have cast our vote. They cannot stop us.'

4　Tamil Eelam is the name given by the Liberation Tigers of Tamil Eelam to the independent state which they seek to establish in the Northern and Eastern portions of

Sri Lanka. Although claimed by the Tamils, the origins of the word Eelam are inevitably disputed between Tamil and Sinhala nationalist historians. Some say it derives from Senhela, an ancient Sinhalese word for the island. The word is also claimed to have its origin in the Tamil term for mother (hence motherland) and the ancient Sanskritic name for the entire subcontinent *Ilavarta*.

5 *The Economist*, 7 February 1998.
6 The lack of a communal or religious ethic in the Sri Lankan conflict may arguably be seen in the way in which the Tamil Tigers have taken to burying rather than cremating their dead, allegedly for propaganda purposes (but perhaps merely to avoid detection), their attempts to recruit descendants of Muslim south Indians to the Tamil cause, and the frequency with which Buddhist monks in Sri Lanka have broken their vows of pacifism.

17 Neo-nationalism and the challenge of democracy

1 Quoted in Rama Lakshmi, 'Rapes Go Unpunished in Indian Mob Attacks: Muslim Women Say Claims Are Ignored', *Washington Post*, 3 June 2002. The 2002 Gujarat anti-Muslim riots were said to be in revenge for an alleged attack on a train bringing Hindu activists home from a visit to Ayodhya (as if this somehow justified them). They were probably also not unconnected to impending state elections, and the then BJP state government was accused of complicity.
2 Hanif, ice-cream vendor, Bombay, quoted in 'Eyewitness to terror', a report on Bombay bombings attributed to retaliation for the anti-Muslim riots of 2002 in Gujarat (*Time Asia*, 26 August 2003).
3 Ibid. The events of 2002–3 were a ghastly echo of similar events seen in 1992 after the initial destruction of the Babri Masjid in Ayodhya.
4 Vajpayee was briefly prime minister for two weeks in 1996, but the BJP failed then to prove its majority in the Lok Sabha.
5 The Indian government itself officially claims there were five devices in Pokhran II (also known as Operation Shakti) tested over two days, the first device being thermonuclear and yielding 43–45 kilotons, two more fission devices yielding 12 and 0.2 kilotons on the 11th, and a further two simultaneous explosions (Shakti IV–V) on the 13th, providing a total yield of more than 60 kilotons. However, two former chairmen of the Indian Atomic Energy Commission have since admitted this was an exaggeration, and the last two tests on the 13th were not seismically detected outside of India. Several scientific estimates (e.g. Wallace 1998) put the total yield on the 11th at no more than 12–25 kilotons whilst others have suggested a more reasonable estimate of $31 + 12 + 0.2$ kilotons. The potency of the Pakistani explosions was consistently exaggerated as well, for reasons on both sides that include the strategic (but probably also as sheer braggadocio).
6 Defence Minister George Fernandes, speech after watching the Agni launch at the Inner Wheeler Island base station near Chandpur-on-Sea, 11 April 1999, as reported by the *Tribune* (New Delhi) on 12 April.
7 Prime Minister Atal Behari Vajpayee, 'Message to the Nation', broadcast in English on Doordarshan TV, India, 11 April 1999.
8 The *Independent* (London), 21 March 2002.
9 *Compounding Injustice: The Government's Failure to Redress Massacres in Gujarat*, Human Rights Watch Report, 19 July 2003, vol. 15, no. 3 (C), pp. 50–51: Human Rights Watch interview with Khalid Noor Muhammad Sheikh, Ahmedabad, 5 January 2003.
10 Scott Baldauf, 'Indian Government Struggles to Maintain Order: Continuing Riots Test Hindu-led Coalition's Credibility', *Christian Science Monitor*, 4 March 2002.
11 *Financial Times* (London), 5 July 2002 interview with L.K. Advani, Indian deputy prime minister.
12 Throughout the 1990s a growing number of candidates came to the polls encumbered

with criminal convictions. Although a law was passed banning such candidates, more than half of the BJP and Shiv Sena candidates in Maharashtra in 2004 were alleged by Maharashtra Election Watch (a citizens' group) to have had criminal charges filed against them, along with approximately one-quarter of the candidates fielded by the Congress and its ally, Sharad Pawar's Nationalist Congress Party. Since the Election Commission firmly required candidates to list all affidavits against them, this information was transparently and clearly available for the first time in 2004.

13 The UPA coalition consists of the Indian National Congress (INC); the Rashtriya Janata Dal (RJD), led by Laloo Prasad Yadav in Bihar; the Dravida Munnetra Kazhagam (DMK) in Tamil Nadu, headed by M. Karunanidhi; the Nationalist Congress Party (NCP), led by Sharad Pawar in Maharashstra; the Pattali Makkal Katchi (PMK), an OBC (Vanniyar) caste party in northern Tamil Nadu; the Telangana Rashtra Samithi (TRS) in Andhra Pradesh; the Jharkhand Mukti Morcha (JMM), led by Shibu Soren in Jharkhand; the Marumalarchi Dravida Munnetra Kazhagam (MDMK) in Tamil Nadu; the Lok Jan Shakti Party (LJNSP), led by Ram Vilas Paswan in Bihar; the Indian Union Muslim League (IUML), whose main stronghold is Kerala; the Jammu and Kashmir Peoples Democratic Party (JKPDP); the Republican Party of India (Athvale) (RPI[A]); the Republican Party of India (Gavai) (RPI[G]); the All-India Majlis-e-Ittehadul Muslimen (AIMIM) in Hyderabad; and the Kerala Congress (KC). This alliance is externally supported by the four left parties: Communist Party of India (Marxist) in Bengal and Kerala; the Communist Party of India; Revolutionary Socialist Party and All-India Forward Bloc. In order to co-ordinate the co-operation, a UPA-Left Coordination Committee was formed.

14 The NDA coalition currently includes the Shiv Sena in Maharashtra; the Janata Dal (United), led by Sharad Yadav, an alliance of the JD(U) and George Fernandes' Samata Party; the Biju Janata Dal in Orissa; the Trinamool Congress in Bengal; Indian National Lok Dal, led by Om Prakash Chautala in Haryana; and the Shiromani Akali Dal in Punjab. The Telugu Desam Party in Andhra Pradesh, led by Chandra Babu Naidu, supports the NDA without formally being part of the coalition. The DMK, PMK and MDMK were formerly allies too, but in 2004 formed the 'Democratic Progressive Alliance', along with the Congress in Tamil Nadu, and are now part of the Congress-led United Progressive Alliance. The Himachal Vikas Congress left the coalition and merged with the Congress in 2004.

15 A survey of the gainers and losers from the reform programme of the NDA government is available in the May 2004 issue of the monthly journal *Seminar* (no. 537, July 2004: available at www.india-seminar.com), and a detailed analysis of the 2004 general election is available in a special issue of *Seminar* for July 2004 (no. 539) and the journal *Economic & Political Weekly*, 18 December 2004.

18 South Asia in the new millennium

1 Siddharth Dube, *In the Land of Poverty: Memoirs of an Indian Family, 1947–1997* (London: Zed, 1998), p. 200. The moving story of a *dalit* family in their own words, plus commentary, since independence.

2 Sanjay Nirupam of the Shiv Sena was reported in 2004 as saying: 'One always hears about AIDS and how it's this big problem. But I have personally never come across anyone with AIDS or seen anyone dying of the disease . . . I think it's just hype (BBC News South Asia [http://news.bbc.co.uk/2/hi/south_asia/], 'Fighting India's AIDS apathy', Wednesday, 14 July 2004. Having introduced compulsory HIV testing of long-term visitors in the late 1980s, the official view was that little more was required since AIDS was a disease of foreigners to which India was immune due to customs of early marriage, the lack of a dating culture, the strength of marriage bonds, and the low divorce rate. However, this ignored the huge sex industry within the subcontinent, which employs some 30,000 to 40,000 in Bombay alone – each of them serving an

average of at least half a dozen clients per day. Large-scale infection inevitably ensued, which has since passed into the wider population. According to UNDP estimates 3.8 million adult Indians were infected by 2001, nearly 1 per cent of the population. The second highest rates are – unsurprisingly – in Nepal, whence a great many workers for the sex industry are sourced.

3 India Planning Commission/UNDP, *India: Human Development Report 2005; CIA World Fact Book, 2006.*

4 It is believed that sampling rather than census returns allows for more accurate returns. On this basis, according to a background paper by Padam Singh for the India Planning Commission's *Vision 2020* report, infant mortality, as well as the under-5 mortality rate in the so-called 'backward' states, continues to be very high. As a result, these states together account for about two-thirds of infant and child deaths. They also have an average fertility rate of 4.2 compared to an overall national rate in 2006 of 3.3 (a bit higher than the CIA's estimate).

5 *The Economist*, 19–25 August 2006, p. 56: 'India's Naxalites: A Spectre Haunting India'. They are known as 'Naxalites' after the district of Naxalbari in West Bengal where they staged an uprising in 1967. They have as many as 9,000 to 10,000 armed fighters and 40,000 full-time supporters, spread across forested areas in the states of Bihar, Chhattisgarh, and Andhra Pradesh.

6 *The Economist*, 5 March 2005, 'A Survey of India and China', p. 6.

7 Ratios between males and females in the population are highest in affluent northern states such as the Punjab, suggesting a toxic combination of new economic realities (the burden of females and higher potential earnings of males) and older cultural preferences.

8 The *Telegraph*, New Delhi, 5 April 2000, p. 10. India was identified by 82 per cent of US companies as their top destination for software outsourcing, according to a World Bank Survey in 2001, and it is believed that remote services (back office, call centres, medical transcription) in the Infotech Industry could employ some 3 million in India within the next ten years.

9 The Hindu-revivalist Bharatiya Janata Party (BJP) came to power partly on the back of a claim that it would put an end once and for all to corruption in the higher echelons of government. The filming of the BJP Party president Bangaru Laxman receiving bribes in an office within the defence ministry from Tehelkha.com journalists, masquerading as arms contractors, in March 2001 persuaded many that moral posturing alone would not right endemic corruption within the political system.

10 Human Rights Commission of Pakistan, *The State of Human Rights in Pakistan in 1999* (Lahore: RCP, 1999); International Labour Organisation–International Program on Elimination of Child Labour (ILD–IPEC), *Mainstreaming Gender in IPEC Activities* (Geneva: ILO, 1999); ILO–IPEC, Karen C. Tumlin, *Overview of Child Trafficking for Labour Exploitation in the Region*, Working Papers on Child Labour in Asia, vol. 2 (Bangkok: ILO, 2001); ILO–IPEC, *Rapid Assessment of Child Labour Situation in Bangladesh* (Geneva: ILO, 1996).

11 *Child Labour In India* by Taha Husein (www.child-labour.freeyellow.com). A comprehensive summary of the statistics on child labour in India is available at www.globalmarch.org/worstformsreport/world/india/html

Bibliography

This bibliography has been created for scholars and students interested in further reading. It is thus wide-ranging and occasionally extends beyond items immediately referenced in the text.

1 History, society and culture of the Indian subcontinent

Ahmad, I. (ed.), *Caste and Social Stratification among Muslims in India* (New Delhi: Manohar, 1978).

Ahsan, Aitaz, *The Indus Saga and the Making of Pakistan* (Karachi: Oxford University Press, 1997).

Alchin, B. and Alchin, A.R., *The Birth of Indian Civilisation: India and Pakistan before 500 B.C.* (London: Penguin, 1968).

Arnold, David, 'Gramsci and peasant subalternity', *Journal of Peasant Studies* 11, 4 (1984), pp. 155–177.

Ballantyne, Tony, *Orientalism and Race: Aryanism in the British Empire* (Basingstoke: Palgrave, 2002).

Barth, Fredrik, 'The system of social stratification in Swat, north Pakistan', in E.R. Leach (ed.), *Aspects of Caste in South India, Ceylon and North-West Pakistan* (Cambridge: Cambridge University Press, 1962).

Bates, Crispin, ' "Lost innocents and the loss of innocence": interpreting advasis in South Asia', in R.H. Barnes, A. Gray and B. Kingsbury (eds), *Indigenous Peoples of Asia* (Ann Arbor, Mich.: American Association for Asian Studies, 1995).

Bates, Crispin, 'Race, caste and tribe in central India: the early origins of Indian anthropometry', in P. Robb (ed.), *The Concept of Race in South Asia* (New Delhi: Oxford University Press, 1996).

Bates, Crispin, 'Introduction', in C. Bates (ed.), *Beyond Representation* (New Delhi: Oxford University Press, 2006).

Bayly, Susan, *Saints, Goddesses and Kings: Muslims and Christians in south Indian society, 1700–1900* (Cambridge: Cambridge University Press, 1990).

Bayly, Susan, *Caste, Society and Politics in India from the Eighteenth Century to the Modern Age* (Cambridge: Cambridge University Press, 1999).

Chatterjee, Partha, *The Nation and Its Fragments* (Princeton, N.J.: Princeton University Press, 1993).

Chaturvedi, Vinayak (ed.), *Mapping Subaltern Studies and the Postcolonial* (London: Verso, 1999).

Chaudhuri, K.N., *Trade and Civilisation in the Indian Ocean* (Cambridge: Cambridge University Press, 1985).

Chaudhuri, K.N., *Asia Before Europe* (Cambridge: Cambridge University Press, 1990).

Cohn, Bernard S., *India: the social anthropology of a civilisation* (Englewood Cliffs, N.J.: Prentice-Hall, 1971).

Dirks, N.B., *Castes of Mind: colonialism and the making of modern India* (Princeton, N.J.: Princeton University Press, 2001).

Dumont, Louis, *Homo Hierarchicus: caste system and its implication* (Chicago: University of Chicago Press, 1980).

Flood, Gavin D., *An Introduction to Hinduism* (Cambridge: Cambridge University Press, 1996).

Fuller, C.J., *The Camphor Flame: popular Hinduism and society* (Princeton, N.J.: Princeton University Press, 1992).

Gilmartin, David and Lawrence, Bruce B. (eds), *Beyond Turk and Hindu: rethinking religious identities in Islamicate South Asia* (Gainesville: University Press of Florida, 2000).

Goswami, Manu, *Producing India: from colonial economy to national space* (New Delhi: Permanent Black, 2004).

Guha, Ranajit, 'Introduction', in R. Guha (ed.), *Subaltern Studies I* (New Delhi: Oxford University Press, 1981).

Guha, Ranajit, *Dominance without Hegemony: history and power in colonial India* (Boston: Harvard University Press, 1997a).

Guha, Ranajit (ed.), *A Subaltern Studies Reader, 1986–1995* (Minneapolis and London: University of Minnesota Press, 1997b).

Guha, R. and Spivak, G.C. (eds), *Selected Subaltern Studies* (New York: Oxford University Press, 1988).

Hock, Hans Heinrich, 'Through a glass darkly: modern "racial" interpretations vs. textual and general prehistoric evidence on arya and dasa/dasyu in Vedic society', in J. Bronkhorst and M.M. Deshpande (eds), *Aryan and Non-Aryan in South Asia* (Cambridge, Mass.: Harvard College, 1999).

Hubel, Teresa, *Whose India?: the independence struggle in British and Indian fiction and history* (London: Leicester University Press, 1996).

Inden, Ronald, 'Orientalist constructions of India', *Modern Asian Studies* 20, 3 (1986), pp. 401–446.

Inden, Ronald, *Imagining India* (Oxford: Blackwell, 1990).

Joshi, B. (ed.), *Untouchable: voices of the dalit liberation movement* (London: Zed, 1986).

Khilnani, Sunil, *The Idea of India* (New York: Farrar Straus Giroux, 1999).

King, Richard, *Orientalism and Religion: post-colonial theory, India and the mystic East* (London: Routledge, 1999).

Ludden, David (ed.), *Reading Subaltern Studies: critical history, contested meaning, and the globalization of South Asia* (London: Anthem Press, 2001).

Ludden, David (ed.), *Making India Hindu: religion, community, and the politics of democracy in India* (New Delhi: Oxford University Press, 2005).

Madan, T.N., *Modern Myths, Locked Minds: secularism and fundamentalism in India* (New Delhi: Oxford University Press, 1998).

Mendelsohn, O. and Vicziany, M., *The Untouchables* (Cambridge: Cambridge University Press, 1998).

Moore-Gilbert, Bart, *Postcolonial Theory: contexts, practices, politics* (London: Verso, 1998).

Peabody, Norbert, *Hindu Kingship and Polity in Precolonial India* (Cambridge: Cambridge University Press, 2003).

Prakash, Gyan, 'Subaltern studies as postcolonial critique', *The American Historical Review* 99, 5 (1994), pp. 1475–1490.

Renfrew, C., *Archaeology and Language: the puzzle of Indo-European origins* (Cambridge: Cambridge University Press, 1990).

Richards, J.F., *The Mughal Empire* (New Cambridge History of India) (Cambridge: Cambridge University Press, 1993).

Robinson, F., *Atlas of the Islamic World since 1500* (Oxford: Phaidon, 1982).

Said, Edward, *Orientalism* (New York: Pantheon, 1978; London: Routledge, 1979).

Said, Edward, *Culture & Imperialism* (New York: Knopf, Random House, 1993).

Sen, Sudipta, *Empire of Free Trade: East Indian Company and the making of the colonial marketplace* (Philadelphia: University of Pennsylvania Press, 1998).

Sen, Sudipta, *A Distant Sovereignty: national imperialism and the origins of British India* (London: Routledge, 2002).

Singh, Khushwant, *History of the Sikhs*, 2 vols (Princeton, N.J.: Princeton University Press, 1963).

Singh, K.S., *Tribal Society in India: an anthropo-historical perspective* (New Delhi: Manohar, 1985).

Spivak, Gayatri Chakravorty, 'Can the subaltern speak?', in C. Nelson and L. Gorssberg (eds), *Marxism and the Interpretation of Culture* (Urbana: University of Illinois Press, 1988).

Spivak, Gayatri Chakravorty, *A Critique of Postcolonial Reason: towards a history of the vanishing present* (Cambridge, Mass.: Harvard University Press, 1999).

Stein, Burton, *Peasant, State & Society in Medieval South India* (New Delhi: Oxford University Press, 1980).

Sugirtharajah, Sharada, *Imagining Hinduism: a postcolonial perspective* (London: Routledge, 2003).

Thapar, Romila, *From Lineage to State Formation: social formations in the mid-first millennium B.C. in the Ganga valley* (New Delhi: Oxford University Press, 1984).

Thapar, Romila, *Interpreting Early India* (New Delhi: Oxford University Press, 1993).

Trautmann, Thomas R., *Aryans and British India* (Berkeley: University of California Press, 1997).

Trautmann, Thomas R. (ed.), *The Aryan Debate* (New Delhi: Oxford University Press, 2005).

Vanaik, Achin, *The Painful Transition: bourgeois democracy in India* (London: Verso, 1990).

Washbrook, D.A., 'Orients and Occidents: colonial discourse theory and the historiography of the British Empire', in R.W. Winks (ed.), *The Oxford History of the British Empire*. Vol V: *Historiography* (Oxford: Oxford University Press, 1999).

Washbrook, D.A. and O'Hanlon, R., 'After Orientalism – culture, criticism, and politics in the Third World.' *Comparative Studies in Society and History* 34, 1 (1992), pp. 141–167.

2 The decline of Mughal India and rise of European dominion

Alam, M., *The Crisis of Empire in Mughal North India* (New Delhi: Oxford University Press, 1986).

Alam, M., 'Aspects of agrarian uprisings in north India', in S. Bhattacharya and R. Thapar (eds), *Situating Indian History* (New Delhi and Oxford: Oxford University Press, 1986).

Alam, M. and Subrahmanyam, S. (eds), *The Mughal State, 1526–1750* (New Delhi and Oxford: Oxford University Press, 1998).

Ali, M. Athar, *The Mughal Nobility Under Aurangzeb* (London: Asia Publishing House, 1966; rev. edn New Delhi: Oxford University Press 1997).

Barnett, R.B., *North India Between Empires: Awadh, the Mughals, and the British 1720–1801* (Berkeley and London: University of California Press, 1980).

Bayly, C.A., *Rulers, Townsmen and Bazaars* (Cambridge: Cambridge University Press, 1983).

Bayly, C.A., *Indian Society and the Making of the British Empire* (New Cambridge History of India) (Cambridge: Cambridge University Press, 1988).

Bayly, C.A., *The Imperial Meridian* (London: Longmans, 1989), introduction and ch. 5.

Blake, Stephen P., 'The patrimonial bureaucratic empire of the Mughals', *Journal of Asian Studies* 39 (November, 1979), pp. 77–94.

Calkins, P., 'The formation of a regionally-oriented ruling group in Bengal, 1700–1740', *Journal of Asian Studies* 29, 4 (1970), pp. 799–806.

Chakrabarty, Dipesh, *Provincializing Europe* (Princeton, N.J.: Princeton University Press, 2000).

Chandra, Satish, *Parties and Politics at the Mughal Court, 1707–1740* (Aligarh: Dept. of History, Aligarh Muslim University, 1959).

Chaudhury, Sushil, *From Prosperity to Decline: eighteenth century Bengal* (New Delhi: Manohar, 1995).

Clarke, J.J., *Oriental Enlightenment: the encounter between Asian and Western thought* (London: Routledge, 1997).

Cohn, Bernard S., 'Political systems in 18th century India: the Banaras region', in *An Anthropologist among the Historians and Other Essays* (New Delhi: Oxford University Press, 1987).

Das Gupta, Ashin, *Indian Merchants and the Decline of Surat* (New Delhi: Manohar 1994; originally Franz Steiner Verlag, Wiesbaden, Germany, 1979).

Fisher, M.H., *The Politics of the British Annexation of India, 1757–1857* (New Delhi and Oxford: Oxford University Press, 1993).

Furber, Holden, *Rival Empires of Trade in the Orient, 1600–1800* (Minneapolis: University of Minnesota Press, 1976).

Gordon, S.N., 'Scarf and sword: thugs, marauders, and state-formation in 18th century Malwa', *Indian Economic & Social History Review* 6, 4 (1969), pp. 403–429.

Gordon, S.N., 'The slow conquest: administrative integration of Malwa into the Maratha empire, 1720–1760', *Modern Asian Studies* 11, 1 (1977), pp. 1–40.

Gordon, S.N., *The Marathas* (New Cambridge History of India) (Cambridge: Cambridge University Press, 1993).

Guha, Ranajit, *A Rule of Property for Bengal* (Paris: Mouton, 1963).

Habib, Irfan, 'Potentialities of capitalistic development in economy of Moghul India', *Journal of Economic History* 29, 1 (1969), pp. 32–78.

Habib, Irfan, *The Agrarian System of Mughal India (1556–1707)* (1st edn Bombay and London: Asia Publishing House, 1963; 2nd rev. edn New Delhi: Oxford University Press, 2000).

Habib, Irfan, *Confronting Colonialism: resistance and modernization under Haider Ali and Tipu Sultan* (London: Anthem Press, 2002).

Haynes, Douglas E., 'From avoidance to confrontation: a contestatory history of merchant–state relations in Surat', in D.E. Haynes and G. Prakash, *Contesting Power* (Berkeley: University of California Press, 1991).

Heesterman, J.C., *The Inner Conflict of Tradition: essays in Indian ritual, kingship, and society* (Chicago and London: University of Chicago Press, 1985).

Hintze, Andrea, *The Mughal Empire and its Decline* (London: Ashgate, 1997).

Khan, A.M., *The Transition in Bengal, 1756–1775: a study of Seiyid Muhammad Reza Khan* (London and Cambridge: Cambridge University Press, 1969).

Kolff, D.H.A., *Naukar, Rajput and Sepoy: the ethnohistory of the military labour market in Hindustan, 1450–1850* (Cambridge: Cambridge University Press, 1990).

Leonard, Karen, 'The Hyderabad political system and its participants', *Journal of Asian Studies* 30, 3 (1971), pp. 569–582.

Leonard, Karen, 'Theory of the decline of the Mughal empire', *Comparative Studies in Society & History* 21 (1979), pp. 151–167.

Ludden, David, *Peasant History in South India* (Princeton, N.J. and Guildford: Princeton University Press, 1985), ch. 3.

MacKenzie, J.M., *Orientalism: history, theory and the arts* (Manchester and New York: Manchester University Press, 1995).

Majeed, Javed, *Ungoverned Imaginings: James Mill's 'History of British India' and Orientalism* (Oxford: Oxford University Press, 1992).

Marshall, P.J., *East India Fortunes: the British in Bengal in the eighteenth century* (Oxford: Clarendon Press, 1976).

Marshall, P.J., *Bengal: the British bridgehead* (New Cambridge History) (Cambridge: Cambridge University Press, 1987).

Moorhouse, Geoffrey, *Calcutta* (London: Pheonix, 1998).

Nightingale, P., *Trade and Empire in Western India* (London: Cambridge University Press, 1970).

Parthasarathi, Prasannan, *The Transition to a Colonial Economy: weavers, merchants and kings in south India, 1720–1800* (Cambridge: Cambridge University Press, 2001).

Peabody, Norbert, *Hindu Kingship and Polity in Precolonial India* (Cambridge: Cambridge University Press, 2003).

Pearson, M., 'Shivaji and the decline of the Mughal empire', *Journal of Asian Studies* 35, 2 (1976), pp. 221–235.

Perlin, Frank, 'Proto-industrialization and pre-colonial South Asia', *Past and Present* 98 (1983), pp. 30–95.

Raychaudhuri, T., *Cambridge Economic History of India*, vol. II (Cambridge: Cambridge University Press, 1983).

Richards, J.F., 'The imperial crisis in the Deccan', *Journal of Asian Studies* 35, 2 (1976), pp. 237–256.

Richards, J.F., *The Mughal Empire* (New Cambridge History of India) (Cambridge: Cambridge University Press, 1993).

Sarkar, Jadunath, *Fall of the Mughal Empire*, vols 1–4 (Calcutta: M.C. Sarkar, 1932–50).

Sen, Sudipta, *Empire of Free Trade: East India Company and the making of the colonial marketplace* (Philadelphia: University of Pennsylvania Press, 1998).

Singh, C., 'Conformity and conflict: tribes and the agrarian system of Mughal India', *Indian Economic & Social History Review* 25, 3 (1988), pp. 319–340.

Stein, Burton, *Peasant, State & Society in Medieval South India* (New Delhi: Oxford University Press, 1980).

Stein, Burton, 'The segmentary state: interim reflections', *Pursartha*, no. 13 (Paris, 1990), pp. 217–238.

Subrahmanyam, S. and Bayly, C. A., 'Portfolio capitalists and the political economy of early modern India', *Indian Economic & Social History Review* 25, 4 (1988), pp. 401–424.

Subramanian, Lakshmi, *Indigenous Capital and Imperial Expansion: Bombay, Surat and the west coast* (New Delhi: Oxford University Press, 1996).

Trautmann, Thomas R., *Aryans and British India* (Berkeley: University of California Press, 1997).

Washbrook, David A., 'Progress and problems: South Asian economic and social history, c. 1720–1860', *Modern Asian Studies* 22, 1 (1988), pp. 57–96.

Wickham, C., 'The uniqueness of the East', in T.J. Byres and H. Mukhia (eds), *Feudalism and Non-European Societies* (London: Frank Cass, 1985).

Wink, André, *Land and Sovereignty in India: agrarian society and politics under the Maratha Svarajya* (Cambridge: Cambridge University Press, 1986).

3 Social and economic change in the early nineteenth century and the 'era of reform'

Arnold, David, *Police Power and Colonial Rule* (New Delhi and New York: Oxford University Press, 1986).

Arnold, David, *Colonising the Body: state medicine and epidemic disease in 19th century India* (Berkeley: University of California Press, 1993).

Bairoch, P., 'International industralization levels from 1750–1980', *Journal of European Economic History* 11 (1982), pp. 269–333.

Bates, Crispin, 'Class and economic change in central India: the Narmada valley, 1820–1930', in C.J. Dewey (ed.), *Arrested Development in India: the historical perspective* (New Delhi: Manohar, 1988).

Bates, Crispin, 'Tribal migration in India and beyond' (with M. Carter), in G. Prakash (ed.), *The World of the Rural Labourer in Colonial India* (New Delhi: Oxford University Press, 1992).

Bates, Crispin, 'Regional dependence and rural development in central India: the pivotal role of migrant labour', in D. Ludden (ed.), *Agricultural Production and Indian History* (New Delhi: Oxford University Press, 1994).

Bates, Crispin, 'Human sacrifice in colonial central India: myth, agency and representation', in *Beyond Representation: constructions of identity in colonial and postcolonial India* (New Delhi: Oxford University Press, 2006).

Bayly, C.A., *Rulers, Townsmen and Bazaars: north Indian society in the age of British expansion, 1770–1870* (Cambridge: Cambridge University Press, 1983).

Bayly, C.A., *Indian Society and the Making of the British Empire* (Cambridge: Cambridge University Press, 1988), chs 4–5.

Bayly, C.A., *Imperial Meridian: the British Empire and the world, 1780–1830* (London: Longman, 1989).

Breckenridge, C.A. and van der Veer, P., *Orientalism and the Postcolonial Predicament* (Philidelphia: University of Pennsylvania Press, 1993).

Chakravarti, Uma, *Rewriting History: the life and times of Pandita Ramabai* (New Delhi: Kali for Women, 1998).

Chakravarty-Kaul, Minoti, *Common Lands and Customary Law: institutional change in north India over the past two centuries* (New Delhi: Oxford University Press, 1996).

Charlesworth, Neil, *British Rule and the Indian Economy* (London: Macmillan, 1982).

Chattopadhyay, Basudeb, *Crime and Control in Early Colonial Bengal, 1770–1860* (Calcutta: K.P. Bagchi, 2000).

Cohn, Bernard S., *An Anthropologist among the Historians and other Essays* (New Delhi: Oxford University Press, 1988).

Cohn, Bernard S., *Colonialism and Its Forms of Knowledge: the British in India* (Princeton, N.J.: Princeton University Press, 1996).

Derrett, J.D.M., *Hindu Law, Past and Present: being an account of the controversy which preceded the enactment of the Hindu code, the text of the code as enacted, and some comments thereon* (Calcutta: A. Mukherjee, 1957).

Derrett, J.D.M., *Religion, Law and the State in India* (London: Faber, 1968; reprinted New Delhi: Oxford University Press, 1999).

Dirks, N.B., 'The invention of caste: civil society in colonial India', *Social Analysis* 25 (1989), pp. 42–52.

Dirks, N.B., 'From little king to landlord: colonial discourse and colonial rule', in N. Dirks (ed.), *Colonialism and Culture* (Ann Arbor: University of Michigan Press, 1992).

Furber, Holden, *John Company at Work* (Cambridge, Mass.: Harvard University Press, 1948).

Gadgil, M. and Guha, R., *This Fissured Land: an ecological history of India* (New Delhi and Oxford: Oxford University Press, 1992).

Guha, Ranajit, *Elementary Aspects of Peasant Insurgency* (New Delhi: Oxford University Press, 1983).

Guha, Ranajit, *A Rule of Property for Bengal: an essay on the idea of permanent settlement* (Paris: Mouton, 1963; repr. Durham, N.C.: Duke University Press, 1996).

Habib, Irfan, 'Studying a colonial economy without perceiving colonialism', *Modern Asian Studies* 19 (1985), pp. 355–381.

Hardiman, David, 'Community, patriarchy, honour: Bhangare, Raghu Revolt', *Journal of Peasant Studies* 23, 1 (1995), pp. 88–130.

Hardiman, David, 'Colonial irrigation, state power and community in the Indus basin', in D. Arnold and R. Guha (eds), *Nature, Culture and Imperialism: essays on the environmental history of South Asia* (New Delhi: Oxford University Press 1996).

Kasturi, Malavika, *Embattled Identities: Rajput lineages and the colonial state in nineteenth-century north India* (New Delhi: Oxford University Press, 2002).

Kling, B., *The Blue Mutiny* (Philadelphia and London: University of Pennsylvania Press, 1966).

Kling, B., *Partner in Empire: Dwarkanath Tagore and the age of enterprise in eastern India* (Berkeley: University of California Press, 1976).

Kopf, D., *British Orientalism and the Bengal Renaissance* (Berkeley: University of California Press, 1969).

Ludden, David, *Peasant History in South India* (Princeton, N.J. and Guildford: Princeton University Press, 1985), chs 4–5.

Ludden, David, 'Orientalist empiricism: transformations of colonial knowledge', in C.A. Breckenridge and P. van der Veer (eds), *Orientalism and the Postcolonial Predicament* (Philadelphia: University of Pennsylvania Press, 1993).

Ludden, David (ed.), *Agricultural Production and Indian History* (New Delhi: Oxford University Press, 1994).

Majeed, Javed, 'James Mill and the *History of British India* and utilitarianism as a rhetoric of reform', *Modern Asian Studies* 24, 2 (1990), pp. 209–234.

Majeed, Javed, *Ungoverned Imaginings: James Mill's 'History of British India' and Orientalism* (Oxford: Oxford University Press, 1992).

Major, Andrea, *Pious Flames: European encounters with Sati 1500–1830* (New Delhi: Oxford University Press, 2006).

Mani, Lata, 'The production of an official discourse on *sati* in early 19th century Bengal', in F. Barker *et al.* (eds), *Europe and Its Others* (Colchester: University of Essex, 1985); also in K. Sangari and S. Vaid (eds), *Recasting Women: essays in colonial history* (New Delhi: Kali for Women 1990).

Mani, Lata, *Contentious Traditions: the debate on 'sati' in colonial India* (Berkeley: University of California Press, 1998).

Metcalf, Barbara D., *Islamic Revival in British India* (Princeton, N.J.: Princeton University Press, 1982), introduction.

Metcalf, Thomas R., *Ideologies of the Raj* (New Cambridge History of India) (Cambridge: Cambridge University Press, 1994).

Mukherjee, S.N., *Sir William Jones: a study in 18th century British attitudes to India* (London: Cambridge University Press, 1968).

Mukhia, Harbans, 'Was there feudalism in Indian history?', in T.J. Byres and H. Mukhia (eds), *Feudalism and Non-European Societies* (London: Frank Cass, 1985); also published as a special issue of the *Journal of Peasant Studies* 12, 2 and 3 (1984).

Nigam, S., 'Disciplining and policing the "criminals by birth", Part 1: the making of a colonial stereotype – the criminal tribes and castes of north India', *Indian Economic & Social History Review* 27, 2 (1990), pp. 131–164.

Padel, Felix, *The Sacrifice of Human Being: British rule and the Khonds of Orissa* (New Delhi: Oxford University Press, 1995).

Pathak, Akhileshwar, *Contested Domains: the state, peasants and forests in contemporary India* (London: Sage, 1994).

Peggs, J., *India's cries to British humanity: an historical account of Suttee, Infanticide, Ghat Murders and Slavery in India*, 2nd edn (London: Seely & Son 1830).

Perlin, Frank, 'Of white whale and countrymen in the eighteenth century Maratha Deccan: extended class relations, rights and the problem of rural autonomy under the old regime', *Journal of Peasant Studies* 5, 2 (1978), pp. 172–237.

Philips, C.H. (ed.), *The Correspondence of Lord William Cavendish Bentinck* (Oxford: Oxford University Press, 1977).

Prakash, G., *Bonded Histories: genealogies of labour servitude in colonial India* (Cambridge: Cambridge University Press, 1990).

Raheja, Gloria Goodwin, 'India: caste, kinship and dominance reconsidered', *Annual Review of Anthropology* 17 (1988), 497–522.

Rocher, R., 'British Orientalism in the eighteenth century: the dialectics of knowledge and government', in C.A. Breckenridge and P. van der Veer (eds), *Orientalism and the Postcolonial Predicament* (Philadelphia: University of Pennsylvania Press, 1993).

Rosselli, J., *Lord William Bentinck: the making of a Liberal imperialist* (London: Chatto & Windus, 1974).

Said, Edward, *Orientalism* (London: Routledge, 1978; Harmondsworth: Penguin Modern Classics, 2003).

Singha, Radhika, *A Despotism of Law: crime and justice in early colonial India* (New Delhi: Oxford University Press, 1998).

Skaria, Ajay, 'Women, witchcraft and gratuitous violence in colonial western India', *Past & Present* 155 (1997), pp. 109–141.

Skaria, Ajay, *Hybrid Histories* (Delhi and Oxford: Oxford University Press, 1999).

Spence, Jonathan D., *The Search for Modern China*, (2nd edn London: W.W. Norton, 1999).

Stein, Burton, *Thomas Munro: the origins of the colonial state and his vision of empire* (New Delhi: Oxford University Press, 1989).

Stokes, Eric, *English Utilitarians and India* (Oxford: Clarendon Press, 1959).

Stokes, Eric, *The Peasant and the Raj* (Cambridge: Cambridge University Press, 1978).

Stokes, Eric, 'Bureaucracy and ideology in Britain and India in the 19th century', *Transactions of the Royal Historical Society*, 5th series, 30, (1980), pp. 131–156.

Trocki, Carl A., *Opium, Empire and the Global Political Economy: a study of the Asian opium trade 1750–1950* (London: Routledge, 1999).

Vishwanathan, G., *Masks of Conquest* (New York: Columbia University Press, 1989; New Delhi and Oxford: Oxford University Press, 1998).

Washbrook, D.A., 'Law, state and agrarian society in colonial India', *Modern Asian Studies* 15, 3 (1981), pp. 649–721.

Washbrook, D.A., 'The golden age of the pariah', in P. Robb (ed.), *Dalit Movements and the Meanings of Labour* (New Delhi: Oxford University Press, 1993).

Yang, A. (ed.), *Crime and Criminality in British India* (Tucson: University of Arizona Press, 1985).

Yang, A., *The Limited Raj* (New Delhi: Oxford University Press, 1989), chs 1 and 4.

4 Peasant resistance, rebellion and the uprising of 1857

Alavi, Seema, *The Company and the Sepoy* (New Delhi and Oxford: Oxford University Press, 1995).

Anon. (probably William Robson), *Origin of the Pindaris, preceded by historical notices on the rise of the different Mahratta States* (London, 1818).

Arnold, David, *Police Power and Colonial Rule: Madras, 1859–1947* (New Delhi and New York: Oxford University Press, 1986).

Ballhatchet, K.A., *Social Policy and Social Change in Western India, 1817–1830* (London: Oxford University Press, 1957).

Ballhatchet, K.A., *Race, Sex and Class Under the Raj: imperial attitudes and policies and their critics, 1793–1905* (London: Weidenfeld & Nicolson, 1980).

Bayly, C.A., *Rulers, Townsmen and Bazaars* (Cambridge: Cambridge University Press, 1983), ch. 8.

Bayly, C.A., *Indian Society and the Making of the British Empire* (Cambridge: Cambridge University Press, 1988), ch. 6.

Bayly, C.A., *Empire and Information: intelligence gathering and social communication in India, 1780–1870* (Cambridge: Cambridge University Press, 1997).

Bayly, C.A., *Origins of Nationality in South Asia: patriotism and ethical government in the making of modern India* (New Delhi: Oxford University Press, 1998).

Bhadra, G., 'Four rebels of 1857', in R. Guha (ed.), *Subaltern Studies IV* (New Delhi: Oxford University Press, 1985).

Brodkin, E.I., 'The struggle for succession: rebels and loyalists in the Indian mutiny of 1857', *Modern Asian Studies* 6, 3 (1972), pp. 277–290.

Broehl, W.G., *Crisis of the Raj: the revolt of 1857* (Hanover, N.H. and London: University of New England, 1986).

Chatterji, B., 'The Darogah and the countryside: the imposition of police control in Bengal and its impact, 1793–1837', *Indian Economic & Social History Review* 18, 1 (1981), pp. 19–42.

Chaudhuri, S.B., *Civil Disturbances During the British Rule in India, 1765–1857* (Calcutta: World Press, 1955).

Cohn, B., 'Representing authority in Victorian India', in T. Ranger and E. Hobsbawm (eds), *The Invention of Tradition* (Cambridge: Cambridge University Press, 1983); also in B. Cohn, *An Anthropologist Among the Historians* (New Delhi: Oxford University Press, 1990).

Dalrymple, William, *The Last Mughal: the fall of a dynasty, Delhi 1857* (New Delhi: Penguin, 2006).

Embree, A.T. (ed.), *India in 1857: the revolt against foreign rule* (New Delhi: Chanakya, 1987).

Farooqui, Amar, *Smuggling as Subversion, Colonialism, Indian Merchants and the Politics of Opium, 1790–1843* (New Delhi: New Age International Publishers, 1998; Lanham, Md.: Rowman & Littlefield, 2005).

Fisher, Michael H., *A Clash of Cultures: Awadh, the British and the Mughals* (Riverdale, Md.: Riverdale Company, 1987).

Fisher, Michael H. (ed.), *The Politics of the British Annexation of India, 1757–1857* (New Delhi: Oxford University Press, 1993).

Germon, Maria, *Journal of the Siege of Lucknow: an episode of the Indian Mutiny*, ed. M. Edwardes (London: Constable, 1958).

Ghosh, B.B., *British Policy Towards the Pathans and the Pindaris in Central India, 1805–1818* (Calcutta: Punthi Pustak, 1966).

Gordon, S.N., 'Scarf and sword: thugs, marauders, and state-formation in 18th century Malwa', *Indian Economic & Social History Review* 6, 4 (1969), pp. 403–429.

Gordon, S.N., *The Marathas* (New Cambridge History of India) (Cambridge: Cambridge University Press, 1993).

Guha, Ranajit, *Elementary Aspects of Peasant Insurgency* (New Delhi and Oxford: Oxford University Press, 1983a).

Guha, Ranajit, 'The prose of counter-insurgency', in R. Guha (ed.), *Subaltern Studies II* (New Delhi: Oxford University Press, 1983b).

Hardiman, David, *Feeding the Baniya: peasants and usurers in western India* (New Delhi: Oxford University Press, 1996).

Majumdar, R.C., *The Sepoy Mutiny and the Revolt of 1857* (Calcutta: K.L. Mukhopadhyay, 1963).

Marx, K. and Engels, F., *The First Indian War of Independence* (Moscow: Progress Publishers, 1959).

Metcalf, Thomas R., *The Aftermath of Revolt* (Princeton, N.J.: Princeton University Press, 1964), chs 4, 5, 8.

Metcalf, Thomas R., *Land, Landlords and the British Raj* (Berkeley: University of California Press, 1969).

Metcalfe, C.T. (ed.), *Two Native Narratives of the Mutiny of Delhi* (Westminster: A. Constable & Co., 1898).

Mohan, Surendra, *Awadh under the Nawabs: politics, culture and communal relations 1722–1856* (New Delhi: Manohar, 1997).

Mukherjee, R., 'The Azamgarh Proclamation and some questions on the revolt of 1857 in the North Western Provinces', in *Essays in Honour of S.C. Sarkar* (New Delhi: India People's Publishing House, 1976).

Mukherjee, R., *Awadh in Revolt* (New Delhi: Oxford University Press, 1984).

Mukherjee, R., ' "Satan let loose upon earth": the Kanpur massacres in the revolt of 1857', *Past and Present* 128 (1990), pp. 92–116.

Pandey, Gyanendra, 'A view of the observable: a positivist understanding of agrarian society and political protest in colonial India', Review of Eric Stokes, *Journal of Peasant Studies* 7, 3 (1980), pp. 375–383.

Ray, Rajat Kanta, *The Felt Community: commonality and mentality before the emergence of Indian nationalism* (New Delhi: Oxford University Press, 2003).

Roy, Tapti, *The Politics of a Popular Uprising: Bundelkhand in 1857* (New Delhi: Oxford University Press, 1985).

Russell, William Howard, *My Indian Mutiny Diary*, ed. M. Edwardes (London: Cassell & Co., 1957).

Sleeman, W., *Ramaseeana, or a Vocabulary of the Peculiar Language used by the Thugs, with an Introduction and Appendix descriptive of the system pursued by that fraternity, and of the measures adopted for its suppression* (Calcutta: G.H. Hattman, Military Orphanage Press, 1836).

Stokes, Eric, *English Utilitarians and India* (Oxford: Clarendon Press, 1959).

Stokes, Eric, *The Peasant and the Raj: studies in agrarian society and peasant rebellion in colonial India* (Cambridge: Cambridge University Press, 1978), chs 1 and 5–8.

Stokes, Eric, *The Peasant Armed: the Indian revolt of 1857* (Oxford: Clarendon, 1986).

Taylor, Meadows Philip, *Confessions of a Thug*, 1st edn in 3 vols (London: Kegan Paul, Trench, Trubner, 1839; New York: Oxford University Press, 1998).

Taylor, P.J.O., *What Really Happened During the Mutiny: a day-by-day account of the major events of 1857–1859 in India* (New Delhi: Oxford University Press, 1997).

Van Woerkens, Martine, *The Strangled Traveller: colonial imaginings and the Thugs of India* (Chicago: University of Chicago Press, 2002).

Yang, A., *The Limited Raj: agrarian relations in colonial India, Saran District, 1793–1920* (Berkeley: University of California Press, 1988).

5 Zenith of empire: economic and social conditions in the late nineteenth century

Amin, S., 'Small peasant commodity production and rural indebtedness: the culture of sugarcane in eastern U.P., *c.* 1880–1920', in R. Guha (ed.), *Subaltern Studies I* (New Delhi: Oxford University Press, 1981).

Amin, S., *Sugarcane and Sugar in Gorakhpur* (New Delhi and New York: Oxford University Press, 1984).

Arnold, David and Guha, Ramchandra (eds), *Nature, Culture and Imperialism: essays on the environmental history of South Asia* (New Delhi: Oxford University Press, 1996).

Bagchi, A.K., *Private Investment in India* (Cambridge: Cambridge University Press, 1972).

Baker, C., *An Indian Rural Economy* (Oxford: Oxford University Press, 1984).

Baker, D.E.U., *Colonialism in an Indian Hinterland: the Central Provinces, 1820–1920* (New Delhi: Oxford University Press, 1993).

Banaji, Jairus, 'Capitalist domination and the small peasantry: Deccan districts in the late nineteenth century', in U. Patnaik (ed.), *Agrarian Relations and Accumulation: the 'mode of production' debate in India* (Bombay: Sameeksha Trust, 1990).

Bannerjee, S., *A Nation in Making: being the reminiscences of fifty years of public life* (1925; repr. Bombay: Oxford University Press, 1963).

Bates, Crispin, 'The nature of social change in rural Gujarat – the Kedha district, 1818–1918', *Modern Asian Studies* 15 (1981), pp. 771–821.

Bates, Crispin, 'Tribalism, dependency and the sub-regional dynamics of economic change in central India', in C.J. Dewey (ed.), *The State and the Market: studies in the economic and social history of the Third World* (New Delhi: Manohar, 1987).

Bates, Crispin, 'Class and economic change in central India: the Narmada valley, 1820–1930', in C.J. Dewey (ed.), *Arrested Development in India: the historical perspective* (New Delhi: Manohar, 1988).

Bates, Crispin, 'Tribal migration in India and beyond' (with M. Carter), in G. Prakash (ed.), *The World of the Rural Labourer in Colonial India* (New Delhi: Oxford University Press, 1992).

Bates, Crispin, 'Regional dependence and rural development in central India: the pivotal role of migrant labour', in D. Ludden (ed.), *Agricultural Production and Indian History* (New Delhi: Oxford University Press, 1995).

Bayly, C.A., *The Local Roots of Indian Politics: Allahabad, 1880–1920* (Oxford: Clarendon Press, 1975).

Bhagavan, Manu, *Sovereign Spheres: princes, education and empire in colonial India* (New Delhi: Oxford University Press, 2003).

Bhatia, B.M., *Famines in India, 1860–1945* (Bombay: Asia Publishing House, 1967).

Blyn, G., *Agricultural Trends in India, 1891–1947* (Philadelphia: University of Pennsylvania Press, 1966).

Bose, S., *Agrarian Bengal* (Cambridge: Cambridge University Press, 1986).

Bose, S. (ed.), *South Asia and World Capitalism* (New Delhi and Oxford: Oxford University Press, 1990).

Chakrabarty, Bidyut, *Subhas Chandra Bose and Middle Class Radicalism: a study in Indian nationalism, 1928–1940* (London: London School of Economics and Political Science, 1990).

Chakrabarty, D., 'Conditions for knowledge of working-class conditions: employers, government and the jute workers of Calcutta, 1890–1940', in R. Guha (ed.), *Subaltern Studies II* (New Delhi: Oxford University Press, 1983).

Chakrabarty, D., 'Trade unions in a hierarchical culture: the jute workers of Calcutta, 1920–50', in R. Guha (ed.), *Subaltern Studies III* (New Delhi: Oxford University Press, 1984).

Chakrabarty, D., *Rethinking Working Class History* (Princeton, N.J.: Princeton University Press, 1989).

Chakravarty, L., 'Emergence of an industrial labour force in a dual economy', *Indian Economic & Social History Review* 15, 3 (1978), pp. 249–328.

Chandavarkar, R., 'Industrialization in India before 1947', *Modern Asian Studies* 19 (1985), pp. 623–668.

Chandavarkar, R., *Origins of Industrial Capitalism in India: business strategies and the working classes in Bombay, 1900–1940* (Cambridge: Cambridge University Press, 1994).

Chandra, Satish, 'The Indian League and the Western India Association', *Indian Economic & Social History Review* 8, 1 (1971), pp. 73–98.

Charlesworth, N., *British Rule and the Indian Economy* (London: Macmillan, 1982).

Charlesworth, N., *Peasants and Imperial Rule* (Cambridge: Cambridge University Press, 1985).

Cohn, Bernard S., 'Representing authority in Victorian India', in E. Hobsbawm and T. Ranger (eds), *The Invention of Tradition* (Cambridge: Cambridge University Press, 1983); also reprinted in B. Cohn, *An Anthropologist Among the Historians and Other Essays* (New Delhi: Oxford University Press, 1987).

Davis, Mike, *Late Victorian Holocausts: El Nino famines and the making of the Third World* (London: Verso, 2001).

Dewey, C.J. (ed.), *Arrested Development in India* (New Delhi: Manohar, 1988).

Digby, William, *'Prosperous' British India: a revelation from official records* (London: T. Fisher Unwin, 1901; repr. New Delhi: Sagar Publications, 1969).

Dirks, Nicholas B., *The Hollow Crown: ethnohistory of an Indian kingdom* (Cambridge: Cambridge University Press, 1987).

Dutt, R.C., *Famines and Land Assessments in India* (London: Kegan Paul, Trench, Trubner, 1900).

Dutt, R.C., *The Economic History of India under Early British Rule: from the rise of the British power in 1757 to the accession of Queen Victoria in 1837* (London: Kegan Paul, Trench, Trubner, 2nd edn, 1906a).

Dutt, R.C., *The Economic History of India in the Victorian Age: from the accession of Queen Victoria in 1837 to the commencement of the twentieth century* (London: Routledge & Kegan Paul, 2nd edn, 1906b).

Fernandes, Lila, *Producing Workers* (Philadelphia: University of Pennsylvania Press, 1997).

Gadgil, D.R., *The Industrial Evolution of India in Recent Times* (Calcutta and London: Oxford University Press, 1942).

Gadgil, M. and Guha, R., *This Fissured Land: an ecological history of India* (New Delhi and Oxford: Oxford University Press, 1993).

Ganguli, B.N., *Dadabhai Naoroji and the Drain Theory* (Bombay: Asian Publishing House, 1965).

Gordon, Leonard A., *Bengal: the nationalist movement, 1876–1940* (New York: Columbia University Press, 1974).

Gordon, Stewart, *Jute and the Empire: the Calcutta jute wallahs and the landscapes of empire* (Manchester and New York: Manchester University Press, 1998).

Greenough, P., *Prosperity and Misery in Modern Bengal* (Oxford and New York: Oxford University Press, 1982).

Grove, R., Damodaran, V. and Satpal, S., *Nature and the Orient: the environmental history of South and Southeast Asia* (New Delhi and New York: Oxford University Press, 1998).

Guha, S., *The Agrarian Economy of the Bombay Deccan* (New Delhi and New York: Oxford University Press, 1985).

Guha, S. (ed.), *Growth, Stagnation or Decline? Agricultural productivity in British India* (New Delhi: Oxford University Press, 1992).

Gupta, Ranajit Das, *Labour and Working Class in Eastern India: studies in colonial history* (Calcutta: K.P. Bagshi & Co., 1994).

Hardiman, David, *Feeding the Baniya: peasants and usurers in western India* (New Delhi: Oxford University Press, 1996).

Hurd, John and Whitcombe, Elizabeth, 'Irrigation and railways', in D. Kumar (ed.), *Cambridge Economic History of India*, vol. 2 (Cambridge: Cambridge University Press, 1983).

Johnson, G., *Provincial Politics and Indian Nationalism: Bombay and the Indian National Congress, 1880–1915* (Cambridge: Cambridge University Press, 1973).

Johnson, G. (ed.), 'The Cambridge Economic History of India and Beyond', *Modern Asian Studies* 19 (1985), pp. 353–354, esp. articles by Habib and Kumar.

Joshi, C., 'Bonds of community, ties of religion: Kanpur textile workers in the 20th century', *Indian Economic & Social History Review* 22, 3 (1985), pp. 251–280.

Kerr, Ian, *Building the Railways of the Raj, 1850–1900* (Delhi: Oxford University Press, 1995).

Kumar, Dharma (ed.), *The Cambridge Economic History of India. Vol. 2: c. 1757–c. 1970* (Cambridge: Cambridge University Press, 1983).

Kumar, N., *Artisans of Benares: popular culture and identity, 1880–1986* (Princeton, N.J.: Princeton University Press, 1988).

Ludden, D. (ed.), *Agricultural Production and Indian History* (New Delhi and New York: Oxford University Press, 1995).

McAlpin, M.D., *Subject to Famine* (Princeton, N.J.: Princeton University Press, 1983).

McLane, J.R., *Indian Nationalism and the Early Congress* (Princeton, N.J.: Princeton University Press, 1977).

Marx, K. and Engels, F., *The First Indian War of Independence (1857–1858)* (Moscow: Progress Publisher, 1959).

Metcalf, Thomas R., *The Aftermath of Revolt: India, 1857–1870* (New Delhi: Manohar, 1990).

Misra, B.B., *The Indian Middle Classes: their growth in modern times* (New Delhi: Oxford University Press, 1961).

Mohapatra, Prabhu, 'Coolies and colliers: a study of the agrarian context of labour migration from Chotanagpur, 1880–1920', *Studies in History*, new series 1, 2 (1985), pp. 247–304.

Morris, M.D., *Emergence of an Industrial Labour Force in India* (Berkeley: University of California Press, 1965).

Morris, M.D., *Indian Economy in the 19th Century: a symposium* (New Delhi: Indian Economic and Social History Association, 1969).

Morris, M.D., 'The growth of large-scale industry to 1947', in D. Kumar (ed.), *Cambridge Economic History of India*, vol. 2 (Cambridge: Cambridge University Press, 1982).

Nanda, B.R., *Gokhale: the Indian moderates and the British Raj* (New Delhi and London: Oxford University Press, 1977).

Naoroji, Dadabai, *Poverty of India* (London: Vincent Brooks, Day & Son, 1878).

Naoroji, Dadabai, *Poverty and UnBritish Rule in India* (London: S. Sonnenschein, 1878; repr. 1901).

Nigam, S., 'Disciplining and policing the criminals by birth', Parts 1, 2, in *Indian Economic and Social History Review* 27, 2 and 3 (1990), pp. 131–165, 257–288.

Prakash, G. (ed.), *The World of the Rural Labourer in Colonial India* (New Delhi and New York: Oxford University Press, 1992), the ch. by Bates and Carter.

Ramusack, B., *The Indian Princes and their States* (Cambridge: Cambridge University Press, 2004).

Rangarajan, Mahesh, *Fencing the Forest: conservation and ecological change in India's central provinces, 1860–1914* (New Delhi: Oxford University Press, 1996).

Ray, R.K., *Industrialization in India: growth and conflict in the private corporate sector, 1914–47* (New Delhi and Oxford: Oxford University Press, 1979), esp. discussion of Bagchi.

Rothermund, D., *An Economic History of India* (New Delhi: Manohar, 1988).

Sen, A.K., *Poverty and Famines: an essay in entitlement and deprivation* (Oxford: Clarendon, 1982).

Simmons, C.P., 'Indigenous enterprise in the Indian coal-mining industry', *Indian Economic & Social History Review* 13, 2 (1976), pp. 189–218.

Stone, Ian, *Canal Irrigation in British India* (Cambridge: Cambridge University Press, 1984).

Timberg, T., *The Marwaris* (New Delhi: Vikas, 1978).

Tomlinson, B.R., *The Economy of Modern India, c. 1860–1970* (New Cambridge History of India) (Cambridge: Cambridge University Press, 1993).

Washbrook, D.A., *The Emergence of Provincial Politics: the Madras presidency 1870–1920* (Cambridge: Cambridge University Press, 1976).

Whitcombe, E., *Agrarian Conditions in Northern India, 1860–1900* (Berkeley: University of California Press, 1972).

Wolpert, S.A., *Tilak and Gokhale* (Berkeley: University of California Press, 1962).

6 Revivalist and reform movements in the late nineteenth century

Ahmad, A., *Islamic Modernism in India and Pakistan* (London: Royal Institute of International Affairs, 1967).

Ahmed, R., *The Bengal Muslims, 1871–1906: a quest for identity* (New Delhi: Oxford University Press, 1981).

Ballhatchet, K., *Race, Sex and Class under the Raj: imperial attitudes and policies and their critics, 1793–1905* (London: Weidenfeld & Nicolson, 1980).

Barnett, M.R., *The Politics of Cultural Nationalism in South India* (Princeton, N.J.: Princeton University Press, 1976).

Barrier, N.G., 'The Arya Samaj and Congress politics in the Punjab, 1894–1908', *Journal of Asian Studies* 26, 3 (1967), pp. 363–379.

Bayly, C.A., 'The pre-history of communalism? Religious conflict in India, 1700–1860', *Modern Asian Studies* 19, 2 (1985), pp. 177–203.

Bayly, C.A., 'Rallying around the subaltern', *Journal of Peasant Studies* 16, 1 (1988), pp. 110–120.

Bayly, Susan, *Saints, Goddesses and Kings: Muslims and Christians in south Indian society, 1700–1900* (Cambridge: Cambridge University Press, 1990).

Bhattacharya, Sabyasachi (ed.), *Education and the Disprivileged: nineteenth and twentieth century India* (New Delhi: Orient Longman, 2002).

Burton, Antoinette, *Burdens of History: British feminists, Indian women and imperial culture* (Chapel Hill, N.C. and London: University of North Carolina Press, 1994).

Carroll, Lucy, ' "Sanskritisation", "westernization" and "social mobility": a reappraisal of the relevance of anthropological concepts to the social historian of modern India', *Journal of Anthropological Research* 33, 4 (1977), pp. 355–371.

Carroll, Lucy, 'Colonial perceptions of Indian society and the emergence of caste(s) associations', *Journal of Asian Studies* 37, 2 (1978), pp. 233–250.

Chandra, Sudhir, *Enslaved Daughters: colonialism, law and women's right* (New Delhi: Oxford University Press, 1998).

Chatterjee, Partha, *The Nation and its Fragments: colonial and post-colonial histories* (Princeton, N.J.: Princeton University Press, 1993).

Cohn, Bernard S., 'The command of language and the language of command', in R. Guha (ed.), *Subaltern Studies IV* (New Delhi: Oxford University Press, 1984).

Cohn, Bernard S., 'Representing authority in Victorian India', in E. Hobsbawm and T. Ranger (eds), *The Invention of Tradition* (Cambridge: Cambridge University Press, 1983); also in B. Cohn, *An Anthropologist Among the Historians and Other Essays* (New Delhi: Oxford University Press, 1990).

Dalmia, Vasudha, *The Nationalization of Hindu Traditions: Bharatendu Harishchandra and nineteenth-century Banaras* (New Delhi: Oxford University Press, 1999).

Dixit, P., 'The political and social dimensions of Vivekananda's ideology', *Indian Economic and Social History Review* 12, 3 (1975), pp. 293–313.

Forbes, Geraldine, *Women in Modern India* (Cambridge: Cambridge University Press, 1996).

Fox, R.G., *Lions of the Punjab: culture in the making* (Berkeley: University of California Press, 1985).

Freitag, S., 'Sacred symbol as mobilizing ideology', *Comparative Studies in Society and History* 22, 4 (1980), pp. 597–625.

Freitag, S., *Collective Action and Community: public arenas and the emergence of communalism in north India* (Berkeley: University of California Press, 1989).

Graham, B.D., *Hindu Nationalism and Indian Politics: the origins and development of the Bharatiya Jana Sangh* (Cambridge: Cambridge University Press, 1990).

Grewal, J.S., *The Sikhs of the Punjab* (New Cambridge History of India) (Cambridge: Cambridge University Press, 1990).

Gupta, Charu, *Sexuality, Obscenity, Community: Women, Muslims and the Hindu Public in Colonial India* (New Delhi: Permanent Black, 2001).

Gupta, Maya and Gupta, Amit Kumar, *Defying Death: struggles against imperialism and feudalism* (New Delhi: Tulika, 2001).

Hardgrave, R.L., *The Dravidian Movement* (Bombay: Popular Prakashan, 1965).

Hardy, P., *The Muslims of British India* (Cambridge: Cambridge University Press, 1972).

Hasan, M., *Communal and Pan-Islamic Trends in Colonial India* (New Delhi: Oxford University Press, 1985).

Hasan, M., *Nationalism and Communal Politics in India, 1885–1930* (New Delhi: Oxford University Press, 1991).

Irschick, E.F., *Politics and Social Conflict in South India: the non-Brahman movement and Tamil separatism, 1916–1929* (Berkeley: University of California Press, 1969).

Irschick, E.F., *Tamil Revivalism in the 1930s* (Madras: Cre-A, 1986).

Jalal, Ayesha, *Self and Sovereignty: individual and community in South Asian Islam since 1850* (London: Routledge, 2001).

Jones, K.W., *Arya Dharm: Hindi consciousness in nineteenth century Punjab* (New Delhi: Oxford University Press, 1976).

Jones, K.W., *Socio-religious Reform Movements in British India* (Cambridge: Cambridge University Press, 1989).

Jordens, J.T.F., *Dayananda Sarasvati: his life and ideas* (New Delhi: Oxford University Press, 1997).

King, Christopher R., 'Forging a new linguistic identity: the Hindi movement in Benares, 1868–1914', in S. Freitag (ed.), *Culture and Power in Benares* (Berkeley: University of California Press, 1983).

King, Christopher R., *One Language, Two Scripts: the Hindi movement in nineteenth century north India* (Bombay: Oxford University Press, 1995).

Kopf, D., *British Orientalism and the Bengal Renaissance* (Berkeley: University of California Press, 1969).

Kopf, D., *The Brahmo Samaj and the Shaping of the Modern Indian Mind* (Princeton, N.J.: Princeton University Press, 1979).

Kumar, Radha, *The History of Doing: an illustrated account of movements for women's rights and feminism in India 1800–1990* (New Delhi: Kali for Women, and London: Verso, 1993).

Lajpat, Rai, *Arya Samaj: an account of its origin, doctrines and activities* (repr. Bombay: Renaissance Publishing House, 1996).

Landau, Jacob M., *The Politics of Pan-Islam: ideology and organization* (New York: Clarendon Press of Oxford University Press, 1990).

Lelyveld, D., *Aligarh's First Generation* (Princeton, N.J.: Princeton University Press, 1978).

Lelyveld, D., 'The fate of Hindustani: colonial knowledge and the project of a national language', in C.A. Breckenridge and Peter van der Veer (eds), *Orientalism and the Postcolonial Predicament* (Philadelphia: University of Pennsylvania Press, 1993).

McLane, John R., *Indian Nationalism and the Early Congress* (Princeton, N.J.: Princeton University Press, 1977).

McLeod, W.H., *The Evolution of the Sikh Community* (New Delhi: Oxford University Press, 1976).

McLeod, W.H., *The Sikhs: history, religion and society* (New York: Columbia University Press, 1991).

Madhya Pradesh Government, *Report of the Christian Missionary Activities Enquiry Committee, Madhya Pradesh, 1956*, vols 1–3 (Indore, 1956–7).

Malik, H., *Sir Sayyid Ahmad Khan and Muslim Modernization in India and Pakistan* (New York: Columbia University Press, 1980).

Metcalf, Barbara D. *Islamic Revival in British India: Deoband, 1860–1900* (Princeton, N.J.: Princeton University Press, 1982).

Nandy, A., *The Intimate Enemy: loss and recovery of self under colonialism* (New Delhi: Oxford University Press, 1983).

Naregal, Veena, *Language Politics, Elites, and the Public Sphere: western India under colonialism* (London: Anthem Press, 2002).

O'Hanlon, R., *Caste, Conflict and Ideology* (Cambridge: Cambridge University Press, 1985).

O'Hanlon, R., 'Issues of widowhood: gender and resistance in colonial western, India', in

G. Prakash and D. Haynes (eds), *Contesting Power* (New Delhi: Oxford University Press, 1991).

O'Hanlon, R., *A Comparison between Women and Men: Tarabai Shinde and the critique of gender relations in colonial India* (New Delhi: Oxford University Press, 1994).

Omvedt, G., *Cultural Revolt in a Colonial Society: the non-Brahman movement in western India* (Bombay: Scientific Socialist Education Trust, 1976).

Omvedt, G., *Dalit Visions: the anti-caste movement and the construction of an Indian identity* (Tracts for the Times 8) (London: Sangam Books, 1995).

Pandey, Gyanendra, 'Rallying round the cow: sectarian strife in the Bhojpuri region, *c.* 1888–1917', in R. Guha (ed.), *Subaltern Studies II* (New Delhi: Oxford University Press, 1983).

Pandey, Gyanendra, ' "Encounters and calamities": the history of a north Indian qasba in the nineteenth century', in R. Guha (ed.), *Subaltern Studies III* (New Delhi: Oxford University Press, 1984).

Pandey, Gyanendra, 'The colonial construction of "Communalism": British writings on Banaras in the nineteenth century', in R. Guha (ed.), *Subaltern Studies VI* (New Delhi: Oxford University Press, 1989).

Pandey, Gyanendra, *The Construction of Communalism in North India* (New Delhi: Oxford University Press, 1990).

Pandian, M.S.S., *Brahmin and Non-Brahmin: genealogies of the Tamil present* (New Delhi: Permanent Black, 2007).

Panikkar, K.N., *Culture, Ideology, Hegemony: intellectuals and social consciousness in colonial India* (New Delhi: Tulika, 1996).

Poddar, Arabinda, *Renaissance in Bengal: search for identity* (Simla: Institute for Advanced Studies, 1977).

Pralay, Kanungo, *RSS's Tryst with Politics: From Hedgewar to Sudorshan* (New Delhi: Manohar, 2002).

Qureshi, M. Naeem, *Pan-Islam in British Indian Politics: a study of the Khilafat movement, 1918–1924* (Leiden: Brill, 1999).

Radice, William (ed.), *Swami Vivekananda and the Modernization of Hinduism* (New Delhi: Oxford University Press, 1998).

Robinson, Francis, *Separatism Among Indian Muslims: the politics of the United Provinces' Muslims, 1860–1923* (London: Cambridge University Press, 1974).

Robinson, Francis, *The Ulema of Firangi Mahal and Islamic Culture in South Asia* (New Delhi: Permanent Black, 2001).

Sen, Amita, *Hindu Revivalism in Bengal, 1872–1905: some essays in interpretation* (New Delhi: Oxford University Press, 1993).

Shastri, Sivanath, *A History of the Brahmo Samaj* (Calcutta: Sadharan Brahmo Samaj, 1912; repr. 1974).

Singh, K.S., *A History of the Sikhs* (Princeton, N.J.: Princeton University Press, 1963).

Sinha, M., *Colonial Masculinity: the 'manly Englishman' and the 'effeminate Bengali' in the late nineteenth century* (Manchester: Manchester University Press, 1994).

Sinha, M., *Specters of Mother India: global restructuring of an empire* (Durham, N.C. and London: Duke University Press, 2006).

Southard, Barbara, *The Women's Movement and Colonial Politics in Bengal: the quest for political education and social reform legislation* (New Delhi: Manohar, 1995).

Titus, M.T., *Indian Islam: a religious history of Islam in India* (London: Oxford University Press, 1930).

Walsh, Judith, *Domesticity in Colonial India: What Women Learned When Men Gave Them Advice* (Lanham, Md.: Rowman and Littlefield, 2004).

Washbrook, D.A., 'Caste, class and dominance: non-Brahminism, Dravidianism and Tamil nationalism', in F.R. Frankel and M.S.A. Rao (eds), *Dominance and State Power in Modern India*, vol. 1 (New Delhi: Oxford University Press, 1989).

Washbrook, D.A. and Baker, C.J., *South India: political institutions and political change, 1880–1940* (Delhi: Macmillan, 1975).

Watt, Carey A., *Serving the Nation: Cultures of Service, Association and Citizenship* (New Delhi: Oxford University Press, 2004).

Wolpert, S.A., *Tilak and Gokhale: revolution and reform in the making of modern India* (1962; repr. Berkeley: University of California Press, 1977; New Delhi: Oxford University Press, 1989).

Yang, A., 'Sacred symbol and sacred space in rural India: the "anti-cow killing" riot of 1893', *Comparative Studies in Society and History* 22, 4 (1980), pp. 576–596.

Zelliot, E., *From Untouchable to Dalit: essays on the Ambedkar movement* (New Delhi: Manohar Publications, 1992).

7 The Swadeshi and Ghadar movements

Arnold, David, 'Rebellious hillmen: the Guden-Rampa risings, 1839–1924', in R. Guha (ed.), *Subaltern Studies I* (New Delhi: Oxford University Press, 1982).

Barrier, N. Gerald, *The Punjab Alienation of Land Bill of 1900* (Durham, N.C.: Duke University Press, 1966).

Basu, Shamita, *Religious Revivalism as Nationalist Discourse: Swami Vivekananda and new Hinduism* (New Delhi: Oxford University Press, 2002).

Bayly, C.A., *The Local Roots of Indian Politics: Allahabad, 1880–1920* (Oxford: Clarendon Press, 1975).

Cashman, Richard, *Myth of Lokamanya: Tilak and mass politics in Maharashtra* (Berkeley: University of California Press, 1974).

Charlesworth, Neil, 'The myth of the Deccan Riots', *Modern Asian Studies* 6, 4 (1972), pp. 401–421; reprinted in D. Hardiman (ed.), *Peasant Resistance in India, 1858–1914* (New Delhi: Oxford University Press, 1992).

Dasgupta, Swapan, 'Adivasi politics in Midnapur, *c.* 1760–1924', in R. Guha (ed.), *Subaltern Studies IV* (New Delhi: Oxford University Press, 1985).

Dilks, David, *Curzon in India*, 2 vols (New York: Taplinger Pub. Co., 1970).

Fox, Richard G., *Lions of the Punjab: culture in the making* (Berkeley: University of California Press, 1985).

Gilmour, David, *Curzon* (London: Murray, 1994).

Goradia, Nayana, *Lord Curzon: the last of the British Moghuls* (New Delhi: Oxford University Press, 1997).

Gordon, Leonard A., *Bengal: the nationalist movement, 1876–1940* (New York: Columbia University Press, 1974).

Guha, Ranajit (ed.), 'Introduction', in *Subaltern Studies I* (New Delhi: Oxford University Press, 1982).

Guha, Ramachandra, 'Forestry and social protest in British Kumaun, *c.* 1893–1921,' in R. Guha (ed.), *Subaltern Studies IV* (New Delhi: Oxford University Press, 1985).

Gupta, Maya and Gupta, Amit Kumar, *Defying Death: struggles against imperialism and feudalism* (New Delhi: Tulika, 2001).

Hardiman, David, 'The Bhils and Shahukars of Eastern Gujarat', in R. Guha (ed.), *Subaltern Studies V* (New Delhi: Oxford University Press, 1987).

Hardiman, David A. (ed.), *Peasant Resistance in India, 1858–1914* (New Delhi: Oxford University Press, 1992).

Haynes, Douglas E. and Prakash, G. (ed.), *Contesting Power: resistance and everyday social relations in South Asia* (New Delhi: Oxford University Press, 1991).

Johnson, Gordon, *Provincial Politics and Indian Nationalism: Bombay and the Indian National Congress, 1880–1915* (Cambridge: Cambridge University Press, 1973).

Johnson, Gordon *et al.* (eds), 'Locality, Province and Nation', a special issue of *Modern Asian Studies* (1973), esp. chs 1 and 5.

McLane, J.R., *Indian Nationalism and the Early Congress* (Princeton, N.J.: Princeton University Press, 1977).

Mansergh, Nicholas (ed.), *Transfer of Power 1942–7: constitutional relations between Britain and India*, vols 1 to 10 (London: HMSO, 1970–83).

Mayo, Katherine, *Mother India* (London, 1927).

Nanda, B.R., *Gokhale, the Indian Moderates and the British Raj* (New Delhi: Oxford University Press, 1977).

Narain, P., *Press and Politics in India, 1885–1905* (New Delhi: Oxford University Press, 1970).

Owen, H.F., 'The Home Rule Leagues, 1915–18', in D.A. Low (ed.), *Soundings in Modern South Asian History* (London: Weidenfeld & Nicolson, 1968).

Pandey, Gyanendra, 'Rallying round the cow: sectarian strife in the Bhojpuri region, *c.* 1888–1917', in R. Guha (ed.), *Subaltern Studies II* (New Delhi: Oxford University Press, 1983).

Pandey, Gyanendra, ' "Encounters and calamities": the history of a north Indian qasba in the nineteenth century', in R. Guha (ed.), *Subaltern Studies III* (New Delhi: Oxford University Press, 1984).

Panikkar, K.N., *Against Lord and State: religion and peasant uprisings in Malabar 1836–1921* (New Delhi: Oxford University Press, 1989).

Puri, Harish K., *Ghadar Movement: ideology, organization and strategy* (Amritsar: Guru Nanak Dev University Press, 1983).

Radice, William (ed.), *Swami Vivekananda and the Modernization of Hinduism* (London: SOAS Studies in South Asia; New Delhi: Oxford University Press, 1998).

Rai, Lajpat, *Unhappy India: being a reply to Miss Katherine Mayo's* Mother India (Calcutta: Banna Pub. Co., 1928).

Ray, Rajat K., *Social Conflict and Political Unrest in Bengal, 1875–1922* (New Delhi: Oxford University Press, 1984).

Raychaudhuri, Tapan, *Europe Reconsidered: perceptions of the West in nineteenth-century Bengal* (Oxford: Oxford University Press, 1988).

Robinson, F., *Separatism Among Indian Muslims: the politics of the United Provinces' Muslims, 1860–1923* (London: Cambridge University Press, 1974).

Sarkar, Sumit, *The Swadeshi Movement in Bengal, 1903–08* (New Delhi: Oxford University Press, 1973).

Sarkar, Sumit, *Modern India, 1885–1947* (New Delhi: Macmillan, 1983).

Sarkar, Sumit, 'The conditions and nature of subaltern militancy: Bengal from swadeshi to non-co-operation, *c.* 1905–22', in R. Guha (ed.), *Subaltern Studies III* (New Delhi: Oxford University Press, 1984).

Seal, Anil, *The Emergence of Indian Nationalism* (Cambridge: Cambridge University Press, 1968).

Singh, K.S., *Tribal Movements in India* (New Delhi: Manohar, 1982).

Singh, K.S., *Birsa Munda and his Movement 1874–1901: a study of a millenarian movement in Chotanagpur* (New Delhi: Oxford University Press, 1983).

Washbrook, D.A., *The Emergence of Provincial Politics: the Madras presidency, 1870–1920* (Cambridge: Cambridge University Press, 1976).

Wolpert, S.A., *Tilak and Gokhale: revolution and reform in the making of modern India* (1962; repr. Berkeley: University of California Press, 1977; New Delhi: Oxford University Press, 1989).

8 Aftermath of the First World War and M.K. Gandhi's rise to power

Amin, Shahid, 'Gandhi as Mahatma: Gorakhpur district, Eastern UP, 1921–22,' in R. Guha (ed.), *Subaltern Studies III* (New Delhi: Oxford University Press, 1984).

Amin, Shahid, 'Agrarian bases of nationalist agitations in India', in D.A. Low (ed.), *The Indian National Congress: centenary hindsights* (New Delhi: Oxford University Press, 1988).

Arnold, David, 'Gramsci and peasant subalternity in India', *Journal of Peasant Studies* 11, 4 (1984), pp. 155–177.

Arnold, David, *Gandhi* (London: Longman, 2001).

Bondurant, Joan, V., *Conquest of Violence* (Princeton, N.J.: Princeton University Press, 1958; repr. 1965, 1969, 1988).

Brown, Judith M., *Gandhi's Rise to Power: Indian politics, 1915–1922* (Cambridge: Cambridge University Press, 1972).

Brown, Judith M., *Gandhi: prisoner of hope* (New Haven, Conn.: Yale University Press, 1989).

Chatterjee, Margaret, *Gandhi's Religious Thought* (London: Macmillan, 1983).

Chatterjee, Partha, 'Gandhi and the critique of civil society', in R. Guha (ed.), *Subaltern Studies III* (New Delhi: Oxford University Press, 1984).

Coates, Tim, *The Amritsar Massacre: General Dyer in the Punjab 1919* (London: Stationery Office, 2000).

Copley, Antony, *Gandhi: against the tide* (Oxford: Blackwell, 1987).

Dalton, Dennis, *Mahatma Gandhi: non-violent power in action* (New York: Colombia University Press, 1993).

Dhanagare, D., *Peasant Movements in India* (New Delhi: Oxford University Press, 1987).

Epstein, S.J.M., *The Earthy Soil: Bombay peasants and the Indian nationalist movement 1919–1947* (New Delhi: Oxford University Press, 1988).

Forbes, Geraldine, *Women in Modern India* (New Cambridge History of India) (Cambridge: Cambridge University Press, 1996).

Gandhi, M.K., *An Autobiography: the story of my experiments with truth* (Boston, Mass.: Beacon Press; 1993 [1st edn 1923]).

Gandhi, M.K., *Collected Works*, vols. 1–100 (Publications Division, Ministry of Information and Broadcasting, Government of India, rev. edn 2001, originally published 1956–94).

Gandhi, Rajmohan, *The Good Boatman* (New Delhi: Viking, 1995).

Guha, Ramachandran, *The Unquiet Woods* (New Delhi: Oxford University Press, 1989).

Guha, Ranajit, 'Introduction', in R. Guha (ed.), *Subaltern Studies I* (New Delhi: Oxford University Press, 1982).

Guha, Ranajit, *Dominance without Hegemony: history and power in colonial India* (Cambridge, Mass.: Harvard University Press, 1997).

Guha, Ranajit (ed.), *A Subaltern Studies Reader* (Minneapolis and London: University of Minnesota Press, 1997).

Guha, Ranajit and Spivak, Gayatri Chakravorty (eds), *Selected Subaltern Studies* (New York: Oxford University Press, 1988), section IV, 'Nationalism: Gandhi as signifier'.

Hardiman, David, *Peasant Nationalists of Gujarat* (New Delhi: Oxford University Press, 1981).

Hardiman, David, 'The Indian "faction": a political theory examined', in R. Guha (ed.), *Subaltern Studies I* (New Delhi: Oxford University Press, 1982).

Hardiman, David, 'Adivasi assertion in south Gujarat: the Devi movement of 1922–23', in R. Guha (ed.), *Subaltern Studies III* (New Delhi: Oxford University Press, 1984).

Hardiman, David, *The Coming of the Devi: adivasi assertion in western India* (New Delhi: Oxford University Press, 1987).

Hardiman, David, 'Power in the forests: the Dangs, 1820–1940,' in D. Arnold and D. Hardiman (eds), *Subaltern Studies VIII* (New Delhi: Oxford University Press, 1996).

Hardiman, David, *Gandhi in His Time and Ours: the global legacy of his ideas* (London: Hurst & Co., 2004).

Huttenback, R.A., *Gandhi in South Africa: British imperialism and the Indian question, 1860–1914* (Ithaca, N.Y.: Cornell University Press, 1971).

Low, D.A. (ed.), *Congress and the Raj* (London: Heinemann, 1977).

Markovits, C., *The UnGandhian Gandhi: the life and afterlife of the Mahatma* (London: Anthem Press, 2004).

Mukherjee, Rudrangshu (ed.), *The Penguin Gandhi Reader* (New Delhi and London: Penguin, 1993).

Nanda, B.R., *Mahatma Gandhi: a biography, complete and unabridged* (New Delhi: Oxford University Press, 1996; originally published in London by G. Allen & Unwin, 1958).

Pandey, Gyanendra, *The Ascendancy of Congress in the United Provinces* (New Delhi: Oxford University Press, 1978).

Pandey, Gyanendra, 'Peasant revolt and Indian nationalism: the peasant movement in Awadh, 1919–1922', in R. Guha (ed.), *Subaltern Studies I* (New Delhi: Oxford University Press, 1982).

Parekh, Bhikhu C., *Gandhi's Political Philosophy: a critical examination* (Basingstoke: Macmillan, 1989).

Patel, Sujata, *The Making of Industrial Relations: the Ahmedabad textile industry 1918–1939* (New Delhi: Oxford University Press, 1987).

Pouchepadass, Jacques, 'Local leaders and the intelligentsia in the Champaran satyagraha (1917): a study in peasant mobilization', *Contributions to Indian Sociology* 8 (1974), pp. 67–87.

Pouchepadass, Jacques, *Champaran and Gandhi: planters, peasants and Gandhian politics* (New Delhi: Oxford University Press, 1999).

Sarkar, S., *'Popular Movements' and 'Middle-Class' Leadership in Late Colonial India* (Calcutta: K.P. Bagchi & Co., 1983).

Seal, Anil, *The Emergence of Indian Nationalism: competition and collaboration in the later nineteenth century* (Cambridge: Cambridge University Press, 1968).

Shah, Ghanshyan, 'Traditional society and political mobilization: the experience of Bardoli satyagraha, (1920–28)', *Contributions to Indian Sociology* 8 (1974), pp. 89–107.

Sissons, R. and Wolpert, S. (eds), *Congress and Indian Nationalism* (Berkeley: University of California Press, 1988).

Swan, Maureen, *Gandhi: the South African experience* (Johannesburg: Ravan Press, 1985).

Tarlo, Emma, *Clothing Matters: dress and identity in India* (London: Hurst, 1996).

9 Non-co-operation and civil disobedience, 1920–39

Ali, Tariq, *The Nehrus and the Gandhis: an Indian dynasty: the story of the Nehru–Gandhi family* (London: Chatto & Windus, 1985).

Ambedkar, B.R., *Dr. Babasahaeb Ambedkar: writings and speeches*, 17 vols, edited by Vasant Moon (Mumbai: Government of Maharashtra, 1979–95).

Amin, Shahid, *Event, Metaphor, Memory: Chauri Chaura 1922–24* (New Delhi: Oxford University Press, 1995).

Anderson, W.K. and Damle, S., *The Brotherhood in Saffron: the RSS and Hindu revivalism* (New Delhi: Vistaar, 1987), ch. 1.

Arnold, David, *The Congress in Tamilnad: nationalists politics in south India, 1919–1937* (London: Curzon Press, 1977).

Azad, M. Abdul Kalam, *India Wins Freedom: the complete version* (New Delhi: Orient Longman, 1988).

Bahl, V., 'Congress attitude towards the working class struggle in India, 1900–1947', in K. Kumar (ed.), *Congress and Classes* (New Delhi: Manohar, 1988).

Baker, C.J., *The Politics of South India, 1920–1947* (Cambridge: Cambridge University Press, 1976).

Baker, C.J., 'Leading up to Periyar', in B.N. Pandey (ed.), *Leadership in South Asia* (New Delhi: Vikas, 1977).

Baker, D.E.U., ' "A serious time": forest satyagraha in Madhya Pradesh, 1919–1939', *Indian Economic & Social History Review* (1984), pp. 71–90.

Battacharya, S., 'The colonial state, capital and labour: Bombay 1919–31', in S. Bhattacharya and R. Thapar (eds), *Situating Indian History* (New Delhi: Oxford University Press, 1986).

Bose, Subhas Chandra, *Congress President: speeches, articles and letters January 1938–May 1939*, vol. 9 in Sisir Kumar Bose and Sugata Bose (eds), *Netaji Collected Works* (New Delhi: Oxford University Press, 1995).

Bose, Sugata, 'The roots of communal violence in Bengal: a study of the Kishoregani riots, 1930', *Modern Asian Studies* 16, 3 (1982), pp. 463–491.

Bose, Sugata, *Agrarian Bengal* (Cambridge: Cambridge University Press, 1986), chs 6–8.

Brown, Judith M., *Gandhi and Civil Disobedience* (Cambridge: Cambridge University Press, 1976).

Chandavarkar, R., *Origins of Industrial Capitalism in India: business strategies and the working classes in Bombay, 1900–1940* (Cambridge: Cambridge University Press, 1994).

Chandra, B., 'Ideological development of revolutionary terrorists in northern India in the 1920s', in B. Chandra, *Nationalism and Colonialism in India* (New Delhi: Orient Longman, 1981).

Chatterji, Basudev, 'Business and politics in the 1930s', in A. Seal *et al.*, *Power, Profit, and Politics*, special issue of *Modern Asian Studies* 15, 3 (1981).

Chatterji, Basudev, *Trade, Tariffs, and Empire: Lancashire and British policy in India, 1919–1939* (New Delhi: Oxford University Press, 1992).

Chatterji, Basudev (ed.), *Towards Freedom: documents on the movement for independence in India, 1938* (New Delhi: Oxford University Press, for the Indian Council of Historical Research, 1999).

Chatterji, J., *Bengal Divided: Hindu communalism and partition, 1932–47* (Cambridge: Cambridge University Press, 1994).

Copland, Ian, *The Princes of India in the Endgame of Empire, 1917–1947* (Cambridge: Cambridge University Press, 2002).

Coupland, R., *The Constitutional Problem in India* (Oxford: Oxford University Press, 1944).

Das, Suranjan, *Communal Riots in Bengal, 1905–47* (New Delhi: Oxford University Press, 1993).

Desai, A.R. (ed.), *Peasant Struggles in India* (Bombay: Oxford University Press, 1979).

Desai, M.V., *The Story of Bardoli: being a history of the Bardoli satyagraha of 1928 and its sequel* (Ahmedabad: Navajivan Press, 1957).

Dhanagare, D., *Peasant Movements in India* (New Delhi: Oxford University Press, 1987).

Dutt, R. Palme, *India Today* (1st edn London: V. Gollancz, 1940; 2nd edn Lahore, 1979).

Forbes, Geraldine, 'The politics of respectability: Indian women and the Indian National Congress', in D.A. Low (ed.), *The Indian National Congress* (New Delhi: Oxford University Press, 1988).

Forbes, Geraldine, *Women in Modern India* (New Cambridge History of India) (Cambridge: Cambridge University Press, 1996).

Gallagher, J., 'The Congress in decline: Bengal 1930–39', in J. Gallagher *et al.*, *Locality, Province and Nation*, a special issue of *Modern Asian Studies* 7, 3 (1973), pp. 589–645.

Gandhi, M.K., *Collected Works*, vols. 1–100 (Publications Division, Ministry of Information and Broadcasting, Government of India, revised edn 2001; originally published 1956–94).

Gopal, Sarvepalli, *Jawaharlal Nehru: a biography*, vol. 1 (London: Cape, 1975).

Gordon, A.D.D., *Businessmen and Politics: rising nationalism and a modernising economy in Bombay, 1918–1933* (New Delhi: Manohar, 1978).

Gould, William, 'Congress radicals and Hindu militancy: Sampurnanand and Purshottam Das Tandon in the politics of the United Provinces, 1930–1947', *Modern Asian Studies* 36, 3 (2002), pp. 619–655.

Graham, B.D., *Hindu Nationalism and Indian Politics: the origins and development of the Bharatiya Jana Sangh* (Cambridge: Cambridge University Press, 1990).

Guha, Ramachandran, *The Unquiet Woods* (New Delhi: Oxford University Press, 1989).

Gupta, Maya and Gupta Amit Kumar (eds), *Defying Death: struggles against imperialism and feudalism* (New Delhi: Tulika, 2001).

Hardiman, David, *Peasant Nationalists of Gujarat* (New Delhi: Oxford University Press, 1981).

Hardiman, David, 'Adivasi assertion in south Gujarat: the Devi movement of 1922–23', in R. Guha (ed.), *Subaltern Studies III* (New Delhi: Oxford University Press, 1984).

Hardiman, David, *The Coming of the Devi: adivasi assertion in western India* (New Delhi: Oxford University Press, 1987).

Hasan, Mushirul, 'The Muslim mass contacts campaign: analysis of a strategy of political mobilisation', in R. Sisson and S. Wolpert (eds), *Congress and Indian Nationalism: the pre-independence phase* (Berkeley: University of California Press, 1988).

Heehs, Peter, *The Bomb in Bengal: the rise of revolutionary terrorism* (New Delhi: Oxford University Press, 1993).

Jaffrelot, Christophe, *Ambedkar: leader of the dalits, architect of the Indian constitution* (London: Hurst, 2001).

Joshi, Bhagwan and Joshi, Shashi, *Struggle for Hegemony in India: the colonial state, the left and the national movement*, vols 1 and 2 (New Delhi: Sage, 1992).

Kanungo, Pralay, *RSS's Tryst with Politics: from Hedgewar to Sudarshan* (New Delhi: Manohar, 2002).

Keer, Dhananjay, *Dr. Ambedkar: life and mission* (Bombay: Popular Prakashan, 1st edn 1954; repr. 1981).

Kishwar, Madhu, *Gandhi and Women* (New Delhi: Prakashan, 1986).

Kumar, Radha, *The History of Doing: an illustrated account of movements for women's rights and feminism in India 1800–1990* (London: Vision, 1993).

Leonard, Gordon A., *Brothers against the Raj: a biography of Indian nationalists Sarat and Subhas Chandra Bose* (New York: Colombia University Press, 1990).

Markovits, Claude, *Indian Business and Nationalist Politics, 1931–1939* (Cambridge: Cambridge University Press, 1985).

Moore, R.J., *The Crisis of Indian Unity, 1917–1940* (Oxford: Clarendon Press, 1974).

Mukherjee, A., *Imperialism, Nationalism and the Making of the Indian Capitalist Class, 1920–1947* (New Delhi: Sage, 2002).

Nehru, Jawaharlal, *An Autobiography: with musings on recent events in India* (London, 1936).

Nehru, Jawaharlal, *A Bunch of Old Letters* (New Delhi, 1958; repr. 1988, 2005).

Omvedt, Gail, *Ambedkar: towards an enlightened India* (New Delhi: Penguin, 2004).

Orsini, Francesca, *The Hindi Public Sphere 1920–1940: language and literature in the age of nationalism* (New Delhi: Oxford University Press, 2002).

Pandey, B.N., *Leadership in South Asia* (New Delhi: Vikas, 1977).

Pandey, Gyanendra, 'Peasant revolt and Indian nationalism: the peasant movement in Awadh, 1919–1922', in R. Guha (ed.), *Subaltern Studies I* (New Delhi: Oxford University Press, 1982).

Pandey, Gyanendra, *The Ascendancy of Congress in the United Provinces* (New Delhi: Oxford University Press, 1978; London: Anthem Press, 2002).

Rasul, M.A., *A History of the All-India Kisan Sabha* (Calcutta: National Book Agency Private Ltd, 1989).

Rothermund, Dietmar, *India in the Great Depression, 1929–1939* (New Delhi: Manohar, 1992).

Sarkar, Sumit, *Modern India: 1885–1947* (Delhi: Macmillan, 1983).

Sarkar, Sumit, *'Popular Movements' and 'Middle-Class' Leadership in Late Colonial India* (Calcutta: Published for Centre for Studies in Social Sciences by K.P. Bagchi, 1985).

Sarkar, Tanika, *Bengal 1928–1934: the politics of protest* (New Delhi: Oxford University Press, 1987).

Shah, Ghanshyam, 'Traditional society and political mobilization: the experience of Bardoli satyagraha, (1920–28)', *Contributions to Indian Sociology* 8 (1974), pp. 89–107.

Toye, Hugh, *The Springing Tiger: a study of a revolutionary* (London: Cassell, 1959).

Vaikuntham, Y. (ed.), *People's Movement in the Princely States* (New Delhi: Manohar, 2004).

Zelliot, E., 'The leadership of Babasaheb Ambedkar', in B.N. Pandey (ed.), *Leadership in South Asia* (New Delhi: Vikas, 1977).

10 Quit India and partition, 1939–47

Ahmed, Akbar S., *Jinnah, Pakistan and Islamic Identity: the search for Saladin* (London: Routledge, 1997).

Aiyar, S., ' "August Anarchy": the partition massacres in Punjab, 1947', *South Asia* 18, special issue on North India: partition and independence (1995), pp. 13–36.

Azad, M. Abdul Kalam, *India Wins Freedom: complete version* (New Delhi: Sangam Books, 1988).

Baig, M.R.A., *The Muslim Dilemma in India* (New Delhi: Vikas, 1974).

Bayly, C.A., 'The pre-history of communalism', *Modern Asian Studies* 19, 2 (1985), pp. 177–203.

Bhalla, A. (ed.), *Stories About the Partition of India* (New Delhi: Indus, 1994).

Bhattacharjea, Ajit, *Unfinished Revolution: a political biography of Jayaprakash Narayan* (New Delhi: Rupa, 2004).

Bose, Sugata, 'The roots of communal violence in Bengal: a study of Kishoreganj riots, 1930', *Modern Asian Studies* 16, 3 (1982), pp. 463–491.

Bose, Sugata, *Agrarian Bengal* (Cambridge: Cambridge University Press, 1986), chs 6–8.

Brass, Paul R., 'Elite groups, symbol manipulation and ethnic identity among the Muslims of South Asia', in D. Taylor and M. Yapp (eds), *Political Identity in South Asia* (London: Curzon Press, 1979).

Brown, Judith, *Modern India: the origins of an Asian democracy* (Oxford: Oxford University Press, 1994).

Butalia, U., *The Other Side of Silence: voices from the partition of India* (New Delhi: Penguin Books, 1998).

Chakrabarty, Bidyut, *Biplabi: a journal of the 1942 open rebellion* (Kolkata: K.P. Bagchi & Co., 2002).

Chatterji, J., *Bengal Divided: Hindu communalism and partition, 1932–47* (Cambridge: Cambridge University Press, 1994).

Chatterji, K., 'Right or charity? Relief and rehabilitation in west Bengal', in S. Kaul (ed.), *The Partitions of Memory: the afterlife of the division of India* (New Delhi: Permanent Black, 2001).

Chopra, P.N. (ed.), *Quit India Movement, British Secret Documents*, vol. 1 (New Delhi: Interprint, 1986).

Chopra, P.N. (ed.), *Historic Judgement on Quit India Movement: Justice Wickenden's report* (New Delhi: Konark Publishers, 1989).

Chopra, P.N. (ed.), *Quit India Movement, British Secret Documents*, vol. 2. *Role of Big Business* (New Delhi: Interprint, 1991).

Cooper, Adrienne, *Sharecropping and Sharecropper's Struggles in Bengal, 1930–1950* (Calcutta: K.P. Bagchi, 1988).

Custers, P., *Women in the Tebhaga Uprising* (Calcutta: Naya Prakash, 1987).

Dalton, Dennis, *Mahatma Gandhi: nonviolent power in action* (New York: Columbia University Press, 1993), ch. 5, 'The Calcutta Fast'.

Damodaran, Vinita, *Broken Promises: popular protest, Indian nationalism and the Congress Party in Bihar, 1935–46* (New Delhi: Oxford University Press, 1992a).

Damodaran, Vinita, 'Azad Dastas and dacoit gangs: the Congress and underground activity in Bihar, 1942–44', *Modern Asian Studies* 26, 3 (1992b), pp. 417–450.

Das, S., 'The crowd in Calcutta violence', in B. Chattopadhyaya *et al.* (eds), *Disssent and Consensus: social protest in pre-industrial societies* (Calcutta: K.P. Bagchi, 1989).

Datta, Pradip Kumar, *Carving Blocs: communal ideology in early twentieth century Bengal* (New Delhi: Oxford University Press, 1999).

Desai, A.R. (ed.), *Peasant Struggles in India* (Bombay: Oxford University Press, 1979).

Dhanagare, D.H., 'Peasant insurrection in Telengana', in *Peasant Movements in India* (New Delhi: Oxford University Press, 1987).

Fay, Peter Ward, *The Forgotten Army: India's armed struggle for independence, 1942–1945* (Ann Arbor: University of Michigan Press, 1993).

Gandhi, Dev Das, *India Unreconciled: a documented history of Indian political events from the crisis of August 1942 to Feb. 1944* (New Delhi: Times of India, 1944).

Gilmartin, David, *Empire and Islam: the Punjab and the making of Pakistan* (Berkeley: University of California Press, 1988).

Gondhalekar, Nandini and Bhattacharya, Sanjoy, 'The All India Hindu Mahasabha and the end of British rule in India, 1939–1947', *Social Scientist*, 27, 7 and 8 (1999), pp. 48–74.

Gopal, Sarvepalli, *Jawaharlal Nehru: a biography* (Oxford: Oxford University Press, 1975), vol. 1.

Gopal, Sarvepalli (ed.), *Anatomy of a Confrontation: the rise of communal politics in India* (New Delhi: Penguin 1991; 2nd edn London: Zed, 1993).

Greenough, Paul R., *Prosperity and Misery in Modern Bengal: the famine of 1943–44* (Oxford: Oxford University Press, 1982).

Greenough, Paul R., 'Political mobilisation and the underground literature of the Quit India movement, 1942–44', *Modern Asian Studies* 17, 3 (1983), pp. 353–386.

Gupta, Partha Sarathi, *Imperialism and the British Labour Movement, 1914–1964* (London: Macmillan, 1975; repr. London: Sage, 2002).

Harcourt, M., 'Kisan populism and revolution: the 1942 disturbances in Bihar and East U.P.' in D.A. Low (ed.), *Congress and the Raj* (London: Heinemann, 1977).

Hasan, Mushirul (ed.), *India's Partition: process, strategy and mobilisation* (New Delhi: Oxford University Press, 1993).

Hasan, Mushirul (ed.), *India Partitioned: the other face of freedom*, vols 1 and 2 (New Delhi: Lotus Collection, 1995).

Hasan, Mushirul, *Legacy of a Divided Nation: India's Muslims since independence* (London: Hurst, and Delhi: Oxford University Press, 1997).

Hasan, Mushirul (ed.), *Inventing Boundaries: gender, politics and the partition of India* (New Delhi: Oxford University Press, 2000).

Hashmi, Taj ul-Islam, *Pakistan as a Peasant Utopia: the communalization of class politics in East Bengal, 1920–1947* (Boulder, Colo. and Oxford: Westview Press, 1992).

Henningham, Stephen, 'Quit India in Bihar and the Eastern United Provinces: the dual revolt', in R. Guha (ed.), *Subaltern Studies II* (New Delhi: Oxford University Press, 1983).

Hodson, H.V., *The Great Divide* (London: Hutchinson, 1969).

Jalal, Ayesha, *The Sole Spokesman: Jinnah, the Muslim League and the demand for Pakistan* (Cambridge: Cambridge University Press, 1985).

Jeffrey, Robin, 'A sanctified label: "Congress" in Travancore politics, 1938–48', in D.A. Low (ed.), *Congress and the Raj* (London: Heinemann Educational, 1977–8).

Kamtekar, Indivar, 'The End of the Colonial State in India, 1942–1947', Unpublished Ph.D. thesis, University of Cambridge, 1988.

Kamtekar, Indivar, 'A different war dance: state and class in India 1939–1945', *Past & Present* 176 (2002), pp. 187–221.

Kaul, S. (ed.), *The Partitions of Memory: the afterlife of the division of India* (Bloomington: Indiana University Press, 2001).

Kuwajima, Sho, *Muslims, Nationalism and the Partition: 1946 provincial elections in India* (New Delhi: Oxford University Press, 1998).

Lalita, K. *et al.*, *'We Were Making History': women and the Telengana uprising* (London: Zed, 1989).

Leonard, Gordon A., *Brothers against the Raj: a biography of Indian nationalists Sarat and Subhas Chandra Bose* (New York: Colombia University Press, 1990).

Low, D.A. and Brasted, H. (eds), *Freedom, Trauma and Continuities: northern India and independence* (New Delhi: Sage, 1998).

Major, Andrew, ' "The Chief Sufferers": abduction of women during the partition of the Punjab', in D.A. Low and H. Brasted (eds), *Freedom, Trauma and Continuities* (New Delhi: Sage, 1998).

Mansergh, P.N.S. *et al.*, *The Transfer of Power*, vols VI–VIII (documents) (London: HMSO, 12 vols, 1970–83).

Mathur, Sobhag, *Hindu Revivalism and the Indian National Movement: ideas and policies of the Hindu Mahasabha, 1939–45* (Jodhpur: Kusumanjali, 1996).

Mathur, Y.B., *Quit India Movement* (New Delhi: Pragati Publications, 1979).

Menon, Ritu and Bhasin, Kamala, *Witness to Freedom: how women experienced the partition of India* (New Delhi: Manohar, 1997).

Menon, Ritu and Bhasin, Kamla, *Borders and Boundaries: women in India's partition* (New Delhi: Kali for Women, 1998).

Menon, V.P., *The Transfer of Power* (London: Longmans, Green & Co., 1957).

Moon, P., *Divide and Quit* (London: Chatto & Windus, 1961).

Moore, Barrington, *Social Origins of Dictatorship and Democracy* (Harmondsworth: Penguin, 1966), ch. 6.

Moore, R.J., *The Crisis of Indian Unity, 1917–1940* (Oxford: Clarendon, 1974).

Moore, R.J., *Escape from Empire: the Attlee government and the Indian problem* (Oxford: Clarendon, 1983).

Omvedt, Gail, *Dalit Visions* (New Delhi: Orient Longman, 1995).

Omvedt, Gail, *Ambedkar: towards an enlightened India* (New Delhi: Penguin, 2004).

Ouwerkerk, Louise and Kooiman, Dick (eds), *No Elephants for the Maharaja: social and political change in the princely state of Travancore, 1921–1947* (New Delhi: South Asia Books, 1994).

Page, D., *Prelude to Partition: the Indian Muslims and the imperial system of control 1920–1932* (New Delhi: Oxford University Press, 1982).

Pandey, Gyanendra, 'Rallying around the cow: sectarian strife in the Bhojpuri region, *c.* 1888–1917', in R. Guha (ed.), *Subaltern Studies II* (New Delhi: Oxford University Press, 1983).

Pandey, Gyanendra (ed.), *The Indian Nation in 1942* (Calcutta: K.P. Bagchi, Centre for Studies in Social Science, 1988).

Pandey, Gyanendra, *The Construction of Communalism in Colonial North India* (New Delhi: Oxford University Press, 1992).

Pandey, Gyanendra, 'The prose of otherness', in D. Arnold and D. Hardiman (eds), *Subaltern Studies VIII: essays in honour of Ranajit Guha* (New Delhi: Oxford University Press, 1994).

Pandey, Gyanendra, *Remembering Partition: violence, nationalism and history in India* (Cambridge and New York: Cambridge University Press, 2001).

Philips, C.H. and Wainwright, M. (eds), *The Partition of India* (London: Allen & Unwin, 1970).

Qureshi, Abdul Saleem (ed.), *Jinnah: the founder of Pakistan* (Karachi: Oxford University Press Pakistan 1998).

Reddy, Arutla Ramachandra, *Telangana Struggle: memoirs* (New Delhi: People's Publishing House, 1984).

Robinson, Francis, 'Islam and Muslim separatism', in D. Taylor and M. Yapp (eds), *Political Identity in South Asia* (London: Curzon Press, 1979).

Roy, Asim, 'Reviews: the high politics of India's partition: the revisionist perspective', *Modern Asian Studies* 24, 2 (1990), pp. 385–415.

Sarkar, Sumit, *Modern India, 1885–1947* (New Delhi: Macmillan, 1983).

Sayeed, K.B., *Pakistan: the formative phase, 1860–1948* (Lahore, 1968).

Sen, Amartya, *Poverty and Famine: an essay on entitlement and deprivation* (Oxford: Clarendon, 1981).

Shaikh, F., *Community and Consensus in Islam: Muslim representation in colonial India, 1860–1947* (Cambridge: Cambridge University Press, 1989).

Shinde, A.B., *The Parallel Government of Satara: a phase of the Quit India movement* (New Delhi: Allied Publishers, 1990).

Singh, A. Inder, *The Origins of the Partition of India, 1936–47* (Oxford: Oxford University Press, 1987).

Singh, A. Inder, 'The Congress and the Hindu–Muslim problem, 1920–47', in D.A. Low (ed.), *The Indian National Congress* (New Delhi: Oxford University Press, 1988).

Sundarayya, Puchalapalli, *Telengana People's Armed Struggle* (Calcutta: Communist Party of India (Marxist), 1972; New Delhi: Rajendra Prasad for NBC, 1985).

Talbot, Ian A., 'The 1946 Punjab elections', *Modern Asian Studies* 14, 1 (1980), pp. 65–92.

Talbot, Ian A., 'Deserted collaborators: the political background to the rise and fall of the Punjab Unionist Party, 1923–1947', *Journal of Imperial and Commonwealth History* 11, 1 (1982), pp. 73–93.

Talbot, Ian A., *Freedom's Cry: the popular dimension in the Pakistan movement and partition experience in north-west India* (Karachi: Oxford University Press, 1996).

Tan, T.Y. and Kudaisya, G., *The Aftermath of Partition in South Asia* (London: Routledge, 2001).

Taylor, D. and Yapp, M. (eds), *Political Identity in South Asia* (London: Curzon Press, 1979).

Thirumalai, Inukonda, 'Peasant class assertions in Nalgonda and Warangal districts of Telengana, 1930–1946', *Indian Economic & Social History Review* 31, 2 (1994), pp. 217–238.

Thirumalai, Inukonda, *Against Dora and Nizam: people's movement in Telangana 1939–1948* (New Delhi: Kanishka, repr. 2003).

Tottenham, Richard, 'Congress responsibility for the disturbances', in *Indian Annual Register for 1942* (Calcutta: Annual Register Office, 1942).

Toye, H., *The Springing Tiger: a study of a revolutionary* (London: Cassell, 1959).

Vaikuntham, Y. (ed.), *People's Movement in the Princely States* (New Delhi: Manohar, 2004).

Wavell, Archibald Percival, *Wavell: the viceroy's journal*, edited by Penderel Moon (London: Oxford University Press, 1973).

Wolpert, S., *Jinnah of Pakistan* (Oxford: Oxford University Press, 1984).

11 Pakistan and Bangladesh, post-1947

Abbas, Hassan and Stern, Jessica, *Pakistan's Drift into Extremism: Allah, the army, and America's war on terror* (New York: M.E. Sharpe, 2004).

Ahmed, Akbar, *Pakistan Society: Islam, ethnicity and leadership in South Asia* (Karachi: Oxford University Press, 1986).

Ahmed, Akbar (ed.), *Pakistan: the social sciences perspective* (Karachi and Oxford: Oxford University Press, 1990).

Ahmed, Rafiuddin, *Religion, Nationalism and Politics in Bangladesh* (New Delhi: South Asian Publishers, 1990).

Ahsan, Aitaz, *The Indus Saga and the Making of Pakistan* (Karachi: Oxford University Press, 1997).

Aijazuddin, F.S., *The White House and Pakistan: secret declassified documents, 1969–1974* (Oxford: Oxford University Press, 2003).

Akbar, M.J., *India: the siege within* (New Delhi: UBS Publishers, 1996).

Akhund, Iqbal, *Trial and Error: the advent and eclipse of Benazir Bhutto* (Karachi and Oxford: Oxford University Press, 2000).

Alamgir, M., *Famine in South Asia: the political economy of mass starvation in Bangladesh* (Cambridge, Mass.: Oelgeschlager, Gunn & Hain, 1980).

Alavi, Hamza, 'The post-colonial state', in K. Gough and H.P. Sharma (eds), *Imperialism and Revolution in South Asia* (New York: Monthly Review Press, 1973).

Alavi, Hamza, 'The politics of ethnicity in India and Pakistan', in H. Alavi and J. Harriss (eds), *South Asia: the sociology of developing societies* (Basingstoke: Macmillan, 1989).

Ali, T., *Can Pakistan Survive?: the death of a state* (Harmondsworth: Penguin 1983).

Barthorp, Michael, *Afghan Wars and the North-West Frontier 1839–1947* (London: Cassell, 2002).

Baxter, Craig, *Bangladesh: from a nation to a state* (Boulder, Colo.: Westview Press, 1997).

Bhutto, Benazir, *Daughter of the East: an autobiography* (London: Hamish Hamilton, 1988).

Bhutto, Z.A., *Great Tragedy* (Karachi: Pakistani People's Party, 1971).

Bornstein, David, *The Price of a Dream: the story of the Grameen Bank* (Chicago: University of Chicago Press, 1997).

Burki, S.J., *Pakistan under Bhutto, 1971–77* (London: Macmillan, 1980).

Chakma, Saradindu Shekhar, *The Untold Story* (Dhaka: Jatiya Grantha Prakashan, 2002).

Choudhury, G.W., *Last Days of United Pakistan* (London: Hurst & Co., 1974).

Cloughley, Brian, *A History of the Pakistan Army* (Karachi: Oxford University Press, 1999).

Cohen, Stephen P., *The Idea of Pakistan* (Washington, DC: Brookings Institution Press, 2004).

Coll, Steven, *Ghost Wars: the secret history of the CIA, Afghanistan, and Bin Laden, from the Soviet invasion to September 10, 2001* (New York: Penguin Press, 2004).

Commonwealth Secretariat, *Pakistan: national and provincial assembly elections, October 2002* (London: Commonwealth Secretariat, 2004).

Cooley, John, *Unholy Wars: Afghanistan, America and international terrorism* (London: Pluto, 2002).

Crow, Ben, *Sharing the Ganges: the politics and technology of river development* (Thousand Oaks, Calif.: Sage, 1995).

Ewans, Martin, *Afghanistan: a short history of its people and politics* (New York: Perennial, 2002).

Gardner, Katy, *Global Migrants, Local Lives: travel and transformation in rural Bangladesh* (Oxford: Clarendon, 1995).

Gauhar, Altaf, *Ayub Khan: Pakistan's first military ruler* (Lahore: Sang-e-Meel, 1993).

Haqqani, Husain, *Pakistan: between mosque and military* (Washington, DC: Carnegie Endowment for International Peace, 2005).

Haque, Tatjana (ed.), *Voices of Women: a new era of political leadership in Bangladesh* (Dhaka: Asia Foundation, 2002).

Harrison, Selig S., *In Afghanistan's Shadow: Baluch nationalism and Soviet temptations* (New York: Carnegie Endowment for International Peace, 1981).

Harrison, Selig S., 'A new hub for terrorism?: in Bangladesh, an Islamic movement with Al-Qaeda ties is on the rise', *Washington Post*, 2 August 2006.

Hartman, A. and Boyce, B., *Needless Hunger: voices from a Bangladesh village* (San Francisco: Institute for Food and Development Policy, 1979).

Hymam, A., Ghayur, M. and Kaushik, N., *Pakistan: Zia and after* (London: Asia Publishing, 1988).

Jaffrelot, Christophe (ed.), *A History of Pakistan and Its Origins* (London: Anthem Press, 2004).

Jahan, Rounaq (ed.), *Bangladesh: promise and performance* (London: Zed, 2000).

Jalal, Ayesha, 'Inheriting the raj: Jinnah and the governor-generalship', *Modern Asian Studies* 19, 1 (1985), pp. 29–53.

Jalal, Ayesha, *The State of Martial Rule: Pakistan's political economy of defence* (Cambridge: Cambridge University Press, 1990).

Jalal, Ayesha, *Democracy and Authoritarianism in South Asia: a comparative and historical perspective* (Cambridge: Cambridge University Press, 1995).

Kakar, M. Hassan, *Afghanistan: the Soviet invasion and the Afghan response, 1979–1982* (Berkeley: University of California Press, 1995).

Kamtekar, Indivar, 'A different war dance: state and class in India 1939–1945', *Past & Present* 176 (2002), pp. 187–221.

Khan, Ayub, *Friends Not Masters: a political autobiography* (London: Oxford University Press, 1967).

Khan, K. (ed.), *Islam, Politics, and the State: the Pakistan experience* (London: Zed, 1985).

Khan, Roedad, *The American Papers: secret and confidential India–Pakistan–Bangladesh documents, 1965–73* (Karachi: Oxford University Press, 1999).

Kramsjo, B., Wood, G.D. and Ahmed, F., *Breaking the Chains: collective action for social justice among the rural poor of Bangladesh* (London: Intermediate Technology Publications, 1992).

Kux, Dennis, *The United States and Pakistan, 1947–2000: disenchanted allies* (Washington, DC: Woodrow Wilson Center Press, 2001).

La Porte, Robert, *Power and Privilege: influence and decision-making in Pakistan* (Berkeley: University of California Press, 1976).

Lifschultz, L., *Bangladesh: the unfinished revolution* (London: Zed, 1979).

Low, D.A. (ed.), *The Political Inheritance of Pakistan* (Basingstoke: Macmillan, 1991).

Ludden, David, 'Forgotten heroes', *Frontline* 20, 15 (19 July–1 August 2003).

Majumdar, Chandrika Basu, *Genesis of Chakma Movement in Chittagong Hill Tracts* (Kolkata: Progressive Publishers, 2003).

Malik, Iftikhar H., *State and Civil Society in Pakistan: politics of authority, ideology and ethnicity* (Basingstoke: Macmillan, 1997).

Malik, Iftikhar H., *Islam, Nationalism and the West: issues of identity in Pakistan* (Basingstoke: Macmillan, 1999).

Maniruzzaman, Talukder, *The Bangladesh Revolution and its Aftermath* (Dhaka: Bangladesh Books International, 1980).

Margolis, Eric, *War at the Top of the World: the struggle for Afghanistan, Kashmir and Tibet* (London: Routledge, 2001).

Mascarenhas, Anthony, *Bangladesh: a legacy of blood* (London: Hodder & Stoughton, 1986).

Mohsin, Amena, *The Chittagong Hill Tracts, Bangladesh: on the difficult road to peace* (Boulder, Colo.: Lynne Rienner Publishers, 2003).

Mumtaz, K. and Shaheed, F., *Women of Pakistan: two steps forward, one step back?* (London: Zed, 1987).

Murshid, T.M., *Sacred and the Secular: Bengal Muslim discourse, 1871–1977* (Calcutta: Oxford University Press, 1995).

Musharraf, Pervez, *In the Line of Fire: a memoir* (London: Simon & Schuster, 2006).

Nations, R., 'The economic structure of Pakistan and Bangladesh', in R. Blackburn (ed.), *Explosion in a Subcontinent* (London: Pelican, 1975).

Noman, Omar, *Pakistan: an economic and social history since 1947* (London: Kegan Paul, 1988).

Rahman, Tariq, *Language and Politics in Pakistan* (Karachi: Oxford University Press, repr. 2003).

Rashid, Ahmed, *Taliban: militant Islam, oil, and fundamentalism in central Asia* (New Haven, Conn.: Yale University Press, 2001).

Rashid, J. and Dardezi, H., *Pakistan, the Roots of Dictatorship: the political economy of a praetorian state* (London: Zed, 1983).

Raza, Rafi, *Zulfikar Ali Bhutto and Pakistan 1967–1977* (New Delhi: Oxford University Press, 1997).

Riaz, Ali, *God Willing: the politics of Islamism in Bangladesh* (New York: Rowman & Littlefield, 2004).

Rubin, Barnett R., *The Fragmentation of Afghanistan* (New Haven, Conn.: Yale University Press, 2002).

Rushdie, S., *Shame* (London: Penguin Books, 1984).

Samad, Yunas, *A Nation in Turmoil: nationalism and ethnicity in Pakistan, 1937–58* (New Delhi: Sage, 1995).

Samaddara, Ranabir, *Paradoxes of the Nationalist Time: political essays on Bangladesh* (Dhaka: University Press, 2002).

Sisson, Richard and Rose, L.E., *War and Secession: Pakistan, India and the creation of Bangladesh* (Berkeley: University of California Press, 1990).

Sobhan, Rahman, *The Crisis of External Dependence: the political economy of foreign aid to Bangladesh* (London: Zed, 1984).

Tahir-Kheli, Shirin and Tahir-Kheli, Shirin R., *India, Pakistan, and the United States: breaking with the past* (New York and Washington: Council on Foreign Relations Press, 1997).

Talbot, Ian, *Provincial Politics and the Pakistan Movement: the growth of the Muslim League in north-west and north-east India, 1937–1947* (Karachi: Oxford University Press, 1988).

Talbot, Ian, *Freedom's Cry: the popular dimension in the Pakistan struggle and partition experience in north-West India* (Karachi: Oxford University Press, 1996).

Talbot, Ian, *Pakistan: a modern history* (London: Hurst, 1998).

Transparency International, *Global Corruption Report 2004* (London: Pluto, 2004).

Umar, Badruddin, *The Emergence of Bangladesh: class struggles in East Pakistan, 1947–1958* (Karachi: Oxford University Press, 2004).

Van Schendel, Willem, *The Bengal Borderland: beyond state and nation in South Asia* (London: Anthem Press, 2005).

Verkaaik, Oskar, *Migrants and Militants: fun and urban violence in Pakistan* (Princeton Studies in Muslim Politics) (Princeton, N.J.: Princeton University Press, 2004).

Wahid, Abu N.M., *The Grameen Bank: poverty relief in Bangladesh* (Boulder, Colo.: Westview Press, 1983).

Waseem, Mohammad, *Politics and the State in Pakistan* (Islamabad: National Institute of Historical and Cultural Research, 1994a).

Waseem, Mohammad, *The 1993 Elections in Pakistan* (Lahore: Vanguard, 1994b).

Weaver, Mary Ann, *Pakistan: in the shadow of Jihad and Afghanistan* (New York: Farrar, Straus & Giroux, 2003).

Weiss, A.M., 'Women's position in Pakistan: sociocultural effects of Islamization', *Asian Survey* 25, 8 (1985), pp. 863–880.

White, Sarah, *Arguing with the Crocodile: gender and class in Bangladesh* (London: Zed, 1992).

Wolpert, Stanley, *Zulfi Bhutto of Pakistan: his life and times* (Oxford: Oxford University Press, 1993).

Zaman, Niaz (ed.), *Under the Krishnachura: fifty years of Bangladeshi* (Dhaka: University Press, 2003).

Ziring, Laurence, *The Ayub Khan Era: politics in Pakistan 1958–69* (Syracuse, N.Y.: Syracuse University Press, 1975).

Ziring, Laurence, *Pakistan in the 20th Century: a political history* (Oxford: Oxford University Press, 1999).

12 The Nehruvian era

Akbar, M.J., *Nehru: the making of India* (London: Viking, 1988).

Ali, Tariq, *The Nehrus and the Gandhis* (rev. edn London: Picador, 1991).

Bagchi, A.K., 'Public sector industry and quest for self-reliance in India', *Economic & Political Weekly* 17 (1982), pp. 615–628.

Bhargawa, Rajeev (ed.), *Secularism and its Critics* (New Delhi: Oxford University Press, 1998).

Brecher, Michael, *Nehru: a political biography* (Oxford: Oxford University Press, 1959).

Brown, Judith, *Nehru* (London: Longman, 1999).

Brown, Judith, *Nehru: a political life* (New Haven, Conn.: Yale University Press, 2003).

Chandra, N.K., 'Role of foreign capital in India', *Social Scientist* 5, 9 (1977), pp. 3–20.

Chatterjee, Partha, *A Possible India: essays in political criticism* (New Delhi: Oxford University Press, 1999).

Chaudhuri, A., *Private Economic Power in India: a study in genesis and concentration* (New Delhi: People's Publishing House, 1975).

Chibber, Vivek, *State-building and Late Industrialisation in India* (Princeton, N.J.: Princeton University Press, 2004).

Choudhury, Golam Wahed, *Pakistan's Relations with India, 1947–1966* (London: Pall Mall Press, 1968).

Committee on the Status of Women in India (CSWI), *Towards equality: report of the Committee on the Status of Women in India* (New Delhi: Goverment of India, Ministry of Education and Social Welfare, Department of Social Welfare, 1975).

Copland, Ian, *The Princes of India in the Endgame of Empire, 1917–1947* (Cambridge: Cambridge University Press, 1997).

Das, M.N., *The Political Philosophy of Jawaharlal Nehru* (London: Allen & Unwin, 1961).

Dey, S.K., *Power to the People?: a chronicle of India, 1947–67* (Bombay: Orient Longmans, 1969).

Dikshit, Sheila (ed.), *Jawaharlal Nehru: centenary volume* (New Delhi: Oxford University Press, 1989).

Gopal, S., *Jawaharlal Nehru: a biography*, vols 2 and 3 (London: Cape, 1979–84).

Harrison, Selig, *India: the most dangerous decades* (Madras: Oxford University Press, 1965).

Hasan, Zoya and Menon, Ritu, *Unequal Citizens: a study of Muslim women in India* (New Delhi: Oxford University Press, 2004).

Herring, Ronald J., *Land to the Tiller: the political economy of agrarian reform in South Asia* (New Haven, Conn.: Yale University Press, 1983).

International Institute for Non-aligned Studies (IINS), *35 Years of Non-aligned Movement: documents, 1961–1996* (New Delhi: IINS, 1997).

Jain, R.K., *The Kashmir Question, etc.: Soviet South Asian relations, 1947–1973* (Oxford: Martin Robertson, 1979).

Jalal, Ayesha, *Democracy and Authoritarianism in South Asia* (Cambridge: Cambridge University Press, 1995).

Jeffery, P. and Jeffery, R., *Population, Gender and Politics: demographic change in rural north India* (Cambridge: Cambridge University Press, 1997).

Khilnani, Sunil, *The Idea of India* (London: Hamish Hamilton, 1997).

King, Robert D., *Nehru and the Language Politics of India* (New Delhi: Oxford University Press, 1997).

Kochanek, S., *The Congress Party of India: the dynamics of one party democracy* (Princeton, N.J.: Princeton University Press, 1968).

Lamb, A., *Kashmir: a disputed legacy, 1846–1990* (Hertingfordbury: Roxford Books, 1991).

Madan, T.N., 'Secularism in its place', *Journal of Asian Studies* 46, 5 (1987), pp. 747–759.

Mahajan, Mehr Chand, *Looking Back: the autobiography of Mehr Chand Mahajan* (Bombay: Asia Publishing House, 1963).

Maxwell, N., *India's China War* (London: Cape, 1970).

Mende, Tibor, *Nehru: conversations on India and world affairs* (New York: G. Braziller, 1956).

Mitra, Asok, *The New India, 1948–1955: memoirs of an Indian civil servant* (Bombay: Popular Prakashan, 1991).

Mukerjee, Hiren, *The Gentle Colossus: a study of Jawaharlal Nehru* (Calcutta, 1964; repr. New Delhi: Oxford University Press, 1992).

Nanda, B.R. (ed.) *Indian Foreign Policy: the Nehru years* (New Delhi: Vikas, 1976).

Nanda, B.R., *Jawaharlal Nehru: rebel and statesman* (New Delhi: Oxford University Press, 1995).

Nehru, J., *Selected Works*, second series edited by Sarvepalli Gopal (New Delhi: Oxford University Press, 1984).

Nehru, J., *Letters to Chief Ministers, 1947–1964*, 4 vols, edited by G. Parthasarathi (New Delhi: Oxford University Press, 1985–9).

Norman, Dorothy (ed.), *Nehru: the first sixty years* (London: The Bodley Head, 1965).

Puri, Balraj, *Kashmir Towards Insurgency* (Bombay: Orient Longman, 1993).

Ramaswamy, Sumathi, *Passions of the Tongue: language devotion in Tamil India* (Berkeley: University of California Press, 1997).

Shankar, Prem, *Kashmir, 1947: rival versions of history* (New Delhi: Oxford University Press, 1996).

Shenoy, Sudha R., *India: progess or poverty? A review of the outcome of central planning in India 1951–69* (London: Institute of Economic Affairs, 1971).

Shepperdson, M. and Simmons, C. (eds), *The Indian National Congress Party and the Political Economy of India 1885–1985* (Aldershot: Avebury, 1988).

Shirokov, G.K., *Industrialisation of India* (Moscow: Progress Publishers, 1973; repr. 1980, New Delhi: People's Publishing House).

Shukul, H.C., *India's Foreign Policy: the strategy of nonalignment* (New Delhi: Chanakya, 1994).

Toye, John, *Public Expenditure and Indian Development Policy 1960–1970* (Cambridge: Cambridge University Press, 1981).

Weiner, M. and Katzenstein, M.F., *India's Preferential Policies* (Chicago: University of Chicago Press, 1981).

Zachariah, Benjamin, *Nehru* (London: Routledge, 2003).

13 Indira Gandhi: progress, poverty and authoritarian rule

Alexander, P.C., *My Years with Indira Gandhi* (New Delhi: Vision Books, 1991).

Ali, T., *The Nehrus and the Gandhis* (rev. edn London: Picador, 1991).

Bannerjee, S., *India's Simmering Revolution* (London: Zed, 1984).

Bardhan, P., *The Political Economy of Development in India* (rev. edn New Delhi: Oxford University Press, 1998).

Baxter, C., *The Jana Sangh: a biography of an Indian political party* (Philadelphia: University of Pennsylvania Press, 1969).

Bayliss-Smith, T.B. and Wanmali, S. (eds), *Understanding Green Revolutions* (Cambridge: Cambridge University Press, 1984).

Brecher, Michael, *Succession in India: a study in decision-making* (Oxford: Oxford University Press, 1966).

Byres, T.J., 'The new technology, class formation, and class action in the Indian countryside', *Journal of Peasant Studies* 8, 4 (1981), pp. 405–454.

Byres, T.J., 'Charan Singh: an assessment', *Journal of Peasant Studies* 15, 2 (1988), pp. 139–189.

Byres, T.J. and Crow, Ben, *The Green Revolution in India* (Milton Keynes: Open University Press, 1983).

Damodaran, A.K. and Bajpai, U.S. (eds), *Indian Foreign Policy: the Indira Gandhi years* (London: Sangam, 1990).

Dandekar, V.M., *Indian Economy, 1947–92*. Vol. 1: *Agriculture* (New Delhi: Oxford University Press, 1994).

Dhar, A.N., *Indira Gandhi, the 'Emergency', and Indian Democracy* (New York: Oxford University Press, 2000).

Etienne, G., *Rural Development in Asia: meetings with peasants* (New Delhi: Sage, 1985).

Franda, M., *Radical Politics in West Bengal* (Cambridge, Mass.: MIT Press, 1971).

Frank, Katherine, *Indira Gandhi: the life of Indira Nehru Gandhi* (London: HarperCollins, 2001).

Frankel, F., *India's Green Revolution* (Princeton, N.J.: Princeton University Press, 1971).

Ghosh, Jayati, 'Development stategy in India: a political-economic perspective', in S. Bose and A. Jalal (eds), *Nationalism, Democracy and Development* (New Delhi: Oxford University Press, 1997).

Glaeser, Bernhard (ed.), *The Green Revolution Revisited: critique and alternatives* (London: Allen & Unwin 1987).

Graham, B.D., *Hindu Nationalism and Indian Politics: the origins and development of the Bharatiya Jana Sangh* (Cambridge: Cambridge University Press, 1990).

Herring, R.J., *'Land to the Tiller': the political economy of agrarian reform in South Asia* (London: Yale University Press, 1983).

Jayakar, P., *Indira Gandhi: a biography* (New Delhi: Viking, 1992).

Jeffery, R. and Jeffery, P., *Confronting Saffron Demography: religion, fertility, and women's status in India* (New Delhi: Three Essays Collective, 2006).

Masani, Z., *Indira Gandhi* (London: Hamish Hamilton, 1975).

Mehta, Ved, *A Family Affair* (New Delhi: Oxford University Press, 1983).

Mitra, Ashok, *Calcutta Diary* (London: Cassell, 1977).

Moraes, Dom, *Mrs. Gandhi* (London: Cape, 1980).

Narayan, Jayaprakash, *Swaraj for the people* (Varanasi: Sarva Seva Sangh Prakashan, 1963).

Nayar, K., *The Judgement: inside story of the emergency in India* (New Delhi: Vikas, 1977).

Ray, R., *The Naxalites and their Ideology* (New Delhi: Oxford University Press, 1988).

Selbourne, D., *An Eye to India: the unmasking of a tyranny* (Harmondsworth: Penguin, 1977).

Sen, E., *Indira Gandhi: a biography* (London: Owen, 1973).

Sharma, Rita and Poleman, Thomas, *The New Economics of India's Green Revolution* (Ithaca, N.Y.: Cornell University Press, 1993).

Tarlo, Emma, *Unsettling Memories: narratives of the 'emergency' in Delhi* (Berkeley: University of California Press, 2001).

Tully, Mark and Satish, Jacob, *Amritsar: Mrs Gandhi's last battle* (Calcutta: Rupa, 1985).

14 Local patriotism and centre–state relations

Akbar, M.J., *Riot after Riot: caste and communal violence in India* (Harmondsworth: Penguin, 1988).

Akbar, M.J., *India: the siege within* (rev. edn New Delhi: UBS Publisher's Distributors, 1996).

Akbar, M.J., *Kashmir: behind the veil* (New Delhi: Roli, 2002).

Ali, S. Mahmud, *The Fearful State: power, people, and internal war in South Asia* (London: Zed, 1993).

Anderson, R.S. and Huber, W., *The Hour of the Fox: tropical forests, the World Bank, and indigenous people in Central India* (Seattle: University of Washington Press, 1988).

Bardhan, P., *The Political Economy of Development in India* (rev. edn New Delhi: Oxford University Press, 1998).

Bardhan, P. and Srinivasan, T.N. (eds), *Rural Poverty in South Asia* (New York: Columbia University Press, 1988).

Baruah, Sanjib, *India Against Itself: Assam and the politics of nationality* (Princeton, N.J.: Princeton University Press, 1999).

Baruah, Sanjib, *Durable Disorder: understanding the politics of northeast India* (New Delhi: Oxford University Press, 2005).

Basu, Amrit and Kohli, Atul (eds), *Community Conflicts and the State in India* (New Delhi: Oxford University Press, 1998).

Bates, Crispin and Basu, Subho (eds), *Rethinking Indian Political Institutions* (London: Anthem, 2005).

Baxi, Upendra and Parekh, Bikhu (eds), *Crisis and Change in Contemporary India* (New Delhi: Sage, 1995).

Béteille, André, *Society and Politics in India: essays in a comparative perspective* (London: Athlone Press, 1991a).

Béteille, André, 'The reproduction of inequality: occupation, caste and family', *Contributions to Indian Sociology* 25, 1 (1991b), pp. 3–28.

Bhagwati, Jagdish N., *India in Transition: freeing the economy* (Oxford: Clarendon, 1993).

Bhattacharjea, A., *Kashmir: the wounded valley* (New Delhi: UBS Publisher's Distributors, 1994).

Bose, Sugata (ed.), *South Asia and World Capitalism* (New Delhi: Oxford University Press, 1990).

Bose, Sumantra, *Kashmir: roots of conflict, paths to peace* (Cambridge, Mass.: Harvard University Press, 2003).

Brass, Paul, 'The Punjab crisis and the unity of India', in Atul Kohli (ed.), *India's Democracy* (Princeton, N.J.: Princeton University Press, 1988).

Brass, Paul, *Ethnicity and Nationalism: theory and comparison* (New Delhi and London: Sage, 1991).

Brass, Paul, *The Politics of India Since Independence* (New Cambridge History of India) 2nd edn (Cambridge: Cambridge University Press, 1994).

Byres, T.J. and Crow, Ben, *The Green Revolution in India* (Milton Keynes: Open University Press, 1983).

Calman, Leslie J., *Protest in Democratic India: authority's response to challenge* (Boulder, Colo.: Westview Press, 1985).

Corbridge, Stuart, 'The ideology of tribal economy and society: politics in the Jharkhand, 1950–1980', *Modern Asian Studies* 22, 1 (1988), pp. 1–42.

Desai, M., 'India: emerging contradictions of a slow economic development', in R. Blackburn (ed.), *Explosion in a Subcontinent* (Harmondsworth: Penguin/New Left Review, 1975).

Devalle, S., *Discourses of Ethnicity: culture and protest in Jharkhand* (New Delhi: Sage, 1992).

Drèze, Jean and Sen, Amartya, *India: economic development and social opportunity* (New Delhi: Oxford University Press 1995).

Duyker, E., *Tribal Guerrillas: the Santals of west Bengal and the Naxalite movement* (New Delhi: Oxford University Press, 1987).

Engineer, A.A., *Secular Crown on Fire: the Kashmir problem* (New Delhi: Ajanta, 1991).

Fox, R.G., *Lions of the Punjab: the Sikhs and British India's culture in the making* (Berkeley: University of California Press, 1985).

Frankel, F.R. and Rao, M.S.A. (eds), *Dominance and State Power in Modern India*, vols 1 and 2 (New Delhi: Oxford University Press, 1989–90).

Gadgil, M. and Guha, R., 'Ecological conflicts and the environmental movement in India', *Development and Change* 25, 1 (1994), pp. 101–136.

Galanter, Marc, *Competing Equalities: law and the backward classes in India* (Berkeley: University of California Press, 1984).

Ganguly, Sumit, *Conflict Unending: India–Pakistan relations since 1947* (New York: Columbia University Press, 2002).

Ganguly, Sumit and Hamilton, Lee H. (eds), *The Crisis in Kashmir: portents of war, hopes of peace* (Cambridge: Cambridge University Press, 1999).

Guha, Ramchandra, 'Chipko: social history of an environmental movement', in R. Guha, *The Unquiet Woods: ecological change and peasant resistance in the Himalaya* (Oxford: Oxford University Press, 1989).

Gupta, Dipankar, *Nativism in a Metropolis: the Shiv Sena in Bombay* (New Delhi: Manohar, 1982).

Hansen, Thomas Blom, 'The vernacularisation of Hindutva: the BJP and Shiv Sena in rural Maharashta', *Contributions to Indian Sociology* 30, 2 (1996), pp. 177–214.

Hansen, Thomas Blom, *The Saffron Wave: democracy and Hindu nationalism in modern India* (Princeton, N.J.: Princeton University Press, 1999).

Hansen, Thomas Blom, *Wages of Violence: naming and identity in postcolonial Bombay* (Princeton, N.J.: Princeton University Press, 2001).

Hardgrave, R.L., *India Under Pressure* (Epping: Bowker, 1984).

Harihar, Bhattacharya, *Communism in Tripura* (New Delhi: Ajanta Publishers, 1999).

Harris, John, 'What is happening in rural west Bengal?: Agrarian reform, growth and distribution', *Economic and Political Weekly* 28 (1993), pp. 1237–1247.

Hasan, Zoya, *Quest for Power: oppositional movements and post-Congress politics in Uttar Pradesh* (New Delhi: Oxford University Press, 1998).

Hewitt, Vernon, *Reclaiming the Past?: the search for political and cultural unity in contemporary Jammu and Kashmir* (Manchester: Manchester University Press, 1997).

Jeffery, R., *What's Happening to India?: Punjab, ethnic conflict, Mrs. Gandhi's death and the test for federalism* (Basingstoke: Macmillan, 1986).

Kapur, R.A., *Sikh Separatism: the politics of faith* (London: Allen & Unwin, 1986).

Karlekar, Hiranmay, *In the Mirror of Mandal: social justice, caste, class and the individual* (New Delhi: Ajanta Publications, 1992).

Katzenstein, Mary F., *Ethnicity and Equality: the Shiv Sena Party and preferential politics in Bombay* (Ithaca, N.Y.: Cornell University Press, 1979).

Kochanek, S., *The Congress Party of India: the dynamics of one party democracy* (Princeton, N.J.: Princeton University Press, 1968).

Kohli, Atul, *The State and Poverty in India* (Cambridge: Cambridge University Press, 1987).

Kohli, Atul (ed.), *India's Democracy: an analysis of changing state–society relations* (Princeton, N.J.: Princeton University Press, 1988).

Kohli, Atul, 'From elite activism to democratic consolidation: the rise of reform communism in west Bengal', in F. Frankel and M.S.A. Rao (eds), *Dominance and State Power in India*, vol. 2 (Oxford: Oxford University Press, 1989).

Kohli, Atul, *Democracy and Discontent: India's growing crisis of governability* (Cambridge: Cambridge University Press, 1990).

Kumar Singh, Ujimal, *Political Prisoners in India* (New Delhi: Oxford University Press, 1998).

Lamb, A., *Kashmir: a disputed legacy, 1846–1990* (Hertingfordbury: Roxford Books, 1991).

Leaf, M., 'The Punjab crisis', *Asian Survey* 25, 5 (1985), pp. 475–498.

Ludden, David (ed.), *Contesting the Nation: religion, community, and the politics of democracy in India* (Philadelphia: University of Pennsylvania Press, 1996).

Mahmood, Cynthia Keppley, *Fighting for Faith and Nation: dialogues with Sikh militants* (Philadelphia: Pennsylvania University Press, 1997).

Malik, Yogendra K., 'The Akali Party and Sikh militancy: move for greater autonomy or secessionism in Punjab?', *Asian Survey* 26, 3 (1986), pp. 345–362.

Mallick, Ross, 'Agrarian reform in west Bengal: the end of an illusion?', *World Development* 20, 5 (1992), pp. 735–750.

Mallick, Ross, *Indian Communism: opposition, collaboration, and institutionalization* (New Delhi: Oxford University Press, 1994).

Marwah, Ved, *Uncivil Wars: pathology of terrorism in India* (New Delhi: Indus, 1995).

Mawdsley, Emma Elizabeth, 'Non-secessionist regionalism in India: the demand for a separate state of Uttarakhand', Unpublished Ph.D. dissertation, University of Cambridge, July 1997.

Mukarji, Nirmal and Arora, Balveer (eds), *Federalism in India: origins and development* (New Delhi: Vikas, 1992).

Nag, Chitta Ranjan, *Post-colonial Mizo Politics, 1947–1998* (New Delhi: Vikas, 1999).

Nossiter, Tom, *Communism in Kerala* (London: Hurst, 1982).

Nossiter, Tom, *Marxist State Governments in India* (London: Pinter, 1988).

O'Connell, J.T. (ed.), *Sikh History and Religion in the 20th Century* (Toronto: University of Toronto Centre for South Asian Studies, 1988).

Pettigrew, Joyce, *The Sikhs of the Punjab: unheard voices of state and guerilla violence* (London: Zed, 1995).

Purandare, Vaibhav, *The Sena Story* (Mumbai: Business Publications, 1999).

Rothermund, D. (ed.), *Liberalising India: progress and problems* (New Delhi: Manohar, 1996).

Rudolph, L.I. and Rudolph, S.H., 'Determinants and varieties of agrarian mobilisation', in M. Desai *et al.* (eds), *Agrarian Power and Agricultural Productivity in South Asia* (Berkeley: University of California Press, 1984).

Saberwal, S., *India: the roots of crisis* (New Delhi: Oxford University Press, 1986).

Saez, Lawrence, *Federalism Without a Centre: The Impact of Political and Economic Reform on India's Federal System* (New Delhi and London: Sage, 2002).

Samanta, Amiya K., *Gorkhaland: a study in ethnic separatism* (New Delhi: Khama, 1996).

Sathyamurthy, T.V., *India since Independence: studies in the development of the power of the Indian state*. Vol. 1: *Centre–State Relations* (New Delhi: Ajanta Publications, 1985).

Sathyamurthy, T.V., *Social Change and Political Discourse in India: structures of power, movements of resistance*. Vol. 3: *Region, Religion, Caste and Gender in Contemporary India* (New Delhi: Oxford University Press, 1996).

Schofield, Victoria, *Kashmir in Conflict: India, Pakistan and the unending war*, 2nd rev. edn (London: I.B. Tauris and Company, 2002).

Sen, Amartya, 'How is India doing?', in Iqbar Khan (ed.), *Fresh Perspectives on India and Pakistan* (Oxford: Bougainvillea Books, 1985).

Sengupta, N. (ed.), *Fourth World Dynamics: Jharkhand* (New Delhi: Authors Guild, 1982).

Shankar, Prem, *Kashmir, 1947: rival versions of history* (New Delhi: Oxford University Press, 1996).

Shiva, Vandana, *The Violence of the Green Revolution: ecological degradation and political conflict in Punjab* (Dehra Dun: Research Inst. for Science and Ecology, 1989).

Singh, K.S. (ed.), *Tribal Movements in India*, vols I and II (New Delhi: Manohar, 1982).

Singh, K.S., *Tribal Society in India: an anthropo-historical perspective* (New Delhi: Manohar, 1985).

Subba, Tanka Bahadur, *Ethnicity, State and Development: a case study of the Gorkhaland movement in Darjeeling* (New Delhi: Har-Anand in association with Vikas, 1992).

Sundar, Nandini, *Subalterns and Sovereigns: an anthropological history of Bastar, 1854–1996* (New Delhi: Oxford University Press, 1997).

Thakur, Sankarshan, *The Making of Laloo Yadav: the unmaking of Bihar* (New Delhi: HarperCollins, 2000).

Tully, M. and Jacob, S., *Amritsar: Mrs Gandhi's last battle* (Calcutta: Rupa, 1985).

Vanaik, Achin, *The Painful Transition: bourgeois democracy in India* (London: Verso, 1990).

Vanaik, Achin, *The Furies of Indian Communalism: religion, modernity, and secularization* (London: Verso, 1997).

Wallace, Paul, 'The Sikhs as a "minority" in a Sikh majority state in India', *Asian Survey* 26, 3 (1986), pp. 363–377.

Wallace, Paul, 'Sikh minority attitudes in India's federal system', in J.T. O'Connell (ed.), *Sikh History and Religion in the 20th Century* (Toronto: University of Toronto Centre for South Asian Studies, 1988).

Wallace, Paul, 'Religious and ethnic politics: political mobilization in Punjab', in Francine Frankel and M.S.A. Rao (eds), *Dominance and State Power in Modern India*, vol. 2 (New Delhi: Oxford University Press, 1990).

Washbrook, David, 'Caste, class and dominance in modern Tamil Nadu', in Francine Frankel and M.S.A. Rao (eds), *Dominance and State Power in Modern India*, vol. 1 (New Delhi: Oxford University Press, 1989).

Weber, Thomas, *Hugging the Trees: the story of the Chipko movement* (New Delhi: Viking, 1985).

Weiner, Myron, *Sons of the Soil* (New Delhi: Oxford University Press, 1988).

Weiner, Myron and Katzenstein, M.F., *India's Preferential Policies* (Chicago: University of Chicago Press, 1981).

Wirsing, Robert G., *India, Pakistan, and the Kashmir Dispute: on regional conflict and its resolution* (New York: St Martins Press, 1994).

Zutshi, Chitralekha, *Languages of Belonging: Islam, regional identity, and the making of Kashmir* (New Delhi: Permanent Black, 2003).

15 Rajiv Gandhi and the demise of the congress system

Ahluwalia, I.J. and Little, I.M.D. (eds), *India's Economic Reforms and Development: essays for Manmohan Singh* (New Delhi: Oxford University Press, 1998).

Allen, Douglas (ed.), *Religion and Political Conflict in South Asia, India, Pakistan and Sri Lanka* (Westport, Conn.: Greenwood Press, 1992).

Anderson, R. and Damle, S., *The Brotherhood in Saffron: the RSS and Hindu revivalism* (Boulder, Colo. and London: Westview Press, 1987).

Arif, K.M., *Khaki Shadows: Pakistan 1947–1997* (Karachi: Oxford University Press, 2001).

Basu, Tapan *et al.*, *Kakhi Shorts and Saffron Flags: a critique of the Hindu right* (New Delhi: Orient Longman, 1993).

Bates, Crispin, 'The development of panchayati raj in India', in C. Bates and S. Basu (eds), *Rethinking Indian Political Institutions* (London: Anthem Press, 2002).

Béteille, André, 'The politics of "non-antagonistic" strata', and 'The future of the backward classes', in A. Béteille, *Society and Politics in India* (London: Athlone Press, 1992).

Bhagwati, Jagdish, *India in Transition: freeing the economy* (Oxford: Clarendon, 1993).

Bhargava, Rajeev (ed.), *Secularism and its Critics* (New Delhi: Oxford University Press, 1998).

Bidwai, Praful, Mukhia, Harbans and Vanaik, Achin (eds), *Religion, Religiosity, and Communalism* (New Delhi: Manohar, 1996).

Bilgrami, A., 'What is a Muslim?: fundamentalist commitment and cultural identity', in G. Pandey (ed.), *Hindus and Others* (New Delhi: Penguin, 1993).

Breman, J., *Patronage and Exploitation* (Berkeley: University of California Press, 1974).

Breman, J., *Of Peasants, Migrants and Paupers* (New Delhi: Oxford University Press, 1985).

Bullion, Alan J., *India, Sri Lanka and the Tamil Crisis, 1976–1994: an international perspective* (London: Pinter, 1995).

Burman, B.K. Roy, *Beyond Mandal and After: backward classes in perspective* (New Delhi: Mittal, 1992).

Cassen, R. and Vijay, Joshi, *India: the future of economic reform* (New Delhi: Oxford University Press, 1995).

Chakravarti, Uma and Haksar, Nandita, *The Delhi Riots: three days in the life of a nation* (New Delhi: Lancer International, 1987).

Chhachhi, Amrita, 'Forced identities: the state, communalism, fundamentalism and women in India', in D. Kandiyoti (ed.), *Women, Islam and the State* (Philadelphia: Temple University Press, 1991).

Das, Veena (ed.), *Mirrors of Violence: communities, riots and survivors in South Asia* (New Delhi: Oxford University Press, 1990).

Elst, Koenraad, *Ram Janmabhoomi vs. Babri Masjid* (New Delhi: Voice of India, 1990).

Engineer, A.A., *Communal Riots in Post-Independence India* (Hyderabad: Sangam Books, 1984).

Engineer, A.A., *The Shah Bano Controversy* (Hyderabad: Orient Longman, 1987).

Engineer, A.A., *Communalism and Communal Violence in India: an analytical approach to Hindu–Muslim conflict* (New Delhi: Ajanta Publications, 1989), intro.

Engineer, A.A., *Mandal Commission Controversy* (New Delhi: Ajanta Publications, 1991).

Forbes, Geraldine, *Women in Modern India* (Cambridge: Cambridge University Press, 1996).

Galanter, M., 'Pursuing equality in the land of hierarchy', in M. Galanter, *Law and Society in Modern India* (New Delhi: Oxford University Press, 1991).

Gandhi, Nandita, 'Impact of religion on women's rights in Asia', *Economic and Political Weekly* 23, 4 (1988), pp. 127–129.

Gandhi, Nandita, *When the Rolling Pins Hit the Streets* (London: Zed, 1996).

George, Rosen, *Contrasting Styles of Industrial Reform: China and India in the 1980s* (Chicago: Chicago University Press, 1992).

Gopal, Sarvepalli *et al.* (eds), *Anatomy of a Confrontation: Ayodhya and the rise of communal politics in India* (a.k.a. *Anatomy of a Confrontation: the Babri Masjid–Ram Janmabhumi issue*) (Harmondsworth: Penguin, 1991).

Gupta, Bhabani Sen, *Rajiv Gandhi: a political study* (New Delhi: Konark Publishers, 1989).

Gupte, Pranay, *Vengeance: India after the assassination of Indira Gandhi* (New York: W.W. Norton & Co. Ltd, 1985).

Hansen, Thomas Blom, *The Saffron Wave: democracy and Hindu nationalism in modern India* (Princeton, N.J.: Princeton University Press, 1999).

Hansen, Thomas Blom and Jaffrelot, Christophe (eds), *The BJP and the Compulsions of Politics in India* (New Delhi: Oxford University Press, 1998).

Hasan, Zoya, 'Minority identity, Muslim Women Bill campaign and the political process', *Economic and Political Weekly* 24, 1 (1989), pp. 44–50.

Hasan, Zoya, *Quest for Power: oppositional movements and post-Congress politics in Uttar Pradesh* (New Delhi: Oxford University Press, 1998).

Jaffrelot, Christophe, *India's Silent Revolution: the rise of the lower castes* (London: C. Hurst, 1999).

Jain, P.C. (ed.), *Indian Economic Crisis: diagnosis and treatment* (New Delhi: Concept, 1992).

Jain, Sharada *et al.*, 'Deorala episode: women's protest in Rajasthan', *Economic and Political Weekly* 22, 45 (1987), pp. 1891–1893.

Jalan, Bimal, *India's Economic Crisis: the way ahead* (New Delhi: Oxford University Press, 1991).

Karlekar, Hiranmay, *In the Mirror of Mandal: social justice, caste, class, and the individual* (New Delhi: Ajanta Publications, 1992).

Katju, Manjari, *Vishwa Hindu Parishad and Indian Politics* (New Delhi: Orient Longman, 2003).

Kochanek, Stanley A., 'Regulation and liberalization theology in India', *Asian Survey* 26, 12 (1986), pp. 1284–1308.

Koenraad, Elst, *Ram Janmabhoomi vs. Babri Masjid: a case study in Hindu–Muslim conflict* (New Delhi: Voice of India, 1990).

Kothari, Smitu and Sethi, Harsh (eds), *Voices from a Scarred City: the Delhi carnage in perspective* (New Delhi: Lokayan, 1985).

Lapierre, Dominique and Moro, Javier, *It was Five Past Midnight in Bhopal*, translated from the French by Kathryn Spink (New Delhi: Full Circle Publishers, 2001).

Lewis, John P., *India's Political Economy: governance and reform* (New Delhi: Oxford University Press, 1995).

Linnemann, H. and Hanumantha Rao, C.H. (eds), *Economic Reforms and Poverty Alleviation in India* (New Delhi: Sage, 1996).

Llewellyn, J.E., *Legacy of Women's Uplift in India: contemporary women leaders in the Arya Samaj* (New Delhi and Thousand Oaks, Calif.: Sage, 1998).

Lucas, R. and Papanek, G. (eds), *The Indian Economy: recent development and future prospects* (Boulder, Colo.: Westview Press, 1988).

Ludden, David, *Contesting the Nation: religion, community, and the politics of democracy in India* (Philadelphia: University of Pennsylvania Press, 1996).

Ludden, David (ed.), *Making India Hindu: religion, community, and the politics of democracy in India* (New Delhi: Oxford University Press, 1999).

Madan, T.N., *Modern Myths, Locked Minds: secularism and fundamentalism in India* (New Delhi: Oxford University Press, 1998a).

Madan, T.N., 'Secularism in its place', *Journal of Asian Studies* 46, 4 (1987), pp. 747–759; also in R. Bhargava (ed.), *Secularism and its Critics* (New Delhi: Oxford University Press, 1998b).

Malik, Yogendra K. and Singh, V.B., *Hindu Nationalists in India: the rise of the Bharatiya Janata Party* (Boulder, Colo.: Westview Press, 1994).

Mehta, V., *Rajiv Gandhi and Rama's Kingdom* (New Haven, Conn.: Yale University Press, 1994).

Mendelsohn, O. and Vicziany, M., *The Untouchables* (Cambridge: Cambridge University Press, 1998).

Morris-Jones, W.H., *The Government and Politics of India*, 3rd edn (London and New York: Hutchinson, 1971).

Mukhopadhyay, Nilanjan, *The Demolition: India at the crossroads* (New Delhi: Indus, 1994).

Nandy, Ashish, *Creating a Nationality: the Ramjanmabhoomi movement and fear of the self* (New Delhi: Oxford University Press, 1995).

Nandy, Ashish, 'Sati in *Kali Yuga*: the public debate on Roop Kanwar's death', in *Return from Exile* (New Delhi: Oxford University Press, 2005), pp. 32–52.

Nugent, N., *Rajiv Gandhi: son of a dynasty* (London: BBC Books, 1990).

Omvedt, Gail, 'Twice born riot against democracy', *Economic and Political Weekly* 25, 39 (1990), pp. 2195–2201.

Omvedt, Gail, *Dalit Visions: the anti-caste movement and the construction of an Indian identity* (New Delhi: Orient Longman, 1995).

Oza, B.M., *Bofors, the Ambassador's Evidence* (New Delhi: Konark Publishers, 1997).

Pandey, Gyanendra (ed.), *Hindus and Others: the question of identity in India today* (New Delhi: Viking, 1993).

Patel, Sujata and Kumar, Krishna, 'Defenders of sati', *Economic and Political Weekly* 23, 4 (1988), pp. 129–130.

Pathak, Zoya and Rajan, R.S., 'Shahbano', *Signs* 14, 3 (1989), pp. 558–582.

People's Union for Democratic Rights/People's Union for Civil Liberties, *Who Are The Guilty?: Report of a joint enquiry into the causes and impact of the riots in Delhi from 31 October to 10 November* (New Delhi, 1984).

Qadeer, Imrana and Hasan, Zora, 'Deadly politics of the state and its apologists', *Economic and Political Weekly* 22, 46 (1987), pp. 1946–1949.

Rajagopal, Arvind, *Politics after Television: Hindu nationalism and the reshaping of the public in India* (Cambridge: Cambridge University Press, 2001).

Rose, Kalima, *Where Women are Leaders: the SEWA movement in India* (London: Zed, 1992).

Rosen, George, *Contrasting Styles of Industrial Reform: China and India in the 1980s* (Chicago: University of Chicago Press, 1992).

Rothermund, D., *Liberalising India: progress and problems* (New Delhi: Manohar, 1996).

Sanjay, Srivastava, *Constructing Post-colonial India: national character and the Doon School* (New York: Routledge, 1998).

Shrivastava, P., *Bhopal: anatomy of a crisis* (Cambridge, Mass.: Ballinger, 1987).

Statesman, Calcutta, *Bofors, the Unfinished Story* (Calcutta: Statesman, 1989).

Tambiah, S.J., *Levelling Crowds: ethnonationalist conflicts and collective violence in South Asia* (Berkeley: University of California Press, 1996).

Thapar, Romila, 'Imagined religious communities?: Ancient history and the modern search for a Hindu identity', *Modern Asian Studies* 23, 2 (1989), pp. 209–239.

Tully, M. and Masani, Z., *From Raj to Rajiv* (London: British Broadcasting Corporation, 1988).

Vaidyanathan, A., *Indian Economy: crisis, response and prospects* (New Delhi: Orient Longman 1995).

Van Dyke, Virginia, 'The anti-Sikh riots of 1984 in Delhi: politicians, criminals and the discourse of communalism', in P. Brass (ed.), *Riots and Pogroms* (Basingstoke: Macmillan, 1996).

Vanaik, Achin, 'Rajiv's Congress in search of stability', *New Left Review* 154 (1985), pp. 55–82.

Vanaik, Achin, *The Furies of Indian Communalism: religion, modernity, and secularization* (London: Verso, 1997).

Van der Veer, Peter, *Religious Nationalism: Hindus and Muslims in India* (Berkeley: University of California Press, 1984).

Van der Veer, Peter, ' "God must be liberated!": a Hindu liberation movement in Ayodhya', *Modern Asian Studies* 21, 2 (1987), pp. 283–301.

16 Colonial and post-colonial Sri Lanka: the dilemmas of national identity

Ames, Michael M., 'Magical-animism and Buddhism: a structural analysis of the Sinhalese religious system', *Journal of Asian Studies* 23, 'Aspects of Religion in South Asia' (1964), pp. 21–52.

Bates, Crispin, 'Introduction', in C. Bates (ed.), *Community, Empire and Migration: South Asians in diaspora* (Basingstoke: Macmillan, 2001).

Dharmadasa, K.N.O., *Language, Religion, and Ethnic Assertiveness: the growth of Sinhalese nationalism in Sri Lanka* (Ann Arbor: University of Michigan Press, 1992).

Gombrich, Richard, *Theravada Buddhism: a social history from ancient Benares to modern Colombo* (London: Routledge, 1991)

Gombrich, Richard and Obeyesekere, Gananath, *Buddhism Transformed: religious change in Sri Lanka* (Princeton, N.J.: Princeton University Press, 1988).

Ismail, Qadri, 'Constituting nation. Contesting nationalism: the southern Tamil (woman) and separatist Tamil nationalism in Sri Lanka', in P. Chatterjee and P. Jeganathan (eds), *Subaltern Studies XI: community, gender and violence* (New Delhi: Ravi Dayal, 2000).

Jayawardena, Kumari, *The Origins of the Left Movement in Sri Lanka* (Colombo: Sanjiva Books, 1980).

Jayawardena, Kumari, *Ethnic and Class Conflict in Sri Lanka: the emergence of Sinhala Buddhist consciousness 1883–1983* (Colombo: Sanjiva Books, 1985).

Jayawardena, Kumari, *Nobodies to Somebodies: the rise of the colonial bourgeoisie in Sri Lanka* (London: Zed, 2002).

Kannangara, A.P., *The Riots of 1915 in Sri Lanka: a study in the roots of communal violence* (Oxford: Past and Present Society, 1984).

Kemper, Steven, *The Presence of the Past: chronicles, politics, and culture in Sinhala life* (Ithaca, N.Y.: Cornell University Press, 1991).

Manor, James, 'The failure of political integration in Sri Lanka', *Journal of Commonwealth and Comparative Politics* 17 (1976), pp. 21–46.

Manor, James (ed.), *Sri Lanka in Change and Crisis* (London: Croom Helm, 1984).

Manor, James, *The Expedient Utopian: Bandranaike and Ceylon* (Cambridge: Cambridge University Press, 1989).

Meyer, E., 'Seeking the roots of the tragedy', in J. Manor (ed.), *Sri Lanka in Change and Crisis* (London: Croom Helm, 1984).

Moore, Mick, 'Thoroughly modern revolutionaries: the JVP in Sri Lanka', *Modern Asian Studies* 27, 3 (1993), pp. 593–542.

Narayan Swamy, M.R., *Tigers of Lanka: from boys to guerillas* (New Delhi: Konark Publishers, 1994).

Nissan, Elizabeth, *Sri Lanka: a bitter harvest* (London: Minority Rights Group, 1996).

Obeyesekere, Gananath, 'The great tradition and the little tradition in the perspective of Sinhalese Buddhism', *Journal of Asian Studies* 22, 2 (1963), pp. 139–153.

Obeyesekere, Gananath, 'The origins and institutionalisation of political violence', in J. Manor (ed.), *Sri Lanka in Change and Crisis* (London: Croom Helm, 1984).

Peebles, Patrick, *The Plantation Tamils of Ceylon* (London: Continuum International Publishing Group/Leicester University Press, 2001).

Ram, Mohan, *Sri Lanka: the fractured island* (New Delhi: Penguin, 1989).

Roberts, Michael, *Exploring Confrontation. Sri Lanka: politics, culture and history* (Chur, Switzerland: Harwood Academic Publishers, 1994).

Roberts, Michael, *Burden of History: obstacles to power sharing in Sri Lanka – a history of ethnic conflict in Sri Lanka: recollection, reinterpretation and reconciliation* (Colombo: Marga Institute, 2001).

Seneviratne, H.L., *The Work of Kings: the new Buddhism in Sri Lanka* (Chicago: Chicago University Press, 1999).

De Silva, K.M., *A History of Sri Lanka* (London: Hurst, 1981).

De Silva, K.M., *Sri Lanka*. Part 1: *The Second World War and the Soulbury Commission, 1939–1945.* Part 2: *Towards Independence, 1945–1948.* British documents on the end of empire, series B, vol. 2 (London: Stationery Office, 1997).

De Silva, K.M., *Reaping the Whirlwind: ethnic conflict, ethnic politics in Sri Lanka* (New Delhi: Penguin, 1998).

De Silva, K.M. and Wriggins, Howard, *J.R. Jayewardene of Sri Lanka: a political biography* (London: Anthony Bland, 1988).

Spencer, Jonathan, *A Sinhala Village in a Time of Trouble: politics and change in rural Sri Lanka* (New Delhi: Oxford University Press, 1990a).

Spencer, Jonathan (ed.), *Sri Lanka: history and the roots of conflict* (London: Routledge, 1990b).

Tambiah, S.J., *Sri Lanka: ethnic fratricide and the dismantling of democracy* (Chicago: Chicago University Press, 1986).

Tambiah, S.J., *Buddhism Betrayed? Religion, politics and violence in rural Sri Lanka* (Chicago: Chicago University Press, 1992).

Tambiah, S.J., *Leveling Crowds: ethnonationalist conflicts and collective violence in South Asia* (New Delhi: Vistaar, 1997).

Thornton, E. and Niththyananthan, R., *Island of Terror: an indictment* (London: Eelam Research Organisation, 1984).

Wickramasinghe, N., *Ethnic Politics in Colonial Sri Lanka* (New Delhi: Vikas, 1995).

Wickramasinghe, N., 'Migration, migrant communities and otherness in twentieth century Sinhala nationalism in Sri Lanka', in C. Bates (ed.), *Community, Empire and Migration* (Basingstoke: Macmillan, 2001).

Wickramasinghe, N., *Sri Lanka in the Modern Age: a history of contested identities* (London: Hurst, 2005).

Wilson, A.J., *Politics in Sri Lanka, 1947–1979* (London: Macmillan, 1979).

Wilson, A.J., *The Break-up of Sri Lanka: the Sinhalese–Tamil conflict* (London: Hurst, 1988).

Wilson, A.J., *Sri Lankan Tamil Nationalism: its origins and development in the nineteenth and twentieth centuries* (London: Hurst, 2000).

17 Neo-nationalism and the challenge of democracy

Abraham, Itty, *The Making of the Indian Atomic Bomb: science, secrecy and the postcolonial state* (London: Zed, 1998).

Akbar, M.J., *Kargil: cross border terrorism* (New Delhi: Mittal Publications, 1999).

Austin, Granville, *The Indian Constitution: cornerstone of a nation* (New Delhi: Oxford University Press, 1999).

Bates, Crispin and Basu, Subho (eds), *Rethinking Indian Political Institutions* (London: Anthem Press, 2005).

Bose, Sumantra, *Kashmir: roots of conflict, paths to peace* (Cambridge, Mass.: Harvard University Press, 2003).

Chakraborty, A.K., *Kargil: inside story* (Noida: Trishul Publications, 1999).

Chandhoke, Neera, *State and Civil Society: explorations in political theory* (New Delhi and London: Sage, 1995).

Chatterjee, Rupa, *Sonia Gandhi: the lady in shadow* (New Delhi: Butala Publications 1998).

Cohen, Stephen P., *India: emerging power* (Washington, DC: Brookings Institution, 2002).

Desai, Jatin, *Kargil and Pakistan Politics* (New Delhi: Commonwealth, 2000).

Engineer, Asghar Ali (ed.), *The Gujarat Carnage* (New Delhi: Sangam Books, 2003).

Ganguly, Sumit, *Conflict Unending? India–Pakistan relations since 1947* (New York: Columbia University Press, 2002).

Ganguly, Sumit and Devota, Neil, *Understanding Contemporary India* (London: Lynne Rienner, 2003).

India Kargil Review Committee (IKRC), *From Surprise to Reckoning: the Kargil Review Committee report, New Delhi, December 15, 1999* (New Delhi: Sage Publications, 2000).

Jaffrelot, Christophe, *India's Silent Revolution: the rise of the lower castes* (London: Hurst, 1999).

Jeffery, Patricia and Jeffery, Roger, *Don't Marry Me to a Plowman!: Women's everyday lives in north India* (Boulder, Colo.: Westview Press, 1996).

Kapur, Ashok, *Pokhran and Beyond: India's nuclear behaviour*, 2nd edn (New Delhi: Oxford University Press, 2003).

Kishwar, Madhu and Vanita, Ruth, *In Search of Answers: Indian women's voices from Manushi* (New Delhi: Manohar, 1996).

Krishna, Ashok and Chari, P.R. (eds), *Kargil: the tables turned* (New Delhi: Manohar, 2003).

Krishna, Sankaran, *Postcolonial Insecurities: India, Sri Lanka and the question of nationhood* (Minneapolis: Minnesota University Press, 1999).

Kumar, Amrita and Bhaumik, Prashun (eds), *Lest We Forget: Gujarat 2002* (New Delhi: Rupa, 2002).

Mallick, Ross, *Development, Ethnicity and Human Rights in South Asia* (New Delhi: Sage, 1998).

Mazari, Shireen M., *The Kargil Conflict: separating fact from fiction* (Islamabad: Institute for Strategic Studies, 1999).

Nuruzzaman, Muhammad, 'SAARC and subregional co-operation: domestic politics and foreign policies in South Asia', *Contemporary South Asia* 8, 3 (1999), pp. 311–322.

Pai, Sudha, *Dalit Assertion and the Unfinished Democratic Revolution: the Bahujan Samaj Party in Uttar Pradesh* (New Delhi and London: Sage, 2002).

Panikkar, P.N. (ed.), *The Concerned Indian's Guide to Communalism* (New Delhi: Penguin, 2003).

Paul, T.V. (ed.), *The India–Pakistan Conflict: an enduring rivalry* (Cambridge: Cambridge University Press, 2005).

Rai, Ajai K., *The Kargil Conflict and the Role of the Indian Media* (New Delhi: Institute for Defence Studies and Analyses, 2001).

Schofield, Victoria, *Kashmir in Conflict: India, Pakistan and the unending war*, 2nd rev. edn (London: I.B. Tauris and Company, 2002).

Talbott, Strobe, *Engaging India: diplomacy, democracy and the bomb* (Washington, DC: Brookings Institution, 2004).

Varadarajan, Siddharth, *Gujarat: the making of a tragedy* (New Delhi: Penguin, 2003).

Wallace, Terry C., 'The May 1998 India and Pakistan nuclear tests', *Seismological Research Letters*, September.

Yadav, Yogendra, 'The elusive mandate of 2004', *Economic and Political Weekly* 39 (2004), pp. 5383–5395.

18 South Asia in the new millennium

Baviskar, Amita, *In the Belly of the River: tribal conflicts over development in the Narmada valley* (New Delhi: Oxford University Press, 1995).

Chandhoke, Neera, *Beyond Secularism: rights of religious minorities* (New Delhi: Oxford University Press, 1999).

Drèze, Jean et al. (eds), *The Dam and the Nation: displacement and resettlement in the Narmada valley* (New Delhi: Oxford University Press, 1997).

Forbes, Geraldine, *Women in Modern India* (New Cambridge History of India) (Cambridge: Cambridge University Press, 1996).

Hasan, Zoya, Sridharan, E. and Sudarshan, R. (eds), *India's Living Constitution: ideas, practices, controversies* (London: Anthem Press, 2005).

Hust, Evelin, *Women's Political Representation and Empowerment in India: a million Indiras now?* (New Delhi: Manohar, 2004).

Jayawardena, Kumari and de Alwis, Mulathi (eds), *Embodied Violence: communalising women's sexuality in South Asia* (New Delhi: Kali for Women, 1996).

Jeffery, P. and Basu, A. (eds), *Appropriating Gender: women's activism and politicised religion in South Asia* (London: Routledge, 1998).

Jenkins, Rob, *Democratic Politics and Economic Reform in India* (Cambridge: Cambridge University Press, 1999).

Kishwar, Madhu and Vanita, Ruth, *In Search of Answers: Indian women's voices from Manushi* (New Delhi: Manohar, 1996).

Kumar, Radha, *The History of Doing: women's movement in India* (London: Zed, 1993).

Misty, Dinshaw, 'India's emerging space program', *Pacific Affairs* 71, 2 (1998), pp. 151–174.

Moog, Robery S., 'Elite–court relations in India: an unsatisfactory arrangement', *Asian Survey* 38, 4 (1998), pp. 410–423.

Roy, Arundhati, *The Cost of Living* (New York: Modern Library, 1999).

Roy, Arundhati, *The Algebra of Infinite Justice* (New Delhi: Penguin/New York: Harper-Collins, 2002).

Sathe, S.P., *Judicial Activism in India: transgressing borders and enforcing limits* (New Delhi: Oxford University Press, 2002).

Sen, Mala, *Death by Fire: sati, dowry death and female infanticide in modern India* (London: Weidenfeld & Nicolson, 2001).

Stern, Robert W., *Changing India: bourgeois revolution on the subcontinent* (Cambridge: Cambridge University Press, 2003).

United Nations Development Programme (UNDP), *Human Development Report 2004* (New York and Oxford: Oxford University Press, 2004).

World Bank, *Wasting Away: the crisis of malnutrition in India* (Washington, DC: World Bank, 1999).

Index

Note: page numbers in **Bold** denote illustrations